Cross-Cultural Studies of Behavior

Cross-Cultural Studies of Behavior

Edited by

Ihsan Al-Issa
University of Calgary

Wayne Dennis
City University of New York

HOLT, RINEHART AND WINSTON, INC.

New York   Chicago   San Francisco   Atlanta   Dallas
Montreal   Toronto   London   Sydney

To Birgitta and Moosa, with Love and Admiration
Ihsan

Copyright © 1970 by Holt, Rinehart and Winston, Inc.
All rights reserved
Library of Congress Catalog Card Number: 76–113056
SBN: 03–083567–4
Printed in the United States of America
0   1   2   3   22   9   8   7   6   5   4   3   2   1

Preface

Today, social science is largely an American concern. American books discussing perception, or intelligence, or child behavior deal primarily with perception, intelligence, and child behavior in the United States. However, a wider view of social science is evolving, in which mankind as a whole is under scrutiny. Until recently, few countries had sufficient data on human behavior, and thus a quasi-world-wide view of human behavior was impossible.

However, many Western social scientists have been conducting research in non-Western countries, and a considerable number of non-Western countries, themselves, now have behavioral scientists trained in research.

The furtherance of research on human behavior in many cultural settings represents a great step forward in the behavioral sciences. This book proposes to introduce the reader (whether he is a student of integrated social science, psychology, sociology, or of any related field in any country) to what can be achieved in human understanding when one steps outside of his own culture.

March 1970·
Ihsan Al-Issa
Wayne Dennis

Contents

Chapter 3: **Cross-Cultural Studies of Personality 153**

Chapter 4: **Cultural Differences in Child Rearing and Child Behavior 235**

Chapter 5: **Psycholinguistics 333**

CHAPTER **1**

CROSS-CULTURAL
STUDIES OF PERCEPTION

1-1

The Puzzle of Color Vocabularies

ROBERT S. WOODWORTH

This selection is one of the earliest comprehensive treatments of a cross-cultural problem and it is therefore placed first. The fact that many languages lacked certain color names was noted in the 1800s and subsequently given many interpretations. Woodworth, one of the elders in American Psychology, wrapped it up, as the present selection shows, and his interpretation has not been challenged.

It was Gladstone (1858) who first called attention to the rather extraordinary vagueness of early color nomenclature. Collating from the Iliad and Odyssey the passages which referred to color, he found such uncertainty and inconsistency in the application of color names as to lead him to deny to the Greeks of Homeric times any clear notions of color whatever. "I conclude," he says, "that the organ of color and its impressions were but partially developed among the Greeks of the heroic age."

This hypothesis of Gladstone (1858) was made more precise and given a definite evolutionary character by Geiger (1880), who, extending the study to many ancient literatures, found them all defective in the same respect; they all showed a lack of any clear term for blue, and the

Reprinted from *Psychol. Bull.*, 1910, **7**, 325–334, by permission of the American Psychological Association.

oldest of them had also none for green. Speaking of the Vedas, Geiger (1880) says:

> "These hymns, consisting of more than 10,000 lines, are nearly all filled with descriptions of the sky. Scarcely any subject is more frequently mentioned; the variety of hues which the sun and dawn display in it, day and night, clouds and lightnings, the atmosphere and the ether, all these are with inexhaustible abundance exhibited to us again and again in all their magnificence; only the fact that the sky is blue could never have been gathered from these poems by any one who did not already know it himself. . . . The *Bible*, in which, as is equally well known, the sky or heaven plays no less a part, seeing that it occurs in the very first verse, and in upwards of 430 other passages besides . . . yet finds no opportunity either of mentioning the blue color.
>
> "The color *green* is met with in antiquity one stage farther back than the blue. . . . The ten books of Rigveda hymns, though they frequently mention the earth, no more bestow on it the epithet green than on the heavens that of blue."

In the very earliest literary remains, according to Geiger, there is not even a name for pure yellow, though there is one for golden or reddish yellow; red appears more firmly entrenched than yellow. And, by aid of etymology, the author believes it possible to go back of even the earliest literature, and "arrive at a still earlier stage, when the notions of black and red coalesce in the vague conception of something colored."

Following his general doctrine that the development of the human mind can be traced by aid of the history of language, Geiger concludes that in an early stage of human development, only a vague sense of indefinite color existed; that red first took on the character of a definite sensation, and that the other colors followed in the order of the spectrum.

The views of Geiger were warmly espoused by Magnus (1877, 1884), who, besides attempting to trace a gradual evolution in the use of color names in Greek literature, took the important step of examining, on a wide scale, both the color vocabularies and the color sense of existing primitive peoples. As a result of a questionnaire, with a set of colors to be named and distinguished, sent out to traders and missionaries, Magnus discovered that most primitive tribes possessed a color nomenclature which was incomplete in about the same way as that of Homer or of the Vedas. But he also found that the limits of color vision were the same among these tribes as among Europeans. They could see and distinguish all the colors from red to violet, though usually they did not possess names for them all. This discrepancy between color vision and the color vocabulary was in itself an important discovery, since it betrayed the weak foundation of the philological method.

This same discrepancy, however, was not only a discovery, but also a problem. Why should color nomenclature not be fairly adequate to the development of the color sense, and why should it be so much further advanced among some peoples than among others? In particular, the uniform character of the deficiency constituted a problem. Magnus (1877, 1884) was able to establish definite laws governing the growth of color vocabularies. Color nomenclature begins, almost always, with red, and spreads to the other colors in spectral order, usually however skipping transitional colors such as orange, blue-green and violet. Practically every language has a name for red; nearly all have a name for yellow; but comparatively few have a conventional word for green, and still fewer have one for blue. Neighboring colors, especially green and blue, are sometimes called by the same name. Where a name for blue is absent, a blue, or at least a saturated blue, is very commonly called by the name which seems primarily to designate black or dark or dull. These results of Magnus's inquiry, which have been generally confirmed by later observations, certainly set a pretty problem in folk psychology.

The observations of Rivers, on both the color vocabulary and the color sense of several primitive groups, are probably the most accurate and important which we possess. He has examined four peoples by a constant method: the Egyptian peasants (Rivers, 1901a), the Papuans of Torres Straits (Rivers, 1901b), the Uralis and Sholagas of India (Rivers, 1903), and the Todas of Southern India (Rivers, 1905); and also a number of whites (English) for purposes of comparison.

Among the natives of Torres Straits he found four stages in the development of a color vocabulary represented in different islands. Some of these stages he has also found exemplified in Egypt and India.

> "In the lowest there appears only to be a definite term for red apart from white and black; in the next stage there are definite terms for red and yellow, and an indefinite term for green; in the next stage there are definite terms for red, yellow and green, and a term for blue has been borrowed from another language; while in the highest stage there are terms for both green and blue, but these tend to be confused with one another."

This highest stage differs but slightly from that of popular language in Europe.

To complete this account of the different stages of color nomenclature, it should be added that some languages have no conventional color names at all. Some American Indian languages show this peculiarity; the color of any presented object will be said to be like that of some other object, and such comparisons are often very accurately made; but there is an absence of fixed usage as to what objects shall constitute the standards for comparison, so that color language remains in a fluid state. Rivers observed much the same fact in the naming of certain colors by the natives of Torres Straits. Probably we shall be right in recognizing several stages in the establishment of a color name: in the first stage comparisons are fluid and there is no fixed usage; in a later stage usage centers about some one comparison, so that all objects having a certain (approximate) color are said to have the color of one particular object; in a later stage, as described by Wundt (1900), the name becomes abstract in the sense that the object is no longer thought of when its name is used as the designation of a color; and later still the name may chance to become obsolete as applied to the object and remain exclusively as the name of the color. Obsolescence of the original usage of the name is probably a purely incidental feature, but is of interest, when it occurs, as showing antiquity of the color meaning.

Fixity of usage depends probably on frequency; where the need for designating a certain color, or range of colors, is infrequent, the fluid condition of color designation will be adequate, and no occasion will arise for stereotyping the name or for dissociating its color meaning from its reference to a particular object. It is evident that growing fixity of usage by no means indicates a finer sensitivity to differences in color, since each stereotyped color name covers a considerable range of discriminable colors. For this reason the original fluid method of color designation persists alongside of the fixed usage, and is employed especially by those who need to designate colors more precisely than is accomplished by the use of the conventional names.

Another fact which has not hitherto been introduced into the discussion of color vocabularies concerns the richness of European languages in names for different parts of the spectrum. The fact is that the English language, for example, is much richer in abstract names for the colors toward the red end of the spectrum than for colors toward the violet end. The following list includes all the color names which I have been able to find in modern English, in which the color reference is thoroughly dissociated, in common usage, from reference to any specific object.

For the reds and yellows and their various shades: red, ruddy, rubicund, russet, roan, auburn, carmine, crimson, scarlet, brown, bay, sorrel, dun, yellow, tawny, sallow, lurid. (To these might be added buff, maroon, vermilion, and perhaps such words as magenta, since the objects to which these names primarily refer are not known by most persons who use the names.)

For the greens, blues and violets: green, verdant, blue, azure, purple, livid.

To the fact that names for red and yellow develop first in the history of a language should therefore be added the fact that they predominate in the European languages. It is further to be noted that many of the names for shades of red and yellow are applied mostly to men and animals. Apparently there is some special demand for names of animal colors. Magnus (1884, p. 9) reports that the Kaffirs have over thirty words and expressions to designate the colors and markings of cattle; and regarding another people of herdsmen, the Ovaherero or Damara of Southwest Africa, his informant makes the following suggestive statement:

> "Colors that coincide with those of cows, sheep and goats, they name without difficulty; but whatever is not a color of cattle, particularly blue and green, they cannot name, although they can distinguish them from the other colors, and when necessary use foreign words to designate them. . . . Those who have not come into contact with foreign culture and foreign names cannot name green and blue, and think it highly amusing that there should be names for these colors."

It would indeed be ridiculous to have names for colors simply because the colors were distinguishable.

With these facts of color language before us, we may turn to the problem of explanation. At the outset, it is clear that no such view as that of Geiger can longer be entertained. The absence of a name for a sensory quality does not point to the absence of the quality. The case of smell is particularly convincing, for certainly many odors are vivid experiences, likely to attract the attention and be, relatively, isolated from a total sensory complex, and often they are practically significant; and yet there is an almost complete absence of abstract odor names from all languages. Taste nomenclature, though better defined than that of smell, presents some striking incongruences with taste sensation, as has been shown by Myers (1904) and by Chamberlain (1903). Many languages do not possess four words to correspond to the four tastes (which, it can hardly be doubted, are the property of all races of men), and even where the language is complete in this regard, common usage often employs one taste word to refer to substances of discrete tastes. In its most rudimentary condition, a taste vocabulary consists simply of words for well-tasting and ill-tasting; and in more developed languages this affective basis of taste nomenclature is still visible. Sweet and mildly saline are often called by one name; and sour and bitter by one name. Even Scotch villagers, examined by Myers, described a weak solution of quinine as having 'a sort of sour' or a 'sort of salty' taste. It is the exception, rather than the rule, when any sensation, either elementary or complex, receives a special name.

Magnus, as the result of his inquiry, was forced to abandon the doctrine of a close correspondence between color sense and the color vocabulary; but it still seemed to him impossible to explain the deficiency of names for green and blue without assuming some underlying sensory defect; and he is inclined to the view that these sensations, though present in primitive folk, were perhaps of recent development and certainly less vivid and impressive than to European eyes. Their lack of vividness, he supposed, was the cause of their remaining nameless.

This more moderate form of the Gladstone-Geiger hypothesis, though practically obsolete for two decades, has come into renewed prominence through the support of Rivers. Though this author admits the existence of other factors in the development of color language, he regards a lack of vividness of the sensation of blue as of great importance. This conclusion seems to him to be indicated by the results of his measurements of the sensitiveness of different peoples to colors. His measurements determined the faintest tint of red, yellow and blue which could be recognized and named. His results on four primitive peoples, as compared with the English, show average thresholds for the five groups which are in fairly close agreement, with the following exceptions. The English have a much lower threshold for yellow and for blue than any of the more primitive groups; and one of his primitive groups (the Murray Islanders) show a much lower threshold for red than either the English or any of the remaining groups.

The only one of these differences which is emphasized by Rivers is the greater sensitiveness of the English for blue. This seems to him of importance as showing that the absence of a name for blue is actually associated with a certain degree of insensitiveness for this color. The low threshold of the English for *yellow* does not impress him as significant, and yet, though it is less marked than their low threshold for blue, it cannot be explained by the probable error of his observations, but is, on the contrary, rather striking. It creates some difficulty in the way of using the facts in explaining color nomenclature, since the name for yellow is present, though the sensitiveness to that color is comparatively blunt.

A more serious difficulty with Rivers' results is that so much depends on the group of 41 educated Englishmen whose average gives the basis for comparison.

The individuals in this group differed greatly from each other in sensitiveness to the colors. Rivers ascribes this variability, in the case of red, to the probable presence in the group of some individuals with a tendency to red-green blindness—though demonstrably color blind individuals were of course excluded—and in the case of blue, to the possibility that some of his Englishmen helped out sensation by inference, calling a glass blue when they did not detect either of the two more easily recognized colors. It is possible, accordingly, that the English threshold for red is too high, and for blue too low, to compare fairly with the thresholds of the primitive groups; and, if so, the corrected result would read simply that the English were able to recognize and name fainter tints than the other races tested. Such a result might well be due to a better adaptation of the educated subjects to the conditions of the test, and to their greater habituation to analyzing and naming pale colors.[1]

Rivers himself accepts the low sensitivity of his primitive groups to blue as a well-established fact, and offers alternative explanations for it. One of his suggestions is new and deserves careful attention. "The Murray Islander," he says, "differs from the Englishman in two important respects; he is more primitive and he is more pigmented, and his insensitiveness to blue may be either a function of his primitiveness or of his pigmentation. In other words, it is possible that his insensitiveness may depend on the lack of development of some physiological substance or mechanism, which acts as the basis of the sensation blue in ourselves, or it may only depend on the fact that the retina of the Papuan is more strongly pigmented than that of the European. There is some reason to think that this latter factor is the more important. We know that the macula lutea in the retina, which contains the region of most distinct vision, is pigmented, and that as a consequence of the reddish-yellow color of its pigment, blue and green rays are more strongly absorbed than red and yellow; we have reason to believe further that the macula of dark races is more pigmented than that of ourselves. The consequence would be that, in dark races, blue and green would be more strongly absorbed, and consequently there would be a certain degree of insensitiveness to these colors, as compared with red and yellow" (Rivers, 1901c).

This suggestion regarding retinal pigmentation is the more deserving of attention since Johnson (1901) has reported his ophthalmoscopic examinations of the fundus oculi in various races, and shown that the color of it ranges from orange-red in fair-haired Europeans to dark chocolate in the Negro. What effect these differences in pigmentation should have on color vision, however, remains to be worked out. Meanwhile, this suggestion by no means contains a full explanation of the peculiar order of growth of color vocabularies, since this order has apparently been the same in light-skinned as in dark-skinned races. Even the Welsh language of today, according to Rivers (1905), has no word for blue. The late appearance of names for green and blue is too wide-spread a phenomenon to be explained in terms of racial differences.

---

[1]That this statement represents the true state of the case, I am strongly inclined to believe, on the basis of tests of several more or less primitive peoples made by Dr. Bruner and myself at the St. Louis Exposition. Publication of the full results of our work has been unduly delayed; and I will simply state that our test called for fine discrimination of color tones, instead of the recognition of pale tints, and is therefore, in strictness, not comparable with that of Rivers. At the same time, we found, clearly enough, that all the primitive peoples were inferior to white Americans, in this test, but that the inferiority was no more marked in the blues than in the reds and yellows. Some of these primitive people, however, possess no names for green and blue.

Now, finally, to make an attempt at a positive explanation of the puzzle of color vocabularies. The matter now appears to me—after several years of consideration—rather simple and devoid of psychological interest, except perhaps from its bearing on the methods of folk psychology. We may fairly assume, with Wundt (1900), that abstract color names are of relatively late introduction into any language, and that they developed out of names for colored objects; so that the question is primarily regarding that hardening and dissociation of linguistic usage of which mention was previously made. What requires explanation is rather the development of this fixity of usage than its absence; some need for it must be pointed out, and this need must, undoubtedly, include frequency of reference to the color.

It is further evident that the color implication of the name of an object would never be dissociated from the whole connotation of the name, if there existed no other object of similar color, to which there was frequent need to refer. A color name can scarcely develop except where there are a variety of objects of the same general color.

A further necessity is brought into view by considering the function of color in practical and primitive life. The color of an object is not a practically important character, except as a ready means, and often the readiest means, of identifying the object and distinguishing it from its background. It is where color serves as the mark of an important object, or condition of an object, that a color name would be most likely to develop. But a color name need not always develop even in these circumstances, for practical tendencies lead us to pass quickly from a sign to the thing signified, and to speak of the thing signified rather than of the sign. We speak of a gray patch in the sky as a cloud, of a red spot on the skin as blood; we speak of a berry as ripe rather than red, of a knife as rusty rather than brown, of meat as well done or underdone rather than as brown or red. In such cases the color is the mark by which the condition of the thing is known, but what is named is the condition rather than the mark.

Such considerations make clear the lack of a need for color names, and account for the widespread poverty of languages in such names. They also help to explain why red and yellow are so much more generously supplied with names than green and blue.

Green and blue, in nature, are predominantly background colors, while red and yellow are usually the colors of small objects contrasting with the background and recognized most readily by their color. More than this, red and yellow are the usual colors of such important objects as ripe fruits, domestic animals, wild animals to be hunted or avoided, blood and flesh. It is as animal colors, and particularly as mammalian colors, that red and yellow, with their darker shades, are most important to primitive man; and it would be hard to point out any equal importance of green and blue. Particularly in distinguishing cattle from one another, for purposes of barter, or for many other purposes of the herdsman, is it necessary to use the color as a mark, and to designate an individual by its color. If cows had affected the blues and greens, the history of color vocabularies would probably have been quite different. It is also true (Rivers, 1901c) that the most accessible and most used pigments are red and yellow, and the use of pigments might easily give rise to a variety of objects alike save in color and needing to be designated by reference to their color. Probably the exact history of names for red and yellow has been different in different tribes.

Needs for the names of red and yellow are thus not far to seek, but the case is different with green and blue. It would be hard to show wherein primitive man suffers inconvenience from lack of names for green and blue. He needs, indeed, to observe and speak of the difference between growing and ripe or dead vegetation, but names for ripe and unripe, fresh and dried, living and dead supply this need admirably, and have the advantage of sticking close to the inner conditions indicated by the color signs. Similarly, primitive man needs to observe and speak of the difference between a blue and a gray sky, but weather names supply this need. We ourselves abandon our color names when speaking of the sky in a practical connection. We are unlikely to refer to it as deep blue, or grayish blue, or mottled blue and gray, or uniformly gray, when what we mean is that it is clear, hazy, fair or overcast. So long as vegetation and the sky are the only objects in which the colors green and blue are of practical importance, no motive can be assigned for the use of special names for these colors. And it is hard to think of other objects of these colors—especially of blue—which are important in primitive conditions. With the introduction of green and blue paints and dyes, these colors become important marks in distinguishing household objects; and it is probably owing to the use of pigments that names for green and blue have become stereotyped in European languages.

References

Chamberlain, A. F. Primitive taste words, *Amer. J. Psychol.*, 1903, **14**, 146–153.

Geiger, L. *Contributions to the history of the human race.* Translated by D. Asher. London: Trubner and Co., 1880.

Gladstone, W. E. *Studies on Homer and the Homeric Age.* Vol. III. Oxford: Oxford University Press, 1858.

Johnson, L. Contributions to the comparative anatomy of the mammalian eye, chiefly based on opthalmoscopic examination, *Philos. Trans. Roy. Soc. London*, 1901. Ser. B., **194**, 1–82.

Magnus, H. *Die geschichtliche entwicklung des farbensinnes.* Liepzig: Veit und Co., 1877.

Magnus, H. *Untersuchungen über den Farbensinn der naturvolker.* Wiesboden: Bergmann, 1884.

Myers, C. S. The taste names of primitive people, *Brit. J. Psychol.*, 1904, **1**, 117–126.

Rivers, W. H. R. Observations on the senses of the Todas, *Brit. J. Psychol.*, 1905, **1**, 321–396.

Rivers, W. H. R. Observations on the vision of the Uralis and Scholagas, *Madras Govt. Mus. Bull.*, 1903, **5**, 1–16.

Rivers, W. H. R. The color vision of the native of Upper Egypt, *J. Anthropol. Inst.*, 1901(a), **31**, 229–245.

Rivers, W. H. R. Introduction and vision. In A. C. Haddon (ed.), *Reports of the Cambridge anthropological expedition to the Torres Straits.* vol. II, Part 1. Cambridge, Eng.: The University Press, 1901(b).

Rivers, W. H. R. Primitive color vision, *Pop. Sci. Mo.*, 1901 (c), **59**, 44–58.

Wundt, W. *Völkerpsychologie*, 1900, Bd. 1, Th. 2., 512–515.

1-2

Human Color Perception and Behavioral Response

VERNE F. RAY

The use of color terms continues to be of interest, as indicated by this article written by an anthropologist. He demonstrates that color vision in "real life" cannot be separated from color significance; i.e., ordinary observers, whether "primitive" or "civilized," do not group colors as a physicist or a sensory psychologist might, but rather according to the uses or meaning of the referents that bear color. For example, green grass, brown grass, yellow grass may all be "grass colors" and blue sea and green sea have "sea color."

In his introductory remarks to a recent symposium on perception Werner (1950) pointed out that the man-in-the-street is quite sure that he sees with his eyes and hears with his ears. Apparently this naive view is shared by anthropologists. It is generally futile to search in an ethnography for so much as a paragraph, to say nothing of a chapter, on the subject of perceptual patterning as affected by the particular culture under discussion. Theoretical or analytical papers on the subject are equally rare. A good start was made by W. H. R. Rivers over forty years

Reprinted from *Trans. N. Y. Acad. of Sci.*, 1953, **16**, 98–104, by permission of the author and the New York Academy of Science.

ago but his stimulating leads were never followed up by his contemporaries or successors.

Psychologists, on the other hand, have always given generous attention to problems of perception. Currently these studies are concerned largely with the projective nature of perception. An attempt is being made to determine the manner in which "the perceived world pattern mirrors the organized need pattern within," as Gardner Murphy (1947) has phrased it.

These studies should be of great interest to the anthropologist; they naturally focus upon the individual but the basic problem is one which demands an analysis of the cultural factors operating before it can be answered. The organized need pattern within the person is based largely upon the organized pattern of his culture, only secondarily upon individually unique learning. Psychologists must usually, if not always, study narrow individual directive states which are mere variations upon a theme. The theme itself and all comparable themes are cultural in character and the notes constituting them, indeed the character of the bars upon which they are written, can only be described and interpreted by anthropologists. In neglecting our duty we not only deprive ourselves of significant insights into man's behavior but we put psychologists at an unfortunate disadvantage, that of working without adequate controls.

Let us take an example from a recent psychological experiment by Bruner and Postman (1950). Subjects at Radcliffe and Harvard were shown, successively, by tachistoscopic exposure, five different playing cards. On one to four of the cards color and suit were reversed; the normal and distorted cards were presented in random order. One interesting result was disruption, that is, gross failure to organize the perceptual field, with consequent frustration and inability to describe that which had been presented. When the subject was able to recognize a normal card in 20 to 50 milliseconds the same subject might despair of describing a distorted card after a hundred or more milliseconds of exposure. Such a state of frustration is brought about by the subject's failure to confirm any of his repertory of experiences. As a consequence, perception fails to produce any kind of meaningful behavior. "Repertory of experiences" and "meaningful behavior" are significant terms here. What repertory of experiences? That which derives from the subject's unique psychological makeup? No; it is rather the repertory of his culture that is the critical factor in his reaction. His conditioning in this respect—and his directive state—are derived from his culture and are shared by his fellows regardless of individual variations in experience.

Meaningful behavior? Here again we are dealing with a notion which has significance at the cultural level. The playing card is a good example of a culturally arbitrary and symbolic object of perception. A person whose culture lacks playing cards would not be perturbed; for him there would be no perceptual disruption because no prescribed and therefore meaningful behavior is elicited by the perception of a black spade or a red diamond.

And thus is pointed the way to anthropologists for significant investigations of perceptual problems, investigations broad in base and experimental in method.

These introductory remarks have had to do with vision simply because the great bulk of work on perception has been concerned with seeing in its various manifestations. The complexity of this phase of perception and the intriguing problems it presents make this predilection understandable but hardly defensible because we are left with a woefully inadequate knowledge of perception via the other senses.

My own experimental and field researches have included studies of auditory perception but the bulk of my work has been in the field of vision. I have attempted to develop an adequate methodology and technique for the anthropological study of human color vision and to advance somewhat our knowledge of that aspect of perception. Toward these ends I have worked from time to time over the last twenty years with subjects, mostly American Indians, representing about sixty linguistically and culturally distinct groups. The diversity is indicated by the fact that approximately twenty linguistic stocks were involved, in terms of the old Powell classification, and six culture areas have been covered. In a recent paper I summarized my recommendations regarding technique and gave some attention to methodology and problems (Ray, 1952). At this time I wish to present some of my experimental data but first it may be wise to repeat a word or two about technique.

After experimenting with spectroscopes and spectrographs and finding them unsatisfactory I sought other means for obtaining perceptual data. I demanded a technique which would permit designation of color quality in terms of wavelength since only in this way would it be possible to convey the results of my findings to fellow workers. Attempts to establish international color standards have failed completely and the reproduction of color samples to accompany a scientific article would be either technically impossible or prohibitively expensive. The most desirable color sample for perceptual research is a pigmented flat surface. Contrary to expectation, it was found possible to produce such samples with a purity and uniformity more than adequate for use in perceptual experiments and at the same time identifiable in terms of wavelength. In experimentation these samples are presented to subjects under rigidly controlled conditions as to quality of light, background, method of exposure, character of responses, recordings of responses—and, of course, the samples are presented in random order. The basic response of the subject is the identification of the color perceived by the appropriate color term in his particular language. In so far as the scientific analysis of the data is concerned color names are dispensed with entirely and wavelength designations used exclusively. However, for purposes of writing and discussion, it is desirable to have a name designation to correspond with each of the wavelength numbers. Standard color names can be used with the understanding that they mean nothing more than a wavelength span. A particular wavelength and name designates a specific point in a continuum, the spectrum. It would be preferable to have the dividing lines between one sample and the two adjacent samples identified but this is impossible with discrete samples, possible only with an elaborate spectroscope or a continuous spectral reproduction; the former is impracticable, the latter is useless for these experimental purposes because of the carry-over or contamination effect of the visible adjacent colors. However, the various samples are arbitrary as to wavelength position, and the number of samples is generally much greater than the basic color-name repertory of the culture. Therefore an approximation of the wavelength position of the dividing lines can usually be made for any particular system. This is significant because the range for a particular cultural designation is sometimes narrow, sometimes broad, and the type or focal point is not always the mid-point—indeed it is often found at one or another extreme.

The accompanying chart (Figure 1) should of course be drawn as a circle or a wheel rather than linearly. The spectral continuum turns back upon itself, so to speak, in all systems in which the classification is extended to include the non-spectral violets, thus joining the two "ends" of the distribution. A circular drawing would avoid the awkwardness involved in repeating one of the violets at the two "ends" of a straight-line scale. But I have found that circular charts are hard to read and to conceptualize and for these reasons the linear presentation is to be preferred.

The position of the color name on the scale indicates the recognized type position for that particular color. The horizontal lines on either side of the color name indicate the range. A color name will sometimes be found opposite the dividing line between two of the segments into which the spectrum has been divided for experimental purposes. This means that the color samples on either side of the line are perceived as equally typical of the color in the culture concerned. It is not, of course, necessary to use color terms to indicate the structures of the various systems; a simple check mark or dot would serve the purpose. However, I have chosen to give the names for the interest that they may hold and for illustration of some factors which are linguistic in character.

The color systems presented are those of ten cultures of north-western America: nine Indian and one American. The cultures vary in character from that of the northwestern United States to that of the Atka Eskimo and from Wishram Chinook to Chilcotin Athapaskan. The lan-

Color	Wave length	English Northwest U.S.	Salish Sanpoil	Sahaptin Tenino	Chinook Wishram	Salish Songish	Athapaskan Chilcotin	Eskimo Atka	Athapaskan Chetco R.	Takelma Rogue R.	Kalapuya Santiam
Violet-red	comp 5600										sa'kwala
Red	6571	red							ɫ'si'k	ãɪ̇c·'ɫ	
Orange-red	6340		qu'ł		da'bã'l	nɑsɑ·'ɡu		u'łu·ðax			utsa·'ła
Red-orange	6230			luɫ'sa'			ʈɛłʈɛ'ł				t's·'łłɪɛ·
Orange	6085	orange		mɔ'kɔ							
Yellow-orange	5390				dagã'c	lɑlɑ'c̑			xa'dɛgii	na'uɑx	
Orange-yellow	5870		kuɲa'i	'pa'a'x		iɑ iɑ cãlis		cu·'mnu'ʔɪx			na'łamɪ
Yellow	5793	yellow			qa'naptsu	nɑkwa'i	ʈɛłtso·'				
Green-yellow	5710										tsk·'łkwu
Yellow-green	5600		qwi'n					cɪ'ðʔɪx			
Green	5164	green				cɪʈ'ałs			ł'su'	gwa'camt	
Blue-green	5050				daptsã'x	sqwa'iux					
Green-blue	4985						ʈɪ·łcã'n				
Blue	4695	blue		lɑ'mt		nɑkwa'i				tɔicɔ·'mt	pɔ·'x
Violet-blue	4455		qwa'i								
Blue-violet	4360			pu'u'x		nɑkwa'i			xa'dɛtsu'		
Violet	4210	violet				kwi'łmɑł				kiyɑ·'x	
Red-violet	comp 4990		xʷ'n		iyaquił sabɑł						
Violet-red	comp 5600										

Figure 1

guages of the ten cultures are mutually unintelligible; several distinct stocks are represented. The cultures are not arranged in geographical order. Such an arrangement is less illuminating than one, as used here, which places together those systems which show the greatest similarity, especially as regards continuity of the horizontal lines which mark the boundaries of color range. The chart has been simplified to show only the standard colors, not the tints, shades or grays. If these were included the complexity of each system would be greatly increased.

This accounts only in part for the apparent simplicity of these systems. The chart shows only the basic color terms and the spectral bands which they designate. Hundreds or thousands of additional color descriptive terms are available to the users of each of these languages. But the significant point is that these are not color terms proper. They do not refer to recognized divisions of the color range conceived abstractly. They are terms such as mauve or chartreuse in English and each one has connotations beyond that of color. Sometimes the color meaning is dominant, other connotations secondary, as in the term scarlet; in other instances the reverse as, for example, smoky. In many cases the number of primary or secondary connotations is considerable; an example is chestnut. It is not uncommon to find true complexes of meaning, as witness sable. Some terms exhibit a fixed linkage of primary and secondary meanings; for instance, sorrel. In the vast majority of cases it is difficult or impossible to determine whether color connotation is primary or secondary; consider chartreuse, mauve, and cardinal, to name but a few.

These examples from English could be duplicated in kind in any one of the languages represented on the chart. Naturally they are more numerous in some languages than others. The primary reason for the variation is cultural tolerance or encouragement, not linguistic structure. Some languages provide mechanisms for the invention of new color terms on the spur of the moment, for example blue-blue-violet. However, these linguistic devices relate to true color terms as opposed to the color descriptive words and phrases that we are now discussing.

The most significant characteristic of color descriptors—to coin a word—is the fact that they form no system; they are merely a random collection of useful words gathered from diverse sources. As such there is an amazing tolerance to their careless usage—one can hardly speak of inaccurate usage—and consequently great variation from person to person.

The perception of colors in descriptive terms is an exceedingly complex phenomenon. When I see a brightly-colored sunset my behavioral response, if linguistic, may not involve color at all but, instead, fire, waves, clouds, dusk, autumn, beauty, music, rest. Or a rose: beauty, odor, loveliness, softness, dew. And if color response be involved it is apt to be in terms of descriptors, not color terms. The latter relate to concepts, the former to things.

Perhaps the significance of what I have called color terms proper and the basic color system is now more clear. Perception of color and behavioral response thereto is our problem; not description of color. The basic color system is the foundation of precise behavior with respect to the world of color. The cultural repertory of experience provides appropriate behavior—utterance of the proper color term, for example—when perception occurs. No individual variation is permitted within the culture in this respect, except it be interpreted as error, and all normal persons perceive nearly equally well.

I have never encountered a culture lacking such a basic system. It is not an easy task to separate proper color terms from words which are merely descriptors, especially when the culture and its language are not too well known. I doubt that it can be done with an acceptable degree of validity without experimentation of the general type which I have described. Such a technique is effective in this respect because it brings out the system without the subject being aware that a system is being sought; he is asked no questions whatsoever. The procedure is quite analogous to that of the linguist who derives the grammar of a language from what the informant thought were random words, phrases and texts. In each case the problem of analysis is considerable and the end product often less than perfect. But the fundamental characteristics of the pattern are clearly exhibited in both instances.

Let us now return to the chart and see what variations in pattern are found. First we may look for instances of cross-cultural uniformity. None is found; the closest approach is in the region of red. Next we see that several cultures, the Tenino, Atka, Chetco, and Kalapuya, exhibit what has been called "blue-green confusion." Before discussing this let us look at the American perceptual pattern. We see that the green band is exceptionally narrow and that the type is immediately adjacent to blue. Only the Chilcotin draw the line where we do. The Tenino, for example, place the boundary just one unit from ours and thereby become guilty of "blue-green confusion" despite the fact that theirs is a more evenly divided system. But they are also victims of "green-yellow confusion" because they are not as "blue-green confused" as, say, the Atka who include all the greens with blue. The conclusion would seem to be that a color system without any "confusion" would have to possess a great number of basic terms—more than the number actually found in any recorded system—and the consequence of that might well be a hopeless individual confusion in perception and response. There is no question but that the Atka perceive broad bands of blue and green as one color just as the Sanpoil perceive orange and yellow to be unitary; the Chilcotin, blue and violet; the Chetco, red and orange; and the Americans ʙa'lamɩ and tskι'ɫkwu (Santiam). We designate the latter two colors by the unitary term yellow. This is the so-called "ʙɑ'lamι–tskι'ɫkwu confusion."

"Blue-green confusion" is often attributed to peoples who, as a matter of fact, perceive more subtly the variations in this region of the spectrum than we do. Instead of a dual division of the spread from the 5600 to 4455 wavelength positions, three divisions are perceived. When the naive investigator or observer notes that the middle segment of this tripartite division includes portions of what we call blue and green he tends to explain this phenomenon as confusion. A good example of the tripartite classification is found in the Songish system, a system which is characterized throughout by the subtlety of its distinctions. By what appears to be an accident of selection of examples, the chart shows only one other example of this pattern which is really quite common; this from the Rogue River.

Even the small amount of evidence presented on the chart demonstrates the low correlation of type and mid-point of range in color perception. In the American system the type for red is found at one end of the spectral range, green at the opposite end of its range. Tenino and Chetco present significant examples of types at one or another extreme of very broad bands. Chilcotin, on the other hand, is consistent in choosing the mid-point even though this culture is Athapaskan in speech as is Chetco. Frequently the type for a color in one system is located exactly where a division between colors is found in another pattern. Examples appearing on the chart are found in the Santiam column, also Wishram, Songish, and Tenino (5600–5164), Tenino and U. S. (4455–4350), Tenino and Sanpoil and others (4210) and in numerous other cases.

It is worthy of note that the number of terms in the basic systems shown varies only from three to eight with the mode at five and the average exactly five; the American pattern is close, with six. These figures would mean little, due to the small number of cases, were it not that they are consistent with most of the results shown by analysis of the total of sixty recorded cultures. These figures throw a new light upon the so-called primitive or simple systems which get along with three basic units. In the arbitrary division of the color continuum into three or eight segments there is a difference of finesse, not of kind, between the two, when it be a question of utility of the system. Behavior differs depending upon the perceptual grading: the person who has but three basic color terms at his disposal must more frequently use color descriptors to express his meaning. But behavior is meaningful in both cases; there is no disruption. Whether perception differs in the two instances is a matter which will be touched upon below.

Attempts to find correlations between the basic number of units in the color perception pattern and complexity of culture or development of art are doomed to failure if the sixty cultures studied are representative.

It is true that the Chilcotin, with three basic terms, is at the same time one of the meagerest cultures represented on the chart but this cannot be said of the Atka. The most complex Indian culture presented is perhaps the Songish and it is also the one with the most numerous color distinctions. But American culture is far and away the most complex and artistically the most highly developed of these examples and we have but six categories to the Songish eight.

A search for environmental explanations is equally fruitless. The Atka have no basic color categories for the violets yet it is precisely these colors which are predominant in their Aleutian environment. The environments of the Songish, Chetco, Rogue and Santiam are virtually identical but their color systems vary as widely as any recorded.

It will be seen that even a small quantity of data, as in this chart, provides numerous illustrations of fundamental aspects of color perception and response. With a few more researchers at work and a few more years of time we should have answers to numerous basic problems of culture and perception. And, in the course of such research, a great many related questions would be answered. Rough form can be given to some of these even now. Here are a few: Does human color perception have a peculiar linear and unidimensional quality, as contrasted to perception in terms of such multidimensional descriptors as those mentioned earlier? If so, is this quality characteristic also of other phenomena sharing this linear quality—in this instance, wavelength—for example, musical tones? Is man's richness of perception limited by behavioral response in terms of pattern? Is man's unique possession, language, a deterrent to full and varied response to his environment since its patterns often provide but few categories—as in color—whereas his physical sensitivity is exceedingly subtle? Does the artist see the world more richly and rewardingly because he divests himself of cultural pattern, and thus becomes less of a human being? Whatever the answer to these last questions may be, we must remember that if language makes possible human patterns, then pattern makes possible science; and also, that man is not a slave to pattern since he can perceive, and even respond in words, to the sunset or the rose as I have suggested is his wont.

Finally, I would like to repeat some of the conclusions which I offered in my earlier paper in advance of presentation of the experimental evidence. I conclude that there is no such thing as a "natural" division of the spectrum. The color systems of man are not based upon psychological, physiological, or anatomical factors. Each culture has taken the spectral continuum and has divided it upon a basis which is quite arbitrary except for pragmatic considerations. None of these systems derives from physiological limitations; none exploits more than meagerly the physiological sensitivity of the human being. The notion of color confusion reflects only the confusion of those expressing the idea.

Color systems serve to bring the world of color sensation into order so that perception may be relatively simple and behavioral response, particularly verbal response and communication, may be meaningful.

REFERENCES

Bruner, J. S. and D. Krech (eds.). *Perception and personality*. Durham, N.C.: Duke University Press, 1950.

Bruner, J. S. and L. Postman. On the perception of incongruity. In Bruner and Krech (eds.), *Perception and personality*. Durham, N.C.: Duke University Press, 1950, 206–223.

Murphy, G. *Personality*. New York: Harper & Row, Publishers, 1950, 351.

Ray, V. F. Techniques and problems in the study of human color perception, *Southwestern J. Anthropol.*, 1952, **8**, 251–259.

1-3

Cultural Differences in the Perception of Geometric Illusions

MARSHAL H. SEGALL
DONALD T. CAMPBELL
MELVILLE J. HERSKOVITS

Does our own culture blind us to the "realities" of the world that are seen by individuals of other cultures? The data presented in this paper from 15 societies show that there are substantial inter-societal differences in the perception of space and in the suscepti-bility to geometrical illusions. It is shown that patterns of responses reflect the acquisition of different habits of perceptual inference which relate to cultural and ecological factors in the environment. The degree of rectangularity in the social surroundings is regarded as a factor affecting the extent of the Müller-Lyer illusion and the Sander Parallelogram. It is suggested that European and American city dwellers have a much higher percentage of rectangularity in their environments than do residents of non-Europeanized cultures; rural residents also live in a less carpentered visual environment than do urban inhabitants because the former are outdoors more often. Furthermore, in non-Western cultures, residents of square houses would have a more rectangular visual environment than would persons living in round-house cultures. Results of the present study

Reprinted from *Science*, 1963, **139**, 769–771, by permission of the authors and the American Association for the Advancement of Science.

show that European groups are more susceptible to the Müller-Lyer illusion and the Sander Parallelogram than non-Western groups living in less carpentered environments.

The Horizontal-vertical illusion is also interpreted ecologically by the authors. This illusion consists of the tendency to perceive the vertical lines as longer than the horizontal when both are of equal length. It is suggested that inhabitants of flat plains would frequently observe horizontal expanses and should tend to infer long, horizontal distances from short vertical retinal images. People living in rain forests and canyons would have tree trunks or mountains extending vertically in front of them; and they should be less likely to foreshorten the vertical. People who have as much experience with horizontal floors as with vertical walls (Europeans) would be in an intermediate position. This study shows that the Toro and Bayonkole people who both live in high open country are the most susceptible to this illusion, while the Bete people of jungle environment are the least, with the European peoples in an intermediate position.

Stimulus materials based upon geometric illusions were prepared in 1956 for standardized administration under varying field conditions in an effort to encourage the collection of cross-cultural data that might bear on the nativist-empiricist controversy concerning space perception (Herskovits, Campbell, and Segall, 1956). Over a 6-year period anthropologists and psychologists administered these tests to 14 non-European samples of children and adults, ranging in size from 46 to 344 in 12 locations in Africa and one in the Philippines, to a sample ($N = 44$) of South Africans of European descent in Johannesburg, to an American undergraduate sample ($N = 30$), and to a house-to-house sample ($N = 208$) in Evanston, Ill. In all, data were collected from 1878 persons. Analysis of these protocols provides evidence of substantial cross-cultural differences in response to these materials. The nature of these differences constitutes strong support for the empiricistic hypothesis that the perception of space involves, to an important extent, the acquisition of habits of perceptual inference.

The stimulus materials to be considered here consisted of 39 items, each one a variation of one of four figures constructed of straight lines, generally referred to in the psychological literature as perceptual, or geometric illusions. These were the Müller-Lyer figure (12 items), the Sander Parallelogram (seven), and two forms of the Horizontal-vertical figure (nine and eleven). For each illusion the discrepancy in length of the segments to be compared varied from item to item so as to permit the employment of a version of the psychophysical method of constant stimuli. As each stimulus was shown to a respondent, his task was simply to indicate the longer of two linear segments. To minimize difficulties of communication, the materials were designed so that the linear segments to be compared were not connected to the other lines, and were printed in different colors. Respondents could indicate choice by selecting one of two colors (saying *red* or *black*) in response to the Horizontal-vertical items, and by indicating *right* or *left* for the other illusions. Other steps taken to enhance the validity of response protocols included the administration of a short comprehension test requiring judgments similar to, but more obvious than, those demanded by the stimulus figures. Nonetheless, since no amount of precautionary measures could insure the elimination of all sources of error (for example, communication difficulties, response sets, and so forth) which could result in artifactually produced cross-cultural differences, an internal consistency check was made and all protocols containing gross departures from orderliness were withheld from analysis. (Another analysis was performed with all 1878 cases included, and the results were substantially the same as those obtained in the analysis of consistent cases only.)

The analysis proceeded as follows: Each respondent's four protocols were first examined for evidence of internal consistency. To be considered consistent, a protocol had to contain no more than one Guttman error (1947). Each consistent protocol was then assigned a score which was simply the total number of times in that stimulus set that the respondent chose the typically over-estimated segment. The mean of these scores was computed for each sample, and differences between pairs of means were evaluated by t-tests with significance levels modified by the Scheffé procedure (Scheffé, 1953) to compensate for the increase in error rate that accompanies nonindependent, multiple comparisons.

On both the Müller-Lyer and Sander Parallelogram illusions the three "European" samples made significantly more illusion-produced responses than did the non-European samples. (The innumerable t ratios resulting can only be sampled here. For example, on the Müller-Lyer illusion, comparisons of the Evanston sample with the non-European samples resulted in t ratios ranging from 7.96 to 15.39. A value of 3.57 is significant at the $p = .05$ level by the Scheffé test.) On the latter two illusions, the European samples had relatively low scores, with many, but not all, of the non-European samples having significantly larger mean scores. (For these illusions, the largest t ratios, up to 17.41, were found between pairs of non-European groups. Comparisons involving the Evanston sample and five non-European groups resulted in t's ranging from 11.04 to 4.69.) When the samples were ranked according to mean number of illusion responses on each illusion, and the rank order correlations among the five illusions factor-analyzed, two orthogonal factors emerged; the Müller-Lyer and Sander Parallelogram illusions loaded highly on one, and the Horizontal-vertical illusions loaded highly on the other. Thus, the overall pattern of intersample differences indicates not only cross-cultural differences in illusion susceptibility, but in addition a systematic variation in those cross-cultural differences over two classes of illusion figures.

Both to illustrate and substantiate the findings which emerged from the analysis just described, proportions of individuals in each sample choosing the typically overestimated segment were computed for each item, separately for each illusion set. Psychophysical ogives were then constructed from these proportions and points of subjective equality (PSE) determined graphically. Table 1 contains PSE scores and mean number of illusion-responses for all samples on each of the illusions. (The scores shown in Table 1 were computed for internally consistent cases only, and, except where otherwise noted, the groups consisted of children and adults combined. In samples containing both children and adults, children typically had higher means and PSE's. Combining children and adults as in Table 1 tends to attenuate some intersample differences.) Figure 1 contains four sets of ogives which illustrate (i) the lesser susceptibility of the combined non-European samples as compared with the combined European samples to the Müller-Lyer and Sander Parallelogram illusions, and (ii) the greater susceptibility to the two Horizontal-vertical illusions shown by one non-European sample group as compared to one European sample, and the lesser susceptibility of another non-European sample. Examples of the four illusions are also presented in Figure 1.

Cross-cultural comparisons made over a half-century ago by Rivers (1901, 1905) also indicated that two non-Western peoples were simultaneously less susceptible to the Müller-Lyer illusion and more susceptible to the Horizontal-vertical illusion than were a group of English respondents. Since the non-European samples uniformly perform better than Europeans on one type of illusion and generally worse on the others, any explanation based on presumed contrasting characteristics of "primitive" and "civilized" peoples is difficult to maintain. Rather, evidence seems to point to cross-cultural differences in visual inference systems learned in response to different ecological and cultural factors in the visual environment. In a monograph which reports the present study in detail (Segall et al., 1966) Rivers' findings as well as our own are shown to be in accord with an empiricistic, functionalistic interpretation which

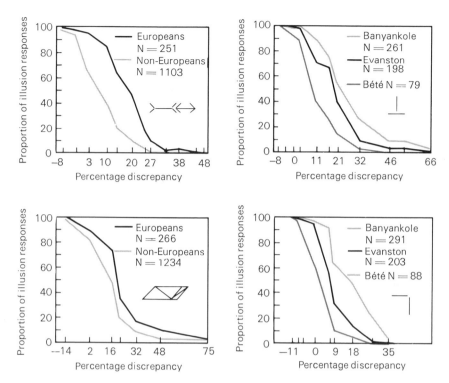

Figure 1. Psychophysical ogives based on proportions of illusion responses to item of varying percentage discrepancy. (Upper left) Müller-Lyer illusion responses plotted for Europeans (three samples combined) and non-Europeans (all other samples combined). (Lower left) Sander Parallelogram illusion responses plotted for same two combined groups. (Upper right) Horizontal-vertical(⊥) illusion responses by one European and two non-European samples. (Lower right) Horizontal-vertical (⌐) illusion responses by same three samples. These graphs are all based on internally consistent cases only.

relates visual response habits to cultural and ecological factors in the visual environment.

An example of a cultural factor which seems relevant is the prevalence of rectangularity in the visual environment, a factor which seems to be related to the tendency to interpret acute and obtuse angles on a two-dimensional surface as representative of rectangular objects in three-dimensional space. This inference habit is much more valid in highly carpentered, urban, European environments, and could enhance, or even produce, the Müller-Lyer and Sander Parallelogram illusions. This interpretation is consistent with traditional explanation of these illusions. Less clearly, the Horizontal-vertical illusion can perhaps be understood

TABLE 1
Points of Subjective Equality and Mean Number of Illusion Reponses

Group	N	PSE (%)	Mean	Group	N	PSE (%)	Mean
Müller-Lyer illusion				*Horizontal-vertical illusion* ($\perp$)			
Evanstonians	188	20.3	5.36	Suku	69	21.0	6.55
*N. U. students**	27	16.2	5.00	Banyankole	261	22.5	6.54
*S. A. Europeans**	36	13.5	4.33	Dahomeans†	57	22.3	6.49
Dahomeans†	40	11.9	4.23	Toro	105	20.0	6.44
Senegalese	125	12.2	4.18	Ijaw School†	46	20.7	6.28
Ijaw School†	54	6.6	3.67	S. A. mineboys*	69	19.3	6.27
Zulu	35	11.2	3.66	Fang	98	19.3	6.18
Toro	86	10.3	3.56	Senegalese	130	22.7	6.11
Banyankole	224	9.3	3.45	Ijaw	86	19.5	6.06
Fang	85	6.2	3.28	Bushmen*	41	19.5	5.93
Ijaw	84	6.5	3.16	*Evanstonians*	198	18.4	5.81
Songe	89	6.2	3.07	Songe	91	18.2	5.80
Hanunoo	49	7.7	3.00	*N. U. students**	29	18.7	5.72
Bete	75	3.2	2.72	Hanunoo	52	15.3	5.46
Suku	61	2.8	2.69	*S. A. Europeans**	42	15.0	5.33
Bushmen*	36	1.7	2.28	Zulu	35	9.5	4.80
S. A. mineboys*	60	1.4	2.23	Bete	79	9.8	4.62
Sander-Parallelogram illusion				*Horizontal-vertical illusion* ($\ulcorner$)			
*N. U. students**	28	19.9	3.54	Dahomeans†	63	19.2	6.52
Evanstonians	196	19.1	3.27	Toro	98	19.5	6.38
Ijaw School†	53	18.3	3.15	Banyankole	291	17.0	6.15
*S. A. Europeans**	42	17.4	2.98	Ijaw School†	57	18.4	6.02
Zulu	67	18.5	2.97	Suku	69	9.0	5.74
Senegalese	198	15.7	2.90	S. A. mineboys*	69	11.5	5.71
Fang	96	17.3	2.86	Songe	95	8.9	5.60
Ijaw	98	16.9	2.74	Ijaw	97	8.9	5.55
Banyankole	262	17.3	2.69	Fang	105	9.1	5.49
Dahomeans†	58	16.0	2.55	Bushmen*	39	8.6	5.15
Hanunoo	52	13.5	2.52	Zulu	74	7.8	5.03
Toro	105	14.3	2.49	*Evanstonians*	203	7.2	4.90
Songe	97	14.7	2.41	*N. U. students**	30	7.2	4.83
Bete	86	12.8	2.37	Hanunoo	53	6.3	4.70
Suku	91	9.7	2.14	*S. A. Europeans**	42	5.0	4.67
S. A. mineboys*	71	8.7	2.06	Senegalese	168	6.0	4.45
(Bushmen not administered this set)				Bete	88	2.0	3.81

*Adults only.
†Children only.

as the result of an inference habit of interpreting vertical lines as extensions away from one in the horizontal plane. Such an inference habit would have more validity for those living in open, flat terrain than in rain forests or canyons. An examination of such factors, and thorough examination of alternative explanations of our findings, are contained in our monograph (Segall, et al., 1966). Whether or not the correct environmental features have been isolated, the cross-cultural differences in susceptibility to geometric illusions seem best understood as symptomatic of functional differences in learned visual inference habits.

REFERENCES

Guttman, L. The Cornell technique for scale and intensity analysis, *Educ. Psychol. Measurement*, 1947, **7**, 247.

Herskovits, M. J., D. T. Campbell, and M. H. Segall. *Materials for a cross-cultural study of perception.* Evanston, Ill.: Northwestern University, program of African studies, 1956.

Rivers, W. H. R. Vision. In A. C. Haddon (ed.), *Reports of the Cambridge anthropological expedition to the Torres Straits.* Cambridge, Eng.: The University Press, 1901. Vol. 2, Part 1.

Rivers, W. H. R. Observations on the senses of the Todas, *Brit. J. Psychol.*, 1905, **1**, 321–396.

Scheffé, H. A method for judging all contrasts in the analysis of variance, *Biometrika*, 1953, **40**, 87.

Segall, M. H., D. T. Campbell, and M. J. Herskovits. *The influence of culture on perception.* Indianapolis: The Bobbs-Merrill Company, Inc., 1966.

1-4

The Trapezoidal Illusion Among Zulus

GORDON W. ALLPORT
THOMAS F. PETTIGREW

The rotating trapezoid illusion is generated by a figure cut in the form of a trapezoid which is attached to a motor and rotates at a constant speed. Panes are cut in the figure and shadows painted on it to give the impression of a window. Most observers tend to report that the rotary figure oscillates to and fro rather than revolves in a complete circle. This effect appears to be dependent on the individual's identifying the object as a rectangular window. The longer edge of the window is interpreted as being nearer and thus it appears to oscillate rather than rotate.

How would the rotating trapezoid be perceived by people with little experience with rectangular forms? The Zulus used in the present study are ideal subjects to demonstrate this effect. They live in round huts which are normally arranged in circles. Their huts have no windows and their cooking implements are round. Their language has words for "round and circle," but no words for "square and rectangle." The hypothesized difference between Western and Zulu subjects was obtained most strongly under binocular viewing at 10 feet, a condition under which it is most difficult to see the oscillation. (The Zulus reported the oscillation less frequently

Reprinted from *J. Abnorm. Soc. Psychol.*, 1957, **55**, 104–113, by permission of the authors and the American Psychological Association.

than did Western subjects.) As the effect became more obvious, the differences between these groups decreased, until under monocular viewing at 20 feet the groups did not differ. The Zulus are, of course, relatively, although not completely, deprived of experience with rectangular objects or right angles. The relative susceptibility to the trapezoidal illusion supports the effect of learning and experience on perception.

Traditionally, theories of the visual perception of movement—with which the present study deals—have been divided into two classes: 1. The *nativistic*, i.e., theories emphasizing the role of retinal and cortical functions relatively unaffected by learning, habit, experience, or meaning; and 2. The *empiricistic*, i.e., theories giving primary weight to the role of experience and learning.

For our purposes it is essential to subdivide empiricistic theories into two groups:

Cumulative habit: Stressing the effects of many types of early, remote, and generalized experience which by transfer or cross conditioning become a major determinant of the perception of movement. Toch and Ittelson (1956) state that "contemporary empiricism" favors this type of approach, offering its explanations of perceived movement in terms of "weighted averages of experiential sediments of all kinds acting inseparably."

Object connotation (meaning): Explaining perceived movement largely in terms of familiar objects. One sees continuous wing motion in an electric sign representing a bird in flight, although the stimulus actually occurs discontinuously in two or in three fixed positions. This theory would hold that our familiarity with birds in flight causes us to fill the gaps with perceived motion. A good statement of this theory of stroboscopic movement may be found in James (1890). This author insisted that "perception is of definite and probable things." In explaining illusions, James leaned heavily upon their resemblance to familiar objects. In so doing he was merely rendering more concrete and specific Helmholtz's theory of "unconscious inferences" and Wundt's "assimilation" theory.

At the present time none of these theories can be defended in their exclusive purity. F. H. Allport (1955) makes this fact abundantly clear. No empiricist, for example, can deny the native physiological substrate of the perception of movement nor its structural properties as represented by Korte's laws governing the phi-movement (Korte, 1915). Conversely, no nativist can deny the contribution that past experience may make to perceived movement. Wertheimer (1925), for instance, admits that "it is certainly correct that past experience can influence the conditions (Verhältnisse) of stroboscopic vision." Von Schiller (1933) makes the suggestion—especially important for the present research—that attitudinal set and expectancy are particularly effective in determining the perception of movement in ambiguous (*alternativ*) situations.

Many authors who have worked with perceived movement, e.g., Neff (1936) and Hall and Earle (1954), have favored an eclectic view. They have concluded that native and experiential factors both contribute, as do likewise momentary set and the previous level of adaptation. And they allow, among experiential factors, for both *cumulative habit* and *object connotation* (meaning).

While the eclectic position is no doubt correct there is, as Toch and Ittelson (1956) insist, still a fundamental question concerning "the relative primacy or importance of learning processes and physiological conditions." Theorists do tend to lean in one direction or the other. The distinction between nativists and empiricists still exists. Among the former, one thinks of Wertheimer (1925), Koffka (1935), Metzger (1936), Michotte (1946); among the latter, of Von Helmholtz (1925), Piéron (1934), Ames (1951), Wundt (1910), Cantril (1950), G. E. Müller (1923), Kilpatrick (1954), and Toch and Ittelson themselves (1956).

THE CROSS-CULTURAL APPROACH

To gain light on this dispute psychologists have often asked, "How about primitive peoples?" If we can find a tribe or a culture where relevant past experience can be ruled out, we could then determine whether the perception resembles that of western peoples. If it does so, then the argument for nativism is presumably stronger. The first extensive attempt to apply this test was made by W. H. R. Rivers (1901) during the Torres Strait expedition in 1898. Rivers presented to the island natives a whole array of visual illusions and compared their reports with western norms. For some of the illusions there were no appreciable differences; for others, the natives seemed on the whole less susceptible than westerners. While Rivers himself does not make the point clearly, his results seem to show that illusions involving object connotation (e.g., a European street scene) are far less compelling to the natives than are illusions having no such object connotation (e.g., the rotating spiral) (Rivers, 1901).

It is not easy for western psychologists to visit primitive tribes, nor to conduct among them adequately controlled experiments. The present article, however, deals with one such attempt. But before we describe it, the theoretical point at issue should be made entirely clear: *We do not claim to be testing the merits of the nativist or empiricist positions directly.* For reasons that will appear in the course of our discussion, we do not believe that comparative perceptual studies on western and on primitive peoples can solve this particular riddle. *We claim only to have illuminated the part played by object connotation (meaning) in the perception of motion as over and against the part played by either nativistic determinants or cumulative habit.* Our experiment is *not* able to distinguish between the role of these last two factors.

The Rotating Trapezoidal Window

Before the days of Gestalt psychology it was customary to regard visual illusions as oddities, as exceptional experiences to be accounted for either in terms of nativistic or experiential constraints. Today, however, we make little distinction between illusions and veridical perceptions, since no illusion lacks veridical elements and no veridical perception is devoid of subjective shaping. So-called illusions are simply instances of perception where the discrepancy between impression and knowledge (whether the knowledge be the subject's or the experimenter's) is relatively striking. It is in such "looser" conditions of perception that theorists often seek to obtain light on the relative weight of factors entering into the normal perceptual process. The reasoning is not unlike that which leads psychologists to study exaggerated functions in psychopathology in order to obtain light on the same but less exaggerated functions of the normal mind.

Our experiment follows this logic, making use of the rotating trapezoidal window described by Ames (1951)—a device that has been called "a dramatic masterpiece of ambiguous stimulation" (Allport, 1955, p. 276). The window is so proportioned that as it rotates, the length of the longer edge is always longer on the retina than is the shorter edge (even when the shorter edge is nearer). The resulting perception is normally one of oscillation or sway; the observer apparently tending to keep the longer edge nearer to him. Instead of seeming to rotate, as it actually does, the window is seen to sway back and forth in an arc of 90 to 180 degrees.

An appended cube and rod add great interest to the illusion, since the perceived *rotating* of these objects conflicts sharply with the perceived *sway* of the window. In consequence, the cube is usually seen to detach itself and swing without support in a ghostly fashion in front of the window (for that period of time when the shorter edge, to which it is attached, is in fact nearer to the subject). Similarly, the rod bends, twists or "cuts through" the mullions in order to accommodate itself to the phenomenal oscillation. The observer finds the bizarre effect both amusing and inexplicable.

The window used in the present experiment is smaller than the original Ames window; length 13¼ inches, height of the long side 12½ inches, height of the short side 9 inches. Ames demonstrated that within limits the ratio of the sides of the trapezoid to one another cannot affect the illusion. The optimum speed of rotation Ames reports as 3 to 6 r.p.m. Our own motor driven window ran slightly less than 2 r.p.m. The original Ames window had mullions dividing it into 15 frames; ours had 6 frames (probably more normal for a "window"). For certain comparisons, we employed also a true rectangular window, 12″ x 10½″.

The explanation Ames gives for the illusion maintains (*a*) that the observer, owing to familiarity with rectangular windows, assumes *this* window to be rectangular; and (*b*) that owing to long experience with doors, windows, and similar objects, the observer has learned to interpret longer retinal stimulations as coming from nearer objects. Hence, the longer edge of the window is interpreted as being nearer, and the window is seen to oscillate rather than to rotate.

Ames (1951) gives a clearly empiricistic explanation with a leaning toward the object connotation version:

> In his past experience the observer, in carrying out his purposes, has on innumerable occasions had to take into account and act with respect to rectangular forms, e.g., going through doors, locating windows, etc. On almost all such occasions, except in the rare case when his line of sight was normal to the door or window, the image of the rectangular configuration formed on his retina was trapezoidal. He learned to interpret the particularly characteristic retinal images that exist when he looks at doors, windows, etc., as rectangular forms. Moreover, he learned to interpret the particular degree of trapezoidal distortion of his retinal images in terms of the positioning of the rectangular form to his particular viewing point. These interpretations do not occur at the conscious level, rather, they are unconscious and may be characterized as *assumptions* as to the probable significance of indications received from the environment.

It should be added that Ames does not insist that object connotation ("windowness") is the sole determinant of the illusion. He himself employed a variety of trapezoidal figures and discovered that even a plane surface of trapezoidal shape arouses the illusion of sway, though to a much less degree than does a "window frame" (Ames, 1951).

The Hypothesis

In order to test the "object connotation" theory, we studied various groups of Zulu children (10–14 years old) in Natal whose own culture is virtually devoid not only of windows, but, to a surprising extent, of angles, straight lines, and other experiential cues that would presumably "cause" the illusion if it were wholly a product of experience. Our hypothesis therefore is:

Zulu children, provided they are unacculturated (amabinca) *will report the illusion of sway in the trapezoidal window less often than will urbanized acculturated Zulu children* (amabunguka) *or than white* (*"European"*) *children.*

The Zulu Culture

Zulu culture is probably the most spherical or circular of all Bantu cultures, possibly the most spherical of all native African cultures (though it would be difficult to prove this contention). The word "zulu" means heavens or firmament, and the aesthetic ideal of round rather than angular styles affects native art, architecture, and speech.

Huts are invariably round (rondavels) or else beehive shaped, whereas in other Bantu tribes they are sometimes square or rectangular. Round huts arranged in a circular form with round stockades to fence in animals, constitutes a typical African homestead (kraal). Fields follow the irregular contours of the rolling land, and never seem to be laid out in the neat rectangular plots so characteristic of western culture.

The typical Zulu hut has no windows, and no word for such an apperture exists. In the more primitive beehive grass huts, doors are merely round entrance holes; in the round mud huts doors are amorphous, seldom if ever neatly rectangular. Cooking pots are round or gourd shaped. In his studies among Zulus, Doob (1957) finds that the less acculturated natives, relative to westernized natives, show a statistically significant preference for circles over squares when they are asked to choose between designs drawn in these shapes (personal communication to the authors).

It is commonly said in Natal that Zulus fresh from reserves cannot plow a straight furrow and are unable to lay out a rectangular flower bed. Such inability is of course overcome with experience and training, but the initial defect would seem clearly related to the circularity that is characteristic of life on the reserves and to the lack of familiarity with straight layouts.

Linguistically, the same bias towards circularity is seen. While it is possible to say "round" in Zulu, there is no word for "square." There is a word for "circle" but not for "rectangle." To speak of window, of square, or of rectangle at all, a Zulu is forced to borrow these terms from Afrikaans or from English—provided he is able to do so.

The Subjects

The experiment required the use of two contrasting groups of subjects (Ss): those who had lived all or most of their lives in western culture, and those who were unacculturated. Even in the Bantu reserves or in Zululand itself it is not possible to make certain that a resident does not know what a window is like. While schools, churches, and health centers are few and far between, they are nevertheless within the possible range of visitation by most native inhabitants, even children. Our experiments at Polela and Ceza took place in health centers, at Nongoma in a court house. The Ss, to be sure, were brought in from remote parts of the reserves by lorry, or came on foot; but they had at least this one-time acquaintance with a rectangular building and windows.

Still, it is possible to say that the experiment dealt with two widely contrasting groups in respect to the degree of experience they had had with western architecture and ways of life. Some members of the more primitive groups, for example, may never have seen windows with rectangular panes of glass prior to the actual experimental situation.

By using herd boys as Ss—mostly between 10 and 14 years of age (few of them knew their age exactly)—we were able to make certain that they had never been off the reserves and had never attended school. Boys of the same age comprised our urban control groups: one group of European boys at Greyville Community Center; another group of Bantu boys at the Lamontville Community Center in Durban. Most of these urban boys were attending school.

Our major experiment thus involved the following groups:

Group A	Urban European boys	(20 cases)
Group B	Urban African boys˙	(20 cases)
Group C	Polela Rural Africans	(20 cases)
Group D	Nongoma Rural Africans	(20 cases)

A rough indication of the cultural differences between the rural and urban groups lies in answers to the question asked at the end of the experiment about the rectangular window, "What does this look like?" The percentage saying "window" or "window frame" among the urban children was 88; among the rural, 45.

Procedure

The procedure involves four conditions, varying two factors bearing on the perception of the illusion: monocular vs. binocular viewing and distance from the stimulus object. Each S saw first the rectangular, and then the trapezoidal window in at least 3 full revolutions under each of the following conditions.

First trial: 10 ft.	binocular
Second trial: 10 ft.	monocular
Third trial: 20 ft.	binocular
Fourth trial: 20 ft.	monocular

It was thought that this order would impose the "hardest" condition first and therefore minimize the effects of suggestion. One might fear that if at 20 feet with one eye a subject easily perceived the illusion he might become accustomed to expecting oscillation in the trapezoidal window at closer distances and under binocular conditions. Conversely, of course, it might be argued that a subject who cannot perceive the illusion at ten feet binocularly would form an expectation that might prevent his obtaining it under easier conditions. We shall refer later to a control experiment (starting at 20 feet monocularly) designed to check on any suggestive effect that might arise from our order of presentation.

The experimenter (E) required the assistance of a second psychologist who kept records of the Ss' reports, also of an interpreter with all African Ss. Care was taken to prevent Ss who had finished the experiment from communicating with Ss who had not.

After being put at ease, the S gave his age (if he knew it) and his degree of education (if any). The S then sat in a chair placed at the proper distance from the window and was told to watch carefully the movement that he would see. After approximately three revolutions the E asked, "How does it seem to you to be moving?" Often the S spontaneously used his hands to indicate the motion until the E was satisfied whether a full rotation or a fluctuation was intended. The use of hand motion by the S proved to be fully convincing, for when he reversed the hand at precisely the right moment for the illusion to occur there could be no question concerning his experience. This device gave a useful check on the accuracy of the translator's report of the S's verbal statements.

After obtaining a report for the rectangular window in each of the positions, the trapezoidal window was inserted in place of the rectangular, and the same method of report employed. In addition, the S was asked to tell whether the motion of the trapezoidal window was "like" that of the first window. This procedure served as a further check on the verbal description and hand report. In nearly all cases it was possible to record a clear and unequivocal judgment of the S's perception. Less than three per cent of all judgments were listed by the E as "uncertain."

Whenever the illusion was reported for the first condition, the bar was inserted and the S asked, "How does the bar move?" and "Does the bar stay straight?" On occasional trials when the S had reported both the sway of the window and the bending of the bar, the cube was attached and the S asked to describe its motion. In these cases there was usually laughter (as with American Ss) and considerable confusion and difficulty manifested in describing so unreal and "spooky" a motion. Because of the difficulty of communicating concerning these complex phenomena we make no further systematic use of the cube and rod in the present study.

At the conclusion of the experiment, the S was asked what the rectangular window "looked like." He also stated his preference for one of two geometrical drawings presented to him in pairs (a circle, square, trapezoid). He then received a slight payment for his services (usually one pound of sugar or a candy bar and sixpence).

RESULTS

GENERAL RESULTS. Table 1 gives the results for the two unacculturated groups (Nongoma and Polela Reserves) and for the two districts within metropolitan Durban, African (Lamontville), and European (Greyville).

Combining all four conditions, there is a very significant tendency for the urban groups to report the illusion more often than the rural groups (corrected 2×2 $X^2 = 15.34$; $p < .001$). This difference is most marked with the first condition (corrected 2×2 $X^2 = 12.38$; $p < .001$). There is also a significant trend with the second condition (corrected 2×2 $X^2 = 4.80$; $p < .05$) and a slight tendency with the third condition (corrected 2×2 $X^2 = 1.87$; $p < .20$) for the rural children to observe the illusion less often than the urban children. Virtually no difference exists with the fourth, 20 feet and one eye condition.

TABLE 1
Number Reporting Illusion*

Condition	Nongoma Rural			Polela Rural			African Urban			Urban European		
	Yes	No	Uncer-tain	Yes	No	Uncer-tain	Yes	No	Uncer-tain	Yes	No	Uncer-tain
First condition (10′, both eyes)	3	17	0	4	14	2	13	7	0	11	9	0
Second condition (10′, one eye)	14	6	0	16	4	0	19	1	0	19	1	0
Third condition (20′, both eyes)	8	12	0	17	1	2	16	3	1	16	4	0
Fourth condition (20′, one eye)	18	2	0	17	2	1	18	2	0	19	0	1
Total	43	37	0	54	21	5	66	13	1	65	14	1

*Boys 10–14 yrs. of age; $N = 20$ in each group.

Table 2 expresses the results in an alternative way. Since four conditions of presentation were used we can determine in how many of these four conditions on the average each of the cultural groups reported the illusion. For the two unacculturated groups combined, the illusion is reported in 2.425 of the four conditions, while for the acculturated groups the average is 3.275. This mean difference has high statistical significance ($t = 3.51$; $p < .001$).

It is evident from Tables 1 and 2 that city dwellers, whether Zulu or European, find the illusion somewhat more compelling than do rural ("primitive") natives. This tendency is especially pronounced at 10 feet with binocular vision—a condition when binocular cues of true depth (in this case, true rotation) are most plentiful. The reader will also note that the results for Polela (rural) stand somewhat between those for the city children and those from Nongoma (rural). At ten feet binocularly, they resemble those of Nongoma; at twenty feet binocularly, those of the city boys. Polela is, in fact, one hundred miles closer to Durban than is Nongoma which lies in the heart of Zululand. There is no doubt that the children in Polela have somewhat more familiarity with western architecture (specifically with windows) than do the children of Nongoma. The results (Table 2) correspond to a continuum of cultures: city children having a maximum of familiarity with western architecture, Nongoma children the least.

TABLE 2
Distribution of Scores

Sample	Number of Yes's					Average
	4	3	2	1	0	
Nongoma	2	4	10	3	1	2.15
Polela	4	10	3	2	1	2.70
Urban African	12	4	2	2	0	3.30
Urban European	11	5	3	0	1	3.25
Total ($N = 80$)	29	23	18	7	3	2.85

PREFERENCE FOR CIRCLES. Following the experiment, all Ss were shown drawings of a square, a trapezoid, and a circle (in pairs), and asked to express a preference. Table 3 indicates that those who expressed a preference for the circle (at least once in the two pairings) tend in the African groups to report the illusion *less* often. This tendency holds for all experimental conditions for all three African groups. The relationship is statistically significant, however, for only the binocular conditions. Circle-preferring Zulu children report the illusion significantly less often than the angle-preferring Zulus in Conditions 1 and 3 (corrected 2×2 $X^2=3.89$; $p < .05$), but the difference in the monocular, second and fourth, conditions is not significant (corrected 2×2 $X^2 = 0.18$, *n.s.*). There are no differences approaching significance between the circle and noncircle-preferring European Ss.

TABLE 3
Percentage of Cases Reporting Illusion among Subjects Preferring
and Not Preferring Circle

Condition	Combined African Groups $N = 60$		European Group $N = 20$	
	Preferring Circle $N = 39$	Not Preferring Circle $N = 21$	Preferring Circle $N = 12$	Not Preferring Circle $N = 8$
10' binocular	28	43	58	50
10' monocular	79	86	100	88
20' binocular	59	86	83	75
20' monocular	87	90	100	88
All conditions	63	76	85	75

Let us assume that the aesthetic preference for circles may provide an index of the subjective closeness of the individual to Zulu culture (since it is, as we have seen, overwhelmingly a circular culture). If we do so we may say that this subjective closeness seems to predispose the S to resist the illusion. Stated in terms of transactional theory, rectangles and trapezoids have less functional significance for him. His perception of the window's rotation is accordingly more frequently veridical.

We have noted that this influence is significant only in the conditions involving *binocular* perception. A reasonable interpretation would be that cultural effects cannot easily change the basic demand character of the illusion monocularly perceived, but may do so when binocular conditions leave more latitude for choice and for interpretation among a greater number of cues.

This result then, so far as it goes, lends some weight to the contention that "cultural significance" is playing an appreciable part in determining the results.

ILLUSION WITH RECTANGLE. Before viewing the trapezoidal window, every S in all four conditions first saw the rectangular window rotating. The purpose was to make sure that the sway (oscillation) reported for the trapezoid was judged to be *different* from the motion of the rectangular window. In most cases, indeed, the S was able to make the distinction clearly, indicating by gesture and by words that the rectangular window went "round and round" whereas the trapezoid oscillated.

There were cases, however, where the rectangular window was reported as oscillating. In fact, nearly one-third of the 80 Ss reported such a phenomenon at one or more of the four conditions. The actual percentage reporting sway in the *rectangular* window at each of the four conditions is:

> First condition   0
> Second condition   8
> Third condition   16
> Fourth condition   28

It is conceivable that this curious and somewhat unwelcomed finding may be a result of a "suggestive" order of presentation. Thus, no S seeing the rectangle before the trapezoid under the first condition (10 feet binocularly) reported the phenomenon. And, with the exception of 3 cases, no S reported the rectangular illusion in the second, third, or fourth condition *unless* he had previously reported the trapezoidal illusion. Altogether, 81 per cent of our Ss reported the illusion monocularly at 20 feet for the trapezoidal window, but only 28 per cent did so for the rectangular window under the same condition. In virtually all these cases the Ss had grown accustomed to seeing oscillation at some previous stage with the trapezoid.

Pastore (1952), however, finds that more than half of his 58 American college Ss reported sway with the rectangle during a three-minute exposure, and at considerable distance from the window (where the retinal angle subtended by the two shapes may be subliminal). He does not tell whether the Ss had grown accustomed to the sway of the trapezoid before they reported sway in the rectangle. We must leave this problem for the time being unsolved.

A CONTROL EXPERIMENT

In order to determine whether unwanted suggestive effects, caused by our order of presentation, were influencing the results at the optimal stage for the trapezoidal illusion (viz., 20' monocularly) we simplified our procedure with entirely new Ss. Urban and rural Africans served as before. To secure the latter, we visited the Ceza Medical Mission in Zululand, approximately 20 miles from Nongoma. Both Ceza and Nongoma are in the deepest part of the native reserves, over 200 miles north of Durban. Polela, as we have said, lies about 100 miles west of Durban and has more European influence (e.g., European-style architecture). This fact, we repeat, seems to explain why, as Tables 1 and 2 show, the Polela Ss report the illusion somewhat more frequently than do Ss at Nongoma or Ceza.

In the control experiment, the S was asked to cover one eye. Sitting at twenty feet from the rotating trapezoidal window he then described its motion (both in words and by hand motion). Later he was seated at ten feet from the object and using both eyes described the motion, comparing it with the previous motion. Finally he was, as in the other groups, asked his preference for the circular, square, or trapezoidal figures. None of these herd boys had ever been to school.

For an urban control group we used a fresh population of Lamontville boys of the same age range.

Results

Table 4 gives the results.

These data are practically identical with those of the Nongoma and urban African samples cited previously. Again, the rural Zulu group reported the illusion significantly less often than the urban Zulu group in 10' binocular condition (corrected 2×2 $X^2 = 11.53$; $p < .001$), but no differences appear at the 20' monocular condition. This similarity of data proves that the order of presentation is not an important variable.

At the Ceza Mission Hospital we tested also a group of eleven expectant mothers, only one of whom had ever left the reserve. Eight reported the illusion at 20' monocularly, two did not, and one was uncertain. None of the eleven, however, reported it at 10' binocularly. These cases confirm the trend in all our tables that "primitives" are less able to perceive the sway in the trapezoidal window illusion under marginal conditions (i.e., at 10' binocularly) than are city dwellers.

TABLE 4
Number Reporting Illusion in Control Experiment

Condition	Ceza (Rural) $N = 24$			Lamontville (Urban) $N = 21$		
	Yes	No	Uncertain	Yes	No	Uncertain
First condition (20', monocular)	22	2	0	20	0	1
Second condition (10', binocular)	2	18	4	14	7	0

TABLE 5
Percentage of Cases Reporting Illusion among Subjects
Preferring Two Circles*

Condition	Preferring Two Circles $N = 15$	Preferring Less than Two $N = 29$
20' monocular	92	97
10' binocular	27	38

*Combined African Groups (Ceza and Lamontville); $N = 44$.

Something should be said concerning the qualitative differences reported by Ss who first reported the illusion at 20′ monocularly and then again at 10′ binocularly. Not infrequently their reports at 10′ binocularly were "mixed," that is to say, sometimes they saw the oscillation and sometimes not. In every case, the S was asked to tell the "difference" if any existed between the movement seen at 20′ monocularly and that at 10′ binocularly. Most Ss claimed that there was a difference; sometimes the window at the closer distance seemed to move faster, sometimes in a bigger arc, sometimes even in the reverse direction. And often, as we have said, the reports at 10′ binocularly were "mixed"— the subjects reporting sometimes a full rotation and sometimes a sway. We record "yes" to the illusion at 10′ binocularly if at any point in the experiment the S reports a clear oscillation. Since the same criteria were applied at both Ceza and Lamontville, no source of error is introduced.

If the reader is acquainted with the illusion he will no doubt recognize this ambiguity in the perception at 10′ when binocular cues are powerful evidence for true rotation, and yet the tendency to see illusory sway likewise exists. Because of this dual tendency we consider 10′ binocularly as a *marginal* condition for the illusion. What is important for our purposes is the finding that under such marginal conditions urban children, who are familiar with western architecture, report the illusion much more frequently than do herd boys on the Zulu reserves.

TABLE 6
Percentage of Subjects Recognizing Stimulus as a "Window"
Who Report the Illusion

Condition	Recognizing "Window" N = 20	Not Recognizing "Window" N = 24
20′ monocular	100	88
10′ binocular	55	29

As in the major experiment our Ss expressed their preference, in three paired comparisons, for a circle, trapezoid, or square. Since only seven cases of the 45 failed to choose the circle at least once, we changed our criterion slightly from that used in Table 3. We determined the occurrence of the illusion among those who chose the circle *twice* as compared with those who chose it only once or not at all. Table 5 shows that in this population likewise, Ss who show a preference for circles tend—particularly in the binocular condition—to report the illusion somewhat less frequently than those who do not. The differences are not statistically significant but are in the same direction as those reported in

Table 3. The implication of this finding, we repeat, seems to be that Ss whose aesthetic preference lies with the circularity of their tribal culture are the more resistant to the illusion.

At the conclusion of the experiment the investigator showed each S the rectangular window and asked, "What is this?" (In order to make certain that the children would have an opportunity to say "window" if they perceived the resemblance, the question was asked in three different ways in the Zulu language.) To one or more of these three questionings 67 per cent of the urban children said "window," but only 26 per cent of the Ceza children gave the same reply. If we combine all cases who said "window" at both Ceza and Lamontville we find an appreciable, though not statistically significant, tendency for them to report the illusion more often than do children who did not recognize the windowness of the stimulus object (corrected 2×2 $X^2 = 2.81$; $p < .10$ when both conditions are combined). So far as it goes, this finding (Table 6) lends support to the object-connotation theory of the perception of movement, especially under the 10' binocular condition.

DISCUSSION

Our most striking finding is that under optimal conditions (monocularly at 20 feet) virtually as many primitive Zulus report the trapezoidal illusion as do urban Zulus or Europeans. Taking this one partial result by itself we can say that the experiment supports either the nativistic or the cumulative habit theory. It does not by itself give us grounds for choosing between them.

Nativists might argue, for example, that whenever a longer and a shorter projection on the retina occur simultaneously the longer will assume a figure character and therewith a frontal position in the perception (other conditions being equal). Thus, some form of isomorphism obtains between retinal-cortical processes and the perception itself.

An empiricist with a "cumulative habit" preference might say that myriad ocular-motor adjustments from infancy have built up a dependable expectancy that longer projections on the retina will betoken nearer objects. One learns through repeated experience that longer retinal images of trees, cattle, people, stand for *nearer* objects (provided, of course, that one assumes such objects to be of equal size whether far or near from the eyes). It is not necessary for the S to have acquaintance with specific objects (in this case a window) in order to make a similar inference. The transfer effect is wide. Even the shadows painted on the rotating window are reminiscent of the S's experience with shadows in nature. Old experiences automatically condition novel experiences even though the latter are only analogous.

One assumption that may play a decisive part in this case is the assumption of "right angularity." From earliest life the child is conditioned to the fact that perpendicular objects best withstand the force of gravity. Circular though his culture is, his basic frame of reference is still one of verticals and horizontals. Seeing an entirely new object (the trapezoidal window) he assumes unconsciously (no less than do people who are familiar with windows) that its shape is rectangular. Just like people in western culture he may make this assumption even if he "knows" that the object is not in reality rectangular. This assumption, together with the assumption that longer objects on the retina are usually nearer objects, would predispose him to perceive that the longer edge of the window is always nearer (thus inducing the perceived oscillation). No less than people in western culture he would fail to "correct" his assumptions of right-angularity and of long-edges-being-near-edges by his "knowledge" of the trapezoidal shape of the stimulus.

Our major result is clearly not compatible with a narrowly conceived object-connotation theory. It is not necessary for the S consciously to assume that the object is a window in order to experience the illusion. True, as Table 6 suggests, the specific object connotation seems somewhat to favor the illusion, but it is clearly not the decisive determinant. Thus, for example, 88 per cent of those who did not consciously recognize the frame as a "window" nevertheless experienced the illusion at 20′ monocularly.

Yet, at the same time, our results show that object connotation cannot be disregarded. It also plays a part. Let us review the evidence:

1. Under all *suboptimal* conditions, as we see in Tables 1 and 4 (10 feet monocularly, and binocularly at 10 or 20 feet) there is a tendency for unacculturated Ss to report the illusion less frequently than do the acculturated.

2. The Ss who recognize the "windowness" of the stimulus object tend to report the illusion somewhat more frequently especially at 10 feet binocularly (Table 6).

3. African Ss expressing a preference for circles (assumed here to indicate a subjective closeness to the rotund Zulu culture) tend to report the illusion less often than those expressing preference for angular figures (Tables 3 and 5).

We conclude that experience with, and identification with, western culture make it more likely that the illusion will be perceived under marginal (suboptimal) conditions.

One fact reported by Ames, and mentioned above, supports our interpretation. He finds that a plane trapezoidal frame yields appreciable oscillation, but that the addition of mullions, panes, and shadows enhances the illusion. In other words, specific "thingness" contributes to the experience though it does not account for it wholly (Doob, 1957, pp.

28–31). And we may again allude to von Schiller's contention that expectancy is effective in determining perceived movement under marginal (*alternative*) conditions.

Brenner (1956) likewise makes the point that when marginal conditions obtain, the S is forced to depend on stimulus *meaning*. On the other hand, when optimal stimulus conditions obtain, even brain-damaged cases report apparent movement to much the same degree as do normal cases.

Several other experiments have dealt with the effects of meaning on apparent movement. Thus, Jones and Bruner (1954) report that in a stroboscopic experiment the line drawing of a man is seen to be in motion more actively than is a nonsense figure. De Silva (1926) had previously established this same fact. Jones and Bruner (1954) conclude that "the more probable and practiced the movement, the more adequately will the movement experience maintain itself under suboptimal conditions." This conclusion is in agreement with our own.

Toch and Ittelson (1956) report an experiment in which drawings of a bomb stroboscopically presented are seen in a downward (falling) motion, whereas drawings of an airplane presented in an identical fashion are seen in an upward (rising) motion. Though this experiment taken by itself favors an object-connotation theory, the authors argue in general for the cumulative-habit theory. They contend, rightly no doubt, that the nativist position cannot be adequately tested short of a longitudinal study of infants from birth. They believe that generalized past experience accounts for our major dispositions to perceive stroboscopic or other illusory movement, but allow that under conditions of ambiguity or equivocation specific meaning connotations will enter to determine the direction and nature of the movement. Here, too, our findings are concordant.

If we leave the field of experimental testing for a moment, we can find many familiar instances of the role of object connotation in resolving perceptual ambiguities. A streak of light in the night sky may be seen as a shooting star, as distant fireworks, or as a jet plane, depending largely on one's expectations. Bartlett tells of the Swazi chieftain who perceived all traffic policemen in London as friendly beings, because in Swazi culture the upraised arm is an amiable greeting. A child in a dentist's chair, more familiar with space-ships than with nitrous oxide, perceives the inhalator as a spaceship toy. Every projective test assumes that ambiguous (multivalent) stimuli will receive subjective structuring on the basis of need, set, expectancy, or habit.

Our experiment does not introduce factors of need or of set, but deals only with the relevance of past experience (meaning) as a determinant of perceived movement. It may, however, be pointed out that among sophisticated observers of the trapezoidal illusion under marginal conditions (e.g., at 10 feet binocularly) a voluntary effort to see or not to see the window as oscillating (or as rotating) can also be effective, especially if the observer picks out some detail of the window to watch during the rotation, thus inhibiting the impression as a whole. Meaning is not the only determinant entering into the resolution of perceptual ambiguity, but it is one of them.

Returning to James's statement that, "Perception is of definite and probable things," we may say that under optimal conditions of stimulation definite structure is conferred by physiological conditions or by deeply ingrained functional habits of spatial adjustment, or by both. But when marginal conditions prevail, an association with the most "probable" object is often called upon to provide the definiteness that is otherwise lacking.

What we have called "marginal" conditions should receive a further word of explanation. We use the term in our experiments to indicate that perceptual conflict is present. Under binocular conditions (especially at 10′) there are many cues that "give away" the true rotation; at the same time there are operating also the assumptions that the window is rectangular and that longer objects are nearer. Under such a condition of conflict our finding is that urban children resolve the conflict with the aid of the supplementary assumption of "windowness." Not being able to draw on this supplementary assumption, the rural children as a rule resolve the conflict in favor of the binocular (or true) evidence. In this particular case, therefore, one might say that the primitive children see things "as they are" more often than do the children of civilization.

CONCLUSION

The perception of motion as represented in the rotating trapezoidal window is governed, under *optimal* conditions, by nativistic determinants or by the unconscious utilization of residual (but not immediately relevant) experience, or by both. (Our experiment does not enable us to decide this issue.) At the same time, object connotation (meaning) based on closely relevant cultural experience helps to determine the nature of the perceived movement under *marginal* conditions.

An adequate theory of perceived movement must therefore allow a place for the subject's specific assumptions of meaning even though it cannot be based solely on this foundation.

REFERENCES

Allport, F. H. *Theories of perception and the concept of structure.* New York: John Wiley & Sons, Inc., 1955.

Ames, A., Jr. Visual perception and the rotating trapezoidal window, *Psychol. Mongr.*, 1951, **65**, No. 7 (Whole No. 324).

Brenner, May W. The effects of brain damage on the perception of apparent movements, *J. Pers.*, 1956, **25**, 202–212.

Cantril, H. *The "why" of man's experience.* New York: The Macmillan Company, 1950.

DeSilva, H. R. An experimental investigation of the determinants of apparent visual movement, *Amer. J. Psychol.*, 1926, **37**, 469–501.

Doob, L. An introduction to the psychology of acculturation, *J. Soc. Psychol.*, 1957.

Hall, K. R. L. and A. E. Earle. A further study of the pendulum phenomenon, *Quart. J. Exp. Psychol.*, 1954, **6**, 112–124.

Helmholtz, H. von. *Physiological optics.* Vol. III, Chaps. 26, 78. Translated by J. P. C. Southall. Optical Society of America, 1925.

James, W. *Principles of psychology.* Vol. II, Chap. 19. New York: Henry Holt, 1890.

Jones, E. E. and J. S. Bruner. Expectancy in apparent visual movement, *Brit. J. Psychol.*, 1954, **45**, 157–165.

Kilpatrick, F. P. Two processes in perceptual learning, *J. Exp. Psychol.*, 1954, **47**, 362–370.

Koffka, K. *Principles of Gestalt psychology.* New York: Harcourt, Brace & World, Inc., 1935.

Korte, A. Kinematoskopische Untersuchungen, *Z. F. Psychol.*, 1915, **72**, 193–206.

Metzger, W. *Gesetze des Sehens.* Frankfurt: Kramer, 1936.

Michotte, A. *La perception de la causalité.* Paris: Vrin, 1946.

Müller, G. E. *Komplextheorie und Gestalttheorie.* Göttingen: Vandenhoeck & Ruprecht, 1923.

Neff, W. S. A critical investigation of the visual apprehension of movement, *Amer. J. Psychol.*, 1936, **48**, 1–42.

Pastore, N. Some remarks on the Ames oscillatory effect, *Psychol. Rev.*, 1952, **59**, 319–323.

Piéron, H. Remarques sur la perception du mouvement apparent, *Année Psychol.*, 1934, **34**, 245–248.

Rivers, W. H. R. Introduction and vision. In A.C. Haddon (ed.), Reports of *Cambridge anthropological expedition to Torres Straits.* Vol. II, Part 1. Cambridge, Eng.: University Press, 1901.

Schiller, P. von. Stroboskopische Alternativversuch, *Psychol. Forsch*, 1933, **17**, 179–214.

Toch, H. H., and W. H. Ittelson. The role of past experience in apparent movement: A revaluation, *Brit. J. Psychol.*, 1956, **47**, No. 3, 195–207.

Wertheimer, M. *Experimentelle Studien über das Sehen von Bewegung. Drei Abhandlungen zur Gestalttheorie.* Erlangen: Verlag d. Phil. Akad., 1925, 1–105.

Wundt, W. *Gründzüge der physiologischen Psychologie.* Vol. II (6th ed.). Leipzig: W. Engelmann, 1910.

1-5

Dominance in Binocular Rivalry in Mexico and the United States

JAMES W. BAGBY

Binocular rivalry and dominance occur when a subject is stereo-scopically shown a pair of different photographs in such a manner that each eye is presented with only one member of the pair. The subject sees only one of the two pictures at a time, or one picture is seen earlier than the other. In the following study, the American subjects tended to recognize pictures with American contents more easily, while the Mexicans tended to recognize pictures with Mexican contents more easily. Two factors seem to be important in these cultural differences of visual recognition. The individual will most readily identify stimuli that are similar in content to his most frequent visual experiences. Furthermore, previous pleasant associations with the stimuli also facilitate recognition.

Only recently has research on binocular rivalry and fusion begun to explore the influence that objects which possess particular significance or meaning for an observer have upon him. Most former work had used

Reprinted from *J. Abnorm. Soc. Psychol.*, 1957, **54**, 331–334, by permission of the author and the American Psychological Association.

abstract figures, circles, squares, colored patches, discrepant lines and the like. Consequently the principles of binocular fusion were elaborated on the basis of studies employing such abstract forms. A recent series of investigations by Engel (1955), which employed photographs of people and objects, has demonstrated that there are important empirical and theoretical consequences when "meaningful" content is introduced in fusion and rivalry experimentation. This work strongly suggests that meaning for the perceiver is influential in the binocular resolutions achieved.

Binocular presentation of materials of disparate content and of varying subjective significance thus appears to be a technique of considerable value for psychology (Bagby, 1955; Bagby, 1956; Engel, 1956). The binocular conflict method offers an approach for ascertaining the role of a variety of factors in the perceptual processes. The nature of the specific resolution of two affectively charged pictures which Engel (1955) presented to his subjects, for example, appeared to derive from an unconscious and spontaneous choice on the part of the subject. Although a large number of resolutions were possible, the perceptual choices were shown to reflect the subject's actual feelings and dispositions. There is need, however, for much further work to clarify the phenomena encountered in such situations of binocular conflict.

The present investigation is concerned with discovering whether the cultural characteristics of conflicting visual presentations are differentially perceived by members of different societies. Presented with a situation of simultaneous binocular rivalry, do subjects perceive more readily and consistently visual presentations of content drawn from their own culture than presentations of similar content from another society? The present study investigated this question with respect to Mexicans and Americans.

METHOD

Subjects

There were two experimental groups, one composed of 12 Mexican Ss, and the other composed of 12 American Ss. Half of each experimental group were males and the other half females. They ranged in age from 16 to 42 years. All of the Ss had 20–20 vision. Each S in the Mexican group was matched with an American counterpart as to sex, age, education, occupation and socioeconomic status. Table 1 presents some characteristics of the matched Ss.

An examination of Table 1 reveals that the Mexican Ss were largely middle-class residents of interior provincial centers and that they possessed superior educational backgrounds. The American Ss were residents from Northeast, Middle Atlantic, and Midwestern states with similar educational and socioeconomic backgrounds. With the exception of one matched pair, no S had traveled outside his own country. Thus, for both Mexican and American Ss, the knowledge of the opposite culture was limited to books, the mass communication media, secondhand experience, and other similar sources.

TABLE 1
Some Characteristics of Mexican and American Ss

Male Ss		Age	Education†		Occupation	SES‡	Geographic Residence
A		32	17		Statistician	Middle	Chihuahua
	A'	30		16	Accountant	Middle	New York
B		19	13		Student	Middle	Durango
	B'	18		13	Student	Middle	Connecticut
C		20	15		English student	Upper	Coahuila
	C'	20		15	English student	Upper	Wisconsin
D		19	13		Mathematics student	Middle	Jalisco
	D'	18		13	Mathematics student	Middle	Pennsylvania
E		20	14		Education student	Middle	Morelia
	E'	20		14	Education student	Middle	New York
F		23	12		Fine artist	Upper	Mexico City
	F'	22		13	Commercial artist	Upper	Massachusetts
Female Ss							
G		27	17		College teacher	Upper	Torreon
	G'	27		16	High school teacher	Middle	Kentucky
H		42	16		Language teacher	Middle	Coahuila
	H'	40		17	Language teacher	Middle	New England
I		33	16		Elementary teacher	Middle	Chihuahua
	I'	32		16	Elementary teacher	Middle	Illinois
J		16	11		Student	Upper	Guadalajara
	J'	17		12	Student	Upper	New Jersey
K		27	12		Artist	Middle	Jalisco
	K'	30		16	Art teacher	Middle	Iowa
L		29	16		Teacher	Middle	Guanajuato
	L'	31		16	Teacher	Middle	Colorado

*Ss matched: A, Mexican—A', American; B, Mexican—B', American, etc.
†Numeral refers to years of formal education. Thus, 11 is equivalent to junior year in high school, 17 is equivalent to one year beyond college graduation etc.
‡SES refers to socioeconomic status in three groupings: upper, middle and lower classes.

Stimulus Material

Ten pairs of photographic slides were presented. In each pair, one photograph was of a typical Mexican scene including one or more persons, and the other was a photograph of a similar American scene. The picture had been reduced or enlarged to occupy a standard 2″ by 2″ area. An attempt was made to attain similarity in the form, contour of major mass, texture, definition, and light and shadow of the paired scenes.

The following were the 10 stereogram slide pairs:

I. An American business man and a Mexican peasant.
II. A blonde American girl and a dark Mexican girl.
III. An old farm woman and an Indian peasant woman.
IV. An old farm man and a Mexican peon.
V. An American miner and a Latin American miner.
VI. An American wedding scene of a bride and groom and a traditional Mexican wedding scene.
VII. An American farm couple and an Indian couple.
VIII. A blonde American mother with children and a dark Indian mother with children.
IX. A baseball scene and a bullfight scene.
X. A young American boy and a Mexican boy.

Apparatus

The stereogram slide pairs were presented to S by means of a prism lens stereoscope enclosed in a light-tight box, like that more fully described by Bagby and Engel (Bagby, 1956; Engel, 1956). Each eye was independently presented with but one photograph of a pair. The slide holder was adjustable to permit the proper setting for a normal binocular fusion of the two stimuli. The intensity of illumination upon either slide could be independently varied, but for the present set of data it was equated.

Procedure

The S was informed that he was to view a series of slides in the apparatus and was to tell E what he saw. The S was cautioned to look with both eyes and to keep his forehead pressed against the metal view piece. When the preliminary questions regarding procedure were answered to S's satisfaction he was placed in viewing position.

The initial presentation was stereoscopic slide 33 of the Titchener series (Titchener, 1942). The S was asked to adjust the setting so the white circle (in one visual field) was centered as nearly as possible in the black circle (presented to the other field). When this had been achieved a slide from the series of Engel's (1955) "male faces" was presented and S was asked what he saw. All described a single male face. The S was then asked if the face appeared in clear focus. Ordinarily there was some minor adjustment to be made in the setting of the apparatus to obtain proper fusion.

At this point S was told that the apparatus was adjusted for his own vision and that the experiment *per se* was to begin. The sequence of Mexican-American stereogram slides was then presented, each being exposed for a 60-sec. viewing period. To control for eye dominance, the left-eye-right-eye positions of the Mexican and American scenes were randomized within the series. In terms of S's running descriptive report of what he saw, E recorded the relative predominance of the right or left stimulus object. The basic data, however, derive from the initial view or first 15-sec. exposure of the slides.

RESULTS AND DISCUSSION

A variety of reports was obtained from Ss:

1. In the simplest (and relatively infrequent) case S reported seeing but one slide of a pair, and solely described its features. This slide could readily be classified as "predominant" or "preferred" by S.

2. In other cases one slide of the pair would be described very thoroughly, after which S would begin to say he saw "something else," gradually describing the features of the other slide while reporting that each picture "comes and goes." In the case of such "rivalry," the preference or predominance of one slide was determined by: (a) the picture first reported, and (b) S's statements as to which picture seemed to be present most of the time.

3. There were also reports of a single picture which was an "admixture" of the two pictures presented. "Admixture" reports were rare for the initial view; usually they came during total exposure after a transition from marked predominance. It was not difficult to determine the preferred slide since S's report of content was definitive.

4. There were also reports of the two pictures being seen at once with one superimposed on the other. This condition was reported for first view on only three occasions.

Table 2 gives the over-all results. The Wilcoxon (1949) test was used for determining the significance of differences between the selections made by the Mexican and American Ss. Significance was at the .01 level of confidence.

Since the initial time interval was rather short, it may be suggested that culturally familiar subject matter was preferentially reported in cases 3 and 4 without the selection being strictly perceptual. This possibility was checked by excluding these cases from the analysis; the over-all results remain unchanged with significance at the .02 level.

TABLE 2

Differential Selection of American Content in Ten Stereograms

Nationality	Number of Ss Selecting American Content in Given Number of Stereograms				Total
	8–10	5–7	2–4	0–1	
Mexican Ss	0	0	5	7	12
American Ss	9	3	0	0	12
Total	9	3	5	7	24

TABLE 3

Over-all Perceptual Predominance in the Ten Stereogram Pairs

	No. Where Mexicans Dominate	No. Where Americans Dominate	Total (6 × 10)
Mexican males (6)	44	16	60
Mexican females (6)	45	15	60
American males (6)	7	53	60
American females (6)	12	48	60

An additional check on the preferential reports for cases 3 and 4 was conducted on all Ss using the same stimulus materials. This consisted of re-exposing the materials and varying the intensity of light on the two pictures (Bagby, 1956). The degree to which illumination of the less preferred picture had to be increased to offset the advantage of the other provided a quantitative measure of perceptual predominance. The direction only, and not the relative strength of the indexes, was used in further support of the predominance report derived from the first-view-in-time. In no instance were the original criteria for determining preference, more especially cases 3 and 4, contra-indicated.

Table 3 gives the results from the intensity variation.

Since the probability of equal perceptual predominance was rejected at the .01 level for both Ss and content, the conclusion seems justified that Ss report scenes of their own culture as predominant in binocular rivalry over scenes from another culture. The national cultural differences appear critical in affecting perceptual predominance in the majority of the stereogram slide pairs. There were only three pairs in which cultural preference was not marked (i.e., I, V, and X). One can only speculate concerning the less marked cultural influence in the latter pairs, which could involve the physical characteristics of the photographs (e.g., greater clarity or better definition of the prints), or possibly greater "appeal" of the particular individuals depicted regardless of cultural setting. However, the major finding is clear.

Various theoretical interpretations are possible for describing the findings of the present investigation. The position here favored, however, is that advanced by Ames, Cantril, and the transactional school who regard perception as being fundamentally determined by previous, rather than present, experience (Ittelson and Cantril, 1954; Kilpatrick, 1952). In transactional perceptual theory the role of meaning is accorded a central position in the perceptual processes. Differences in ways of perceiving come about as a consequence of differences in past experiences and purposes. These in turn emerge from influences in the home, in the school, and in the various groups with which an individual identifies. Thus, under conditions of perceptual conflict as found in the binocular rivalry situation, those impingements possessing the more immediate first-person meaning would be expected to predominate in visual awareness. The findings of the present experiment seem accountable in these terms. While greater familiarity with the objects and scenes from the S's own culture provided a more dominant set for perceiving those materials in preference to the relatively less familiar, other variables such as mood, need, and self-reference values undoubtedly entered into the actual selections. The best explanation of the present data, therefore, would seem to be in terms of past experience. The accumulated past experience of the individual within the characteristic settings and with typical individuals of his own culture should make pictorial scenes from his own culture possess greater personal significance at the visual level than that possessed by the less familiar situations and individuals of another society.

SUMMARY

Twelve Mexican and twelve matched American subjects were simultaneously presented with a series of ten stereogram slide pairs of similar scenes, one from Mexico and one from the United States. Under these conditions of experimentally induced binocular rivalry, it was found that scenes from the S's own culture tended to be perceptually predominant. The findings were accounted for in terms of the demonstrable role of personal significance in perceptual processes.

REFERENCES

Bagby, J. W. The relative roles of information and action in the genesis of a perception. Doctor's dissertation, Columbia University, 1955.

Bagby, J. W. A perceptual study of cross-cultural attitudes in Mexico and the United States. Advance report, Psychol. Dept., Princeton University, March 1956.

Engel, E. Binocular conflict and resolution. Doctor's dissertation, Princeton University, 1955.

Engel, E. The role of content in binocular resolution, *Amer. J. Psychol.*, 1956, **69**, 87–91.

Ittelson, W. and H. Cantril. *Perception: A transactional approach.* New York: Doubleday and Company, Inc. 1954.

Kilpatrick, F. P. Human behavior from the transactional point of view. Hanover, N. H.: Institute for Associated Research, 1952.

Titchener Series. *Stereoscopic slides.* Chicago: C. H. Stoelting Company, 1942.

Wilcoxon, F. *Some rapid approximate statistical procedures.* New York: American Cyanamid Company, 1949.

1-6

Pictorial Depth Perception in African Groups

W. HUDSON

One dominant feature of Western literate society is the two-dimensional representation of three-dimensional objects. At an early age, children in this culture are exposed to pictures, photographs, and motion pictures; and they are encouraged to make two-dimensional drawings themselves. Perceptual inference from graphic material is taken for granted in the West. However, this type of perception may not come naturally to people who are not accustomed to graphic representation. The present study shows that illiterate African children find it difficult to perceive pictorial depth. School children, on the other hand, are able to see pictures as being three-dimensional. Experience with pictures and photographs at home and school appears to help in employing depth cues and seeing pictures and photographs in three dimensions.

Western culture is book-learned, characterized by dependence upon the written word, illustration, diagram, photograph. Visual presentation is a common mode in the classroom. Educational and training programes, advertisements, safety, and health propaganda, and much

Abridged from *J. Soc. Psychol.*, 1960, **52**, 183–208, by permission of the author and The Journal Press.

current didactic literature make use of pictorial material. Certain characteristic perceptual habits have become normal for Western culture, and for the groups professing it. Pictorial representation of a three-dimensional scene requires the observance and acceptance of certain artistic or graphic conventions. Pictorial depth perception depends upon response to these conventional cues in the two-dimensional representation. There are three such cues concerned with form only, viz., object size, object superimposition or overlap, perspective. In the visual world, of two objects of equal size, that object nearer the observer is larger. When one object overlaps another the superimposed object is nearer to the observer. Parallel lines tend to converge with distance from the observer. In the two-dimensional representation of the three-dimensional scene, foreground objects are depicted larger than background items. Superimposed objects are perceived as nearer. Pictorial structuring by perspective technique is accepted as a convention for depicting distance. The incidental evidence furnished by African samples indicates that these pictorial conventions are not familiar to such subcultural groups. The present investigation is limited to the study of the perception of three dimensions in pictorial material by subcultural groups in southern Africa.

METHOD

Test Material

Test material was constructed to isolate the pictorial depth cues of object size, object superimposition and perspective. Six outline drawings and one photograph were constructed. The experimental situation is simple to construct. Pictures 1–6 were designed to obtain the responses of observers to depth cues of size, overlap, and perspective in horizontal pictorial space. Each picture is similarly structured. The elephant is positioned centrally between a human figure and an antelope. In this "hunting scene," the elephant is depicted smaller than the antelope. This object size depth cue occurs in each of the six pictures. Pictures 2 and 3 carry the additional depth cue of overlapping. Pictures 4, 5 and 6 have perspective lines representing a road vanishing in a horizon. In all pictures the hunter's assegai is aligned on both elephant and antelope.

A similar picture was made using modeled objects. Human figure, elephant, and antelope were modeled to scale and subsequently photographed to reproduce a scene similar to Picture 1.

Testing Procedure

Pictures were presented separately to individual candidates in the given order. Questioning was done orally in whatever tongue was mutu-

Figure 1. Horizontal pictorial space.

ally intelligible to both candidate and tester. Where this practice was not feasible (with illiterate samples from different territories in southern Africa), an interpreter was used. Answers were recorded seriatim. Complete picture sets were not administered to the first four samples.

Candidates were asked the following questions while viewing each picture:

1. What do you see?
2. What is the man doing?
3. Which is nearer to the man, the elephant or the antelope?

In addition candidates were required to identify each object in each picture, viz., man, assegai, elephant, tree, hill, antelope.

If a candidate reported that the man was aiming or throwing the spear without specifying his quarry, an additional question was asked to clarify whether he was aiming at elephant or antelope. In the majority of cases, this additional question was unnecessary.

Scoring Method

For reasons to be discussed later, responses to Question 3 were taken as indicative of the type of dimensional pictorial perception possessed by a candidate. If candidates reported the antelope in the "hunting scene" to be nearer the man than the elephant, their responses were classified as three-dimensional (3D). Similarly, for Question 2, if candidates reported the hunter to be aiming at the antelope, these responses were classified as three-dimensional. All other responses in the scenes were characterized as two-dimensional (2D).

Samples

The test was administered to 11 samples. Characteristics of these samples are given in Table 1. Samples fell into two main types, a nonschool-attending group (Sample *a-e*) and a school-attending group (Sample *f-k*). The nonschool-attending group contained no children and consisted of four black and one white sample. The school-going group consisted of children mainly except for one sample of adult teachers. Three of the samples in this group were black, and three white. All samples were tested in the Union of South Africa. Samples *a-d* contain candidates whose territorial origins cover the Union of South Africa, South West Africa, High Commission territories, Federation of Rhodesias and Nyasaland, East Africa, Mozambique, and Angola. Age and educational data are lacking for two cases in Sample *e*.

RESULTS

Intersample Differences in Depth Perception for Outline Drawings

For each of the 11 samples the percentage number of candidates giving 3D responses are listed in Table 2. 3D responses are fairly consistent per sample over the pictures.

Intersample Differences in Depth Perception for Photographs

Percentage number giving 3D responses to Question 3 with respect to the photograph are listed for samples taking this test (Table 3).

Illiterate mine workers do not see the photograph three-dimensionally. The remaining samples, where a high proportion of candidates perceive three-dimensionally, are all school-going samples, both black and white. There are minor differences within this second group. White school beginners and black pupils at the end of their primary course perceive the photograph three-dimensionally less frequently than

TABLE 1
Characteristics of Samples

		Age				Education			
	n	Under 14	14-20	21-40	Over 40	Illiterate	Primary	Higher	Graduate
a. Mine laborers (Illiterate) (Black)	57	—	36	19	2	57	—	—	—
b. Mine laborers (Primary) (Black)	54	—	23	29	2	—	54	—	—
c. Mine clerks (High school) (Black)	48	—	3	34	11	—	—	48	—
d. Mine laborers (Illiterate) (Black)	45	—	12	29	4	45	—	—	—
e. White laborers	60	—	2	29	27	10	46	2	—
f. School children (Grades & Std. 1) (White)	42	42	—	—	—	—	42	—	—
g. School children (Grade 1–Std. 6) (White)	113	113	—	—	—	—	113	—	—
h. School children (Std. 6) (Black)	34	—	34	—	—	—	34	—	—
i. Teachers (Graduate) (Black)	25	—	—	22	3	—	—	—	25
j. School children (Stds. 8 & 10) (Black)	52	—	47	5	—	—	—	52	—
k. School children (Stds. 5 & 6) (White)	32	32	—	—	—	—	32	—	—

TABLE 2
Percentage Candidates with 3D Responses

		Horizontal Space					
Samples	n	Size P_1	Superimposition P_2	Superimposition P_3	Perspective P_4	Perspective P_5	Perspective P_6
a	57	0	0	—	0	0	0
b	54	0	0	—	2	0	2
c	48	23	40	—	31	17	20
d	45	—	—	2	—	—	—
e	60	13	20	23	8	15	13
f	42	26	31	69	29	33	26
g	113	47	57	93	57	63	51
h	34	50	68	76	53	50	65
i	25	56	76	80	60	68	60
j	52	69	69	94	62	73	63
k	32	75	88	100	81	97	78

TABLE 3
Percentage Candidates with 3D Responses

Samples	n	Percentage
d	45	0
f	42	72
g	113	85
h	34	76
i	25	92
j	52	81
k	32	100

do white pupils at the end of their primary course. But the main intersample difference in depth perception in photographs lies between the illiterate black sample and the school-going group, both black and white.

Object Identification as a Factor in Dimensional Perception

Since pictorial depth perception depends upon the perception of the appropriate cues there must be a direct relationship between object identification and dimensional perception.

In all pictures, except Picture 3, the man and the animals were correctly identified. In Picture 3, the depth cue of overlap was introduced and as can be seen from Figure 1 (p. 59), objects were superimposed over the central figure of the elephant in order to enhance the perception of depth. With the illiterate Sample *d*, this technique defeats its own object by complicating the representation of the elephant to such an extent as to render it unrecognizable to the candidates. This finding does not apply to Picture 2 where overlap is also used. In this instance superimposition is restricted to contour lines, so that the animals and objects retain their definition.

DISCUSSION

White and black school-going samples perceive depth more frequently in pictorial material than do illiterate black samples, and samples, both black and white, which have terminated their school course and live in isolation from the dominant cultural norm. As expected there is a direct relationship between incorrect identification of items, in the drawings and two-dimensional perception, but correct identification does not predicate three-dimensional perception. Outline drawings making use of perspective depth cues are less frequently seen three-dimensionally than those using overlap or size depth cues. This finding holds particularly in the case of white primary school pupils. School-going samples perceive three-dimensions in a photograph more readily than in an outline drawing, but this finding does not apply to illiterate samples. Intersample differences are less pronounced with photographic material than with outline drawings.

There are three hypotheses which can be set up on these results: (1) that the results are artifacts of the test, (2) that the results are culturally determined, (3) that the results are genetically determined.

Test Artifacts in Dimensional Pictorial Perception

This hypothesis has two aspects to it: (a) How far has the perceptual structure of the test influenced results? (b) How far has the semantic structure of the test influenced results?

Outline drawings were used to provide the simplest and least graphically contaminated medium for the representation of the appropriate depth cues in a standard scene. Such drawings have representational drawbacks. Perspective cues in particular tend to become symbolic and unrealistic and the high proportion of incorrect identifications, particularly in the illiterate samples, lends support to this view. But responses to the photographic reproduction of the same pictorial scene modeled show that with that form of two-dimensional representation, which is least symbolic and most realistic of three-dimensions, the illiterate sample continues to perceive two-dimensionally. Work by Smith et al. (1958) on perceived distance as a function of the method of representing perspective showed that judgments of distances in drawings do not vary with the amount of detail included. They also concluded that the perception of depth did not differ in perspective line drawings and in photographs. These findings corroborate the evidence in the present study and on these grounds the hypothesis that test results are an artifact of the perceptual structure of the test can be rejected.

What do candidates understand the tester to mean when he asks the question—Which is nearer to the man, elephant or antelope? There is evidence to show that 2D responses are not semantically dependent on the wording of the question. With all samples except high school pupils (black) and graduate teachers (black) responses, whether 3D or 2D, were immediate. With the two samples specified hesitation in responding was noticeable and was particularly pronounced with the graduate teachers some of whom took as long as one hour per picture to respond. Part of this hesitation may be due to occupational cautiousness or insecurity, but part of it was exposed by introspection as a problem in perceptual organization. Candidates asked the tester for information on the mode of perception because there were to them two possibilities, viz., 2D or 3D, which means that to them "nearness" was semantically unstable in the questionnaire. For the less highly educated and illiterate samples which perceived the pictures two-dimensionally in a majority of cases, there is additional evidence. Following their identification of objects in the pictures candidates were asked what the hunter was aiming at in the "hunting scene," prior to being questioned on relative proximity of animals to hunter. Candidates in all samples, choosing the elephant as the hunter's quarry, were those who perceived the elephant as nearer the hunter than the antelope. This means that the whole manifest content of the picture tended to be perceived two-dimensionally, and appropriately interpreted. The occurrence of this phenomenon is considered to be a function of perceptual organization and not merely a semantic evaluation. The hypothesis postulating the influence of the semantic structure of the test on candidates' responses is rejected.

Cultural Factors in Dimensional Pictorial Perception

There are two levels of cultural factors to be considered, viz., (a) formal education, (b) informal training.

The white primary groups (Samples *f, g, k*) 3D perception is associated with educational level. The higher the educational standard, the more frequent is the occurrence of 3D pictorial perception.

This finding does not apply to black samples, otherwise markedly superior performances would be expected from black high school pupils (Sample *j*) and graduate teachers (Sample *i*). Candidates in Sample *b* (mine laborers) possess a primary school level of education, but their pictorial perception is entirely two-dimensional and does not differ from that of the illiterate mine workers. In addition the 3D perception of the white laborers (Sample *e*), the majority of whom have had primary schooling, is markedly inferior to that of the white school beginners (Sample *f*).

Training in pictorial perception is not included in the formal school curriculum. It is gradually acquired by white children between the ages of 6 and 12 years (Samples *f, j, k*). During that period, there is an informal process of almost continuous exposure to pictorial material in the school and in the home, so that by the age of 12 years, most white children have learned to perceive pictures three-dimensionally.

But pictorial depth perception is not learned by the white laborers in Sample *e*, although they attended school. Mundy-Castle and Nelson (1960) have described this subculture elsewhere. It is an isolated group living under conditions of sheltered employment, closely intermarried, and centripetal. Families are large, and homes are poorly supplied with pictures, books, magazines, and newspapers. Consequently school-going children are not exposed in the home to the informal training necessary for the three-dimensional perception of pictorial material. School is equal-ly isolated, and, as an agency by which the outside world may attempt to invade the community, is resisted by the elders of the group. There is little opportunity for scholars, unstimulated perceptually in the home, to acquire new depth perceptual organization with respect to pictures.

The black samples are also isolated. This is particularly true of Samples *a-d*, which are migratory and rurally orientated. The black urban Samples (*h, i, j*) are ethnocentrically isolated. They have been urbanised for one generation only. Homes, even of graduates, are poorly furnished with pictures and illustrated reading matter. The women-folk seldom read and then mainly literature in the vernacular. Most books owned by the men are of the nature of textbooks. Daily and monthly magazines are taken, but most of these are sparsely illustrated with photographs. During the early years, however, when the white child is obtaining his informal training in pictorial material, the black child, even in an urban home, suffers from lack of exposure to pictures. He may acquire the skill at a later stage, but there is little opportunity for stimulation, particularly where formal schooling is presided over by teachers, many of whom perceive pictorial material two-dimensionally. Hence it does occur that a black graduate of London University perceives a picture flat. It also happens that a black teacher sees a picture flat, and his pupil perceives it three-dimensionally.

Such results are not unexpected. African art is essentially volumet-ric. Where it is pictorial as in wall decorations or body tattooing, it is either diagrammatic or two-dimensional naturalistic. Haselberger (1957) reports on a long continuous history of two-dimensional mural art in Africa. Jeffreys (1957) describes tattooing in Nigeria as the African counterpart to abstract pictorial art in Europe and America. Such evi-dence emphasizes that the critical feature for pictorial depth perception appears to be adequate exposure to the appropriate experience.

SUMMARY

Pictures constructed to provide self-evident responses of 2D or 3D perception on the depth cues of object size, superimposition, and per-spective were given to 11 samples, six of them school-going (3 white, 3 black) and five of them nonschool-going (1 white, 4 black). School-going samples saw predominantly three-dimensionally, the others almost entire-ly two-dimensionally both in outline drawings and on a photograph. The hypothesis that their dimensional perception was an artifact of test construction was rejected. Formal schooling and informal training com-bined to supply an exposure necessary for the development of 3D perception. Cultural isolation was effective in preventing or retarding the process, even in candidates possessing formal education of an advanced level.

REFERENCES

Haselberger, H. Die Wandmalerei der afrikanischen Neger, *Zeitschrift für Ethnographie*, 1957, **82**, 209–237.

Jeffreys, M. D. W. Negro abstract art or Ibo body patterns, *S. African Mus. Bull.* 1957, **6**, 219–229.

Mundy-Castle, A. C. and G. K. Nelson. Intelligence, personality and brain rhythms in a socially isolated community, *Nature*, 1960, **185**, 484–485.

Smith, O. W., P. C. Smith, and D. Hubbard. Perceived distance as a function of the method of representing perspective, *Amer. J. Psychol.*, 1958, **71**, 662–674.

CHAPTER 2

CROSS-CULTURAL STUDIES OF INTELLECTUAL FUNCTIONING

2-1

Social Factors in Recall

FREDERIC CHARLES BARTLETT

A culture sensitizes its members to certain objects and events in their environment and these cultural experiences could have noticeable influence on the thinking of these members. British students studied by Bartlett remembered, organized, and elaborated on a story from another culture to fit their own previous cultural experiences and their own view of the world. The Swazi chiefs were able to remember the English policemen regulating traffic in London because this action is in accord with their native experience. To these chiefs, the uplifted arm of the policeman has the pleasant associations of warmth and friendliness.

EXPERIMENTS ON REMEMBERING:
THE METHOD OF REPEATED REPRODUCTION

I have selected for special consideration a story which was adapted from a translation by Boas (1901) of a North American folk-tale. Several reasons prompted the use of this story.

First, the story as presented belonged to a level of culture and a social environment exceedingly different from those of my subjects. Hence it seemed likely to afford good material for persistent transforma-

Reprinted from *Remembering*. Cambridge, Eng.: Cambridge University Press, 1932, by permission of author and the publisher.

ion. I had also in mind the general problem of what actually happens when a popular story travels about from one social group to another, and thought that possibly the use of this story might throw some light upon the general conditions of transformation under such circumstances. It may fairly be said that this hope was at least to some extent realized.

Secondly, the incidents described in some of the cases had no very manifest interconnection, and I wished particularly to see how educated and rather sophisticated subjects would deal with this lack of obvious rational order.

Thirdly, the dramatic character of some of the events recorded seemed likely to arouse fairly vivid visual imagery in suitable subjects.

Fourthly, the conclusion of the story might easily be regarded as introducing a supernatural element, and I desired to see how this would be dealt with.

The original story was as follows:

The War of the Ghosts

One night two young men from Egulac went down to the river to hunt seals, and while they were there it became foggy and calm. Then they heard war-cries, and they thought: "Maybe this is a war-party." They escaped to the shore, and hid behind a log. Now canoes came up, and they heard the noise of paddles, and saw one canoe coming up to them. There were five men in the canoe, and they said:

"What do you think? We wish to take you along. We are going up the river to make war on the people."

One of the young men said: "I have no arrows."

"Arrows are in the canoe," they said.

"I will not go along. I might be killed. My relatives do not know where I have gone. But you," he said, turning to the other, "may go with them."

So one of the young men went, but the other returned home.

And the warriors went on up the river to a town on the other side of Kalama. The people came down to the water, and they began to fight, and many were killed. But presently the young man heard one of the warriors say: "Quick, let us go home: that Indian has been hit." Now he thought: "Oh, they are ghosts." He did not feel sick, but they said he had been shot.

So the canoes went back to Egulac, and the young man went ashore to his house, and made a fire. And he told everybody and said: "Behold I accompanied the ghosts, and we went to fight. Many of our fellows were killed, and many of those who attacked us were killed. They said I was hit, and I did not feel sick."

He told it all, and then he became quiet. When the sun rose he fell down. Something black came out of his mouth. His face became contorted. The people jumped up and cried.

He was dead.

Each subject read the story through to himself twice, at his normal reading rate. Except in the case which will be indicated later, the first reproduction was made 15 minutes after this reading. Other reproductions were effected at intervals as opportunity offered. No attempt was made to secure uniformity in the length of interval for all subjects; obviously equalizing intervals of any length in no way equalizes the effective conditions of reproduction in the case of different subjects. No subject knew the aim of the experiment. All who were interested in this were allowed to think that the test was merely one for accuracy of recall.

I shall analyze the results obtained in three ways:

First, a number of reproductions will be given in full, together with some comments;

Secondly, special details of interest in this particular story will be considered;

Thirdly, certain general or common tendencies in the successive remembering of the story will be stated and discussed more fully.

SOME COMPLETE REPRODUCTIONS TOGETHER WITH COMMENTS

After an interval of 20 hours subject H produced the following first reproduction:

The War of the Ghosts

Two men from Edulac went fishing. While thus occupied by the river they heard a noise in the distance.

"It sounds like a cry," said one, and presently there appeared some men in canoes who invited them to join the party on their adventure. One of the young men refused to go, on the ground of family ties, but the other offered to go.

"But there are no arrows," he said.

"The arrows are in the boat," was the reply.

He thereupon took his place, while his friend returned home. The party paddled up the river to Kaloma, and began to land on the banks of the river. The enemy came rushing upon them, and some sharp fighting ensued. Presently someone was injured, and the cry was raised that the enemy were ghosts.

The party returned down the stream, and the young man arrived home feeling none the worse for his experience. The next morning at dawn he endeavoured to recount his adventures. While he was talking something black issued from his mouth. Suddenly he uttered a cry and fell down. His friends gathered round him.

But he was dead.

In general form (1) the story is considerably shortened, mainly by omissions; (2) the phraseology becomes more modern, more "journalistic," e.g., "refused, on the ground of family ties"; "sharp fighting ensued"; "feeling none the worse for his adventures"; "something black issued from his mouth"; (3) the story has already become somewhat more coherent and consequential than in its original form.

In matter there are numerous omissions and some transformations. The more familiar "boat" once replaces "canoe"; hunting seals becomes merely "fishing"; Egulac becomes Edulac, while Kalama changes to Kaloma. The main point about the ghosts is entirely misunderstood. The two excuses made by the man who did not wish to join the war-party change places; that "he refused on the ground of family ties" becomes the only excuse explicitly offered.

Eight days later this subject remembered the story as follows:

The War of the Ghosts

Two young men from Edulac went fishing. While thus engaged they heard a noise in the distance. "That sounds like a war-cry," said one, "there is going to be some fighting." Presently there appeared some warriors who invited them to join an expedition up the river.

One of the young men excused himself on the ground of family ties. "I cannot come," he said, "as I might get killed." So he returned home. The other man, however, joined the party, and they proceeded in canoes up the river. While landing on the banks the enemy appeared and were running down to meet them. Soon someone was wounded, and the party discovered that they were fighting against ghosts. The young man and his companion returned to the boats, and went back to their homes.

The next morning at dawn he was describing his adventures to his friends, who had gathered round him. Suddenly something black issued from his mouth, and he fell down uttering a cry. His friends closed around him, but found that he was dead.

All the tendencies to change manifested in the first reproduction now seem to be more marked. The story has become still more concise, still more coherent. The proper name Kaloma has disappeared, and the lack of arrows, put into the second place a week earlier, has now dropped out completely. On the other hand a part of the other excuse: "I might get killed," now comes back into the story, though it found no place in the first version. It is perhaps odd that the friend, after having returned home, seems suddenly to come back into the story again when the young man is wounded. But this kind of confusion of connected incidents is a common characteristic of remembering.

EXPERIMENTS ON REMEMBERING:
THE METHOD OF SERIAL REPRODUCTION

Methods for studying remembering often deal with factors influencing individual observers. They help to show what occurs when a person makes use of some new material which he meets, assimilating it and later reproducing it in his own characteristic manner. Already it is clear, however, that several of the factors influencing the individual observer are social in origin and character. For example, many of the transformations which took place as a result of the repeated reproduction of prose passages were directly due to the influence of social conventions and beliefs current in the group to which the individual subject belonged. In the actual remembering of daily life the importance of these social factors is greatly intensified. The form which a rumor, or a story, or a decorative design, finally assumes within a given social group is the work of many different successive social reactions. Elements of culture, or cultural complexes, pass from person to person within a group, or from group to group, and, eventually reaching a thoroughly conventionalized form, may take an established place in the general mass of culture possessed by a specific group. Whether we deal with an institution, a mode of conduct, a story, or an art-form, the conventionalized product varies from group to group, so that it may come to be the very characteristic we use when we wish most sharply to differentiate one social group from another. In this way, cultural characters which have a common origin may come to have apparently the most diverse forms.

The experiments now to be described were designed to study the effects of the combination of changes brought about by many different individuals. The results produced are not entirely beyond the range of experimental research, as I shall show, and the main method which I have used is best called *The Method of Serial Reproduction.*

In its material form this method is simply a reduplication of *The Method of Repeated Reproduction.* The only difference is that A's reproduction is now itself reproduced by B, whose version is subsequently dealt with by C, and so on. In this way chains of reproduction were obtained: (1) of folk-stories, (2) of descriptive and argumentative prose passages and (3) of picture material. The folk-stories were used, as before, because they are predominantly a type of material which passes very rapidly from one social group to another; because most subjects regard them as interesting in themselves; because stories can easily be chosen which were fashioned in a social environment very different from that of any social group that is likely to yield subjects for a given experiment; and because, both as to form and as to content, they undergo much change in the course of transmission. The descriptive and argumentative passages were used because they represent a type of material with which all the subjects of these experiments were already familiar, so that they would provide some kind of check, or control, upon the results with the folk-tales. The picture material was used, because the transmission of picture forms has constantly occurred in the development of decorative and realistic art, and in order to see whether the same principles of change would operate in spite of the difference of medium dealt with.

In the case of the verbal passages, each subject read the material twice through, to himself, at his normal reading pace. Reproduction was effected after a filled interval of 15–30 minutes. In the case of the picture forms, a subject was allowed adequate time for observation, and he effected his reproduction after a similar interval.

So far as the two chains of reproduction already considered go, it appears that, under the conditions of the experiment, the following are the main types of transformation likely to occur:

1. There will be much general simplification, due to the omission of material that appears irrelevant, to the construction gradually of a more coherent whole, and to the changing of the unfamiliar into some more familiar counterpart.
2. There will be persistent rationalization, both of a whole story and of its details, until a form is reached which can be readily dealt with by all the subjects belonging to the special social group concerned. This may result in considerable elaboration.
3. There will be a tendency for certain incidents to become dominant, so that all the others are grouped about them.

It also seems probable that a cumulative form of story favors the retention of the general series of incidents with little change, and that whatever causes amusement is likely to be remembered and preserved. It may be to this last factor that the preservation of the novel in a commonplace setting is largely due.

SOCIAL PSYCHOLOGY AND THE
MATTER OF RECALL

First, then, I propose to consider a few typical cases in which memory appears to be directly influenced by social facts. I shall discuss the psychological explanation of these instances, and, following this, I shall draw certain tentative conclusions bearing upon the psychological significance of social organization, so far as remembering is concerned.

Some years ago the Paramount Chief of the Swazi people, accompanied by several of his leading men, visited England for the purpose of attempting to obtain a final settlement of a long-standing land dispute. When the party returned, there was naturally some curiosity among the British settlers in Swaziland concerning what were the main points of recall by the native group of their visit to England. The one thing that remained most firmly and vividly fixed in the recollection of the Swazi chiefs was their picture of the English policeman, regulating the road traffic with uplifted hand.

Why should this simple action have made so profound an impression? Certainly not merely because it was taken as a symbol of power. Many other illustrations of power, far more striking to the European mind, had been seen and, for all practical purposes, forgotten. The Swazi greets his fellow, or his visitor, with uplifted hand. Here was the familiar gesture, warm with friendliness in a foreign country, and at the same time arresting in its consequences. It was one of the few things they saw that fitted immediately into their own well-established social framework, and so it produced a quick impression and a lasting effect.

I take another case from the same community. Even acute observers often assert of the Swazi the same kind of observation that has been made of the Bantu in general: "The Bantu mind is endowed with a wonderful memory (Junod, 1927)." Yet this sort of statement never seems to have been submitted to any careful experimental test. If such tests were carried out, it would most certainly be found that individual differences are about as pronounced as they are in a European community, and, a fact more to our present purpose, that the lines of accurate and full recall are very largely indeed, just as they are with us, a matter of social organization, with its accepted scales of value.

I myself, having listened to numerous stories about the marvelous word-perfect memory of the Swazi from his childhood up, and having been credibly informed that I could test these stories, with complete certainty of confirmation, upon any person I liked, arranged a simple experiment. Choosing at random a boy of eleven or twelve years of age, a native interpreter and myself concocted a brief message of about twenty-five words which the boy was to take from one end to another of a village. The journey took him about two minutes. The message was given to him very carefully twice over, and he did not know that he was being kept under observation. He was given a lively inducement to be accurate. He delivered the message with three important omissions, doing certainly no better than an English boy of the same age might do. Several times also I tried, with natives of varied ages and both sexes, common observation and description tests, something like the ones I have already recorded in this book, but with modifications so as to make them of greater intrinsic interest to a native observer. The results were much the same as they would have been for similar tests in a typical European group, neither better nor worse.

Nevertheless, it is not difficult to show that the common belief has some ground. For example, once, when I was talking with a prominent Scottish settler in Swaziland who has an extensive and sound knowledge of the native, he repeated the usual stories of exceedingly accurate and detailed memory. I told him of my own tests, and he at once agreed that his assertions held good only provided the native were taken in his own preferred fields of interest. Now most Swazi culture revolves around the possession and care of cattle. Cattle are the center of many of the most persistent and important social customs. The settler himself suggested a test case. He guaranteed that his herdsman would give me a prompt and absolutely literal description of all the cattle which he, the owner, had bought a year earlier. The herdsman had been with him while the transactions were completed, and had then driven the beasts back to the main farm. Immediately after the purchase, the cattle had been dispersed to different places and the herdsman had seen them no more. The settler himself had his own written records of the deals, and naturally could not himself remember the details without looking them up. It was arranged that he should not himself look at his records, or interview the herdsman. At the moment, the native was found to be at a "beer-drink," and inaccessible in more ways than one. The next day, however, the man was sent to me. He walked some twenty miles and brought with him the sealed book of accounts, which, in any case, he was not able to read. He knew nothing whatever of the reason for his journey. I asked him for a list of the cattle bought by his employer the year previously, together with whatever detail he cared to give. Squatting on the ground, apparently wholly unmoved, he rapidly recited the list. This was as follows:

From Magama Sikindsa, one black ox for £ 4;

From Mloyeni Sifundra, one young black ox for £ 2;

From Mbimbi Maseko, one young black ox, with a white brush to its tail, for £ 2;

From Gampoka Likindsa, one young white bull, with small red spots, for £ 1;

From Mapsini Ngomane and Mpohlonde Maseko, one red cow, one black heifer, one very young black bull for £3 in all;

From Makanda, one young gray ox, about two years old, for £ 3;

From Lolalela, one spotted five year old cow, white and black, for £ 3, which was made up of two bags of grain and £ 1;

From Mampini Mavalane, one black polly cow, with gray on the throat, for £ 3;

From Ndoda Kadeli, one young red heifer, the calf of a red cow, and with a white belly, for £ 1.

My notes, made at the time, say that the herdsman, a native of something over forty years, "showed no hesitation, no apparent interest, and certainly no excitement. He seemed to be reciting a well-known exercise and in no way reconstructing the deals on the basis of a few definitely remembered details."

The list was correct in every detail but two. The price of the second black ox mentioned was £ 1. 10s., and the "black" heifer from Mpohlonde Maseko was described in the book as "red." Against these trifling errors, it must be remembered that the herdsman had himself no say in the price of the beasts, and had merely overheard the bargains made by his master; and further that native color names are apt to be rather widely ambiguous.

It seems certain that this was in no way an isolated and remarkable case. The Swazi herdsman has generally an accurate and prodigiously retentive capacity to recall the individual characteristics of his beasts. An animal may stray and get mixed up with other herds. It may be away for a very long time. However long the interval, if the owner comes with a description of the missing beast, his word is almost never questioned, and he is peaceably allowed to drive the animal back. It is true, that, in spite of this, cattle were formerly all earmarked—a custom that appears to have fallen into disuse except in the case of the Royal herds—but altogether apart from these special marks, by common consent, the native herdsman always remembers his beasts individually.

And why should he not? Just as the policeman's uplifted hand was noteworthy because of the familiar social background, so the individual peculiarities of the cattle can be recalled freshly and vividly, because herds, and all dealings with them, are of tremendous social importance.

We can now see the general psychology underlying the way in which social conditions settle the matter of individual recall. Every social group is organized and held together by some specific psychological tendency or group of tendencies, which give the group a bias in its dealings with external circumstances. The bias constructs the special persistent features of group culture, its technical and religious practices, its material art, its traditions and institutions; and these again, once they are established, become themselves direct stimuli to individual response within the group. Perhaps, in some so far unexplained way, the social bias of the group may work its way, by actual inheritance, into at least some of the individual members; perhaps all that happens is that it appears in the individual through the pervasive influence of one of the many forms of social suggestion. In any case, it does immediately settle what the individual will observe in his environment, and what he will connect from his past life with this direct response. It does this markedly in two ways. First, by providing that setting of interest, excitement and emotion which favors the development of specific images, and secondly, by providing a persistent framework of institutions and customs which acts as a schematic basis for constructive memory.

SOCIAL PSYCHOLOGY AND THE MANNER OF RECALL

I shall state briefly three principles. I do this with great hesitation. Others could perhaps be derived from the general discussion. In an uncharted realm like the present one, any tentative expression of laws can do no more than form a basis for a further exploration of the relevant facts. The principles, such as they are, must stand or fall as more facts become known. What is beyond dispute is that remembering, in a group, is influenced, as to its manner, directly by the preferred persistent tendencies of that group.

1. In whatever field, where social organization has no specifically directed organizing tendencies, but only a group of interests, all about equally dominant, recall is apt to be of the rote racapitulatory type. This very often is the case over a wide field of daily happenings in the primitive group.

2. Whenever there are strong, preferred, persistent, specific, social tendencies, remembering is apt to appear direct, and as if it were a way of reading off from a copy, and there is a minimum of irrelevance. It may perhaps be that this is due to the adoption of a direct image type of recall, supplemented by the help of prevailing social "schemata" which take the form of persistent customs.

3. Whenever strong, preferred, persistent, social tendencies are subjected to any form of forcible social control (e.g., are disapproved by an incoming superior people, or are opposed to the general immediate trend of social development in the group), social remembering is very apt to take on a constructive and inventive character, either wittingly or unwittingly. Its manner then tends to become assertive, rather dogmatic and confident, and recall will probably be accompanied by excitement and emotion.

Each of these principles has found illustration in the preceding discussion. Obviously they all stand in need of further differentiation before, some day, the whole story of the social control of remembering can be written.

REFERENCES

Boas, F. Kathlamet texts, *Bureau of American Ethnology*, 1901, 182–184.
Junod, H. A. *The life of a South African tribe.* Vol. II. London: The Macmillan Company, 1927.

2-2

Comparisons of Word
Association Responses
in English, French,
German, and Italian

MARK R. ROSENZWEIG

The Kent-Rosanoff word association test consists of 100 common words, mostly adjectives and nouns. The subject is instructed to give the first response he can think of to the stimulus word presented to him. There appears to be a commonality of response (norms for frequency of occurrence) to these word stimuli among Western subjects. Studies of these norms taken at different periods show that there have been systematic changes toward greater commonality of responses over the past 50 years (Dörken, 1956; Jenkins and Palermo, 1965; Jenkins and Russell, 1960). These trends were attributed to the greater mass communication and uniformity in modern society. It was assumed that these environmental conditions lead to the formation of more universal verbal habits. In the present paper, Rosenzweig shows that there is generality in word associations across language; that is, the most frequent responses in one language tend to be similar in meaning to the most frequent responses in other languages. There seems to be some universality in the associative strength of stimulus words.

Reprinted from *Amer. J. Psychol.*, 1961, **74**, 347–360 by permission of the author and University of Illinois Press.

REFERENCES

Dörken, H. Frequency of common association, *Psychol. Rep.*, 1956, **2**, 407–408.

Jenkins, J. J., and D. S. Palermo. Further data on changes in word-association norms, *J. Pers. Soc. Psychol.*, 1965, **1**, 303–309.

Jenkins, J. J., and W. A. Russell. Systematic changes in word-association norms: 1910–1952, *J. Abnorm. Soc. Psychol.*, 1960, **60**, 393–404.

It has now become possible to compare directly word-association responses among several languages, since recent studies in France, Germany, and Italy have .employed translations of the list of Kent and Rosanoff which has long been used in America. An initial comparison was made between English and French primary responses (*i.e.* the response given most frequently to each stimulus-word), and it was found that for about half the items the primary responses of the two languages were equivalent in meaning (Rosenzweig, 1957). Next, it was found that the greater the frequency of the primary response in one language, the more likely it is to be equivalent in meaning to the corresponding primary response in the other language (Rosenzweig, 1959). From these results it was hypothesized that associative habits tend to be held in common among different language-communities. In the present report, this hypothesis is tested by comparing the primary responses in English, French, German, and Italian, and a smaller amount of material in Navaho.

METHOD

The English primary responses were obtained from the study of Russell and Jenkins (1954). They administered the stimulus-words of Kent and Rosanoff (1910) as a paper-and-pencil test to students at the University of Minnesota in 1952. One thousand and eight complete protocols were obtained. No breakdown of Ss by sex was given.

For comparison of primary responses of the two sexes in English, reference will be made to the study of Tresselt, Leeds, and Mayzner (1955). They tested individually 114 men and 115 women. The Ss were all between 18 and 25 yr. of age; they were of a variety of occupations and from several regions of the United States.

A French translation of the list of Kent and Rosanoff was administered to students at the Sorbonne and at Paris *lycées* in 1955–1956

(Rosenzweig, 1957). The same procedures were employed as those used by Russell and Jenkins. Two hundred eighty-eight complete protocols were obtained, 184 from women and 104 from men. The responses of the two sexes were tabulated separately. Although the results for the two sexes were quite similar, in the preparation of the composite table of primary responses the frequencies were so weighted that the men counted as much as the women in determining the final results.

A German translation of the list of Kent and Rosanoff was given to students at the University of Würzburg and at high schools in Würzburg and nearby cities by Russell and Meseck (1959). The same procedures were followed as in the study of Russell and Jenkins. Thirty-one complete protocols were obtained from women and 300 from men; the responses of the two sexes were pooled.

An Italian translation of the list of Kent and Rosanoff was administered to Ss in Italy by Levi (1949). The Ss were chosen to be fairly representative of the Italian population in age and social class, although the majority were students. About two-thirds of the 229 Ss were men; responses of the two sexes were pooled. Ninety-seven of the Ss were tested in Turin with a paper-and-pencil test such as those used in the other three languages. The 132 Ss tested in Rome heard the stimulus-words from a phonograph record and responded on a sheet with numbered blanks. The responses of these two subgroups were generally similar and were pooled to give a single set of norms. Only primary responses that were given by at least 9% of the Ss were reported. For 11 stimulus-words the primary response was given by less than 9% of the Ss, and these 11 responses are not available. The responses reported were English translations of the Italian responses.

RESULTS

To compare primary responses in the four languages, a table was prepared which included the stimulus-words, the primary responses, and the percentage of Ss giving each response. A judgment was then made as to the equivalences of meaning among the responses for each item, and these judgments were entered as the final column of the table. Because of limitations of space the entire table is not given here, but selected items are given as examples in Table 1.

It will be noticed that the Italian responses are given in English, since this is the way in which they were reported. Where no primary response was reported in Italian, as for Item 10, a question mark is shown in the table. The Italian primary response was not reported for Items 10, 17, 43, 45, 53, 57, 58, 83, 90, 93, and 100. (Except for some of these 11 items, all the items specifically mentioned in the text will be found in Table 1.)

TABLE 1

Stimulus-Words, Primary Responses, and Their Percentages for Word-Association Tests in English, French, German, and Italian

Stimulus-words (English, French, German, Italian)	Primary responses, their percentages, and agreements among four languages				
	English	French	German	Italian	
1. table, table, Tisch, tavola	84 chair	53 chaise	29 Stuhl	23 chair	E-F-G-I
2. dark, somber, dunkel, scuro	83 light	45 clair	44 hell(e)	18 light	E-F-G-I
3. Music, musique, Musik, musica	18 song‡	16 note‡	9 Tone‡	10 beautiful	F-G
4. sickness, maladie, Krankheit, malattia	38 health	10 santé	15 Gesundheit	13 serious	E-F-G
5. man, homme, Mann, uomo	77 woman‡	66 femme	52 Frau	39 woman	E-F-G-I
6. deep, profond, tief, profondo	32 shallow	12 creux	49 hoch	16 sea	–
7. soft, mou, wiech, morbido	45 hard	39 dur(e)	39 hart	14 hard, pillow	E-F-G-I
8. eating, manger, Essen, mangiare	39 food	39 boire	23 trinken	30 drinking	F-G
9. mountain, montagne, Berg, montagna	27 hill‡	13 plaine	35 Tal	17 high	–
10. house, maison, Haus, casa	25 home	14 toit	14 Hof	?	–
12. mutton, agneau,* Hammelfleisch, montone	37 lamb	15 brebis	7 Rindfleisch, Essen	18 sheep	–
3. woman, femme, Frau, donna	64 man‡	29 homme†	40 Mann	22 man	E-F-G-I
9. beautiful, belle, schön, bello	21 ugly	18 femme	27 hässlich	31 ugly	E-G-I
2. sheep, mouton,* Schaf, pecora	20 wool	25 laine	15 Wolle	18 wool	E-F-G-I
0. square, carré, Quadrat, piazza	37 round	30 rond	14 Viereck	10 large	E-F

*The French stimulus-word and responses for Items 12 and 62 were, as explained in the text, interchanged in the tabulation.
†Incorrectly given as 26% in Rosenzweig's paper in 1957 and also, consequently, in Russell and Meseck's.
‡Singular or plural.

TABLE 2
Numbers of Agreements in Meaning between Primary Responses
among Pairs of Languages

A. *All items* (100)

	French	German	Italian
English	48	48	(35)
French	–	45	(36)
German	–	–	(36)

B. *Items where Italian response is known* (89):

	French	German	Italian
English	43	43	35
French	–	41	36
German	–	–	36

The final column of the table indicates which responses have been judged to be equivalent in meaning; *e.g.* the notation E-F-G-I for Item 1 means that all four responses are equivalent, while the dash in this column opposite Item 6 means that no response is equivalent to any other. In the rare cases when two responses are tied for primary rank, as are the Italian responses for Item 7, an agreement was counted if either of the two was equivalent to the primary response of another language. When the Italian response is not available, as for Item 10, it is, of course, considered not to be equivalent to any other response.

AGREEMENT BETWEEN PAIRS OF LANGUAGES. Table 2 gives the number of primary responses judged equivalent in meaning when any pair of languages is compared. The upper half (A) of the table includes all 100 items. The numbers of agreements between English and German and between French and German are the same as those reported by Russell and Meseck. For the comparison between English and German, however, they reported 47 cases of agreement while we find 48. The numbers of agreements found between Italian and the other languages is clearly biased by the omission of 11 responses from the Italian norms. To make an unbiased comparison, the lower half (B) of Table 2 was prepared. Here only the 89 items were used for which the Italian responses had been reported. Even in Part B it is the Italian responses which show the smallest numbers of agreements with other languages. It should be remembered that the Italian study differed from the other three in using a more varied group of Ss and in employing an auditory presentation of the stimulus-words for a large proportion of the Ss. Both of these factors may have made the Italian responses somewhat different from those of the other groups.

The agreement among the four languages is impressive, almost half the comparisons in any pair of languages yielding agreements. As a yardstick, we may note the amount of agreement between two samples of Ss drawn from the same population. Where the responses of the two sexes have been tabulated separately for a study, we have two samples tested alike and selected alike in every respect but sex. The primary responses of French men and women agree for 75 out of 100 items. The English data of Tresselt et al. (1955) show 82 agreements between the primary responses of men and women. There is little evidence of real sex-differences in either study. Rather, as we shall discuss later, the men and women can be considered simply as two samples drawn from the same language-community. For a further comparison, we can note the agreements between the independent English studies of Tresselt et al. (1955) and of Russell and Jenkins (1954). For this purpose, the responses of men and women from the former paper have been pooled. This procedure allows us to compare groups that were tested somewhat differently and that differed in occupation and educational status, both groups however including the two sexes. The primary responses in these two studies agree in 82 out of the 100 cases. Thus, the number of agreements between pairs of Western European languages is only about three-fifths as great as the number of agreements between samples drawn from the same language.

For 21 stimulus-words, the responses of all four languages are equivalent in meaning. If only English, French, and German are considered, there are 36 items for which all primary responses agree. (Russell and Meseck (1959) judge that there are 34 cases in which the three primary responses agree.) Moreover, when the primary responses do not agree, the primary response of one language is often equivalent to the secondary response of the other language. Russell and Meseck (1959) have found this relationship in comparing English and German, and the same result has also been reported in the initial comparison of English and French responses (Rosenzweig, 1957).

The degree of similarity among the languages is probably even greater than appears from these results, since any inadequacies of translation of the stimulus-words inevitably lead to differences of response. Thus, Items 12 and 62, 'mutton' and 'sheep', should both be translated as 'mouton' in French. To avoid repeating a stimulus-word, 'agneau' ('lamb' in the sense of 'the young of the sheep') was used for Item 62. The responses to Item 12 showed that 'mouton' was understood in the sense of 'sheep'; therefore 'mouton' and its primary response 'laine' (wool) are tabulated as Item 62. 'Agneau' and its response are placed as Item 12 ('mutton'), and agreement cannot be expected here. In the case of Item 80, 'square,' the English responses show that the word was taken in the sense of a geometrical shape. The French and German stimuli were chosen to conform to this sense, but the Italian translation was 'piazza' (a public square), thus making it certain that the Italian primary response could not agree with those of the other languages.

DISTRIBUTION OF AGREEMENTS. Are these cases of agreement distributed randomly through the list, or is there any regularity in their distribution? A generalization has already been suggested by comparison of French and English primary responses.

> If we take the 25 associations with the highest frequency in French, 22 are equivalent to the corresponding American association. In successive sets of 25 French associations by declining frequency, there were 12, 10, and 4 agreements with the American associations. . . . Thus, the most frequently given associations are shared by the two languages, while the less frequent associations tend to differ (Rosenzweig, 1959).

A similar comparison was made among the four languages. Using the 89 items for which the Italian response is known, the primary responses of a language were divided into halves according to the relative frequency with which they were given. The responses were also categorized according to whether they agreed with zero, one, two, or three corresponding responses of the other languages. The results of this analysis are given in Table 3. Let us examine the distribution of agreements between English and the other three languages. Among the 46 English primary responses at or above the median frequency, only 7 do not agree with any of the corresponding primary responses of the other three languages, 9 agree with one of the corresponding responses, 12 agree with two other responses, and 18 agree with all three responses of the other languages. Among the 43 English primary responses whose frequency is below the median, the trend is just the reverse: 24 do not agree with a single other corresponding response, 7 agree with one response, 9 agree with two, and only 3 agree with all three responses of the other languages. Within each language, the more frequent responses show many more agreements than do the less frequent responses. The relationship between frequency of response and number of agreements is significant at better than the 0.1% level in English, in French, and in Italian, as tested by χ^2; in German the effect is significant at better than the 1% level. The distributions for all four languages were then cumulated to give a total distribution. A response in the upper half of the total frequency-distribution agrees, on the average, with 1.81 other responses; a response in the lower half agrees, on the average, with only 0.81 other responses. Of the responses that agree with all three corresponding responses in the other languages, 84.53% are in the upper half of the frequency-distribution; of responses that agree with no corresponding response, only 29.85% are in the upper half of the frequency distribution.

It can also be shown that the mean percentage of response varies monotonically with the number of agreements. The results of this analysis are displayed in Figure 1. For each language, the responses that agree

TABLE 3

Agreements with Primary Responses of Other Languages, among the
89 Items where the Italian Response Is Known

		Number of Agreeing Primary Responses				
Language	Percentage	0	1	2	3	Σ
English	≥ 33	7	9	12	18	46
	< 33	24	7	9	3	43
French	≥ 18	12	3	14	18	47
	< 18	21	10	8	3	42
German	≥ 18	11	5	10	17	43
	< 18	21	10	11	4	46
Italian	≥ 17	10	9	7	18	44
	< 17	28	7	7	3	45
Over-all	≥ Mdn.	40	26	43	71	180
	< Mdn.	94	34	35	13	176
	Σ	134	60	78	84	356

with none of the corresponding responses of the other languages have a mean percentage only about half as great as that of responses that agree with all three corresponding responses. There is only one minor exception to the monotonic rise of frequency with agreements: in German, the mean percentage for zero agreements is two more than the percentage found for one agreement. When the primary responses of a language were thus classified according to the number of agreements with primary responses of other languages, about one-fourth of the total variance of response-frequencies was accounted for by the variance between classes. The correlation ratios between response-frequency and number of agreements were 0.54 for English, 0.57 for French, 0.48 for German, and 0.45 for Italian. Each of these correlation ratios was significant at better than the 0.1% level of confidence.

Figure 1 also brings out the much greater frequency of primary responses of the American Ss as compared to the European Ss. This difference has previously been reported for French (Rosenzweig, 1959) and for German (Russell and Meseck, 1959). It now appears that all three European groups have rather similar frequencies of primary responses and that the communality of response among American Ss is almost twice as great.

RESPONSE CLASS AND AGREEMENTS. Can classification of the responses according to the relation between stimulus and response aid in predicting agreements among languages? Two frequently used categories were analyzed first, *opposites* (*e.g.* dark-light, sickness-health) and *coördinates* (*e.g.* table-chair, man-woman). Throughout this section

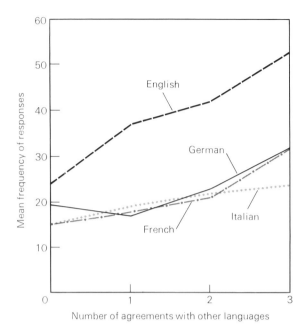

Figure 1. Mean frequencies of primary responses.

we will consider only the 89 items for which the Italian response is known. Among the four languages the *opposite* and *coördinate* classes account for 23 and 37%, respectively, of all primary responses.

(1) Opposite Responses. The opposite responses were tabulated for each language as in Table 3, both according to the number of agreements with the corresponding responses of the other languages and according to whether their frequency was above or below the median. The separate distributions for the four languages were then cumulated, and the results are given in Table 4A. For every language, most of the opposite responses are above the median in frequency; over-all, 77% are above the median. As would be expected of a group of responses with generally high frequency, the opposite responses show a rather high mean number of agreements with the corresponding primary responses of the other three languages—2.18, as compared with only 1.31 for all responses taken regardless of classification. Among the opposite responses, the factor of relative frequency of response exerts a significant effect ($\chi^2 = 4.73$, $df. = 1$, $P < 0.05$). The small number of opposite responses below the median frequency makes it necessary to group together the categories 0, 1, and 2 which probably reduces the obtained significance. Those opposite responses that are above the median in frequency show a mean number of 2.34

TABLE 4
Agreements with Primary Responses of Other Languages,
According to Categories of Responses

	Number of Agreeing Primary Responses						
Frequent response	0	1	2	3		Σ	M
A. Opposite responses:							
$\geq$ Mdn.	5	3	21	35	64		2.34
$<$ Mdn.	5	2	7	5	19	83	1.63
							2.18
B. Coördinate responses:							
$\geq$ Mdn.	12	14	18	27	71		1.85
$<$ Mdn.	31	15	12	1	59	130	0.70
							1.33
C. Adjective-adjective responses							
$\geq$ Mdn.	5	5	17	35	62		2.32
$<$ Mdn.	6	5	2	5	18	80	1.33
D. Noun-noun responses:							2.10
$\geq$ Mdn.	23	17	22	33	95		1.69
$<$ Mdn.	57	21	27	7	112	207	0.86
							1.24

agreements with the corresponding responses of the other languages. This value is considerably higher than the mean of 1.81 found for all responses above the median, regardless of classification. Those opposite responses with a frequency below the median show a mean number of 1.63 agreements, which is considerably greater than the mean of 0.81 agreements found for all responses below the median in frequency. Thus, the opposites of high and of low frequency show considerably more agreements than do responses of high and low frequency in general.

(2) Coördinate Responses. Table 4B presents the results for the coördinate responses. Unlike the opposite responses, the coördinate responses show no strong tendency to be high in frequency, only 55% being above the median. Their mean number of agreements with primary responses of other languages is 1.33, compared with 1.31 for unselected responses. Thus, the fact that a response is in the coördinate class does not help in predicting the number of agreements it will have with corresponding primary responses of other languages. Among the coördinate responses, the factor of relative frequency of response exerts a highly significant effect ($\chi^2 = 32.93$, $df. = 3$, $P < 0.001$).

Inspection of the opposite responses shows that among the 83 opposites, for all four languages, 73 are adjective-adjective pairs, *i.e.* both stimulus- and response-words are adjectives. Names of colors are considered to be adjectives here. These 73 responses in turn account for almost all of the 80 adjective-adjective pairs found among the primary responses of the four languages. Thus, almost the same result is obtained whether one classifies according to the relational category of opposition or according to the grammatical category, adjective-adjective (A-A).

(3) Adjective-Adjective Pairs. The tabulation of A-A responses by frequency and by number of agreements with responses of other languages (Table 4C) is very similar to that of opposite responses (Table 4 A). A χ^2-test shows that the effect of frequency on number of agreements is significant for A-A responses ($\chi^2 = 13.02$, *df.* = 2, *P* < 0.01). The A-A responses, as a group, show a rather high mean number or agreements with other languages, 2.10. This number is very similar to the mean of 2.18 found for opposite responses and is well above the mean for all responses, taken without regard to category.

While the category of opposite responses tends largely to be composed of A-A responses, there is an equally strong tendency for the category of coördinate responses to be composed of noun-noun (N-N) pairs.

(4) Noun-Noun Pairs. Of the 130 coördinate responses, 114 are N-N pairs. Only five coördinate responses are A-A pairs, and these are all pairs of colors. In turn, the 114 N-N coördinate responses make up more than half of the total of 207 N-N responses. Tabulation of the N-N responses by frequency and by number of agreements (Table 4 D) gives a distribution somewhat similar to that for coördinates (Table 4 B). As was true for coördinate responses, the more frequently given N-N responses have significantly more agreements with the responses of other languages than do the less frequent N-N responses ($\chi^2 = 31.02$, *df.* = 3, *P* < 0.001). While the N-N responses of above-median frequency show a mean of 1.69 agreements with responses of other languages, those of below-median frequency show a mean of only 0.86 agreements. The N-N responses, as a group, have a mean of 1.24 agreements with the responses of other languages. This is similar to the mean for coördinate responses and is slightly below the mean for all responses, without regard to category.

DISCUSSION

In what terms can we attempt to account for the relation between agreements of primary responses among languages, on the one hand, and frequencies or categories of responses, on the other? Let us consider first the role of frequency, employing the following model: Suppose two random samples are taken from the word-association responses made to a single stimulus by the members of a language community. If the population gives one particular response with far greater frequency than any other response, then both samples will tend to show that response as their primary one. If, on the other hand, the primary and secondary responses of the population are not very different in frequency, then the two samples may well show different primary responses. If the statistics of the population are not known, one can nevertheless predict from one sample to another. The more the frequency of the primary response for an item exceeds the frequency of the secondary response in one sample, the more likely it is that the same response will be primary in another sample. This model predicts quite well the occurrence of the agreements between primary responses of women and men on the French test of word-association. If we take the 25 primary responses with the highest frequencies among the women, all 25 agree with the corresponding primary responses of the men; of the next 25, 23 agree; of the third set of 25 responses, 15 agree; of the 25 responses of lowest frequency among the women, only 12 agree with the primary responses of the men. When a similar analysis is made for the English data of Tresselt et al. (1955), the respective numbers of agreements are 25, 23, 21, and 13. Thus, the more frequent the primary response is in one sample, the more stable is it from sample to sample. (The somewhat greater agreement between the sexes in English than in French is consistent with the generally higher frequencies of primary responses in English as compared to French.) While division by sex does not give random samples, there is little evidence of significant difference in the associations of the two sexes, and the results for each language fit the model well. A further test is provided by the distribution of agreements between the English studies of Russell and Jenkins (1954) and that of Tresselt et al. (1955). Of the 25 most frequent primary responses found by Russell and Jenkins, all 25 agree with the corresponding primary responses found by Tresselt et al. (1955). In successive groups of 25 responses, arranged by decreasing frequency, there are, respectively, 25, 22, and 10 agreements. Again the obtained distribution follows the prediction of the model.

Thus far we have shown that the probability of agreement of primary responses among samples from the same population should be related to the extent to which the primary response exceeds the secondary response in frequency. Only for English have complete norms been published, however, so that the differences in frequencies between primary and secondary responses are readily available only in English. For French, German, and Italian, only the frequencies of primary responses have been published. To see how well the frequency of the primary response could serve as an index of the difference in frequencies between primary and secondary responses, the correlation was obtained between these two values for all 100 items in the English and French norms. The respective coefficients were 0.97 and 0.94, indicating that we are fully justified in using the frequency of the primary response in place of the difference in frequencies between primary and secondary responses.

To apply the model across languages requires the hypothesis that there is a cross-cultural community which shares verbal associations and meanings, even though verbal forms are different. If this hypothesis is limited to western European languages, then it is clearly supported by the results we have obtained. That is, the more frequently a primary response is given in one language, the more stable is the meaning of the response in other languages. It is as if each of the languages we have considered is a sample of a more general language-system.

It is tempting to try to extend the hypothesis to all languages, but data do not yet exist to test adequately this broad form of the hypothesis. A limited and preliminary test can be attempted with a small amount of Navaho material. The material on Navaho word-association was obtained by Ervin and Horowitz in 1956 (unpublished material). Their test was composed of 114 items, 42 of which were equivalent to items on the list of Kent and Rosanoff. The test was administered individually and orally in Navaho to 38 adult Ss, about two-thirds of whom were women, and most of whom spoke only Navaho. In view of the small size of the Navaho sample and of the difficulties of translation, comparisons with the Navaho material cannot have more than suggestive value. For 3 of the 42 items, the Italian response is not known, so comparisons can be made across all five languages for 39 items. In many cases the Navaho primary response is equivalent to that of the other languages (*e.g.* man-woman, soft-hard, hand-foot, long-short, heavy-light). In other cases, a cultural difference is apparent (*e.g.* bitter-chili pepper, river-canyon, beautiful-horse). The Kent-Rosanoff items included in the Navaho test tend to be predominantly selected from among items showing rather high inter-language agreement among the four European languages. To compare the number of agreements among the primary responses of the five languages, each language was considered in turn and the number of agreements with the responses of the other languages was tabulated for each of the 39 items. The English responses showed a mean number of agreements per item of 2.41; French, 2.05; German, 2.08; Italian, 2.03; Navaho, 1.69. Thus Navaho clearly shows fewer agreements with the European languages than each of the European languages shows with the other four. Nevertheless, the number of agreements between Navaho and any single European language is substantial. It ranges from 21 cases of agreement (out of 39) with English down to 14 cases of agreement with German. This extent of agreement offers support for the hypothesis that speakers of all languages share many verbal associations, even though their verbal forms are different.

In indicating why frequent responses tend to show strong agreement among languages, our model may also help to indicate why opposite or A-A responses show relatively high agreement among languages. If a stimulus has a clear opposite, this response tends to be given with much greater frequency than other responses, as Karwoski and Schachter found: "not all words have opposites; usually there is only one good opposite. When a stimulus-word has a common opposite word, the tendency is for the responses to pile up on that one word." Karwoski and Schachter (1948) did not mention grammatical categories, but it appears that adjectives are more likely to have opposites than are nouns. This is certainly the case in dictionary-citations. Thus adjectives are likely to have clear opposites, and if an opposite response exists it tends to be given with considerably greater frequency than other responses. As we have shown, such predominance of one response is the condition in which agreements among primary responses of different languages are to be expected.

If associative habits were completely general among languages, we would expect to find as many agreements of primary responses between two languages as between two samples from the same language. We have seen that this is not the case. Between English and French, for example, there are 48 cases of agreement, while between French men and women there are 75 cases of agreement. Is the entire difference between these figures to be accounted for by differences in English and French associative habits? There are at least two other factors to be considered:

(*a*) Part of the difference appears to arise from an artificial cause—difficulties of translation. In at least 10–15 cases, the French stimulus-word was not an exact equivalent of the English, and about the same proportion seems to hold for German and Italian. We have mentioned above the difficulties with 'sheep' and 'mutton' in French and with 'square' in Italian. In several other cases, the word translated was not of the same grammatical form as the English word. There is a strong tendency for response-words to be of the same grammatical form as the stimulus-word. Thus, changing the form of the translated word from that of the English makes it unlikely that the responses in the two languages will agree.

(*b*) In some cases, a difference occurred when the primary response in one language was one of completion, *i.e.* a complex of which the stimulus-word is a part. This is a type of associative habit, but of a special nature that deserves separate mention. It is extremely rare that two languages share the same completion-response, even though their other associations to the stimulus-word are similar. Thus, the English primary response to 'whistle' is 'stop' ('whistle-stop'). French does not have this compound term. The French primary response is 'train,' which is the secondary response in English. Each of the four languages has two or three cases in which the primary response is one of completion. Thus, between a pair of languages, about five disagreements will arise from this cause.

We can then apportion the cases of disagreement of primary responses between a pair of languages as follows: (a) About 25 cases are due to instability of the primary response, even samples from the same language failing to agree in this many cases. (b) In another 10–15 cases, the translation of the stimulus-word is inexact, so the similarity of association between languages is not tested adequately. (c) In about 5 cases, one language shows a completion-response and a similar complex does not exist in the other language. Thus, between a pair of western European languages, there seem to remain not more than perhaps 10 cases in which cultural factors give rise to a substantial difference in associations.

One strong qualification must be attached to our hypothesis that speakers of different languages tend to share the same associative habits—it holds only among adults. Comparison of responses of American children with those of American adults have shown very different types of responses (Woodworth, 1938). It would be interesting to see whether children speaking other languages respond similarly to American children, as we have shown adults of other languages to respond similarly to American adults. Such a study could help in the search for general factors operating in the learning of language in all cultures and tending to produce similar associative habits regardless of the forms of particular languages.

SUMMARY

Comparisons were made among primary responses to the word-list of Kent and Rosanoff and to its translations in French, German, and Italian. There was a strong tendency for primary responses to corresponding stimulus-words to be equivalent in meaning. In each language, the greater the frequency with which a particular primary response was given, the more likely was that response to agree in meaning with the corresponding primary responses of the other languages. When both stimulus- and primary response-words were adjectives or when the response was opposite in meaning to the stimulus-word, there also was high agreement among languages. (The two categories, 'opposite' and 'adjective-adjective' had seven-eighths of their cases in common.)

The results can be accounted for on the assumption that, across languages, similar associations tend to occur among words of similar meaning, regardless of differences in verbal forms among the languages.

Within a single language, the more a particular response tends to predominate in one sample of responses to a given word, the more likely it is that the same response will be primary in another sample. If associative tendencies are shared among languages, then the more a particular response predominates among the responses to a given stimulus-word in one language, the more likely it is that an equivalent response will be primary in another language.

REFERENCES

Karwoski, T. F. and J. Schachter. Psychological studies in semantics: III. Reaction times for similarity and difference, *J. Soc. Psychol.*, 1948, **28**, 103–120.

Kent, G. H. and A. J. Rosanoff. A study of association in insanity, *Amer. J. Insanity*, 1910, **67**, 37–96, 317–390.

Levi, M. An analysis of the influence of two different cultures on responses to the Rosanoff free association test. Unpublished Master's thesis, University of Chicago, 1949.

Rosenzweig, M. R. Etudes sur l'association des mots, *Année Psychol.*, 1957, **57**, 23–32.

Rosenzweig, M. R. Comparisons between French and English word association norms, *Amer. Psychologist*, 1959, **14**, 363.

Russell, W. A. and J. J. Jenkins. The complete Minnesota norms for responses to 100 words from the Kent-Rosanoff Word Association Test, 1954.

Russell, W. A. and O. R. Meseck. Der Einfluss der Association auf das Erinnern von Worten in der Deutschen, Französischen, und Englischen Sprache, *Z. Exp. Angew. Psychol.*, 1959, **6**, 191–211.

Tresselt, M. E., D. S. Leeds, and M. S. Mayzner. The Kent-Rosanoff Word Association Test: II. A comparison of sex differences in response frequencies, *J. Genet. Psychol.*, 1955, **87**, 149–153.

Woodworth, R. S. *Experimental Psychology*. New York: Holt, Rinehart and Winston, Inc., 1938.

2-3

Abstract and Concrete Modes of Classification in Nigeria

D. R. PRICE-WILLIAMS

Western intelligence tests often show African people as having a lower level of abstraction than Western groups. Can these cultural differences between African and Western subjects be reduced with the use of culturally appropriate test material? Instead of using conventional classification tests (Goldstein-Scheerer cube test, the Wechsler Bellevue version of the Kohs Block Test), Dr. Price-Williams made an ingenious effort to use test material from the Tiv environment in Nigeria. He also tried to communicate certain concepts such as triangle and square in the absence of these configurations as abstract shapes in the Tiv language. His study shows the effects of literacy, education, and the availability of linguistic expression for certain concepts on the development of abstract abilities. It seems that the assumption that non-Western people lack these abilities is contrary to the results of the present study. The same assumption is not in line with the general observation that indigenous laws and family and tribe organization require a high level of abstraction. In their discussion of this problem, Hunt and Cofer (1944, p. 1018) stated that "One should not expect primitive

Reprinted from *Brit. J. Educ. Psychol.*, 1962, **32**, 50–61, by permission of the author and the British Psychological Society.

peoples to lack the basic capacity to acquire our adult forms of organization. They lack them because these forms did not exist in the cultures that nurtured them. Moreover, they would have great difficulty acquiring ours at adulthood because of habit interference between their own and ours."

REFERENCES

Hunt, J. McV. and C. Cofer. Psychological deficit. In J. McV. Hunt (ed.), *Personality and the behavior disorders*. Vol. II. New York: The Ronald Press Company, 1944.

I.—INTRODUCTION

There have been several kinds of evaluations of the cognitive abilities of underdeveloped peoples. The first kind is best exemplified by Carothers (1953) who, on the basis of little relevant evidence, claimed that the African does not have sound abstraction. Also Haward and Roland (1954, 1955a, 1955b), in a series of papers in an anthropological journal, which sparked off highly critical responses by anthropologists, drew attention to what they termed the concreteness of the Nigerian's mental approach. This conclusion was inferred from the application of a somewhat inadequate (for this purpose) instrument, namely the Goodenough Draw-a-Man Test. A second kind of assessment, one which comes to the same conclusions although somewhat modified, has been that expressed by Wintringer (1955). The difference is that the latter has based his conclusions on a considerable number of relevant tests by other investigators. Wintringer writes:

"L'infériorité intellectuelle du noir s'explique donc par un comportement mental profondément conditionné par une attitude concrète, intuitive, et rivée à la perception syncrétique de la réalité sensible. Par conséquent la presque totalité des noirs est incapable d'effectuer une opération mentale selon le procédé classique de l'abstraction et de manier simultanément des relations conceptuelles opposées."

On the other hand, McConnell (1954), in his study among the Tepehuan Indians, using an adaptation of the Wechsler-Bellevue version of the Kohs Block Test, found marked evidence of ability to abstract. However, both these studies are similar in that actual experiments were performed, and the conclusions drawn are not sweeping generalisations.

Comparing them one might come simply to the conclusion that while Africans do not have the ability to abstract, Tepehuan Indians have.

A third kind of assessment starts off from the premise that *degree* of abstraction is the relevant factor, and has gone on to make the highly important inquiry as to whether there is a difference between acculturated and literate *versus* unacculturated and illiterate natives. Jahoda (1956), for instance, using the Goldstein-Scheerer Cube Test on adolescent boys in or near Accra, found that "boys from literate homes performed significantly better than those from illiterate ones." Maistriaux (1955), in a whole series of investigations in the Belgian Congo, found large differences between bush and school Africans. His general conclusions are that, while qualitatively the thought processes of the African Negro are similar to those of Europeans, their rate of development in this direction is lower.

All of these studies, performed within various age ranges, but generally on adolescents and young adults, have used tests of abstract ability which are similar to those used in American or European cultures. Jahoda, in the same article, maintains that these are no more 'culture-free' than tests of intelligence, which are clearly recognised as not being so. This statement provides a starting-off point for the present study which is different from those listed above inasmuch as it employs material which is indigenous to those to whom it is applied. The question can then be directly tested, whether the difference between bush subjects and subjects with school education, still persists.

The subjects of the research were children of the Tiv tribe, of Benue Province, Nigeria. The investigation was carried out while the writer was living, in the manner of an anthropologist, in a native hut of a particular compound. Experiments were carried out either in this hut, or anywhere else in the compound, or in other compounds or in the nearby Bush Junior Primary School. The study might be described as ecological, a type of research which Leeper (1951) has advocated in his chapter on Cognitive Processes. Though it is recognised that properly conducted laboratory studies are methodologically more rigorous, there is much to be said for this kind of research where the instructions are carried out in the native language and where experimental results are assessed in the context of everyday living conditions. Tiv are a tribe of subsistent farmers; their interests lie in animals, plants and matters of agriculture generally. Therefore, the material used for the research were exemplars of animals and plants with which they were familiar. The purpose of the research was to see to what extent and in what kind of way Tiv children could categorise this material. The results are assessed in the framework of abstraction *versus* concreteness of approach.

As with so many psychological terms, 'abstract' and 'concrete' suffer from a lack of precision. The various definitions given to them in the literature designate two widely contrasted attitudes. To Lévy-Bruhl (1926), in his writings on the so-called pre-logical mentality, concreteness had meant dependency on particular objects, with the consequent inability to select and classify independently, attributes from the objects. To Goldstein and Scheerer (1941) in their classic monograph, concreteness of thinking indicated 'immediacy of claim' of one particular aspect of an object, which might be experienced as sensory impressiveness, or as sensory cohesion, or as situational belongingness. Whatever the nature of the claim, the individual is unable to detach himself from the uniqueness of the object and fails to see it as a representative of a class. This dependency results in rigidity and 'lack of shifting.' Conversely, the abstract attitude forms the basis for being able to shift reflectively from one aspect of a situation to another or to hold in mind simultaneously various objects. Hanfmann and Kasanin (1942) entertain similar definitions, while Humphrey (1951), treating abstraction more as a process than an attitude, nevertheless defines it as the selection of some particular feature of a situation to the exclusion of others.

Generalising from these descriptions, abstraction will be regarded as being steps away from a 'zero-level' of complete sensory immediateness and object dependency. A simple measurement device for scoring responses on this basis will be described later.

II.—METHODOLOGY

(1) *ASSUMPTIONS.* On the assumption that (*a*) the continuum abstract-concrete has some value, particularly when considered in the setting of non-Western children undergoing Western education, and (*b*) that tests, standardised in the West, are inadequate for testing abstract ability, experiments were devised which involved problems of abstraction on 'natural' phenomena. These experiments were done with children who attended a Bush Junior Primary School and children who did not attend any school. The homes of both groups of children were identical. Both lived in compounds around the school and, with the exception of those children whose fathers were teachers (two children only), their parents were illiterate. There was one factor which could not be controlled, and that is bilingualism. Of the four classes in a Bush Primary School, the first three are taught as much in English as in their own language. Although all these experiments were carried out in the vernacular, at first with the help of translators (teachers), and afterwards by the investigator himself, 75 per cent. of the literates could speak and understand varying degrees of English. Although some of the illiterates in their turn could speak English, this was of the pidgin variety and did not go very far.

(2) *DESIGN.* The material consisted of animals and plants. The difficulty of language (for the investigator) and the desire not to complicate the task inordinately, led to very simple methods of enquiry, which were requests for classification and requests for sorting. On the one hand, a selection of material was put before the subject with the request to select those that belonged together. This is the simplest variant of what Vinacke (1951) has labelled the problem-solving method involved in concept formation experiments. On the other hand, three or four objects were put before a subject, one of which was different from the others on some basis: the subject was merely asked to say which one. In both methods reasons were sought as to the basis of classification and differentiation.

(3) *AGE SAMPLING.* This was a considerable problem as *absolute* age was very difficult to ascertain, but it was easier if *relative* age was taken as a basis. A convenient starting point for age sampling was the Bush Junior Primary School, which was divided into four classes. With the aid of its teachers, the classes were ascribed a somewhat rough estimate of age as follows:

Class I	6½ years approx.
Class II	8 years approx.
Class III	9½ years approx.
Class IV	11 years approx.

This estimation was based on the average of each class, but was given somewhat more precision by taking out (for reasons of sampling in testing) any particular boy or girl whom the teachers knew to be clearly older or younger than the estimated average age. For example, an 11-year-old (estimated) boy who was in Class III would be relegated, for testing only, to Class IV. With this as a base-line illiterates could be classified by the simple device of asking each child whether he was older or younger than a selected boy whom he knew in school, and again whether he was older or younger than another illiterate. Generally, there could be found illiterates living side by side with literates, and although their absolute ages were always in doubt, the importance of age grading in the Tiv, and the importance of seniority in the family, determined fairly well the required comparisons.

The number of schoolchildren in the classes varied, but for convenience of tabulating the number of subjects was taken as 20 for each. This was done by leaving out the surplus around the centre of each class, again with the advice of the teachers. Collecting the same number of illiterates was a formidable task, partly on account of the continual movement of Tiv children, so the total number of illiterates equivalent to each literate class was less, namely 15. This gave a total of 80 literate subjects and 60 illiterates.

III.—LINGUISTIC BACKGROUND

It is necessary to include a relevant digression on the classifications of animals and plants in the Tiv language, although none of the children tested overtly used them. Abraham (1940) noted that there was a mixture of abstraction and concreteness in the Tiv language. The verb to break, for example, has no generic term but differs according to whether one is breaking something into pieces, or breaking it across and so forth. On the other hand, the linguistic classification of animals separates clawed animals from the cloven-hoofed and ruminants, and domestic animals from wild. Nevertheless, concreteness is also in evidence by the dependency on colour or situation: crabs are divided into red or black, fish into those that swim on the surface or those which frequent the river bed. Plants tend to be categorised functionally in the language. Bohannan (1954) reports that staple crops are termed faeces-forming food while the remainder are termed urine-forming food. Abraham (1940) again comments that there is, for example, a separate classification for plants from which soup can be made.

According to my informants in the area, the linguistic classification of plants is twofold. This is not mentioned in the published literature nor did I hear of it from missionaries in the area who were familiar with the language and culture of the Tiv.

I. *Sham i yer.* This is roughly translatable as 'plants as seeds.' The term *sham* refers to the seed actually in the plant, while *yer* means 'to conceal.' The classification includes such plants as guinea-corn, millet, bean, ground nut, rice and benniseed.

II. *Atam a yer.* Roughly translatable as plants with roots. *Atam* is the plural of *ityamegh*, meaning fruit. This includes cassava, potatoes, and two plants, untranslatable, called *alum* and *mongolo*.

The first group has a sub-classification:

(a) *Ishange mom.* 'Ishange' is the term given to a grain of seed. 'Mom' merely means 'one.' This refers to the actual seed leaf, which is visible. It could be translatable into our own botanical nomenclature as monocotyledon. It includes millet and guinea-corn.

(b) *Asange ahar.* This is the plural form, and can be called 'two-leaf' or dicotyledon. It includes ground-nut, bean.

It is interesting to note that whereas this sub-classification is pheno-typical, its superordinate is genotypical.

Although these classifications may be a modernised Tiv version (as I never came across other than educated Tiv who used them) the *idea*, of some plants having one seed-leaf and others two, was certainly entertained. Besides this some plants, distinguishable overtly from the language, were classified according as to whether they lay beside a stream or on a hill, and again some plants were classified in sex terms (*ihura nomso, ihura kwase*: *ihura* being the name of the plant and the other two terms being male and female). This did not imply any biological connection between the plants; it was only that each was used in a male or a female ceremony.

IV.—CLASSIFICATION EXPERIMENTS

PROCEDURE AND SCORING. A collection of either animal examples or plant examples was arranged before each subject with instructions to put into rows those which belonged together. He was asked to do this in as many different ways as he could. A simple scoring device was to list the number of alternative ways which each subject employed, together with the reason for them. This was done on the commonly held assumption that the ability to 'shift,' that is of alternative ways of classification, is a measure of ability to abstract. The reasons were given a qualitative grading on a scale ranging from concreteness to abstraction, a zero score being a classification in terms of sensory immediateness or object-dependency, while scores above zero signified varying steps away from the particular and immediate towards generality and abstraction. As there is always an arbitrariness about such qualitative scores these results are considered as secondary in significance to the number of shifts.

(1) *Animal Material.* Toy animals were used, all familiar to Tiv children, as follows:

2 Black Cocks.
2 Brown Cocks.
2 White Hens.
2 Black Hens.
2 Brown Horses.
2 Black-and-white Cows.
2 Brown Goats.
2 Grey Elephants.[1]
2 Green Snakes.
2 White Sheep.
2 Brown Birds (unspecified variety).
2 Brown Rats.

[1]There were no elephants in the area, but the animal was known.

In addition to this, I collected two dead black beetles and a fish known to the Tiv. The whole collection was displayed to each child at one time.

The following reasons of classification were given:
A. Individual creatures according to name.
B. Colour.
C. Size.
D. Number of Legs.
E. Situations. Example, fish in water, snake in bush, cocks and hens in compound, bird in air.
F. Domesticity *versus* Wildness.
G. Edibility.
H. Odd choices. Example, Some have marks, some are bright, etc.

Quantitative responses are given in Tables 1 and 2. As more than one classification was selected, Table 2, which shows the percentages of reasons for classifications, takes only the initial choice.

(2) *Plant Material.* The following plants and leaves were collected from the area and displayed for classification:

guinea-corn,
millet,
benniseed,
ground-nut,
cassava,
yams,
leaves of *mongolo*,
three other types of plants, non-edible and untranslatable.

This whole collection was also displayed to each child at one time. Qualitative responses were based on the following:

A. Edibility.
B. Size.
C. Coming from the earth or from trees.
D. Roots *versus* non-Roots.
E. Situation, e.g., near river or on top of hill.
F. Seed-leaves.

Results with the plant experiments are seen in Tables 3 and 4. Table 4 again takes the initial choice of classification for the basis of scoring the reasons.

TABLE 1
Average Number of Shifts per Age Group

	Literates	Illiterates
Class I	3.0	3.2
Class II	3.5	3.6
Class III	4.8	5.0
Class IV	6.1	5.8

TABLE 2
Percentage of Qualitative Responses per Age Group,
According to Previous Categories, First Choice

	Literates								Illiterates							
	A	B	C	D	E	F	G	H	A	B	C	D	E	F	G	H
Class I	80	15	5	—	—	—	—	—	87	7	7	—	—	—	—	—
Class II	80	10	5	5	—	—	—	—	80	7	7	—	—	—	—	7
Class III	65	15	5	5	—	—	5	5	73	7	—	—	—	13	—	7
Class IV	60	5	5	5	5	—	15	5	67	7	—	—	7	13	7	—

TABLE 3
Average Number of Shifts per Age Group

	Literates	Illiterates
Class I	2.2	2.4
Class II	2.8	3.0
Class III	4.5	4.5
Class IV	5.4	5.6

TABLE 4
Percentage of Qualitative Responses per Age Group, According to
Previous Categories, First Choice

	Literates						Illiterates					
	A	B	C	D	E	F	A	B	C	D	E	F
Class I	85	5	5	—	5	—	87	7	7	—	—	—
Class II	80	5	5	—	10	—	80	13	7	—	—	—
Class III	70	—	10	5	10	5	73	7	7	7	7	—
Class IV	65	—	20	5	5	5	67	—	13	7	7	7

V.—SORTING EXPERIMENTS

PROCEDURE AND SCORING. The qualitative responses given by subjects on the preceding classification experiments were made the basis for sorting experiments. The procedure involved was very simple: a variety of items was put before each subject with the statement that one was different. Each subject was asked which one was different and to give the reason. A preliminary test was carried out with sizes of leaves. Four leaves were set on the ground, one of which was very big, while the others were quite small. Scoring was done in percentages of correctness of responses. A response was judged correct if both the response and the reason for it accorded with the experimenter's choice. The following list shows the material used:

(1) Animal Material.
  (*a*) Three animals with four legs, one of two legs.
  (*b*) Three domestic animals, one wild animal, as recognised by Tiv.
  (*c*) Three edible (by Tiv) animals, one non-edible.
(2) Plant and leaves Material.
  (*a*) Three plants with roots, one without.
  (*b*) Three plants with two seed leaves, one with one seed-leaf.
  (*c*) Three plant-leaves from the earth, one from a tree.

All material was selected to be as individually different from one another as possible except for the chosen criterion. For example, where model animals were used, all four objects were different colours, all were different sizes, and so forth.

RESULTS. Table 5 shows the percentage responses of both groups according to the material employed.

TABLE 5
Percentage of Correct Responses in Sorting Experiments

Basis		Literates				Illiterates		
	I	II	III	IV	I	II	III	IV
(1) Animals:								
(*a*) Legs	75	80	90	100	60	73	93	93
(*b*) Domesticity	45	60	75	80	53	73	73	73
(*c*) Edibility	55	55	65	90	60	67	80	93
(2) Plants:								
(*a*) Roots	45	50	60	70	53	60	67	80
(*b*) Two-leafed	55	55	60	70	60	67	73	80
(*c*) From earth	65	70	85	95	67	73	93	100

VI.—ANALYSIS OF REASONS FOR CLASSIFICATION

In the Introduction it was stated that sensory immediateness and object dependency formed the 'zero-level' of the idea of concreteness. In relation to the actual responses noted in Tables 2 and 4, this means that any answer given in terms of an immediate sensory impression, such as colour, shape or size will be given a zero mark. Responses by name qualify also for a zero mark as this is evidence of object-dependency, that is the inability to conceive of the object as a member of a class. Where there is clear evidence of a movement away from the immediate situation, to make some classification on a basis of a dichotomy like edibility *versus* non-edibility, or domesticity *versus* wildness, a mark of 2 will be given. This still leaves responses concerning classifications on the basis of number of legs in animals, and roots and seed-leaves of plants to be considered. These qualify for sensory immediateness inasmuch as the exemplars are there in front of the classifier, yet there is some attempt to select from each example a feature which is common to the set, and on this basis to form a class. These responses will be given an intermediate mark of 1. The scoring system is summarised as follows:

Score 0. *Animal Classifications:* Name, Colour, Size, Situation.
          Plant and Leaf Classifications: Size, Coming from earth or trees Situation.

Score 1. *Animal Classifications:* Number of legs.
          Plant and Leaf Classifications: Roots *versus* non-roots, number of seed-leaves.

Score 2. *Animal Classifications:* Domesticity *versus* wildness. Edibility.
          Plant and Leaf Classifications: Edibility.

Table 6 gives the comparison of the four groups of literates and illiterates in terms of the scoring system, expressed as percentages. Odd choices are not scored.

TABLE 6
Scoring of Qualitative Responses

Score	Lit. I	Illit. I	Lit. II	Illit. II	Lit. III	Illit. III	Lit. IV	Illit. IV
				Animals				
0	100	100	95	94	85	80	75	80
1	—	—	5	—	5	—	5	—
2	—	—	—	—	5	13	15	20
				Plants				
0	15	13	20	20	20	20	25	20
1	—	—	—	—	10	7	10	13
2	85	87	80	80	70	73	65	67

VII.—DISCUSSION

A highly relevant feature involved in analysing the process of classification in non-Western people is that of interest or motivation. Where there is little incentive in forming different kinds of categories, it is not surprising to find apparent dependency upon the concrete. Yet only a casual acquaintance with the monographs of anthropologists should convince one that the simplest of peoples often have social categories of kinship, marriage, property and law which call for abstraction of a fairly complex order. It is in relation to *objects* that the concrete is dominant, or appears dominant and it may be, as Rollings (1960) has recently pointed out, that there is a radical difference between Europeans and Africans in relation to the perception of objects and to people. However, with reference to the present theme, it need only be said that there is little interest in forming classification of objects. Where there *is* interest, as is seen in the figures for plants in Table 6, then an abstract classification is appreciably formed. The lack of a classification on the grounds of edibility and domesticity *versus* wildness in animals needs to be explained. In the particular area in which this research was conducted, there were, in fact, very few wild animals. Most of the land had been cultivated and the game killed. Also the majority of food-stuffs came from plants. Chickens, goats and occasionally sheep were the only animal foods eaten. This factor of interest is relevant again when studying those Tables relating to shift of classifications and those in which the qualitative responses of the first choice are noted. For, in those cases where the first choice is clearly of a concrete nature, it is only by probing the individual that the interrogator receives an abstract classification. For example, with the animal material, it is only by the last or one but last shift of classification that a category of wildness *versus* domesticity comes. It does not come readily. Nevertheless, the fact that it comes at all indicates that the Tiv child can abstract. Even if the qualitative scoring system presented here is arbitrary, the number of shifts shown in Tables 1 and 3 shows that the Tiv child is quite capable of moving from one category to another. Granted that this is so, a comparison of literates and illiterates was arranged in order to see whether the small amount of formal abstraction which literate Tiv children receive in school would influence their classification of natural phenomena. A comparison of the number of shifts (Tables 1 and 3) shows hardly any difference between the groups in any of the classes. Neither does a comparison of the qualitative responses (Tables 2 and 4). The sorting experiments (Table 5) show similar results. It is difficult to comment upon this finding. The available evidence does not indicate whether the lack of difference shows a similarity of potential for abstraction, or whether the type of training in schools, up to the age tested, does not encourage an abstract attitude, or whether the type of material used for experiments fails to discriminate between the groups.

With both literates and illiterates there is a tendency for less dependence upon the concrete as the children grow older. Experiments with animals show both a decrease of the purely concrete reasons for classifications and an increase in the more abstract reasons (Table 6). An exception to this trend appears in the figures for edibility in the plants experiments. Here Class I (literates and illiterates) returned a higher percentage than the three other classes, and there is a gradual decline from Class I to Class IV, although in all groups the abstract reasons (Score 2) were the most frequent. Again, in the sorting experiments, the figures suggest (Table 5) that there is a consistent increase over the years in the ability to determine what exemplars make a group, although these figures do not show any significant difference between the kinds of exemplars chosen by the experimenter.

One point needs to be made regarding the position of language. It has been said that there was little reference to the formal system of classification reported by ethnographers. For example, the term for a domestic animal is 'ilev.' Of the responses noted as domesticity *versus* wildness of animals, very few children actually used the term 'ilev.' The distinction was eked out by circuitous descriptions of animals that one found in the compound and which could be left to roam about on their own, which did not attack one and the like. It was clear here that the category of 'domestic animal' was uppermost although the actual term was not used. The findings reported, therefore, are not fully determined by the existing linguistic classification. It was also noted that linguistic terms could be constructed if, in fact, there was no corresponding term in the language. For example, there is no Tiv term for 'triangle.' When (in other perceptual experiments which the writer performed) this figure was drawn, it was labelled a 'three-cornered square.' Actually, there is really no term for square either, but a drawing of a square proper or a rectangle was called after the native term for that shaped hut—'gondo.' A three-cornered 'gondo' was merely an extension, constructed to fill a lacuna in their own language. That the experimenter has now introduced the *concept* of triangularity into the Tiv tribe is a philosophical point which he feels unqualified to amplify.

The discussion has so far been focussed on the rather more clinical connotation of the verb 'to abstract.' In the Introduction it was noted that the word, as far as psychologists employ it, has two aspects: that of attitude and that of process. As far as the former is concerned, we hope to have shown that there is little difference between these African children tested and European children. When we come to consider the results viewing abstraction as a process, it is necessary to use a framework other than the clinical one. It is doubtless a confusion of the two aspects that has given rise in the past to such statements as that Africans show a schizophrenic rigidity in their thinking. A convenient framework comes from the general works of Piaget. Using this framework, Maistriaux found that his adolescent and young adult African subjects, both bush and literates, only reached the most primitive of Piaget's rational stages, i.e., the period of concrete operations (see Duijker and Frijda, 1960, summary). Now the age range of the subjects used in the present study comes under the period of the third stage—the period of concrete operations. It is within this period, according to Piaget, that the idea of classes properly arises. As Berlyne (1957) puts it: "The concept of a 'class' or the operation of 'classification' is an internalised version of the action of grouping together objects recognized as similar. Having learned to pick out all the yellow counters in a heap and *place* them together in one spot, the child acquired the ability to *think* of all yellow objects together and thus form the concept of the 'class of all yellow objects'." The transition from perception to conception can be picked up from our analysis of the qualitative responses (Table 6). Leaving aside the edibility aspect of plants, there does seem to be a deficiency of the ability to form abstract classes below Class III. Now Class III, as has been noted, had an average age of 9½ years; and Class II's mean age was 8 years. Even allowing for the difficulty of absolute precision in age reckoning, it would seem that there is a little lag in years for this period of 'concrete operations.' That these African children reach it, whether literate or illiterate, is certainly the case. However, our figures suggest that, in comparison with European standards, already there is a difference, on the assumption that we can equate the material used with those of other workers. If valid, this is an important finding because there is no difference between literates and illiterates when not using material upon which the factor of training would be likely to influence differences, i.e., blocks and designs. Using familiar material which they have had an opportunity of manipulating, the evidence suggests that the growth in the capacity to reach the state of 'concrete operations' proceeds at a similar rate in both school and illiterate children.

SUMMARY

1. Past investigations of the cognitive processes of primitive peoples are reviewed, with special reference to the continuum of abstract and concrete. It is pointed out that these studies have used Western type tests in reaching their conclusions. The present study differs in using indigenous material; the author, having lived among the subjects in the

manner of an anthropologist, and speaking (inexpertly but sufficiently) the native language.

2. Bush and primary school children, living in the same area, were compared in their ability to classify and to sort (*a*) models of animals known in the area, (*b*) plants actually picked in the neighbourhood. The ability to shift from one classification to another and the basis of classification were investigated. The linguistic background relevant to the classifications is described.

3. Using familiar material there was found no difference between the two sets of children, of an age range from approximately 6½ to 11 years. The results are discussed in the light of the general ability to abstract, in the sense of shifting from one class to another, and in the framework of the transition of the process of abstraction during this age period which comes under Piaget's period of "Concrete Operations."

REFERENCES

Abraham, R. C. *The Tiv people.* Second ed., London: Crown Agents for the Colonies, 1940.

Berlyne, D. E. Recent developments in Piaget's work, *Brit. J. Educ. Psychol.*, 1957, **27**, 1–12.

Bohannan, P. *Tiv farm and settlement.* London: H.M.S.O., Colonial Research Studies, No. 15, 1954.

Carothers, J. C. *The African mind in health and disease.* Geneva: World Health Organisation, 1953.

Duijker, H. C. J., and N. H. Frijda. *National character and national stereotypes.* Confluence: Surveys of Research in the Social Sciences. Vol. 1. Amsterdam: North-Holland Publishing Co., 1960.

Goldstein, K., and M. Scheerer. Abstract and concrete behavior. An experimental study with special tests, *Psychol., Monogr.*, 1941, **53**, No. 2.

Hanfmann, E., and J. Kasanin. *Conceptual thinking in schizophrenia.* New York: Nervous and Mental Disease Monographs, No. 67, 1942.

Haward, L. C. R., and W. A. Roland. Some inter-cultural differences on the Draw-a-Man test: Goodenough scores, *Man*, 1954, **54**, 86–88.

Haward, L. C. R., and W. A. Roland. Some inter-cultural differences on the Draw-a-Man test: Part II, Machover scores, *Man*, 1955(a), **55**, 27–29.

Haward, L. C. R., and W. A. Roland Some inter-cultural differences on the Draw-a-Man test. Part III, conclusion, *Man*, 1955(b), **55**, 40–42.

Humphrey, G. *Thinking.* London: Methuen and Co., Ltd., 1951.

Jahoda, G. Assessment of abstract behavior in a non-western culture, *J. Abnorm. Soc. Psychol.*, 1956, **53**, 237–243.

Leeper, R. Cognitive processes. In S. S. Stevens (ed.), *Handbook of experimental psychology.* New York: John Wiley and Sons, Inc., 1951.

Lévy-Bruhl, L. *How natives think.* English translation. London, 1926.

Maistriaux, R. La sous-évolution des noirs d'Afrique. Sa nature, ses causes, ses remèdes, *Revue de Psychologie des Peuples*, 1955, **10**, Part I, 167–189; Part II, 397–456.

McConnell, J. Abstract behavior among the Tepehuan, *J. Abnorm. Soc. Psychol.*, 1954, **49,** 109–110.

Rollings, P. J. A note on the cultural direction of perceptual selectivity, *Proc. 16th Int. Congr. of Psychol.*, 1960.

Vinacke, W. E. The investigation of concept formation, *Psychol. Bull.*, 1951, **48,** 1–31.

Wintringer, G. Considérations sur l'intelligence du noir africain, *Revue de Psychologie des Peubles*, 1955, **10,** 37–55.

2-4

The Intelligence of English Canal Boat Children

HUGH GORDON

Traditional intelligence tests emphasize, to a great extent, cognitive abilities (vocabulary, general information) that are obviously developed by education. The strength of the relationship between IQ and educational deprivation or lack of intellectual stimulation is well illustrated by the present study of Canal Boat children. Gordon demonstrates that the IQ scores of these underprivileged children do not reflect their native abilities but are due to the inadequacy of their educational opportunities. Moreover the decrease in their IQ with age does not mean that these children become progressively duller. It only reflects that the influence of lack of formal education on IQ scores increases with age.

In order to test the effect of a lack of schooling on the responses to "intelligence" tests, a school was chosen attended by children who had had little or no schooling—a special school for Canal Boat children.

The following quotations from a report on living-in on canal boats gives a good description of the life and education of these children. The

Abridged from *Mental and scholastic tests among retarded children*, Educational Pamphlet, No. 44, London: Board of Education, 1923, by permission of the controller of Her Britannic Majesty's Stationery Office.

report was drawn up in May 1921, and contains many facts of interest in connection with the present investigation.[1]

Referring to the Canal Boat population generally, the report states:

. . . but the majority of witnesses have agreed that, so far as health, cleanliness, morality, feeding and clothing are concerned, they are fully equal, if not superior, to town dwellers of a similar class.

In reference to the health of the children, it further says:

. . . but taking the evidence as a whole, we cannot assert that the health of Canal Boat children is worse than that of those who live in the crowded dwellings of our large cities. Probably the open-air life during the day does something to counteract the conditions at night. Certainly the children do not appear to be nearly so liable to infectious diseases as those who live on shore, and this is in accordance with what we should naturally expect, as they must be less exposed to infection.

As regards child labour the Committee considers that without doubt these children are useful to the boatmen, particularly when they are 12 years of age and upwards.

As to education, the report continues:

There remains the question of education, and here the evidence is overwhelming and practically unanimous that under the present circumstances Canal Boat children are scandalously under-educated. When their manner of life is considered, it is not surprising; their only opportunities for schooling occur when the boats are tied up for loading or discharging, and the fact that many of the adult boat population are themselves unable to read or write has a tendency to make them lax in seeing that their children take full advantage of their opportunities.

It was calculated that in one part of the system half the children had not put in twenty half-day attendances in the year. From other statistics it appeared that 532 children averaged only forty-six half-day attendances during a period of sixteen months, and that if those children who lived on shore part of the time were eliminated the average of the remaining 354 was only twenty-two half-days. How small this attendance really is may be well judged when it is compared with the 360 half-day attendances in the year of the child in the ordinary Elementary School.

From the registers of the school under review it appears that the children only attend about once a month for one to perhaps two and a half days. The maximum continuous attendance of any child was five half-days, and such a number of attendances was very exceptional. It is true that in between their attendances here they have the opportunity of

[1](Report of the Departmental Committee on Living-in on Canal Boats. 1921, Ministry of Health.)

attending other schools, e.g., in Birmingham and elsewhere. It is unnecessary to emphasise the difficulties of teaching such children.

In referring to the future careers of the children, the report adds:

> It may be pointed out in this connection that want of education practically ties these children down to the occupation of their fathers, and, however useful this may be from the point of view of the industry, we cannot bring ourselves to consider it as a serious argument in comparison with the prospects of the children.

As to the number of Canal Boat children statistics are very meagre. It was estimated by the Board of Education that for the year 1919 there were 1,112 children of school age. In another estimate the number of children was given as 1,343, of whom 726 were of school age. Of these, 629 had either never been to school or had practically no education; there appeared to be only 97 whose education could be considered good or fair.

The following additional information, which seems to be reliable, may be of interest. The Canal Boat population, as a rule, is born, lives and dies on the boats. It is stated that at least £4 a week is earned on an average, even in bad times; at other times considerably more. Some of the men even own their own boats. These people appear to live very isolated lives with very little social intercourse. To quote once more from the report:

> Life on board these boats appears to be of an almost patriarchal character, and there was a general agreement among witnesses that the presence of the wife and mother on board helps to preserve a high standard of morality among the men, and a kindly but efficient discipline among the children.

When the boats remain in a town for loading and unloading, the children do not appear to mix readily with other children; they attend places of entertainment, such as cinemas, etc., and have money to spend. Many of the children are well dressed, clean and appear fairly intelligent, although some of the older ones are undoubtedly very dull. The majority were found to be anxious to talk, but it was often difficult to understand what they said owing to their indistinct articulation and their use of unrecognisable words. As can be well imagined, the teacher of such a school has a most difficult task, for on one day she may have thirty children aged from 5 to 14 years, half of whom can neither read nor do the simplest calculation; on the next day she may have but one pupil. The discipline during the inspections was excellent; the children were interested, and anxious to do their best.

To sum up, these children in respect to health, cleanliness, morality, feeding, etc., are fully equal, if not superior, to town dwellers of a similar character. That they are not mentally defective, as is generally understood by that term, is shown by the life and wages of their parents, who in many cases have had no education and can neither read nor write. Their intellectual life, on the other hand, is of a most meagre description, owing to their lack of education and also owing to their social isolation.

THE TESTS

The tests used in these investigations were those described by L. M. Terman, in his "Measurement of Intelligence," 1919. They are called "The Stanford Revision and Extension Tests" and are based on the Binet-Simon Scale, but with considerable revisions and extensions. Full details and explanations are given in the book. The instructions and scoring in the book and record booklet were followed as closely as possible. A few necessary changes were made. For example, in VIII_3 (c), "What's the thing to do if a playmate hits you without meaning to do it?" for "playmate," "boy" or "girl," as the case may be, was substituted; in III_4 (b), "An apple and a peach. In what way are they alike?" for "peach" was substituted "orange"; in XIV_6 "Change places" was substituted for 'trade places." In IX_3, "pennies" was substituted for "cents"; the absurdity of the question as thus altered was never noticed; it was thought better, however, to keep the questions arithmetically as near as possible to the original. In the same question "shopkeeper" was used in place of "storekeeper."

In the first school tested (School B) the "abbreviated scale" was used. As the results were interesting, and unexpectedly subnormal, the full scale was used for School A. All the children present in the two schools were tested. The results of the two scales were carefully compared, and it was found on calculation that there was on the average a difference of less than a week in M.A. between them. Throughout the following report by the term "intelligence" is meant "intelligence" as found by the tests—nothing more unless otherwise stated. Whether this is real intelligence as is understood by the common use of the term is quite another matter.

In addition to these Stanford revision tests, standardised tests in the speed of reading (discontinuous), in the speed of adding, and in the speed of subtracting were given to all. These tests, standardised for age, were the only ones available when the investigation was begun. A full account of them is given in "Mental Tests" by P. B. Ballard (1920, pages 136, 187). They are one-minute tests and occupy very little time. The first line of the one-minute test in reading consists of the following words:

is me on at by so us an it or be.

A printed sheet containing the words is given to the child, and he is told to read the words as quickly as possible until he is stopped. The following examples are given to show the simplicity of the one-minute tests for addition and subtracting:

Addition Test	Subtraction Test
(1) $1 + 2$	(1) $2 - 1$
(2) $4 + 1$	(2) $3 - 1$
(3) $2 + 2$	(3) $5 - 1$
(4) $2 + 4$	(4) $6 - 2$
(5) $3 + 2$	(5) $5 - 3$
etc.	etc.

RESULTS OF THE TESTS

Two facts became very evident as the tests proceeded:
(i) The lowness of the "intelligence" of these children.
(ii) The decided decrease of "intelligence" with an increase of age.

Mental and Scholastic Quotients

In Table 1 are given the results obtained in this school.

TABLE 1

Average Mental and Educational Quotients
of Those Who Could Do All the Educational Tests

	No.	I.Q.	E.Q.*
Boys	14	77.6	70.8
Girls	22	67.6	70.1
Boys and Girls	36	71.5	70.4

*The "educational quotient" (E.Q.) is the average of the three subjects: Reading, Adding, and Subtracting.

The average I.Q. for the remaining 40 children was 67.9.

The correlation between the mental and educational quotients for the 36 children was 0.715, P. E. $\pm$ 0.054. For 57 per cent of the children the difference between the I.Q. and educational quotient was only five points or less, and for 83 per cent ten points or less.

The average I.Q. (69.6) for the 76 children is very low; it is, in fact, only a little higher than that found by Burt in schools for mentally defective children (63.3). As in the schools for physical defectives, the girls test considerably lower than the boys (65.6 compared with 75.1). This difference, however, is probably to a large extent due to the girls being more than a year older than the boys on an average, *i.e.*, 9 years 10 months, compared with 8 years 9 months of boys, for, as has already been explained, the older the children the worse they tested. The educational quotients of the thirty-six children who could be tested in reading, adding and subtracting was 70.4; slightly less than their I.Q., 71.5. In spelling the quotient (63.0) was considerably less than that of any of the other tests, the girls being especially weak in this subject, although they were slightly better than the boys in reading. The I.Q. of the forty children, who had no scholastic attainments, was 67.9, a quotient that is slightly lower than that of the other children.

It is evident that the low educational quotient is due to the lack of schooling. It is not so clear, however, why the I.Q. is so much below that of ordinary Elementary School children, unless the majority are "mentally defective," or unless the "intelligence" tests used depend on school attainments, or on the mental exercises given in schools.

Before, however, considering this question further, it is necessary to deal more precisely with the question of age and "intelligence." The correlation between the I.Q.'s and age—*i.e.*, the correlation by rank, the children in order of ages, the oldest first and the youngest last—was as follows:

No.	Observed Correlation	P.E.
ρ (calc. from) 76 . .	$-.755$ . .	$\pm .033$

That is to say, the older the child the less his "intelligence." This negative correlation is remarkably high, but still more remarkable is the result shown in Table 2, in which are given the ages and I.Q.'s of children in the same family. There are twenty-two cases in which two or more children of the same family are attending this school—eleven families with two children, six with three children and five with four children.

With one or two exceptions, an increase of age is found to be associated in the same family with a decrease in I.Q. Family No. 9 is one of the exceptions; the children are dirty and of a low-grade type, and all are very dull. The oldest (12–1) could read a little (reading age 6–10), could add 1 + 2 and 4 + 1 but could get no further, and could not take 1 from 2. The other two in the family could not read any of the words in the list, neither could they add or subtract any of the numbers given in the tests. One significant fact is noticeable in many of the families, and it is that in the same family the mental ages are practically the same, although the chronological ages differ very considerably, *e.g.*, 7–0, 6–3, 6–0; 5–6, 5–6; 6–9, 6–6; 6–0 and 6–3. This peculiarity seems to indicate that for children associating only with uneducated brothers and sisters there is a tendency to equalisation of mental ages.

TABLE 2

I.Q.'s and Ages of Children in the Same Family*

Family	Sex and Age	I.Q.	Sex and Age	I.Q.	Sex and Age	I.Q.	Sex and Age	I.Q.
1	g. 13–1	59	b. 10–1	72	g. 8–0	75	b. 6–4	98
2	b. 10–6	74	g. 8–4	72	g. 6–5	74	b. 4–7	87
3	g. 10–7	38	b. 9–1	71	g. 7–5	64	g. 5–1	79
4	g. 12–9	78	g. 10–0	62	g. 8–5	82	g. 5–8	79
5	g. 13–8	58	g. 11–6	65	b. 9–6	76	b. 7–3	100
6	g. 12–1	43	b. 10–10	64	b. 6–10	84	—	—
7	g. 12–2	67	g. 8–7	78	g. 6–2	93	—	—
8	b. 10–1	70	b. 7–7	82	b. 6–2	97	—	—
9	g. 12–1	58	b. 10–9	41	g. 9–7	38	—	—
10	b. 12–1	58	b. 10–0	62	g. 7–10	70	—	—
11	g. 12–8	75	b. 9–10	79	g. 5–1	83	—	—
12	g. 11–6	65	b. 8–4	72	—	—	—	—
13	g. 10–7	68	b. 6–6	96	—	—	—	—
14	g. 9–3	70	b. 6–11	90	—	—	—	—
15	b. 13–6	51	g. 11–4	68	—	—	—	—
16	g. 11–0	68	b. 9–7	90	—	—	—	—
17	b. 11–1	63	g. 5–9	82	—	—	—	—
18	b. 7–5	77	g. 4–11	76	—	—	—	—
19	g. 13–0	51	g. 10–3	63	—	—	—	—
20	g. 13–11	43	g. 9–11	63	—	—	—	—
21	g. 11–11	55	g. 8–3	70	—	—	—	—
22	g. 14–0	33	b. 6–5	85	—	—	—	—

*g. = girl; b. = boy. Age is given in years and months.

Figure 1 gives these results graphically. The average age and I.Q. of all the oldest children were calculated and then entered at the appropriate point—there were twenty-two, their average age was 11.6

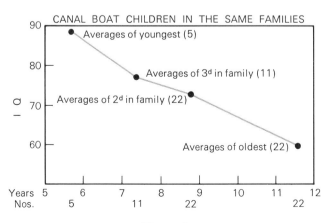

Figure 1

years, their average I.Q. was 60: so with the second children in a family, etc. Again, in the case of the youngest of four in a family: there were five such children, with an average age of 5.7 years and an average I.Q. of about 87.

SUMMARY AND CONCLUSIONS

1. Life, habits and education of Canal Boat children. Canal Boat population live an isolated life, almost patriarchal in character. In health, morals, etc., they compare favourably with town dwellers of the same class. The children are "scandalously under-educated"; their attendance at school averages about 4 to 5 per cent., compared with the 88 per cent. of children in ordinary Elementary Schools.

2. The abbreviated scale of the Stanford revision tests was used, together with standardised tests in the speed of reading, adding and subtracting, and at a subsequent period a standardised test in spelling.

3. The average I.Q. of the seventy-six children tested was 69.6—a very low I.Q. when compared with those found in ordinary Elementary Schools. In a very superior (socially) school the I.Q. is 112; in a very poor school, 87; in schools for physically defective children, 85; and in schools for mentally defective children, 63.

4. The boys tested considerably higher than the girls, the latter being roughly a year more retarded than the boys. This retardation, however, may be accounted for, at all events in part, by the greater average age of the girls (9 years 10 months, against 8 years 9 months of the boys), for it has been shown that the older the children the less their "intelligence" as found by the tests.

5. The educational quotient of the thirty-six children who could do the simple scholastic tests was only slightly lower than the I.Q. (70.4 and 71.5 respectively); the educational quotients of both boys and girls was practically the same (70.8 and 70.1). Whereas in the case of the girls their educational quotient was slightly higher than their I.Q.; in the case of the boys it was considerably lower.

6. Spelling was the weakest subject, especially among the girls, whose spelling quotient was 60.9 compared with 66.0 of the boys.

7. The correlation (r) between the mental and educational quotients was .715, P.E. .054—a high correlation.

8. The correlation between "intelligence" (test) and age was −.755, P.E. ± .033— a very high negative correlation, indicating unquestionably that with an increase of age there was a corresponding decrease in "intelligence." The same conclusion was to be drawn from a comparison of the I.Q. of the children in the same family. Here also it is evident that even in the same family the older the child the less "intelligence" he has.

This result makes it almost certain that the low average "intelligence" of the children in this school is not due to heredity, seeing that the youngest children test more or less normally, *i.e.*, are of average "intelligence."

CONCLUSIONS

The fact that there is a marked decrease in "intelligence" with an increase of age, and that this is especially noticeable among children in the same family, suggests very convincingly that the low average "intelligence" of these children is not due to heredity. It may be due to environment, or to the lack of schooling, or to both combined. But as it has been shown that the correlation between the results of the mental and scholastic tests is very high, and further that the average quotients for these two sets of tests are approximately the same, it may be assumed with some reasonableness that the lack of schooling has affected both "mental" and scholastic attainments to the same extent. In other words, without education (schooling) children are very much handicapped when tested by the "intelligence" tests used in this investigation—in fact, to nearly the same extent as when tested by purely scholastic tests. It is clear, however, that for very young children there cannot be any educational tests, as such children have, as a rule, no so-called scholastic attainments, and for this reason the "mental" tests are necessarily not of the same character as those for older children, and in consequence the children test normally. Without the mental effort or mental exercises associated with schooling it would appear that there has been very little mental development on the intellectual side. How far there has been a similar lack of development among these children in connection with problems touching their own especial environment, it is difficult to say and, without tests especially devised and standardised for childern in such surroundings, impossible to measure.

2-5

A Trans-Decade Comparison of the IQ's of Tennessee Mountain Children

LESTER ROSIN WHEELER

Studies in the U.S. comparable to those done on Canal Boat children of England were carried out by Wheeler in the Mountain regions of Eastern Tennessee. Here the evidence also points to the intellectually depressing effects of barren and isolated living conditions and the lack of adequate educational facilities. Improvement in educational facilities and other cultural contacts had much to do with raising the children's intellectual status. The study, however, shows that after a decade, these children are still retarded in comparison with the samples on whom intelligence tests had been standardized. It is obvious that mental potentialities are greatly depressed by the absence of educational stimulation.

Certain trends in the investigations of the intelligence of rural and mountain children raise questions of vital importance to education. Does the deviation of these children from the normal distribution indicate that they are inherently inferior? Are they by training and experience made

Reprinted from *J. Educ. Psychol.*, 1942, 33, 321–323, by permission of the author and Abrahams Magazine Service, Inc.

less capable of dealing with intelligence tests than children in other environments? To what extent do intelligence ratings vary as a result of improving environmental conditions? Is the decrease in IQ with an increase in chronological age due to defects in the process of maturation of intelligence, or to the increasing influence of poor cultural conditions?

Although investigators agree that variations do occur in the IQ, there is much controversy concerning the causes of these discrepancies. The *Thirty-ninth Yearbook* of the National Society for the Study of Education (1940) sequential to the *Twenty-seventh Yearbook* (1928), reviews the investigations and presents the nature-nurture discussion from various points of view. All the studies but one indicate that rural children make lower scores on intelligence tests than city children; the Scottish Council for Educational Research (Scottish Council for Research in Education, 1933) reports that no difference in intelligence is found between the rural and urban children of Scotland, and offers the explanation that, "nowhere has scholastic opportunity been more evenly equated than in Scotland—99.7 per cent of Scottish teachers are fully trained." Most investigators feel that environmental differences influence the lower ratings of rural children.

INTELLIGENCE OF MOUNTAIN CHILDREN

In 1930 we made a study of the intelligence of East Tennessee Mountain children (Wheeler, 1932). The Dearborn IA and IIC Intelligence Tests were given to eleven hundred forty-seven children in Grades I–VIII from twenty-one mountain schools, and the Illinois Intelligence Test was given to five hundred sixty-four of these cases in Grades III–VIII. The median IQ was 82 on the Dearborn and 78 on the Illinois Test. The IQ on the Dearborn Test was 95 at age six, and decreased to 74 at age sixteen. A marked school retardation was evident, from one-and-a-half years in the first grade to over two years in the eighth grade. The conclusions reached were: (1) The results of both tests were materially affected by environmental factors, (2) the mountain children were not as far below normal intelligence as the tests indicated, and (3) with proper environmental changes the mountain children might test near a normal group. It was noted that

> The growing educational opportunities in the mountains are materially changing the isolated sections. The State is providing modern and adequate schools in the very heart of the mountains, and is sending well-trained teachers, many of whom are holding or working toward college degrees, into these schools to teach the mountain children. . . . Educational opportunities of the mountains have advanced with the improvement of roads, thus enabling consolidation of schools in a number of sections. As

this is only a recent development, it will be interesting to note the influence of better schools on the results of later intelligence test data on the same groups of children (Wheeler, 1932, p. 354).

Ten years have elapsed since this initial study was made, and we have retested the same mountain areas. The data for this second investigation were gathered during the Spring and Fall of 1940. Obviously we could not retest the same children, but we have repeated the same test on children in the same areas and largely from the same families; ninety-one per cent of the families represented in this study have been life-residents of the area, eight per cent have moved into the areas since 1930 from adjacent Appalachian Mountain sections, leaving only one per cent shifting into the mountains from undetermined areas. The overlapping of a majority of the family names in the two studies agrees with this general trend, and the data indicate that any major changes found in the results of the intelligence tests are due to other factors than population shift.

SOME ENVIRONMENTAL CHANGES IN THE MOUNTAIN AREA

During the past decade there have been many changes in the economic, social and cultural life of these mountain people. The State has completed an excellent road system which gives every community access to progressive areas outside of the mountains, and has developed transportation facilities for schools and industry. Our data show about sixty per cent of the families in one county and forty per cent in another had one or more members working in industrial plants. In 1930 neither State nor county provided transportation; in 1940, two thousand three hundred sixteen children were transported daily to and from school. This probably accounts for much of the seventeen per cent increase in enrollment in 1940, and for the thirty-two per cent higher average daily attendance. Basing the allotment of State money to county schools on the basis of average daily attendance now stimulates the teachers and community to keep the children in school. Hot lunches are served regularly in all the larger schools.

There has been a general shift from the one-room to larger schools, a reorganization made possible by improved roads. An improvement is also indicated in the types of school buildings. Many schools now have adequate playgrounds and fairly well equipped gymnasiums. A circulating library, maintained by the State and counties, makes available around fourteen thousand volumes for these schools, and free textbooks are furnished for the first three grades. While a decade ago the average training of the teachers was less than two years of college work, today it is about three years. A majority of the teachers are either college graduates or receiving training-in-service from accredited teacher-training colleges. New teachers employed are required to have four years of college training. Well-trained, progressive college graduates have displaced the politically appointed county superintendents of a decade ago. An excellent supervisory program is provided for the area with well-trained county supervisors and a State regional supervisor who assists in coördinating instruction. Schools have been improved by the innovation of a State rating system based on points for improved instruction, additional books and materials, provision for health facilities and general equipment.

During the past ten years the rapid growth of industry in the area enables the families to supplement its agricultural livelihood with ready cash through employment in the rayon, lumber, pottery and other industrial plants. Farming methods have materially changed; pasture lands now replace many of the corn fields on the rough mountain slopes, and stock raising and dairy farming is proving profitable. Small but modern frame houses located on or near the main highways have replaced many of the log cabins and small rough-board houses. There has been unusual development in the area, and the improvement in roads, schools, agriculture and the economic life of the communities has materially changed the general environment of these people.

In the 1930 investigation nine hundred forty-six children were tested from twenty-one different schools. In 1940 all the children in these schools, and an additional two thousand cases in nineteen other mountain schools, were tested in order to increase the statistical reliability of the study. Comparisons were made between the original and additional schools, and, when no significant differences were found between the distribution of intelligence in the two groups, the data were combined for subsequent treatment. Apparently any significant changes in IQ are not due to the additional cases. The median IQ for the original twenty-one schools is 87.6 ± .34, and for the additional schools, 87.2 ± .32. The administration and scoring of the tests was under the same supervision as in 1930.

The average mountain child is eight months younger for his grade than ten years ago, as shown in Table 1 and Figure 1. The differences in chronological age range from three months in Grade I to fifteen months in Grade V. There is a consistent difference in favor of the 1940 group in each grade and a significant difference in most of the grades, substantiating other investigations which indicate that age-grade retardation decreases with improvement in instruction and general educational opportunities. There seems to be a tendency for the other children to leave the elementary school earlier than they did ten years ago, probably due to better opportunities for high-school attendance and industrial employment. The degree of age-grade retardation in the Tennessee mountains is practically the same as that reported by Edwards and Jones (1938) for Georgia mountains. Sherman and Key (1932) found a larger amount among Virginia mountain children, and the Appalachian areas in general appear to have a much greater problem of retardation than the Iowa rural schools studied by Baldwin (Baldwin et al., 1940).

INCREASE IN MENTAL AGE DURING LAST DECADE

Table 1 and Figure 1 show a comparison of the median mental ages. An average mental age for all grades shows the 1940 group has gained about nine months over the 1930 group, or nearly one mental month a year for ten years. In other words, the average mountain child in 1940 is

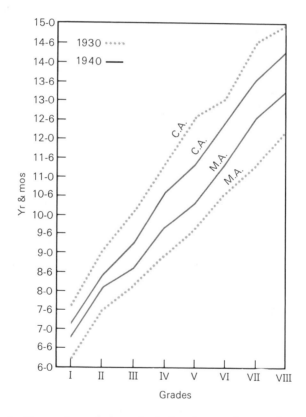

Figure 1. Comparison of chronological and mental ages of mountain children according to grade, 1930 and 1940 groups.

TABLE 1

Comparision of Mental Ages of Mountain Children According
to Grades and Chronological Ages

	Median CA	Median MA		Median MA
Grade I			Six-year-olds	
1930	7-5	6-3	1930	6-1
1940	7-2	6-10	1940	6-8
Difference	0-3	0-7	Difference	0-7
Grade II			Seven-year-olds	
1930	9-2	7-6	1930	6-10
1940	8-5	8-1	1940	7-6
Difference	0-9	0-7	Difference	0-8
Grade III			Eight-year-olds	
1930	10-2	8-2	1930	7-7
1940	9-3	8-7	1940	8-6
Difference	0-11	0-5	Difference	0-11
Grade IV			Nine-year-olds	
1930	11-4	8-11	1930	8-2
1940	10-7	9-8	1940	9-2
Difference	0-9	0-9	Difference	1-0
Grade V			Ten-year-olds	
1930	12-7	9-8	1930	8-10
1940	11-4	10-4	1940	9-7
Difference	1-3	0-8	Difference	0-9
Grade VI			Eleven-year-olds	
1930	13-1	10-7	1930	9-3
1940	12-5	11-5	1940	10-9
Difference	0-8	0-10	Difference	1-6
Grade VII			Twelve-year-olds	
1930	14-6	11-4	1930	10-2
1940	13-7	12-7	1940	11-3
Difference	0-11	1-3	Difference	1-1
Grade VIII			Thirteen-year-olds	
1930	15-0	12-3	1930	10-7
1940	14-4	13-4	1940	11-11
Difference	0-8	1-1	Difference	1-4
			Fourteen-year-olds	
			1930	10-11
			1940	12-4
			Difference	1-5
			Fifteen-year-olds	
			1930	11-4
			1940	12-7
			Difference	1-3
			Sixteen-year-olds	
			1930	12-2
			1940	13-3
			Difference	1-1

TABLE 2

Comparison of IQ's of Mountain Children According to Grades

	No. Cases	Median IQ	PE	Q-1	Q-3	Q	Range
Grade I							
1930	115	84.10	1.14	74.91	94.42	9.76	45 to 115
1940	371	95.14	.57	86.08	103.73	8.83	50 to 165
Difference	—	11.04	1.27	—	—	—	—
Grade II							
1930	87	85.40	1.04	77.08	92.66	7.79	45 to 125
1940	282	95.66	.74	84.69	104.58	9.95	50 to 166
Difference	—	10.26	1.27	—	—	—	—
Grade III							
1930	103	83.96	1.27	72.92	93.54	10.32	45 to 150
1940	500	92.84	.64	80.67	103.62	11.48	35 to 160
Difference	—	8.88	1.42	—	—	—	—
Grade IV							
1930	172	81.50	1.18	69.30	94.17	12.44	45 to 135
1940	491	92.38	.71	79.83	104.83	12.50	45 to 160
Difference	—	10.88	1.37	—	—	—	—
Grade V							
1930	137	76.10	1.13	67.58	88.75	10.59	50 to 125
1940	465	91.36	.74	78.66	104.19	12.77	50 to 160
Difference	—	15.26	1.35	—	—	—	—
Grade VI							
1930	117	81.90	1.17	73.63	93.84	10.12	55 to 125
1940	458	92.41	.68	80.66	103.78	11.56	50 to 160
Difference	—	10.51	1.35	—	—	—	—
Grade VII							
1930	128	79.50	1.00	73.23	91.36	9.07	50 to 130
1940	360	92.63	.75	81.75	104.44	11.35	50 to 150
Difference	—	13.13	1.25	—	—	—	—
Grade VIII							
1930	87	84.80	1.13	73.25	90.14	8.45	55 to 120
1940	325	93.23	.76	82.78	104.80	11.01	40 to 150
Difference	—	8.43	1.36	—	—	—	—
All Grades							
1930	946	82.40	.40	72.70	92.62	9.96	45 to 150
1940	3252	92.22	.25	81.47	104.22	11.38	35 to 166
Difference	—	10.82	.15	—	—	—	—

three-fourths of a year mentally superior for his grade than the average mountain child in 1930 was. The greatest differences between the two groups occur in the seventh and eighth grades, and the smallest in Grade III. Figure 1 shows that mental age increases fairly consistently from grade to grade, but falls below the chronological age level. The 1930 group was definitely older chronologically but younger mentally than the

1940 group; the difference between MA and CA of the 1940 group is about a third of that found ten years ago. There is still a tendency for the increments of mental growth to decrease with an increase in chronological age. During the first and second grades mental ages of the 1940 group lack only four months of normality.[1] This increases to eight months in Grade III, eleven months in Grade IV, and twelve months in Grades V–VIII. While the 1940 group is perfectly normal at ages six, seven and eight,[2] the mental age falls below the chronological age in Grades I, II and III as a result of overageness and age-grade retardation. Beginning at age nine, the 1940 mental age falls from four months below normal to twenty-five months at fourteen years. The average difference between MA and normal CA is about a third as great as it was in 1930. These trends are shown also in the comparison in Table 3.

The distributions of IQ's for the 1930 and 1940 groups are shown in Table 2. The median IQ for the 1930 group, 82 ± .40, has increased over ten points to 93 ± .25 in 1940. This gain is further shown by a study of the percentage of overlapping: Seventy-four per cent or about three-fourths of the 1930 cases are below the 1940 median. In 1930 the median IQ classified the children as a dull group, while in 1940 the group is within the normal classification. The wider range in 1940 is largely due to the increased number of cases.

Since 1930 there has been a noticeable IQ gain in all types of schools. In 1930 there was a greater tendency for the IQ to increase with the size of school. This trend was also shown in Baldwin's study (Baldwin et al., 1940) where Iowa farm children in one-room schools had a median IQ of 91.7, against 99.4 in the consolidated schools. The fact that there is less difference in the IQ among different types of schools in Tennessee mountain areas than in rural Iowa may indicate there is more uniformity of instruction and educational facilities in the mountain areas; perhaps the one-room schools are not so poor nor the larger schools as good as the consolidated schools in Iowa. Greater uniformity in instructional practices in 1940 may also be a factor in decreasing the differences among the various types of schools in the mountain area.

Table 3 shows the median IQ of the 1940 group is consistently higher at all ages. The differences are statistically significant at all ages except sixteen, where the limited number of cases tends to increase the PE's. Similar trends are seen in comparing the ranges of the two groups, and the first and third quartiles. Both groups show a decline in IQ with increasing chronological age.

[1]Median CA, Table 4 less median MA, Table 5.

[2]CA of 6-6, 7-6, 8-6, represents normal age for Grades I, II, III, etc.

TABLE 3

Comparison of IQ's of Mountain Children According to CA

	No. Cases	Median IQ	PE	Q-1	Q-3	Q	Range
Six-year-olds							
1930	33	94.68	2.03	89.06	107.75	9.34	75 to 115
1940	188	102.56	.64	95.34	109.38	7.02	75 to 165
Difference	—	7.88	2.12	—	—	—	—
Seven-year-olds							
1930	62	90.90	1.38	81.25	98.61	8.68	55 to 125
1940	244	99.85	.66	91.38	107.77	8.19	65 to 160
Difference	—	8.95	1.54	—	—	—	—
Eight-year-olds							
1930	60	88.88	1.09	82.33	95.90	6.78	40 to 110
1940	322	99.18	.70	90.50	110.71	10.10	60 to 160
Difference	—	10.30	1.29	—	—	—	—
Nine-year-olds							
1930	94	86.38	1.79	79.95	95.22	7.72	60 to 145
1940	324	96.44	.74	85.73	107.07	10.67	55 to 160
Difference	—	10.06	1.93	—	—	—	—
Ten-year-olds							
1930	99	84.25	1.64	74.29	94.75	10.23	50 to 125
1940	383	91.44	.73	81.33	104.04	11.36	45 to 160
Difference	—	7.19	1.79	—	—	—	—
Eleven-year-olds							
1930	102	80.00	1.49	70.19	94.32	12.06	50 to 130
1940	358	93.87	.88	80.36	106.95	13.30	50 to 150
Difference	—	13.87	1.73	—	—	—	—
Twelve-year-olds							
1930	107	81.41	1.06	74.25	91.88	8.81	50 to 135
1940	365	90.17	.80	75.67	100.13	12.23	35 to 150
Difference	—	8.76	1.33	—	—	—	—
Thirteen-year-olds							
1930	109	77.61	1.22	66.56	86.97	10.21	45 to 120
1940	319	87.75	.87	75.30	100.04	12.37	50 to 145
Difference	—	10.14	1.48	—	—	—	—
Fourteen-year-olds							
1930	125	74.72	1.09	63.39	82.80	9.71	45 to 115
1940	257	85.06	.75	74.05	93.33	9.64	50 to 125
Difference	—	10.34	1.32	—	—	—	—
Fifteen-year-olds							
1930	61	73.44	1.39	65.56	82.93	8.71	59 to 95
1940	116	81.33	1.13	73.00	92.50	9.75	50 to 110
Difference	—	7.89	1.79	—	—	—	—
Sixteen-year-olds							
1930	29	73.50	2.41	64.06	84.81	10.37	45 to 95
1940	34	80.00	2.08	68.12	87.50	9.69	40 to 110
Difference	—	6.50	3.18	—	—	—	—

OVER-AGENESS AND DECLINE IN IQ

The study of mountain children in 1930 showed a consistent de-crease in IQ with increase in chronological age from 94.7 at age six to 73.5 at age sixteen, a decline of 1.9 points a year. The study in 1940 shows a similar decline from 102.6 at age six to 80 at age sixteen, an average of two points each year. The total decrease in IQ in 1930 was 21.3 points, and in 1940, 22.6 points. In 1930 the children were within the normal intelligence group at age six; the 1940 data definitely show that the children are normal at age six. Some investigators explain this decline in IQ and the low average intelligence of mountain children as due to a poor heredity, caused by inbreeding and the superior families leaving the mountains for better economic and educational opportunities in other sections. Others base their explanations on the theory that the mind develops with stimulation, maintaining that, since the rural environment is less stimulating, there occurs a general decline in the rate of mental growth as the children become older chronologically. It has also been suggested that the relative placement of the items of tests standardized on urban children does not adequately measure the development of the rural child, especially in the older age-levels.

Over-ageness and age-grade retardation among rural and mountain children has been observed by various investigators, and presents a serious problem in the rural schools of Tennessee (Wheeler, 1940). In order to study the influence of this factor on the decline of the IQ, in Table 4 all children who were over-age one and two-or-more years were eliminated from each grade.[3] In Grade I nearly half the children are over-age, and the retardation increases to seventy-three per cent in Grade VIII. For the normal-age groups the IQ remains normal at each grade level. The over-age group definitely lowers the total average for each grade. The effect of this age-grade retardation on the median IQ is shown in Table 5. The retarded cases lower the IQ from four points at age seven and eight to 14.83 ± 1.53 points at age twelve. As over-ageness increases, and retardations accumulate from grade to grade, there occurs a corresponding decline in IQ, indicating that age-grade retardation causes the median IQ to decline with increasing chronological age. The IQ decreases with an increase in the amount of age-grade retardation.

The decline of the IQ with increase in chronological age is the same as it was a decade ago except that it is on a higher IQ level. Over a period of ten years the general level of intelligence of these mountain

[3]Normal age for Grade I, 6 to 7; Grade II, 7 to 8; etc.

TABLE 4

Showing the Effect of Over-ageness on the Distribution of IQ's

	Per Cent of Cases	Median IQ	Range
Grade I			
6-year-olds	51.3	102.56	75 to 165
7-year-olds	30.8	92.82	65 to 120
8 years and over	17.9	90.04	50 to 115
All ages	100.0	95.14	50 to 165
Grade II			
7-year-olds	44.6	104.00	75 to 166
8-year-olds	30.2	94.00	60 to 150
9 years and over	25.2	88.98	50 to 140
All ages	100.00	95.66	50 to 166
Grade III			
8-year-olds	40.5	103.28	75 to 160
9-year-olds	25.7	91.79	65 to 155
10 years and over	33.8	83.45	35 to 130
All ages	100.0	92.84	35 to 160
Grade IV			
9-year-olds	34.7	104.13	55 to 160
10-year-olds	26.1	90.33	45 to 135
11 years and over	39.2	82.68	45 to 133
All ages	100.0	92.38	45 to 160
Grade V			
10-year-olds	35.6	102.17	70 to 160
11-year-olds	25.8	92.91	50 to 130
12 years and over	38.6	79.00	50 to 125
All ages	100.0	91.36	50 to 160
Grade VI			
11-year-olds	32.8	103.44	60 to 160
12-year-olds	31.3	93.09	65 to 130
13 years and over	35.0	80.70	50 to 120
All ages	100.0	92.41	50 to 160
Grade VII			
12-year-olds	30.0	105.00	65 to 150
13-year-olds	31.2	93.18	60 to 145
14 years and over	38.8	79.80	50 to 130
All ages	100.0	92.63	50 to 150
Grade VIII			
13-year-olds	27.0	101.00	60 to 150
14-year-olds	32.2	90.17	60 to 125
15 years and over	40.8	88.52	40 to 115
All ages	100.0	93.23	40 to 150

children has been rasied ten IQ points. We have shown that although this investigation throws further light on the data and interpretations presented ten years ago, more research with other groups in other areas is

TABLE 5

Showing the Effect of Retardation on the Decrease in IQ
with Increasing CA

	No. of Cases	Median IQ	PE
Seven-year-olds			
1. Retarded cases eliminated	124	104.00	1.00
2. All cases	244	99.85	.66
3. Difference	—	4.15	1.19
Eight-year-olds			
1. Retarded cases eliminated	178	103.28	.83
2. All cases	322	99.18	.70
3. Difference	—	4.10	1.08
Nine-year-olds			
1. Retarded cases eliminated	148	104.13	.98
2. All cases	324	96.44	.74
3. Difference	—	7.69	1.22
Ten-year-olds			
1. Retarded cases eliminated	146	102.17	1.30
2. All cases	383	91.44	.73
3. Difference	—	10.73	1.49
Eleven-year-olds			
1. Retarded cases eliminated	128	103.44	1.21
2. All cases	358	93.87	.88
3. Difference	—	9.57	1.49
Twelve-year-olds			
1. Retarded cases eliminated	94	105.00	1.31
2. All cases	365	90.17	.80
3. Difference	—	14.83	1.53
Thirteen-year-olds			
1. Retarded cases eliminated	76	101.00	1.47
2. All cases	319	87.75	.87
3. Difference	—	13.25	1.70

needed before reaching any final conclusions as to the relative influence of nature and nurture on IQ changes. A check study should also be made to determine whether children in the general population score higher today on the Dearborn Tests than they did a decade ago. However, the general trends found in these mountain studies and in other investigations of rural children present a challenge for education: Large environmental changes appear to influence the IQ. In contrast to other social philosophies, our democratic ideals depend upon the opportunities each child has for developing his individual abilities.

SUMMARY

(1) There is a general agreement among investigators that urban children rate higher on intelligence tests than rural or mountain children.

(2) The majority of studies indicate a decrease in IQ with an increase in chronological age.

(3) There are diverse opinions concerning the factors which cause rural-urban differences and the decline in IQ.

(4) During the Spring and Fall of 1940, intelligence tests were given to three thousand two hundred fifty-two children in forty mountain schools of East Tennessee, and the results are compared with a similar study made ten years ago.

(5) During the decade there has been definite improvement in the economic, social and educational status of this mountain area.

(6) Today the average mountain child is about eight months younger chronologically and nine months older mentally for his grade than the average child of ten years ago.

(7) The difference between the chronological and mental age of the average mountain child is now about one-third as great as it was a decade ago.

(8) The 1940 group of mountain children is mentally superior to the 1930 group at all ages and all grades, as measured by the same tests.

(9) The average mountain child has gained ten points in IQ, or nearly one point a year during the past ten years.

(10) The average mountain child's I.Q. decreases about two points each year from age six to sixteen. This is about the same rate of decline as was found ten years ago.

(11) Over-ageness, or age-grade retardation, among mountain children appears to be the predominating cause of the decline in IQ with increase in chronological age.

(12) The results of this investigation give further light on the findings of the 1930 study, and indicate that intelligence, as measured by these tests, may be improved with an improvement in educational and general environmental conditions.

REFERENCES

Baldwin, B. T., E. A. Fillmore, and L. Hadley. *Farm children*. Chapter 13, pp. 231–263. New York: Appleton-Century-Crofts, 1940.

Edwards, A. S. and L. Jones. An experimental and field study of North Georgia mountaineers, *J. Soc. Psychol.*, 1938, **9,** 317–333.

National Society for the Study of Education. *Nature and nurture: Their influence on intelligence.* Twenty-seventh Yearbook, Parts I and II. Bloomington, Ill.: Public School Publishing Co., 1928.

National Society for the Study of Education. *Intelligence: its nature and nurture.* Thirty-ninth Yearbook, Parts I and II. Bloomington, Ill.: Public School Publishing Co., 1940.

Scottish Council for Research in Education. *The intelligence of Scottish Children: A national survey of an age-group.* London: University of London Press, 1933.

Sherman, M. and C. B. Key. The intelligence of isolated mountain children, *Child Devel.,* 1932, **3,** 279–290.

Wheeler, L. R. The intelligence of East Tennessee Mountain children, *J. Educ. Psychol.,* 1932, **23,** 351–371.

Wheeler, L. R. and Others. Reports on Unicoi County: Educational surveys, *Res. Bull. East Tenn. Educ. Assoc.,* Vol. I, Chaps. I and II. Edgar M. Cook (ed.). Carson-Newman College, Jefferson City, Tennessee, 1940.

2-6

Goodenough Scores, Art Experience, and Modernization

WAYNE DENNIS

Psychological tests often prove not to be valuable for their intended purpose, but nevertheless may be valuable for other purposes. This is true of the Goodenough Draw-a-Man Test. It was proposed as a test of "native" intelligence. It is now certain that there is no "intelligence" test that is unaffected by experience. Experience affects the answers to any test question. Thus, the ability of children to draw a man, when various groups are compared, turns out to be an index of modernization or of artistic backgrounds.

A. INTRODUCTION

Florence Goodenough published "The Measurement of Intelligence by Drawings" in 1926, only ten years after the appearance of the Stanford-Binet. It was published at a time when there was considerable confidence on the part of psychologists that mental tests measured differences due primarily to heredity, rather than to environment. This

Reprinted from *J. Soc. Psychol.*, 1966, **68**, 211–228, by permission of The Journal Press.

interpretation was applied to differences between groups as well as to individual differences.

As a possibly "culture-free" test, the Draw-a-Man Test had much to recommend it. It is nonverbal, it has little relationship to academic subject matter, and the referent to be drawn is universally familiar.

Goodenough, in 1926, the same year in which her book appeared, reported large differences between groups of American children of different racial and ethnic origins. While some effect of environment was acknowledged, these findings were given an interpretation which was chiefly biological.

But doubts soon arose that "intelligence" tests could be "culture-free." Doubts became stronger when some groups were found to test higher than American whites. We believe we were the first to report such a finding in respect to the Draw-a-Man Test (Dennis, 1942). Hopi Indian boys, aged 8 to 11 years, were found to have a mean Goodenough *IQ* of 123. We suggested that this mean was due to the high development of certain kinds of representational art among Hopi men and to the early involvement of Hopi boys in this art. Havighurst et al. (1946) confirmed our findings in respect to Hopi scores and in addition reported that boys of several other southwestern Indian groups also had high Goodenough means. In general, southwestern Indian girls who play a lesser role than boys in southwestern Indian art, tested significantly lower than the boys.

In a review of research on children's drawings, Goodenough and Harris (1950, p. 339) said: "The present writers would like to express the opinion that the search for a culture-free test, whether of intelligence, artistic ability, personal-social characteristics, or any other measurable trait is illusory, and that the naive assumption that mere freedom from verbal requirements renders a test equally suitable for all groups is no longer tenable. The studies by Dennis and by Havighurst point the moral very clearly so far as the Draw-a-Man Test is concerned." Since 1950 a considerable body of additional data have corroborated the view expressed above (see Harris, 1963).

But it does not suffice to deny that the Draw-a-Man Test, or any other test, is a test of native ability. If differences in scores are not due to biological causes, they must be due to other causes. These other causes should be found. While environment is the alternative to heredity, a specific accounting for agents producing environmental differences is necessary.

It is proposed in this paper that differences between societies in children's Goodenough scores are due primarily to group differences in their experience with, and participation in, representational art. It is further proposed that in many societies Goodenough scores are indirect indices of modernization, since for many groups Western civilization and modern education provide to children their chief experiences with representational art.

Let us state these hypotheses in detail. It is proposed that groups of children differ greatly in respect to Goodenough scores because of differences in their acquaintance with representational art and in their stimulation to produce it. But the differences in drawing performances are not due entirely to differences in acquaintance with Western art. Groups having little experience with Western art nevertheless show wide contrasts in Goodenough scores. This is because some non-Western groups have reached a high level of achievement in respect to several forms of art, such as wood carving, sculpture, decorated pottery, masks, or sandpainting. In such groups we would expect children to earn high Draw-a-Man scores. That is, in societies in which children have had little or no exposure to Western mass media, the Draw-a-Man scores will reflect the level of native representational art.

In Western societies there is today a great amount of representational art presented in visual mass media, such as newspapers, magazines, picture books, textbooks, comic books, billboards, placards, movies, and television programs. These influences impinge upon almost all Western children. They also impinge upon children in some non-Western societies, but the exposure differs according to the degree of modernization.

Usually when groups are exposed to newspapers, placards, photographs, etc., they are at the same time exposed to other Western influences, such as urbanization, technological changes, medical care, sanitation, education, etc. It is therefore proposed that in societies which had few visual arts of their own prior to Western contacts there will be a progressive increase in their Draw-a-Man scores as acculturation occurs, an improvement which will provide a rough index of cultural change.

These propositions do not deny that individual differences in Goodenough scores within a group that is relatively homogeneous in culture are due largely to heredity or to other biological causes. The present paper presents no data on this problem; it is concerned only with differences between groups that differ considerably in respect to native art or in respect to modernization, or in respect to both. It is limited to a consideration of data obtained from the Draw-a-Man Test. Analogous data could probably be presented in respect to group differences on other "intelligence" tests. Few tests, however, are likely to be so directly related to exposure to representational art as is the Goodenough test.

We will first present data from groups which differ considerably in Goodenough scores and will then attempt to determine whether these differences are related to representational art and acculturation as proposed above. Alternative explanations of group differences will be considered, and the effect of social change will be explored.

B. SOURCES OF DATA, AND PROCEDURE
IN GATHERING DATA

The Draw-a-Man Tests to be considered come in part from a collection of children's drawings which we have accumulated over a period of years. In making the collection we have aimed at obtaining drawings from groups which are diverse in culture. Three continents and 11 countries have contributed drawings. Nevertheless, the subjects who contributed to the collection are by no means a random sample of the world's children.

Most of the subjects were tested while attending school. A few results are presented from communities not having schools.

The majority of the data to be reported were collected under our own auspices, but use is made of some data published by others.

The data obtained under our supervision were, for the most part, obtained in our presence. To English-speaking subjects, we gave the instructions ourselves. To non-English-speaking subjects, the instructions were dictated to an assistant who was competent in English and in the native language. The instructions were those used by Goodenough (1926b).

In the case of some groups we were not present when data were gathered. In all such instances the drawings were obtained by a person thoroughly briefed in respect to Goodenough procedures. No drawings were obtained by teachers or by school officials, although such persons were sometimes present in the classrooms which were being tested.

In collecting data for this study, we have usually tested all children in grades 1–5, inclusive, who were attending school on a given day. In rural communities and villages, this means we obtained 100 per cent samples of pupils in attendance on that day. In towns with two or three schools, we often tested grades 1–5 in all of the schools. In large cities, 100 per cent samples of an entire city were not feasible. Here we tested grades 1–5 in one or more schools in a poor neighborhood and one or more schools in well-to-do neighborhoods. The results of such testing are presented separately for the two socioeconomic groups. It is felt that nearly all children in what are called poor neighborhoods were classifiable as lower class and that those in neighborhoods called well-to-do were primarily middle-class. Urban schools in which children are from diverse socioeconomic origins are not represented in our data.

The classification of a neighborhood as poor or well-to-do was based upon information supplied by local informants and by inspection of the neighborhood.

No effort was made to obtain "upper-class" groups, although there were a few upper-class children in schools described as middle-class. A "private school" is attended chiefly by upper-middle-class pupils but usually a small number of upper-class children also attend the school.

The term "group" as used in this paper refers to those children attending school in a particular community, village, town, or urban neighborhood. It is not used in a sociological sense, although some of our groups may have constituted social groups as defined by others.

We have chosen to present data primarily for six-year-olds, although some data will be presented for older children. Our choice of six-year-olds as the primary source of data for this paper was based upon the desire to minimize the direct effect of education upon Goodenough scores. In most communities, nearly all six-year-olds are in school, but they have been in school only for a short time. Hence differences between groups of six-year-olds cannot be due in major part to differences in amount of schooling. Nevertheless, since testing was done at various times during the school year, some six-year-olds had been in school longer than others at the time they were tested. Later we shall show that the Goodenough mean *IQ* of six-year-olds seldom differs by more than a few points from the mean *IQ* of seven-year-olds tested at the same time, and who, for the most part, have received an additional year of schooling.

In some communities, children enter kindergarten or first grade at age five, or even earlier. It might be thought that if we wished to avoid school influences, we should present data for children in their first year of school, whatever their ages. In fact, we tried this procedure but found a systematic difference in Goodenough *IQs* in favor of five-year-olds as compared to six-year-olds. This is probably due to selection; *i.e.*, it is likely that the bright child is considered more suitable for entering kindergarten than the ordinary child or dull child. In any case, we wished where possible to obtain 100 per cent samples and since school attendance is seldom compulsory before age six, 100 per cent samples cannot be obtained before that age.

In a few schools in which the usual age at entering school is greater than six years we have used data from older groups. In small schools, the data from two or more age levels were combined to obtain an adequate number of subjects. We have attempted to obtain in each group at least 25 children, but this was not always possible.

Boys and girls are separated in presenting our data, except for groups in which the numbers of boys or of girls of the desired age were too small to justify separate presentation.

The age-data necessary for computing *IQs* were obtained, when possible, from records in the school files. When date of birth was not available in the school files, age was determined by questioning the child or the teacher. When age was reported in terms of years (i.e., "I am six years old"), a report of this kind was understood to mean that the child was between 6.0 and 6.99, and hence the midpoint of this interval, 6.5, was used in computing the *IQ*.

In addition to new data, we have made use of some data previously published. Where this has been done the author and the date of the original source are shown in Table 1 immediately following the name of the group. If such a reference does not appear, the item refers to new data.

TABLE 1

Mean IQs of Various Groups

Group	Sex	Age	N	IQ	SD	Date of Testing
1. Larned, Kansas	BG	6	25	125	27.2	1957
2. Kyoto, Japan	G	6	13	124	13.9	1958
3. Kyoto, Japan	B	6	12	123	13.9	1958
4. Rockville, Maryland (Whites)	G	6	25	119	19.4	1957
5. Armenian priv. sch., Beirut [Dennis (1957)]	BG	6	16	116	21.0	1955
6. Coastal villages, Japan	G	6-7	25	115	13.9	1958
7. Navaho Indians	B	6-7	14	115	22.6	1936
8. Hopi Indians [Dennis (1942)]	B	6-7	18	112	20.1	1941
9. Mountain village, Japan	G	6	16	112	15.6	1958
10. Brooklyn, Yeshiva	B	6	25	111	18.5	1959
11. Coastal villages, Japan	B	6-7	19	109	13.4	1958
12. Rockville, Maryland (Whites)	B	6	25	109	17.3	1957
13. Mountain village, Japan	B	6	18	107	12.4	1958
14. Nashville, Tennessee (Negroes)	BG	6	28	105	16.8	1957
15. Hopi Indians [Dennis (1942)]	G	6-8	18	104	20.1	1941
16. Rockville, Maryland (Negroes)	B	6	26	101	17.2	1957
17. Rockville, Maryland (Negroes)	G	6	21	101	15.7	1957
18. Pennsylvania Amish	BG	6-7	14	100	13.4	1958
19. Port Said, Egypt [Dennis (1957)]	BG	6	37	94	12.0	1955
20. Univ. school, Beirut [Dennis (1957)]	B	6	15	93	13.0	1955

TABLE 1 (*Continued*)

Mean IQs of Various Groups

Group	Sex	Age	N	IQ	SD	Date of Testing
21. Villages near Cairo, Egypt [Fahmy (1955)]	BG	6	132	92	15.0	c. 1955
22. Navaho Indians	G	6-7	14	91	16.3	1936
23. Poor Armenian neighborhood, Beirut [Dennis (1957)]	B	6-7	15	91	13.0	1955
24. Merida, Mexico	B	6-7	13	89	7.4	1931, 1936
25. Poor neighborhood, Tehran	G	7	25	89	12.1	1959
26. Poor Armenian neighborhood, Beirut [Dennis (1957)]	G	6	16	87	13.0	1955
27. Urban Negroes, Natal So. Africa [Hunkin (1950)]	B	6	300	85	—	1949
28. Sidon, Lebanon [Dennis (1957)]	G	6	32	84	13.0	1955
29. Villages in India [Menzel (1935)]	B	6	91	83	—	1932
30. Villages in India [Menzel (1935)]	G	6	37	82	—	1932
31. E. Zoutar, Lebanon	B	7	15	82	24.4	1959
32. Virginia mountaineers [Sherman and Key (1932)]	BG	6-8	12	80	—	1929
33. Brooklyn Hassidim	B	9-11	26	79	11.9	1960
34. Urban Negroes, Tennessee & Louisiana [Goodenough (1926)]	BG	6-9	613	79	17.5	1925
35. St. Helena, South Carolina (Negroes) [Peterson and Telford (1930)]	BG	6	24	78	—	1928
36. Remhala, Lebanon	B	6-7	7	77	23.2	1959
37. Kakiet, Lebanon	B	7	25	76	15.0	1959
38. Chamula Indians, Mexico	BG	5-9	23	75	18.0	1962
39. Bedouins, Syria [Dennis (1960)]	B	6-7-8	28	56	8.3	1959
40. Primitive Shilluk, Sudan [Fahmy (1956)]	BG	7-13	c. 180	53	—	c. 1954

C. RESULTS AND HYPOTHESES

The chief data to be discussed in this paper are contained in Table 1, which gives for each of 40 groups the number of cases, the mean score, and the standard deviation, except that in some instances in which data were obtained from published sources the standard deviations were not available. In Table 1 the groups are arranged from high to low according to their Goodenough means. The name of each group provides an indication of its geographic location, and usually provides information concerning its race, its ethnic affiliation, and its religion. Often further information concerning a group will be provided in connection with the discussion of the results. Each group name is followed by B, G, or BG to show that it consists of boys or girls or both, and by a figure which indicates the age of the group. For each group Table 1 shows the year in which the group was tested.

The statistical treatment of the data in Table 1 was performed by Professor Solomon Weinstock, to whom we are greatly indebted. Footnote 1,[1] prepared by Professor Solomon Weinstock of Brooklyn College, explains the procedure which was used. It is a conservative procedure which takes into account the number of possible group comparisons which are possible in Table 1, and which makes allowances for the probability of finding "significant" differences because so many comparisons have been made. Professor Weinstock's general finding is that any two groups in Table 1 with Ns of 25 are significantly different at the 5 per cent level if their means differ by as much as 20 points. In groups involving larger Ns, smaller differences are significant at the 5 per cent level of confidence. The level of confidence in respect to differences greater than 20 points is considerably greater. Since the mean IQs exhibited in Table 1 vary from 125 to 53, it is obvious that a considerable number of the differences which are represented by Table 1 are significant at 5 per cent level by the procedure employed by Professor Weinstock.

[1] When Kramer's modification is used (Kramer, 1956), differences between two group means M_i and M_j are declared significant if $M_i - M_j$ (assuming M_i larger than M_j) is larger than $3.90 \sqrt{MS_{w6}} \sqrt{1/n_i + 1/n_j}$. When all the groups are the same size the procedure is the same as Tukey's procedure. The value 3.90 was obtained from a table presented by Acton (1959, p. 186). The sums of squares for all groups were pooled and the mean square within groups, MS_{w6}, was computed as 281.1053. Thus, differences greater than $65.39 \sqrt{1/n_i + 1/n_j}$ were reported as significant.

A procedure proposed by Tukey [see Scheffe (1959)] to provide a 5 per cent "experimentuise" error rate was used to determine which of the differences in Table 1 were statistically significant. The procedure was modified, following a suggestion of Kramer (1956), to deal with unequal n's in the groups. The results of the "multiple comparisions" procedure are presented in Table 2.

TABLE 2

Results of Tukey's Multiple Comparison Procedure

Group	Highest Ranking Group*
1	14
2-4	19
5-7	21
8-12	25
13-15	27
16-17	29
18	34
19	37
20-38	39

*The entries in this column are the "highest ranking groups" from which the groups in the first column differ significantly. All lower ranking groups also differ significantly from the indicated group.

We shall now consider the extent to which the data in Table 1 support or negate the propositions which were proposed in the introductory section. The first proposal to be evaluated is that high scores are made by groups which have a high local development of representational art or which are high in respect to exposure to modern visual media. Among the high means will be found those of two Japanese groups. The highest Japanese means are 124 for girls and 123 for boys in Kyoto, an ancient center of Japanese culture which contributed greatly to Japanese art. However, two Japanese coastal villages, which have limited communication with urban centers, have means of 115 for the girls and of 109 for the boys. In a Japanese mountain village, which also is somewhat isolated, the girls have a mean of 112 and the boys a mean of 107. The means mentioned above are not significantly different from each other, but are significantly different, respectively, from all groups whose means are lower by 20 points or more.

Japan has a long history of art achievement, of which Kyoto was one of the centers. This art tradition was not limited to the upper classes. Woodblock printing, which was introduced about 1750, made possible a widespread distribution of prints, illustrated books, and picture books. An article in the 1956 edition of the Encyclopedia Britannica (Vol. 12, p. 964) states ". . . perhaps in no country has fine taste been so widely diffused. The color prints of the 18th century were produced by men of the artisan class solely for a public of the same class."

Popular art is widely diffused in Japan today. But Western influences also are great at the present time. The respective Japanese scores may, therefore, reflect a combination of native and Western influences, and it seems reasonable to believe that the differences between urban and rural Japanese means may represent the direction of movement of both influences from urban cultural centers to the hinterland.

Not far from the top of Table 1 are Navaho Indian boys whose mean score at ages six and seven is 115. Navaho girls of the same ages in the same schools have a mean score of only 91, significantly lower than the Navaho boys. The data here presented were gathered by Steggerda in 1936, when, in general, the Navaho lived under more primitive conditions than they do today, although primitive conditions persist at the present time in some parts of the Navaho reservation.

In 1936 the majority of adult Navaho were illiterate, and for the most part each family lived in a one-room dwelling, and were little affected by Western influences. In order to attend school the young children tested in 1936 were moved from their homes to boarding schools operated by the U.S. Indian Bureau. Before coming to these boarding schools at six or seven years, most of these children had never seen paper, pencil, books, or pictures, nor electric lights, piped water, beds and sheets.

Anthropologists from an early date have noted the high artistic development of the Navaho as shown by their chants and rituals, which involve masks, dances, sand-paintings, and recitatives replete with visual imagery. The performers in ceremonies are men. In addition men also do silverwork and leatherwork. The art work performed by women, which is geometric, consists of the weaving of blankets and rugs. The findings with respect to the Navaho are therefore in accord with our hypotheses.

The Hopi Indians are neighbors of the Navaho, but they live in villages. Because it is easier to enforce compulsory education under village conditions than under nomadic conditions, the Hopi received education earlier than did the Navaho. The parents of the children tested by us (Dennis, 1942) had, for the most part, attended school, and their education could indirectly have affected the art of their children. The Hopi boys score about the same as Navaho boys, but Hopi girls score above the Navaho girls. Hopi girls presumably have been more subject than Navaho girls to Western influences.

As Table 1 shows, the Hopi boys' mean score in 1942 was 112; the girls, 104. Havighurst et al. (1946) also found similar and significant sex difference among the Navaho and the Hopi. Among the Hopi, as among the Navaho, the artistic activities belong primarily to the men. Boys begin to participate in these activities at an early age. Hopi women do not engage in representational art. For example, Hopi pottery is made by women but is decorated by men.

Table 1 contains two American white groups—Larned, Kansas; and Rockville, Maryland—whose scores are as high as those of any other group; i.e., equivalent to those of Kyoto boys and girls, and to Navaho and Hopi boys. Each of these towns is a county seat, which contains a large proportion of the highly educated persons in the county. Almost all homes in these towns contain newspapers, illustrated magazines, illustrated children's books, pictures, photographs, art objects, television, crayons, pencil and paper, coloring books, drawing books, and a variety of visual play materials.

In Rockville, Maryland, Negro boys score eight points lower than white boys; and Negro girls, 18 points below white girls. The latter difference is not quite significant. From no other city do we have both Negro and white children, but Table 1 shows that Rockville, Maryland, Negroes score 101 and Negroes in Nashville, Tennessee, in 1958 had a Goodenough mean of 105. These results are significantly different from the mean of 79 which Goodenough obtained from Negro children in several Southern towns in 1925 (see item 34 in Table 1). In other words, from the evidence at hand it appears that urban Negroes today test as high on the Goodenough as urban whites did about thirty years ago, although it is not appropriate to generalize from our samples to the United States as a whole.

The visual art stimulation provided by Negro homes today is undoubtedly greater than it was in 1925. The exposure of white children has also increased. It seems likely that the Goodenough scores of many groups have improved over the intervening period of time. Quite possibly the scores of Navaho and Hopi boys have not improved, since their participation in native "visual displays" may have decreased. But because of the increase in Western influences, the scores of Navaho and Hopi *girls* probably have increased.

In 1958 we tested five one-room rural schools near Lancaster, Pennsylvania (Group 18). All but two pupils in these schools were children of Amish farmers. The Amish homes do not have television. They have few illustrated magazines or children's books. The Amish do not attend movies. However, the public schools which they attend have the usual illustrated textbooks, placards are on the walls, and some drawing assignments are given. The teachers in the schools are non-Amish because until recently the Amish have refused to send their children beyond the eighth grade, and hence Amish young people cannot meet the state educational qualifications for teaching. In view of the nature of the Amish home environment, it is not surprising that the Amish mean is 100, more than 25 points lower than Larned, Kansas, and Kyoto, Japan, and about the same as American Negro groups that we tested.

We did not attempt to obtain data from culturally deprived American communities. They are numerous, and it is certain that many would earn Goodenough means below 100. We centered our attention chiefly on groups which, in terms of our hypothesis, we expected to be appreciably above or below 100. For this reason, the mid-region of Table 1 contains relatively few groups. This is undoubtedly a result of our selection of groups to be tested.

In the groups listed in Table 1, the next group after the Amish is Port Said (Group 19). Port Said is a relatively modern city. The schools which we tested were probably representative of Port Said, yet the mean score of six-year-olds in 1955 was only 94, a value significantly different from all means above 114 and below 74.

Since several Middle Eastern groups are represented in the remainder of Table 1, some general comments should be made about the historical influences upon representational art in Arab, chiefly Moslem, countries.

In the Middle East, there was until recently little development of representational art. This was due in part to a general retardation of cultural progress in Moslem countries. But the low Goodenough scores are due primarily to the consequences of an Eastern religious tradition against making graven images, which was interpreted as prohibiting the making of images of man. Today this interpretation has been widely abandoned. But because of the long duration of the taboo upon the representation of human beings, realism in painting and drawing in the Middle East has been slow in developing.

As a consequence, the group differences among Draw-a-Man scores in the Middle East seem closely related to the degree of Western influence. Children of educated parents in Beirut have scores near Goodenough's American norms. In fact an upper-middle-class progressive Armenian school scored 116 (Group 5). An elementary school associated with the American University of Beirut operated for Arabic-speaking children has a mean score of 93 (Group 20). Villages near Cairo have means respectively of 94 and 92 (Group 21). Sidon, Lebanon, has a mean of 84. Three poor villages in Lebanon, whose access to Beirut is only by poor roads and in which schools were only recently built, have means of 82, 77, and 76 (Groups 31, 36, 37). We are familiar with all of these communities. In our judgment, their scores reflect accurately the amount of contact, respectively, that these groups have had with modern visual mass media and modern civilization in general.

In Beirut boys attending an Armenian private school, the fathers of whom were primarily business and professional men (Group 5), scored 116. The boys and girls in a very poor Armenian section of Beirut scored respectively only 91 and 87 (Groups 23 and 26), significantly lower than the Armenian private school but not different from the Arab private school.

A lower-class group in Merida, Mexico, in 1931–1936 (Group 24) had a mean of 89, as did girls from a poor neighborhood in Tehran in

1959 (Group 25). Urban Negroes in Natal, South Africa (Group 27), scored 85 in 1949. It would appear that for many underprivileged urban groups the usual mean for six-year-olds is between 85 and 90.

Generally speaking the mean scores of underprivileged rural groups represented in Table 1 are lower than those of urban children. Sherman and Key obtained data from a very isolated Virginia mountain community in 1932 (Group 32). Only 12 children six-eight years old were tested. The mean was only 80; the mean of older children was lower than 80.

This community had little contact with newspapers, books, or magazines. Most adults were illiterate. The schooling of the children was minimal. At about the same date, rural Negroes on a relatively isolated island (St. Helena) off the South Carolina coast earned a mean score of 79 (Group 35). Rural hamlets in Lebanon and Mexico (Groups 36, 37, 38) are not significantly different from many other poor rural groups, having means of 77, 76, and 75 respectively.

But such low scores are not limited to rural conditions. Distance from urban centers is not the only barrier between children and modern representational art. Of this fact, the Hassidim in the Williamsburg area of Brooklyn provide an instructive example.

The Hassidim constitute an ultraconservative Jewish group which migrated to Brooklyn from Hungary after World War II [see Poll (1962) for fuller details]. This group attempts to maintain Jewish orthodox traditions as it conceives them to have been many centuries ago. To this end, it prevents contacts between Hassidic children and other Jewish children as well as with Gentile children. It prohibits contact with most modern mass media, such as radio, television, and non-Hassidic publications. All Hassidic children attend Hassidic parochial schools. Certain courses in secular education are required by the State of New York, but the chief emphasis in these schools is upon religious training.

In connection with Goodenough scores, the chief point of interest in respect to the Hassidim is that they have perpetuated the ancient Middle Eastern tradition against the making of images. This is interpreted to proscribe for the Hassidim not only illustrations, movies, and television, which we have mentioned before, but also photographs and drawings. Of course, in a modern city, this prohibition cannot be 100 percent success- ful, since in passing along the city streets Hassidic children must neces- sarily see placards, billboards, movie entrances, magazine covers, the front pages of tabloids, and even drawings of children on sidewalks and walls.

We obtained drawings from Hassidic children through a former student of ours, a teacher of secular subjects at an Hassidic school (few if any Hassidim can qualify as secular teachers). Some Hassidic children refused to draw a man; several said they had never drawn a man before but complied with the request. A total of 26 drawings was obtained from boys aged nine to 11 years, the boys in the classroom of the cooperating teacher (Group 33). The mean Goodenough *IQ* was 79, which is not significantly different from the results obtained from South African Negroes, Negroes in the American South between 1925 and 1928, and poor villages in India, Lebanon, and Mexico. This low score in an urban group seems to be due to its self-imposed insulation from modern mass media. It is not likely that this will continue through another generation.

Two groups only remain to be discussed (Groups 39 and 40). They are the Syrian Bedouins (Dennis, 1960) and the Shilluk group of Sudanese (Fahmy, 1956). Their respective means are 56 and 53. These scores are approximately 20 points lower than the next higher group and significantly different from this group and all other groups.

The Bedouins and the Shilluk are the only groups who were not attending school when tested. Their entire communities were illiterate. Before being tested, these children had not used pencil and paper. They had probably never seen pictures of men, except perhaps in stray copies of newspapers or occasional packages of cigarettes or other packaged goods. The results obtained from these groups seem to indicate that mean scores of about 50 can be earned by children who have had almost minimal exposure to representational art. It will be recalled that this mean is approximately 75 points less than the highest means which we obtained.

In brief, all of the significant differences between groups in Table 1 seem attributable to differences in exposure to representational art, which are often related to differences in modernization.

D. A CONSIDERATION OF ALTERNATIVE HYPOTHESES

We shall now inquire as to whether or not some alternative hypothesis or hypotheses explain equally well the large differences observed in Table 1. Several alternative hypotheses occur to us.

1. Alternative Hypothesis I

Large group differences in Goodenough scores are due primarily to heredity or to other biological factors. This is, of course, the hypothesis which was popular when Goodenough's test was developed. We have no doubt that brain damage and other pathological conditions can affect Goodenough scores, nor do we doubt that *within* a group with homogeneous experience large differences due to heredity will be apparent. But we have been dealing with large differences in scores among biologically normal persons, living in functioning groups. There is no reason to believe that any community can function adequately if the mean "biological" intellectual capacity of the group is equal to or below that of a Western moron. It seems more likely that in these groups biological differences are not being measured.

An environmental rather than a biological interpretation of group differences is supported by our findings concerning sex differences. In many groups, sex differences in Goodenough scores are nonexistent or small. In the rural Japanese communities, girls score higher than boys although not significantly so. In Southwestern Indian groups, boys score significantly higher than girls. Such reversals of sex differences do not seem to be compatible with a biological interpretation.

Further evidence against a biological interpretation of most of the differences shown in Table 1 is derived from the fact that large differences exist between pairs of groups that presumably have much the same heredity. Among such pairs are American Negroes in 1925 and American Negroes in 1956, Hassidic Jews in Brooklyn and Brooklyn Yeshiva students, Arab Bedouins and Arab urban dwellers.

2. Alternative Hypothesis II

Group differences are due chiefly to differences in schooling. We mentioned earlier that six-year-olds and seven-year-olds tested in the same school at the same time seldom differ by more than a few points. From 11 schools we have assembled data for six- and seven-year-olds tested on the same day. The median group scores are identical for the two age groups. Since six- and seven-year-olds in the same schools do not differ in Goodenough scores, the differences in amount of schooling among six-year-olds fail to account for the large differences between groups in Table 1.

3. Alternative Hypothesis III

Differences between groups are due primarily to the fact that urban populations make better scores than do rural populations. While in many countries urban children may enjoy a test-superiority, urban residence accounts for only a few of the differences shown in Table 1. Of the high-scoring groups in Table 1, many are "rural" or village or small town in character. This is true of the three highest white American groups, of four of the six Japanese groups, and of the Navaho and Hopi boys. Nor are all metropolitan groups high-scoring. The Hassidic Jewish group, living in Brooklyn, a city of three million persons, averages 36 points below Navaho boys who have never seen a city. Also there are low-scoring groups in Beirut, in Tehran, and in Natal, all of which are sizeable cities. City groups are often exposed to representational mass media, but this is not true of all urban groups. In contrast, some primitive communities have extensive native art. Our hypothesis seems to fit the data better than does the rural-urban hypothesis.

4. Alternative Hypothesis IV

Group differences are due largely to the literacy and education of the children's parents. Parental education often accompanies exposure to representational art and modernization. But many facts indicate that parental education is not a necessary causal agent. Most of the parents of the high-scoring Navaho boys were uneducated and illiterate. Furthermore, the Navaho parents who produced high-scoring boys produced girls who scored much lower. The fathers of the low-scoring Hassidic boys are literate in Yiddish, Hebrew, and Hungarian and have much religious knowledge, but their sons' mean Goodenough *IQ* is only 79.

In short, no alternative hypothesis which has occurred to us seems to be as satisfactory as the hypotheses which have been proposed by us to account for the differences presented in Table 1.

E. THE EFFECTS OF CULTURAL CHANGE

In this section we will review the evidence that in the case of societies which, prior to contact with Western civilization, developed little or no representational art, Goodenough scores increase as exposure to Western influences increases. This will to some extent repeat what has already been said, but will focus upon Goodenough scores as indicators of cultural change.

Let us start with the Bedouins, who are among the two lowest scoring groups. The Bedouins live a simple nomadic pastoral life, moving their flocks from place to place in an arid environment in search of pasture. This pattern of life has been followed for centuries, and those who are Bedouins today are probably much like the Bedouins of many hundreds of years ago. Because the pastoral cultural pattern has remained constant, it seems likely that Bedouins living centuries ago would have made human figure drawings like the Bedouins of today.

But through the centuries there has been in Arab lands, as elsewhere, a migration of population from rural areas to urban centers. Many of the people in Arab villages, towns, and cities today are descendants of Bedouins. In the most primitive Lebanese villages—as in Remhala, E. Zoutar, and Kakaiet—the mean Goodenough scores are much higher than the Bedouins' average of 56. In modern Beirut it is higher still. It would seem that as Arab culture has incorporated representational art, and other Western influences, the Goodenough score has improved accordingly.

Jews, whose early cultural background was very similar to that of the Arabs, have followed a similar course of development. We have no data on Hebrew shepherds, the counterparts of the Arab Bedouins, but we have data on children of ultraconservative Hassidim now living in Brooklyn. In this group the relative isolation from modern influences is self-imposed. Presumably because of self-imposed restrictions, the Hassidic mean is only 79. Other Jews, living in Brooklyn, who have abandoned the taboo on human representations, have mean test scores of 100 or above. The difference in scores between the children of Hassidic and other American Jews appears to be a matter of cultural change.

The reader is reminded that scores appear to have changed considerably in recent years among American Negroes. Goodenough (1926a) reported the results of testing 613 Negro children in segregated schools in Chattanooga and Mt. Pleasant in Tennessee and in Natchitoches, Louisiana. The mean obtained was 79. Peterson and Telford (1930) testing a rural group of Negroes in St. Helena Island, South Carolina, found a mean of 78. In 1957 we obtained data on six-year-olds in the then-segregated schools of Nashville, Tennessee, and of Rockville, Maryland. The Nashville mean was 105; the Maryland Negroes had a mean score of 101. Since the earlier and later scores were not obtained from the same communities, the evidence is not conclusive, but it suggests that a significant increase of 20 points or more may have taken place in Negro scores since 1926, even under segregated conditions.

The data just discussed are consistent with the interpretation that cultural influences affect Draw-a-Man scores. However, retests of communities tested many years ago could provide direct confirmation. It is hoped that such direct evidence will be obtained soon.

F. SUMMARY AND CONCLUSIONS

The mean Goodenough scores of 40 groups differing widely in original culture and in degree of modernization have been presented. The data were obtained primarily from six-year-olds who were in their first year of school, but some data from some older children and from children not in school have been included. The Goodenough "IQ" means varied from 53 to 125.

It was proposed that the independent variable most directly related to the diversity of group means is the amount of experience with representational art, and in encouragement to engage in it. Variation in exposure to representational art may be due to differences in development of native art or to the degree of exposure to Western art, or to both. Since exposure to Western visual mass media is usually accompanied by exposure to other aspects of Western civilization, it was hypothesized that in the case of groups with little indigenous art, Goodenough scores reflect different degrees of acculturation to Western civilization.

Examination of the data presented seems to support these interpretations more strongly than they support alternative hypotheses.

Evidence has been adduced that Goodenough means of formerly low-scoring populations have increased as their modernization has increased.

The Goodenough test, originally designed to measure "hereditary" differences, may be found useful as an index of what have variously been called degrees of acculturation, Westernization, modernization, and social change.

REFERENCES

Acton, F. S. *The analysis of straight-line data.* New York: John Wiley & Sons, Inc., 1959.

Dennis, W. The performance of Hopi children on the Goodenough Draw-a-Man Test, *J. Comp. Psychol.*, 1942, **34**, 341–348.

Dennis, W. Performance of Near Eastern children on the Draw-a-Man Test, *Child Devel.*, 1957, **28**, 427–430.

Dennis, W. The human figure drawings of Bedouins, *J. Soc. Psychol.*, 1960, **52**, 209–219.

Fahmy, M. *Draw-a-Man Test in an Egyptian rural community.* Cairo: Egypt Publication House, *ca.* 1955.

Fahmy, M. Initial exploring of the Shilluk intelligence. Cairo: Dar Misr Printing House, *ca.* 1956.

Goodenough, F. L. Racial differences in the intelligence of school children, *J. Exper. Psychol.*, 1926(a), **9**, 388–397.

Goodenough, F. L. The measurement of intelligence by drawings. Yonkers-on-Hudson, N.Y.: World Book, 1926(b).

Goodenough, F. L. and D. B. Harris. Studies in the psychology of children's drawings: II. 1928–1949, *Psychol., Bull.*, 1950, **47**, 369–433.

Harris, D. B. *Children's drawings as measures of intellectual maturity.* New York: Harcourt, Brace & World, Inc., 1963.

Havighurst, R. J., M. K. Gunther, and I. E. Pratt. Environment and the Draw-a-Man Test: The performance of Indian children, *J. Abnorm. Soc. Psychol.*, 1946, **41**, 50–63.

Hunkin, V. Validation of the Goodenough Draw-a-Man Test for African children, *J. Soc. Res.* (Pretoria), 1950, **1**, 52–63.

Kramer, C. Y. Extension of multiple range tests to group means with unequal numbers of replications, *Biometrics*, 1956, **12**, 307–310.

Menzel, E. W. The Goodenough Intelligence Test in India, *J. Appl. Psychol.*, 1935, **19**, 615–624.

Peterson, J. and C. W. Telford. Results of group and of individual tests applied to practically pure-blood Negro children on St. Helena Island, *J. Comp. Psychol.*, 1930, **11**, 115–144.

Poll, S. *The Hassidic community of Williamsburg.* New York: The Free Press, 1962.

Scheffe, H. *The analysis of variance.* New York: John Wiley & Sons, Inc., 1959.

Sherman, M. and C. B. Key. Intelligence scores of isolated mountain children, *Child Devel.*, 1932, **3,** 279–290.

CHAPTER 3

CROSS-CULTURAL
STUDIES OF PERSONALITY

3-1

Culture and Motivation

RUTH BENEDICT

Ruth Benedict was a brilliant anthropologist, noted chiefly for her interpretations of cultures. In this selection she described how great, in her opinion, is the wealth of possible human motivations, and indicated that each culture selects for emphasis only a few of the motives that can activate mankind. Thus, in a sense, culture rather than human nature determines a man's motives and drives. To put it another way, every man has many potential interests and goals, but society to a large extent determines which will be actualized. Mozart could not have been a musician if he had been a devout Quaker, nor Napoleon a conqueror if he had been an Eskimo.

In culture we must imagine a great arc on which are ranged the possible interests provided either by the human age-cycle or by the environment or by man's various activities. A culture that capitalized even a considerable proportion of these would be as unintelligible as a language that used all the clicks, all the glottal stops, all the labials, dentals, sibilants, and gutturals from voiceless to voiced and from oral to nasal. Its identity as a culture depends upon the selection of some segments of this arc. Every human society everywhere has made such

Reprinted from *Patterns of culture*, Boston: Houghton Mifflin Company, 1934, by permission of the publisher.

selection in its cultural institutions. Each from the point of view of another ignores fundamentals and exploits irrelevancies. One culture hardly recognizes monetary values; another has made them fundamental in every field of behavior. In one society technology is unbelievably slighted even in those aspects of life which seem necessary to ensure survival; in another, equally simple, technological achievements are complex and fitted with admirable nicety to the situation. One builds an enormous cultural superstructure upon adolescence, one upon death, one upon after-life.

The great arc along which all the possible human behaviors are distributed is far too immense and too full of contradictions for any one culture to utilize even any considerable portion of it. Selection is the first requirement. Without selection no culture could even achieve intelligibility, and the intentions it selects and makes its own are a much more important matter than the particular detail of technology or the marriage formality that it also selects in similar fashion.

The vast proportion of all individuals who are born into any society always and whatever the idiosyncrasies of its institutions, assume, as we have seen, the behavior dictated by that society. This fact is always interpreted by the carriers of that culture as being due to the fact that their particular institutions reflect an ultimate and universal sanity. The actual reason is quite different. Most people are shaped to the form of their culture because of the enormous malleability of their original endowment. They are plastic to the moulding force of the society into which they are born. It does not matter whether, with the Northwest Coast, it requires delusions of self-reference, or, with our own civilization, the amassing of possessions. In any case the great mass of individuals take quite readily the form that is presented to them.

They do not all, however, find it equally congenial, and those are favored and fortunate whose potentialities most nearly coincide with the type of behavior selected by their society.

For example, trance is an abnormality in our society. Even a very mild mystic is aberrant in Western civilization. In order to study trance or catalepsy within our own social groups, we have to go to the case histories of the abnormal. Therefore the correlation between trance experience and the neurotic and psychotic seems perfect. As in the case of the homosexual, however, it is a local correlation characteristic of our century. Even in our own cultural background other areas give different results. In the Middle Ages when Catholicism made the ecstatic experience the mark of sainthood, the trance experience was greatly valued, and those to whom the response was congenial, instead of being overwhelmed by a catastrophe as in our century, were given confidence in their pursuit of it. Individuals who were susceptible to trance, therefore, succeeded or failed in terms of their native capacities, but since trance experience was highly valued, a great leader was very likely to be capable of it.

Among some primitive peoples, trance and catalepsy have been honored in the extreme. Some of the Indian tribes of California accorded prestige principally to those who passed through certain trance experiences. Not all of these tribes believed that it was exclusively women who were so blessed, but among the Shasta this was the convention. Their shamans were women, and they were accorded the greatest prestige in the community. They were chosen because of their constitutional liability to trance and allied manifestations. One day the woman who was so destined, while she was about her usual work, fell suddenly to the ground. She had heard a voice speaking to her in tones of the greatest intensity. Turning, she had seen a man with drawn bow and arrow. He commanded her to sing on pain of being shot through the heart by his arrow, but under the stress of the experience she fell senseless. Her family gathered. She was lying rigidly, hardly breathing. They knew that for some time she had had dreams of a special character which indicated a shamanistic calling, dreams of escaping grizzly bears, falling off cliffs or trees, or of being surrounded by swarms of yellow-jackets. The community knew therefore what to expect. After a few hours the woman began to moan gently and to roll about upon the ground, trembling violently. She was supposed to be repeating the song which she had been told to sing and which during the trance had been taught her by the spirit. As she revived, her moaning became more and more clearly the spirit's song, until at last she called out the name of the spirit itself, and immediately blood oozed from her mouth.

When the woman had come to herself after the first encounter with her spirit, she danced that night her first initiatory shaman's dance. For three nights she danced holding herself by a rope that was swung from the ceiling. On the third night she had to receive in her body her power from the spirit. She was dancing, and as she felt the approach of the moment she called out, "He will shoot me, he will shoot me." Her friends stood close, for when she reeled in a kind of cataleptic seizure, they had to seize her before she fell or she would die. From this time on she had in her body a visible materialization of her spirit's power, an icicle-like object which in her dances thereafter she would exhibit, producing it from one part of her body and returning it to another part. From this time on she continued to validate her supernatural power by further cataleptic demonstrations, and she was called upon in great emergencies of life and death, for curing and for divination and for counsel. She became, in other words, by this procedure a woman of great power and importance.

It is clear that, far from regarding cataleptic seizures as blots upon the family escutcheon and as evidences of dreaded disease, cultural approval had seized upon them and made of them the pathway to authority over one's most respected social type, the type which functioned with most honor and reward in the community. It was precisely the cataleptic individuals who in this culture were singled out for authority and leadership.

Warfare is another social theme that may or may not be used in any culture. Where war is made much of, it may be with contrasting organization in relation to the state, and with contrasting sanctions. War may be, as it was among the Aztecs, a way of getting captives for the religious sacrifices. Since the Spaniards fought to kill, according to Aztec standards they broke the rules of the game. The Aztecs fell back in dismay and Cortez walked as victor into the capital.

There are even quainter notions, from our standpoint, associated with warfare in different parts of the world. Only our familiarity with war makes it intelligible that a state of warfare should alternate with a state of peace in one tribe's dealings with another. The idea is quite common over the world, of course. But on the one hand it is impossible for certain peoples to conceive the possibility of a state of peace, which in their notion would be equivalent to admitting enemy tribes to the category of human beings, which by definition they are not even though the excluded tribe may be of their own race and culture.

On the other hand, it may be just as impossible for a people to conceive of the possibility of a state of war. Rasmussen tells of the blankness with which the Eskimo met his exposition of our custom. Eskimos very well understand the act of killing a man. If he is in your way, you cast up your estimate of your own strength, and if you are ready to take it upon yourself, you kill him. If you are strong, there is no social retribution. But the idea of an Eskimo village going out against another Eskimo village in battle array or a tribe against tribe, or even of another village being fair game in ambush warfare, is alien to them. All killing comes under one head, and is not separated, as ours is, into categories, the one meritorious, the other a capital offence.

3-2

Emotional Expression in Chinese Literature

OTTO KLINEBERG

No doubt there are universal facial expressions, such as, for example, crying and smiling. But there are also facial expressions that have become part of a culture and that are learned by the children of the culture. Klineberg presents an example by citing the differences in facial expressions as described in Chinese and English literature.

The fact that the expression of the emotions is at least to some extent patterned by social factors is probably known to all psychologists. Even in our own society there is considerable evidence that this is so. When we turn to the descriptions of other cultures, instances of this patterning occur frequently. One of the most striking examples is the copious shedding of tears by the Andaman Islanders and the Maori of New Zealand when friends meet after an absence, or when two warring parties make peace. Another is the smile with which the Japanese responds to the scolding of his superior, or which accompanies his announcement of the death of his favorite son.

This paper represents part of a more extensive study of emotional

Reprinted from *J. Abnorm. Soc. Psychol.*, 1938, **33**, 517–520, by permission of the author and the American Psychological Association.

expression among the Chinese. Among the various techniques employed, it seemed valuable in the case of a civilization as articulate as the Chinese to examine at least a portion of the Chinese literature for the light it might throw on this problem. There is not much precedent for the reading of novels as a technique of psychological investigation, but in this case it seemed warranted at least as an introduction to more objective methods.

Before turning to the question of the kind of expression involved, a word should be said as to the related question of the amount of expression which the culture permits. There are, for example, many admonitions—especially to the young girl—not to show emotion too readily. In the Chinese book *Required Studies for Women* we find such warnings as the following: "Do not show your unhappiness easily and do not smile easily"; also, "Do not let your teeth be seen when you smile," that is, your smile must be so circumspect that the teeth do not show. On the other hand, there are many occasions on which the emotion of grief has to be displayed. One piece of advice from the same volume reads, "If your father or mother is sick, do not be far from his or her bed. Do not even take off your girdle. Taste all the medicine yourself. Pray your god for his or her health. If anything unfortunate happens cry bitterly."

The alleged inscrutability of the Chinese, which as a matter of fact has been greatly exaggerated, completely breaks down in the case of grief. Not only is grief expressed, but there is an elaborate set of rules and regulations which insure that it shall be properly expressed. One of the Chinese classics is *The Book of Rites*, a considerable portion of which is devoted to the technique of the mourning ceremonial, with elaborate instructions as to just what procedure should be followed in order that the expression of the grief may be socially acceptable.

The most extreme degree of patterning of emotional expression is found on the Chinese stage, and is illustrated by the following examples from a Chinese *Treatise on Acting*. There is an occasional pattern which does conform closely to our own; for example, "taking the left sleeve with the right hand and raising it to the eyes as if to wipe the tears" is clearly an expression of sorrow. There are others, however, that are not so clear. To "draw one leg up and stand on one foot" means surprise. To "raise one hand as high as the face and fan the face with the sleeve" means anger, as does also to "blow the beard to make it fly up." Joy or satisfaction is represented by stretching "the left arm flatly to the left and right arm to the right." To "move one hand around in front of the middle of the beard and touch your head with the fingers of the other hand" means sorrow, while to "put the middle part of the beard into the mouth with both hands and bite firmly" indicates that one has come to a decision. To "raise both hands above the head with the palms turned outwards and the fingers pointing up, let the sleeves hang down behind the hands, then walk towards the other person, shake the sleeves over, and let the hands fall" means love.

There were two long novels which were read for this study: one, *The Dream of the Red Chamber*, was read in Chinese, with considerable help from Miss Wu T'ien Min, a graduate student at Yenching University, and the other, *All Men are Brothers*, in Pearl Buck's English translation. These represent two of the three most famous Chinese novels, the third being *The Romance of the Three Kingdoms. The Dream of the Red Chamber* is a love story; *All Men are Brothers* is a tale of swashbuckling adventure dealing with the so-called "bandits" who are among the most picturesque figures of Chinese legend and history. Besides these, several modern stories were also consulted.

In some cases the descriptions of emotional expression correspond closely to our own. When we read (D.R.C.), for example, that "everyone trembled with a face the color of clay," there can be little doubt that fear is meant. The same holds for the statement that "every one of his hairs stood on end, and the pimples came out on the skin all over his body," (from *Married Life Awakening the World*). Other descriptions of fear (A.M.B.) are the following: "A cold sweat broke forth on his whole body, and he trembled without ceasing"; "it was as though her two feet were nailed to the ground and she would fain have shrieked but her mouth was like a mute's"; "they stood like death with mouths ajar"; "they were so frightened that their waters and wastes burst out of them." In general, it may be said that fear is expressed in very much the same way in the Chinese literature as in our own. As far as other emotions are concerned, in the sentence, "He gnashed his teeth until they were all but ground to dust," we recognize anger; "He was listless and silent" suggests sorrow; "His face was red and he went creeping alone outside the village" clearly indicates shame. There is no doubt of the frequent similarity between Chinese and Western forms of expression.

There are also differences, however. When we read "They stretched out their tongues" (D.R.C.), most of us would not recognize this description as meaning surprise, except for the context. This phrase as an expression of surprise occurs with great frequency, and it would be easy to give many examples. The sentence, "Her eyes grew round and opened wide," would probably suggest to most of us surprise or fear; to the Chinese it usually means anger. This expression, with slight variations, also occurs very often. In the form "He made his two eyes round and stared at him" (A.M.B.), it can mean nothing but anger. "He would fain have swallowed him at a gulp" (A.M.B.) implies hatred; "I could eat you up!" has a somewhat different significance. "He scratched his ears and cheeks" would probably suggest embarrassment to us, but in the *Dream of the Red Chamber* it means happiness. "He clapped his hands" (D.R.C.) is likely to mean worry or disappointment.

The case of anger appears to be particularly interesting. We have already noted the expressions connected with "round eyes," "eyes wide open," "staring," etc. We find in addition descriptions like these: "He laughed a great ho-ho," and "He smiled a chill smile," and "He looked at them and he smiled and cursed them" (A.M.B.). Both the laugh and the smile of anger or contempt occur in our own culture, but apparently not nearly so frequently as in China and the Chinese literature. More curious still is the phrase "He was so angry that several times he fainted from his anger" (A.M.B.). This expression occurs frequently. When I showed wonder as to why this should be, Chinese friends said that they in turn could never understand why European women fainted so frequently in the mid-Victorian literature with which they were acquainted. Certainly the delicately nurtured young women of not so long ago did faint with astonishing ease and regularity; there were even etiquette books which taught them how to faint elegantly. Such a custom is certainly no less surprising than that the Chinese should faint in anger. The conclusion seems clear that fainting, like tears, may be conditioned by social custom to appear on widely varying occasions.

Most striking of all perhaps, is the indication in the literature that people may die of anger. "His anger has risen so that he is ill of it and lies upon his bed, and his life cannot be long assured," " 'To-day am I killed by anger' . . . and when he had finished speaking he let his soul go free." (A.M.B.). This phenomenon incidentally, mysterious though it may sound, is reported as still occurring, and I saw one patient in a hospital in Peiping whose father was said to have died of anger after losing a lawsuit. It is important to note that a death of this kind cannot be explained as due to anything like an apoplectic stroke; it does not occur suddenly as a stroke would. When someone is very angry but is forced to suppress his anger because there is nothing he can do about it, he may become ill, faint many times and take to his bed; death may follow after the lapse of some days or weeks. The only explanation is in terms of suggestion; the belief that people die of anger when they can do nothing about it may succeed in actually bringing on the death of an impressionable person. There is the parallel case of the Polynesian native who inadvertently eats the tabooed food of the chief, remains perfectly well as long as he does not know it, but may die when he learns what he has done.

These examples indicate that, although there are many similarities between the literary descriptions of the emotions in China and in the West, there are also important differences which must be recognized if Chinese literature is to be read intelligently. When the literary pattern is such that the expression alone is described but not labeled, real misunderstanding may arise. When I first read, for instance, "They stretched out their tongues," I did not know that surprise was meant. Our own literature is of course also rich in these unlabeled expressions. We read, "His jaw dropped"; "He gnashed his teeth"; "His lip curled"; "His eyes almost popped out of his head"; "He clenched his fists," etc., and in each case we know at once what emotion is indicated. These expressions are a part of language and must be learned in order to be understood.

The question arises as to the degree to which these Chinese literary expressions are related to expression in real life. Caution must certainly be exercised in inferring from one to the other. A Chinese reader of our literature, for instance, might conclude that laughter was dangerous to Westerners, in view of the frequency with which he read the expression "I nearly died laughing." I think I may say, however, on the basis of information obtained by methods other than the reading of novels, that the Chinese patterns which I have described do appear not only in the literature but also in real life. I may add that photographs illustrating these literary expressions are judged more easily by Chinese than by American subjects.

3-3

Transcultural Variables
and Conceptual Equivalence

ROBERT R. SEARS

One of the main aims of psychologists is to find empirical relationships between variables and thus formulate general principles of behavior. Are variables investigated in one culture comparable across several cultures? Dr. Sears is dealing in this paper with transcultural variables in studying personality. In the field of personality, psychologists are generally concerned with constructs (concepts) that subsume various kinds of acts and behavior. These constructs cannot be described or measured directly, they can only be defined. Dr. Sears thinks that these constructs can be investigated transculturally if they are regarded as representing the motivational state of the person or the goal responses of his motives. It is the goal responses of motives and their relationship to different cultural backgrounds that lend themselves to cross-cultural investigations. Behaviors that are indices of motivational states may be culture-specific.

Transcultural variables are variables that can be measured in all cultures. They are universal properties of man or of his environment. By

Reprinted from B. Kaplan (ed.), *Studying personality cross-culturally*, New York: Harper and Row, Publishers, Inc., 1961 by permission of the author and publisher.

no means all the variables used in American researches on personality have this quality. For example, value dimensions such as those measured by the Allport-Vernon scale, or occupational interests as defined by the Strong inventory, are probably local to Western culture. These kinds of culture-bound variables may be of considerable value either for engineering purposes or for actual theory construction, but only within their own culture area. For cross-cultural research which is designed to develop personality theory that will be universally applicable, variables are required that can be measured everywhere.

THE PURPOSES OF CROSS-CULTURAL RESEARCH

The reasons for this rest on the two functions of cross-cultural research. One of these functions is to provide a population sample, for testing hypotheses, that offers greater extremes on relevant variables, and broader variation among irrelevant variables, than can be obtained within a single culture. Cross-cultural research done with these aims in mind normally makes use of the modal behavior of a reasonably homogeneous culture group (the primary sampling unit, or PSU) as the unit. This procedure contrasts with ordinary research methods on personality in which the modal behavior of an individual person is the unit. The works of Murdock (1949) and of Whiting and Child (1953) offer examples.

The second function is to provide appropriate conditions for the systematic variation of factors that cannot be varied within a single culture. If some cultural characteristic such as "authoritarian government" or "sororal polygyny" is believed to have interacting effects on the variables between which relational principles are being sought, then the testing of the hypotheses must be done in different cultures that can provide for such interaction. This is sometimes spoken of, rather inexactly, as "varying the background factors."

Whichever purpose is the basis for a given cross-cultural research venture, the variables used must be transcultural. They must be measurable in whatever culture is chosen, whether the culture be a unit of the sample population or a source of systematic variation of an interaction variable.

CONCEPTUAL EQUIVALENCE AND OPERATIONAL
DEFINITIONS

The first requirement for testing any hypothesis, or for discovering any empirical relationship, is to have two or more variables which can be precisely defined. These definitions must be in sufficiently operational terms that actual measurements can be made of the variables. These are obvious rules for any investigative procedure, and they could go without saying except for the fact that they create a special problem in cross-cultural research, the problem of *conceptual equivalence.*

In most natural science research and even in much behavioral science research, crucial variables are defined by reference to a direct operation of measurement. A given variable is represented by a single operation. Thus a principle that states the relationship between (X) duration of dark adaptation and (Y) visual threshold in the human eye is a statement about the relationship between two exactly specified measurement operations, one based on amount of time under conditions of non-illumination, and the other on a precise psychophysical measurement of responses to light stimuli of different intensities. In the field of personality, however, the variables with which we seem usually to concern ourselves are once removed from a perceptually unique measurement operation. They are constructs that subsume several kinds of instigating situations or actions. For example, the behavior concept of *aggression* cannot be measured by any single operation; it may be defined in terms of the relative number of homicides in a society, the frequency of insults, the intensities of physical injuries as judged by some *a priori* scale, or any one of a dozen other kinds of action. Likewise, an antecedent variable like frustration may be measured by reference to interference with a host of different action systems.

There is nothing intrinsically wrong with using each of these many separate "aggression" or "frustration" items as a single variable, except that to do so would be inefficient. For the sake of economy, it is desirable that we have as few behavior variables as will conveniently provide adequate predictability of the entire scope of behavior that we consider a suitable subject matter for science. From the standpoint of measurement, on the other hand, single behavior items that permit single measurement operations provide the greatest precision in the statement of relationships.

A solution to this dilemma can sometimes be found in a compromise. For example, in the problem of dark adaptation, mentioned above, there are three different psychophysical methods for measuring visual threshold. Any one of these can be used for determining a general principle that states the relation between time of adaptation and visual threshold. They all give the same principle. The actual threshold values obtained will vary, of course, depending on the method. All three measures are indices of a more general concept, *viz.,* visual threshold. Another way of saying the same thing is that there are three interchangeable operational definitions of this concept. The compromise between economical, but unmeasurable, "globality" of concepts, and uneconomical, but measurable, operationism lies in the discovery of the exact relationships between the various indices of a given concept. When indices are interchangeable, and provide the same $X \rightarrow Y$ principles, they display *conceptual equivalence*.

There is one difficulty to be kept in mind, however. When we are dealing with spontaneous behavior, *i.e.*, actions that are elicited by the natural environment and the person's internal sources of instigation, we find that there is sometimes systematic interaction between the items of behavior that we believe should be used as indices. In the case of aggression, for example, overt and displaced aggression have a very complex non-linear relationship that prevents us from using one kind as an index interchangeable with the other. There may be other instances, as in the defense mechanisms, in which two behaviors seemingly comparable as "anxiety reducers" are actually alternatives. This means that $X \rightarrow X$ and $Y \rightarrow Y$ relationships must be examined carefully before $X \rightarrow Y$ relationships are sought.

This problem is hard enough to solve when one is working with a single construct like *aggression* in a single and quite homogeneous culture group. Over the last two decades, considerable labor has been expended in the study of just what behavior items are conceptually equivalent within the aggression system. So far, at least, one can say that most of this research effort has not seriously questioned whether aggression itself is a useful and desirable concept within the American culture. But that is about as far as one can go. Research has not yet provided more than a minimal start toward a study of the actual equivalence and functional interactions of different types of aggressive action (Berkowitz, 1958).

From a cross-cultural standpoint, a more primitive question must be raised. Is *aggression* itself a good behavior concept? Is this a unitary kind of behavior that exists in the behavior repertories of all peoples, regardless of the cultures in which they are reared?

TRANSCULTURAL DETERMINANTS

To the extent that there are universal characteristics of people as biological organisms and universal characteristics of environment, to that extent there are likely to be transcultural properties of behavior. In other words, we presume that when a given kind of organism has to interact with a given kind of environment, all organisms having the same general property will develop behavior repertories that can be conceptualized in the same way. This reasoning rests explicitly on the assumption that not only are there universal biological qualities in man, but that the basic characteristics of the learning process, including the acquisition of motives, are universal, too.

Biologically, there are a number of universals in man. Some of these can be specified by reference to what are commonly called the primary drives, while others are referrable to common structural characteristics. Primary drives relate mainly to the biological integrity of the individual. For his own maintenance, man must eat, drink water, eliminate waste products, maintain a certain range of body temperature, avoid damaging injury to his body wall, sleep and rest, exercise his muscles, and breathe air. If the species survives, obviously most men engage in sexual activity also.

Structurally and functionally there are other universal qualities which are of importance. Man is a warm-blooded mammal, hairless over most of his body; he is ground living, with neither wings nor tail nor strong arms to take him into the air or into tree tops; he is omnivorous, but with neither the digestive system of a ruminant nor the teeth and claws of carnivora; he is big brained, lacks a good smell sense but has excellent vision and audition; he has a capacity for the use of spoken language. Perhaps as important as anything is the fact that he has an organismic growth rate that requires several years of direct physical care of the young by mature animals.

It is difficult to specify the universalities in the human environment. There are two aspects of it that need separation. First is the physical or nonhuman environment. One could point to such facts as that food never grows on man's body itself, but always must be sought by hunting or fishing or climbing or agriculture. The same is true of water, in the sense that it exists on the earth's surface independently of the biological organisms that also exist there. There are few places in which man can live without at least occasional activity related to maintaining body temperature within its proper limits. There are many dangerous objects that can injure him. There are cliffs to trip him, lightning to fell him, the dangers of fire, falling objects, sharp pointed objects, wild beasts and smothering caves; and there are poisonous snakes, fruits, fish and springs.

The second aspect of the environment is the human. The same universal qualities that establish universal behavior repertories also create environmental universals for other men. Every human being lives in a world in which there are others who are also seeking food and water, others who become fatigued and sleep, others who become enraged and destructive because of pain or injury, and so on. The basic biological and physical environmental universals create certain universal qualities in man, and since there are always many men as part of the environment, these learned behavioral qualities also become universal parts of the environment. There are, in other words, what might be called *derivative* or *secondary* universals.

It seems evident that there are two broad general classifications of transcultural variables, one monadic and the other dyadic. Monadic variables are those that are constructed in the individual's behavior repertory by experiences that do not involve any regularized interaction with other people. Some such variables may be characteristic of the person as a biological organism (i.e., they are unlearned), while others may be a function of inevitable universal experiences.

Dyadic variables are those that depend upon universal interactions with other persons. They involve mutual expectancies and mutual reinforcements. There are obviously some dyadic variables related to behavior that is initially established in the individual by his interaction with one or perhaps two other people (e.g., dependency in relationship to the mother, or competition among peers), and eventually become behavioral properties of the person more or less independent of any one other individual but related to his functioning as a member of a social system. This would be the case, for example, with such a concept as *aggression anxiety* or *inhibition of aggression*.

Another distinction to keep in mind is that between antecedent and consequent variables. The *conditions* for establishing transcultural behavioral variables belong in the category of antecedents. In man, with his potentialities for learning new motives and expectancies, these antecedents create transcultural consequent variables. These may play the logical role, in some instances, of intervening variables, as is the case with "anticipation of success or failure." Such a concept may then be used, for all practical purposes, as an antecedent of action. In other cases, the consequent variable produced by these universal antecedents is an abstraction of some action quality. Aggression or competition or status-striving are examples.

These abstractions point up the problem of conceptual equivalence. Take aggression as an example. A distinction must be made between the instrumental acts that are indices of aggression (e.g., hitting, insulting, nonco-operating) and the hypothetical "goal response" of the aggression motive (perceiving another person's reactions to injury). It is the latter that one would expect to find transculturally. The aggressor's instrumental activities that serve to hurt someone else—and thus enable him to perceive reactions to injury in his victim—will differ from one culture to another. The form of an insult, for instance, depends on the values held by the insulted one. Or to take another example: automobile racing and football can be instrumental activities for competition only if the society has automobiles and knows how to play football.

It seems doubtful that there are very many transcultural variables at the level of description of the instrumental act. Societies differ too much both in their structure and in the natural resources they have available to permit identity of instrumental actions across cultural lines. Of course, there are a few instrumental acts that are almost inevitably transcultural. Such aggressions as hitting, kicking, stabbing and biting probably create pain responses in others (the *Beta* persons in dyadic relationships) no matter what culture is involved. But such universal instrumental acts appear to be rare.

At the goal response level of description, however, the actions are essentially descriptive of what the motivational system is. The actions are defined in terms of the Environmental Events they tend to produce. In other words, securing the unsharable goal, perceiving nurturant orientation, and perceiving pain responses refer to the Environmental Events that are brought about by motivated actions. The details of the actions that bring about such Environmental Events will differ radically from culture to culture, but the events themselves should be identical.

These action "abstractions" are only one type of variable that may be transcultural. Since it is possible that the methods of discovering useful variables may be different, depending on the kind involved, it is worth listing what seem to be different types. There are various ways in which one can conceptualize action or learning, and the following terms are representative of but one (Sears, 1951).

1. *Environmental Events.* As indicated above, these are the occurrences in the environment that a motivated action system seeks to produce. It is assumed that the person, Alpha, develops an *expectancy* of such events, through the process of motive acquisition, and that their occurrence is the necessary condition for his gratification. They are often a form of behavior in another person, Beta. They can be defined at either a phenomenal or a genotypic level. Presumably only the latter would be transcultural.

2. *Goal responses (or action abstractions).* These are the hypothetical actions that occur in Alpha when the appropriate Environmental Events occur. They are "consummatory" responses. In the case of acquired motives, they may prove to be useless concepts, since in fact all we ever know about, or can observe, are the Environmental Events and the instrumental acts that produce them.

3. *Instrumental acts.* Underlying the phenomenal multiplicity of behavior that produces Environmental Events, there are genotypic qualities that are likely to be transcultural. That is, "aggressive" acts are designed to produce a pain response in Beta. In many instances, the form of aggression will not be transcultural, but the genotypic quality of "aggression" will be.

4. *Learning situations.* These have been discussed above.

5. *Action instigators.* Once an action system has been formed, there must be instigators to set it off. These can presumably be transcultural.

6. *Intervening mechanisms of response.* Such processes as displacement, retroactive inhibition, repression, projection, etc., are essentially statements of complex relations between antecedents and consequents. They appear to have the logical status of intervening variables, and are among the general laws of learning and action that are here presumed to be universal. Their identification transculturally will doubtless involve the same problems as those related to antecedents and consequents, plus the additional one of determining, for each culture, the special dimensions of stimulus similarity unique to the culture.

MOTIVATIONAL SYSTEMS

At present we know little about what motivational systems may prove to be transcultural. Three examples that seem likely candidates are aggression, dependency and competition. Brief descriptions will indicate why.

Aggression

Aggression may be defined as a goal response to instigation to injure an organism or an organism-surrogate. While a rage response appears to be a native characteristic of mammals, elicitable by various types of frustration even in early infancy, the peculiar quality of aggression involves perception of pain responses in another person. One hypothesis to account for its development requires that it would occur in all human beings. This reasoning rests on the fact that all people can feel pain, and respond to it by expressive movements that are perceivable by a child. One of the commonest reactions to pain is an attempt to remove its source. When this source is another person who is making demands on one, this attempt is likely to be in the form of a compliance with those demands. In other words, the young child can secure compliance from his mother or older siblings by hurting them, and because their signs of pain reaction are associated with the gratifications of his needs, he develops a secondary motivational system for which the goal response is perceiving another person's signs of being hurt. (For a more extended discussion, see Sears et al., 1957.)

The problem of securing transculturally usable indices of aggression is probably not too serious. What is required is that we be able to identify the Environmental Event (pain responses) for all cultures. With overt physical aggression, this is simple, for the signs of pain are themselves of a universal reflex character. More subtle forms of aggression, such as insults and techniques of injuring someone's ego or pride, may be more difficult to equate cross-culturally. The defensive character of people's responses to these more subtle forms of injury tends to hide direct indications of pain. To identify aggression of this kind, then, it may be necessary to examine what transcultural motives there are in people that can provide for pain when they are frustrated. For example, if it turns out that we can deduce the universal existence of such a motive as pride, we will need only to discover, for each culture, of what things any individual is ordinarily proud. The behavior of someone else that interferes with a person's pride in these things can then be identified as a form of aggression.

Dependency

The dependency drive can be defined as instigation to be oriented toward and cared for by another person. Since man has such a long period of physical dependency, he has a tremendous number of reinforcements of maternal orientation toward him, accompanied by primary drive gratification. As a consequence, it may be assumed that this orientation, and other signs of caretaking behavior, become the appropriate Environmental Events for the gratification of a secondary drive of dependency. Again, as with aggression, the manifestations will vary from one culture to another, depending in this case upon the characteristic forms of caretaking that have been applied to the child in early childhood. Behavior connected with food offerings is probably important. There seems to be no alternative to simple empirical investigation of different cultures in order to discover the commonest forms of orientation toward the child and of the latter's techniques for securing such orientation. The techniques that will work for him will differ from culture to culture.

Competition

The competition drive may be defined as instigation to secure an unsharable goal. There seems no doubt that competitive behavior is a transcultural variable. In the very nature of family living the attention and help of the mother or other major caretaker is to some degree unsharable among the various people who want it. As a consequence, children from a fairly early age are forced to seek such goals in the presence of similar striving from other persons (competitors). To the extent that such competitive efforts are successful for a particular youngster, to that extent he should develop a competition drive which would lead him to respond to almost any goal as an unsharable one. The qualities of competition, then, would enter into his behavior in connection with attempting to secure the goal.

CRITERIA OF CONCEPTUAL EQUIVALENCE

Since action categories such as aggression, dependency and competition describe the reference events in which we are ultimately interested, attention should be given to discovering which ones are transcultural.

The criteria for determining conceptual equivalence of responses are not at all clear. However, the problem is probably no worse at the cross-cultural level than at the inter-individual. For example, one might ask what criteria there are for defining both a street fight and the telling of malicious gossip as indices of aggression. We seem to accept this identity on some intuitive basis and without critical examination of the criteria involved. Equally, we have to this point accepted reasonably obvious similarities cross-culturally, doubtless on the same intuitive basis. Actually, of course, intuition is merely a word to indicate that our reasoning and observations on this matter have been unsystematic. If we are to go beyond the few concepts which many students of behavior have been examining and working with for many years, however, these criteria must be formalized. Perhaps it will help get us started if we try to analyze the implicit criteria we have been using in the past.

1. *Is there a universal learning situation?* In the case of aggression and dependency, at least, we appear always to have rested the case for conceptual equivalence, in part, on the fact that we could imagine the transcultural existence of the learning conditions. For aggression, this was the capacity of Beta to feel pain and to comply with directions for future behavior when she did. Alpha was presumed to have the capacity for producing pain stimulation. For dependency, the learning situation was the long period of physical dependency in infancy, together with Alpha's presumed capacity for developing a strong object cathexis.

To use this criterion, we must be able to specify in detail what the exact antecedents of any given response are. Have we any present evidence that mothers *do* comply with children's demands when these are accomplished by pain-inducing acts? *Does* such (presumed) compliance occur in association with grimaces of a standard and oft-repeated kind? *Are* these (presumed) grimaces uniquely indicative of the occurence of pain stimulation?

2. *Can the appropriate Environmental Event be identified?* Since this Event is the "goal" of the action which is being studied, it must be recognizable. For aggression it has been defined as Beta's expression of pain-response. For dependency, it is nurturant orientation from the adult caretaker.

3. *Are there discoverable instrumental acts that produce these*

Environmental Events? These acts will differ, of course, from person to person and from culture to culture. However, the measurement of the action category depends upon our finding quantifiable forms of behavior that are regularly used for producing the specified Environmental Events. The relation between such actions is a major unknown even in our own culture. Some appear to be alternatives to one another, as is the case with positive and negative attention-getting in young children. Others appear to be positively related, as are the frequencies (under some circumstances) of overt and fantasy aggression.

It seems likely that a great deal of work needs doing on the mechanisms of development of instrumental activity before we can go far with this criterion. The mechanisms of projection and displacement, for example, suggest that sheer correlational studies of consequent-consequent measures are covering up elaborate mechanisms that relate these responses to one another in regular but very complex ways.

4. *Are the same antecedent-consequent relations demonstrable in all cultures?* The methodological implications of this criterion are both vast and expensive. If the first criterion (universal learning situations) is met, and if the assumption is valid that the laws of learning and action laws are universal, this criterion would automatically be met. However, there is good reason to examine it separately, for we find it difficult to be satisfactorily rigorous about any of these matters as yet. A good many psychologists have assumed that the frustration-aggression relationship is universal, but Bateson (1941) has expressed doubt that this holds true in Bali.

There would be some value in knowing whether certain of the other relationships that we find in American culture are as valid elsewhere. This can be done by replication of experiments. But at this point, the reasoning turns back to the original problem itself, for one of the purposes of cross-cultural research is simply this—to discover whether certain antecedent-consequent relations are universal!

References

Bateson, G. The frustration-aggression hypothesis and culture, *Psychol. Rev.*, 1941, **48**, 350–355.

Berkowitz, L. The expression and reduction of hostility, *Psychol. Bull.*, 1958, **55**, 257–283.

Murdock, G. P. *Social structure.* New York: The Macmillan Company, 1949.

Sears, R. R. A theoretical framework for personality and social behavior, *Amer. Psychol.*, 1951, **6**, 476–483.

Sears, R. R., E. E. Maccoby, and H. Levin. *Patterns of child rearing.* New York: Harper and Row, Publishers, 1957.

Whiting, J. W. M. and I. Child. *Child training and personality: A cross-cultural study.* New Haven: Yale University Press, 1953.

3-4

Social Distance Among Greek and United States College Students

HARRY C. TRIANDIS
LEIGH MINTURN TRIANDIS

Social psychologists long have been interested in the study of social distance and ethnic stereotypes. Bogardus (1925) was one of the first to design a social distance scale for measuring and comparing attitudes toward different nationalities. The scale is comprised of several statements to indicate the subject's degree of acceptance of various nationalities. The statements progress from one implying willingness to accept a close relationship with the nationality group, such as "to close kinship and marriage," to one implying unwillingness to accept any relationship, such as "would exclude from my country."

Katz and Braly (1933) have similarly constructed a checklist scale for the study of ethnic stereotypes; subjects are asked to give the five traits that they consider most characteristic of different ethnic groups or nationalities. The traits are to be selected from 84 adjectives, although subjects are allowed to add any trait they like to attribute to these nationalities.

One important contribution of Drs. Triandis and Triandis is to point out the methodological limitations of the above scales and

Abridged from *Psychol. Monogr.*, 1962, **76**, No. 540, by permission of the authors and the American Psychological Association.

attempt to refine them for the study of cultural groups. In his recent review, Dr. H. C. Triandis (1964) points out that the use of a single word such as "Negro" or "Irishman" limits the interpretations of the results. When a word such as "Negro" or "Irishman" is presented to a subject, he may be responding either to race, occupation, religion, nationality, or a combination of these factors. In the same review, Dr. Triandis (1964) comments on the checklist method of studying stereotypes. He indicates that certain adjectives tend to be differently correlated with evaluation; for example, the adjective "aggressive" may be regarded as "good" in one culture but as "bad" in another. In the present study Drs. Triandis and Triandis attempted to overcome these methodological difficulties. They studied social distance and ethnic stereotypes by the use of complex stimuli (Portuguese miner, Negro of the same religion) to be judged by American and Greek students on the evaluative scales of the semantic differential (see Selection 5–3) and on social distance scales standardized in America and Greece.

REFERENCES

Bogardus, E. S. Measuring social distance, *J. Appl. Sociol.*, 1925, **9**, 299–308.
Katz, D. and K. W. Braly. Racial stereotypes of 100 college students, *J. Abnorm. Soc. Psychol.*, 1933, **28**, 280–290.
Triandis, H. C. Cultural influences upon cognitive processes. In L. Berkowitz (ed.), *Advances in experimental social psychology*. Vol. 1. New York: Academic Press, 1964.

The notion that social distance exists between an individual and others has been discussed in the social-psychological literature for some time. For instance, Bogardus (1928) offered a scale of social distance; Lewin (1936) discussed the social distance between individuals in the United States and in Germany, arguing that the average social distance seemed smaller in the United States, so far as the "peripheral regions" of the personality were concerned. More recently, several writers have used this concept, although they have not employed the term "social distance." For instance, much of the work of Peak (e.g., Peak et al., 1960) utilizes distances; Fiedler's (1958) notion of assumed similarity is a special case of social distance. Finally, most of the research on prejudice is a special case of the research on social distance (Triandis, 1961).

Social distance is here defined as that distance that is indicated by a person to exist, between himself and another person, by means of endorsement of certain statements. Minimal social distance would include endorsement of the statement, "I would like him as an intimate friend." Progressively larger distances are implied by endorsement of, "I would like to go dancing with him (her)," "I would like to take a trip in the same car with him (her)," "I would exclude him from my neighborhood," and maximal distance by endorsement of, "I would gladly participate in his lynching."

It is clear that it is possible to obtain satisfactory measures of social distance. The next task is twofold: on the one hand we have to consider the determinants of social distance, and on the other hand its consequences. This present paper deals with the determinants.

In a previous study (Triandis and Triandis, 1960) an equal-interval social distance scale and 16 stimuli consisting of imaginary people were utilized. The 16 people were chosen so that they had characteristics consisting of combinations of one of two levels of race (Negro-white), occupation (high prestige or low prestige), religion (same as the subject or different from that of the subject), and nationality (with high-low social distance in Bogardus' studies). For instance, one of the stimuli was "A Portuguese Negro physician of the same religion as you"; another was "A white Swedish truckdriver of a different religion." The stimuli were chosen according to a factorial design; this permitted the estimation of the percentage of the total variance in social distance scores controlled by each of the characteristics (race, occupation, religion, nationality).

The results of this study indicated that about 77% of the variance in the social distance scores was accounted for by race, about 17% by occupation, 5% by religion, and 1% by nationality. Separate analyses of variance for individuals of various backgrounds showed substantial differences in emphasis on these factors. For instance, upper-class individuals emphasized religion more than did lower-class individuals; middle-class individuals emphasized occupation, and lower-class individuals emphasized race more than did others. Subjects whose parents came from Southern and Eastern Europe emphasized occupation and religion more than those subjects whose parents came from Northern and Western Europe; the latter emphasized race more than the former. In short, differences were found in both absolute amounts of social distance and in the relative emphasis placed on the four determinants used in the study, between subjects of various socioeconomic, religious, and ethnic backgrounds.

The findings of the first study and a review of the literature suggested that three concepts are central to the understanding of the determinants of social distance: conformity to group norms, cognitive dissonance, and insecurity. Conformity concerns the adoption of the values of the ingroup. Every society has established norms concerning the social distance that is "correct" towards various classes of people. These norms may specify that a certain amount of social distance is correct towards all people, except one's family and established friends; and may, in addition, specify what is the appropriate distance towards people with certain characteristics, e.g., age, sex, occupation, race, nationality, political views, philosophic views, religion, people who are friends of your friends, adversaries of your friends, neighbors, people who have various physical disabilities, etc. The list of the characteristics is rather large and so far only a few have been explored[1] (Triandis, 1961; Triandis and Triandis, 1960). Exactly how the various characteristics interact with one another is also interesting.[2] Thus, the average social distance obtained from the members of a given social group is determined, in part, by the norms of the group. However, individuals in a group vary in the amount of emphasis they place on the various determinants of social distance. Some individuals emphasize race, others occupation, etc.

The investigator of social distance must concern himself first with what is an ingroup for the particular person being studied, and second with the norms of this ingroup. The size of the ingroup may specify different norms. Thus, if the ingroup is very narrow, for instance, if it consists of "my white neighbors," the norms of this group concerning social distance may involve large amounts of social distance towards Negroes. On the other hand, if the ingroup is very wide, for instance, if it is no smaller than mankind itself, then there would be no social distance towards any person because of differences in race, religion, or nationality. At the present stage of knowledge we cannot exclude the possibility, also, that a person may be aware of different ingroups at different times. This makes the concept of an ingroup similar to that of a reference group. It is also likely that a person may be aware of several ingroups arranged in concentric circles, for instance, his professional group, neighborhood, social class, state, nation, and "the white race." His social distance norms may be influenced by all these ingroups, in various degrees. Research in social distance is in effect dealing, in part, with individual differences in the size and influence of ingroups.

Persons in most complex cultures are subjected to conflicting values and norms. For instance, equalitarian democratic, and religious values coexist with norms specifying a considerable amount of social distance, or economic, sexual, and prestige gains (Dollard, 1957) of one cultural group in relation to another (e.g., a minority group; Myrdal, 1944). Individuals subjected to such conflicting norms experience a certain amount of cognitive dissonance (Festinger, 1957), which they feel com-

[1]Triandis, H. C. Factors affecting employee selection in two cultures. *Journal of Applied Psychology*, 1963, 47, 89–96.
[2]Triandis, H. C. A study of cognitive interaction. In preparation.

pelled to reduce. Negative stereotypes toward minority groups arise in the process of reduction of this cognitive dissonance. They involve beliefs that groups of inferior social status actually deserve that status, that equalitarian responses are inappropriate towards people who are somehow not fully human (Dollard, 1957, p. 372), etc. Such stereotypes support and may accentuate the social distance towards minority groups.

Finally, *prejudice* (i.e., high social distance towards some social groups) is particularly likely to occur among people who are insecure. This is true both because such people may not be able to tolerate cognitive dissonance as much as others, and also because insecure people prefer the status quo and thus are more likely to adopt a nonequalitarian, conservative view than an equalitarian, change-requiring view. Actually, what they must do is adopt one of the conflicting views—either extreme equalitarianism, or prejudice. The notion that extreme liberals and extreme bigots have similar cognitive systems is supported by Taylor's (1960) data. The complete discrediting of the "opposing view" permits reduction in the cognitive dissonance.

In addition, people who are insecure cannot tolerate the dissonance produced by disagreement with people who have different values or cognitive systems (Rokeach, 1960), and hence would avoid people who are likely to be different from themselves.

From these considerations a number of hypotheses were developed:

1. Different cultures have different norms about social distance.

2. The greater the value conflict in a given culture, the more negative the stereotypes towards individuals with various characteristics: since, when there is much conflict there is much dissonance, and negative stereotype responses occur in order to reduce this dissonance. (This hypothesis will only be confirmed in those cultures where democracy, Christianity, or some other philosophicoethical system, at least in theory, has propagated strong equalitarian values.)

3. Within a culture, the more insecure and anxious an individual is, the higher the amount of social distance he will feel towards people who are not like him.

4. Child training practices which have been found to produce insecure adults will be found more frequently in the life histories of individuals showing large social distances than among individuals showing small social distances.

To test these hypotheses we selected two cultures with which we are quite familiar: Greece and the United States. From our knowledge of these cultures we predicted that in Greece there would be much more emphasis on nationality and on religion and much less emphasis on race as a determinant of social distance, and that since Greece has a very homogeneous population (97% are Greek Orthodox and speak Greek, there is little immigration and a great deal of emigration, and there are very few Negroes), there would be less negative stereotyping in Greece than in the United States. Finally, we hoped that Hypotheses 3 and 4 would be supported by the evidence in both the cultures.

METHOD

Subjects

Questionnaires were administered to 100 University of Athens students and 100 University of Illinois students. The characteristics of the two groups of subjects were as follows: All subjects were white males. All individuals in the Greek sample were native Greeks and reported no other ancestry. All were Greek Orthodox. The Illinois students indicated Old American, Central European, Northern, Western, and Eastern European backgrounds (in that order). The father's occupation and education were distributed in about the same way in both samples. Only those subjects who clearly understood and followed all instructions were included in the study. This excluded 22 Greeks and 9 American subjects. Thus, the results described below are based on 78 Greek and 91 American subjects.

Standardization of the Social Distance Scale

Fifty statements referring to various degrees of social distance were administered to 100 Greek high school seniors. A graphic form of the Thurstone successive intervals procedure was used, as described by Edwards (1957). Fifteen statements with satisfactory interquartile ranges were selected to be used in the study. Nine of these statements were exact translations of statements in the standardized American scale used by Triandis and Triandis (1960). The other six were only suitable for Greece, since some of the words used had specific Greek connotations. The rank-order correlation between the scale values of the common statements as standardized in Greece and the United States was .933. Some of the statements that showed very large interquartile ranges, and hence were not used in Greece (though they were used in the American scale, since they are perfectly satisfactory), include, "I would not permit this person to live in my neighborhood," "I would be willing to participate in the lynching of this person," and "I would not permit this person's attendance at our universities." These statements were confusing to the Greeks since neighborhoods are not zoned, lynchings are unknown, and there are no non-Greek students at the universities.

The same Greek high school seniors also ranked 16 occupations on the degree of prestige attached to them; and 15 nationalities, 4 races, and

6 religions on the degree of liking for them. The mean ranks are shown in Table 1.

TABLE 1

Prestige of Occupations and Liking for Nationalities, Religions, and Races as Reflected in the Mean Rankings of 100 Greek High School Seniors

Occupation		Nationality		Religion		Race	
University		Greece	1.22	Greek		White	1.04*
professor	3.21	United States		Orthodox	1.11*	Negro	2.49†
Civil engineer	3.84	(white)	5.91	Roman		Redskin	3.12
Bank manager	4.33*	Italy	5.92	Catholic	2.12	Yellowskin	3.28
Physician	4.65	France	6.05*	Protestant	3.28		
Superintendent		Germany	7.05	Jewish	4.66†		
of schools	5.82	Canada	7.61	Moham-			
Lawyer	6.52	United States		medan	4.78		
Army captain	7.43	(Negro)	7.98	Buddhist	5.15		
School teacher	7.94	Sweden	8.15				
Electrician	8.78	Holland	8.33				
Postman	10.63	Denmark	8.37				
Farmer	11.06	Norway	9.27				
Grocer	11.58	Portugal	9.48†				
Carpenter	11.71	Serbia	11.03				
Miner	12.32†	England	11.47‡				
Barber	12.86	Syria	12.11				
Ditch digger	13.44						

*Chosen for high stimulus.
†Chosen for low stimulus.
‡Probably low because of Cyprus controversy.

Questionnaires

The questionnaires were identical for the two samples, except as described below, and were translated by the senior author, whose mother tongue is Greek. In order to use exactly the same stimuli in both questionnaires we had to compromise. For instance, the studies of occupational prestige in the United States do not place university professors at the top of the prestige hierarchy, as does the Greek study; physicians are very high in the United States but not quite as high in Greece. Bank manager was chosen as a stimulus that occupied approximately the same point in the occupational hierarchy in both cultures. Similar considerations prompted the choice of the remaining stimuli, as indicated in Table 1. For the American ranking data the studies of Welch (1949) and Bogardus (1928) were used. For religions, Christian and Jewish were used in the Greek study and "the same religion as you" and "different religion from yours" in the American study, with the same instructions as in the 1960 study. The latter device permits the inclusion of Jewish subjects in the American study, and permits the American study to be a replication of the Triandis and Triandis (1960) study.

Thus, the questionnaires consisted of 16 stimulus persons (Table 2), each of whom was characterized by a particular combination of high or low race, occupation, religion, and nationality. Each of these 16 stimuli were judged on 16-statement social distance scales separately standardized in each culture. The scoring was done as in the Triandis and Triandis (1960) study. Following this, 16 Semantic Differential scales (Osgood, et al., 1957) were included for each of the concepts French, Portuguese, white, bank manager, etc., and their combinations. These permitted a detailed stereotype analysis and a study of cognitive interaction.

Part II of the questionnaires obtained data about the sex, age, ethnic background, social class, political preferences, etc., of the subjects. It also included five questions, to be checked as true or false, concerning the behavior of the subject's mother, and five concerning the behavior of the subject's father. The subjects then rated the home atmosphere of their childhood on 12 Semantic Differential scales (such as cold-warm, child-centered-child-subordinating, affectionate-hostile, etc.). The subjects

TABLE 2

Mean Social Distance, on A 100-Point Scale, Expressed Towards Stimuli by Two Groups

Stimulus	American (N = 91)	Greek (N = 78)
French bank manager, white, same religion	11.1	22.9
Portuguese bank manager, white, same religion	12.1	23.4
French miner, white, same religion	12.0	26.3
Portuguese miner, white, same religion	12.8	25.6
French bank manager, white, different religion	14.0	30.6
Portuguese bank manager, white, different religion	16.2	31.5
French miner, white, different religion	17.8	32.6
Portuguese miner, white, different religion	19.0	32.5
French bank manager, Negro, same religion	26.5	28.6
Portuguese bank manager, Negro, same religion	27.1	29.8
French miner, Negro, same religion	30.0	31.4
Portuguese miner, Negro, same religion	27.0	30.6
French bank manager, Negro, different religion	29.0	32.7
Portuguese bank manager, Negro, different religion	28.8	32.9
French miner, Negro, different religion	31.5	32.4
Portuguese miner, Negro, different religion	37.1	33.4

were also questioned about the frequency of various kinds of parental disciplinary techniques and the frequency of anxiety symptoms during childhood. Fifty-five other questions about the child-training practices of their parents were asked. This set of questions dealt with parental severity, conflict with the parents, overprotection and rejection by parents, disagreements between the parents, which parent had the most influence on the subject during his upbringing, the kind of aggression training obtained from the parents, the degree of understanding of parental norms during childhood, etc.

Part III of the questionnaire included 19 statements from the Taylor (1953) Manifest Anxiety scale.

SCORING. The scoring was done as in Triandis and Triandis (1960) and according to the standard ways used for scoring the various scales. Where some difference was introduced it will be described in the Results section below.

RESULTS

Relative Importance of the Characteristics of the Stimulus Persons in the Two Cultures

Combining the information from Tables 2 and 3, it is clear that all white, same religion stimuli were accepted as friends and close kin by marriage in both cultures. However, white, different religion (Jewish) persons were not as desirable from the point of view of the Greeks. While the average American subject indicated that he was willing to have such a person as a close kin by marriage, the Greeks did not accept him as such. They were willing, however, to accept him as a member of their social group, provided he had compensating characteristics, such as a high prestige occupation. Finally, the Greeks indicated that they might invite such a person to dinner, but in Greece this is a formal situation that may involve a good deal of social distance.

Turning now to Negro, same religion persons, we find that the average American subject was willing to accept them as roommates, but not as close kin by marriage. A Negro miner was not even acceptable as a roommate, but might be accepted in the club of the average American subject. By contrast, the Greek subjects showed much less social distance toward such a person, and indicated willingness to accept him in their *parea* (social group of intimate kind). Negroes of a different religion, however, experienced much more social distance. The American subjects on the average accepted them as neighbors, but not much more. The Greeks again would invite them to dinner, a situation that might involve

TABLE 3

Scale Values of Statements Used in the Two Cultures

Statement	American Scale Value	Greek Scale Value
I would marry this person.	0.0	0.0
I would accept this person as an intimate friend (in Greek: "best friend").	11.1	13.5
I would accept this person as a close kin by marriage.	21.5	28.5
I would accept this person as a roommate.	29.5	—
I would accept this person as a member of my social group (in Greek: parea).	—	31.1
I would accept this person as a personal chum in my club.	31.1	—
I would accept this person as my family's friend.	40.9	24.0
I would accept this person as a neighbor.	38.7	—
I am going to invite this person to dinner.	—	33.3
I would live in the same apartment house with this person.	49.4	—
I would rent a room from this person.	57.5	42.8
I would accept this person as a speaking acquaintance.	52.4	45.6
I would accept this person as a step-father.*	—	46.1
I would exclude this person from my country.	95.0	82.6
I would be willing to participate in the lynching of this person.	97.2	—
As soon as I have a chance I am going to kill him.	—	100.0

*For brevity, not all of the statements used in the study are included in the table.

a good deal of social distance, but would not go much further. Thus, it is clear that the Americans responded to race much more than the Greeks and the Greeks responded to religion much more than the Americans. The Greeks showed a fair amount of social distance towards all the persons used as stimuli in this study. However, we do not interpret this to mean that the Greeks showed more social distance towards "people in general" than did the Americans. Instead, we think this indicates that the Greeks show social distance towards all people who are not Greek, although the amount of this distance is relatively small.

The two cultures use about the same range of the social distance scale, but their social distance is determined by very different factors: in Illinois, race, occupation, and religion are the determinants of social distance, with race being by far the most important. In Greece, nationality and religion are the determinants of social distance, with nationality being the most important.

A comparison of the 1960 study and the present study, for the American samples, shows that occupation controlled more variance in the former study. However, the 1960 study used physician as the high prestige occupation, while the present study used bank manager. Since physician is more prestigeful than bank manager, it is likely that the difference between the two studies can be accounted for by this difference in the high prestige stimulus.

The social distance due to race and religion was computed for each of the subjects and plotted on a graph whose x axis represented distance towards Negroes and whose y axis represented distance towards people with a different religion. In accordance with the findings of the California studies (Adorno et al., 1950), this plot suggested a correlation between anti-Semitism and anti-Negro biases in the Greek sample, but surprisingly, there was a negligible correlation in the American sample.

Stereotypes in the Two Cultures

The Semantic Differential judgments obtained in the two cultures were analyzed to obtain information about the stereotypes of the subjects. The evaluative dimensions of the differentials were used to obtain a score for the eight concepts used in this study on the evaluative factor (Osgood, Suci, & Tannenbaum, 1957). The results for the Greek sample indicate that the concept Christian had the highest evaluation (1.05), bank manager the next highest (.90), then white (.75), French (.70), Portuguese (.50), Negro (.15), and Jew (.10); coal miner had a negative evaluation loading (−.15). In this analysis the difference on evaluation is largest in the case of occupation (1.05), next largest in the case of religion (.95), followed by race (.60), and with nationality the least important (.20).

The evidence here suggests that social distance is not a direct function of the affect towards the stimulus object, but is determined by a combination of affect and concepts about what is "proper" behavior in a society. Thus, coal miner is a concept involving negative affect yet a coal miner is acceptable as close kin by marriage, while Jew involves slightly positive affect but a Jew is not acceptable.

A comparison of the Greek Semantic Differentials for the eight concepts shows that a bank manager, compared to a coal miner, is more important, bad, active, cold, heavy, optimistic, egotistic, old, and sociable. The most discriminating scales are optimistic-pessimistic and egotistic-altruistic. A Christian, compared to a Jew, is seen as more important, good, soft, light, grateful, successful, warm, sociable, young, optimistic, and masculine. The most discriminating scales are warm-cold, sociable-unsociable, young-old, optimistic-pessimistic, and masculine-feminine, with the latter poles descriptive of the Jews. A white person, as opposed to a Negro, is seen as more important, fast, active, successful, cold, positive, feminine, egotistic, sociable, light, optimistic, and old, with important-unimportant, fast-slow, active-passive, and successful-unsuccessful as the most discriminating scales. There were no important differences between the stereotypes of the Portuguese and the French.

In comparing the Greek and the American stereotypes we distinguished Greeks and Americans who were High or Low in social distance. The comparisons were made between Greek Highs and Lows, American Highs and Lows, Greek and American Highs, and Greek and American Lows. All comparisons were made using the Mann-Whitney U test and the .05 level of significance. Since many tests of significance were run, some of the differences may be significant by chance. Thus, the reader should look for trends rather than for specific results.

WHITE-NEGRO. For this set of stereotypes the Greek Highs, compared with the Greek Lows, did not differ in their perception of whites, but did differ in their perception of Negroes. The Highs saw Negroes as more slow, ungrateful, weak, and egotistic than did the Lows. The American Highs saw the white man as faster and younger than the American Lows, and the Negro as more hot, heavy, less genuine, and older than did the American Lows. Comparing the Greek and American Highs, we found that the Greeks saw the white man as heavier and less genuine than did the Americans, and the Negro as lighter, more grateful, genuine, and weak. Finally, comparing the Greek and American Lows, we found the Greeks thinking of the white man as more important and faster than did the Americans, and the Negro as more grateful than did the Americans. Using Osgood's evaluation, potency, and activity factors (Osgood et al., 1957), the Greek Highs saw the Negro as a more positively evaluated concept and with less potency than did the American Highs. At the same time, the Greek Highs evaluated Negroes less positively and attributed less potency and activity to them than did the Greek Lows. Greek Lows, compared to Highs, gave a higher evaluative score to both Negroes and whites. The Greeks gave a higher evaluation score than did the American Lows on both concepts, and the same as the American Highs for the concept white. The potency factor differentiated Highs from Lows in both cultures, with the Negro seen as lower in potency by the Greek and higher in potency by the American Highs. This may be restated as: "For the Greek Highs the Negro is unimportant, unsuccessful, weak, etc., but for the American Highs he is threatening." This suggests a difference in the quality of the stereotype in the two cultures.

SAME VERSUS DIFFERENT RELIGION. The Greek subjects responded to the dichotomy Jewish-Greek Orthodox, since they were all

Greek Orthodox. The American subjects rated a different kind of "different religion" (for exact instructions see Triandis and Triandis, 1960).

In the case of this stereotype we found no difference in the perception by the Highs and the Lows in either culture, except that the Greek Highs saw the Jews as more active than the Greek Lows. The Greek Highs, in comparison with the American Highs, thought of Christianity as softer and more optimistic, but of Judaism as more active. A comparison of the Greek and American Lows again showed no difference. On the Osgood factors there was an insignificant tendency for the Greeks to see Christianity as lower in potency than Judaism. Judaism was seen higher on the activity factor by the Greek Highs than by the Greek Lows.

FRENCH VERSUS PORTUGUESE. Again, the stereotypes were extremely similar for all four groups (Greek, American, High, Low) with the exception that the Greek Highs saw a Frenchman as more active and successful than the American Highs; and the Portuguese as more fast, active, positive, light, optimistic, young, and sociable than did the American Highs. The Greek Lows also tended to see the Portuguese as faster, better, more active, more positive, and more sociable than the American Lows.

BANK MANAGER VERSUS COAL MINER. No significant differences were found between the four groups. On the Osgood factors the Greek Highs saw the bank manager as better and less powerful than the American Highs.

The overall picture is one of great similarity between the two cultures. There are more differences between Highs and Lows within culture than between the corresponding Highs or Lows between cultures. There is about as much difference between the Highs and the Lows in Greece as in America.

Personality Scales

The Manifest Anxiety scale gave no difference in the American sample; however, in the Greek sample one set of t values (between the No Variance group and the other three groups) was significant ($p \leq .01$), with the No Variance group being lower in manifest anxiety. (In both cultures, there were substantial groups who showed no social distance toward any of our 16 stimulus persons. These were designated as the 'No Variance' groups.)

Following Soueif's (1958) findings and interpretations of extreme checking style as a measure of anxiety and intolerance for ambiguity, we counted the number of +3 and −3 responses to 11 seven-point Semantic

Differential scales, on which the subjects described their parental home atmosphere. The probability that an American Low will check one of the extreme categories is .136, that an American High will do so is .227, that a Greek Low will do so is .255, and that a Greek High will do so is .344. Checking style, then, seems to be more extreme for the Highs than for the Lows in both cultures, and the Greeks seem more extreme than the Americans. Another way of analyzing checking style is to consider the percentage of the subjects in each group who used an extreme category when checking these 11 Semantic Differential scales. We checked whether the percentages of the High groups were higher than the percentages of the Low groups. In the case of the Americans seven of the percentages of the High group were higher, four were identical, and none were lower than the percentages of the Low group. Ignoring the identical ones, seven out of seven cases support the hypothesis. The binomial test gives a $p <$ .016. In the case of the Greeks nine supported the hypothesis and two were identical. The binomial gives a $p < .004$. Thus, it is clear that either way the result is the same; the Highs are higher on intolerance to ambiguity than the Lows in both cultures.

Comparison of Highs with Lows in Both Cultures on the Child Training Questions

The frequency distributions of the answers of the High and the Low social distance subjects in both cultures to questions concerning the child training practices of their parents were recorded. The subjects in the top 27% of the distribution of social distance scores were compared with the subjects in the bottom 27% of this distribution. This permitted the use of Flanagan's (1939) tables to compute the correlation between a given pattern of responses and the amount of social distance.

More Greek Highs than Greek Lows had been subjected to physical punishment as the most frequently used socialization technique ($p <$ .02 by chi square). There is evidence that the mothers of the Greek Highs tended to overprotect their children ($p < .001$), and also that the fathers were the chief socializers and used physical punishment as a frequent technique. The Greek Lows indicated that their mothers were the important socializers, and reported that their fathers left much to be desired. The Greek Highs, as compared to the Lows, reported that they did not have a clear understanding of what was expected of them when they were children ($p < .07$), their parents did not explain to them what it was that they had done wrong ($p < .05$), and they were often punished without any explanation ($p < .05$). The Lows, on the other hand, as compared with the Highs, indicated that though their parents disagreed with each other ($p < .10$), they did explain to them what was right and wrong, and never ridiculed them ($p < .05$).

The American Highs and Lows were different on the warmth dimension. The Highs reported that their homes were colder than the Lows ($p < .001$), that their parents tended to withdraw help ($p < .01$) and to let them go to the movies by themselves earlier than did other children ($p < .001$), and that their mothers did not protect them from disappointments ($p < .05$) or difficult situations ($p < .05$), and tended to reject them at times. Highs also reported that their parents subjected them to inconsistent punishment ($p < .05$), and were not as good in explaining behavior norms as was indicated by the Lows ($p < .05$). Again, the father was reported as the important influence in the socialization process by the High social distance subjects and the mother by the Low social distance subjects ($p < .05$).

Thus, although on the warmth dimension the Highs in Greece and Illinois seem to be at the opposite poles of the continuum, in at least two respects they report strikingly similar practices, compared to the Lows. In both cultures the Highs reported that their fathers influenced them more, the Lows that their mothers did; and the Highs reported inconsistent punishment and poor explanations of parental norms while the Lows reported consistent punishment and clear explanation of norms.

DISCUSSION

Three of the main hypotheses of the present study were generally confirmed. A number of qualifications, however, seem to be necessary.

The first hypothesis, that different cultures have different norms about social distance, was confirmed. Though the rank-order correlation of the mean social distance scores obtained from the Greek and American subjects (Table 2) is .71 and highly significant (beyond the .01 level), there is considerable difference in the emphasis placed on the various factors, with the Greeks emphasizing religion and nationality and the Americans emphasizing race. There is a Western norm (possibly a "white norm") operating and causing the above-mentioned correlation, and in addition a regional norm which produces regional differences in emphasis.

In addition, our data suggest differences in the kind of outgroup-ingroup boundaries in the two cultures. The best description of this finding is that the social distance towards outgroups is equivalent in the two cultures, but the definition of an outgroup is different. The Greek outgroup consists of non-Greeks; the American outgroup consists of people of a different race. The great homogeneity of Greek society may be instrumental in this definition of an outgroup, while the very heterogeneity of American society may cause a line to be drawn between ingroup and outgroup that splits the society into two parts.

The second hypothesis was that the greater the value conflict (or heterogeneity) of a society, the more negative would be the stereotypes of individuals who have characteristics differing from the characteristics of the ingroup. The analysis of the stereotypes of the two cultures did not support this hypothesis.

The third hypothesis stated that the more insecure and anxious an individual is, the higher the amount of social distance that he will experience towards people who are not like him. Our analysis of extreme checking styles confirmed this view in each of the cultures, but the Taylor Manifest Anxiety scale did not discriminate the Highs from the Lows in the American sample, although it did discriminate the No Variance group from the other three groups in the Greek sample. The No Variance (extreme liberal) Greeks showed less manifest anxiety than the other Greek groups.

Our fourth and final hypothesis was that child training practices which may be expected to produce insecure adults will be found more frequently in the life histories of individuals showing large social distances than among individuals showing small social distances. This hypothesis was confirmed. In both cultures the Highs reported inconsistent punishment and poorer explanations of parental norms than did the Lows, a state of affairs that leads to confusion and insecurity. Another difference was that the High social distance subjects reported that their fathers influenced them more than their mothers; the Low social distance subjects reported the reverse.

In addition, there were some differences between the High and the Low social distance subjects that reached statistical significance in only one culture. Thus, the Greek Highs reported that they were overprotected, but also said that they were punished physically more frequently than did the Greek Lows. The American Highs reported that their home atmospheres were cold and their parents indifferent or rejecting, which is the opposite of what was reported by the American Lows. There is probably some equivalence in the use of physical punishment and the rejecting home atmosphere, but the differences in child training practices between the cultures are, in some respects, so striking that it is not possible to show exactly the same processes operating and causing large social distances. Thus, in the Greek family the authoritarian parents used physical punishment and at the same time overprotected their children. In the American family the authoritarian parents did not use physical punishment but nevertheless rejected their children. The overall impression made by the statistically significant results obtained from the child training questionnaire was that the Greeks were more satisfied with their homes than were the Americans. There seem to be a number of findings that suggest that the American parent is trying to be "equalitarian," to use textbook techniques of child rearing, to be rational, to explain why certain behaviors are improper, etc., and yet that he somehow does not succeed. By contrast, the "no nonsense" procedures of the Greek parent result in the perception of more rationality and less emotionality than do the techniques used by the American parents. The data suggest that the American subjects may have had an idealized frame of reference from the perspective of which their homes were anxious, emotional, contentious, and not very rational; while the Greeks did not have as high a set of expectations and consequently saw their homes as rational, concordant, and objective. If this is true, a behavior which would appear to the Greek as "normal" might appear to the American, when viewed within his idealized frame of reference, as cold, emotional, etc. Since it is inevitable that parents will at times feel "fed up" with their children and say so, it can be argued that the nonidealized Greek frame of reference is a "protection" against perceiving such acts as emotional, contentious, etc. The notion that Americans tend to idealize while Greeks use a no nonsense approach is also suggested by the data of Triandis and Osgood (1958). On the other hand, it is possible that the Greek perception of the home is reflecting the usual authoritarian glorification of home and parents.

The present research is consistent with the view that a good deal of the variance in social distance scores is attributable to conformity to the norms of one's society. There is also little doubt that some of the variance is accounted for by personality factors, such as personal insecurity and intolerance for ambiguity. The results on the differences in child training practices reported by Greek and American Highs and Lows are consistent with previous research, reviewed by Triandis and Triandis (1960), and with the findings of Martin and Westie (1959) and of Saarbourg (1958). The latter two studies dealt with child training practices of tolerant and intolerant individuals in Indianapolis and in Germany.

An explanation of the mechanism connecting child training practices and authoritarianism is suggested by the work of Henry (1954). In Western society the mother is the nurturant agent, as far as the children are concerned. This is not only true from an objective point of view, but is also clear to the children, as Kagan and Lemkin (1960) have shown. When the mother is the chief disciplinarian she is the cause of the frustrations associated with punishment. If the child were to turn his aggression towards her, after a particular punishment, the flow of nurturance coming from her would be endangered. Thus, when the mother is the chief disciplinarian, the child has good reasons to develop internal controls for his behavior. When the father is the chief disciplinarian the child can afford to aggress against him without losing the mother's nurturance, and thus is more likely to require external controls of his behavior. Saarbourg (1958) has also shown that when the mother is the chief disciplinarian the child is likely to become intrapunitive, while if the father is the chief disciplinarian he is more likely to become extra-punitive.

Also, children subjected to a harsh home environment are not likely to feel that they will lose much if they aggress against their parents, and hence are likely to require external controls and develop extrapunitive orientations. In addition, when the behavior norms are not explained by the parents the children do not know what controls to internalize.

It has already been stated that most Western societies have norms requiring large social distances towards people who are ideologically and racially different. A person whose behavior is externally controlled is more likely to conform to these norms, if these norms are the most salient, than a person whose behavior is internally controlled. A person with strong internal controls is likely to "think for himself" and avoid fanatical adoption of any norms. Furthermore, a person who is extrapunitive is more likely to blame minority groups for frustrations that he is experiencing than a person who is intrapunitive. Thus, many of the findings of the present study seem to be accounted for by the mechanism of the source and kind of discipline and nurturance.

The overall impression derived from the examination of the results of the present study is that there exists a "white" norm concerning social distance, which is shared by Greeks and Americans. On this norm are superimposed national norms; the Greek norm emphasizes nationality and religion as determinants of social distance, and the American norm emphasizes race. Insecure, externally controlled subjects in both cultures are particularly likely to adopt these norms and behave accordingly. The relative heterogeneity of each of the cultures leads to differences in the definition of outgroups. Finally, the child training practices of Greece and the United States are such that there should be greater conformity to the social distance norms in Greece than in the United States. However, since the Greek social distance norms exclude outgroups only from marriage and intimate friend relationships (specify relatively small degrees of social distance) the net result is that we find less absolute amounts of social distance in Greece than in the United States.

The Triandis and Triandis (1960) study found higher social distance responses among American subjects with Old American, Northern, or Northwestern European ethnic backgrounds than among American subjects with Southern or Eastern European backgrounds. This difference was entirely accounted for by differences in the amount of social distance toward Negroes found among these groups. The present study suggests the probable cause of this finding. The Old Americans and probably also the Northern Europeans emphasize race as a determinant of social distance, while the Southern Europeans emphasize other criteria. Naturalistic observation of the behavior of Italians, French, and Portuguese toward Negroes suggests that their social distance norms are similar to those of Greece. The findings of the Triandis and Triandis (1960) study suggest that though the norms of the American subjects of Southern European background are more similar to the American than to the Greek norms, they are more similar to the Greek norms found in the present study than those of the American subjects of Northern European background. Further research with new immigrants, second generation Americans, etc., is here suggested. It would be most interesting to find out the speed with which immigrants acquire the norms of their new environment concerning social distance. It is most likely that the acquisition of new norms curve will be asymptotic, i.e., it will take many generations for people of immigrant background to acquire exactly the same norms as those of the majority of Americans.

The general conclusion of the present study is that the social distance experienced by an individual towards outgroups is much more a function of the norms of his social group, concerning appropriate behavior towards outgroups, than a function of his particular personality, though certain kinds of personality characteristics function to accentuate conformity to norms. Furthermore, since in most societies different groups have somewhat different norms concerning social distance, people with a given kind of personality may choose as their reference groups those groups which permit them to express hostilities toward outgroups. Thus, the social distance that a given individual experiences towards outgroups is a complex function of his social distance norms and personality.

SUMMARY

Seventy-eight Greek students and 91 Illinois college students rated 16 stimuli, consisting of imaginary people with characteristics involving different combinations of race, social class, religion, and nationality, on an equal-interval social distance scale. The stimuli were chosen according to a factorial design, which permitted the computation of the percentage of variance accounted for by race, religion, social class, and nationality. The responses of the subjects to several personality and attitude scales, as well as to a questionnaire investigating the child training practices of their parents, were obtained. The data were analyzed in terms of the differences between cultures and between subjects high, medium, and low in social distance towards minority group members in each culture. The stereotypes concerning Negroes, Jews, etc., in the two cultures were compared by means of the Semantic Differential.

The data suggest that nationality and religion were the two most important variables for the subjects in the Greek sample, and race and religion for the subjects in the American sample. This suggests that different cultural norms are operating in the two cultures. However, a rank order correlation of .71 between the responses of the Greek and the American subjects for the 16 stimuli used in the study suggests that norms of considerable generality within Western culture are also operating. It was also found that insecure individuals in each culture were particularly likely to experience large social distances towards minority groups. A number of differences in the child training practices of parents of High and Low social distance subjects were observed. In both cultures the father was the chief disciplinarian in the case of the High social distance subjects, and the mother in the case of the Low social distance subjects. In both cultures the Highs experienced conflicting, inconsistant punishment and unclear explanations of parental norms compared to the Lows. In Greece the Highs experienced more physical punishment than the Lows, and in the United States the Highs were subjected to a colder, more rejecting environment than the Lows. These findings were incorporated into a theory of prejudice which was suggested in Triandis and Triandis (1960) and which utilizes conformity to group norms, cognitive dissonance produced by value inconsistencies, and insecurity of the individual as some of the key variables.

REFERENCES

Adorno, T. W., Else Frenkel-Brunswick, D. J. Levinson, and R. N. Sanford. *The authoritarian personality.* New York: Harper and Row, Publishers, 1950.

Bogardus, E. S. *Immigration and race attitudes.* Boston: D. C. Heath and Company, 1928.

Dollard, J. *Caste and class in a southern town.* New York: Anchor, 1957.

Edwards, A. L. *Techniques of attitude test construction.* New York: Appleton-Century-Crofts, 1957.

Festinger, L. *A theory of cognitive dissonance.* New York: Harper and Row, Publishers, 1957.

Fiedler, F. E. *Leader attitudes and group effectiveness.* Urbana: University of Illinois Press, 1958.

Flanagan, J. C. General considerations in the selection of test items and a short method of estimating the product-moment coefficient from the tails of the distribution, *J. Educ. Psychol.*, 1939, **30**, 674–680.

Henry, A. F. and J. F. Short, Jr. *Suicide and homicide.* New York: The Free Press, 1954.

Kagan, J. and Judith Lemkin. The child's differential perception of parental attributes, *J. Abnorm. Soc. Psychol.*, 1960, **61**, 440–447.

Lewin, K. Social-psychological differences between the United States and Germany, *Charact. Pers.*, 1936, **4**, 265–293.

Martin, J. G. and F. R. Westie. The tolerant personality, *Amer. Sociol. Rev.*, 1959, **24**, 521–528.

Myrdal, G. *An American dilemma: The Negro problem and modern democracy.* New York: Harper and Row, Publishers, 1944.

Osgood, C. E., G. J. Suci, and P. H. Tannenbaum. *The measurement of meaning.* Urbana: University of Illinois Press, 1957.

Peak, Helen, Barbara Muney, and Margaret Clay. Opposites structures, defenses, and attitudes, *Psychol. Monogr.*, 1960, **74**(8, Whole No. 495).

Rokeach, M. *The open and closed mind: Investigations into the nature of belief systems and personality systems.* New York: Basic Books, Inc., 1960.

Saarbourg, E. A. Frustration und autoritarismus. Doctoral dissertation, University of Köln, 1958.

Soueif, M. I. Extreme response sets as a measure of intolerance of ambiguity, *Brit. J. Psychol.*, 1958, **49**, 329–333.

Taylor, I. A. Similarities in the structure of extreme social attitudes, *Psychol. Monogr.*, 1960, **74** (2, Whole No. 489).

Taylor, Janet A. A personality scale of manifest anxiety, *J. Abnorm. Soc. Psychol.*, 1953, **48**, 285–290.

Triandis, H. C. A note on Rokeach's theory of prejudice, *J. Abnorm. Soc. Psychol.*, 1961, **62**, 184–186.

Triandis, H. C. and C. E. Osgood. A comparative factorial analysis of semantic structures of monolingual Greek and American college students, *J. Abnorm. Soc. Psychol.*, 1958, **57**, 187–196.

Triandis, H. C. and Leigh M. Triandis. Race, social class, religion, and nationality as determinants of social distance, *J. Abnorm. Soc. Psychol.*, 1960, **61**, 110–118.

Welch, M. K. The ranking of occupations on the basis of social status, *Occupations*, 1949, **27**, 237–241.

3-5

German and American Traits Reflected in Popular Drama

DONALD V. MCGRANAHAN
IVOR WAYNE

One of the many ways of comparing cultures is to compare the content of the successful plays produced by each culture. This method can be criticized, as the authors acknowledge. Perhaps authors, not nations, are being compared. But plays are produced for profit, and it seems likely that over the years the producers have learned to give the audiences what they want.

INTRODUCTION

If Germans and Americans have not behaved alike in recent years, this may be because of differences in immediate circumstance, or because of differences in basic psychological traits ("national character"). Empirically, there is no way to find out how Americans would have behaved if subjected to all the circumstances to which Germans were subjected in their recent history. We cannot plant the American people in the middle

Abridged from *Human Relations*, 1948, **1**, No. 4, 429–455, by permission of the authors and Plenum Publishing Co., Ltd.

of Europe at a given historical date, immerse them in German surroundings, and then see if they would react like Germans to the same stimuli. In fact, we could not logically equate external circumstances for the purposes of comparison without making Germans and Americans alike in the first place, since one important external circumstance influencing any given individual is the nature of the personalities of those about him. We can try, however, to rule out the influence of *temporary* circumstances, like the National Socialist regime, by comparing peoples of successive periods of history. If we find that certain differences between Germans and Americans actually endure through variations of historical circumstance, if these differences turn up in the more propitious years of the Weimar Republic, as well as in the pre- and post-Weimar days, then we shall have much firmer ground for arguing the theory of national character. Such a theory need not imply stereotyped uniformity within a nation. We are concerned only with the statistical distribution of psychological traits. Nor need it imply racism. Enduring and distinctive traits may depend upon basic social environmental conditions that persist with relatively little change through the ups and downs of political and economic fortune.

The following study is an experimental attempt to compare German and American traits reflected in the 45 most popular plays in each country in 1927. This was, in each country, a year of relative prosperity and of political democracy. The theatres were free to produce what they pleased and the audiences free to attend what they pleased.

A smaller sample of popular German and American plays from the period 1909–10 has also been used for comparison. This, too, was a relatively prosperous period in both countries, but Germany differed politically in being an empire under the Kaiser. In this older period, however, there was no recent military defeat to distinguish the German situation from that of the United States.

Our first assumption in this study is that popular drama can be regarded as a case of "social fantasy"—that the psychological constellations in a dramatic work indicate sensitive areas in the personalities of those for whom the work has appeal; their needs, assumptions and values are expressed ("projected") in the drama. The successful play must be attuned to the audience. There can be no claim that dramatic material reflects the total personality of the individual who enjoys it. Analysis of popular songs, poetry, art, humor, novels and short stories, propaganda, advertising, religious writings, public activities, statistics on crime and mental disease, etc., may well reveal other psychological facets of a historical population that is not accessible to direct study.

Our analysis of the plays is clearly limited by the fact that the play-going audience is not a proper sample of the national population. It represents primarily an educated, urban segment. However, the German and American audiences are roughly comparable. If significant psychological differences can be shown between corresponding segments of two national populations, then this indicates a real difference in national character, unless one rejects a statistical definition of that concept and reserves it only for nationally uniform traits. Whether the traits expressed in the plays actually extend to other parts of the population must be determined by study of other sources.

METHODS AND PROCEDURE

As a first step in choosing the sample for each country, all reported productions for the calendar year 1927 (including productions first staged in the last weeks of December, 1926) were examined, and musical comedies, operas, revues and follies were eliminated. From the remaining plays, which relied on story content and characters for appeal, were eliminated all revivals and all foreign importations, so far as these could be determined. Austrian, Sudetan and Swiss-German plays were excluded from the German sample. This left about 135 first productions ("try-outs") for each country.

An attempt was then made to select the 45 most popular plays in each country. Once the 45 plays for each country were chosen on the basis of popularity estimate, summaries of their contents were written down. The summaries were based upon reading of the play or of an abridged form of the play, or upon an examination of several independent reviews, since a single reviewer could not be relied upon to give an adequate digest. An element of unconscious bias may have crept into the summarizing of some of the plays, although a careful attempt was made to obtain accurate digests. The summarized contents were then subjected to various types of analysis by three judges. There is no established psychological method of content analysis in handling dramatic material. The three judges independently gravitated toward categories that followed the traditional lines of break-down in drama: the nature of the setting, of the central characters, of the plot, and of the conclusion. An attempt was made by each of the judges to use the categories used in analysis of the Thematic Apperception Test, but the material did not lend itself easily to this type of analysis. A method seemed required by which each plot could be treated as a unit. Furthermore, exploratory attempts at analysis indicated that it would be wiser to let the categories emerge from the material so far as possible, rather than superimpose categories.

It was found that the structure of nearly all the dramas could be described in terms of the pattern of conflict, the interplay of opposing forces, that underlay the plot: conflict between youthful lovers and parents, between honest folk and criminals, between revolutionary and reactionary political forces, between moral and immoral impulses within the individual, etc. Once the patterns of conflict in the different plays were established, it was further found that these conflicts could be classified into six major groups or categories, called the "love theme," the "morality theme," the "idealism theme," the "power theme," the "career theme," and the "outcast theme." These major categories were then defined in some detail according to their typical ingredients (the definitions are given in the following section).

In view of the ease with which prejudice and preconception operate in the field of national psychology, it was felt that the judgments of the two authors should not be the sole basis for determining German-American differences in terms of these categories, since the authors knew which plays were German and which were American. For this reason, seven additional judges were used. The summaries of the plays were arranged in a random order, authors and titles were deleted. A number of the German plays were already set in the United States, England, Russia, or some other non-Germanic country and had non-Germanic characters. These summaries were left in their original form. In the case of the remaining German plays, the settings and the names of the central characters were transformed into American settings and names, with but five exceptions: in one case, a French setting was substituted, and in the remaining four cases the German settings and characters could not be changed without changing the basic content of the play. To off-set the latter situation, four American plays were given German settings and names. The seven independent judges were then provided with the ninety summaries (each summary averaging a third of a single-spaced typewritten page in length), the detailed definitions of the basic themes, and directions to classify a play under a given thematic category "only if the theme is central to the plot; that is, if the theme could not be eliminated without significantly changing the essential nature of the plot and leaving it logically or psychologically incomplete. If a love theme, for example, is merely thrown in for incidental interest, this is not to be counted." Subjects were told a play might contain only one, or it might contain several of the basic themes.

In addition to this thematic analysis, the judges were asked to classify each play "according to whether the ending is (1) happy, (2) unhappy (tragic), or (3) ambiguous (mixed); also according to whether the play is primarily *personal* in content and import (concerned with private affairs of individuals), or primarily *ideological* (concerned with political, social, national or international issues)." The judges were told that the purpose of the experiment was to test the reliability of the categories used.

Each of the authors also classified the plays independently so that there were nine judges all told. In computation of the results, a play was reckoned to fall under a given category if five or more of the nine judges agreed in placing it there. In only seven of the ninety plays did the majority fail to find any one basic theme applying. There is no standard formula for measuring the reliability of categories of content analysis such as used in this study, but inspection of the data indicates that the love theme and the idealism theme were employed with the greatest agreement among judges, the morality and power themes with least agreement. For example, when the majority of the judges agreed on the presence of the love or idealism theme in a given play, this majority was more often a majority of all nine of the judges than a majority of eight, seven, six, or five judges; whereas a majority agreement in the case of the morality and power themes was more frequently a majority of only five or six of the judges. Agreement on the level of action (personal versus ideological) and the nature of the ending of the play (happy, unhappy, ambiguous) was also fairly high, in the sense that when there was majority agreement, it was most frequently universal agreement.

In the statistical results presented, the procedure of defining the presence of a given category by the majority agreement of the nine judges applies only to the data on the basic themes. In the case of the level of action, and the nature of the endings, the results represent majority agreement among only seven judges (because of pressure of time, two of the judges were not asked to use these categories). All other data represent the analysis of the two authors only.

DEFINITIONS OF THE BASIC THEMES

The following are the detailed definitions of the basic themes as given to the judges who analyzed the plays.

THE LOVE THEME: This category includes only heterosexual love of the boy-girl, husband-wife, master-mistress variety. It does not include family love—unless incest is clearly indicated—or love of any non-sexual object. However, plays dwelling on the problems married people have in getting along with each other are to be ordinarily included, even if romantic love is not highlighted. In plays falling under the love theme, dramatic interest usually centers about the question whether two lovers, or potential or would-be lovers, will be united in the end. Opposed to the love relationship may be any number of factors: parents, personal misunderstandings and grievances between the lovers, career ambitions, character defects, higher ideals of one form or another.

These forces must be overcome or reconciled before the happy union can ensue. Love may, of course, lose to any of the forces conflicting with it.

THE MORALITY THEME: Plays built around a morality theme deal with the problems that arise from the moral standards of society and human weakness or sinfulness in falling below these standards. Morality is used here only in the sense of *conventional personal* morals such as are treated in the Bible and in western criminal law. We are not here concerned with good and bad philosophies of life, political faiths or social systems, but with specific individual behavior. Typical immoralities or sins are: personal crimes of any sort, individual dishonesty, sexual looseness, intentional injury to other persons. Opposed are such virtues as: law-abidingness, honesty, "true love," kindness, and consideration of others. The good and evil forces may be represented externally by good and evil men (e.g., honest folk and criminals) or internally by good and evil impulses. In plays with a basic morality theme (as here defined) the moral is assumed to be the conventional, the expected, the normal behavior of the social majority; the immoral is the deviant, the behavior of the man who falls below the social norm. Indeed, the moral is often treated as having the force of society and perhaps even of "nature" behind it, while the immoral is unsocial, unwholesome, and unnatural. Ordinarily, in plays with a basic morality theme, the guilty person who falls below the social norm *must either reform* (i.e., readjust to society and nature) or *suffer punishment* (or both). The play clearly implies the superiority of virtue, both as desirable and as necessary. Finally, it is assumed in these plays that the choice between good and evil paths of actions is a matter of free choice between possible alternatives, that the individual is therefore responsible for his morality or immorality. Plays of the morality type may be said to provide the spectator with a certain excitement by dramatizing immoral impulses but at the same time they provide him with a moral lesson to the effect that "crime does not pay." Because nearly all plays involve crimes or immoralities of one sort or another, it is desirable to define the morality type negatively and indicate the kinds of plays that do not fall under this category: (1) plays that present illicit love-making as charming or amusing, and involve no moral judgment, no character reform or punishment, fall only under the love theme; (2) plays that justify an ordinarily immoral or criminal act in the name of a higher ideal or value (patriotism, "liberalism," art, etc.) or treat ordinary morality as petty and narrow, in comparison with the hero's higher vision, or present a hero who stands far above a corrupt and evil world, fall under the category of "idealism"; (3) plays that present merely a primitive conflict in which moral forces play no role fall only under the power theme; (4) if the central character is a criminal or other deviant type and the play presents him sympathetically, or makes it clear that he is not responsible for his sins, but society or fate is responsible, then the play belongs under the outcast theme.

THE IDEALISM THEME: Plays featuring the idealism theme have a central character who is consciously attempting to pursue a set of high principles. He may be a revolutionary idealist, a humanitarian idealist, or a devoted supporter of the old regime; a nationalistic patriot or an internationalist; a free-thinking liberal, a priest or an art-lover. The important point is that his motives and his character set him apart from, and above, the masses of the people. He is not merely seeking to live an average, conventional private life, and he does not behave in a manner that can be expected of the average citizen. In the pursuit of his principles, he may have to sacrifice some conventional personal value—his reputation, his life, love, social acceptance, personal happiness, normal creature comforts. He may very well commit some act against conventional morals, as in the case of the patriot who kills his friend for the sake of his country. The idealist theme is thus concerned with the conflicts engendered by those who stand above the ordinary; the morality theme with conflicts engendered by those who fall below the ordinary. Unlike the moral individual, the idealist has convention and normality usually arraigned against him. Idealism plays often imply the desirability of reforming society as a whole, of redefining values, or of preventing a social change that is under way. The idealist typically has to fight against materialism, conventional moral scruples, self-interest, prejudice, pettiness, stupidity, weakness of character, personal desires, lesser loyalties, conflicting systems of ideals. These forces may be external or within himself. Included under idealism are plots that stress an extraordinary sense of duty, loyalty or patriotism, or a single-minded devotion to a "cause."

THE POWER THEME: The power theme deals with the problems that arise from the conflict between two individuals or groups for the same object, territory, position of authority, or controlling influence over a situation. It includes personal conflicts for power, class conflicts, ideological conflicts, revolutions, war, etc. Also included are plays in which a central character seeks power against such obstacles as his own inferiority or his more tender impulses. Frequently the struggle involves the use of violence, ruthlessness, trickery or cold-bloodedness on the part of one or both adversaries. In power conflicts, the more powerful side usually comes to dominate the situation; but it is not necessarily the better side that wins—in fact, the reverse is true if the worse side is stronger. Plays that are principally structured and resolved in terms of who is right and who is wrong, or who is good and who is bad, do not, of course, fall under the power category. Power may be represented by a number of different factors: physical or material means, strength of character, ruthlessness of purpose in pursuit of a goal, lack of "soft" emotions, courage, cunning, trickery.

THE CAREER THEME: In career themes a central character is attempting to win personal success in his occupation, to make money, create a work of art, or advance his professional status. The goal is personal achievement, not the success of an ideal, system, way of life, nation or other super-individual institutions. Various obstacles block the path to success.

THE OUTCAST THEME: In a number of plays we find as a central character a person who is placed outside normality or normal society by some handicap, abnormality, inferiority or stigma. This may be a physical handicap—deformity or extreme ugliness or illness; a mental handicap—some form of mental disease; a political handicap—the condition of being an exile; or any one of a number of social handicaps, such as being a criminal, prisoner, outlaw, vagabond, pauper, Negro, bastard, prostitute. The play dwells upon the relationship of this person to normal society, his reactions to society or society's reactions to him. It may show, for example, how he seeks normal love and acceptance, how he reacts with cunning or brutality to his outcast status, how he is not himself responsible for his status, how society misunderstands and abuses him. Sometimes the outcast has a superior perspective and is also an idealist. *If a criminal or other outcast is the central character of a play, the play ordinarily falls under the outcast theme.* But if the central character is clearly a normal individual and the criminal is his adversary, representing evil forces, then the play is to be classified under the morality theme, since the interest here is not in portraying the problems of the outcast, but the conflict between good and evil. Not included in this category are plays in which the suspicion or accusation of say, murder, is falsely attributed to innocent persons, and the action of the plot is centered about revelation of the true situation. The outcast status must be real, recognized as such by both society and the individual. Plays are not included in which a person, nominally a deviant, enjoys popularity because of his deviance.

RESULTS

American plays are primarily concerned with love and personal morals. The German plays are considerably more preoccupied with idealism, power, and the problems of the abnormal or outcast. Little difference appears in personal career themes.

The love and morality themes often go together—10 of the 20 plays that contain morality themes (U.S. and German combined) were also scored as having love themes. Similarly, idealism and power tend to go together: 5 of the 16 plays considered to express power conflicts were also considered to contain the idealism theme.

German plays are strikingly more pre-occupied with social and political problems than are the American plays. Their level of action is primarily ideological; the basic conflict is between forces that represent divergent social, political or economic interests, or divergent philosophies of life. The problems portrayed in the American plays, on the other hand, are overwhelmingly personal—love affairs, family affairs, difficulties and hostilities on a non-ideological level. The German ideological emphasis is obviously tied up closely with the emphasis on the idealism theme.

The German plays also have more unhappy endings than do the American plays. Connected with this is the fact that the side of virtue consistently wins out in the American plays, but the unsympathetic side often comes out on top in the German. Frequently in the German plays the central character is a ruthless, treacherous, or egoistic individual who wins success because of these very qualities.

The German central characters tend to be older and more often males than is the case in the American plays. More noteworthy than these statistics, however, is the difference in the type of woman who plays a central role. When a female carries the burden of the plot in American drama, she tends to possess in eminent degree qualities that are considered feminine—beauty, emotionality, charm, tenderness, softness, motherliness, etc. But when a female is the central character in a German play, she tends to be strong, and an aggressive type of person who outdoes men in their own territory—she defeats men in economic competition, ruthlessly exploits male weakness, rejects lovers who have too soft a character, refuses to give way to love because this would interfere with her more serious purposes, etc. In short, femininity as such may be as important as masculinity in the American plays, but rarely in the German plays where female equality of importance seems to be possible only by achieving masculine qualities and values.

In keeping with the fact that more of the German plays are on a social level there is a further distinction at once apparent—the German central characters are more frequently social types; that is, their social status or role plays an important part in the logic of the plot. They behave as they do because they are proponents of a cause, princes, rulers, generals, political functionaries, exiles, typical representatives of a social class, etc. The American central characters, on the other hand, are more "ordinary people" whose role or status has less critical bearing on the plot—their occupation could be changed without basically altering the plot. The social type that seems to be favored as the central character in the American theatre of 1927 is the entertainer or artist, although the detective-policeman and the man of great wealth also turn up.

On the basis of what the authors and critics in their respective countries called "light" and "serious" plays, there was no national difference in relative frequency. In both countries the ratio was approximately two light plays to three serious plays. This ratio also holds if we consider not the specific samples chosen but the total number of dramatic productions in each country in 1927. Marked differences appear, however, in the time and place of the action presented in the plays.

The figures reflect a German predilection for historical plays. Seventeen plays out of our sample, and thirty-four per cent of the total German drama production in 1927, fall into this category. But the German drama also takes leave of the contemporary domestic scene through legends and fantasies, and through foreign settings. One curious result is the fact that in the year 1927 more plays on a subject of American history were produced in Germany than in the United States. The German departure from the contemporary scene, however, must not be taken as evidence of a flight from current social problems. It indicates rather a German tendency to view these problems *sub specie aeternitatis*. Such plays appear designed to have a deep meaning for the present.

ANALYSIS OF THEMATIC CONTENT

Not only do the German plays differ from the American plays in the percentages falling under the various basic themes; German plays under a given theme also differ in specific content from the American plays under the same theme. German love plots differ from American love plots. The patterns of conflict found in the U.S. plays with a basic morality theme are not the patterns found in the German morality theme plays, and so with the other major categories.

The Love Theme

There are three types of love plot in the American plays that can be fairly easily identified.

The first presents a pattern of conflict between youthful lovers, on the one hand, and parents who oppose or interfere with this love, on the other hand. The parents are usually pictured as well-meaning but ill-advised individuals, who do not want to lose their sons or daughters; but sometimes they appear immoral, even criminal, in their opposition. A father may murder or attempt to murder his daughter's suitor. A mother, unfaithful to her husband, may vie with her daughter for a young man. Possibly related psychologically are several American plays in which a criminal individual in a position of authority threatens to break up youthful love.

The second common type of love plot in the U.S. plays has a hero or heroine who is faced with an inner conflict and must decide between wholesome, "true love," on the one hand, and unwholesome, false love, on the other hand (love based on mere sensuality, thrills, money, security, prestige, love outside the marriage pattern, etc.) The plot builds up to the act of decision; if true love is chosen, the ending is happy; if not, or if the decision comes too late, there is punishment and suffering. These plays are pre-occupied with the problem of sexual immorality, but in the end teach the lesson that one ought to be good.

The third type of love plot that would appear to captivate an American audience involves a pattern in which two lovers or potential lovers become estranged through some misunderstanding or petty annoyance, and the problem of the plot is how to effect emotional readjustment and bring them happily together again at the end. Included here are stories of the boy-meets-girl, boy-loses-girl, boy-wins-girl variety; but husbands and wives are also frequently getting separated and re-united in the American plays. The circumstance that causes the friction varies from play to play: relatives, financial difficulties, minor or suspected infidelities, occupational success of one of the lovers. The lovers usually become reconciled because one of them (sometimes both) is persuaded to a change of mind by some dramatic circumstance, such as a slap on the face, an act of special ingenuity, a sudden danger, sickness or accident to the other.

It is a striking fact that no German play of 1927 with a basic love theme clearly falls into any of these three common American classes. There is no case of youthful lovers in conflict with parents.

There are several German plays of 1927 that picture idealistic-romantic lovers in rebellion, not against parents, but against petty bourgeois norms in general. In the name of modern "liberalism," religious mysticism, or some other set of values superior to those prevailing, lovers find a basis for lasting unity.

But if lovers are united in German plays because they embrace a common value system superior to conventional norms, it is also true that love may fail because it comes into conflict with higher values and ideals.

The German audience would seem relatively little interested in the problem of how couples are to readjust and reunite once a point of friction has developed—at least, there are no German plots of the popular American variety in which lovers become estranged, then kiss and make up. On the other hand, there are several German cases but no American examples in our data of love that is complicated by the abnormality or outcast status of the central character. In both German and American plays there are a few cases where love is complicated by career ambitions, or by the fact that one of the lovers is a delinquent. In general, the American lovers end up in each other's arms in the overwhelming majority of all plays containing minor as well as major love themes. Statistically, however, the chances do not seem to favor the final union of German lovers.

The Morality Theme

As already indicated, the morality theme frequently appears in union with the love theme. It often appears as a minor theme in love plots where the judges did not consider it important enough to receive an independent rating. Under the morality theme fall also a number of American plays in which detectives, policemen, ordinary honest folk (brothers and sisters, young couples in love, kindhearted elders) are pitted against evil men—crooks, gangsters, corrupt attorneys, criminal maniacs, etc. The evil side consistently has the initial advantage but the side of virtue is consistently triumphant.

One thing that stands out in the American plays is the emphasis given to *character reform* as the solution to the basic problems of human conduct. The central character who has sinned usually reforms, taking a new and wholesome attitude. Criminals frequently reform. The alternative is certain defeat and punishment. Two American plays are in good part devoted to the problems of reformed criminals. Or criminals may confess at the very end and thereby assure the happiness of the hero and heroine. Plays stressing character reform merge into those in which there is a less fundamental change in personality, but in which, nevertheless, a change in attitude of some individual or group is a critical part of the plot. For example, parents who oppose young lovers may change their attitude, realizing they were ill-advised in their opposition, or a husband may realise he has been neglecting his wife. Such change hardly deserves to be called character reform, and plays of this kind do not fall under the morality theme, yet they illustrate a basic principle that underlies a great many American plays—the principle that the solution to conflict and difficulties in life can be obtained through personal re-orientation. The capacity of individuals to change often provides a basis for happy endings. It should be noted that in the case of U.S. plays featuring murder trials, an impartial tribunal of justices when presented with persuasive evidence changes its mind as to who is guilty. Furthermore, once a delinquent has suffered and reformed, then society must re-cast its attitude toward him and welcome him back.

Of the four German plays classified by the judges under the morality theme, none has such a clear-cut opposition between moral and immoral forces as found in the American plays. By and large, the German central characters do not reform or change their minds in the way of solution to the basic dilemmas of life. Criminals do not reform. In five of the six cases where criminals play important roles in the German plays, they are unreformed yet more or less sympathetic characters who battle, not virtue and decency, but smug, petty society. There are, it is true, a number of German plays in which men who have sinned confess their crimes at the end. But in no case does the confession make either the guilty party or any one else happy. It merely confirms the certainty of punishment, sometimes adding a touch of self-immolation to the general gloom.

The German plays have different ways of handling the problem of personal sin or crime. (1) The responsibility for a crime may be removed from the perpetrator and placed upon society as a whole, which should do the reforming. We find, for example, a play in which a poverty-stricken woman who has murdered her crippled and cynical husband is portrayed as not responsible for this act; rather the social system that forced a sordid slum life upon her is held responsible. (2) An act against conventional morality may be interpreted as a courageous, praiseworthy act in terms of a new set of values. There is a strong current of protest in the German plays against conventional values that are considered petty, narrow, mean and confining—what the Germans like to call "Philistin-ism." (3) Conventional sins, like murder of a beloved person, while not condoned as such, may be justified under the tragic necessity of fulfilling a noble ideal. (4) Finally, the good man who faces powerful forces of evil may, overwhelmed, fall into a state of apathetic resignation or commit suicide.

The Idealism Theme

According to the 1927 plays, where the American is a moralist, the German tends to be an idealist. In his pursuit of high ideals, the German hero comes into conflict with two sorts of obstacles: those arising from without, and those arising from within his own personality.

The most striking pattern of conflict in the German plays of 1927 presents a social or political idealist opposed by ruthless, materialistic forces.

In several of the German plays classified under idealism, the ideal-ist is opposed not so much by selfish, materialistic interests, as by the stupidity, narrow conventionality or Philistinism of the masses who fail to appreciate higher values.

In order to succeed in this world, the German idealist must exercise great "strength of character," which often means that he must overcome tender personal sentiments of love and affection. Several German plays portray conflict between patriotic idealism and personal love. Others directly point the moral that a weak or soft character spells failure.

There was only one American play in 1927, although a very popular one, that approximated the German conflict between humanitarian idealism and ruthless materialism.

The Power Theme

The power theme is implicit in most of the German plays of 1927 classified under idealism and five plays were considered by the judges to feature equally the idealism theme and the power theme. The power theme also turns up in a number of German plays in which the central character is an outcast, oppressed by some stigma or inferiority, who compensates for his status by a striving for power or dominance. But we find other central characters as well, who are beset by a strong drive to achieve power as a goal, sometimes with apparent approval of the dramatist. We also find assorted power conflicts between individuals, social classes or nations.

Characteristically enough, the only American play judged to have a basic power theme concerns a conflict between a young man and the father of the girl he loves, the older man attempting unsuccessfully to get the younger one killed. Those individuals in the American drama who seek dominance or employ ruthless techniques, are consistently outwitted, in contrast to the German exponents of ruthless power.

The Outcast Theme

In German plays that contain idealist-heroes in 1927, the majority of these idealists become exiles (i.e., outcasts) or suicides at the end. Some, moreover, start off as weak, sickly or abnormal. In addition to such plays, there are eight German plays, in which the theme of the outcast or abnormal in conflict with normal society quite dominates the plot. These plays are primarily concerned with showing how the condition of being an unloved outcast or abnormal results in criminal, violent, ruthless, or power-seeking behavior on the part of the outcast; or how society itself is heartless in relation to the outcast.

The Career Theme

Although there is little difference between the number of German and American career themes, it should be noted that the German plays place career ambitions primarily in a context of power-seeking or inferiority compensation; while the American plays connect career ambitions primarily with love problems (career success may either upset or insure love), and, to a lesser extent, with moral problems and with revolt against family authority.

THE PLAYS OF 1909–10

Samples of German and American plays from 1909–10 were examined to check on the possibility that the differences found in the 1927 plays may have been due largely to the German defeat in the first World War, and the distress and inflation that followed. It was possible to locate only seventeen popular plays for each country in this older period. Hence our conclusions here must be rough and tentative.

The German predilection for historical plays and plays with a foreign setting is maintained in the older period, with almost exactly the same ratios. The German preference for masculine central characters is likewise maintained, and such females as occupy the center of the stage are strong and man-like. A somewhat smaller proportion of the older German plays, in comparison with the 1927 plays, appear to be ideological in nature and unhappy in outcome; but the German-American differences in these respects are still apparent. So far as the basic themes are concerned, the picture remains much the same with regard to German-American differences in morality, idealism and power. There are relatively more German love plots in the older period, but also more American love plots, so that the German-American difference is consistent. The outcast theme appears less sharply defined in the older German plays, though still present to a greater degree than in the American plays. One striking change, however, is found in the much larger proportion of older American plays falling under the career theme (there is no change in the German plays in this respect). We find a number of American dramas in which a young man from a country town goes to the big city to win success, falls in with evil companions (e.g., actresses), but eventually overcomes temptation and returns to his native town to achieve success there and marry the girl he has always loved.

In the American plays of 1909–1910, we find the same conflict between moral and immoral or unwholesome love; but the conflict between youthful lovers and parents is less pronounced, and there is a greater tendency for the parents to be morally right in such conflicts, as in stories of the prodigal son who associates with bad women against his parents' desire. The same general tendency to structure personal conflicts in terms of right and wrong is apparent, and likewise the tendency to resolve conflict through character reform or change of attitude. In the older German plays we find the same conflict as in 1927 between love and patriotism; also the same plot concerning two men of art who love the same woman but become firm friends because they love art more (the wife in this case commits suicide). The conflict between moral and immoral impulses (or individuals) figures no more prominently in the older German plays than in the 1927 plays. As in 1927, acts contrary to conventional personal morals tend to be justified or excused because the perpetrator is a person of high ideals, broad vision, or great strength of character, capable of going beyond the petty strictures of conventional morality.

SUPPLEMENTARY EVIDENCE

The data of this study show clear differences between the German and the American drama, and lend support to the theory that there are real and persistent German-American psychological differences—or, if you will, differences in "national character." But it is still possible that our results are due to certain peculiar factors in the drama situation. For example, German public ownership or subsidy vs. American private ownership may be the explanation. This question can only be settled by other types of evidence. In favor of a broader interpretation of our results are the following considerations:

1. The results are consistent with German-American differences found historically in other realms, such as philosophy and politics. From our data it is not difficult to see how Germans could be led into National Socialism, with its peculiar combination of power politics and folk idealism. (It does not follow at all, however, that Fascism is the only political system that will fit the German traits here indicated, that the Germans are "Fascists at heart," with all the moral connotations of that phrase. If one wants to be evaluative, one should note that according to our data the Germans would appear capable of great personal dedication and unselfishness, of humanitarian idealism as well as jingoism, of a certain nobility of thought and deed, and of a deeper concern for basic social problems than is found among Americans).

2. The results of the present study are consistent with other comparative studies of Germans and Americans, using other types of data (Lewin, 1947; McGranahan, 1946).

3. A limited check on our U.S. play data is offered by the study by Jones (1942) of one hundred American films in 1941–1942. Jones used a different method of analysis, attempting to isolate the "wants" of the central characters, but certain of her results permit comparison. She found that 68.1% of the central characters of the films primarily wanted "love," while we found that 60% of the American plays had basic love themes. The other categories of wants found in the films (fame, reputation or prestige—26.1%, safety—15.9%, a way of life—13.8%, money or material goods—9.6%, rightness—9.0%, etc.) do not correspond to any of our molar categories of analysis of the dramatic plots; our morality theme, for example, might include plots in which the central character

primarily wanted reputation, safety or rightness. But it should be noted that these wants that Jones found are primarily personal rather than ideological. 61.2% of all major characters in the films "were indulged with respect to all their 'wants' at the end of the picture," 10.1% were wholly deprived. Our data show that 67% of the American plays of 1927 ended happily, 9% ended unhappily. 33% of the central characters in the films were female, not far different from the plays. In general, where the evidence permits comparison, it points to a much higher degree of similarity between the U.S. plays and the U.S. films than between the latter and the German plays.

4. The general principle that German and American audiences do have different likes and dislikes with regard to drama is supported by independent data. During the occupation period, various American plays have been presented in German theatres. Experience has shown that a number of these productions have been equally popular in both countries; some, however, quite popular in the United States have been poorly received by German audiences, while still others that achieved relatively little success in this country have turned out to be hits in Germany.

5. During the war, a series of American motion pictures (about 15 in all) were pre-tested on 200–300 German prisoners of war. Although the prisoners were selected anti-Nazis, it is interesting to note their reactions and their major criticisms of the American films. In general, the majority considered the American films they had seen to be inferior in content to German films.

SUMMARY AND CONCLUSIONS

1. The 45 most popular new plays in Germany and the United States in 1927 were analysed for psychological content. A smaller sample from 1909–10 were also examined. Independent judges, from whom the difference in national origin was concealed, were used to classify the 1927 plays according to certain major categories of analysis.

2. The German plays are considerably more ideological, philosophical, historical and social-minded than the American plays; the latter dwell on private problems, the difficulties of achieving love and virtue in daily life.

3. The German hero tends to be an individual with a distinct role who stands above or outside of normal society: a visionary pursuing a cause, a prince more far-seeing and liberal than his subjects, a social outcast. The American hero tends to be a more ordinary person from society's midst.

4. The central character is less frequently a woman in the German plays than in the American; and where women do have central roles in

the German drama, they tend to take over masculine characteristics and masculine types of action—"femininity" as commonly understood, feminine qualities and feminine emotional reactions, do not get the attention they receive in the American drama.

5. In American love plots, the emphasis is upon the working out of a solution to conflicts and difficulties arising from external obstacles (e.g., parents, criminals) or from the lovers themselves (e.g., misunderstandings, immoral impulses). The path of love is precarious until some final adjustment is made. In the German plays, two individuals may be deeply united in "idyllic" love by virtue of sharing common ideals; or a physical scene or locale, charged with emotion and meaning, may provide a context for idyllic love. The German lovers, however, may be once and for all cut asunder when higher (deeper) values so dictate. The German plays do not feature the love relationship as dependent upon the solution of emotional difficulties in personal relations.

6. The American orientation is essentially moralistic, the German orientation idealistic. The American hero must struggle against immoral or anti-social tendencies in himself or in other specific individuals; such tendencies are portrayed as interfering with the normal realization of personal happiness. The German hero who stands above the masses and is pursuing an ideal goal, a blue-print for society, may have to struggle against the normal practices of society itself. The value pattern expressed in the American plays enjoins the individual to be considerate of the welfare of other specific individuals; at the same time he must watch out for his own welfare. The German idealistic hero, on the other hand, in order to be successful, must consider neither his own welfare nor the welfare of other specific individuals. He must consider only the fulfilment of his high aim.

7. Personal ambitions and satisfactions, which are sanctioned in the American plays, are frequently portrayed as the root obstacle in the German plays, the "materialism" against which the idealist must fight. Similarly, conventional moral standards which in the American plays promote success and happiness, often appear in the German drama to be petty, hypocritical, mean and confining; the German hero must frequently fight against "Philistinism" as well as materialism.

8. Personal crimes and sins, which pose basic problems in the American plays, are frequently excused or justified in the German plays. Society is pictured as responsible, rather than the individual; or an act judged wrongly by society is interpreted as good because society's judgment is petty and narrow; or a criminal act, though not approved *per se,* is necessitated by Fate and the logic of the German idealism. We find, for example, various murders of beloved persons consciously carried out by sympathetically portrayed characters in the German plays. The American hero, placed in the same type of dilemma into which the German hero

falls, might well make the same choice of action—but he does not get into the same dilemma.

9. While the American plays carry the lesson that virtue has pragmatic sanction, the lesson to be found in the German plays is that success in worldly conflicts is won through power and ruthlessness. Without power, idealism is doomed to failure. The German drama accordingly places great emphasis upon strength of character, the determined, even ruthless pursuit of long-range goals. The strong and ruthless national idealist was a German favorite of 1909–10, the humanitarian idealist overwhelmed by strong, ruthless enemies a favorite of 1927.

10. The good side usually wins in the resolution of conflicts in the American drama because some individual in a critical position changes his mind. The hero or heroine who has sinned may undergo character reform, an opposing parent, a criminal or an estranged lover may change his attitude, or, in the last analysis, an independent tribunal of law or public opinion may be persuaded to change its opinion and recognize truth and justice. The reform of attitude or character is usually brought about through some persuasive argument or evidence, rational or irrational, such as legalistic evidence, humanitarian reasoning, a dream occasioned by eating a piece of cheese, a slap on the face, a wife's leaving her husband, the presence of a baby, sympathetic love, sickness or injury, strokes of fortune, sudden consequences that teach a lesson. Acts of ingenuity are often the means by which the compelling evidence is marshalled. The assumption that there is a reliable fundament of good will and good sense in society open to persuasion, that human beings can and will change, provided the proper argument is brought to bear upon them, this assumption of educability and reform pervades the American drama, but is relatively lacking in the German drama. There it is assumed, on the contrary, that human beings are inflexible, uncompromising; they are narrow in their vision, petty and rigid in their interpretation of their status and their adherence to the canons of respectability. Even the law does not serve as an ultimate recourse, for it, too, may operate in a petty, narrow manner. It is consistent with this view of human nature and human society that conflicts are not resolved in the German drama so much through the marshalling of evidence to change attitudes, as through power techniques.

11. Both the German and American plays express rebellion against authority: the American, against parents and others who interfere in the individual's life happiness; the German, against political superiors, classes, or society itself. The American rebels in the name of his personal right to happiness. This right is a positive value, and forces opposed to it are portrayed as immoral, evil, or at least ill-advised. There is no such right to individual happiness clearly presumed to justify rebellion against authority in the German plays. When a German rebels, he must do so, not

in self interest, but in the name of an ideal, a set of values that are superior to those of the authority against which he is rebelling. Each individual German rebellion thus tends to be an ideological movement. A solution to the American rebellion is provided—the individual who is wrong, whether the rebel or the authority, can admit his guilt and reform. But the German rebel cannot reform, since his is the superior position; and authority will not reform. Hence there is no solution in the way of redintegration; the losing side must depart or die or drink its bitter cup in silence.

REFERENCES

Jones, D. B. Quantitative analysis of motion picture content, *Publ. Opin. Quart.*, 1942, **6**, 411–428.

Lewin, H. S. A comparison of the aims of the Hitler Youth and the Boy Scouts of America, *Human Relations*, 1947, **1**, 206–227.

McGranahan, D. V. A comparative study of social attitudes among American and German youth, *J. Abnorm. Soc. Psychol.*, 1946, **11**, 245–257.

3-6

Intergroup Attitudes in South Africa and Southern United States

THOMAS F. PETTIGREW

Cultural norms are the rules and standards that specify appropriate and inappropriate behavior of members of a society. Punishment and reward are used to enforce these norms. Does racial prejudice reflect these norms or is it only a manifestation of the individual personality? Dr. Pettigrew shows that personality factors alone are not sufficient to explain prejudice. Social prejudice also represents the conformity of the individual to community norms.

I. INTRODUCTION

Along the continuum of prejudice theories, two extreme positions have been popular. One strongly emphasizes the personality of the bigot and neglects his cultural milieu; the other views intolerance as a mere reflection of cultural norms and neglects individual differences. Recent evidence lends little support to either pole. As further data are gathered with more refined research tools, it becomes increasingly apparent that

Reprinted from *J. Confl. Resol.*, 1958, 2, 29–42, by permission of the author and the University of Michigan Press.

the psychological and sociological correlates of prejudice are elaborately intertwined and that both are essential to provide an adequate theoretical framework for this complex phenomenon.

Carrying this viewpoint further, Smith, Bruner, and White (1956, pp. 41–44) have delineated three functions that attitudes may serve for an individual. First, there is the *object-appraisal* function; attitudes aid in the process of understanding "reality" as it is defined by the culture. Second, attitudes can play a *social-adjustment* role by contributing to the individual's identification with, or differentiation from, various reference groups. It should be noted that both these functions—object appraisal and social adjustment—are important reflections on the personality level of sociocultural conditions. But the most studied function of attitudes, *externalization*, is somewhat unique. "Externalization occurs when an individual, often responding unconsciously, senses an analogy between a perceived environmental event and some unresolved inner problem . . . [and] adopts an attitude . . . which is a transformed version of his way of dealing with his inner difficulty." Such a process may serve to reduce anxiety. The principal psychological theories of prejudice—frustration-aggression (Dollard, et al., 1939), psychoanalytic (McLean, 1946), and authoritarianism (Adorno, et al., 1950)—all deal chiefly with this third process.

External expression of inner conflict is relatively more independent of sociocultural factors than are the other functions of attitudes. Indeed, a heuristic distinction between externalized personality variables and sociological variables contributes to our understanding of much that is known about intergroup conflict.

Minard's observations of race relations in the coal-mining county of McDowell, West Virginia, serve as a direct illustration of the point (Minard, 1952). The general pattern in this region consists of white and Negro miners being integrated below the ground and almost completely segregated above the ground. Minard estimates that roughly 60 per cent of the white miners manage to reverse roles almost completely; they can accept Negroes as equals in the mines but cannot accept them as equals elsewhere. Furthermore, he feels that, at one extreme, about 20 per cent accept the black miners as equals in both situations, while, at the other extreme, about 20 per cent never accept them in either situation. In our terms, the behavior of the majority of these whites studied by Minard can be predicted largely by sociocultural expectations, and the behavior of the consistent minorities can be accounted for largely by externalized personality variables.

The research literature abounds with further examples in which a separation of psychological and sociological factors is helpful. The many papers on interracial contact in housing (Deutsch and Collins, 1951; Wilner, et al., 1952), at work (Harding and Hogrefe, 1952), and in the army (Stouffer, et al., 1949) show the marked effects that can be brought about by certain changes in the social situation between races. But personality factors are still operating. Usually these studies report that some individuals hold favorable attitudes toward minorities even before the contact and that other individuals still hold unfavorable attitudes after the contact. Many of these studies also find that the changes brought about by the contact are quite specific and delimited in nature. That is, the intergroup changes occur only under a narrow range of conditions, since the basic personality orientations of the participants have not changed fundamentally. Thus white department-store employees become more accepting of Negroes in the work situation after equal status contact but not in other situations (Harding and Hogrefe, 1952). And the attitudes of white army personnel toward the Negro as a fighting man improve after equal status contact in combat, but their attitudes toward the Negro as a social companion do not change (Stouffer, et al., 1949).

Desegregation findings furnish further illustrations where the distinction is useful. Social demands for racial desegregation and the irresistible trend of the times are counteracting personality predispositions in many communities. Thus a 1954 public opinion survey in Oklahoma found an overwhelming majority of the residents sternly against desegregation, and yet today mixed schools have become accepted throughout most of the state without incident (Jones, 1957). And in Wilmington, Delaware, two years after successful school integration without apparent public opposition, a poll indicated that only a minority approved of the school desegregation decision of the Supreme Court (Jones, 1957). Indeed, this discrepancy between opinions and demands is a general phenomenon throughout the border states. Hyman and Sheatsley (1956) report that only 31 per cent of the white population in those border areas that have already integrated their school systems indorse desegregation.

This conflict between authority-supported cultural changes and personal preferences is underscored by another finding that public opinion polls have uncovered in the South. Several investigators have independently shown that respondents themselves make a distinction between what they individually favor and what they expect to happen in their community. Thus the huge majority of southern whites favor racial segregation, but most of them also feel that desegregation is inevitable (Hyman and Sheatsley, 1956; Pettigrew, 1957).

Finally, the work originally done by LaPiere (1934) in 1934 and more recently replicated in different contexts by Saenger and Gilbert (1950) and by Kutner, et al. (1952) furnishes further justification for a theoretical separation of social and externalization aspects of intergroup conflict. These investigations illustrate the results of conflicting personality predispositions and actual social situations with minority-group members; frequently the face-to-face conditions override previous practices.

Such work has led several authorities in the field to make the sociocultural and personality differentiation. Psychologist G. W. Allport (1954) discusses the two classes of factors separately in his definitive volume, *The Nature of Prejudice,* and sociologist Arnold Rose makes a similar distinction in a recent theoretical article on intergroup relations (Rose, 1956).

The present paper is a summary report on research conducted chiefly to gain cross-national perspective on these two sets of prejudice factors. The studies were made in two parts of the world where racial conflict today is highlighted and cultural sanctions of intolerance are intense and explicit: the Union of South Africa and the southern United States. First, a more detailed report of previously unpublished data will be presented on the South African study. Following this, a comparison will be made with the southern United States based on a summary of data presented in detail elsewhere (Pettigrew, 1959).

II. RACIAL PREJUDICE IN THE UNION OF SOUTH AFRICA

The limited evidence available supports the general belief that white South Africans are unusually prejudiced against Africans (Hellmann, 1949; MacCrone, 1937; Malherbe, 1946). This raises the intriguing question as to whether this increased hostility represents (*a*) more externalizing personality potential for prejudice among South Africans, (*b*) the effects of different cultural norms and pressures, or (*c*) both of these.

To provide a tentative answer, a questionnaire study was undertaken of the racial attitudes of students at the English-speaking University of Natal in the Union of South Africa. A non-random sample of 627 undergraduates—approximately one-third of the entire university—completed an anonymous instrument containing three scales and a number of background items. The three scales are a thirteen-item measure of authoritarianism (F scale) whose statements are shown in Table 2, a sixteen-item measure of social conformity (C scale) whose statements are shown in Table 3, and an eighteen-item measure of anti-African attitudes (A scale) whose statements are shown in Table 8. Background information includes place of birth, political party preference, father's occupation, and ethnic-group membership.

Taken as a group, these students evidence considerable hostility toward Africans, accepting in large degree the white-supremacy ideology so adamantly propounded by the present government of their country. Thus 72 per cent of the sample agree that "there is something inherently primitive and uncivilized in the native, as shown in his music and extreme aggressiveness"; and 69 per cent agree that "manual labor seems to fit the native mentality better than more skilled and responsible work." And yet their F-scale responses are roughly comparable to those of American student populations. Thus these South Africans are sharply prejudiced against blacks without possessing any greater externalizing personality potential for intolerance than peoples in more tolerant areas.

In addition, authoritarianism correlates with anti-African attitudes at a level comparable to relationships between authoritarianism and prejudice in other parts of the world. Table 1 shows that the A and F scales correlate + 0.56 among the Afrikaans-speaking members of the sample and + 0.46 among the English-speaking members. Similar scales typically correlate in the fifties in American college samples. The C-scale measure of social conformity—employed for the first time in this investigation—relates to the A-scale scores significantly, too, in both ethnic groups (Table 1).

TABLE 1

Correlations between Anti-African Scale (A) and Authoritarianism (F) and Conformity (C) Scales*

Variables	Ethnic Group†	
	Afrikaners	English
N	50	513
A and F	+0.56	+0.46
A and C	+0.42	+0.46

*All four of these product-moment correlations are significantly different from zero at better than the 1 per cent level of confidence. The scale scores that were correlated vary between 0 and 10. They were calculated on the basis of +4 for agree strongly, +3 for agree, +2 for omitted response, +1 for disagree and 0 for disagree strongly for each item, and then the total scores were collapsed into the 0–10 categories for machine analysis.
†Separate analyses by ethnic group are made necessary by the sharply divergent A-scale means of the two groups (see Table 7).

More detailed analyses of the F and C scales' relationships with anti-African attitudes are provided in Tables 2 and 3. Each of the thirteen authoritarian statements separates the less and more prejudiced halves of the sample in the predicted direction, seven of the differences proving to be significant at better than the 0.001 level of confidence. The sixteen C-scale items predict almost as well; the more anti-African students in every case agree more often than the less prejudiced. Perhaps the conforming attitude of the bigots is capsuled in the first item of Table 3. While only a third of the tolerant members of the group agree with the statement, over half the prejudiced students feel that "it's better to go along with the crowd than to be a martyr."

TABLE 2
Anti-African Prejudice and F-Scale Items

F-Scale Item	Percentage Agreement*		2 × 2 χ^2	p
	Less Prejudiced Half	More Prejudiced Half		
(a) Nowadays when so many different kinds of people move around and mix together so much, a person has to be especially careful not to catch an infection or disease from them.	13.6	33.2	33.5	0.001
(b) There is hardly anything lower than a person who does not feel a great love and respect for his parents.	52.6	70.5	21.2	.001
(c) People can be put into two distinct classes: the weak and the strong.	23.5	37.8	15.1	.001
(d) Most of our social problems would be solved if we could somehow get rid of the immoral, crooked, and feebleminded people.	45.4	60.6	14.8	.001
(e) The most important thing a child should learn is obedience to his parents.	79.8	90.2	13.2	.001
(f) Every person should have faith in some supernatural power whose decisions he obeys without question.	46.7	60.9	13.0	.001
(g) When a person has a problem or worry, it is best for him not to think about it, but to keep busy with more cheerful things.	39.4	53.2	11.8	.001
(h) Nowadays more and more people are prying into matters that should remain private and personal.	63.5	74.5	8.6	.01
(i) If people would talk less and work more, everybody would be better off.	67.8	78.2	8.3	.01
(j) An insult to our honor should always be punished.	31.8	40.3	4.7	.05
(k) No sane, normal person would ever think of hurting a close friend or relative.	67.9	76.6	4.3	.05
(l) Science has its place, but there are many important things that can never possibly be understood by the human mind.	80.7	85.8	2.9	0.10
(m) Some day it will probably be shown that astrology can explain a lot of things.	44.4	48.0	0.9	n.s.

*The respondent was given four categories: agree strongly, agree, and disagree, and disagree strongly. Percentage agreement is calculated by combining the first two of these replies.

TABLE 3

Anti-African Prejudice and C-Scale Items

| | Percentage Agreement[*] | | | |
C-Scale Item	Less Prejudiced Half	More Prejudiced Half	$2 \times 2\ \chi^2$	p
(a) It's better to go along with the crowd than to be a martyr.	34.8	53.2	21.8	0.001
(b) When almost everyone agrees on something, there is little reason to oppose it.	16.6	31.1	18.5	.001
(c) Adherence to convention produces the best kind of citizen.	31.8	46.8	14.9	.001
(d) To be successful, a group's members must act and think alike.	45.7	60.0	12.5	.001
(e) It is important for friends to have similar opinions.	28.5	42.2	12.1	.001
(f) It is more important to be loyal and conform to our own group than to try to co-operate with other groups.	25.6	38.5	11.7	.001
(g) We should alter our needs to fit society's demands rather than change society to fit our needs.	42.4	55.1	11.4	.001
(h) A good group member should agree with the other members.	21.2	33.2	11.1	.001
(i) It is best not to express your views when in the company of friends who disagree with you.	23.8	32.9	6.1	.02
(j) Before a person does something, he should try to consider how his friends will react to it.	54.6	63.1	4.4	.05
(k) To become a success these days, a person has to act in the way that others expect him to act.	33.2	41.5	4.2	.05
(l) A group cannot expect to maintain its identity unless its members all think and feel in very much the same way.	59.3	66.8	3.9	.05
(m) It is one's duty to conform to the passing demands of the world and to suppress those personal desires that do not fit these demands.	43.7	51.1	3.4	.10
(n) A person should adapt his ideas and his behavior to the group that happens to be with him at the time.	45.7	52.6	3.1	.10

TABLE 3 (*Continued*)

Anti-African Prejudice and C-Scale Items

| | Percentage Agreement* | | | |
| | Less Prejudiced Half | More Prejudiced Half | | |
C-Scale Item			2×2 χ^2	p
(*o*) It is extremely uncomfortable to go accidentally to a formal party in street clothes.	78.5	83.1	2.0	.20
(*p*) To get along well in a group, you have to follow the lead of others.	27.2	31.1	1.1	0.30

*Percentage agreement calculated as in Table 2.

These personality relationships suggest (*a*) that personality factors are as important correlates of prejudice in this sample as they are in other, non-South African samples; (*b*) that social conformity (as measured by the C scale) is a particularly crucial personality variable in this sample's attitudes toward Africans; and (*c*) that personality components do not in themselves account for the heightened intolerance of this sample.

We must turn to sociocultural factors to explain the extreme prejudice of these respondents, and the unusual importance of these variables is made clear by the data. For instance, the 560 students who were born on the African continent are significantly more intolerant of Africans than the remaining 65, but they are *not* more authoritarian. Table 4 shows that those not born in Africa are much less likely to fall into the most prejudiced third of the distribution than other sample members. And yet the two groups do not differ significantly in their F-scale scores. More thoroughly influenced throughout their lives by the culture's definition of the white man's situation in Africa, students born on the Dark Continent are more anti-African without the usual personality concomitants of ethnocentrism.

Another such relationship involves students who support the Nationalist party—the pro-*Apartheid* political faction that is presently in power. Table 5 indicates that these respondents score significantly higher on the A scale than their fellow undergraduates, but these two groups do not differ on the F scale. Again a prejudice difference is not accompanied by a personality potential difference. These relationships with political party preference and prejudice hold for each of the major ethnic groups—Afrikaners and English—considered separately.

TABLE 4

Place of Birth and Anti-African Prejudice*

Anti-African Attitudes†	N	Born on African Continent	Not born on African Continent
		560	65
Least prejudiced	176	28%	29%
Medium prejudiced	246	38%	54%
Most prejudiced	203	34%	17%

*2 × 3 chi-square = 9.33; $p < 0.01$.
†The least prejudiced are the students who rated A-scale scores from 0 through 4 by disagreeing with a heavy majority of the items; the medium prejudiced received scores of either 5 or 6 by agreeing with roughly half of the 18 A-scale items; and the most prejudiced obtained scores of 7 through 10 by agreeing with a majority of the statements.

TABLE 5

Political Party Preference and Anti-African Prejudice*

Anti-African Attitudes	N	Political Party Preference† Nationalist Party	Other Parties
		72	483
Least prejudiced	157	8%	35%
Medium prejudiced	210	26%	36%
Most prejudiced	188	66%	29%

*2 × 3 chi-square = 38.60; $p < 0.001$.
†Seventy-two of the 627 students did not indicate any political preference.

Two other comparisons yield statistically significant differences in both authoritarianism and anti-African prejudice. Table 6 indicates that those sample members whose fathers are manually employed are significantly more intolerant of the African than those whose fathers are non-manually employed. The two groups differ in the same manner in their F-scale scores. But when authoritarianism is controlled for, the groups still differ significantly in their attitudes toward blacks. In other words, the children of manual fathers are more prejudiced and more authoritarian than other students, and they remain more prejudiced even after the difference in authoritarianism is partialed out of the relationship. These upwardly mobile students must be carefully in step with the mores to establish firmly their rise in the social structure, and the mores of South Africa lead to intolerance.

TABLE 6

Father's Occupational Status and Anti-African Prejudice*

Anti-African Attitudes	N	Father's Occupational Status†	
		Manual	Nonmanual
		146	417
Less prejudiced half	280	34%	55%
More prejudiced half	283	66%	45%

*2 × 2 chi-square = 18.90; $p < 0.001$.
†Sixty-four of the 627 students did not indicate their fathers' occupations.

Table 7 shows the sharp difference between the Afrikaner and English subjects in the sample. Afrikaners are both more anti-African and more authoritarian, and, when the F-scale differences are corrected for, they remain significantly more hostile to the African. These 50 students are directly subject to the national ethos and have no conflicting national reference, as many English-speaking South Africans have in Great Britain. Like the upwardly mobile, they are in roles that demand unusual conformity.

Table 8 clarifies further the ethnic differences in attitudes toward the African. Sixteen of the A scale's eighteen statements significantly separate the Afrikaners from the English, the former scoring higher in all cases. And, moreover, there is a definite trend in these differences. The five items which discriminate poorest between the ethnic groups (items *n* through *r*) are all stereotyped-belief statements; they refer to the standard traits frequently associated with Africans—lazy, primitive, happy-go-lucky, and bad-smelling. Conversely, five of the six best discriminators (items *b* through *f*) are all exclusion-discrimination statements; they deny equal rights to Africans in employment, housing, and voting. Afrikaans-speaking and English-speaking students, then, do not differ sharply in the degree to which they harbor the traditional stereotype of the African, but they do possess markedly divergent views on discrimination against the African. A key to these differences may be provided in the lone exception to this trend, item *a*. Seven out of every ten Afrikaners, as compared with only a third of the English, believe that the "natives will always have a greater tendency toward crimes of violence than Europeans." Strong projection may be operating for those agreeing with this statement, but, in any event, it suggests that physical fear of the black man is especially prevalent among our Afrikaans-speaking respondents and that this may be the fundamental motivation for their emphasis on excluding and discriminating against the African.

All these findings point to the crucial role of the cultural milieu in shaping the attitudes of the white South African toward the blacks in his

TABLE 7

Ethnic Group and Anti-African Prejudice*

| Anti-African Attitudes | N | Ethnic Group† | |
		Afrikaners	English
		50	513
Less prejudiced half	264	14%	50%
More prejudiced half	299	86%	50%

*2 × 2 chi-square = 23.7; $p < 0.001$.
†Ethnic group is determined by both the student's own ethnic identification and the principal language spoken in his home. Sixty-four of the students identified with other groups (e.g., Jewish, French, German) and are not included in this analysis.

midst. While externalizing personality factors do not account for the students' unusually prejudiced attitudes concerning Africans, variables which reflect the dominant norms of the white society prove to be important. Students who are especially responsive to these norms—those who were born in Africa, those who identify with the Nationalist party, those who are upwardly mobile, and those who have been molded by the conservative traditions of the Afrikaans-speaking people—tend to be intolerant of Africans to some degree, regardless of their basic personality structure.

III. RACIAL PREJUDICE IN THE SOUTHERN UNITED STATES

Similar considerations led to an earlier comparative study of anti-Negro prejudice in the southern and northern United States. While considerable evidence indicates that white southerners are typically more intolerant of the Negro than white northerners (Hyman and Sheatsley, 1956; Myrdal, 1944; Prothro, 1952; Samelson, 1945; Sims and Patrick, 1936; Stouffer, et al., 1949), little work has been focused on the factors underlying this difference. But, like the South African data, the scant data available suggest that sociocultural and not externalization factors may be the crucial determinants of the contrasting regional attitudes toward the Negro.

Thus, if the South did have more externalizing personality potential for prejudice than other American areas, it should also be more anti-Semitic. But Roper (Roper, 1946; Roper, 1947) has twice found in his national polls that the South is one of the most tolerant regions toward Jews, and Prothro (1952) has noted that 40 per cent of his adult white Louisiana sample is at the same time favorable in its attitudes toward

Jews and highly anti-Negro. Furthermore, there is no evidence that the stern family pattern associated with "prejudiced personalities" (Adorno, et al., 1950; Harris, et al., 1950) is more prevalent in the South than in the North (Davis, et al., 1941; Dollard, 1937). And, finally, the few white southern populations that have been given the F scale have obtained means that fall easily within the range of means reported for non-southern populations (Adorno, et al., 1950; Milton, 1952; Smith and Prothro, 1957).

Rose categorically concludes: "There is no evidence that 'authoritarian personality' or frustration-aggression or scapegoating, or any known source of 'prejudice' in the psychological sense, is any more prevalent in the South than in the North" (Rose, 1956). And Prothro adds: "Situational, historical and cultural factors appear to be of considerable, perhaps major, import in addition to personality dynamics" in determining anti-Negro attitudes in the South (Prothro, 1952).

In testing these ideas in the two regions, different methods were employed than those used in South Africa. Public opinion polling techniques were utilized with 366 randomly selected white adults in eight roughly matched communities in the North and South. The four small southern towns, located in Georgia and North Carolina, were chosen to have Negro population percentages ranging from 10 to 45 per cent, while the small northern towns, all located in New England, have less than 1 per cent Negroes each.

The interview schedule contained a ten-item measure of authoritarianism (F scale), an eight-item measure of anti-Semitism (A-S scale), and a twelve-item measure of anti-Negro prejudice (N scale), together with numerous background questions. The poll purported to be concerned with the effects of the mass media upon public opinion, and it seems largely due to this guise that the blatantly phrased prejudice statements caused no interview breakoffs.

Of greatest immediate interest is the striking similarity in these results with those of the South African investigation. First, the southern sample is considerably more anti-Negro than the northern sample but is *not* more authoritarian. Similar to the Afrikaner-English differences (Table 8), the southerners respond in the more prejudiced direction on each of the N-scale statements but are most unique in their extreme attitudes concerning excluding and discriminating against the Negro. That is, southerners and northerners in the samples both share in large degree the lazy, primitive, happy-go-lucky, and bad-smelling stereotype of the Negro, but southerners far more than northerners wish to deny equal rights to the Negro in employment, housing, and voting. And yet there is no difference in the externalization potential for intolerance; the F-scale means of the two samples are almost identical.

TABLE 8

Ethnic-Group Differences on A-Scale Items

A-Scale Items	Percentage Agreement[*]		$2 \times 2 \chi^2$	p
	Afrikaners	English		
(a) Because of their primitive background, natives will always have a greater tendency toward crimes of violence than Europeans.	70.0	34.9	33.6	0.001
(b) Native musicians are sometimes as good as Europeans at swing music and jazz, but it is a mistake to have mixed native-European bands.	86.0	54.2	18.8	.001
(c) Most of the natives would become officious, overbearing, and disagreeable if not kept in their place.	80.0	48.3	18.2	.001
(d) Laws which would force equal employment opportunities for both the natives and Europeans would not be fair to European employers.	74.0	44.2	16.2	.001
(e) The natives have their rights, but it is best to keep them in their own districts and schools and to prevent too much contact with Europeans.	86.0	63.7	9.9	.01
(f) The natives do not deserve the right to vote.	64.0	41.3	9.5	.01
(g) The natives will never have the intelligence and organizing ability to run a modern industrial society.	42.0	23.2	8.7	.01
(h) As the native will never properly absorb our civilization, the only solution is to let him develop along his own lines.	68.0	46.3	8.6	.01
(i) Manual labor seems to fit the native mentality better than more skilled and responsible work.	88.0	68.9	8.0	.01
(j) Seldom, if ever, is a native superior to most Europeans intellectually.	72.0	52.2	7.1	.01
(k) The natives tend to be overly emotional.	66.0	46.5	7.1	.01
(l) Because of his immaturity, the South African native is likely to be led into all sorts of mischief and should therefore be strictly controlled in his own best interests.	92.0	75.6	6.9	.01
(m) The granting of wide educational opportunities to natives is a dangerous thing.	36.0	19.9	6.9	.01

TABLE 8 (*Continued*)

Ethnic-Group Differences on A-Scale Items

A-Scale Items	Percentage Agreement[*]		$2 \times 2 \chi^2$	p
	Afrikaners	English		
(n) Most natives are lazy and lack ambition.	60.0	44.1	4.6	.05
(o) There is something inherently primitive and uncivilized in the native, as shown in his music and extreme aggressiveness.	86.0	72.1	4.4	.05
(p) Due to the differences in innate endowment, the Bantu race will always be inferior to the white race.	54.0	39.6	4.0	.05
(q) Most of the natives are happy-go-lucky and irresponsible.	70.0	60.0	1.9	0.20
(r) In spite of what some claim, the natives do have a different and more pronounced body odor than Europeans.	84.0	81.5	0.2	n.s.

[*]Percentage agreement calculated as in Table 2.

Further similarities to the South African data support the contention that personality dynamics, such as authoritarianism, are not responsible for the sharp North-South divergence in attitudes toward the Negro. When age and education are partialed out, the N and F scales correlate to a comparable degree in the two populations. Moreover, with age and education partialed out again, the N and A-S scales relate at equivalent levels in the two regional samples. In other words, the externalizing prejudiced personality as tapped by the F and A-S scales does not account for any more of the anti-Negro variance in the southern sample than it does in the northern sample. This finding, combined with the previously mentioned fact that the two groups do not differ in their F-scale responses, indicates that externalization factors do not explain the heightened bigotry of the southerners. As with the South African results, we must turn to social variables in an effort to account for the regional discrepancy in attitudes toward the Negro.

All six of the sociocultural dimensions tested yield meaningful relationships with Negro prejudice in the southern sample: sex, church attendance, social mobility, political party identification, armed service, and education. These variables reflect southern culture in a manner similar to the social variables tested in the South African study. And as in South Africa, those southerners, who by their roles in the social structure can be anticipated to be conforming to the dictates of the culture, prove to be more prejudiced against Negroes than their counterparts. For example, females, the "carriers of culture," are significantly more anti-Negro than men in the southern sample but *not* in the northern sample.

Two other groups of southerners who manifest conforming behavior in other areas are also more intolerant of Negroes. Respondents who have been to church within the week are significantly more anti-Negro than those who have not been within the month, and there is a tendency (though not statistically significant) for the upwardly mobile to be more anti-Negro than others in the non-manual occupational class. The latter result recalls the finding in the South African study that students whose fathers are manual workers tend to be more anti-African (Table 6). In the northern sample, no such trends appear. Protestant churchgoers in the North tend to be more tolerant of the Negro than Protestant non-attenders, and no relationship between upward mobility and attitudes toward Negroes is discernible. Conformity to northern norms—unlike conformity to southern or South African norms—is not associated with hostility for the black man.

In contrast to the conformers, southerners who evidence deviance from the mores in some area of social life tend to be *less* anti-Negro. Non-attenders of church furnish one example. Another example are respondents who explicitly identify themselves as political independents, which also represents a degree of deviance: they tend to be considerably more tolerant of the Negro than are southerners who consider themselves either Democrats or Republicans. Again, no such discrepancy occurs in the northern population.

Downward mobility has been noted by other investigators to be positively related to intolerance in the North (Bettelheim and Janowitz, 1950; Greenblum and Pearlin, 1953), and this finding is replicated in the present northern data. But in the southern data a striking reversal occurs. The downwardly mobile in the South are much less anti-Negro than other manually employed respondents, though the two groups do not differ in authoritarianism. Perhaps in a culture that emphasizes status and family background, that makes a sharp distinction between "poor whites" and "respectable whites," and that cherishes its aristocratic traditions (Cash, 1941; Davis et al., 1941; Dollard, 1937), the downwardly mobile southern-er learns to reject much of his culture. And rejecting the culture's stress on tradition and status makes it easier to reject also the culture's dicta concerning the Negro.

Two groups of southerners—armed service veterans and the highly educated—are potential deviants from southern culture simply because their special experience and study have brought them into contact with other ways of life. And, as we might expect, we find that both veterans and college-educated southerners are considerably more tolerant of the Negro than non-veterans and the poorly educated. Veterans in both regions prove to be more authoritarian than non-veterans, and, consistent with this, northern veterans are less tolerant of Negroes than northerners who had not served. Education is negatively related to N-scale scores in the northern sample, too, but significantly less than in the southern sample. Exposure to non-southern culture leads to deviance from the strict southern norms concerning the Negro; little wonder that southerners who have been out of the region for any considerable length of time are generally viewed as suspect by their neighbors upon return.

These consistent relationships with social factors in the southern data have been interpreted in terms of conformity and deviance from the narrowly prescribed mores of small-town southern life. Evidence for such an analysis comes from a final intra-southern difference. Southern communities with high Negro population ratios (38 and 45 per cent) have significantly higher N-scale means than the other communities sampled in the South with low Negro ratios (10 and 18 per cent), though they are *not* different in authoritarianism or anti-Semitism. In southern areas with the most intensely anti-Negro norms, prejudice against the black southerner is greater, even though there is not a greater amount of externalizing personality potential for prejudice.

Though limited by the restricted samples employed, this evidence indicates that sociocultural factors—as in the South African sample—are indeed the key to the regional difference in attitudes toward the Negro. In spite of the marked contrast in samples and method between the two investigations, both the South African and the southern results underline the unique importance of social variables in prejudice that is sanctioned by the cultural norms.

IV. SUMMARY AND CONCLUSIONS

Finely interwoven personality and sociocultural variables together form the foundation upon which a broad and satisfactory theory of racial prejudice must be built. Neither set of factors can be neglected, but a heuristic separation between the relatively culture-free externalization factors and social factors aids analysis. The present paper uses this distinction to interpret prejudice data from two parts of the world with tense racial conflict—the Union of South Africa and the southern United States.

Externalization factors such as authoritarianism are associated with prejudice in both the South African and the southern samples at levels roughly comparable with other areas. Data from the South African students hint, however, that susceptibility to conform may be an unusually important psychological component of prejudice in regions where the cultural norms positively sanction intolerance. In addition, there is no indication in either of these samples that there is any more externalizing personality potential for prejudice in these areas than in more tolerant parts of the globe.

The extensive racial prejudice of the South African and southern groups seems directly linked with the antiblack dictates of the two cultures. Sociocultural factors which reflect the mores consistently relate to prejudice—place of birth, political party preference, upward mobility, and ethnic-group membership in the South African data and sex, church attendance, social mobility, political party identification, armed service, and education in the southern data. The pattern is clear: conformity to South African or southern mores is associated with racial intolerance, while deviance from these mores is associated with racial tolerance.

Taken together with other published work, these limited results suggest a broad, cross-cultural hypothesis:

In areas with historically imbedded traditions of racial intolerance, externalizing personality factors underlying prejudice remain important, but sociocultural factors are unusually crucial and account for the heightened racial hostility.

Should future, more extensive, research support such a hypothesis, its implications for prejudice theory would be considerable. Regions or peoples with heightened prejudice against a particular outgroup would not necessarily be thought of as harboring more authoritarianism; the special conflict may reflect the operation of particular historical, cultural, and social factors. Such a prospect may be encouraging to many action programs—efforts which typically are more successful at changing a person's relation to his culture than they are at changing basic personality structure. Desegregation is a case in point. The success of the movement in the South does not depend—this hypothesis would contend—on changing the deeply ingrained orientations of prejudice-prone personalities; rather, it rests on the effectiveness with which racial integration now going on in the South can restructure the mores to which so many culturally intolerant southerners conform.

A second implication of the hypothesis is that personality factors such as authoritarianism and susceptibility to conform cannot be overlooked in understanding bigotry even in parts of the world like the Union of South Africa and the southern United States. Most psychological approaches to prejudice, it has been noted, are concerned chiefly with the externalization function of attitudes. Perhaps, as the object-appraisal and social-adjustment functions of attitudes are studied in more detail, the direct personality concomitants of cultural pressures will be isolated and better understood.

REFERENCES

Adorno, T. W., Else Frenkel-Brunswik, D. J. Levinson, and R. N. Sanford. *The authoritarian personality.* New York: Harper & Row, Publishers, 1950.

Allport, G. W. *The nature of prejudice.* Reading, Mass.: Addison-Wesley Publishing Co., 1954.

Bettelheim, B., and M. Janowitz. *Dynamics of prejudice.* New York: Harper & Row, Publishers, 1950.

Cash, W. *The mind of the South.* New York: Alfred A. Knopf, 1941.

Davis, A., B. Gardner, and Mary Gardner. *Deep South.* Chicago: University of Chicago Press, 1941.

Deutsch, M., and M. Collins. *Interracial housing.* Minneapolis: University of Minnesota Press, 1951.

Dollard, J. *Caste and class in a Southern town.* New Haven, Conn.: Yale University Press, 1937.

Dollard, J., L. Doob, N. Miller, O. Mowrer, and R. Sears. *Frustration and aggression.* New Haven, Conn.: Yale University Press, 1939.

Greenblum, J. and L. Pearlin. Vertical mobility and prejudice: A socio-psychological analysis. In R. Bendix and S. Lipset (eds.), *Class, status, and power,* pp. 480–491. New York: The Free Press, 1953.

Harding, J. and R. Hogrefe. Attitudes of white department store employees toward Negro co-workers, *Journal of Social Issues,* 1952, **8,** No. 1, 18–28.

Harris, D. B., H. G. Gough, and W. E. Martin. Children's ethnic attitudes. II. Relationship to parental beliefs concerning child training, *Child Devel.,* 1950, **21,** 169–181.

Hellmann, Ellen (ed.). *Handbook on race relations in South Africa.* Cape Town, South Africa: Oxford University Press, 1949.

Hyman, H. H. and P. B. Sheatsley. Attitudes toward desegregation, *Scientific American,* 1956, **195,** 35–39.

Jones, E. City limits. In D. Shoemaker (ed.), *With all deliberate speed,* pp. 71–87. New York: Harper & Row, Publishers, 1957.

Kutner, B., Carol Wilkins, and Penny Yarrow. Verbal attitudes and overt behavior involving racial prejudice, *J. Abnorm. Soc. Psychol.,* 1952, **47,** 649–652.

La Piere, R. T. Attitudes versus actions, *Social Forces,* 1934, **13,** 230–237.

McLean, Helen V. Psychodynamic factors in racial relations, *Annals Amer. Acad. Pol. and Soc. Sci.,* 1946, **244,** 159–166.

MacCrone, I. D. *Race attitudes in South Africa.* London: Oxford University Press, 1937.

MacCrone, I. D. Ethnocentric ideology and ethnocentrism, *Proc. S. African Psychol. Assoc.,* 1953, **4,** 21–24.

Malherbe, E. G. *Race attitudes and education.* Johannesburg, South Africa: Institute of Race Relations, 1946.

Milton, O. Presidential choice and performance on a scale of authoritarianism, *Amer. Psychol.,* 1952, **7,** 597–598.

Minard, R. D. Race relations in the Pocahontas Coal Field, *Journal of Social Issues*, 1952, **8**, No. 1. 29–44.

Myrdal, G. *An American dilemma.* New York: Harper & Row, Publishers, 1944.

Pettigrew, T. F. Desegregation and its chances for success: Northern and Southern views, *Social Forces*, 1957, **35**, 339–344.

Pettigrew, T. F. Regional differences in anti-Negro prejudice, *J. Abnorm. Soc. Psychol.*, 1959, **59**, 28–36.

Prothro, E. T. Ethnocentrism and anti-Negro attitudes in the Deep South, *J. Abnorm. and Soc. Psychol.*, 1952, **47**, 105–108.

Roper, E. United States anti-Semites, *Fortune*, 1946, **33**, 258–260.

Roper, E. United States anti-Semites, *Fortune*, 1947, **36**, 5–10.

Rose, A. M. Intergroup relations vs. prejudice: Pertinent theory for the study of social change, *Social Problems*, 1956, **4**, 173–176.

Saenger, G. and Emily Gilbert. Customer reactions to the integration of Negro sales personnel, *Intern. J. Opin. and Attitude Res.*, 1950, **4**, 57–76.

Samelson, Babette. The patterning of attitudes and beliefs regarding the American Negro: An analysis of public opinion. Unpublished doctoral dissertation, Radcliffe College, 1945.

Sims, V. M. and J. R. Patrick. Attitude towards the Negro of Northern and Southern college students, *J. Soc. Psychol.*, 1936, **7**, 192–204.

Smith, C. U., and J. W. Prothro. Ethnic differences in authoritarian personality, *Social Forces*, 1957, **35**, 334–338.

Smith, M. B., J. S. Bruner, and R. W. White. *Opinions and personality.* New York: John Wiley & Sons, Inc., 1956.

Stouffer, S. A., E. A. Suchman, L. C. DeVinney, Shirley A. Star, and R. M. Williams, Jr. *The American soldier: adjustment during Army life.* Vol. I: Studies in Social Psychology in World War II. Princeton: Princeton University Press, 1949.

Wilner, D. M., R. P. Walkley, and S. W. Cook. Residential proximity and intergroup relations in public housing projects, *Journal of Social Issues,* 1952, **8,** No. 1, 45–69.

CHAPTER 4

CULTURAL DIFFERENCES IN CHILD REARING AND CHILD BEHAVIOR

4-1

Swaddling in Eastern Europe

RUTH BENEDICT

Many cultural practices are symbolic rather than functional. Thus it is difficult to claim that immersion versus sprinkling as a form of baptism has any but a symbolic effect upon those baptized. Burial versus cremation makes no difference to the deceased, but it does matter to the onlookers.

There is much evidence that swaddling during the early months has little influence upon infant development, but the myths surrounding swaddling mean much to the parents.

Systematic study of national character is an investigation into a special and paradoxical situation. It must identify and analyze continuities in attitudes and behaviors yet the personnel which exhibits these traits changes completely with each generation. A whole nation of babies have to be brought up to replace their elders. The situations two different generations have to meet—war or peace, prosperity or depression—may change drastically, but Americans, for instance, will handle them in one set of terms, Italians in another. Even when a nation carries through a revolution or reverses fundamental state policies, Frenchmen do not cease to be recognizable as Frenchmen or Russians as Russians.

Reprinted from *Amer. J. Orthopsychiat.*, 1949, **19**, No. 2, 342–350, by permission of the American Orthopsychiatric Association Inc.

The cultural study of certain European nations on which I am reporting[1] has taken as one of its basic problems the ways in which children are brought up to carry on in their turn their parents' manner of life. It accepts as its theoretical premise that identifications, securities, and frustrations are built up in the child by the way in which he is traditionally handled, the early disciplines he receives, and the sanctions used by his parents. The study has been carried on in New York City by a staff of interviewers who have supplemented their work with historical, literary, journalistic and economic materials. The aims of the research have been to isolate exceedingly fundamental patterns and themes which can then be tested and refined by study of local, class, and religious differences. It is believed that such preliminary hypotheses will make future field work in the home countries more rewarding, and such field work in the Old World is already being carried out under other auspices by students who have taken part in this research.

The Project has necessarily seen its work as a comparative study of cultures. It has blocked out large culture areas and their constituent subcultures. When a great area shares a generalized trait, the particular slants each subarea has given to these customs are diagnostic of its special values and the range of variation gives insight which could not be obtained from the study of one nation in isolation. This culture area approach commits the student, moreover, when he is working outside his own cultural area, to a detailed study of behaviors which, since they are not present in his own experience, have not been incorporated into his own theoretical apparatus. It is therefore a testing ground for theoretical assumptions and often involves a rephrasing of them.

The custom of swaddling the baby during its first months of life in Central and Eastern Europe illustrates well, in the field of child rearing, the methodological value of a culture area approach. It illustrates how the comparison of attitudes and practices in different areas can illuminate the characteristics of any one region that is being intensively studied, and the kind of inquiry which is fruitful. Specifically I shall try to show that any such student of comparative cultures must press his investigation to the point where he can describe *what is communicated* by the particular variety of the widespread technique he is studying. In the case of swaddling, the object of investigation is the kind of communication which in different regions is set up between adults and the child by the procedures and sanctions used.

[1]Research in Contemporary Cultures, government-aided Columbia University Research Project sponsored by the Psychological Branch of the Medical Sciences Division of the Office of Naval Research. The Russian material was collected and organized under the leadership of Geoffrey Gorer and Margaret Mead, and I am especially indebted to Mr. Gorer's skill and insights; Prof. Conrad M. Arensberg directed the group gathering Jewish material, and Dr. Sula Benet organized the information on Poland. Thanks are due to these leaders and to all their co-workers.

Because of our Western emphasis on the importance of the infant's bodily movement, students of child care who discuss swaddling in our literature often warn that it produces tics. Or with our stress on prohibition of infant genitality, it is subsumed under prevention of infant masturbation. Any assumption that swaddling produces adults with tics ignores the contradictory evidence in the great areal laboratory where swaddling occurs, and the assumption that it is simply a first technique to prevent a child from finding pleasure in its own body is an oversimplified projection of our Western concern with this taboo. Any systematic study of the dynamics of character development in the swaddling area is crippled by these assumptions. Infant swaddling has permitted a great range of communication.

Careful studies of mother-child relations in this country have abundantly shown the infant's sensitivity to the mother's tenseness or permissiveness, her pleasure or disgust, whether these are expressed in her elbows, her tone of voice or her facial expression. Communications of these sorts take place from birth on, and when a particular form of parental handling is standardized as "good" and "necessary" in any community, the infant has a greatly multiplied opportunity to learn to react to the traditional patterns. Local premises, too, about how to prepare a child for life will be expressed in modification of procedure in swaddling, and these detailed differences are means of communication to the child, no less than his mother's tone of voice. Any fruitful research in national character must base its work upon such premises and utilize them as basic principles in comparative study.

Swaddling is tightest and is kept up longest in Great Russia. The baby's arms are wrapped close to its sides and only the face emerges. After tight wrapping in the blanket, the bundle is taped with criss-cross lashings till it is, as Russians say, "like a log of wood for the fireplace." Babies are sometimes lashed so tight that they cannot breathe, and are saved from strangling only by loosening the bindings. The bundle is as rigid as if the babies were bound to a cradleboard, and this affects carrying habits and the way a baby is soothed in an adult's arms. It is not rocked in the arms in the fashion familiar to us, but is moved horizontally from right to left and left to right.

The swaddling in Russia is explicitly justified as necessary for the safety of an infant who is regarded as being in danger of destroying itself. In the words of informants, "It would tear its ears off. It would break its legs." It must be confined for its own sake and for its mother's. In the '30's the Soviet regime made a determined effort to adopt Western customs of child rearing and to do away with swaddling. Young women were trained to instruct mothers that a baby's limbs should be left free for better muscular development and exhibitions of pictures of unswaddled baby care were distributed widely. But swaddling persisted. Informants who have recently lived in Russia say constantly "You couldn't carry an unswaddled baby." "Mothers were so busy they had to make the child secure." Several hundreds of pictures of babies available at the Sovfoto Agency show the prevalence of swaddling; photographs taken in 1946 and 1947 still show the completely bunted baby with only the face exposed. This physical restriction of the baby is traditionally continued for nine months or longer. It is not accompanied by social isolation. Babies are kept where adults are congregated, and their little sisters and grandmothers act as nurses; they are talked to and their needs are attended to.

In many ways the infant apparently learns that only its physical movement is restricted, not its emotions. The Russian emphasis upon the child's inherent violence appears to preclude any belief among adults that its emotions could be curbed. The baby's one means of grasping the outside world is through its eyes, and it is significant that in all Russian speech and literature the eyes are stressed as the "mirrors of the soul." Russians greatly value "looking one in the eyes," for through the eyes, not through gestures or through words, a person's inmost feelings are shown. A person who does not look one in the eyes has something to conceal. A "look" also is regarded as being able to convey disapproval more shattering than physical punishment. Throughout life the eyes remain an organ which maintains strong and immediate contact with the outside world.

The baby's physical isolation within its bindings appears to be related to the kind of personal inviolability Russians maintain in adulthood. It is difficult for foreigners to appreciate the essential privacy accorded the individual in Russian folk life, for their pattern of "pouring out the soul," would be in most cultures a bid for intimacy, and their expressive proverb, "It is well even to die if there are plenty of people around," seems a vivid statement of dislike of isolation. These traits, however, coexist in Russia with a great allowance for a personal world which others do not, and need not, share. "Every man," they say, "has his own anger," and the greatest respect is given to one who has taken his own private vow—either in connection with a love affair or with a mission in life. Whatever an individual must do in order to carry out this personal vow, even if the acts would in other contexts be antisocial, is accepted. He must be true to himself; it is his *pravda.*

The Russian version of swaddling can also be profitably related to the traditional Russian attitude that strong feeling has positive value. Personal outbreaks, with or without intoxication, are traditionally ascribed to the merchant class and to peasants, but they were characteristic of all classes. Official pressure at present attempts to channel this strong feeling toward foreign enemies, but the uses of violence to the individual psyche seem to be stressed in traditional fashion in this modern propaganda.

Not only is violence in itself a means to attain order, but it is also relatively divorced from aggression against a particular enemy. In Czarist days "burning up the town," breaking all the mirrors, smashing the furniture on a psychic binge were not means of "getting even" or of avenging one's honor; they were "in general." Even the peasants characteristically fired the home of a landowner other than the one on whom they were dependent. This trait is prepared for in the first years of life by the relative impersonality of the swaddling. Even in the villages of Great Russia, moreover, there is constant use of wet nurses and *nyanyas*, older women who are engaged to care for the baby; there is consequently a much more diffuse relationship during the first year of life than in societies where the child's contact is more limited to that with its own mother. It is characteristic of Russia, also, that poems and folk songs with the theme of mother love are practically nonexistent. The Great Russian mother is not specifically a maternal figure; she is quite sure of her sex without having to produce children to prove that she is female—as the man also is sure of his sex.

The Polish version of swaddling is quite different from the Russian. The infant is regarded not as violent, but as exceedingly fragile. It will break in two without the support given by the bindings. Sometimes it is emphasized that it would be otherwise too fragile to be safely entrusted to its siblings as child nurses; sometimes that the swaddling straightens its bent and fragile legs. Swaddling is conceived as a first step in a long process of "hardening" a child. "Hardening" is valued in Poland, and since one is hardened by suffering, suffering is also valued. A man does not demean himself by retailing his hardships and the impositions put upon him. Whereas an Italian, for instance, will minimize his dissatisfactions and discouragements and respect himself the more for so doing, Poles characteristically tend to prove their own worth by their sufferings. A usual peasant greeting is a list of his most recent miseries, and Polish patriots have exalted Poland as "the crucified Christ of the Nations." From infancy the importance of "hardening" is stressed. In peasant villages it is good for a baby to cry without attention, for it strengthens the lungs; beating the child is good because it is hardening; and mothers will even deny that they punish children by depriving them of dessert and tidbits, because "food is for strengthening; it would be no punishment to deprive them of any food."

Another theme in Polish swaddling has reference to the great gulf fixed between clean and dirty parts of the body. The binding prevents the infant from putting its toes into its mouth—the feet are practically as shame-ridden as the genitals in Poland—or from touching its face with its fingers which may just before have touched its crotch or its toes. When the baby is unswaddled for changing or for bathing, the mother must prevent such shameless acts. Whereas the Russian baby is quite free during the occasional half-hour when it is unswaddled, the Polish baby must be only the more carefully watched and prevented. Polish decency is heavily associated with keeping apart the various zones of the body.

Although it was possible to sketch Russian infancy without describing details of nursing and toilet training, which are there warm and permissive, in Poland this is impossible. The high point of contrast is perhaps the weaning. In Russia supplementary food is given early; a very small swaddled baby has a rag filled with chewed bread tied around its neck; this is pushed down on its mouth as a "comforter" by anyone present. The baby is eating many foods long before it is weaned. In Poland, however, weaning is sudden. It is believed that a child will die if it is nursed beyond two St. John's Days of its life—or the day of some other saint—and therefore, when the child is on the average eighteen months old, the mother chooses a day for weaning. The child is not given an opportunity beforehand to accustom itself to eating solid food; the sudden transition is good because it is "hardening." It is further believed that a twice-weaned child will die and though many mothers relent because of the child's difficulties, it is necessarily with guilt.

Another contrast with Russia is a consequence of the strong feeling about the evil eye in Poland. Only the mother can touch the baby without running the danger of harming it; in the villages even the baby's aunts and cousins fall under this suspicion. Certainly no woman except the mother can feed the baby at the breast. During the spring and summer months the babies are left behind at home with three and four-year-olds since all older children go to help their parents in the fields. In house after house neglected children are crying and women incapacitated for the fields might advantageously care for them. But this is regarded as impossible.

The Polish child gets nothing from crying. He is hurried toward adulthood, and the steps which reach it are always ones which "harden" him; they are not pleasant in themselves. As a child he has tantrums, but the word for tantrums means literally "being struck," "deadlocked." He does not cry or throw himself about as the Jewish child in Poland does; he sits for hours with rigid body, his hands and his mouth clenched. He gets beaten but he takes it without outcry or unbending. He knows his mother will not attempt to appease him. His defense of his honor in his later life is the great approved means of unburdening himself of resentments and turning them into personal glory. There are many Polish proverbs which say idiomatically and with great affect: Defend your honor though you die. The long process of childhood "hardening" lies back of their insult contest and their spirited struggles in lost causes.

The swaddling of the Jewish baby, whether in Poland or the Ukraine, has characteristics of its own. The baby is swaddled on a soft pillow and in most areas the bindings are wrapped relatively loosely around the baby and his little featherbed. The mother sings to the baby as she swaddles it. The specific stress is upon warmth and comfort, and the incidental confinement of the baby's limbs is regarded with pity and commiseration. People say in describing swaddling, "Poor baby, he looks just like a little mummy," or "He lies there nice and warm, but, poor baby, he can't move." Swaddling is also good, especially for boys, because it insures straight legs. There is no suggestion that it is the beginning of a process of "hardening" or that it is necessary because the baby is inherently violent. Rather, it is the baby's first experience of the warmth of life in his own home—a warmth which at three or four he will contrast with the lack of comfort, the hard benches, the long hours of immobility and the beatings at the *cheder*, the elementary Jewish school where he is taught Hebrew. In strongest contrast to the experience of the Gentile child, swaddling is part of the child's induction into the closest kind of physical intimacy; within the family the mother will expect to know every physical detail of her children's lives and treats any attempts at privacy as a lack of love and gratitude. The pillowed warmth of his swaddling period apparently becomes a prototype of what home represents, an image which he will have plenty of opportunity to contrast with the world outside, the world of the *goy*.

It is profitable also to relate Jewish swaddling to another pattern of Eastern European Jewish life: its particular version of complementary interpersonal relations. I am using "complementary" in a technical sense as a designation of those interpersonal relations where the response of a person or group to its vis-a-vis is in terms of an opposite or different behavior from that of the original actors. Such paired actions as dominance-submission, nurturance-dependence, and command-obedience are complementary responses. The Jewish complementary system might be called nurturance-deference. Nurturance is the good deed—*mitzvah*—of all parents, elders, wealthy, wise and learned men toward the children, the younger generation, the poor, and the still unschooled. In interpersonal relations these latter respond to the former with deference, "respect," but not with *mitzvah*. One never is rewarded in a coin of the same currency by one's vis-a-vis, either concurrently with the act or in the future. Parents provide for all their children's needs, but the obligation of the child to the parent does not include support of his aged parents when he is grown, and the saying is: "Better to beg one's bread from door to door than to be dependent on one's son." The aged parent feels this dependence to be humiliating, and this is in strongest contrast to the non-Jews of Poland, for instance, among whom parents can publicly humiliate their children by complaining of nonsupport. Among the Jews, a child's obligation to his parents is discharged by acting toward his own children, when he is grown, as his parents acted toward him. His aged parents are cared for, not by a son in his role as a son, but in his role as a wealthy man, contributing to the poor. Such impersonal benefactions are not humiliating to either party.

The swaddling situation is easily drawn into this Jewish system of complementary relations. The personnel involved in swaddling is necessarily complementary; it includes the binder and the bound. The bound will never reciprocate by binding the binder, and the Jewish binder conceives herself as performing a necessary act of nurturance out of which she expects the child to experience primarily warmth and comfort; she is rather sorry for the accompanying confinement but she regards random mobility as a sign of the baby's being uncomfortable. She is not, like the Polish mother, "hardening" the baby or preventing indecencies, or like the Russian mother, taking precautions against its destroying itself. She is starting the baby in a way of life where there is a lack of guilt and aggression in being the active partner in all complementary relationships and security in being the passive partner.

In swaddling situations the communication which is then established between mother and infant is continued in similar terms after swaddling is discontinued. Diapering of older babies is understood by Jewish mothers as contributing to the baby's comfort, and by Polish non-Jewish mothers as preventing indecencies by insuring that the baby's hands do not come in successive contact with "good" and "bad" parts of his body. In Rumania, where all informants from cities and towns stressed first, last and always that swaddling was necessary to prevent masturbation, the infant's hands, when he is too old to be swaddled, are tied to his crib, incased in clumsy mittens and immobilized by special clothing. His nurse or mother spies on him and punishes any slip.

The different kinds of swaddling communication which are localized in Central and Eastern Europe make it clear that the practice has been revamped to conform to the values of the several cultural groups. As in any culture area study, investigation discloses the patterning of behavior in each culture. The diversities do not confuse the picture; they enrich it. And the detailed study of this one widespread trait, like any other, throws light on the individuality of each cultural group, while at the same time it emphasizes the kinship among them.

Discussion

MARGARET MEAD. I speak as a member of the research group on the basis of whose work Dr. Benedict has presented these results so that I find it most appropriate to comment on some of the theoretical implications of our experience.

We have attained considerable clarification, we think, of the problems of how to think about the way in which the child's experiences within a culture mould his character. Students of culture who have used child development as a way of describing the culture have recognized for a good many years that the Freudian model of pregenital development, especially in the systematic form relevant to cross-cultural comparisons elaborated by Erikson (Erikson, 1937, 1946; Homburger, 1937), provided us with many clues, when we applied it to an exploration of which zones and which modes at which stages were frustrated, indulged or ignored in the course of child rearing. If a model of development like the Gesell-Ilg (Mead, 1947) was used, it also provided us with important clues to understanding differences in character formation in different societies. We also found that it was not possible to make any simple cross-cultural statement, such as that permissive toilet training or long nursing or sudden weaning would have a single predictable effect in later character. Whenever any single practice was followed cross-culturally, a confusing number of contradictions were found, such as would have been the result if, to the material which Dr. Benedict presented today, we had applied a simple hypothesis that swaddling could be relied upon to produce a single set of effects. It has become increasingly clear over the last few years that it was necessary to include a variable, loosely described as "tone of voice" or the quality of the interpersonal relationship within which a given zone or stage of locomotion or mode of behavior was indulged and frustrated (Mead, 1946; Fries, 1947). I think that the research of the last six months makes it possible to proceed one step further and to advance the hypothesis that within the general framework of biological development the significant specific character-forming elements will be those through which the adults attempt to communicate with the child. This communication need not be an articulate type of "character education" but it is affect-laden and emphatic. Early toilet training followed out for some casual reason of household arrangement will have a very different, and possibly almost negligible effect, while toilet training at an age when it might be conceived to be less traumatic and more appropriate to the developmental stage may, because of the weight given it by the adult, have far stronger effects. By examining the system of communication between parent and child against a theoretical ground plan provided by the body itself, the pattern of family relationships in the society, and the tempo and rhythm of biological growth, we can distinguish those nuances of emphasis—as in the Russian communication to the baby that it is dangerously strong, the Polish that its body must be thought of as divided into good and bad parts, the Jewish that close warmth will defend it against a harsh outer world, and the Rumanian urban and town baby that touching its own body is a pleasure which his parents are concerned to deny him—all within the practice of swaddling during the early months of life.

There is also an aspect of our procedure in this research on contemporary cultures which has, I believe, important implications for psychiatry. In each of our areal groups members of the cultures being studied have worked as collaborators, and the research workers have been forced to take the trouble to phrase their results in ways which were not only scientifically satisfactory but were also culturally acceptable to those who were at one time both subjects and collaborators. This is a step which we felt no need to take as long as we described preliterate people who were unable to read our results. The psychiatrist has not yet faced the problem of how to phrase a diagnosis so that it is acceptable to the patient. Medical secrecy has made it possible to talk about the patient in ways which the patient would find intolerable. Furthermore, it has retarded any revision of a psychiatric vocabulary developed in the day when the early research workers, appalled by what they found in the unconscious, embodied their own repulsion in the vocabulary. The persistence of these practices can only serve to impede public acceptance of psychiatric concepts, and it should be possible to look forward to a time when psychiatric concepts will have such a degree of gentleness and inclusiveness that the patient could sit in at a staff conference where his own case was described.

REFERENCES

Erikson, E. H. Figure 1, a chart of modes and zones. In Leonard Carmichael (ed.), *Manual of child psychology;* p. 670. New York: John Wiley and Sons, Inc., 1946.

Homburger, E. *Configurations in Play-Clinical Notes.* Psychoan. Quart., 1937, **6**, 139–214.

Mead, Margaret. On the implications for anthropology of the Gesell-Ilg approach to maturation, *Amer. Anthropol.*, 1947, **49**, 69–77.

Mead, Margaret. Research on primitive children. In Leonard Carmichael (ed.), *Manual of psychology.* New York: John Wiley & Sons, Inc., 1946.

Fries, Margaret. Diagnosing the child's adjustment through age level tests, *Psychoan. Rev.*, 1947, **34**, 1–31.

4-2

Child Rearing in the Lebanon

EDWIN TERRY PROTHRO

Swaddling or no swaddling, there can be no doubt that *some* child rearing practices must affect the child, otherwise how can one account for the marked differences between the behavior of children in different societies!

Lebanon, a small country, is quite varied in respect to ethnic groups. It encompasses in its small geography a great cultural diversity, and hence is an almost ideal area for research in child development.

Prothro's monograph, of which only a small part can be reproduced here, illustrates some of the modern methods of studying the effects of child rearing.

Since there is general agreement that the family is the keystone of Arab society, it may seem strange that Arab scholars have neglected this area. There are several explanations for this neglect. Among Arabs, as among Western scholars, the study of man lagged behind the study of stars, stones, and states. Family life seemed less important than the study of tangible external phenomena. Moreover, the Arabs developed an antipathy for discussing events in the home. For many, the mention of one's wife or female children was considered an impropriety. Family life

Reprinted from *Child Rearing in the Lebanon*, Cambridge, Mass.: Harvard University Press, 1961, by permission of the author and publisher.

was women's business, and few women had the training and leisure to examine such matters. Finally, in a reasonably stable, tradition-oriented culture, matters of child rearing did not seem open to question. They were simply the natural way that human beings behaved when confronted with the natural event of childbirth. Where no problem was perceived, no analysis or study was called for.

Scholarly interest in Lebanese family and village life is almost entirely a twentieth-century event. This interest has been produced by the general growth of social science in the West, and the reflection of this growth in the work of native scholars whose intellectual orientation is toward the West. As early as 1910, a work appeared on Lebanese customs relating to birth and infancy, written in French by an Arab (Chemali, 1910). Since that time, many sociologists and anthropologists have treated questions of Lebanese family life. Several detailed studies of Lebanese villages have appeared (Touma, 1958; Ayoub, 1955; Williams, 1958) and several psychological studies have been carried out on Lebanese children (Dennis, 1957a, 1957b, 1960). In none of these studies, however, has there been an attempt to gather detailed data on child rearing in the urban center, Beirut, or in the Beqaa Valley area, which is so similar to other parts of the Middle East. Neither has there been careful attention given to child rearing in Armenian communities. If it is true in Lebanon as elsewhere in the Middle East that "on n'a d'existence que par sa famille et pour sa famille" (Weulersse, 1946, p. 216), such studies are as much to be desired by the student of Lebanon and the Middle East as by the student of child psychology.

SOME QUESTIONS TO BE EXPLORED

From what has been said about the current status of studies of child rearing, and of studies of Lebanese people and society, it can be seen that the field is "white unto the harvest." The first task confronting the psychologist who wishes to serve as harvester is the selection of an area or areas of concentration. No one person can hope to do an adequate job over the whole field. A few questions have therefore been posed as guides in the delineation of the area of investigation.

These studies will seek information of use to behavioral scientists in attempting to answer three broad questions, or groups of questions.

I. Are there relationships among elements of maternal or child behavior which are found in non-Western as well as in Western culture? More specifically, are there correlations among those behavior variables which hold among Lebanese Arabs and Armenians as well as among Americans? We know that certain relations hold among Americans. Do they hold among Lebanese? American children, for example, are more likely to have weaning problems if weaned indecisively than if weaned decisively. Is this a general characteristic of children, perhaps related to universal principles of maturation and learning, or is this a finding produced by the peculiar customs of American society? If a relationship such as this one holds in quite different cultures, it gains considerably in significance, even though it does not thereby achieve complete universality. And if such a relationship does not hold among Middle Easterners, we can then begin to look for those cultural elements which have produced it in Americans. The careful study of American mothers carried out by Sears, et al. (1957) yielded many insights into the interrelations of elements of the behavior of mothers and children, and these insights can be checked by obtaining similar information on Lebanese mothers and children. By varying culture, we can apply the "agreement and difference" methods of J. S. Mill to the problems of child psychology.

II. Are there general norms of child rearing which can be related meaningfully to general norms of child (or even of adult) behavior, so that we can speak of a harmony between cultural norms of child rearing and modal personality types? Some cultural anthropologists have argued that cultures form more or less integrated wholes, configurations, or Gestalts. They believe that if a culture is to maintain its integration, it must produce—at least in part by the training of its children—personalities which fit into that culture. Thus child rearing is important as a mechanism for the transmission of culture, and its study is important as a clue to the configuration or Gestalt which characterizes the culture. Now this point of view is far too intricate to be tested by empirical data from a single culture. Nevertheless, such data must be the elements out of which generalizations of this sort arise. Consequently, it is important in any study of child rearing to see whether there are any wide patterns in the behavior of mothers, whether these are related to general patterns in the behavior of their children, and whether any or all of these seem to be reflected in the general behavior of members of the culture. In short, are differences in child rearing the key to differences among peoples?

Anthropologists interested in this question have often followed Freudian lines and have focused on the emotional, affective life of the child. Questions of strictness and permissiveness in weaning, toilet training, sex, and dependency have received much attention. Recently, however, a group of psychologists has focused attention on another motive—the need for achievement (McClelland et al., 1953). They found that individuals differed widely in their need for achievement when the achievement was for its own sake and not for external reward. They also found some relationship between mother-child relations and the amount of achievement need in the children. Some ethnic groups, such as Jews, were found to have far more achievement need than other groups, and it was suggested that ethnic differences in child rearing might account for this. The hypothesis then emerged that differences in rate of economic development in different countries might be attributable not to natural resources, available investment capital, or technological skills alone, but also to the amount of achievement motive found in the inhabitants of that nation.

Lebanon has a rapidly developing economy. Is this development related to the needs and motives of the people? Moreover, it has been observed that Christians play a greater role in this development than do Moslems (Meyer, 1959, p. 43). Can we relate this difference to differences in child rearing? Here again we are confronted with important questions regarding patterns of child rearing and possible personality types of adults, and again we find Lebanon suited to the pursuit of the problem.

III. Do the group differences which have been found in American studies of parent-child behavior exist in a dissimilar society? In the United States, there are certain kinds of responses which are characteristic of the middle class, and others characteristic of the lower class. In the same way, there are identifiable differences between urban and rural parents. Yet there are few differences which can be linked to ethnic origin. Are these results peculiar to mid-century America, or are there class, ethnic, and urban-rural differences which transcend the time and place of the original studies? Are there class differences in child rearing in a culture where family ties include both rich and poor? Are there urban-rural differences where many city people maintain strong emotional ties with their village of origin? Do ethnic differences emerge where there is a mosaic of distinct groups rather than a melting pot blending all together? These questions, too, lend themselves to study in Lebanon because of the peculiar structure of that society.

THE RESEARCH TECHNIQUE

This investigation is deliberately modeled after selected American studies so that results obtained can be compared with those previously obtained in the United States. The most important of these models was the interviewing schedule evolved by the staff of the Laboratory of Human Development of the Graduate School of Education of Harvard University, for use with mothers in two Boston suburbs. This schedule, with the results obtained from its use, was described in detail in *Patterns of Child Rearing* (Sears et al., 1957). It covered a wide range of maternal behavior and explored most of the facets of child rearing considered important by contemporary psychologists.

The second model for the child-rearing study was a series of experiments on the achievement motive (Atkinson, 1958). In this series, techniques for the measurement of the strength of the achievement need in children were set forth (Aronson, 1958; Knapp, 1958), and the child-rearing attitudes of mothers were related to the amount of achievement need in their children (Winterbottom, 1958). It was therefore possible to use these guides in the examination of this important motive in Lebanon.

The third model in the child-rearing study was test situations which psychologists had found to be useful in giving insight into similarities and differences of cultures. One of these, the Draw-a-Man Test (Good-enough, 1926) had been used in the Middle East (Dennis, 1957a), and the other, known as the Uses Test, had been evolved in an attempt to compare Middle Eastern children and adults with persons elsewhere (Dennis, 1957b).

From these three models were evolved interviewing schedules in Arabic and Armenian for use with Lebanese mothers, and a series of tests for use with their children. These formed the research instruments of the study.

PROCEDURE

Communities

The communities, or "primary social units" (Whiting et al., 1953, p. 47), were selected after considering the various geographical, demographic, and related factors. It was decided to draw some of the subjects from the large, comparatively modern and cosmopolitan, coastal city of Beirut and some from the Beqaa Valley, where modernization was less advanced and where the culture was more similar to that of other Middle Eastern countries. The next decision was to draw subjects from three sects: Sunni Moslem, Greek Orthodox Christian, and Gregorian Christian. Members of the first two sects are Arabs; the Gregorians are Armenians. The Sunnis are the largest Moslem group in Lebanon and in the Middle East; the Gregorians are the largest Armenian group in Lebanon and in the Middle East; the Greek Orthodox are the second largest Christian group in Lebanon and the largest in the Middle East.

In order to minimize problems of "minority status" and possibilities of cultural assimilation, an effort was made to choose communities where religion of the subjects was that of the majority in that locality. In Beirut, the Greek Orthodox subjects were drawn largely from the northwestern part of the city where the Christians are a clear majority. This area is also the most "Western" part of the city, for it is the site of the American University and of the embassies of the United States, Britain, and France. The Armenian subjects were drawn largely from the "Armenian quarter" known as Zoukak el Blatt. The Sunnis were drawn almost entirely from the Moslem area known as "the Basta." At the time that this selection was first made in 1958, the demarcation of the Basta was fairly clear, for it was surrounded by barbed wire and largely cut off from the Christian quarters of the city.

In the Beqaa Valley, the Sunnis were drawn from Baalbek, the largest Moslem town in the valley, the Orthodox from Zahle, the largest Christian town in the valley, and the Gregorians from Anjar, the only Armenian village in the valley. All of these localities are in the central plain and no two are more than twenty-five miles apart. Fairly large communities, rather than small villages, were selected in order to make it possible to find a sizable number of mothers in each who met our selection criteria.

Interviewers

Six young women served as interviewers. Three were married, and two of these had children of their own. All were Lebanese, all spoke English and Arabic fluently, and all held at least the Bachelor of Arts degree or its equivalent. One held a Master of Arts from an American university, and one a *licence* from a French university. Five of the six had had previous experience in interviewing.

Of the six interviewers, four were natives and residents of the community where the interviews were conducted. The interviewer for Anjar lived in a town eight or nine miles away, but had been for several years a teacher in Anjar's village school. All five of these interviewers were of the same religious sect as that of the mothers being interviewed.

It was not possible to find a native of the Basta quarter of Beirut who was sufficiently trained to conduct the interviews there. The Baalbek interviewer, however, was of a family which had its winter home in that part of Beirut. Thus she knew the area well and conducted most of the interviews there. As the study drew toward its close, however, it became clear that she could not complete the Beirut Sunni sample without help. A graduate student in psychology, from a nearby part of the city, was therefore assigned to complete that group of interviews. This student, a Christian, knew the area and its people, though she was not of them. With that exception, however, all interviewers were members of the community where they conducted their interviews.

Interviews and Tests

There were two parts to the child-rearing study: an interview with the mother and a session with the child.* The interview with the mother was a modification of the Harvard interview (Sears et al., 1957), which

*Editor's note: all subjects were five years of age.

was evolved in two months of preliminary investigation in Lebanon. One item on the Harvard schedule pertained to television and was deleted. Another asked about sex play among children, and about behavior in the bathroom which showed sex interests. This group of items was deleted, and in its place we asked whether the child had any idea about where babies came from, and where he had acquired such information. Many other items were modified to make them more suited to the culture.

Questions were also asked about many items which had not been of concern to the Massachusetts investigators. Swaddling was discussed, as was thumb-sucking. The mother's idea of a "good child," and her hopes for his future were also explored. A series of questions was asked regarding the mother's demands and expectations in areas relating to the child's independence. In choosing these questions, we used all of those which had been found in America to be related significantly to the need for achievement (Winterbottom, 1958, pp. 468–469).

After each interview with a mother, the investigators filled out a sheet on "socio-economic status evaluation." This sheet called for information about the home: type of construction, number and size of rooms, bathroom facilities, existence of running water, kind and amount of furniture and appliances, presence or absence of reading matter, general appearance of the house, number of servants, and general location in the town or city. This information, together with information on occupation, was used to make a general classification of the class status of the family.

The interview with the child was largely a series of psychological tests. The first of these was our version of the Uses Test (Dennis, 1957b). For each of a series of familiar items, the child was asked "What is it for?" Thus, the first asked "What is a mouth for?" and the last item asked "What is money for?" The version employed was adapted to make it simple enough for the young children being interviewed. It was found in the pre-testing period to be one of the few tests simple enough to elicit culturally relevant information from young children.

Next the child was given a pencil and a piece of paper and asked to draw a man. Standard procedures for this test were followed (Goodenough, 1926). This test has been widely used as a crude measure of functioning intelligence, although it is by no means a measure of innate, "culture-free" intellectual ability (Dennis, 1957a).

The third task the child was asked to do was to reproduce on a sheet of paper some or all of a group of scribbles shown to him. This test, called a test of graphic expression, has been used as a measure of achievement need (Aronson, 1958). The test itself is quite simple. On each of two cards there is a standard set of designs or "scribbles." Each card is shown to the child for a few seconds and he is asked to reproduce the scribbles after the card is taken away. It was found that young children could execute this task if given ample opportunity (approximately ten seconds) to look at each card.

The child's color preference was next ascertained. It has been proposed (Knapp, 1958) that preference for certain colors over others is related to achievement need. The child was therefore presented with a box of twelve colored pencils. Each pencil had a lead and corresponding external color different from every other pencil. In the box there were two red, one orange, one yellow, two green, two blue, one white, one black, and two brown pencils. Where there were two pencils of one hue, one was light and one more saturated in color. When the child took the graphic expression test, he was allowed to work with the colored pencils, using any or all that he wished. After that test he was told that he could keep the pencils, and was asked which color or colors he preferred.

After the testing, the interviewer added any comments or observations she could make on the child's behavior or on his interaction with his mother. The interview with the mother was from one and a half to two hours in length on the average, and the interview with the child usually lasted about an hour.

SUMMARIES OF FINDINGS

Warmth

It was possible to assign reliable ratings to each interview with respect to the amount of warmth, demonstrative love, or affectionate attention the mother expressed for the five-year-old child. These ratings, together with the mothers' replies to several of the specific questions, were interpreted as pointing to a marked reduction in indulgence between the first and fifth year of the child's life. Boys were treated with greater warmth than were girls. Ordinal position in the family was not related to warmth, nor was the use of servants in child care related. Orthodox mothers were more often rated as high in warmth, and Gregorian mothers were least often rated as high. City mothers were more often rated high than were mothers in the valley. In the city, middle-class mothers were more often rated high than were lower-class mothers. City-valley and class differences were interpreted as pointing to greater warmth of the more "modern" mothers. Although the most modern and most traditional mothers had resembled each other in greater than average indulgence for infants, they were dissimilar in warmth given the five-year-old.

Anal Character

In discussing the indulgence of the infant with respect to feeding, and the sharp break he experienced in general nurture and affection at the time of weaning, it was pointed out that this and other training produced a child greatly concerned with food, well suited to living in a culture where food played an important part in all social events. Is there any similar harmony between the culture and toilet-training practices?

To the knowledge of the writer, no student of Lebanon has ever commented on any exceptional fastidiousness of Lebanese children on matters relating to evacuation. Nor is the culture noted for its emphasis on toilet facilities. Fields, vacant lots, and courtyards are often used as outdoor toilets. Virtually any wall serves as a urinal. Apparently the early efforts at toilet training do not produce any inhibitory effect on the child. Nor is this early effort an aspect of a general cultural stress on proper toilets and toilet behavior. Bathrooms are rare among peasants.

It has sometimes been asserted that strict toilet training is a part of a general cultural emphasis on cleanliness, so that the child toilet-trained early and severely will become misophobic, i.e., obsessed with cleanliness. The mother is indeed concerned with tidiness in the children, but the evidence is that the child himself has not absorbed the emphasis on cleanliness. Moreover, the taking of baths is by no means as much a part of the traditional culture as it is in Europe and America. Bathrooms occur only in middle-class homes. The culture gives no evidence of obsessive fear of dirt.

Freudians have suggested that strict and early toilet training may produce an "anal character." Such a person is not only concerned with cleanliness. He also exhibits a miserly frugality, a petulant obstinacy, and a compulsiveness that expresses itself in "orderliness, tidiness, punctuality, meticulousness and propriety." To those who know Lebanon, or who have read studies of the Lebanese, this list is startling in its inappropriateness. Perhaps some evidence could be adduced for emphasis on tidiness and on propriety, but most observers have borne out the writer's impression that the Lebanese are generous within their means (in a socially-determined fashion), flexible to the point of inconsistency, and non-compulsive to the point of fatalism. "Anal character" would indeed be a poor way to describe the Lebanese modal personality.

Conscience

The relation between disciplinary technique used and the presence or absence of conscience is particularly important because disciplinary techniques were one of the chief correlates of conscience in the Harvard Study (Sears et al., 1957, p. 386). In America, too, they found that reasoning produced high conscience and physical punishment produced low conscience more often than would have been expected by chance.

To summarize, the Lebanese child was more likely to exhibit behavior considered to show a strong degree of conscience if he had a warm mother who used explanations and reasoning when he did wrong, who did not use a great deal of physical punishment, and who did not ignore his positive achievements. In this sense the Lebanese child was similar to the American child. Conscience was not a product of sex, class, sect, or place of residence.

The Changing Maternal Role

A study of child-rearing practices is a study of aspects of the role of the mother, so much of this report is a description of the maternal role. One aspect of it has not been treated elsewhere, however: how has the role changed in recent years? A brief exploration into this question was made by posing the following questions: "Now if we compare the method your mother used in rearing you, and the method you use in rearing X, how much do they resemble each other? (If different) Which method is better?"

It would appear that there has been considerable change in the past generation. The number of mothers giving each reply were: much alike, 12; generally similar, 165; different, 216; greatly different, 22; do not know, 46. For those mothers with an opinion, a majority thought their own practices differed from the practices of the previous generations. The mothers who thought things had changed were overwhelmingly in favor of the new technique. Only 35 preferred the older method, and 202 preferred their own way of bringing up children. The preference for current practices was found in all groups.

Because most of the Gregorian mothers were born during the turbulent twenties, a decade marked by great upheaval and hardship for Armenians of the Middle East, it is hardly surprising that they say that things have changed since their childhood. There were 117 Gregorian mothers who said their child-rearing practices were different from those of their own mothers, and 32 Gregorian mothers who said they were about the same.

The most traditional group of mothers also described themselves as transitional. Of 73 Sunni mothers in the valley who expressed an opinion, 51 said the present method was different. The more modern Beirut Orthodox group, on the other hand, said in most cases that child rearing was about the same today as when they were young. Of 75 with an opinion, only 18 said that they differed from their own mothers. These data indicate that changes must have taken place in recent years at a more noticeable rate among the more traditional mothers than among the more modern.

In what ways do mothers of today differ in their treatment of children from the mothers of twenty or thirty years ago? Although we did not ask for a list of these differences, many mothers cited one or two.

Those mothers who felt that the previous generation had done better usually mentioned some personal quality in which they felt inferior to their own mothers: patience, endurance, absence of "nervousness" or irritability. Those who felt that things were being handled better today usually adduced goals or aims of current practices: education, freedom for growth, and happiness and adjustment of the child.

If the comments of the mothers are a valid clue to the direction in which changes are leading, and the rate at which changes are taking place, then it would appear that the differences between "traditional" and "modern" mothers of Lebanon are decreasing. If this were the case, we could expect for the future a more homogeneous culture—with respect to these practices at least. In any event, it is important to note that the group we call most traditional sees itself as transitional, while the group we call modern sees itself as carrying on the practices of the last generation.

Child-Rearing Practices and Achievement

One of the basic tenets of modern psychology is that reinforcement of any behavior, by presenting appropriate stimuli (e.g., praise or affection) at the right moment, will make that behavior more likely to recur. In order to produce enterprise, striving, or an urge to achieve in children it would appear that the reinforcement of acts of achievement would be the soundest approach. As was pointed out earlier, American studies of children agree on the value of this approach. Do Lebanese mothers of high-achieving groups also stand out from their countrywomen in the way they make use of reward?

There were definite class and sectarian differences in the patterns of reinforcement. The lower-class mothers did nothing at all if the child ate well, or performed some task, while the middle class usually rewarded the child in some way. There were some mothers who were generally non-rewarding, and these occurred more often in the lower class, in the valley, and among the Moslems. With respect to systematic rewarding of good behavior, a majority of both Gregorian and Orthodox mothers said they did so, and a majority of the Sunni mothers said they did not. The Sunni mothers, on the other hand, described themselves more often than did other mothers as depending on threats—which threats they often failed to carry out. If the assumption that middle-class Beirut Christians are the "high achievers" among the groups we studied be granted, then our data confirm the American finding that the frequent use of rewards for accomplishing approved tasks characterizes the child-rearing practices of mothers in high-achieving groups.

American psychologists have also stressed maternal expectations of independence as a factor producing high achievement need. By "independence" they do not refer to reactions to dependency, but to the carrying of independent responsibility. The Beirut Orthodox mothers stand out with respect to this kind of independence, and particularly when it relates to competitive achievement. Moreover, the Orthodox groups in general emphasized discussion and reasoning more than did other mothers, and this is a type of discipline which places responsibility on the child. The Gregorians did not stand out from other groups with respect to early age of independence, but they did stand out with respect to the amount of personal responsibility they expected the child to assume in the home. Gregorian children were expected to behave well, even without reward. They were expected more than Arab children to carry out home tasks regularly and to look after their own cleanliness. Yet their mothers kept a close watch on them. These mothers seem to fit the paradoxical description emerging from American studies, of mothers dominant and intrusive but nevertheless demanding a kind of independent activity. In separate fashions both the Beirut Orthodox and the Gregorians seem to foster independence in their young children, thus confirming the hypothesis that such training characterizes groups of high achievers.

One American study described the fathers of high-achieving children as remote and non-interfering, and one American observer of Turkish economic life has even speculated (Bradburn, 1960) that the authoritarian control exercised by Moslem fathers may cause the low achievement motivation in that country. Our data throw serious doubt on the stereotype of the Moslem father as a strict, dominating disciplinarian, but apart from the issue is there merit in the hypothesis that the father is less likely among high-achieving groups than among low to be dominant and interfering? The information which our study provides on this issue applies to young children, and does not deal with the father's control of the adolescent or young adult.

The Gregorian fathers and the Beirut Orthodox fathers play a lesser role in the disciplining of the young child than do other Lebanese fathers in general, and particularly less than do the Sunni fathers in the valley. In the high-achieving groups, the father is a more remote figure than in other groups, in charge of decisions outside the home, but little concerned with controlling the daily activities of the young child. In Lebanon, as in America, lower paternal control is found in groups of higher achievement.

On the whole it may be concluded that those Lebanese groups which show outstanding achievement are characterized by mothers who reward successful accomplishment, who foster independence, and who predominate over the father in the control of the young child. Our data thus confirm the assertions of American investigators that there is a relation between child-rearing practices of a group and the level of achievement of that group.

TOWARD FUTURE RESEARCH

The insights which this investigation has provided into family life in Lebanon and into some of the patterns of child rearing and child behavior found there would appear to justify the belief that the research techniques of child psychology can be applied profitably to cross-cultural research. Not only have we learned something about Lebanese mothers and children, we have also learned much about mother and child behavior in general. This study is only a first step, however, and points to the need for more research with other groups. Only after the accumulation of far more data will we be able to make with any confidence the generalizations and predictions so sorely needed by those offering counsel on child care. In view of the certainty that counsel will be called for, and given, on a basis of the fragmentary knowledge now available, the demand for further research appears acute.

In calling for further cross-cultural research, recognition must be given also to the importance of initial analyses of behavior made in one culture. The studies of significant elements of child rearing in America provided the model for this investigation in Lebanon. In order to build up a general picture of behavior, it is first necessary to analyze the elements and dimensions of behavior, and to devise instruments for assessing such behavior. As such analyses move forward, additional cross-cultural studies become possible. These studies can in turn provide clues for further analysis. Through such an interplay between intensive analysis and extensive cross-validation may arise generalizations worthy of a science of behavior which attempts to embrace mankind.

REFERENCES

Aronson, E. The need for achievement as measured by graphic expression. In J. W. Atkinson (ed.), *Motives in fantasy, action, and society*, pp. 249–265. Princeton: D. Van Nostrand Co., Inc., 1958.

Atkinson, J. W. (ed.). *Motives in fantasy, action, and society.* Princeton: D. Van Nostrand, Co., Inc., 1958.

Ayoub, V. Political structure of a Middle East community. Unpublished Ph.D. thesis, Harvard University, 1955.

Bradburn, N. M. The managerial role in Turkey: a psychological study. Unpublished Ph.D. thesis, Harvard University, 1960.

Chemali, B. Naissance et premier age au Liban, *Anthropos.*, 1910, **5**, 734–737.

Dennis, W. Performance of Near Eastern children on the Draw-a-Man Test, *Child Devel.*, 1957(a), **28**, 427–430.

Dennis, W. Uses of common objects as indicators of cultural orientations, *J. Abnorm. Soc. Psychol.*, 1957(b), **55**, 21–28.

Dennis, W. Arab and United States children: Some psychological comparisons, *Trans. N.Y. Acad. Sci.*, 1960, **22**, pp. 589–605.

Goodenough, Florence L. *Measurement of intelligence by drawings.* Chicago: World Book Co., 1926.

Knapp, R. H. An achievement and aesthetic preference. In J. W. Atkinson (ed.), *Motives in fantasy, action, and society,* pp. 367–372. Princeton: D. Van Nostrand, Co., Inc., 1958.

McClelland, D. C., J. W. Atkinson, R. A. Clark, and E. L. Lowell. *The achievement motive.* New York: Appleton-Century-Crofts, 1953.

Meyer, A. J. *Middle Eastern capitalism: nine essays.* Cambridge, Mass.: Harvard University Press, 1959.

Sears, R. R., Eleanor E. Maccoby, and H. Levin. *Patterns of child rearing.* New York: Harper and Row, Publishers, 1957.

Touma, T. *Un Village de montagne au Liban: Hadeth el Jabbe.* Paris: Mouton, 1958.

Weulersse, J. *Paysans de Syrie et du Proche-Orient.* Second Ed. Paris: Gallimard, 1946.

Whiting, J. W. M. et al. *Field manual for the cross-cultural study of child rearing.* New York: Social Science Research Council, 1953.

Williams, H. H. Some aspects of culture and personality in a Lebanese Maronite village. Unpublished Ph.D. dissertation, University of Pennsylvania, 1958.

Winterbottom, Marian R. The relation of need for achievement to learning experiences in independence and mastery. In J. W. Atkinson (ed.), *Motives in fantasy, action, and society,* pp. 453–478. Princeton: D. Van Nostrand Co., 1958.

4-3

Kibbutz Adolescents

ALBERT I. RABIN

The Kibbutzim, Israeli semi-communal communities, have drawn much attention because they are unique in their organization of social and family life. Much research has been devoted to the psychological effects upon a child of being reared in a Kibbutz. Rabin's studies are among the best on this topic. It is now well-established that Jewish children who grow up in a Kibbutz differ in several respects from the Jewish children of Tel Aviv or Haifa, or Brooklyn.

Two previous reports were concerned with comparisons, along several psychological dimensions, between different age groups of Kibbutz-reared children and their non-Kibbutz age peers. Our findings were that the infants in the Kibbutz setting lagged in some aspects of their development behind the non-Kibbutz infants (Rabin, 1958). However, no residues of this slower start in ego development were noted in the comparative study of Kibbutz ten-year-olds. As a matter of fact, it appeared that these children gave indications of more mature ego development than the ten-year-olds raised outside the Kibbutz structure (Rabin, 1957). In a subsequent report (Rabin, 1959) we have also pointed out that the Kibbutz educational setting does not affect adversely

Reprinted from *Amer. J. Orthopsychiat.*, 1961, 31, 493–504, by permission of the author and the American Orthopsychiatric Association, Inc.

the children's attitudes to parents and family. On the contrary, the findings were that more Kibbutz children had positive attitudes to the family than did the non-Kibbutz controls.

In the present paper we will follow the pattern or design of the previous studies and report its application to groups of adolescents. We shall attempt a comparison between Kibbutz and non-Kibbutz adolescents with respect to a number of pertinent and relevant psychological variables. More specifically, we shall address ourselves to two broad questions: (1) Are the gains in ego strength observed in Kibbutz preadolescents, as measured by our instruments, also maintained during the adolescent period? (2) What are the qualitative differences in terms of fantasy content and inferred dynamics, in social and family interrelationships, in heterosexual attitudes, and in goals and future perspectives, between the Kibbutz-reared adolescents and a similar age group reared in the conventional family setting?

PROCEDURE

In order to try to obtain some answers to these questions two groups of 30 Kibbutz and 25 non-Kibbutz 17-year-olds, roughly equally divided between the sexes, were examined by means of several projective methods. The numbers of individual tests vary somewhat owing to absence or incompleteness of record in a few instances. The Kibbutz children were drawn from four different Kibbutzim, while the non-Kibbutz adolescents resided in three different villages of the conventional variety. All subjects were at the time pupils of the twelfth grade in their local high schools. Group and individual examinations took place in special rooms designated for the purpose in the school buildings through the cooperation of the local authorities.

The projective techniques employed were: the Rorschach, the Sentence Completion Test, which was an expanded version of the one used with the younger children (Rabin, 1959), and the Thematic Apperception Test. The Rorschach was administered individually, while the other two tests were administered in small groups.

Limitations of space would prevent us from reporting the complete results obtained with each of these methods. Consequently, only the data which are more or less directly relevant to the questions which we have raised in the introductory section of this paper will be summarized and discussed. Thus, only some of the Rorschach indices will be included; the response patterns to several of the 52 incomplete sentences will be noted; and the analysis of TAT cards 1, 2, and 4 only will be reported.

RESULTS

The Rorschach Test

The first aspect of this test that may be noted is that of productivity, i.e., the number of responses given to the inkblots. The median number of responses for both groups combined is 31, which is consistent with the usual expectancies. However, the Kibbutz group tended to be more productive. Sixty-two per cent of the Kibbutz subjects exceeded the 31 responses, whereas only 36 per cent of the non-Kibbutz group did so. This difference approaches statistical significance ($p = .08$).

Another interesting index is "first reaction time." This refers to the time it takes the subject to give a response after the card is presented. On eight of the ten cards the average first reaction time of the Kibbutz adolescents is shorter than that of the parallel group. In the remaining two (V and VII) the difference is negligible in the opposite direction. Moreover, the differences on the first card are very significant statistically ($p = .02$). Generally, the Kibbutz group reacts more immediately, with less anxiety and inhibition (see Table 1).

TABLE 1

Median Reaction Times for the Rorschach Cards (in Seconds)

	I*	II	III	IV	V	VI	VII	VIII	IX	X
Kibbutz	6.8	12.2	11.0	17.0	8.0	20.0	16.5	11.5	22.5	24.8
Non-Kibbutz	19.0	17.0	11.5	19.5	7.0	37.5	16.0	12.0	32.5	30.0

*Difference significant at the .02 level.

Since Rorschach's movement response is assumed to reflect fantasied behavior, we followed the notion that some need is expressed in its content. As our guide in classifying the movement content, we followed Kaplan (1954), who employed Murray's classification of needs. We utilized only 8 of the 17 categories listed by Kaplan, for only a negligible number of responses was classifiable in the omitted categories (see Table 2).

The most outstanding difference between the groups is with respect to the "play" category. Nearly 70 per cent of the Kibbutz subjects have it in their records as compared with 32 of the non-Kibbutz adolescents. The other differences are less striking. The non-Kibbutz group includes more

TABLE 2

Themes Represented in the Movement (M) Responses
of the Rorschach Records of the Two Groups

	No. of Subjects		Percentages	
Needs	K	NK	K	NK
Play*	18	7	69	32
Achievement	7	7	27	32
Aggression	4	7	15	32
Activity	12	8	46	36
Cognizance	6	5	23	23
Affiliation	5	4	19	18
Orality	5	1	19	4.5
Passivity	17	14	65	63

*$Chi^2 = 6.80$; $p < .005$.

individuals who utilize the "aggression" category, and the Kibbutz young-sters have more in the "orality" category. However, the differences on these and the remaining categories are not statistically significant.

Lastly, an index of what may be called "general adjustment" was applied to the Rorschach data. Davidson (1950) reported a series of "signs of adjustment," based on the Rorschach, which she found useful in her investigations. We employed 15 of the suggested 17 signs; these are least susceptible to subjective judgment. The range of adjustment signs for individuals in both groups is from 4 to 11. The average number of signs for the Kibbutz and non-Kibbutz group is 8.04 and 7.95 respectively. This is obviously a small and insignificant difference. The two groups do not differ on this index of adjustment or lack of emotional disturbance.

If we are to summarize the Rorschach data only provisionally, for we shall return to integrate them with the findings on the other tests, we can state as follows: The Kibbutz adolescents are more productive and less inhibited in responding to the test; they emphasize more play and orality themes and less aggression themes in the content; their over-all adjustment, i.e., freedom from signs of deviation, is similar to that of the control group.

The Sentence Completion Test

This instrument is an extended version of the test used with the ten-year-olds (Rabin, 1959) and was obtained from the same source (Sacks and Levy, 1950). The 52 sentence roots deal with 13 different areas—four sentences for each area. Consonant with our present limited

TABLE 3

Global Combined Ratings of Family, Father and Mother Areas
Based on Sentence Completion Responses

	Family		Father		Mother	
	Positive	Other	Positive	Other	Positive	Other
Kibbutz	11	17	12	16	14	14
Non-Kibbutz	11	13	9	15	8	17

objectives, we shall deal with 6 of these areas in the present context—Family, Father, Mother, Sexuality, Goals, and Future.

The first three areas were assessed globally, i.e., the four completions in each area were rated as a whole in terms of the positiveness of the attitude which they express. The results are based on a combination of the ratings of two judges working independently. See Table 3.

No significant differences between the groups with respect to the incidence of "positiveness" of attitude to Family, Father and Mother were reflected in the findings. Very similar proportions of both groups indicate positive attitudes in these three areas. In terms of relative numbers, more of the Kibbutz adolescents indicate positive attitudes to Father and Mother. This is a mere trend, however, since the differences are not great enough to be statistically significant.

In the area of sexuality one sentence (out of four) yielded significant group differences. The sentence reads: "If I had sexual relations. . . ." The vast majority of the Kibbutz group rejected this idea unequivocally. "I would discontinue" or "Not at my age" were some of the most frequent responses. About one third of the non-Kibbutz adolescents also rejected the idea. However, most of them indicated positive or neutral attitudes to this hypothetical possibility. The differences between the groups were highly significant statistically ($p < .01$).

In the areas of Future and Goals, three of the eight items yielded interesting and significant differences between the two groups (see Table 4). On item 16 ("I would be definitely satisfied if . . .") more of the Kibbutz group are concerned about being "a good pupil" or "if I am permitted to continue to study," whereas the non-Kibbutz subjects stated more specific goals—"if I were able to be a pilot," for example. On item 29 ("My secret ambition in life . . .") more of the non-Kibbutz group indicate specific personal ambitions ("to be a successful farmer" or "to be a literary man"), while the Kibbutz adolescents are less specific ("continue living in the Kibbutz") or deny having such ambitions altogether. In a similar vein, responses to item 30 ("One of these days, I . . .") show that the non-Kibbutz group have by-and-large long-range goals, being a teach-

TABLE 4

Significant Differences between the Groups
on Future and Goals Items

	Item 16			Item 29			Item 30	
	K	NK		K	NK		K	NK
School	14	3	Personal ambition	7	14	Long range	12	18
Other	10	12	Other	18	9	Trivial	12	4
Chi²	5.40			5.42			4.98	
p	<.02			<.02			<.03	

er, building a farm, etc. Half of the Kibbutz group have similar long-range perspectives, but the other half mention short-range or trivial aims, such as going home, climbing a mountain, and so on. Even the greater interest of the Kibbutz group in school (see item 16) is not an expression of any specific long-range goals; there is no implication of preparation for something specific.

A provisional summary of this material would seem to indicate that the Kibbutz adolescents do not differ from the controls with respect to intrafamilial attitudes, that they reject sexual relations at an early age, and that their goals and future aspirations are less specific (and probably less mature) than those of their non-Kibbutz peers.

The Thematic Apperception Test

Since we did not have a direct measure of the intellectual level of our subjects, we attempted to use the TAT stories, written by them, as a basis for such an evaluation. A psychologist, a native Israeli, was asked to classify the complete records without knowing to which group they belonged. On the basis of facility in the use of language and style, he placed the subjects in three categories—below average, average and superior. The Kibbutz adolescents were nearly evenly divided between the superior and the other two categories combined. Only 5 of the non-Kibbutz group placed in the superior category, while the remaining 18 subjects were put in the average or below average categories (see Table 5).

Productivity on the three TAT cards, in terms of word count per story, was also calculated. The Kibbutz group was on the average consistently more productive, on each card, than the control group. These findings are quite consistent with the higher Rorschach productivity referred to above.

TABLE 5

Productivity and Estimates of Intelligence
Based on TAT Stories

	Productivity (Mdn. No. Words)			Intelligence (Subjects Rated)		
	Card 1	Card 2	Card 4	Low	Average	Superior
Kibbutz	94	102	90	2	11	10
Non-Kibbutz	84	60	55	3	15	5

In comparing the content of the TAT stories, i.e., the fantasy material of the subjects, we attempted to employ some of the categories reported in normative studies with adults (Eron, 1950; Rosenzweig and Fleming, 1949). However, with our small samples of adolescents this was only partially applicable. The final classifications that evolved were most meaningful for, and were dictated by, the material itself.

CARD 1. Murray (1943) describes this picture as that of "a young boy [who] is contemplating a violin which rests on a table in front of him."

The stories in response to this card were analyzed in terms of the dominant characteristics of the hero and in terms of the major themes contained in them. The vast majority of the Kibbutz adolescents describe the hero as "a child who has a violin" or "a pupil." Most of the non-Kibbutz adolescents see either a talented child or one who is in the process of obtaining a violin despite economic limitations. Most of the non-Kibbutz themes involve ambition and high motivation for achievement whereas the Kibbutz themes involve more ambivalence about practice and rejection of the musical endeavor altogether. They view playing the violin as not self-motivated, but as a result of pressure exercised by parents and teachers. Examples of the two types of stories are as follows:

> *Kibbutz–Card 1.* Violin pupil–not anxious about playing. His parents are pressing him to do this. He is before some boring exercise. He has no desire to play. He is thinking of his friends' games outside.
> At the end the pupil will begin to understand the music and love playing, although it will not become the center of his life.

> *Non-Kibbutz–Card 1.* In this picture I see a lad with ambitions and stirrings to be a great violinist. The lad played and played, then got tired and put the violin on top of the music notes. He is looking at the music notes and the violin and is thinking that these two things are his entire life. Slowly he sinks into thought and pictures his future for himself.

CARD 2. "Country scene: in the foreground is a young woman with books in her hand; in the background a man is working in the fields and an older woman is looking on."

The "latent stimulus demand" of this picture, according to Henry (1956) involves the "eliciting feelings toward interpersonal interaction, toward parent-child relations, and toward heterosexual relations"; also "the contrast between the new and the old . . . girl going off for education as opposed to the farm folk." Wittenborn (1949) states that it "may reveal yearnings for independence, ambition . . . the conflict of the socially mobile student."

The relationship between the characters portrayed in the stories and the themes involved were of paramount interest in the present context. More than 90 per cent of the non-Kibbutz adolescents see blood relationships between two or all characters; most often they are seen as members of one family. This is in contrast with the Kibbutz group; 64 per cent of this group see such a relationship. The themes are even more revealing of the differences between the groups. (See Table 6.)

About two thirds (68%) of the non-Kibbutz stories on this card have conflict as their major theme—conflict with parents or internal conflict over leaving the farm and going to the city, over changing occupational status, etc. Less than one fifth of the Kibbutz adolescents project this theme in their stories. They merely describe the pastoral scene, but comparatively rarely see conflict between "new and old," farm and city, and so on.

Examples of contrasting stories follow:

Kibbutz—Card 2. Illana loved to go out every evening to the field and landscape to be acquainted with and know and feel the country, the soil, the fatherland. As usual, also, this evening Illana went up among the rocks on the side of the village, at twilight, looking as she is absorbed in thoughts and ideas. The village is peaceful and quiet; tractors and machines do not disturb the peace and quiet. And the thoughts flow and well up in her—thoughts of love and tenderness—love for the entire world, nature, quiet and peace, for the plowing horse and the man who is walking in his footsteps and for his and everybody's landscape—for all the country folk in the world. How beautiful!

Non-Kibbutz—Card 2. The family is a simple agricultural family and have no connection with education. Agriculture is the magic of the life of the family. But the daughter is dissatisfied with such a narrow outlook. She leaves agriculture and turns to the city. The father terminated his relations with her and does not speak to her. He is tired of all the persuasion which was useless, but mother has not yet given up—looking at father and daughter. She is hoping for an answer from both of them. The daughter does not give in, leaves home and goes away.

TABLE 6

Characters and Major Themes in TAT Stories*

Descriptions of Hero and Major Themes in Response to Card 1

Hero	K	NK	Theme	K	NK
Talented child	4	26	Ambition-motivation	17	65
Tries to obtain violin	17	56	Ambivalence-rejection	61	17
Has violin	78	17	Other (incl. damage to violin)	22	17

Identification of Characters and Major Themes in Response to Card 2

Characters	K	NK	Theme	K	NK
Members of one family	55	68	Conflict over aspirations	18	64
Not related	36	9	Economic frustration	5	9
Two related	9	23	Description	68	18
			Love triangle	9	9

Characters and Major Themes in Response to Card 4

Characters	K	NK	Themes	K	NK
Husband and wife	35	47	Infidelity	10	52
Two in love	35	47	Aggression	50	11
Fellow and girl	30	5	Rejection of love	30	5
			Miscellaneous	10	32

Action	K	NK
Prevent separation	35	74
Prevent aggression	40	21
Embrace	25	5

*Percentage of groups.

CARD 4. "A woman is clutching the shoulders of a man whose face and body are averted as if he were trying to pull away from her." There is also a hazy image of another woman in the background, not mentioned in the standard description in the manual.

Henry (1956) feels that "attitudes toward heterosexual relationship are . . . of course the central issue of importance in this card." "Refusal to see the sexual implications of this picture," according to Wittenborn (1949) "is particularly indicative of a type of immature psychosexual adjustment common in young men."

Some differences in the nature of the main characters portrayed may be noted. Ninety-five per cent of the non-Kibbutz stories specify the relationship of the man and the woman as "married" or "in love." This is true to a lesser degree in the Kibbutz stories, of which 70 per cent delineate this relationship, but 30 per cent mention no close relationship—just "a fellow and a girl." (See Table 6—part 3.)

The differences become more salient when we turn our attention to the themes involved. More than half of the non-Kibbutz stories deal with the issue of infidelity. This theme is represented to a negligible extent (10%) in the Kibbutz stories. Instead, half of the stories have aggression as their major theme, and 30 per cent deal with outright rejection of love and heterosexuality (usually male rejecting female). The "action" involved parallels closely the themes described. The following are two kinds of stories which correspond to the contrasts just discussed:

> *Kibbutz—Card 4.* He is a worker and she is on a farm. They met after a short time that they have not seen each other. They met accidentally at the entrance to one of the movies which described prostitution. They went into the movie with their thoughts. After it is over the woman asks the man to kiss her; she sees it in the film, she sees the couples kissing each other. But, something else entirely different than joy pierces the mind of the worker. He is not joyous, but analyzes and thinks about the problems in the movie—the problem of unemployed workers who find their satisfaction by going to houses of ill fame. Can that go on for long? No—I will change the situation. I will unite the workers around the condition of their brethren. I will bring out workers full of consciousness among them.

> *Non-Kibbutz—Card 4.* In this picture the man is seen between the arms of his wife and the arms of sin. We see him at home.
>
> When he got married he considered himself happy and loved his wife very much; but, accidentally, on one occasion he met a dancer in a cheap club; she attracted him and he fell in love with her. His wife, who felt that something was the matter, tried to stop him and he, still in love with her, did not know what to decide. In the picture we see them together; he wants to go and meet the other one and his wife is holding him back. We

see the prostitute in the background, the one he fell in love with, as if she is coming out of his head. It is impossible to know what he will decide.

The major trends elicited from the TAT stories may now be pulled together. The Kibbutz adolescents appear to be less achievement oriented and less motivated. Their stories tend to be less populated with family-related characters. They also see less conflict between the parents and their children. There is also a greater tendency to reject heterosexuality altogether and also not to see infidelity as a possible problem.

Perhaps important sex differences may also be gleaned from these data. However, this will take us too far afield. We shall address ourselves to this issue on another occasion.

COMMENT

We shall attempt to gather the several strands of evidence and try to integrate them, see their dynamic interrelationship and relate the differences that have evolved from the material to known differences in the experiences of the two groups of adolescents.

We may note, especially from the Rorschach data, that there are no marked differences between the groups with respect to over-all "adjustment." There are a few deviant and tense individuals in both groups, but the over-all picture with respect to what we might infer as ego development is essentially the same for the vast majorities of Kibbutz and non-Kibbutz adolescents. The evidence points to a greater degree of spontaneity (productivity on Rorschach and TAT; first reaction times) in the Kibbutz group. Moreover, there is also some justification for rating the Kibbutz adolescents somewhat higher on the continuum of intellectual development. The quality of the Kibbutz *Mosad* (high school) and the relatively sophisticated intellectual atmosphere in most Kibbutzim must be in part responsible for this fact.

Two problems which are part of the *Sturm und Drang* period of adolescence have been stressed by various authors (Ausubel, 1954; Spiro, 1958)—heterosexuality and independence or emancipation. With respect to the first problem, we note a fairly consistent puritanical trend in the Kibbutz group. Whether it is immaturity or suppression is a question not easily settled. There are three sources of information that may be considered. In the first place there is some evidence of the lesser oedipal intensity in Kibbutz children (Rabin, 1958); also, that little emphasis on sexual segregation is placed in Kibbutz rearing—boys and girls sleep in the same rooms, take showers together, etc. Finally, with all that, there are fairly rigid rules involving adult disapproval and group ostracism with respect to sex play and premarital sexual intercourse. Thus, there is relatively little of the sexual curiosity noted in adolescents who are not brought up in the Kibbutz (Spiro, 1958); less of it is involved in the fantasy of the Kibbutz adolescents as noted in the TAT. Fewer Kibbutz adolescents deal with love and sex in their stories of card 4. The picture has less potency for them in this respect; thus, they include more themes of aggression and the role of the woman as the peacemaker. In most stories of Kibbutz adolescents in which heterosexuality is the major theme, rejection occurs, probably because of the cultural taboos.

Because of the relative independence of the children from their parents from the very beginning, in the Kibbutz setting, the issue of emancipation is not a crucial one. Thus, very few Kibbutz adolescents see the conflict between the generations, between agriculture and culture and education, which is noted by the majority of the non-Kibbutz respondents to card 2 of the TAT. This fact, perhaps, accounts for the tendency of the Kibbutz group to involve fewer parents and relations in their TAT stories. The parental figures are less fraught with conflict and less represented in fantasy. The relatively conscious attitudes to the parents as expressed in the Sentence Completion Test are, by and large, positive and not different from those of the control group.

In considering the data relative to goals and ambitions, two major differences between the two groups, emanating from differences in the family vis-à-vis the socioeconomic structure of the settlements, should be scrutinized. In the first place, as Eisenstadt (1950) has pointed out, there is a discontinuity of roles in the Kibbutz rearing process from childhood to adulthood. By that is meant that until the child becomes eligible for membership in the Kibbutz (following graduation from high school) he virtually has no economic responsibilities. Whatever work he does is primarily educational—not "work" in the economic sense of the adult. Thus, in this respect there is a discontinutiy in roles in the Kibbutz as contrasted with the continuity in the role of the village child who begins to participate in the adult economic workaday world at a relatively young age.

Another relevant difference is that Kibbutz education is geared toward perpetuation of the Kibbutz, i.e., membership in it. This means general personality attributes, but no specific occupational specialization or achievement in the broader "outside" world. This is in contrast with the village child who is reared in the tradition of "rugged individualism" and is preparing for a competitive society.

Bearing these points in mind, the contrast between the groups regarding ambitions, goals and future perspective becomes readily understood. The high emphasis on play in the Rorschach movement content, less emphasis on long-range goals and specific occupational aspirations reflected in the sentence completion material, and the low incidence of themes of ambition and motivation in response to TAT card 1, are all characteristics of the Kibbutz sample which converge on the same point. It involves a shortening of the future perspective as a personal outlook, for the longer future perspective is dependent primarily on the social context and structure, on the peer group, on the collectivity as a whole—the Kibbutz.

If we were to attempt the delineation of a composite picture of the Kibbutz adolescent, we would state that he has an adequately developed ego, is probably above average in intelligence, and is on fairly good terms with his parents, who, however, do not figure importantly in his fantasy, and with whom he is in relatively little conflict. He is relatively less concerned with heterosexuality than the non-Kibbutz age peers and consciously accepts the taboos of his society upon premarital or premature sex play and sexual intercourse. He is not very ambitious or achievement oriented in the world of occupations; in this respect his childhood is prolonged. His goals are not very specific, for they do not require precise definition by the society, and for the social structure, which he expects and is expected to perpetuate.

SUMMARY

In an attempt to tease out some of the psychological differences between Kibbutz-reared adolescents and adolescents (controls) reared in the conventional family and social setting, three projective techniques (Rorschach, Sentence Completion and TAT) were administered to two parallel groups of 17-year-olds. From the data presented, it was concluded that the Kibbutz adolescent is at least as well adjusted as his non-Kibbutz counterpart; there is some evidence that he is more spontaneous and at least as intelligent. The Kibbutz adolescent does not seem to differ from the control with respect to positiveness of attitude to parents; also, he tends to be less in conflict with them and to involve them less in his fantasy productions. He is more rigidly concerned with taboos on premarital sexuality, less self-motivated and less "ambitious" in our conventional sense.

The results were discussed and related to differences in life experience, stemming from differences in the social structure, to which the two groups have been exposed.

REFERENCES

Ausubel, D. P. *Theory and problems of adolescent development.* New York: Grune & Stratton, Inc., 1954.

Davidson, Helen H. A measure of adjustment obtained from the Rorschach protocol, *J. Proj. Tech.,* 1950, **14**, 31–38.

Eisenstadt, S. N. *Studies in social structure:* I. *Age groups and social structure —A Comparison of some aspects of socialization in the cooperative and communal settlements in Israel.* Jerusalem, April 1950.

Eron, L. D. A normative study of the Thematic Apperception Test, *Psychol. Monogr.*, 1950, **64,** No. 9.

Henry, W. E. *The analysis of fantasy.* New York: John Wiley and Sons, Inc., 1956

Kaplan, B. A. *A study of Rorschach responses in four cultures.* Papers of the Peabody Museum, 1954, **42,** 2, 3–44.

Murray, H. A. *Thematic apperception test manual.* Cambridge, Mass.: Harvard University Press, 1943.

Rabin, A. I. Personality maturity of Kibbutz (Israeli collective settlement) and non-Kibbutz children as reflected in Rorschach findings, *J. Proj. Tech.*, 1957, **21,** 148–153.

Rabin, A. I. Infants and children under conditions of "intermittent" mothering in the Kibbutz, *Amer. J. Orthopsychiat.*, 1958, **28,** 577–586.

Rabin, A. I. Some psychosexual differences between Kibbutz and non-Kibbutz Israeli boys, *J. Proj. Tech.*, 1958, **22,** 328–332.

Rabin, A. I. Attitudes of Kibbutz children to family and parents, *Amer. J. Orthopsychiat.*, 1959, **29,** 172–179.

Rosenzweig, S. and Edith Fleming. Apperceptive norms for the thematic apperception test II. An empirical investigation, *J. Pers.*, 1949, **17,** 483–503.

Sacks, J. M. and S. Levy. The sentence completion test. In L. E. Abt and L. Bellak (eds.), *Projective psychology,* pp. 357–402. New York: Alfred A. Knopf, 1950.

Spiro, M. E. *Children of the Kibbutz.* Cambridge, Mass.: Harvard University Press, 1958.

Wittenborn, J. R. Some thematic apperception test norms and a note on the use of the test cards in guidance of college students, *J. Clin. Psychol.*, 1949, **5,** 157–161.

4-4

A Cross-Cultural Survey of Some Sex Differences in Socialization

HERBERT BARRY, III
MARGARET K. BACON
IRVIN L. CHILD

The Human Relations Files, located at Yale University, are the world's largest repository of organized and codified anthropological data. Using these files, the authors of the following selection attempted to find whether there is a world-wide difference in the child care given to boys and girls. It appears that some differences in the training and treatment of boys and girls are well-nigh universal. The question remains as to whether this is due to a ubiquitous tradition, established early in man's history, or whether it is due to the strength of men and the child-bearing of women.

In our society, certain differences may be observed between the typical personality characteristics of the two sexes. These sex differences in personality are generally believed to result in part from differences in the way boys and girls are reared. To the extent that personality differ-

Reprinted from *J. Abnorm. Soc. Psychol.*, 1957, **55**, 327–332, by permission of the authors and the American Psychological Association.

ences between the sexes are thus of cultural rather than biological origin, they seem potentially susceptible to change. But how readily susceptible to change? In the differential rearing of the sexes does our society make an arbitrary imposition on an infinitely plastic biological base, or is this cultural imposition found uniformly in all societies as an adjustment to the real biological differences between the sexes? This paper reports one attempt to deal with this problem.

DATA AND PROCEDURES

The data used were ethnographic reports, available in the anthropological literature, about socialization practices of various cultures. One hundred and ten cultures, mostly nonliterate, were studied. They were selected primarily in terms of the existence of adequate ethnographic reports of socialization practices and secondarily so as to obtain a wide and reasonably balanced geographical distribution. Various aspects of socialization of infants and children were rated on a 7-point scale by two judges (Mrs. Bacon and Mr. Barry). Where the ethnographic reports permitted, separate ratings were made for the socialization of boys and girls. Each rating was indicated as either confident or doubtful; with still greater uncertainty, or with complete lack of evidence, the particular rating was of course not made at all. We shall restrict the report of sex difference ratings to cases in which both judges made a confident rating. Also omitted is the one instance where the two judges reported a sex difference in opposite directions, as it demonstrates only unreliability of judgment. The number of cultures that meet these criteria is much smaller than the total of 110; for the several variables to be considered, the number varies from 31 to 84.

The aspects of socialization on which ratings were made included:

1. Several criteria of attention and indulgence toward infants.

2. Strength of socialization from age 4 or 5 years until shortly before puberty, with respect to five systems of behavior; strength of socialization was defined as the combination of positive pressure (rewards for the behavior) plus negative pressure (punishments for lack of the behavior). The variables were:

(*a*) Responsibility or dutifulness training. (The data were such that training in the performance of chores in the productive or domestic economy was necessarily the principal source of information here; however, training in the performance of other duties was also taken into account when information was available.)

(*b*) Nurturance training, i.e., training the child to be nurturant or helpful toward younger siblings and other dependent people.

(*c*) Obedience training.

(*d*) Self-reliance training.

(*e*) Achievement training, i.e., training the child to orient his behavior toward standards of excellence in performance, and to seek to achieve as excellent a performance as possible.

Where the term "no sex difference" is used here, it may mean any of three things: (*a*) the judge found separate evidence about the training of boys and girls on this particular variable, and judged it to be identical; (*b*) the judge found a difference between the training of boys and girls, but not great enough for the sexes to be rated a whole point apart on a 7-point scale; (*c*) the judge found evidence only about the training of "children" on this variable, the ethnographer not reporting separately about boys and girls.

SEX DIFFERENCES IN SOCIALIZATION

On the various aspects of attention and indulgence toward infants, the judges almost always agreed in finding no sex difference. Out of 96 cultures for which the ratings included the infancy period, 88 (92%) were rated with no sex difference by either judge for any of those variables. This result is consistent with the point sometimes made by anthropologists that "baby" generally is a single status undifferentiated by sex, even though "boy" and "girl" are distinct statuses.

On the variables of childhood socialization, on the other hand, a rating of no sex difference by both judges was much less common. This finding of no sex difference varied in frequency from 10% of the cultures for the achievement variable up to 62% of the cultures for the obedience variable, as shown in the last column of Table 1. Where a sex difference is reported, by either one or both judges, the difference tends strongly to be in a particular direction, as shown in the earlier columns of the same table. *Pressure toward nurturance, obedience, and responsibility is most often stronger for girls, whereas pressure toward achievement and self-reliance is most often stronger for boys.*

For nurturance and for self-reliance, all the sex differences are in the same direction. For achievement there is only one exception to the usual direction of difference, and for obedience only two; but for responsibility there are nine. What do these exceptions mean? We have reexamined all these cases. In most of them, only one judge had rated the sexes as differently treated (sometimes one judge, sometimes the other), and in the majority of these cases both judges were now inclined to agree that there was no convincing evidence of a real difference. There were exceptions, however, especially in cases where a more formal or systematic training of boys seemed to imply greater pressure on them toward

TABLE 1

Ratings of Cultures for Sex Differences on Five Variables of
Childhood Socialization Pressure

Variable	Number of Cultures	Both Judges Agree in Rating the Variable Higher in		One Judge Rates No Difference, One Rates the Variable Higher in		Percentage of Cultures with Evidence of Sex Difference in Direction of		
		Girls	Boys	Girls	Boys	Girls	Boys	Neither
Nurturance	33	17	0	10	0	82	0	18
Obedience	69	6	0	18	2	35	3	62
Responsibility	84	25	2	26	7	61	11	28
Achievement	31	0	17	1	10	3	87	10
Self-reliance	82	0	64	0	6	0	85	15

responsibility. The most convincing cases were the Masai and Swazi, where both judges had originally agreed in rating responsibility pressures greater in boys than in girls. In comparing the five aspects of socialization we may conclude that responsibility shows by far the strongest evidence of real variation in the direction of sex difference, and obedience much the most frequently shows evidence of no sex difference at all.

In subsequent discussion we shall be assuming that the obtained sex differences in the socialization ratings reflect true sex differences in the cultural practices. We should consider here two other possible sources of these rated differences.

1. The ethnographers could have been biased in favor of seeing the same pattern of sex differences as in our culture. However, most anthropologists readily perceive and eagerly report novel and startling cultural features, so we may expect them to have reported unusual sex differences where they existed. The distinction between matrilineal and patrilineal, and between matrilocal and patrilocal cultures, given prominence in many ethnographic reports, shows an awareness of possible variations in the significance of sex differences from culture to culture.

2. The two judges could have expected to find in other cultures the sex roles which are familiar in our culture and inferred them from the material on the cultures. However, we have reported only confident ratings, and such a bias seems less likely here than for doubtful ratings. It might be argued, moreover, that bias has more opportunity in the cases ambiguous enough so that only one judge reported a sex difference, and less opportunity in the cases where the evidence is so clear that both judges agree. Yet in general, as may be seen in Table 1, the deviant cases are somewhat more frequent among the cultures where only one judge reported a sex difference.

The observed differences in the socialization of boys and girls are consistent with certain universal tendencies in the differentiation of adult sex role. *In the economic sphere, men are more frequently allotted tasks that involve leaving home and engaging in activities where a high level of skill yields important returns;* hunting is a prime example. Emphasis on training in self-reliance and achievement for boys would function as preparation for such an economic role. Women, on the other hand, are more frequently allotted tasks at or near home that minister most immediately to the needs of others (such as cooking and water carrying); these activities have a nurturant character, and in their pursuit a responsible carrying out of established routines is likely to be more important than the development of an especially high order of skill. Thus training in nurturance, responsibility, and, less clearly, obedience, may contribute to preparation for this economic role. These consistencies with adult role go beyond the economic sphere, of course. Participation in warfare, as a male prerogative, calls for self-reliance and a high order of skill where survival or death is the immediate issue. *The childbearing which is biologically assigned to women, and the child care which is socially assigned primarily to them, lead to nurturant behavior and often call for a more continuous responsibility than do the tasks carried out by men.* Most of these distinctions in adult role are not inevitable, but the biological differences between the sexes strongly predispose the distinction of role, if made, to be in a uniform direction. For data and interpretations supporting various arguments of this paragraph, see Mead (1949), Murdock (1937), and Scheinfeld (1944).

The relevant biological sex differences are conspicuous in adulthood but generally not in childhood. If each generation were left entirely to its own devices, therefore, without even an older generation to copy, sex differences in role would presumably be almost absent in childhood and would have to be developed after puberty at the expense of considerable relearning on the part of one or both sexes. Hence, a pattern of child training which foreshadows adult differences can serve the useful function of minimizing what Benedict (1938) termed "discontinuities in cultural conditioning."

The differences in socialization between the sexes in our society, then, are no arbitrary custom of our society, but a very widespread adaptation of culture to the biological substratum of human life.

VARIATIONS IN DEGREE OF
SEX DIFFERENTIATION

While demonstrating near-universal tendencies in direction of difference between the socialization of boys and girls, our data do not show perfect uniformity. A study of the variations in our data may allow us to see some of the conditions which are associated with, and perhaps give rise to, a greater or smaller degree of this difference. For this purpose, we classified cultures as having relatively large or small sex difference by two different methods, one more inclusive and the other more selective. In both methods the ratings were at first considered separately for each of the five variables. A sex difference rating was made only if both judges made a rating on this variable and at least one judge's rating was confident.

In the more inclusive method the ratings were dichotomized, separately for each variable, as close as possible to the median into those showing a large and those showing a small sex difference. Thus, for each society a large or a small sex difference was recorded for each of the five variables on which a sex difference rating was available. A society was given an over-all classification of large or small sex difference if it had a sex difference rating on at least three variables and if a majority of these ratings agreed in being large, or agreed in being small. This method permitted classification of a large number of cultures, but the grounds for classification were capricious in many cases, as a difference of only one point in the rating of a single variable might change the over-all classification of sex difference for a culture from large to small.

In the more selective method, we again began by dichotomizing each variable as close as possible to the median; but a society was now classified as having a large or small sex difference on the variable only if it was at least one step away from the scores immediately adjacent to the median. Thus only the more decisive ratings of sex difference were used. A culture was classified as having an over-all large or small sex difference only if it was given a sex difference rating which met this criterion on at least two variables, and only if all such ratings agreed in being large, or agreed in being small.

We then tested the relation of each of these dichotomies to 24 aspects of culture on which Murdock has categorized the customs of most of these societies and which seemed of possible significance for sex differentiation. The aspects of culture covered include type of economy, residence pattern, marriage and incest rules, political integration, and social organization. For each aspect of culture, we grouped Murdock's categories to make a dichotomous contrast (sometimes omitting certain categories as irrelevant to the contrast). In the case of some aspects of culture, two or more separate contrasts were made (e.g., under form of marriage we contrasted monogamy with polygyny, and also contrasted sororal with nonsororal polygyny). For each of 40 comparisons thus formed, we prepared a 2 x 2 frequency table to determine relation to each of our sex-difference dichotomies. A significant relation was found for six of these 40 aspects of culture with the more selective dichotomization of over-all sex difference. In four of these comparisons, the relation to the more inclusive dichotomization was also significant. These relationships are all given in Table 2, in the form of phi coefficients, along with the outcome of testing significance by the use of χ^2 or Fisher's exact test. In trying to interpret these findings, we have also considered the nonsignificant correlations with other variables, looking for consistency and inconsistency with the general implications of the significant findings. We have arrived at the following formulation of results:

1. Large sex difference in socialization is associated with an economy that places a high premium on the superior strength, and superior development of motor skills requiring strength, which characterize the male. Four of the correlations reported in Table 2 clearly point to this generalization: the correlations of large sex difference with the hunting of large animals, with grain rather than root crops, with the keeping of large rather than small domestic animals, and with nomadic rather than sedentary residence. The correlation with the unimportance of fishing may also be consistent with this generalization, but the argument is not clear. Other correlations consistent with the generalization, though not statistically significant, are with large game hunting rather than gathering, with the hunting of large game rather than small game, and with the general importance of all hunting and gathering.

2. Large sex difference in socialization appears to be correlated with customs that make for a large family group with high cooperative

TABLE 2

Culture Variables Correlated with Large Sex Difference
in Socialization, Separately for Two Types of Sample

Variables	More Selective Sample		More Inclusive Sample	
	ϕ	N	ϕ	N
Large animals are hunted	.48*	(34)	.28*	(72)
Grain rather than root crops are grown	.82†	(20)	.62†	(43)
Large or milking animals rather than small animals are kept	.65*	(19)	.43*	(35)
Fishing unimportant or absent	.42*	(31)	.19	(69)
Nomadic rather than sedentary residence	.61†	(34)	.15	(71)
Polygyny rather than monogamy‡	.51*	(28)	.38†	(64)

*$p < .05$.
†$p < .01$.
‡The variables have been so phrased that all correlations are positive. The phi coefficient is shown, and in parentheses, the number of cases on which the comparison was based. Significance level was determined by χ^2, or Fisher's exact test where applicable, using in all cases a two-tailed test.

interaction. The only statistically significant correlation relevant here is that with polygyny rather than monogamy. This generalization is, however, supported by several substantial correlations that fall only a little short of being statistically significant. One of these is a correlation with sororal rather than nonsororal polygyny; Murdock and Whiting (1951) have presented indirect evidence that co-wives generally show smoother cooperative interaction if they are sisters. Correlations are also found with the presence of either an extended or a polygynous family rather than the nuclear family only; with the presence of an extended family; and with the extreme contrast between maximal extension and no extension of the family. The generalization is also to some extent supported by small correlations with wide extension of incest taboos, if we may presume that an incest taboo makes for effective unthreatening cooperation within the extended family. The only possible exception to this generalization, among substantial correlations, is a near-significant correlation with an extended or polygynous family's occupying a cluster of dwellings rather than a single dwelling.

In seeking to understand this second generalization, we feel that the degree of social isolation of the nuclear family may perhaps be the crucial underlying variable. To the extent that the nuclear family must stand alone, the man must be prepared to take the woman's role when she is absent or incapacitated, and vice versa. Thus the sex differentiation cannot afford to be too great. But to the extent that the nuclear family is steadily interdependent with other nuclear families, the female role in the household economy can be temporarily taken over by another woman, or the male role by another man, so that sharp differentiation of sex role is no handicap.

The first generalization, which concerns the economy, cannot be viewed as dealing with material completely independent of the ratings of socialization. The training of children in their economic role was often an important part of the data used in rating socialization variables, and would naturally vary according to the general economy of the society. We would stress, however, that we were by no means using the identical data on the two sides of our comparison; we were on the one hand judging data on the socialization of children and on the other hand using Murdock's (1937) judgments on the economy of the adult culture. In the case of the second generalization, it seems to us that there was little opportunity for information on family and social structure to have influenced the judges in making the socialization ratings.

Both of these generalizations contribute to understanding the social background of the relatively small difference in socialization of boys and girls which we believe characterizes our society at the present time. Our mechanized economy is perhaps less dependent than any previous economy upon the superior average strength of the male. The nuclear family in our society is often so isolated that husband and wife must each be prepared at times to take over or help in the household tasks normally assigned to the other. It is also significant that the conditions favoring low sex differentiation appear to be more characteristic of the upper segments of our society, in socioeconomic and educational status, than of lower segments. This observation may be relevant to the tendency toward smaller sex differences in personality in higher status groups (cf. Terman and Miles, 1936).

The increase in our society of conditions favoring small sex difference has led some people to advocate a virtual elimination of sex differences in socialization. This course seems likely to be dysfunctional even in our society. Parsons, Bales et al. (1955) argue that a differentiation of role similar to the universal pattern of sex difference is an important and perhaps inevitable development in any social group, such as the nuclear family. If we add to their argument the point that biological differences between the sexes make most appropriate the usual division of those roles between the sexes, we have compelling reasons to expect that the decrease in differentiation of adult sex role will not continue to the vanishing point. In our training of children, there may now be less differentiation in sex role than characterizes adult life—so little, indeed, as to provide inadequate preparation for adulthood. This state of affairs is likely to be especially true of formal education, which is more subject to conscious influence by an ideology than is informal socialization at home. With child training being more oriented toward the male than the female role in adulthood, many of the adjustment problems of women in our society today may be partly traced to conflicts growing out of inadequate childhood preparation for their adult role. This argument is nicely supported in extreme form by Spiro's (1956) analysis of sex roles in an Israeli kibbutz. The ideology of the founders of the kibbutz included the objective of greatly reducing differences in sex role. But the economy of the kibbutz is a largely nonmechanized one in which the superior average strength of men is badly needed in many jobs. The result is that, despite the ideology and many attempts to implement it, women continue to be assigned primarily to traditional "women's work," and the incompatibility between upbringing or ideology and adult role is an important source of conflict for women.

NOTE ON REGIONAL DISTRIBUTION. There is marked variation among regions of the world in typical size of sex difference in socialization. In our sample, societies in North America and Africa tend to have large sex difference, and societies in Oceania to have small sex difference. Less confidently, because of the smaller number of cases, we can report a tendency toward small sex differences in Asia and South America as well. Since most of the variables with which we find the sex difference to be significantly correlated have a similar regional distribution, the question arises whether the correlations might better be ascribed to some quite different source having to do with large regional similarities, rather than to the functional dependence we have suggested. As a partial check, we have tried to determine whether the correlations we report in Table 2 tend also to be found strictly within regions. For each of the three regions for which we have sizable samples (North America, Africa, and Oceania) we have separately plotted 2 x 2 tables corresponding to each of the 6 relationships reported in Table 2. (We did this only for the more inclusive sample, since for the more selective sample the number of cases within a region would have been extremely small.) Out of the 18 correlations thus determined, 11 are positive and only 3 are negative (the other 4 being exactly zero). This result clearly suggests a general tendency for these correlations to hold true within regions as well as between regions, and may lend further support to our functional interpretation.

SUMMARY

A survey of certain aspects of socialization in 110 cultures shows that differentiation of the sexes is unimportant in infancy, but that in childhood there is, as in our society, a widespread pattern of greater pressure toward nurturance, obedience, and responsibility in girls, and toward self-reliance and achievement striving in boys. There are a few reversals of sex difference, and many instances of no detectable sex difference; these facts tend to confirm the cultural rather than directly biological nature of the differences. Cultures vary in the degree to which these differentiations are made; correlational analysis suggests some of the social conditions influencing these variations and helps in understanding why our society has relatively small sex differentiation.

REFERENCES

Benedict, Ruth. Continuities and discontinuities in cultural conditioning, *Psychiatry*, 1938, **1**, 161–167.

Mead, Margaret. *Male and female.* New York: William Morrow and Company, Inc. 1949.

Murdock, G. P. Comparative data on the division of labor by sex, *Social Forces,* 1937, **15**, 551–553.

Murdock, G. P., and J. W. M. Whiting. Cultural determination of parental attitudes: The relationship between the social structure, particularly family structure and parental behavior. In M. J. E. Senn (ed.), *Problems of infancy and childhood: Transactions of the Fourth Conference,* March 6–7, 1950, pp. 13–34. New York: Josiah Macy, Jr. Foundation, 1951.

Parsons, T., R. F. Bales, et al. *Family, socialization and interaction process.* New York: The Free Press, 1955.

Scheinfeld, A. *Women and men.* New York: Harcourt, Brace, and World, Inc., 1944.

Spiro, M. E. *Kibbutz: Venture in Utopia.* Cambridge: Harvard University Press, 1956.

Terman, L. M. and Catherine C. Miles. *Sex and personality.* New York: McGraw-Hill, Inc., 1936.

4-5

The Development in Children of the Idea of the Homeland and of Relations to Other Countries

JEAN PIAGET

Piaget has devoted most of his life to understanding the thinking of children, and he has been eminently successful. Piaget, who is Swiss, is undoubtedly the most brilliant child psychologist of this generation, and the most productive. The number of his books and other publications increases almost daily and hence any estimate of his output is soon outdated.

In recent years, several books attempting to summarize Piaget's work have appeared, but to accomplish such a task is probably impossible—perhaps even for Piaget himself.

We therefore have included only one selection from him for the purpose of giving the flavor of his contribution.

I

Any psychological and sociological study of tensions presupposes some acquaintance with certain findings of child psychology. We may begin by enquiring whether, in view of their particular method of

Reprinted from *Intern. Soc. Sci. J.*, 1951, 3, No. 3, 561–578, by permission of the author and UNESCO.

development, the cognitive and affective attitudes associated with loyalty to the homeland and initial contacts with other countries may not be at the root of subsequent international maladjustments. Even if this theory does not at first glance appear to be borne out by facts, we should next proceed to investigate why the child, as he grows, does not acquire enough objectiveness and understanding of others, or readiness to give and take, to withstand those influences for tension or maladjustment that are brought to bear upon him in adolescence or adult life.

These were the two points of view on which the survey described below was based. From the very outset, we were struck by the fact that, whilst children, in the initial stages of their development, did not appear to display any marked inclination towards nationalism, a slow and laborious process in developing a faculty for cognitive and affective integration was necessary before children attained an awareness of their own homeland and that of others; this faculty, being far more complex than would appear on first consideration, is accordingly precarious and liable to be upset by later impacts. For the purpose of studying social and international tensions in general, it is therefore worth giving close consideration to the development and nature of this faculty for integration, since subsequent disturbances will, in the last resort, depend on its strength—or its weakness.

Admittedly, our survey covered only Swiss or foreign children living in Geneva, and, in interpreting the data assembled, some allowance should be made for the influence of the children's adult environment. But, even if we make this allowance, and pending confirmation of our findings by surveys in other areas, we are faced with a paradox which, though it may be peculiar to a particular part of Europe, is none the less indicative.

This paradox may be summed up as follows: the feeling and the very idea of the homeland are by no means the first or even early elements in the child's make-up, but are a relatively late development in the normal child, who does not appear to be drawn inevitably towards patriotic sociocentricity. On the contrary, before he attains to a cognitive and affective awareness of his own country, the child must make a considerable effort towards "decentration" or broadening of his centres of interest (town, canton, etc.) and towards integration of his impressions (with surroundings other than his own), in the course of which he acquires an understanding of countries and points of view different from his own. The readiness with which the various forms of nationalist sociocentricity later emerge can only be accounted for by supposing, either that at some stage there emerge influences extraneous to the trends noticeable during the child's development (but then why are these influences accepted?), or else that the same obstacles that impede the process of "decentration" and integration (once the idea of homeland takes shape) crop up again at all levels and constitute the commonest cause of disturbances and tensions.

Our interpretation is based on the second hypothesis. The child begins with the assumption that the immediate attitudes arising out of his own special surroundings and activities are the only ones possible: this state of mind, which we shall term the unconscious egocentricity (both cognitive and affective) of the child is at first a stumbling-block both to the understanding of his own country and to the development of objective relationships with other countries. Furthermore, to overcome this egocentric attitude, it is necessary to train the faculty for cognitive and affective integration; this is a slow and laborious process, consisting mainly in efforts at "reciprocity," and at each new stage of the process, egocentricity re-emerges in new guises farther and farther removed from the child's initial centre of interest. These are the various forms of sociocentricity—a survival of the original egocentricity—and they are the cause of subsequent disturbances or tensions, any understanding of which must be based on an accurate analysis of the initial stages and of the elementary conflicts between egocentricity and understanding of others ("reciprocity").

We shall set forth under three separate headings the facts we have been able to assemble; in the first section we shall study the cognitive and affective development of the idea of homeland (between four and five and 12 years of age); in the second section we shall analyse the reactions of children towards countries other than their own, while the third section will deal with the problem of cognitive and affective understanding of others ("reciprocity").

Over 200 children between four and five and 14 and 15 years of age were questioned.

The child's gradual realization that he belongs to a particular country presupposes a parallel process of cognitive and affective development. This is not surprising, since any mental attitude is always a blend of cognitive and affective components (the cognitive functions determine the "pattern" of behaviour, whilst the affective functions provide its "dynamism," or driving force, which is responsible for the net result by which behaviour is judged). But there is more than interdependence between the two: the cognitive and affective aspects may be said to be parallel or isomorphous, since the very young find the intellectual concept of "reciprocity" as difficult to grasp as affective "reciprocity" when this passes beyond the range of their immediate practical experience.

Cognitive Aspect

We came across normal children who, until they were seven or eight years old, had none of the basic knowledge essential to understanding the idea of their country. One boy of seven was positive that Paris was in Switzerland because the people there spoke French, and that Berne was not in Switzerland. As a rule, very young children, up to five or six years of age, are apparently unaware that Geneva is in Switzerland. At the outset, then, children have only a simple notion of the territory in which they live (e.g., their home town), a notion comprising a more or less direct knowledge of certain characteristics (approximate size, main language spoken, etc.), but these ideas are mixed up with verbal notions such as "canton," "Switzerland," etc., which they can neither understand nor fit into a coherent picture. Among these verbal notions picked up from other children or adults, one finally becomes rooted in their minds at about five or six years of age: this is that "Geneva is in Switzerland." But the interesting point is whether this piece of acquired knowledge immediately affects their attitude.

Until they are about seven or eight, though children may assert that Geneva is part of Switzerland, they none the less think of the two as situated side by side. When asked to draw the relationship between Geneva and Switzerland by means of circles or closed figures, they are not able to show how the part is related to the whole, but merely give a drawing of juxtaposed units:

Arlette C. 7;6. (This is the abbreviation for 7 years 6 months). Have you heard of Switzerland? *Yes, it's a country.* Where is this country? *I don't know, but it's very big.* Is it near or a long way from here? *It's near, I think.* What is Geneva? *It's a town.* Where is Geneva? *In Switzerland* (the child draws Geneva and Switzerland as two circles side by side).

Mathilde B. 6;8. Have you heard of Switzerland? *Yes.* What is it? *A canton.* And what is Geneva? *A town.* Where is Geneva? *In Switzerland* (the child draws the two circles side by side). Are you Swiss? *No, I'm Genevese.*

Claude M. 6;9 What is Switzerland? *It's a country.* And Geneva? *A town.* Where is Geneva? *In Switzerland* (the child draws the two circles side by side but the circle for Geneva is smaller). *I'm drawing the circle for Geneva smaller because Geneva is smaller. Switzerland is very big.* Quite right, but where is Geneva? *In Switzerland.* Are you Swiss? *Yes.* And are you Genevese? *Oh no! I'm Swiss now.*

We see that these children think of Switzerland as comparable to Geneva itself but situated somewhere outside. Switzerland is of course "near" Geneva and "bigger." But they do not understand, either geographically or logically, that Geneva is in Switzerland. Geographically, it is alongside. Logically, there are Genevese, and not Swiss, or "Swiss now" (like

Claude) but no longer Genevese—which in both cases shows inability to understand how the part is included in the whole.

At a second stage (7–8 to 10–11 years of age), children grasp the idea that Geneva is enclosed spatially in Switzerland and draw their relationship not as two juxtaposed circles but as one circle enveloping the other. But the idea of this spatial enclosure is not yet matched by any idea that logical categories can be included one in another.

Whilst the category of Genevese is relatively concrete, that of Swiss is more remote and abstract: children, then, still cannot be Swiss and Genevese "at the same time."

Florence N. 7;3. What is Switzerland? *It's a country.* And Geneva? *It's a town.* Where is Geneva? *In Switzerland* (drawing correct). What nationality are you? *I'm from Vaud.* Where is the canton of Vaud? *In Switzerland, not far away* (the child is made to do another drawing showing Switzerland and the canton of Vaud. Result correct). Are you Swiss as well? *No.* How is that, since you've said that the canton of Vaud is in Switzerland? *You can't be two things at once, you have to choose; you can be a Vaudois like me, but not two things together.*

Pierre G. 9;0. (The child replied correctly to our first questions and did the drawing properly.) What is your nationality? *I'm Swiss.* How is that? *Because I live in Switzerland.* You're Genevese too? *No, I can't be.* Why not? *I'm Swiss now and can't be Genevese as well.* But if you are Swiss because you live in Switzerland, aren't you also Genevese because you live in Geneva? . . .

Jean-Claude B. 9;3. You've heard of Switzerland, I suppose? *Yes, it's a country.* And what is Geneva? *A town.* Where is this town? *In Switzerland* (the drawing was correct). What is your nationality? *I'm Bernese.* Are you Swiss? *Yes.* How is that? *Because Berne is in Switzerland.* So you can be Bernese and Swiss at the same time? *No, I can't.* Why not? *Because I'm already Bernese.*

The reader can see how these children hesitate: some, like Florence, deny the possibility of being "two things together," although they have just asserted and illustrated with their drawings that Geneva and Vaud are in Switzerland; others, influenced by statements heard repeatedly in their family or in school, hesitate to admit that they belong both to their home town (or canton) and to their country, and don't really believe they can: Jean-Claude, after first admitting it, hastens to add that it is impossible when he hears the words "at the same time"; and Pierre, who says he is Swiss and not Genevese, can only justify his statement by an argument that applies to Geneva as well ("because I live in Switzerland"). It may be said that their real loyalty is to the canton and not to their country. But we find the same response in children who are not living in or do not even know their canton, as well as in Genevese who know they belong there. We have met children who hardly know their home canton, yet stoutly declare they belong to it, out of attachment to their family. The fact is, that at this stage the homeland is still only an abstract notion: what counts is the town, or the family, etc., and the statements heard there; but the children do not yet synthesize these statements into any coherent system.

However, at 10–11 years of age, children enter upon a third stage, in the course of which their ideas are finally synthesized correctly.

Micheline P. 10;3. (The child replies correctly to the first questions and makes an accurate drawing.) What is your nationality? *I'm Swiss.* How is that? *Because my parents are Swiss.* Are you Genevese as well? *Naturally, because Geneva is in Switzerland.* And if I ask someone from Vaud if he is Swiss too? *Of course, the canton of Vaud is in Switzerland. People from Vaud are Swiss, just like us. Everyone living in Switzerland is Swiss and belongs to a canton too.*

Jean-Luc L. 11;1. (The child replied correctly to our first questions and makes no mistakes with the drawing.) What nationality are you? *I'm from St. Gallen.* How is that? *My father is from St. Gallen.* Are you Swiss too? *Yes, St. Gallen is in Switzerland, even though the people there talk German.* Then you are two things at once? *Yes, it's the same thing, since St. Gallen is in Switzerland. All people from Swiss cantons are Swiss. I'm from St. Gallen and still Swiss, and there are others who are Genevese or Bernese and still Swiss.*

It is only at this stage that the notion of country becomes a reality and takes on the idea of homeland in the child's mind. The problem is then to determine whether this development is merely the outcome of a cognitive correlation (inclusion of the part in the whole); whether the age at which these correlations are understood depends on affective factors; or whether both sets of factors evolve side by side.

Affective Aspect

Obviously, the child's emotions cannot be analysed in the course of a simple conversation of the kind used for ascertaining his logical make-up. Nevertheless, though no absolute significance can be ascribed to the actual content of his value judgments, and although, in particular, the importance of affective reactions he cannot put into words must not be overlooked, it is still possible, through comparison of replies made at different ages to quite commonplace questions (what country do you prefer, etc.) to draw some conclusions as to both the type of motivation and the real but unexpressed motives. It is a striking fact that the three stages briefly described above correspond, as regards affective evaluations, to three stages in a clearly marked process of "decentration," starting from motives essentially bound up with subjective or personal impressions (of the most fleeting or even accidental kind) and progressing towards acceptance of the values common to the group, first to the family group and then society as a whole.

During the first stage, the child who is asked for a value judgment does not even think of voicing any preference for Switzerland. He likes any country that appeals to his fancy at the moment and, if Switzerland is chosen, it is for some such reason. The following are the preferences actually expressed by three Swiss youngsters.

Evelyne M. 5;9. *I like Italy. It's a nicer place than Switzerland.* Why? *I was there these holidays. They have the loveliest cakes, not like in Switzerland, where there are things inside that make you cry. . . .*

Denise S. 6;0. *I like Switzerland because it has such pretty houses. I was in the mountains and they were all full of chalets. It's so pretty, and you can get milk there.*

Jacques G. 6;3. *I like Germany best because my mummy just got back from there to-night. It's ever so big and far away an' my mummy lives there.*

These childish affective reactions are analogous to the difficulty, usually experienced by children during this first stage, of integrating their country, canton or town in one logical concept. The question then arises whether it is because it does not yet represent an affective reality that the country is merely juxtaposed to the canton or town, instead of being included in it as part of a whole, or whether it is because the idea of inclusion cannot be logically grasped that the country does not yet arouse any real affective response. A third solution is obviously possible: as reality is centered around their own particular doings and immediate interests, children at stage I lack the requisite logical "decentration" to conceive of their town or canton as enclosed in a larger whole; nor have they a sufficient degree of affective "decentration" to grasp collective realities outside their narrow individual or inter-individual circle: at this level, their failure to grasp the idea of their country or homeland, either on the cognitive or on the affective plane, thus represents two interdependent and parallel aspects of the same spontaneous, unconscious egocentricity—the original obstacle to any integration of logical relationships and affective values.

Next we give the typical reactions at stage II to the same questions of preference or choice.

Denis K. 8;3. *I like Switzerland because I was born there.*
Pierrette F. 8;9. *I like Switzerland because it's my own country. My mummy and daddy are Swiss, so I think Switzerland's a nice place.*
Jacqueline M. 9;3 *I like Switzerland. It's the loveliest country for me. It's my own country.*

The reader senses immediately that, despite the persistence of the same ego-centric statements as at stage I, the motivation is quite different: family loyalties and traditions now begin to predominate over purely personal motives. The country becomes the *terra patria*, and, though there is still difficulty in arranging the town, canton and nation in an exact order, this is unimportant: their common and therefore undifferentiated affective appeal is based on family feeling. Thus we have here a close parallel between the inability to make logical distinctions (e.g., the idea of spatial or spatio-temporal inclusion is accepted, but not that of the inclusion of one class of ideas in another) and the inability to make affective distinctions, so that the different conceptions are reduced to a single emotional factor—that of family tradition. To be more precise, considerable progress has been made in both directions at once; we find the beginnings of logical "decentration," enabling the child to subordinate his territory (town or canton) to a larger unit in which it is enclosed; and, at the same time, the beginnings of affective "decentration," enabling him to subordinate his egocentric motives to collective values beyond his personal interests. But, in both cases, this process of "decentration" has only just begun and is restricted by the above-mentioned inability to differentiate (due to the remnants of egocentricity surviving in more extensive form in the new field of consciousness recently mastered).

At the third stage, finally, the motivations once again change and are more or less adjusted to certain collective ideals of the national community:

Juliette N. 10;3. *I like Switzerland because we never have any war here.*
Lucien O. 11;2. *I like Switzerland because it's a free country.*
Michelle G. 11;5. *I like Switzerland because it's the Red Cross country. In Switzerland, our neutrality makes us charitable.*

Neutrality, freedom, a country spared by war, the Red Cross, official charity, and so on: it sounds like a naïve summary of patriotic village speeches! But the very banality of these motivations is revealing: the most general collective ideals are those which make the strongest appeal to the child. Merely to state that he repeats what he has been told at school is not enough to explain why he repeats it and, more especially, why he understands it; he gives these reasons because, beyond his personal feelings and the motives of family loyalty, he is finally realizing that there exists a wider community with its own values distinct from those of the ego, the family, the town and visible or concrete realities. In brief, he is attaining to a scale of values culminating in relatively abstract virtues, and at the same time he is succeeding in integrating spatio-temporal and logical relationships into the invisible whole formed by the nation or the country: here, once more, we have parallelism between the processes of logical "decentration" or integration, on the one hand, and affective or ethical "decentration" or integration on the other.

II

We shall now give a brief account of this second part of our investigation, considered from the following two standpoints. First of all, we wished to determine whether ideas or feelings about other countries, or peoples of other nationalities (as far as the child was acquainted with any such) develop along the same lines as those referred to in the first section, or whether there is an appreciable difference between the two types of concepts. Our second, and more important aim, was to lead up to the analysis of "reciprocity" which is presented in the third section. For whether the child's ideas and affective reactions regarding his own and other countries develop along similar or different lines, it will be instructive to discover how, in the light of those attitudes, he arrives at that intellectual and ethical "reciprocity" which is, essentially, the faculty for social awareness and international understanding. Admittedly, the "decentration" we have just described, in contrast with the initial egocentricity during stages I-III may, in part, result from active relationships set up by the child, and in that case will necessarily lead to a certain degree of reciprocity: or, to be more precise, it will constitute an integral part of that reciprocity, of which it will be both the effect and the cause. But such "decentration" may also result, to some extent, from the pressure of the social environment: in that case, it will not automatically lead to an attitude of reciprocity, but is just as likely to transform egocentricity into sociocentricity as into real understanding. It is thus essential to make a further study—for the purpose of gathering preliminary data, and by using a process of interrogation similar to those previously adopted—of the child's reactions towards countries other than his own, before presenting him with the problem of reciprocity as such. But, in view of the similarity we have noted, from the intellectual standpoint, between the new reactions and those we have just described, it is pointless to examine separately the development of logical concepts, on the one hand, and the affective aspect of the replies, on the other hand, since the latter alone present any fresh interest.

The children at stage I are found to have the same intellectual difficulty about including the part in the whole in regard to other countries as in regard to their own, and the same judgments, based on subjective and fugitive considerations:

Arlette. 7;6 (Genevese). Do you know any other countries, foreign countries? *Yes, Lausanne.* Where is Lausanne? *In Geneva* (juxtaposed circles).

Pierre G. 9;0. (cf. Section I, stage II) Do you know any foreign countries? *Yes, France, Africa and America.* Do you know what is the capital of France? *Lyons, I think, I was there with daddy, it's in France* (juxtaposed circles, Lyons touching France *"because the city of Lyons is on the edge of France"*). And what are the people who live in Lyons? *Frenchmen.* Are they Lyonese too? *Yes. . . . no, they can't be. They can't have two nationalities at once.*

Monique C. 5;5. Are there any people who don't live in Geneva? *Yes, there are the people living in the Diablerets.* How do you know? *I was on holidays there.* Are there people who don't live either in Geneva or in the Diablerets? *Yes, there is Lausanne. My aunt lives there.* Is there any difference between the people of Geneva and other people? *Yes, the others are nicer.* Why? The people who don't live in Geneva are nicer than the people who do? *Oh yes, in the Diablerets I always get chocolate to eat.*

Bernard D. 6;3. Have you heard of any people who are not Swiss? *Yes, there are the people of the Valais* (Valais, as everyone knows, is one of the 22 Swiss cantons, and the child himself is a native of Valais). And have you heard of other countries too? Are there any differences between the countries? *Oh yes, there isn't a lake everywhere.* And are the people the same? *No, people don't all have the same voice and then they don't all wear the same pullovers. At Nax, I saw some lovely pullovers, all embroidered in front.*

Herbert S. 7;2. Are there any differences between the different countries you know and the different people living there? *Oh yes.* Can you give me an instance? *Well, the Americans are stupid. If I ask them where the rue du Mont Blanc is, they can't tell me.*

It is superfluous to stress the analogies between the reactions of this stage as recorded above and those described in the first section: their concurrence is the less surprising since most of these children are unaware of belonging to their own particular country (cf. Bernard once again).

The reactions of children at stage II, on the other hand, reveal that their ideas of other countries have developed in exactly the same way as those concerning their own, but frequently with an antagonism between the two types of affective ideas or reactions. Identical development in the first place: in both cases, there has been a "decentration" of the original egocentric attitude, which has now given way to an acceptance of the ideas or traditions of the child's immediate environment, especially those of his family. But thereafter—and the possible antagonism originates here—the child's reactions towards other nationalities may be guided into the most varied channels, according to whether his social environment is understanding, critical, or even censorious of foreigners. Here are some instances of these acquired attitudes, the last of them shedding light on the degree of logic to which the child has attained:

Murielle D. 8;2. Have you heard of foreigners? *Yes, there are Germans and French.* Are there any differences between these foreigners? *Yes, the Germans are bad, they're always making war. The French are poor and everything's dirty there. Then I've heard of Russians too, they're not at all nice.* Do you have any personal knowledge of the French, Germans or Russians or have you read something about them? *No.* Then how do you know? *Everyone says so.*

Francois D. 9;0. Have you heard of such people as foreigners? *Yes, Italians, Germans, the French and the English.* Are there any differences between all these people from all these different countries? *Of course.* What difference? *The language, and then in England everyone's sick.* How do you know? *Daddy told Mummy.* And what do you think of the French? *They went to war and they haven't got much to eat, only bread.* And what do you think of the Germans? *They're nasty. They quarrel with everyone.* But how do you know that? Have you been to France or Germany? *Yes, I've been to the Salève.* And it was there that you saw that the French have practically nothing to eat? *No, we took our food with us.* Then how do you know what you've told us? *I don't know.*

Michel M. 9;6. Have you heard of such people as foreigners? *Yes, the French, the Americans, the English. . . .* Quite right. Are there differences between all these peoples? *Oh yes, they don't speak the same language.* And what else? *I don't know.* What do you think of the French, for instance? Do you like them or not? Try and tell me as much as possible. *The French are not very serious, they don't worry about anything, an' it's dirty there.* And what do you think of the Americans? *They're ever so rich and clever. They've discovered the atom bomb.* And what do you think of Russians? *They're bad, they're always wanting to make war.* And what's your opinion of the English? *I don't know . . . they're nice. . . .* Now look, how did you come to know all you've told me? *I don't know . . . I've heard it . . . that's what people say.*

Claudine B. 9;11. Do you know any other countries besides Switzerland? *Yes, Italy, France and England. I know Italy quite well, I was on holidays there with Mummy and Daddy.* What town were you in? *In Florence* (drawn correctly). What nationality is a child living in Florence? *He's Italian.* Is he a Florentine too? *Oh yes, Florence is in Italy. . . .* Do you know any town in France? *Yes, Paris and Lyons* (Drawn correctly). And what are the people living in Paris? *French.* And are they Parisians too? *Yes, oh no, you can't be two things at once.* Is Paris a country? *No, a town.* So you can't be Parisian and French at the same time? *No, I don't think so, you can't have two names. . . . Oh yes, Paris is in France.*

It is easy to perceive the mechanism of such reactions. Whilst the "decentration" of attitudes towards adoption of family traditions may lead to the beginnings of a healthy patriotism, it may also give rise to a kind of tribal outlook, with values based on the disparagement of other social groups. In discarding his fugitive subjective judgments, and replacing them by the judgments of his environment, the child is, in a sense, taking a step forward, since he is projecting his mind into a system of relationships which broaden it and give it increased flexibility. But two courses then lie open to him: acquiescence (with its positive and negative aspects) and reciprocity, which requires independence of judgment in those concerned. Now none of the remarks just quoted give any impression of dawning independence or "reciprocity": everything suggests that, on discovering the values accepted in his immediate circle, the child felt bound to accept that circle's opinions of all other national groups.

It is evident, of course, that harsh judgments are not the unbroken rule, and that favourable estimates are accepted like the others. But even in the latter case, we are faced with the psychological problem that results from any action by the social group and, for that matter, from any form of education: is the spirit of understanding engendered by the content of the ideas inculcated, or simply by the process of exchange? In other words, if a child receives his opinions—even the soundest opinions—ready-made, does he thereby learn to judge for himself, and does he acquire the faculty for integration which will enable him, if need be, to rectify deviations and to overcome tensions?

Let us again see what are the typical reactions of children at stage III, when their intellectual and affective progress seems to come nearer to independence in the formation of logical judgments and estimates and to the attitude of reciprocity inseparable therefrom:

Jean-Luc L. 11;1 (cf section I, stage III). Do you know any foreign countries? *Yes, lots, France, Germany.* And any foreign cities? *Paris*

Where is this city? *In France, it's the capital of France.* (Drawn correctly.) And what nationality are the people who live in Paris? *They're French.* And what else? *They're Parisians, too, because Paris is in France.*

Martin A. 11;9 (mentions a very large number of foreign countries). Is there any difference between all those people? *Yes, they don't all talk the same language.* And are there any other differences? Are some better, more intelligent, or more likable? *I don't know. They're all much the same, each has his own mentality.* What do you mean by mentality? *Some like war and others want to be neutral. That depends on the country.* How do you know that? *I've heard people say so and you hear it on the wireless, and at school, the teacher explained that Switzerland is a neutral country.*

Jacques W. 13;9 (mentions a very large number of foreign countries). Are there any differences between all those people? *Yes, they're not all of the same race and don't have the same language. And you don't find the same faces everywhere, the same types, the same morals and the same religion.* But do all these differences have any effect on the people? *Oh yes, they don't all have the same mentality. Each people has its own special background.*

Jean B. 13;3 (mentions a very large number of foreign countries). Are there any differences between all those countries? *There is only a difference of size and position between all these countries. It's not the country that makes the difference, but the people. You find all types of people everywhere.*

But the same problem confronts us here as when we were considering stage II: is the progress achieved to be attributed to an increasing conformity between the child's judgments and those of his environment, accompanied by a tendency to reject exaggerated views and to prefer a middle and moderate course; or is it the result of new liberation from his immediate surroundings, which favours a wider outlook? We have already observed (section I), in connexion with this same stage III, how the child's mind can arrive simultaneously at a logical conception of whole units and an affective awareness of the larger unit represented by the national group as compared with the more immediate environment, ranging from the family to the town. It would therefore seem that these reactions—unlike those of children at stage II, who are apt to stress the contrast between the homeland and foreign countries—are progressing towards an attitude of "reciprocity". But how far can this be assumed to go?

The general conclusion of this section, as compared with that of the previous section, is, therefore, as follows: the mastery of the concept of the homeland may be interpreted as the culmination of a gradual "decentration," correlative with a process of integration which is applied to a succession of ever larger units. But study of children's reactions towards other countries shows us that this "decentration" may take either of two possible forms: egocentricity, defeated on one plane, may reappear on another plane in the form of a sociocentricity ranging from the naive to the extremely subtle; or, on the contrary, the conquest of egocentricity may mean an advance towards "reciprocity". At this point, we should try to find out whether it is possible to assess the strength of this latter factor.

For the purpose of analysing the understanding of reciprocity as such, while still keeping to the subject of relations between the homeland and other countries, we put two types of question to the same children, 4–5 and 11–12 years of age. To investigate the formation of logical connexions, which, as we have seen, go far to reveal the stage of development of the nationalist concept, we asked each child what a foreigner was, and whether he himself could become a foreigner in certain circumstances (travel, etc.). From the point of view of affective motivations and attitudes, we put the following questions, which lent themselves to illuminating comparisons: "If you had been born without any nationality, what country would you choose, and why?" and "If I asked a little French boy the same question, what country would he choose, and why?"

On this crucial point of reciprocity, as in previous respects, we found an exact parallel between intellectual development and affective understanding. As for the formation of logical concepts, the replies at stage I reflected the notion of the foreigner as something absolute, and an inability to grasp the meaning of reciprocity, that is to say, of the essential relativity of this relationship: foreigners are people belonging to other countries (   ), whereas the Swiss (or Genevese, etc.) cannot be regarded as foreigners, even outside their own country. In the matter of affective motivations, children at this same stage thought that, if they had no homeland, they would choose their present one, but could not understand that French or English children would also choose their respective countries. At stage II, the two types of question call forth intermediate replies, showing the beginnings of reciprocity, together with obvious remnants of egocentricity; and, at stage III, reciprocity gains the upper hand in regard to both types of question.

Intellectual Aspect: The Idea of the Foreigner

As we found in section I, in connexion with the idea of the homeland at this same stage, a certain fund of knowledge is essential if the child is to understand the actual question put to him. Until the child knows the exact meaning of the word "foreigner," it is pointless to present him with the problem of "reciprocity," as the responses would only be something like the following:

Georges G. 6;10. What is a foreigner? *I don't know.* Have you ever seen any? *Oh yes.* How did you know they were foreigners? *By their clothes mostly. They wear old clothes. They're always going off to the country.*

Corrine M. 6;11. Do you know what foreigners are? *I don't know, but I've seen some. They're soldiers.*

However, once the word is understood, the question of reciprocity may be raised, but at stage I, the response is usually negative.

Georges B. 7;5. What nationality have you? *I'm Swiss.* Are you a foreigner? *No.* Do you know any foreigners? *Yes.* Who, for instance? *People living a long way off.* Now imagine you were travelling in France, could you also become a foreigner in certain ways? *No, I'm Swiss.* Could a Frenchman be a foreigner? *Of course a Frenchman is a foreigner.* And is a Frenchman a foreigner in France? *Naturally.*

Ivan M. 8;9. What nationality have you? *I'm Swiss.* Are you a foreigner in Switzerland? *No, I'm Swiss.* And if you go to France? *I stay Swiss, just as before.* Do you know any foreigners? *Yes, the French.* And is a Frenchman a foreigner when he comes to Switzerland? *Yes, he's a foreigner.* And a Frenchman who stays in France? *He stays a foreigner just as before.*

Marie B. 8;0. What nationality have you? *I'm from Geneva.* Are you a foreigner? *No.* Do you know any foreigners? *Yes, the people of Lausanne.* If you go to Lausanne, do you become a foreigner? *No, I'm Genevese.* And is a person from Lausanne a foreigner? *Yes, he lives in Lausanne.* And if he comes to Geneva, does he stay a foreigner or not? *He's still a native of Lausanne, so he's a foreigner.*

Before we conclude that these reactions reflect a failure to grasp the essence of "reciprocity," two possible objections should be discussed. Firstly, it might be argued that it is a mere verbal misunderstanding: it is the word "foreigner" and not the idea which, in this case, gives rise to confusion. To put it differently, the word "foreigner" could be wrongly interpreted as "not Swiss" or not "Genevese," etc., thus giving the impression of non-reciprocity, even though the child might actually be capable of true reciprocity. But this objection may be readily countered by the facts. The replies quoted above are, in fact, typical of a category of very general reactions up to seven or eight years of age and persisting even longer in relation to certain classes of ideas. Thus it is quite common for a boy at this level to assert that he has a brother, but that his brother has none; or children may correctly put out their right or left hand, but cannot tell which is which in the case of a person sitting opposite; or they may have neighbours but do not regard themselves as these people's neighbours, and so on. It is not mere chance, then, if relative concepts become absolute in their minds: this is due to the lack of any power to construct logical relationships or to attain to reciprocity in practice.

A second objection may then be made: could it not be a mere deficiency in reasoning power—affecting the sense of relativity itself—and not a lack of reciprocity as an attitude of mind? There are two answers to this objection. Firstly, relativity (in this particular case the "symmetrical" character of the relationships under consideration) is the result of an operation: the deduction that A=B means the same as B=A, is a conversion operation and, from the psychologist's point of view, the operation is the cause and the relationships deduced are the effect. Any failure to grasp the relativity of a concept is therefore due to a lack of adequate operational equipment. Now the operations producing a sense of relativity are tantamount to a system of reciprocity. Secondly, the surest proof that we have to do with a deep-rooted mental attitude and not merely with logical results is, as we shall see later, that this failure to grasp the meaning of reciprocity is matched by an egocentric motivation in the values themselves.

During stage II, we find a series of reactions midway between those described above and reciprocity, as instanced by the following:

Jacques D. 8;3. Do you know what foreigners are? *Yes, they're the people who come from Valais. I have an aunt from Valais and when she comes to Geneva, she's a foreigner.*

Elaine K. 8;9. What nationality have you? *I'm Swiss.* And what are you in Switzerland? *Swiss.* Are you a foreigner? *No.* And if you go to France? *I'm still Swiss.* Are you a foreigner? *No.* Is a Frenchman a foreigner? *Yes.* And what is a Frenchman in Switzerland? *French, but a little bit Swiss, too, if he's here.* And a Frenchman in France? *He's French.*

Jean-Jacques R. 8;8. What nationality have you? *I'm Swiss.* What is a Swiss when he's in Switzerland? *He's Swiss.* Is he a foreigner? *No.* And what is a Swiss who goes to France? *He's a foreigner and Swiss, because he's Swiss.* And what is a Frenchman? *A foreigner.* What is a Frenchman who comes to Switzerland? *He's Swiss because he comes to Geneva.* And if he stays in France? *He's French.* Is he a foreigner too? *Yes.* And when the Frenchman is in Switzerland, is he a foreigner then too? *No, he's in Switzerland.*

Jules M. 8;9. Do you know what a foreigner is? *Yes, they're the people who come from other countries. There's a foreigner in my class, he comes from France.* Can a Swiss become a foreigner? *Oh no.*

Monique B. 9;4. What nationality are you? *I'm from Vaud.* What is a Swiss in Switzerland? *He's Swiss.* Is he a foreigner? *No.* If a Swiss goes to France, what is he? *A foreigner and a Vaudois at the same time.* Why? *Because the French don't know us properly and look on us as foreigners.* And what is a Frenchman? *A foreigner.* What is a Frenchman who comes to Switzerland? *He's a foreigner, but a little bit Swiss too.* Why? *Because he's come to Switzerland.* What is a Frenchman who stays in France? *A Frenchman and a foreigner.* And if I asked a little French boy the same question, what would he tell me? *That he's French.* He'd tell me that he's a foreigner as well? *No, he's French.*

It is interesting to compare these reactions with our observations on children at the same stage II, recorded in sections I and II. It will be recalled that in their judgments on their homeland and other countries, these children reflected an attitude that might be described as bipolar, if not equivocal: there is a certain degree of logical activity, testifying to progress beyond the egocentricity of the first stage towards "decentration" and integration; but there is also a certain lack of independence, reflected in an acceptance of family opinions, thus transforming the initial egocentricity into sociocentricity, as opposed to "decentration." Here we come across the same bipolarity, but in terms of reciprocity—the new attitude to which we should no doubt look for an explanation of the above reactions. On the one hand, the child has progressed sufficiently far beyond his immediate standpoint not to claim that a Swiss living in another country can never be a foreigner, etc.; this is certainly a development towards reciprocity. But this reciprocity may be said always to stop midway, since there nevertheless remains an undercurrent of sociocentricity tantamount to the assertion that a Swiss (or Genevese, etc.) is not exactly comparable with other people. It is surely the precarious nature of this incipient faculty for integration that accounts for this type of inconsistency.

However, at stage III, the problem appears to be entirely mastered:

Murielle F. 10;6. Do you know what a foreigner is? *It's someone in a country other than his own.* Could you become a foreigner? *Not for the Swiss, but I could for others if I don't stay in my country.*

Robert N. 11;0. You know what a foreigner is? *Yes, they're all the people who are not from the same country as ourselves.* And could you become a foreigner? *Yes, for all the other people who are not Swiss, as I was born in a different country from them, so I'd be a foreigner.*

Marion B. 12;4. What is your nationality? *I'm Swiss.* What is a Swiss person living in Switzerland? *Swiss.* Is he a foreigner? *No, not for* *the Swiss.* What is he if he goes to France? *He's still Swiss, but he'd become a foreigner for the French.* And what is a Frenchman in France? *French.* And what is he if he comes to Switzerland? *He's French, but for us he's a foreigner.*

Pierre F. 12;6. What nationality are you? *I'm Swiss.* What nationality is a Swiss in Switzerland? *He's Swiss.* Is he a foreigner? *No, or perhaps he's a foreigner for foreigners.* What do you mean? *For the French and Germans, for instance, the Swiss are foreigners.* Quite right. Now if a Swiss person went to France, what would he be? *For the French he's a foreigner, but for us he isn't, he's still Swiss.* What is a Frenchman living in France? *He's French and not a foreigner for the French, but for us he's a foreigner.*

Thus, as regards the formation of logical concepts and relationships no further obstacle to reciprocity is discernible at this level. Is the same true from the affective standpoint?

Affective Motivation

Although there appears to be no direct relationship between the question which country children would choose were they to lose their nationality, and whether they themselves are always foreigners to other people because others are foreigners for them, we found a striking concurrence between the corresponding reactions at the three stages considered.

At stage I, not only does the child choose his own country, but he also imagines that a national of another country would likewise choose Switzerland, as though no one could fail to recognize this objective pre-eminence. Here are a few sample remarks made towards the end of stage I (before then, the question is meaningless, as the children are at first quite unaware of their own nationality):

Christian K. 6;5. If you were born without belonging to any country, which would you choose? *I'd like to become Swiss.* (The child is Swiss.) Why? *Because. . . .* Say you could choose between France and Switzerland, would you choose Switzerland? *Yes.* Why? *Because the French are nasty. The Swiss are nicer.* Why? *Because the Swiss didn't go to war.* If I asked a little French boy the same question as I asked you just now and said to him: now look, imagine you were born without any nationality and that now you can choose what you like, what do you think this child would choose? *He'd want to be Swiss.* Why? *Because he just would.* And if I were to ask him who is nicer, the Swiss or the French, or whether they're both as good as each other, what would he say? *He would say that the Swiss are nicer than the French.* Why would he? *Because . . . they know the Swiss are nicer.*

Charles K. 6;11. If you were born without any nationality and you were allowed to choose what nationality you liked, which would you choose? *I'd become Swiss.* Why? *Because there's more to eat.* Do you think the French are nicer or not so nice or just the same as the Swiss? *The Swiss are nicer.* Why? *I don't know.* If I were to say to a little German boy, for instance, "Now imagine you were born without any nationality and you could choose what nationality you like," what do you think he would choose? *He'd say that he'd like to be Swiss.* Why? *Because we're better off in Switzerland.* And if I asked him who was nicer? *He'd say the Swiss are.* Why? *Because they didn't go to war.*

Brian S. 6;2 (English). If you were born without any nationality and you could now choose whichever you liked, what country would you choose? *English, because I know lots of them.* Do you think the English are nicer, not so nice, or just the same as the Swiss? *The English are nicer.* Why? *The Swiss are always quarrelling.* If a Swiss child were given a free choice of nationality, what do you think he would choose? *He'd choose English.* Why? *Because I was born there.* He couldn't choose any other country? *Yes, France perhaps.* Why France? *It's a lovely country. I've been there on holidays at the seaside.* And who do the Swiss think are nicer, the Swiss or the English? *The English.* Why? *Because. . .* Why? *Because they just are.*

It is surprising to find that, as soon as the question is understood, children at this stage voice nationalist feelings that were apparently absent in the children at stage I, described in section I. But apart from the fact that, towards the end of stage I, children begin to be influenced by remarks they pick up (as they will be to an increasing extent during stage II), a factor associated with the actual interrogation should be borne in mind: the first question asked refers to the nationality of the child questioned, and thus has the force of a deliberate suggestion, whereas in section I, his attention was not drawn to this point at the outset.

During stage II, reciprocity appears as a "symmetrical" choice attributed by the child to others of different nationality:

Marina T. 7;9. (Italian). If you were born without any nationality and you were now given a free choice, what nationality would you choose? *Italian.* Why? *Because it's my country. I like it better than Argentina where my father works, because Argentina isn't my country.* Are Italians just the same, or more, or less intelligent than the Argentinians? What do you think? *The Italians are more intelligent.* Why? *I can see the people I live with, they're Italians.* If I were to give a child from Argentina a free choice of nationality, what do you think he would choose? *He'd want to stay an Argentinian.* Why? *Because that's his country.* And if I were to ask him who is more intelligent, the Argentinians or the Italians, what do you think he would answer? *He'd say the Argentinians.* Why? *Because there wasn't any war.* Good. Now who was really right in the choice he made and what he said, the Argentinian child, you or both? *I was right.* Why? *Because I chose Italy.*

Jeannot P. 8;0 (St. Gall) (Bright child). If you had no nationality and you were given a free choice of nationality, what would you choose? *I'd choose to be St. Gallois.* Why? *I don't know.* Who is nicer, an Italian or a St. Gallois, or are they just the same? What do you think? *The St. Gallois are nicer.* Why? *Because I know.* And who is more intelligent? *The St. Gallois are more intelligent.* Why? *Because my Daddy is a St. Gallois.* If I were to give an Italian a free choice of nationality, what do you think he would choose? *Italy.* Why? *Because I know a boy at school who is an Italian, and he wants to stay Italian.* And if I were to ask this boy who is nicer, a St. Gallois or an Italian, what would he say? *I don't know what he thinks, but perhaps he would say Italian.* Why? *I don't know.* And if I were to ask him who is more intelligent? *He'd say Italian.* Why? *Because he has a Daddy too.* Now what do you really think? Who was right, you or the Italian? You haven't answered the same thing, now who do you think gave the best answer? *I did.* Why? *Because the St. Gallois are more intelligent.*

Maurice D. 8;3 (Swiss). If you didn't have any nationality and you were given a free choice of nationality, which would you choose? *Swiss nationality.* Why? *Because I was born in Switzerland.* Now look, do you think the French and the Swiss are equally nice, or the one nicer or less nice than the other? *The Swiss are nicer.* Why? *The French are always nasty.* Who is more intelligent, the Swiss or the French, or do you think they're just the same? *The Swiss are more intelligent.* Why? *Because they learn French quickly.* If I asked a French boy to choose any nationality he liked, what country do you think he'd choose? *He'd choose France.* Why? *Because he is in France.* And what would he say about who's the nicer? Would he think the Swiss and the French equally nice or one better than the other? *He'd say the French are nicer.* Why? *Because he was born in France.* And who would he think more intelligent? *The French.* Why? *He'd say that the French want to learn quicker than the Swiss.* Now you and the French boy don't really give the same answer. Who do you think answered the best? *I did.* Why? *Because Switzerland is always better.*

We see that while the child is induced to choose his own country (as at stage I) he is then easily made to place himself in the position of children from other countries. We thus have a relative parallelism with our observations concerning the intellectual "structuration" typical of stage II. But—and this further strengthens the parallel—at the end of the conversation, we only have to add "but who is really right?" to break down this incipient reciprocity and to bring the child questioned round to an attitude resembling that adopted during stage I. Lastly, at stage III, children show a genuine understanding of the "reciprocity" of points of view, and some resistance to the final suggestion.

Arlette R. 12;6 (Swiss). If you had no nationality and you were given a free choice of whatever nationality you liked, which would you choose? *Swiss nationality.* Why? *Because I was born in Switzerland and this is my home.* Right. Who do you think is nicer, the French or the Swiss, or do you think they are just the same? *Oh, on the whole, they're the same. There are some very nice Swiss and some very nice French people, that doesn't depend on the country.* Who is more intelligent, a Swiss or a French person? *All people have their good points. The Swiss don't sing too badly and the French have some great composers.* If I were to give a Frenchman a free choice of nationality, what do you think he would choose? *French.* Why? *Because he was born in France and that's his country.* And who would seem nicer to a French girl, a French or a Swiss boy? *I don't know, perhaps the French for her but you can't be sure.* Which of you would be right? *You can't tell. Everyone is right in his own eyes. All people have their opinions.*

Janine C. 13;4. Choice of nationality. *I'd choose to be Swiss.* Why? *Because it's my country and I love it.* Who do you think are nicer, the Swiss or the French? *They're just the same as each other. It doesn't depend on the country, but on the people.* And who are more intelligent, the Swiss or the French? *That's the same thing too. France is bigger, so there are more people to think, but we have our scholars and professors in Switzerland too.* What would a French person choose? *He would choose France.* Why? *It's his country and he loves it.* Whom do you think he would find more intelligent, the Swiss or French? *That's difficult to tell. Perhaps he would say they're just the same or he might say the French are, because there are more people in France to think.* Now who do you really think is right and has given the best reply? *You can't say, as that depends on everyone's mentality, but there are all types of people, intelligent and stupid, good and bad.*

We see how, despite the inevitable superficiality of the questions to which we were forced to confine ourselves, the broad outline of this development may be clearly traced. We may thus draw two main conclusions. One is that the child's discovery of his homeland and understanding of other countries is a process of transition from egocentricity to reciprocity. The other is that this gradual development is liable to constant setbacks, usually through the re-emergence of egocentricity on a broader or sociocentric plane, at each new stage in this development, or as each new conflict arises. Accordingly, the main problem is not to determine what must or must not be inculcated in the child; it is to discover how to develop that reciprocity in thought and action which is vital to the attainment of impartiality and affective understanding.

4-6

Animism and Related Thought
Tendencies in Hopi Children

WAYNE DENNIS

In many areas of ideas, Piaget has described "stages" of development. For example, in respect to what referents are living, Piaget has described four stages in the development of the child's ideas concerning what is alive and what is not. Piaget is not very explicit in describing to what extent the child's position on this scale of animism is maturational and to what extent it is experiential. The present study reveals that experience plays a large role in the development of the child's thinking.

INTRODUCTION

Almost all of the investigations of children's ideas which have been based on the work of Piaget have been conducted in Western civilizations and have made use of Indo-European languages. The question arises, therefore, as to what extent the thought tendencies of the child are the result of particular cultural and linguistic influences and to what extent

Reprinted from *J. Abnorm. Soc. Psychol.*, 1943, **38**, 21–36, by permission of the American Psychological Association.

they are universal outcomes of child experience and of incomplete mental development.

In order to answer these questions it will be necessary to have extensive data, gathered by Piaget's methods, on children in other cultures. It is for that reason that the following data on Hopi children are presented. In undertaking this research there was no assumption that the Hopi are a particularly valuable group for such research. The Hopi happened to be a group with whom we had an opportunity to work. While it has turned out that they do provide some valuable information with regard to thought tendencies, it is likely that many other groups would yield results just as interesting.

Before research of this type in a society other than our own can be interpreted, it is necessary to know the intellectual world of the adults of that society, the methods of child rearing of the group, and the nature of the language. Fortunately, for the Hopi, the first and second types of information are available. Pueblo ideas concerning cosmology, magic, and religion have been extensively studied, and the results for all the Pueblo groups, including the Hopi, have been summarized by Parsons (1939). The Beagleholes (1935) and the present writer (Dennis, 1940) have described child care, and Simmons (1942) has edited an autobiography of a Hopi which contains much material on children. Unfortunately, practically no material on the Hopi language is available in print. The late Benjamin J. Whorf, a brilliant student of language, gathered extensive materials on the Hopi language, which it is hoped may be published soon. We had the good fortune to attend Mr. Whorf's seminar on the Hopi language and to be with him for a short time in the field. However, our own work with regard to the language has been limited almost entirely to an attempt to explore the vocabulary and meanings associated with animistic concepts. A wider knowledge of Hopi would be most helpful to the interpretation of the data to be presented and would be almost a prerequisite to more intensive work on the development of concepts in Hopi children.

When intelligent adult Hopi, well acquainted with English, are questioned with regard to objects in nature which the Hopi consider to be living, it is found that they do not by any means limit life to plants and animals.

The Hopi include among living objects the sun, the moon, the stars, the wind, the clouds, permanent springs of water, permanent rivers, and fire. They do not include as living a rainstorm, a flash of lightning, or an arroyo which carries water only after a rain, or a temporary or intermittent spring. These events are brief and transient. Mechanical devices are not living, and sand, stone, and bare earth are not living because they do nothing by themselves. Perhaps one can best describe the quality which causes the Hopi to classify objects as living as some sort of enduring power.

In the Hopi language, there are two verbs which express the idea of being alive or having life. They are "tayta" and "kata." The third person singular nominative pronoun "pum" is used for both sexes and also for neuter objects. Thus "it (or she or he) is living" may be expressed as "pum kata" or "pum tayta." The verb is made negative by the prefix "ka." Consequently, "it is not living" is stated in Hopi as "pum kakata" or "pum katayta." The pronoun is very commonly omitted.

The linguistic situation with reference to animism is complicated by the fact that both of these verbs have more than one meaning. "Tayta" means to look or to peer intently, as well as to live; but "tayta" also means "moving by itself," "in working condition," or "capable of normal activity," in much the same way that our words "live" and "dead" are used when we speak of a live battery and a dead motor. Thus our informants stated that a watch and an automobile are "tayta" when they are working, but they are not "really living." The third meaning of the word indicates "alive in the same way that people are," and this, as we indicated earlier, is said of heavenly bodies, rivers and springs (if permanent), fire and wind, in addition to plants, animals, and supernaturals.

"Kata" has the meaning "to sit" or "to be resting on the ground." In this sense it can be used to describe any object or person. It also has a meaning identical with the third meaning of "tayta" (*i.e.*, really alive), but "kata" in this sense is used properly only with reference to plants and animals, including man. There is no implication that life is restricted to animals and man—the word is synonymous with "tayta"—but it is improper to use "kata" to refer to objects, whereas "tayta" can be used for objects as well as for plants, animals, and man.

In reviewing these Hopi concepts it will be seen that the Hopi adult stage is quite different from the adult stage in our own culture. The stages distinguished by Piaget are as follows: Stage I: everything which is useful, unbroken, and in good condition is alive; Stage II: only things which move are alive; Stage III: only things which can move themselves are alive; Stage IV: only plants and animals are alive. However, one meaning of "tayta" is very close to Piaget's Stage III, if not identical with it. In Stage III, everything is living which is thought to move by itself. This is true with one usage of "tayta." All examples which we secured of "tayta" in this sense referred to manufactured objects, such as automobiles, batteries, and windmills. It seems likely that this usage is a recent metaphorical extension of "tayta" to cover new mechanical objects brought in by white people.

It will be noted that neither "tayta" or "kata" are used by Hopi adults to express meanings similar to the Stage I and Stage II degrees of animism.

THE ANIMISM INTERVIEW

In questioning Hopi children with regard to their conceptions of animation, it was decided to question them in English. A major factor in this decision was the inadequacy of the investigator, who, while he could probably have understood simple answers in Hopi, could not have coped with unusual answers. It is hoped that examinations in the Hopi language may be conducted at a later time. Even apart from the limitations of the experimenter, it seemed best, since the subjects were bilingual, to explore first their responses in English.

All Hopi children learn first the Hopi language and seldom hear English until they enter school at six years of age. The Hopi, even the most highly educated ones, converse with each other in their native language. Aside from the school situation, they use English only when talking to a white person or to a Navajo or to some other non-Hopi Indian. On the reservation, the need for speaking English arises only seldom. Consequently, English has the status of an auxiliary language. It is likely that most Hopi, when employing English, definitely translate from their native language. That is, we believe that they do not have two independent sets of language habits. It is our conviction that if the interviews had been conducted in Hopi the results would have been the same.

The standardized procedure devised by Russell and Dennis (1939) had to be modified for use among the Hopi, since the original procedure was not designed to reveal the concept of the Hopi adults. In order to make it possible to detect this concept certain items of the earlier list of twenty objects were replaced by other objects, the total number of items in the new list as well as the old list being twenty.

The items previously employed by Russell and Dennis (1939) and also used with the Hopi subjects, numbered according to their position in the Hopi list, were (1) knife, (2) mirror, (3) stone, (4) broken button, (5) comb, (6) broken dish, (7) watch, (10) lightning, (12) pencil, (13) clouds, (14) moon, (17) wind, (19) dog, (20) tree. The following original items were removed from the list to make room for new objects: Chair, river, bird, bug, flower, grass. These were replaced by (8) automobile, (9) smoke, (11) windmill, (15) a spring of water, (16) fire, (18) soil in a garden.

In giving the animism interview, each child was taken to a room occupied only by the interviewer and the child. The first seven objects lay on the table at which the child and the interviewer sat. No example of a living or a dead object was given. Although this had been done in some of the earlier work (Russell and Dennis, 1939), it was omitted here because this part of the original procedure had been found to be unnecessary (Russell and Dennis, 1941). After saying "Good morning" or "Good afternoon" to the child and asking him to sit at the table, the interviewer began the interview by remarking, "You know what it means to say that something is living, don't you?" If the subject said "Yes," the examiner proceeded as indicated below. If the subject answered in the negative, the interviewer first said, "How do you say in Hopi, 'I am living'?" or he said, "If you were talking about a sheep, how would you say in Hopi, 'It is living'?" With the exception of one girl, who refused to answer any questions, the subjects all gave "kata" or "tayta" in response to one of these questions. After being assured in this manner that the child understood the questions, the examiner continued with the remainder of the interview.

The remainder of the procedure was identical with that outlined by Russell and Dennis (1939). That is, with reference to each object each subject was asked, "Is the . . . living or is it dead?" and after an answer was obtained the child was asked to give a reason by being asked "Why?" or "How do you know?", "Why do you think so?", "How can you tell?"

If the child stated that some of the objects among the first six were living because they could be used and that others were dead because they were broken, it was unnecessary to carry the interview further since the child was obviously in Stage I. On the other hand, if all of the first six objects were said to be dead because they could not move, further questioning was, of course, necessary. This questioning followed the procedure previously described.

The classification of the answers into stages was accomplished in the usual way, except that two Stage IV's were provided: a Stage IV-P (Piaget) and a Stage IV-H (Hopi). If, in the list of twenty test objects, only the dog and the tree were said to be alive, the subject was classified as IV-P. If, in addition, the clouds, moon, spring, fire, and wind were said to be living while all other objects were said to be dead, the subject was assigned to Stage IV-H.

SUBJECTS

The subjects interviewed comprised all of the Hopi children of First Mesa and Third Mesa between the ages of 12 and 17, inclusive, who were in school when the examinations were conducted, which was between December 16 and December 24, 1941. All Hopi children of First Mesa who were of these ages and who were in the first seven grades were interviewed at the Polacca Day School on First Mesa. Tewa children of First Mesa were excluded because the treatment of animism categories in the Tewa dialect of First Mesa is unknown to us. All First Mesa school children who were at a grade level beyond grade seven were attending the Hopi High School at Oraibi and were examined there; all Third Mesa children were, of course, interviewed on Third Mesa, either at Hotavila or at Oraibi; Second Mesa was omitted from the investigation purely because of lack of time.

In all, 98 subjects, 43 girls and 55 boys, were interviewed; 44 of these were between 12.0 and 13.9 years; 32 were between 14.0 and 15.9, and 22 were between 16.0 and 17.9.

Subjects below twelve years were not interviewed because we wished to select subjects who would be certain to comprehend the questions which were asked in English. By twelve years of age most Hopi children have spent six years in school, and hence can be expected to have little difficulty with the language of the interview.

Beyond age 14 not all Hopi children attend school. We have no information on the type of selection which determines which of the older children remain in school, but there is no reason to believe that the duller ones remain. Almost the entire population of First and Third Mesa between age 12 and age 14 was interviewed and hence we believe we have a representative sample of this age level of Hopi children.

RESULTS OF THE ANIMISM INTERVIEW

Of the 98 subjects, one would not answer at all, one answered only a few questions, and one said, "Don't know," to all questions. Hence 95 usable sets of answers were obtained. Since we do not know whether the three exceptions were merely recalcitrant or whether they were in the "no concept" stage, they will be omitted from our percentages. All three were in the 12.0–13.9 age group.

Only one subject, a fourteen-year-old boy, displayed a special concept. For him things that made themselves were living. This category included, in addition to the dog and tree, lightning and clouds, since he conceived of the clouds as making themselves and of the lightning as coming from the clouds. All other answers were typical of one of the four stages described previously.

Only two subjects were in Stage IV-P; one of these was in the 12.0–13.9 group and one was in the oldest group. More striking still, only two subjects displayed the adult *Hopi* concept of life. These two were distributed in age as were the two mentioned just previously. Furthermore, only seven subjects were in Stage III.

In other words, 83 of the 95 subjects who have meaningful answers were in Stages I and II. These were approximately equally divided between the two stages (45 in Stage I, 38 in Stage II). The older subjects had a slightly smaller proportion of subjects in Stage II than did the younger, but the difference was not reliable. The results in full are shown in Table 1.

TABLE 1

Hopi Cases in Each Stage at Each Age Level

Age Group	Stage				
	I	II	III	IV	SC
12.0–13.9	19	18	2	2	0
14.0–15.9	18	10	3	0	1
16.0–17.9	8	10	2	2	0

These results are very different from the results of Russell (1940) on white children. Russell's study gives data on children in the elementary grades, so that a representative sample was obtained by him only up to age 14. His data, therefore, can be compared with our data only for the age group 12.0–13.9 years. Russell studied three groups, as follows: "F," a Massachusetts urban group; "S," a Virginia suburban group, and "R," a Virginia rural group. The figures for these groups are compared with the Hopi data in Table 2.

This table shows that, even in comparison with the least-advanced white group, the "S" group, the Hopi twelve- and thirteen-year-olds are considerably retarded. Only 11 per cent of the Hopi are in Stages III and IV, whereas these stages are characteristic of 24 per cent of the "F" group. These differences are highly significant.

The differences between Hopi and white subjects at the high-school level are even greater. The Hopi subjects of advanced ages are not different from the Hopi twelve- and thirteen-year-olds, whereas Russell (1942) has found that the majority of white high-school pupils are in Stage IV. (Of the 54 Hopi children between 14.0 and 17.9 years, only two were in Stage IV.)

Discussion of the probable reasons for the retardation of the Hopi subjects will be postponed until data on related concepts have been presented.

TABLE 2

Percentage of Cases in Each Stage at Ages 12.0–13.9 Years

Group	Stage				
	I	II	III	IV	SC
"F"	24	13	34	27	2
"S"	31	45	11	13	0
"R"	31	30	24	13	2
Hopi	47	40	7	4	1

ATTRIBUTION OF CONSCIOUSNESS TO THINGS

Since the attribution of life was found to be so widespread among Hopi children, it seemed advisable to attempt to see whether other human qualities were also extended to inanimate objects. This was done by Piaget (1929) by determining whether or not children attributed consciousness to various objects. The same procedure in a standardized form has been employed by Russell (1940). Both Piaget and Russell found that children frequently conceive as conscious many objects which adults think of not only as lacking in consciousness but also as lacking life.

The preferred procedure in the present instance would have been to employ Russell's standardized technique. However, our time among the Hopi was limited and, since Russell's procedure requires individual interview, its use was out of the question in the time which was available. Consequently, a group test was tried. It was given to grades seven, eight, and nine, at the Hopi High School, comprising a total of 69 subjects distributed as follows: ages 12.0–13.9, 14; ages 14.0–15.9, 42; ages 16.0–17.9, 11. One subject was 11 years of age and one was 18. Each grade was tested separately.

The examiner distributed to each student in the classroom a mimeographed sheet containing the name of each object used in the animism test. A space was provided after each name for the student's response.

The examiner said:

> "I want to ask you some more questions like the ones I asked you the other day. But first I want to ask you a question about yourselves. Do you know where you are? Where are you? (The examiner waited for several oral replies, such as "Oraibi," "In school.") Now tell me (the examiner held up the knife used in previous animism interview) does the knife know where it is? Don't tell me aloud, but write down your answer, yes or no, on the first line on your paper, after the word 'knife.' Do not show anybody your answer." The question, "Does the . . . know where it is?" was repeated for each object on the list.

We did not believe it was feasible to ask the Hopi subjects to write out a reason for each answer. The only data on the answer sheets, therefore, were a series of "yes" and "no" responses. Stage I answers can be distinguished fairly well in the absence of reasons supplied by the subject, since in Stage I the broken button and the broken dish are said not to know where they are because they are broken or because they are dead, whereas all other objects, with the possible exception of the stone, are said to be aware of their location. Twelve of the 69 papers definitely belonged in Stage I. Stages II and III could not be distinguished, since the answers did not show which objects were considered to move spontaneously. However, 34 of the papers belonged either to Stage II or to Stage III. Fourteen papers exhibited answers which could not be readily classified on the basis of the simple "yes" and "no" responses.

The point most relevant to our results on the animism interview is the fact that only *nine* papers limited "knowing" to the dog alone (the only animal on the list). Thus the widespread animism of Hopi children is corroborated by these questions on the attribution of consciousness to things.

Of the 12.0–13.9 group, three, or 21 per cent, limited consciousness to animals (Stage IV). The only comparable data are Russell's (1940) data on Virginia children. In his group, 50 per cent of children aged 12.0–13.9 were in Stage IV, the adult stage. Thus, the investigation of the attribution of consciousness to inanimate objects shows an even greater difference between white and Hopi children than was revealed by the animism examination.

MORAL REALISM

The third topic concerning which we questioned Hopi subjects was that of moral realism, and, in particular, immanent punishment. This interview was given to each subject immediately following the animism interview.

Our procedure was modeled after one used by Piaget (1932) and is similar to procedures employed by Lerner (1937, 1938) and also by Abel (1941). Our modifications were in the direction of insuring that the incident described would seem natural in the Hopi environment.

Our procedure consisted in telling the subject the following:

> I am going to tell you a story and then I am going to ask you some questions about it. Some boys went to an orchard and stole some fruit. They ate the fruit and then started home. On the way home they came to a bridge. The bridge broke and the boys fell. Now tell me, why did the bridge break?

Regardless of whether the child gave to this question (question 1) a naturalistic answer or an answer indicating a belief in moral realism, the child was next asked (question 2) "Did the bridge know that the boys had been stealing?"

If the answer to question 1 had been naturalistic, such as "The boys were too heavy," or "The bridge was old," and if the answer to question 2 was "no," then no further questions were asked. Such a record was classified as naturalistic.

If the answer to question 2 was "yes" (*i.e.*, the bridge knew the boys had been stealing) then we asked further, "Is that why the bridge broke?" If the answer to this question was "yes," and if the answer to question 1 had been to the effect that the bridge broke because the boys stole, then no further questions were asked, and the subject was classified as showing moral realism in this interview. (More than moral realism is involved, but this word is used as a shorthand term for the belief that the bridge knew of the misdemeanor and that the breaking of the bridge was a form of punishment.)

In the few cases in which answers to questions 1 and 3 appeared to contradict each other, the child was asked a final question, "Now tell me, what do you really believe? Why did the bridge break?" These cases were classified on the basis of this last answer. In the 98 sets of responses, there were only 25 such papers. In other words, the majority of the children gave consistent clear-cut answers.

As is usual in his work, Piaget in reporting interviews similar to the one described above does not tell the number of cases which he questioned at any age level. However, he does report that one of his collaborators, Mlle. Rambert (Piaget, 1932, 251), questioned a total of 167 children between ages 6 and 12. Of the eleven- and twelve-year-olds (numbers not stated) 34 per cent gave answers indicating moral realism.

The chief data on white subjects available for comparison with our Hopi results are those of Lerner (1937). Lerner used an analogous but not an identical procedure. His oldest subjects ranged approximately from 10.0 to 12.0 years. Thus they were younger than our youngest subjects. Nevertheless, Hopi subjects aged 12.0 to 13.9 years gave a larger percentage of moral realism responses than did Lerner's ten- and eleven-year-old subjects. While the percentage of moral realism answers among the youngest Hopi subjects was 64, the percentage of moral realism responses among the ten- and eleven-year-olds in Lerner's area A, an underprivileged area, was 31; in his high socio-economic area, area B, it was only 15. The 64-percent record of the Hopi twelve- and thirteen-year-olds is almost exactly equivalent to that of Lerner's six- and seven-year-olds from the more favorable environment and is approximately equivalent to that of Piaget's eight-year-olds.

The moral realism of the Hopi subjects decreased markedly with age. Among the fourteen- and fifteen-year-olds it was 47 per cent of the total answers; among the sixteen- and seventeen-year-olds it was only 9 per cent. The numbers of subjects involved in the three Hopi groups were respectively 44, 32, and 22. Only five subjects failed to give classifiable answers, and these five were scattered among all three age groups.

In this connection it is interesting to note that Abel (1941) has found a high degree of moral realism among institutionalized feebleminded girls of ages 15 to 21. Eighty-five per cent of her subjects showed a belief in immanent punishment. The moral realism of these defective subjects was much greater than that of our Hopi subjects of comparable chronological ages.

DISCUSSION

The results presented in this paper show that twelve- and thirteen-year-old Hopi children, in comparison with white children of average intelligence and of the same age level as the Hopi subjects, much more often have concepts characteristic of the first two stages of animism, much more often attribute consciousness to inanimate objects, much more often believe that a bridge may break because of childish misdeeds, and much more often believe that the bridge is conscious of these misdeeds. The comparisons between Hopi and white children of greater age than thirteen years are less complete but are in the same direction. For brevity, we shall refer to these differences as differences in animism, although it is understood that not all of the differences have reference to animism in its strictest sense.

It is known that mental retardation causes animistic ideas, and also moral realism, to persist to advanced chronological ages (Abel, 1941; Granich, 1940; Lane and Kinder, 1939; Prothro, 1943; Russell et al., 1940). Therefore, the question must be raised as to whether the greater animism of Hopi children in comparison with white children is due to a native difference in intelligence. This theory is difficult to test, since the Hopi would obviously have an environmental handicap in most mental tests and hence an observed difference could not be attributed to native inferiority. Foreseeing this weakness in most intelligence tests as applied to primitive groups, we chose to test Hopi children by means of the Goodenough Draw-a-man test, believing that this test would place the Hopi at little or no disadvantage. In line with our guess, we found that on this test Hopi children show no inferiority to white norms (Dennis, 1942). The Hopi boys, in fact, are superior to white norms. There is no indication of a native inferiority in intelligence on the part of the Hopi, and an explanation of their more extensive animism cannot be given in terms of low intelligence.

The explanation must, therefore, be sought in terms of environment, and no doubt in the cultural environment rather than in terms of the physical environment. The differences in social environment between the Hopi child and the white American child are numerous. Since we cannot vary these social factors one at a time, we cannot find which ones are contributing to the difference in animism. It is very likely that several cultural factors are reinforcing each other. For one thing, the Hopi have a simple material culture, whereas American material culture is the most mechanized in the world. This difference in acquaintance with mechanical artifacts may affect the development of animistic ideas. Furthermore, apart from mechanics, the American culture has a tradition for naturalistic explanation of events, whereas in Hopi culture the naturalistic, the magical, and the supernatural are seldom separated (Parsons, 1939). Even the cultivating of corn has animistic as well as naturalistic elements for the Hopi (Forde, 1931). We may mention also the fact that the Hopi subjects were bilingual, while most of the white subjects were monolingual. The effort involved in learning two languages may very well cause the child to be preoccupied with linguistic problems to such an extent as to preclude much attention to natural-science explanations. There is also the pertinent fact that the adult concept itself attributes life very widely, and this fact may make it difficult for the Hopi child to discover his error. These suggestions do not exhaust the possibilities of accounting for the Hopi-white differences which we have observed but merely serve to call attention to the complexity of the problem. At the present time we can see little likelihood of our being able to isolate the various factors which may be involved. It should be noted that at Zuni, which possesses a culture closely related to the Hopi, a high degree of child animism has also been observed (Dennis and Russell, 1940).

Attention to the differences in the extent of animism between Hopi and white children should not cause us to overlook a fact which is probably more important. This is that the animistic answers, while not equal in frequency in the two societies, were identical in kind. We found practically no answers among the Hopi which are not common among white children. While we did not test very young Hopi children, the facts presented concerning older children indicate that probably Hopi and white children at all ages possess the same types of pre-adult ideas, but that white children give up these childish ideas at a faster rate than do the Hopi.

It is doubtful that the earliest ideas of children differ at all from society to society. The early childhood notions of the sort described by Piaget probably are world-wide. It is likely that they develop out of universal experiences, such as the experiences of self-movement, of visual movement, of frustration and success, of sleeping and waking— experiences which are common to the children of all societies. As we have argued elsewhere (Dennis, 1942), it would seem that these ideas are autogenous, *i.e.*, developed by each individual independently of communication with others. Society affects the fate of these ideas, but not their origin.

One piece of research needs to be examined in detail because it seems to contradict the hypothesis just advanced. We refer to the study by Mead (1932) which concluded that animism is absent among the Manus children of the Admiralty Islands. Mead therefore proposed that child animism is the outcome of certain kinds of cultural influences.

We cannot accept Mead's finding that animism is absent among Manus children because we believe her methods of attempting to discover it were unsatisfactory. In justice to Mead it should be pointed out that her field work was done in the winter of 1928–29, before the appearance of Piaget's *Child's Conception of the World,* on which the recent research on animism has been based.

Mead presented four types of evidence for the absence of animistic thought among the Manus children. We shall describe each of these and then comment briefly on each. (*a*) Mead found that Manus children did not spontaneously construct animistic explanations of natural phenomena in play and in ordinary life situations. Piaget has not used this method because children's explanations are seldom stated clearly or fully unless they are brought to light by the questioning of the investigator. (*b*) In a large series of drawings, there were no personified natural phenomena or humanized inanimate objects; neither are there in the drawings of Hopi children, who are very animistic. The child has no way of expressing in a drawing the fact that the object pictured is alive. Mead has here confused animism with personification. (*c*) No animistic responses were given to ink-blot tests. It is difficult to see how animistic ideas could be expressed in this connection. If a child in Stage I says a blot looks like a table, he does not volunteer that the table is alive: to the child that is taken for granted. Questioning is necessary to elicit such information. (*d*) Various tests were used, none of these identical with Piaget's procedures. They were concerned with the following things: (1) the attribution of malicious intent to a canoe which was drifting away; (2) the attribution of communication to Chinese glass chimes; (3) the explanation of the movements of a doll; (4) the attribution of malicious intent to a pencil with which the child had made a poor drawing; (5) the explanation of the action of a typewriter; (6) the explanation of the opening of Japanese paper flowers placed in water. These tests would seem more appropriate for the investigation of notions of causality (Piaget, 1930) than they are for the study of animism. We need not discuss these situations in full. We need only remark that it appears that not once was a child asked the direct question, "Is this living or is it dead?" Since Piaget's methods were not used, there is no evidence that his methods would reveal an absence of animism among Manus children. Mead's results, therefore, do not negate our hypothesis.

SUMMARY

Ninety-eight Hopi children between the ages of twelve and eighteen years were given a standardized interview with respect to animism and also a standardized interview with regard to moral realism, and 69 of them were further questioned with respect to the attribution of consciousness to objects. The Hopi subjects were more animistic and expressed more belief in the consciousness of objects and in moral realism than do white American subjects of the same ages. The concepts of the Hopi children, however, are of the same types as those found among white children.

It is proposed that the differences in the rate at which early ideas are abandoned in Hopi and white communities may be due to a variety of cultural factors which at present cannot be separated.

It is further proposed that the earliest ideas of children are uniform in all societies and are the product of universal child experiences and of mental immaturity. Mead's evidence which is apparently contradictory to this hypothesis has been analyzed and has been shown to be inconclusive, since the evidence was not derived by the use of the methods which have been employed by Piaget and others.

References

Abel, T. M. Moral judgments among subnormals, *J. Abnorm. Soc. Psychol.,* 1941, **36,** 378–392.

Beaglehole, E. and P. Beaglehole. Hopi of Second Mesa. *Mem. Amer. Anthrop. Ass.,* 1935, **44,** 65.

Dennis, W. *The Hopi child.* New York: Appleton-Century-Crofts, 1940.

Dennis, W. Piaget's questions applied to a child of known environment, *J. Genet. Psychol.,* 1942, **60,** 307–320.

Dennis, W. The performance of Hopi children on Goodenough's Draw-a-Man Test, *J. Comp. Psychol.,* 1942, **34,** 341–348.

Dennis, W. and R. W. Russell. Piaget's questions applied to Zuni children, *Child Development,* 1940, **11,** 181–187.

Forde, C. D. Hopi agriculture and land ownership, *J. Roy. Anthrop. Inst.,* 1931, **61,** 357–405.

Granich, L. A qualitative analysis of concepts in mentally deficient schoolboys, *Arch. Psychol., N. Y.,* 1940, No. 251.

Lane, E. B. and E. F. Kinder. Relativism in thinking of subnormal subjects as measured by certain of Piaget's tests, *J. Genet. Psychol.,* 1939, **54,** 107–118.

Lerner, E. *Constraint areas and the moral judgment of children.* Menasha, Wis.: Banta Publishing Co., 1937.

Lerner, E. Observations sur le raisonnement moral de l'enfant. (*Cahiers pédegog. Exper. et psychol, de l'enfantifi,* No. 11.) Geneva: Palia Wilson, 1938.

Mead, M. An investigation of the thought of primitive children with special reference to animism, *J. Roy. Anthrop. Inst.,* 1932, **62,** 173–190.

Parsons, E. C. *Pueblo Indian religion.* 2 vols. Chicago: University of Chicago Press, 1939.

Piaget, J. *The child's conception of the world.* New York: Harcourt, Brace, and World, Inc., 1929.

Piaget, J. *The child's conception of physical causality.* New York: Harcourt, Brace, and World, Inc., 1930.

Piaget, J. *The moral judgment of the child.* New York: Harcourt, Brace, and World, Inc., 1932.

Prothro, E. T. Egocentrism and abstraction in children and in adult aments. *Amer. J. Psychol.,* 1943, **56,** 66–77.

Russell, R. W. Studies in animism: II. The development of animism, *J. Genet. Psychol.,* 1940, **56,** 353–366.

Russell, R. W. Studies in animism: IV. An investigation of concepts allied to animism, *J. Genet. Psychol.,* 1940, **57,** 83–91.

Russell, R. W. Studies in animism: V. Animism in older children, *J. Genet. Psychol.,* 1942, **60,** 329–335.

Russell, R. W. and W. Dennis. Studies in animism: I. A standardized procedure for the investigation of animism, *J. Genet. Psychol.,* 1939, **55,** 389–400.

Russell, R. W. and W. Dennis. Note concerning the procedure employed in investigating child animism, *J. Genet. Psychol.,* 1941, **58,** 424–425.

Russell, R. W., W. Dennis, and F. E. Ash. Studies in animism: III. Animism in feeble-minded subjects, *J. Genet. Psychol.,* 1940, **57,** 57–63.

Simmons, L. W. (ed.). *Sun chief.* New Haven: Yale University Press, 1942.

4-7

Child Training Practices
and the Achievement Motivation
Appearing in Folk Tales

DAVID C. MCCLELLAND
G. A. FRIEDMAN

It is hoped that by this time the reader will have discovered that cross-cultural studies employ many different research techniques. There is no single approach to the understanding of cultural differences.

This selection utilizes a technique not previously illustrated in this book—the content analysis of folk tales. Folk tales are told in even the most sophisticated societies. If these stories influence children, and they probably do, they reveal to the child the trends of thinking in his society.

The publication of the present selection has stimulated research using other methods to investigate the achievement motive in different cultures. McClelland and his associates (1953) related the achievement motive to childhood socialization by using the Thematic Apperception Test (c f. introduction to Chapter 6, Selection 5). It is found that the achievement motive is associated with parental child rearing practices that stress competition, excellence of performance in addition to positive reinforcement for doing well and negative reinforcement for failure. Although this association has been

Reprinted from T. M. Newcomb, E. L. Hartley, and G. E. Swanson (eds.), *Readings in social psychology*, New York: Holt, Rinehart and Winston, Inc., 1952, by permission of the authors and the publishers.

documented in many cultures (c f. Prothro, Chapter 4, Selection 2), there are some exceptions to the conclusions arrived at by Mc-Clelland and his associates. The development of research in this area in Western as well as non-Western cultures is well documented by De Vos (1968).

The use of folk tales in the study of the achievement motive has been further developed and revised by McClelland (1961) in his book *The achieving society.*

REFERENCES

De Vos, G. A. Achievement and innovation in culture and personality. In E. Norbeck, D. Price-Williams, and W. M. McCord (eds.), *The study of personality: An interdisciplinary appraisal.* New York: Holt, Rinehart and Winston, Inc., 1968.

McClelland, D. C. *The achieving society.* Chapter 3. Princeton, N.J.: D. Van Nostrand Company, 1961.

McClelland, D. C., J. W. Atkinson, R. A. Clark, and E. L. Lowell. *The achievement motive.* New York: Appleton-Century-Crofts, 1953.

It is generally accepted in modern psychological theory that the motives which direct most of the daily behavior of men are acquired during the life experience. Yet systematic empirical investigation into such matters as the conditions under which they are acquired has long been hindered by the lack of an acceptable method of measuring their motives.

Recently steps have been taken to remedy this defect. Two traditional but quite different approaches to the problem of measuring motivation have been combined in a program of research aimed at developing a valid measure of human motivation. The first of these approaches is that adopted by the clinical psychologist who assumes, on the basis of years of successful clinical experience from Freud to Murray, that free association, fantasy, and other such imaginative processes reflect most sensitively the inner motivational states of the human personality. The other approach is that adopted by the animal psychologist who has worked with motivation primarily by arousing it in the laboratory through the manipulation of external conditions such as hours of food deprivation, amount of electric shock, etc. The new research program follows the lead of the experimentalist in arousing the motives in the laboratory and the lead of the clinician in measuring their effect on imaginative processes.

After demonstrating that changes in the content of short imaginative stories written by persons deprived of food for different periods of time (and therefore presumed to differ in hunger) could be coded and quantified in a way which would provide a rough index of hunger motivation (Atkinson and McClelland, 1948), the task of developing a similar measure of achievement motivation was undertaken. Changes in imaginative stories associated with experimentally produced increases in achievement motivation were noted (McClelland, et al., 1949). The plots of stories written following variations of the now fairly standard laboratory procedures for "ego-involving" or heightening the achievement motivation of subjects were compared with stories written under more relaxed conditions and were found to contain many more instances of characters in the story *competing with standards of excellence,* or in more simple terms, *trying to do well* in relation to some achievement goal. A variety of categories of response, corresponding to aspects of the instigation-action or problem-solving sequence commonly used as a model in the analysis of overt behavior, were found to increase with increasing intensity of achievement motivation. Among these were statements of the need to achieve, instrumental acts directed toward achievement, obstacles to be overcome, anticipations of success or failure, and positive or negative affective reactions accompanying the success or failure of the enterprise.

An estimate of the strength of an individual's motivation to achieve has been obtained by counting the number of such achievement-related response categories in his stories. This measure, the n Achievement score, has been related to perception (McClelland and Liberman, 1949), memory (Atkinson, 1951), performance on various activities, level of aspiration, learning, and academic accomplishment (McClelland, et al., 1953). The relationships discovered have confirmed the hypothesis that the n Achievement score is a measure of motivational strength.

While most of these studies have been accomplished with male, mostly middle-class college students, as subjects, other studies with subjects of high-school age (Veroff, 1950; McClelland, et al., 1953) or even from another culture (Navajo) have shown that the method of obtaining the n Achievement score is not just applicable to the selected portion of the population represented in college nor is it culture-bound. For example, a significant increase in mean n Achievement score has been obtained between stories written under conditions of low achievement arousal and higher achievement arousal even among the Navajo.

Having reason to believe that the n Achievement score is actually a measure of motivation, both on the basis of its sensitivity to experimental arousal procedures and its meaningful relations to a variety of behavioral measures, let us turn to the question of how the individual differences in motive intensity that have been observed come about. Are the backgrounds of individuals differing in strength of achievement motivation different in any important respects?

On theoretical grounds we would expect to find important background differences since we have argued that all motives are learned.

According to the definition of an Achievement-related response, as defined in our directions for scoring fantasy products, we should expect that individuals who have more often been held up to competitive achievement standards, either personal or impersonal, should show higher achievement motivation. In addition, the increased frequency of affective anticipations and affective responses accompanying success and failure in imaginative stories concerning achievement lead us to expect that individuals who have experienced more changes in affective arousal resulting from rewards and punishments in connection with problem-solving and mastery in childhood will develop stronger motivation to achieve.

Several investigations have been undertaken which throw light on this problem. The one to be reported here involves a cross-cultural study of the relationship between child-training practices in various North American Indian cultures and strength of the achievement motive as reflected in folk tales told by members of the cultures.

In searching for the factors which might lead to the development of achievement motivation, we were led, both by our general theory and by the positive results of our Navajo study, to believe that there are certain common recurrent problem-solving situations involving achievement which enter into the relationship between any parent and child. All children have to learn to walk, talk, and master other such problems as hunting, sewing, fishing, reading, or writing. We know that parents differ in the amount of pressure they place on their children for early mastery of such skills and in the amount of reward and punishment (producing changes in effective arousal) meted out for success or failure. Furthermore, there are modal differences from culture to culture in the amount of stress placed by parents on achievement. Thus we can test the hypothesis that stress in the achievement area of learning is associated with higher *n* Achievement either among cultures or among families within a culture. We can relate measures of the importance of achievement training in various cultures to *n* Achievement scores for those cultures, and we can relate measures of the importance of achievement training in various families of a given culture to the *n* Achievement scores of individuals from those families.

How can an *n* Achievement score be obtained for a culture? The answer to this question involves a method of measurement which is somewhat different from the one ordinarily used in these studies. We decided to use folk tales rather than actual stories obtained experimentally for several reasons. (1) It would have been prohibitively expensive and time-consuming, though not impossible, to obtain actual stories in the field. (2) Even if we had obtained stories in the field, our subjects would very likely have been partly acculturated (i.e., Americanized) especially if we had taken them from our usual age groups. Folk tales on the other hand, since they are passed on by word of mouth within the cultures, are usually viewed as less altered, "purer" reflections of cultural orientations. (3) A folk tale represents a kind of summation of the common thought patterns of a number of individuals and as such may be considered the rough equivalent of a statistically modal or average story obtained from a sample of stories told by different individuals. Thus it may take the place of testing a large number of individuals from the culture. Such a hypothesis is supported by Bartlett's (1932) laboratory experiments on serial reproduction.

Starting with these assumptions, G. A. Friedman, working with the assistance of Dr. J. W. M. Whiting and Dr. John Roberts, collected twelve brief stories from each of eight American Indian cultures: Navajo, Ciricahua Apache, Western Apache, Comanche, Flatheads, Hopi, Paiute, and Sanpoil. Stories were collected by them in advance of any knowledge on their part of the n Achievement scoring system. In order to reduce variability as much as possible, the stories all concerned the same central character, Coyote, who figures as a trickster hero in many of the folk tales told by North American Indian tribes. Stories were fairly comparable in length and were as unitary with regard to plot as possible—that is, longer stories were broken up into episodes with a beginning, middle, and end. The stories were then scored in the usual way for n Achievement. The fact that no additional assumptions were necessary to perform this feat may be regarded as evidence of the generality of the scoring system.

The major difference between these stories and those of our college students was the infrequency of evidence of "general long-term achievement involvement." Career or occupational concern did not appear in the Coyote stories—perhaps because of the circumstances in which they had been told. Achievement imagery in the form of wanting to do well, however, frequently appeared. Interestingly enough, the themes of tales from different cultures were frequently the same, though they differed in the amount of achievement "embroidery" included. Compare these two stories, for example:

A Comanche Tale

Coyote was always knocking about hunting for something. He came to a creek, where there was nothing but green willows. Two little yellow-birds were playing there. He came up to them. Laughing, they pulled out their eyes and threw them on the trees, while they stood below. "Eyes, fall!" they said. Then their eyes fell back into their sockets. Coyote went to them. *He greatly admired their trick.* "Oh, brothers! I wish to play that way, too." "Oh, we won't show you, you are too mean. You would throw your eyes into any kind of a tree and lose them."—"Oh, no! I would do just like you." At last *the birds agreed to show him.* They pulled out his eyes, threw them up, and said, "Eyes, fall!" They returned to their places. "Let us all go along this creek!" said the birds. "*Other people will see us and take a fancy to us.*" They went along playing. Coyote said, "I am going over there. I know the trick well now." He left them. He got to another creek. A common willow tree was standing there. "*There is no need to be afraid of this tree.* I'll try it first." He pulled out his eyes, and threw them at the tree. "Eyes, fall!" he shouted. His eyes did not fall. He thus became blind. He tied something around his eyes, and left.

A Paiute Tale

Coyote was walking along. He heard someone laughing. "Come in," they said. Wild Cat and some others were sitting there. I think Skunk was there too. Coyote asked them, "What shall I do?" "Take out your eyes. Throw them in the air. Then hold your head back, and they will fall in again." Coyote tried to take out his eyes. He took them both out and threw them up, but not very far. He held back his head, and the eyes fell right in the sockets. Everybody laughed. Then Wild Cat tried it again. *He threw his eyes way in the air, and they came back. Everybody laughed* and told Coyote to try it again. "Throw them way up in the air this time," they said. He did it. One had a stick in his hand. When Coyote's eyes were coming down, he knocked them to one side. Then everybody ran away. They took Coyote's eyes with them.

In both tales the central idea is the same, but—we will not go into the details of the scoring method—it is obvious that the first version, from a high achievement culture, contains far more achievement imagery than the second. Some of the achievement-related portions have been italicized in each story to make the contrast clearer. According to the Comanche, Coyote wants very much to perform this unusual feat with his eyes, is at first blocked, finally succeeds with the help of the birds, is proud of his skill, etc. In the Paiute version, the theme has been so changed that it appears the other animals are now primarily interested in playing a practical joke on Coyote, who is not portrayed on the other hand as having any particular achievement concern. Nevertheless, even in this story some hints of achievement imagery appear, and they were scored here and in other similar instances on the ground that some of the finer nuances of meaning may have been lost in translation.

An n Achievement score was next computed for each of the eight cultures by summing algebraically the number of different types of achievement imagery appearing in each of the twelve stories (with doubtful stories scored 0 and unrelated, -1). The question of interest is whether these "cultural" n Achievement scores are related to differences in the amount of emphasis placed on achievement training in the various cultures. Fortunately, ratings on various child-training practices in these tribes were available. They had been obtained by Whiting and Child for another study from ethnographic data contained in the Human Relations Area File at Yale University (Murdock, et al., 1950) and consisted of the averages of judgments by three judges working independently from the same source material. They covered five areas of training: nursing and weaning, toilet training, sex training, independence training, and aggression control. In each training area three variables were rated. A description of the three variables as rated for independence training follows:

Initial Indulgence—the degree to which the parent responds with nurturance and caretaking to dependency needs whenever the child cries or seems to need attention or want affection. This refers to the period before training starts. (Rated on a 7-point scale.)

Age of Training—the age at which independence training starts.

Severity—the suddenness of training, strength and frequency of punishment for nonindependence, signs of emotional conflict in the child during independence training. (Rated on a 7-point scale.)

Of all the areas rated, independence training is most nearly related to what we have been calling achievement training. A child who is forced to be "on his own" and to give up being nurtured by adults is also one who will have to master his own problems and get along by himself. Furthermore, parents who insist on independence are likely to stress self-reliance and individual achievement and to punish their children for inability to do something without help. We therefore predicted that emphasis on independence training as measured by any of the three variables would be positively associated with the n Achievement score obtained from the folk tales. It is particularly fortunate that ratings took into account "signs of emotional conflict" since such signs of affective arousal give the evidence demanded by our theory (McClelland, et al., 1953) that the opportunity for motive formation had frequently occurred.

The results are given in Table 1. All three measures of stress on independence in the child are related significantly to cultural n Achievement score—that is, the less the initial indulgence, the earlier the age at which the child is put on his own, and the greater the severity of punishment for dependence, the higher the n Achievement score for the culture tends to be. The relationship is particularly close for the second two variables, and when their ranks are combined, the probability of such an agreement between two rank orders arising by chance, as computed by Kendall's (1948) tau, is less than .0005 even with only eight cases. From inspection it can be seen that there is only one inversion in rank order and one tie which prevent the relationship from being perfect. Since the raw achievement scores in the case of the inversion are well

TABLE 1

Rank Correlations (Tau) Between n Achievement Scores Obtained from Folk Tales in Eight Cultures and Ratings of Child Training in Those Cultures

Culture	n Achievement		Independence-Training Rank			Age and Severity	Nursing and Weaning	Ranks of Severity of Training		
		Score Rank	Init. Indulg.	Age	Severity			Toilet	Sex	Aggression
Navajo	19	1	3.5	1	1	1	1	4.5	4.5	7
C. Apache	15	2	8	4	2	2	5	2.5	1	2.5
Hopi	13	3	7	2	6.5	4	5	4.5	6.5	2.5
Comanche	12	4	3.5	3	5	3	5	6.5	8	8
Sanpoil	9	5	6	5.5	3.5	5.5	3	1	3	5
W. Apache	5	6	3.5	5.5	3.5	5.5	2	8	2	6
Paiute	2	7	3.5	7	6.5	7	7	6.5	4.5	1
Flatheads	1	8	1	8	8	8	8	2.5	6.5	4
Tau	—	—	−.56	+.84	+.64	+.91	+.42	+.16	+.16	−.18
P values	—	—	.05	.005	.05	.0005	.15	.40	.40	.35

within scoring error, it is clear that the relationship is a very close one indeed. It is especially impressive in view of some of the methodological considerations involved. (1) The person who scored the folk tales had no accurate knowledge of the independence-training ratings when he was scoring them. In any case, his scoring was highly objective, since he obtained a coefficient of agreement of .91 when he rescored all the stories. (2) Many of the folk tales were collected in adverse circumstances. It was not always possible to get twelve stories that were accurately recorded according to the best field techniques. (3) The dates at which the stories were recorded varied roughly from 1890–1940; the child-training ratings were based on observations made approximately during this same period, but there was no certainty that the date of the folk tale and the date of the observations coincided. From all this we might conclude that the relationship we are measuring is so gross that it can be picked up even with such imperfect instruments.

We are not necessarily arguing for a simple cause-and-effect relationship between emphasis on independence training in childhood and high achievement motivation in a culture. A more likely hypothesis is that a general emphasis on achievement in the culture influences both child training and the kind of stories which are told in the culture—particularly since the stories may often be used to educate the young. The only other child-training variable in the table approaching a significant relationship with n Achievement is severity of weaning. This is not surprising. Weaning severity and independence training were found to be positively correlated in Whiting and Child's study (unpublished manuscript) and, in fact, could not easily be distinguished by the raters since one of the criteria for insistence on independence was age of weaning.

The general implications of this study may be briefly summarized:

1. It illustrates the usefulness of data collected in the Human Relations Area File for testing hypotheses about relationships between culture and personality.

2. It shows how the folk tales of a culture can be used to diagnose the modal motivations of members of the culture, much as stories produced by many individuals may be used to diagnose group tendencies in motivation.

3. It shows that achievement motivation apparently expresses itself fairly universally in fantasy in the same ways or conversely that the scoring system devised is applicable fairly universally for measuring achievement motivation.

4. Finally, it suggests that cultures which are concerned with achievement are likely to stress independence training in childhood, which in turn produces a higher level of achievement motivation in members of the culture, at least as reflected in their folk tales. These stories in turn reinforce the achievement orientation which leads to a

stress on independence training and so on in a chain of mutually reinforcing events which illustrates nicely what anthropologists mean by such terms as "culture pattern" or "cultural value orientation."

References

Atkinson, J. W. Recall of successes and failures related to differences in need for achievement, *Amer. Psychol.*, 1951, **6,** 315 (abstract).

Atkinson, J. W. and D. C. McClelland. The projective expression of needs. II. The effect of different intensities of hunger drive on thematic apperception, *J. Exp. Psychol.*, 1948, **38,** 643–658.

Bartlett, F. C., *Remembering: A study in experimental and social psychology.* Cambridge, Eng.: Cambridge University Press, 1932.

Kendall, M. G. *Rank correlation methods.* London: Charles Griffin and Co., Ltd., 1948.

McClelland, D. C., J. W. Atkinson, R. A. Clark, and E. L. Lowell. *The achievement motive.* New York: Appleton-Century-Crofts, 1953.

McClelland, D. C., R. A. Clark, T. B. Roby, and J. W. Atkinson. The projective expression of needs. IV. The effect of the need for achievement on thematic apperception, *J. Exp. Psychol.*, 1949, **39,** 242–255.

McClelland, D. C. and A. M. Liberman. The effect of need for achievement on recognition of need-related words, *J. Personality*, 1949, **18,** 236–251.

Murdock, G. P., C. S. Ford, A. E. Hudson, R. Kennedy, L. W. Simmons, and J. W. M. Whiting. *Behavior science outlines.* Vol. I: *Outline of cultural materials.* Third rev. ed. New Haven: Human Relations Area Files, Inc., 1950.

Veroff, J. A projective measure of the achievement motivation of adolescent males and females. Unpublished A. B. thesis, Wesleyan University, 1950.

Whiting, J. W. M. and I. L. Child. Child training practices and theories of disease: A cross-cultural study of personality development. Unpublished manuscript.

CHAPTER 5

PSYCHOLINGUISTICS

5-1

The Fitness of Names to Drawings in Tanganyika

R. DAVIS

Sometimes words appear to be arbitrarily assigned to objects without any necessary relation between the two. However, some words because of their physiognomic characteristics seem to be more appropriate for certain objects than do other words. Some visual characteristics of objects tend to be associated with the auditory characteristics of their names. In the present study by Davis there is agreement between children in Tanganyika and English children in matching nonsense words (names) and abstract drawings. This suggests that there is a generality in the association of names and characteristics of objects across cultures.

The fitness of words to their referents has long been a subject for discussion. In Plato's dialogue 'Kratylus' two principles of correct naming are described, one of which may be called an 'associative' principle, the other might be called a 'structural' principle. Whenever any name is applied to a new referent we may consider whether this application is appropriate to its derivation and the ideas it evokes. For example, is 'radio' or 'wireless' the more appropriate name, in view of the associations

Reprinted from *Brit. J. Psychol.*, 1961, **52**, 259–268, by permission of the author and the British Psychological Society.

produced by these words or their components? This is an example of the 'associative' principle in naming. The 'structural' principle involves the relation between the actual speech sounds and their referents. Does 'large' seem a more appropriate sound than 'tiny' to describe large objects because of the actual nature of the speech sounds themselves? The specific structural relationship between speech sounds and their referents has come to be known as 'phonetic symbolism' following Sapir (1929), and in a recent review of the literature, Brown (1958) refers to the other principle as 'metaphor'.

Historically we may trace two distinct types of experiment which have attempted to investigate structural principles in naming. The first of these derives from Jespersen's (1922) studies of the size implications of the vowels in languages of the Indo-European group. A series of experiments on phonetic symbolism, comparing a wide variety of different languages has been critically considered by Brown (1958) in his comprehensive review: He concludes that no sound-meaning correlation has been satisfactorily demonstrated in the lexicon of any language. On the other hand, some studies, such as those of Brown, et al. (1955) indicate that it is probable that most speakers of a given language find similar symbolic implications in an unfamiliar phonetic sequence. In these experiments subjects were asked to indicate which of two opposed meanings a spoken word in an unfamiliar language might have, and their choices were compared with the actual meanings in the unfamiliar language. Further reviews of recent experiments on phonetic symbolism may be found in Brown and Nuttall (1959) and in Slobin (1960).

The earliest example of the other type of approach is probably an experiment by Uznadze (1924) in which subjects were asked to match made-up nonsense syllables with abstract drawings. Uznadze does not reproduce the drawings he used and it is difficult to recover the exact technique from his account. However, there are sufficient subsequent experiments of a similar type to have confidence in the results. Fox (1935) describes an extensive series of experiments of this sort, one of which consisted of asking the subjects to allot Köhler's (1929) pair of nonsense names 'Baluma' and 'Takete' to one or other of a pair of drawings, a predominantly angular drawing and a predominantly rounded one. The results supported Köhler's views: seventy-four out of seventy-eight subjects alloted 'takete' to the angular drawing. When 'baluma' was altered to 'malumba' to avoid the similarity with 'balloon' and the possible association of balloon with the rounded drawing, thirty-six out of thirty-seven subjects responded in the expected way. These results were further confirmed by Irwin and Newland (1940), who used several sets of nonsense words and drawings, including 'takete' and 'maluma', the form finally adopted by Köhler (1947). In a developmental study they showed that significant differences from a chance allocation were clearly established in their subjects by the age of 9 years.

It is clear, however, that associative principles are not entirely ruled out by such experiments. The argument for excluding them has usually been that when subjects were subsequently interrogated about the reasons for their choice, even when they gave associative reasons, these were so disparate that they could hardly account for the uniformity in the results. Hall and Oldfield (1950), on these grounds, considered that structural principles accounted for some of the matches in their experiments, even though meaningful concepts were being matched with fairly complicated drawings. Further evidence for a 'structural' relationship could be obtained by using the same nonsense syllables and drawings in completely different language and culture groups. If the same matches were made this would be strong evidence in favour of the structural explanation. This is what the present author attempted, and the experiments will be described below.

An extreme case of what appears to be a structural relationship is found in synaesthesia, in which the qualities normally appropriate to one mode of perceiving are attributed to a different mode. The writings of the Symbolists are full of such allusions, and Galton (1883) was probably the first person to make a systematic survey of cases of 'coloured hearing', which may take the form of attributing different colours to the notes of a musical scale. Although the extreme cases, in which the actual sensory qualities of the different mode appear to be present to the observer, show considerable variability among subjects, various writers have argued that there is a continuity between synaesthesia and ordinary forms of thinking. Karwoski, Odbert and Osgood (1942) showed that when an unselected group of subjects were asked to represent a 15 sec. melodic line played on a clarinet, their drawings were similar in form to the drawings of a group of 'photistic visualizers' who habitually 'saw' music in the form of visual patterns. Osgood (in Osgood et al., 1957) reports a comparison of Navajo drawings to a simple melodic line in which he found striking similarities to the drawings of Dartmouth students, but this preliminary study is the only one of its type known to the present author. Osgood (1960) has produced an extensive cross-cultural survey of 'synaesthetic thinking', but the words to be matched against pairs of drawings denoted meaningful concepts and he was concerned with analysing relationships which we have called 'associative' by means of the semantic differential technique. Although Osgood found similarities among the different cultural groups in the associative relations of concepts (such as 'man', 'good') to pairs of drawings representing opposites (such as 'up', 'down'), it is necessary to be cautious about interpreting some of his results. All the subjects had some knowledge of English, and the Japanese subjects 'were either staff or students at the University of Illinois, but had been in this country (U.S.A.) less than 2 years'. Clearly, it would be an advantage to have more data on monolingual subjects in completely different cultures.

An opportunity for investigating 'structural' relationships between words and drawings in a completely different cultural group occurred in the summer of 1959 when the author was a member of the Oxford University Tanganyika expedition. The region was an isolated peninsula on the eastern shore of Lake Tanganyika (the Congo-Tanganyika border). The inhabitants were cut off from their place of origin in the Congo by the Lake, which was rarely crossed, and from the rest of Tanganyika by the Mahali mountains (8250 ft.). The only communication with other areas was by way of the lake, or mountain passes. European influence was slight, the main source being the Mission stations to north and south, some hundred miles distant by boat. The other main sources of external influence were the Arab traders who moved between the Lakeshore villages.

The main tribes in the area were the Mholoholo and the Mtongwe, but they were no longer distinct and the district was organized by villages. Each village usually contained members of both tribes as well as a sprinkling of others, and the headman had authority over all members of his village. The lingua franca was Swahili, but for domestic purposes Kitongwe (a Bantu type dialect) was used. For the main investigation the subjects were children from about 8 to 14 years old in the native schools of the larger villages. They spoke Kitongwe (or other dialects) as their first language and were learning Swahili at school. No English was taught (or understood) except in the senior classes of the larger Mission and Government schools, which were not included in the analysis.

II. EXPERIMENTAL METHOD

Since everything had to be carried from place to place, either by small boat, or on foot, experimental equipment had to be reduced to a minimum, and consisted of a set of pencils and some sheets of paper. It was decided to use drawings similar to Köhler's (1947) pair, but 'maluma' was changed to 'uloomu', following Hochberg & Brooks (1956), when it was discovered that 'Malume' in certain Bantu dialects meant 'mother's brother'. 'Takete' seemed to have no immediate reference.

The author's knowledge of Swahili was extremely limited, so that instructions were given through an interpreter in a sentence by sentence translation. A group of children were equipped with pencils and paper and then told that we were interested in comparing African children's drawings with drawings by European children. No mention was made of naming at this point.

Introductory Experiment

In order to get the children used to this rather strange situation, an introductory experiment was carried out using another pair of drawings. These consisted of 'pinmen', one with a circular head and one with a square head, which were drawn on a blackboard by the author. The children were then asked to copy these drawings and when they were finished they were told 'let us suppose that one of these is a man and the other is a woman. Write "man" (Swahili "mume") under the one you think is a man, and "woman" (Swahili "mwanamke") under the one you think is a woman'. It was emphasized that there were no right or wrong answers; we just wanted to see what each of them thought about the drawings. The drawings were made 18–24 in. high by the author and were placed side by side, drawing the 'head' (square or circle) first and adding the 'body', which was identical for the two figures, afterwards (Figure 1). They were copied onto small sheets of note-paper by the children. The right-left placing of the two figures was alternated with successive groups of children and in the verbal instructions 'man' always preceded 'woman'. The relation of the sequence of verbal instructions to the left-right position of the figures is of some importance and will be discussed below.

A   B

Figure 1A. Drawings used in the introductory experiment.
Figure 1B. Drawings used in the main experiment.

Takete-Uloomu Experiment

When the introductory experiment was completed the children were asked to turn over their papers and were told that they would be given two more drawings to copy. The Köhler-type figures were then drawn side by side on the blackboard. These invariably caused some

amusement—or astonishment, and great care was devoted to their reproduction. When everyone had completed his or her copy, two slightly
different procedures were used.

CONDITION A. The drawings on the board were rubbed out and
the words 'takete' and 'uloomu' were written on the board in English
capitals with 'takete' immediately above 'uloomu' (the Swahili alphabet
is similar to the English alphabet). It was explained that we would like to
give names to the drawings and that here were two possible names. The
whole group then repeated the names aloud several times, following the
author's pronunciation, with the main stress on the middle syllable. The
order was always 'takete' followed by 'uloomu'. When everyone seemed
to have grasped how the names were pronounced they were told to look
at their drawings, decide which was the best name for each, and write
the name they chose, under the appropriate drawing. With successive
groups of children the left-right arrangement of the two drawings was
reversed.

CONDITION B. To avoid direct association of the visual pattern of
the written word with the drawing, which has been a possible defect in
most of the previous experiments on word-name matching, in this condition no names whatsoever were written down by the experimenter. The
children were told that we had two names and these were pronounced by
the author over and over again, always in the order 'takete-uloomu', and
the group repeated them aloud until everyone seemed to have grasped
them. They were then told to allot one name to each drawing, as above,
and not to worry how the words were spelt, but to guess the spelling as
well as they could.

In this condition also, the left-right arrangement of the two drawings
was reversed with successive groups of children.

Control Experiments

In view of the fact that most previous experiments on name-drawing
matching have involved presenting the name visually (Irwin & Newland,
1940, is the only exception the author has discovered), a group of control
experiments on English children was carried out. Both the introductory
experiment and the Köhler-type drawings were used and the technique
was exactly the same as with the African children, except that condition
A (names written down) was omitted. Miss Helen Ross carried out the
experiments on 163 East London school children between the ages of 11
and 14, and Mrs. Susie Robinson used the same procedure on 118 school
children aged 13–14, in Wheatley, a village in Oxfordshire.

III. RESULTS. TAKETE–ULOOMU EXPERIMENT

The results of the experiment using the Köhler-type drawings will be considered first.

CONTROL GROUPS. The results of the control groups are shown in Table 1. The order of presentation in which the angular figure was on the left and the rounded figure on the right has been called 'positive'. The names were always spoken in the order 'takete'–'uloomu', so that if a subject followed a 'dictation stereotype' procedure of merely allotting the name first spoken to the drawing on the left, in the case of a positive presentation this would produce the same result as a genuine allocation on the basis of 'fitness'. In the 'negative' presentation the angular drawing was on the right and the same order of names was used, so that a tendency to write the names from left to right in the order they were pronounced would oppose a genuine allocation.

It seemed particularly important to include this control in a cross-cultural study, in which the possibility always existed that the subjects might not have understood the instructions and therefore were trying to do something consistent in their responses, no matter what.

Results are presented as a total frequency of allocation of name to drawing, with both positive and negative orders of presentation combined, and then separately for each order of presentation. χ^2 for the difference between the observed frequencies and the chance frequency of allocation is shown, together with the confidence level reached. The results for boys and girls are presented separately, although the actual groups on which the experiment was performed were mixed.

The results in Table 1 show that 'takete' is allotted to the angular figure very consistently, even though the names were never presented visually—a useful confirmation of earlier results. There is some effect of the order of presentation, notably for the Wheatley boys, for whom the negative order reduced the value of χ^2 to a level not significant at $P = 0.05$. Unfortunately, for practical reasons, the numbers of subjects in different conditions were not equal, which makes it difficult to estimate the magnitude of the order effect. Nevertheless, the results suggest that it exists. Despite this effect, however, there is overwhelming evidence of the uniformity of allocation of 'takete' to the angular figure in the control groups.

AFRICAN CHILDREN. In Table 2 (p. 344) are shown the results for the African children.

TABLE 1

English school children. Köhler-type drawings*

	Combined score				Positive order				Negative order			
	For	Against	χ^2	P	For	Against	χ^2	P	For	Against	χ^2	P
East London												
Boys	57	20	16.8	< 0.001	30	11	8.0	< 0.01	27	9	8.0	< 0.01
Girls	80	6	61.9	≪ 0.001	38	0	—	—	42	6	25.5	< 0.001
Wheatley												
Boys	42	11	16.9	< 0.001	25	3	15.8	< 0.001	17	8	2.6	N.S.
Girls	62	3	59.4	≪ 0.001	31	1	23.8	< 0.001	31	2	23.8	< 0.001

*Showing frequencies for and against the hypothesis that 'takete' would be allotted to the angular drawing.

Table 2A deals with condition A in which the words were actually written down. Here, a positive presentation means that the angular drawing was presented on the left, and a negative presentation that the rounded drawing was presented on the left. In all cases 'takete' was written *above* 'uloomu' after the drawings had been erased from the board (though, of course, each child had his own copy).

Table 2B deals with the condition in which the words were only spoken, always in the order 'takete'—'uloomu', and positive and negative presentations have the same significance as in the control experiment.

IV. CONCLUSIONS. TAKETE–ULOOMU EXPERIMENT

The overall effect is quite clear. The African children match names and drawings in the same way as the English controls, thus providing strong evidence that it is the relation of appropriateness between the actual speech sounds and the perceived shapes which determines the choice, rather than meaningful associations with specific objects. Of course, the results could have been produced through a coincidence of meaningful associations in the two cultures but such a coincidence seems highly improbable—much more improbable than a coincidence of meaningful associations within a particular cultural group.

In no condition were the relative frequencies of allotting names to drawings by the African children opposed to the expected difference, although their agreement is not as high as among the English children, and when the conditions are examined separately some of the differences do not reach a statistically significant level. The effect of order of presentation is clearly demonstrated, particularly by the African girls, which suggests that some of them may not have understood the instructions. As a group they were much more withdrawn than the boys (who seemed to enjoy what they were doing) and some of the more retiring girls needed considerable encouragement before they could get anything at all down on paper.

On the whole the African groups were slightly younger and certainly educationally less advanced than the English children. Irwin and Newland (1940) showed that in their subjects (U.S.A. schoolchildren) consistent allocation of names to their figures, which included the Köhler pair, did not reach the 5% level of confidence until 9 years of age and above. The exact age range of the African children is difficult to determine but certainly the groups included children younger than this. According to teachers' estimates most of them were in the age range 8–14 years, but there were a few younger and a few older than this. The obvious procedure of asking a child to say how old he was produced very odd results. In one group there was a boy who stated that he was 3 years

TABLE 2

African children. Köhler-type drawings*

	Combined score				Positive order				Negative order			
	For	Against	χ^2	P	For	Against	χ^2	P	For	Against	χ^2	P
A. *Words written down*												
Boys	75	32	33.0	≪ 0.001	41	4	47.0	≪ 0.001	34	28	0.40	N.S.
Girls	As for positive order		—	—	21	3	12.0	< 0.001	No data		—	—
B. *Words spoken only*												
Boys	82	33	20.0	< 0.001	49	7	30.7	≪ 0.001	33	26	0.6	N.S.
Girls	50	39	1.1	N.S.	26	15	2.44	N.S.	24	24	0	N.S.

*Showing frequencies for and against the hypothesis that 'takete' would be allotted to the angular drawing.

old and another thought he was 21, although both looked to be at a similar stage of development and their teacher put them as being between 8 and 10 years. Further inquiries among their families produced equally erratic and contradictory stories so the attempt to produce any precise statement of age was abandoned.

V. RESULTS. INTRODUCTORY EXPERIMENT

Although the main intention behind the introductory experiment was to get the African children used to an unfamiliar situation, the results are worth considering as they have some bearing on the issue of whether pictorial symbols have a universal significance, or whether their meaning is specific within a particular culture.

CONTROL GROUPS. The results for the East London and the Wheatley children are shown in Table 3. 'Positive' order of presentation means that the figure with the square head was placed to the left of the figure with the round head, 'negative' order means the reverse arrangement. In giving the instructions 'man' was always mentioned before 'woman'.

A sex difference is immediately obvious in the results, which far outweighs any effect of the order of presentation. Although all the girls gave highly significant results in the expected direction, associating 'man' with the square-headed figure, the London boys (though not the Wheatley boys) gave significant results in the opposite direction. The reason for this was revealed in some of the spontaneous comments which were added to the drawings. 'Square' is used in jazz language to denote someone outside the group, who has the wrong kind of attitudes. As boys of this age tend to look down on girls and their activities, the girls may be considered 'squares'. An indication of this was provided by the boy who wrote 'square' next to the square-headed figure and 'a real cat' next to the round-headed figure.

This tendency was not evident in the children from rural Wheatley, although the Wheatley boys were less consistent in allotting 'man' to the square-headed figure than the girls, for whom there was no exception in sixty-five cases.

AFRICAN CHILDREN. The results for the African children are shown in Table 4.

There is a very clear overall effect in the expected direction. An order effect is also present in the results of the boys, reducing the differences to an insignificant level for the negative order of presentation.

TABLE 3

English school children. Man–woman drawings*

	Combined score				Positive order				Negative order			
	For	Against	χ^2	P	For	Against	χ^2	P	For	Against	χ^2	P
East London												
Boys	24	53	10.2	<0.01	11	25	4.6	<0.05	13	28	4.8	<0.05†
Girls	73	13	40.5	$\ll0.001$	44	4	31.7	$\ll0.001$	29	9	9.5	<0.01‡
Wheatley												
Boys	35	18	4.8	<0.05	18	7	4.0	<0.05	17	11	0.89	N.S.
Girls	65	0	—	—	33	0	—	—	32	0	—	—

† All significant in *opposite* direction to expected

‡ All significant in expected direction.

*Showing frequencies for and against hypothesis that 'man' would be allotted to the figure with a square head.

TABLE 4

African children. Man–woman drawings

	Combined score				Positive order				Negative order			
	For	Against	χ^2	P	For	Against	χ^2	P	For	Against	χ^2	P
Boys	155	76	26.3	<0.001	102	29	39.6	$\ll0.001$	53	47	0.5	N.S.
Girls	73	12	42.4	$\ll0.001$	27	3	17.7	<0.001	46	9	23.6	<0.001

*Showing frequencies for and against the hypothesis that 'man' would be allotted to the figure with the square head.

This does not appear with the girls who are somewhat more consistent than the boys, although presumably not for the same reasons as the London children!

VI. CONCLUSIONS. INTRODUCTORY EXPERIMENT

In this experiment there is an association between drawing and name which seems not to be determined by the structural similarity of the name and the drawing, but by some kind of meaningful association between them. In fact the structural properties of the names would tend, if anything, to produce the opposite allocations. Thus, the Swahili for 'man' is 'mume', and for 'woman' is 'mwanamke'. Structural factors might tend to produce an allocation of the more 'angular' word 'mwanamke' (often abbreviated to 'mke') to the more angular figure—the square head. In this case, however, the meaningful associations were predominant over the slight differences in structure. This may be important when the order in which the experiments were done is considered. The choices made in the introductory experiment would tend, if anything, to produce a bias against a structural allocation in the main experiment. The fact that such an allocation was found in the main experiment makes the evidence for structural factors in this experiment even stronger.

VII. GENERAL CONCLUSIONS

The main experiment had many aspects which tended to reduce the possibility of matching in the expected direction:

(1) The subjects chosen were children who were only learning the language in which the instructions were given (Swahili).

(2) The age of the children was not much above the age level below which differences became insignificant in Irwin and Newland's (1940) study of Philadelphia children. Indeed, the ages of a number of the African children were certainly below this level and their average age was probably a year or two less than the control groups of English children.

(3) The nonsense words were spoken by the experimenter and not written down, so that there was no possibility of an association between the visual pattern of the word and the drawing.

(4) The left-right arrangement in which the drawings were presented was alternated in order to overcome the possible effects of a 'dictation stereotype', a tendency to write down the first spoken name on the left. This was shown to exist, but was not strong enough to invalidate the results. It suggests that, in other cross-cultural studies using this kind

of design, 'dictation stereotypes' should be allowed for. In written languages in which the order of writing is from right to left, or from below upwards, we might well expect to find the opposite stereotype.

Despite all these factors, however, there was a clear tendency among the African children to make allocations in the expected direction. We may therefore state with considerable confidence that purely structural factors do have some influence in naming objects.

As Brown (1958) points out, this conclusion does not necessarily imply the existence of innate universal intersensory associations. Such relations could be learned from the correlations of sense data that exist in those aspects of the nonlinguistic world which are similar for men of all cultures. For example, small drums make high sounds, large drums make deep sounds. As Brown suggests: 'The sensible attributes of the nonlinguistic world may tend to cluster and man could symbolize the visible or tactile attributes of such a cluster with auditory attributes from the same cluster. In this way we could learn a principle of intersensory appropriateness to use in naming.'

Such an assumption would be sufficient to account for the results of the present investigation.

REFERENCES

Brown, R. *Words and things*. New York: The Free Press, 1958.

Brown, R., A. H. Black, and A. E. Horowitz. Phonetic symbolism in natural languages, *J. Abnorm. Soc. Psychol.*, 1955, **50**, 388–393.

Brown, R. and R. Nuttall. Method in phonetic symbolism experiments, *J. Abnorm. Soc. Psychol.*, 1959, **59**, 441–445.

Fox, C. W. An experimental study of naming, *Amer. J. Psychol.*, 1935, **47**, 545–579.

Galton, F. *Inquiries into human faculty and its development*. London: The Macmillan Co., 1883.

Hall, K. R. L. and R. C. Oldfield. An experiment study of the fitness of signs to words, *Quart. J. Exp. Psychol.*, 1950, **2**, 60–70.

Hochberg, J. and V. Brooks. *An item analysis of physiognomic connotation*. Unpublished study, privately distributed, 1956.

Irwin, F. W. and E. Newland. A genetic study of the naming of visual figures, *J. Psychol.*, 1940, **9**, 3–16.

Jespersen, O. *Language: Its nature, development, and origin*. London: George Allen and Unwin, Ltd., 1922.

Karwoski, T. F., H. S. Odbert, and C. E. Osgood. Studies in synesthetic thinking: II. The role of form in visual responses to music, *J. Gen. Psychol.*, 1942, **26**, 199–222.

Köhler, W. *Gestalt Psychology*. Second ed. New York: Liveright Publishing Corp., 1947.

Osgood, C. E. The cross-cultural generality of visual-verbal synesthetic tendencies, *Behav. Sci.*, 1960, **5,** 146–169.

Osgood, C. E., G. J. Suci, and P. H. Tannenbaum. *The measurement of meaning.* Urbana: University of Illinois Press, 1957.

Sapir, E. *Language.* New York: Harcourt, Brace and World, Inc., 1929.

Slobin, D. I. *Antonymic phonetic symbolism in three natural languages.* Unpublished B.A. Honors thesis, University of Michigan, 1960.

Uznadze, D. Ein experimenteller Beitrag zum Problem der psychologischen Grundlagen der Namengebung, *Psychol. Forsch.*, 1924, **5,** 24–43.

5-2

Phonetic Symbolism in Four Languages

ROGER N. BROWN
ABRAHAM H. BLACK
ARNOLD E. HOROWITZ

The sound of some words indicates their meanings. These are called "onomatopoetic," "echoic," or "imitative" words. This phenomenon, which is known as *phonetic symbolism,* has interested psychologists for some time. Thorndike (1946) illustrates phonetic symbolism in the English language with the following example, "How many of these ten words would Arabs, Finns or Chinese define correctly from merely hearing them—blob, chatter, chuckle, flick, giggle, ping, slap, swish, thump, yap? Per contra, a slight, even an imagined, similarity of a word's sound to its meaning may make the meaning easier to get and remember. It may seem as fit and proper that maladroit persons should bungle and that ebullient persons blurt, that dogs should bow-wow and cannons boom. The mere sounds of bungle and blurt may help to carry their meanings as much as do the mere sounds of bow-wow and boom" (pp. 614–615). Is this relationship between sound and meaning universal? Does sound play some role in determining the meaning of words in all languages? The present study shows that certain sounds are associated with certain meanings across languages that come from the same family (English–Czech, English–

Reprinted from *J. Abnorm. Soc. Psychol.*, 1955, **50**, 388–393, by permission of the authors and the American Psychological Association.

Hindi) or from different families (English–Chinese). However, the same sound may be associated with different meanings in different languages (Taylor, 1963). Phonetic symbolism may be more clearly demonstrated when baby talk is examined across languages and cultures (Ferguson, 1956).

REFERENCES

Ferguson, C. A. Arabic baby talk. In *For Roman Jakobson.* The Hague: Mouton and Co., 1956.

Taylor, I. K. Phonetic symbolism re-examined, *Psychol. Bull.*, 1963, **60**, 200–209.

Thorndike, E. L. The psychology of semantics, *Amer. J. Psychol.*, 1946, **59**, 613–632.

In our experiments native speakers of English guessed the meanings of words from unfamiliar languages. The subjects (Ss) agreed very well on the meanings likely to be attached to these strange phonetic sequences. This agreement suggests a culturally acquired phonetic symbolism derived from experience with a common native language. However, the semantic judgments of our Ss were also correct more often than would be expected by chance, and this suggests that there may be some features of phonetic symbolism which have a universal validity. It is possible that speech originated in symbols imitative or somehow suggestive of their meanings and that traces of these "appropriate" linkages survive in all languages today.

NONLINGUISTIC PHONETIC SYMBOLISM

In 1929 Sapir (1929) conducted experiments using pairs of "nonlinguistic words" built on the CVC model. Within a pair the two words were matched for the initial and final consonants while the vowels were varied in the range from "a" to "i" (e.g., "Mal"–"Mil"). Sapir asked his Ss to judge which member of a pair symbolized the larger reference. He found a strong tendency to consider the reference larger for the word that included a vowel nearer the "a" end of the scale.

In 1933 Newman (1933) further analyzed Sapir's data and discovered systematic relationships between the size judgments and such factors as the position of the tongue in forming the vowels, the frequencies of the principal acoustic formants, and the size of the oral cavity created in pronunciation. Newman also discovered the magnitude implications of English consonants and investigated the symbolic values of the vowels and consonants for the dimension "bright to dark."

Bentley and Varon (1933) used nonlinguistic words like those of Sapir and Newman together with some English words and standard nonsense syllables. Their Ss were simply asked to come up with a free associate for each item on a mixed list of such materials. The authors report no tendency to match reference magnitudes with nonlinguistic words in the manner that we should anticipate from the work of Sapir and Newman. From experimental variations Bentley and Varon learned that the reference value had to be forced out of the words by the suggestion of a scale of magnitude.

Bentley and Varon questioned the relevance of all this work to the study of language. Both volume and brightness were known to be among the attributes of pure tones. Sapir and Newman might be said to have demonstrated that these same dimensions could be applied to complex vocal tones. Where in all this was there any justification for speaking of the "symbolic" value of "nonlinguistic words"? It had not been demonstrated that phonetic symbolism actually occurred in natural languages.

PHONETIC SYMBOLISM IN NATURAL LANGUAGES

Tsuru (1934) wrote an unpublished paper called "Sound and Meaning" in which he described an experiment in phonetic symbolism. Tsuru compiled a list of 36 pairs of Japanese antonyms. His Ss were 57 Harvard and Radcliffe undergraduates who spoke English as their native language and disclaimed any knowledge of Japanese. Seated in a group, Ss first saw a pair of Japanese words printed in Romish characters. The English equivalent pair was then written on the board, the order of the words within the pair being randomly related to the order within the Japanese pair. From the back of the room a native Japanese pronounced the words twice, reversing the order the second time. The Ss then attempted to match English-Japanese synonyms with one minute allowed for each pair. Table 1 indicates that they were able to average 69% correct guesses.

Tsuru had demonstrated that someone who knows both English and Japanese can find Japanese words whose meanings will be correctly guessed in a single alternative situation by Ss who know English but not Japanese. Although English and Japanese are believed to be historically unrelated, it would surely be possible to find some synonyms which sound alike. Tsuru's findings, then, could be consistent with the view that symbols are arbitrarily assigned in natural languages. If his Ss had learned in childhood to connect certain sounds in English with their arbitrary meanings they would be able to translate correctly Japanese words if these words were selected for their resemblance to the English. Tsuru's list does not appear to have been selected in this fashion, but the fact that he made his selection with full knowledge of both languages leaves this possibility uncontrolled. The work of Müller (1935) with words from Swahili and Bantu suffers from the same difficulty.

Gordon Allport (1935) made the necessary improvement in an unpublished experiment. He had a native speaker of Hungarian translate Tsuru's list into that language. This Finno-Ugric tongue is historically unrelated to either English or Japanese. Because the translator simply translated the list he was given, there was no opportunity to select words in the foreign language for their resemblance to English equivalents. The results appear in Table 1. Subjects performed somewhat less well than Tsuru's original group but were still above the chance level of 50 per cent.

In 1953 Susannah Rich (1953), an undergraduate at Radcliffe College, wrote a senior honors thesis which bears in part on our problem. She used 25 pairs of words and had them translated into Japanese and Polish. Native speakers of the two languages recorded their pronunciations of the words. The Ss were 44 Radcliffe girls. The results appear in Table 1 and again are above the level to be expected by chance.

Neither Tsuru nor Allport conducted a test for the significance of the departure from chance represented by their results. Rich reported the mean percentages correct for both Polish and Japanese to be significantly better than chance ($p \leq .005$). In general the results in Table 1 encourage the belief that there are significant traces of phonetic symbolism in natural languages.

TABLE 1

Percentages of Correct Translations in Three Studies

Author	Languages	N	% Correct
Tsuru	Japanese	57	69
Allport	Hungarian	68	56.6
Rich	Japanese	44	57.2*
Rich	Polish	44	64.8*

*Reported to be significantly larger than chance ($p < .005$).

THE EXPERIMENT

English antonyms were selected from the Thorndike-Lorge word list with two considerations in mind. (*a*) The words should name sense experiences (e.g., warm–cool, heavy–light). (*b*) The members of a pair should both fall in the frequency range of 100 or over per million. The final list of 21 pairs consisted of those on which the three authors could agree. We were all completely ignorant of the languages into which the list was to be translated—Chinese, Czech, and Hindi.

The English lists were presented for translation to native speakers or scholars of the particular languages. None of the translators was aware of the purpose of the study. They were asked to render the list into the familiar foreign equivalents—preserving the opposition within a pair. They then recorded their pronunciation of the pairs with five seconds between words and ten seconds between pairs.

The Ss were 86 Harvard and Radcliffe students in an undergraduate laboratory in social psychology. They participated in sections of about 20 students each. Our Ss were told that they were to take part in a study of sound symbolism in which meanings of foreign words were to be guessed from the sounds. Ranged down one side of a page were pairs of English antonyms. On the other side appeared foreign language antonyms matched pair by pair with the English. Words within a pair were randomly arranged so that while Ss knew that a given English word translated into one or the other of two foreign words he could not tell from the arrangement which of the two it was. The Ss heard the words pronounced in the same order as they appeared on the sheet and were then allowed ten seconds in which to match the two English words with their foreign language equivalents. The languages were presented in five random orders. All Ss were asked to describe their previous experience with the three languages. One S was disqualified by his knowledge of Chinese.

Preliminary analysis convinced us that the men and women did not show any significant differences in performance and consequently we combined their data. The results are presented in Table 2 in a form comparable to that used by earlier authors and summarized in Table 1. The mean percentages all depart significantly from chance. This calculation is made with reference to the binomial distribution. From these

TABLE 2

Percentages of Correct Translations for Three Languages in
Experimental Condition A

Language	No. of Ss	% Correct	Significance of Departure from Chance
Chinese	86	58.9	.001
Czech	86	53.7	.001
Hindi	85	59.6	.001

statistics we cannot tell whether all pairs on the list are judged with somewhat better than chance success or whether the average result is produced by combining a few words that are nearly always translated correctly with many that are at the chance level or below.

The results have therefore been computed in a different fashion. The performance on each pair of words for each language has been separately determined. We can then ask concerning each item whether more Ss answered it correctly than would be expected by chance. These findings are summarized in Tables 3 and 4 as experimental condition A. On a given pair when there is agreement on 64 per cent of the judgments this result is significant at the .01 level. The great majority of the words in all three languages meet this criterion. It is clear that Ss shared a conception of the more appropriate meaning for most of the words presented. We are interested in knowing how often this conception was correct. There must be 64 per cent correct judgments to reach the .01 level of significance. There are at least nine such pairs in all languages. There are only half as many significant results in the wrong direction. In other words our Ss' conceptions of the proper translation were right twice as often as they were wrong.

The foregoing analysis describes the performance on each pair of words but it does not tell us how the performances of individual Ss were distributed. Table 5 (p. 360) shows that most Ss correctly translated over half the words in a given list. There were 70 Ss for Chinese, 61 for Czech, and 67 for Hindi who had scores of 11 or better out of 21.

Allport's data have been subjected to the same kinds of analyses. Of his 36 pairs of Hungarian words 16 showed positive results significant at the .01 level; 53 of the 68 Ss correctly translated over half of the words.

Possible Causes of the Obtained Results

How are Ss able to arrive at so many correct translations? We suspect that the ability derives from a suggestive power in the phonetic sequences, but there are two other possibilities to be considered.

DIFFERENTIAL LENGTH OF WORDS WITHIN A PAIR. Zipf (1935) has demonstrated for samples of English, Plautine Latin, Peipingese Chinese, and several American Indian tongues that word frequency is related to word length, with the more common words tending to be shorter. It is possible that English words are correlated with their foreign language counterparts in both frequency and length. If this were so, an S need only match the longer English word with the longer foreign language word in each pair to achieve better than chance results. As a first precaution against this possibility we equated our English words for frequency range in the Thorndike-Lorge list. This step does not

TABLE 3

Percentage of Correct Translations for Each Pair in Three
Languages for Experimental Condition A and B

English	Chinese	% Correct A	% Correct B	Czech	% Correct A	% Correct B	Hindi	% Correct A	% Correct B
1. beautiful	mĕi	88*	70	krása	57	31	khubsurat	64*	50
ugly	ch'oŭ			ošklivost			badsurat		
2. blunt	tuñ	78*	70	tupý	81*	83*	gothil	68*	83*
sharp	k'uài			špičatý			tez		
3. bright	liang	67*	90*	svetlý	64*	77	chamakdar	51	90*
dark	àn			tmavý			drundhala		
4. coarse	ts'ŭ	65*	70	hrubý	21†	44	mota	48	31
fine	hsi			drobný			achha		
5. down	hsià	10†	31	dolů	56	50	niche	75*	83*
up	shàng			nahoru			upar		
6. drunk	tsùi	66*	50	opilý	21†	70	nashe men	80*	77
sober	hsĭng			střízlivý			sanjida		
7. dry	kān	72*	70	suchý	44	50	sukha	42	44
wet	shĭh			mokrý			bhiga		
8. fast	k'uài	83*	83*	rychlý	87*	83*	tez	27†	57
slow	màn			pomalý			sust		
9. fat	féi	31†	57	tlustý	69*	77	mota	66*	57
thin	shoŭ			tenký			patala		
10. gold	chīn	57	57	zlato	19†	57	sona	42	64
iron	t'iĕh			železo			loha		
11. bad	huài	34†	64	zlý	62	57	kharab	64*	31
good	haŏ			hodný			achha		

English	Chinese			Czech			Hindi		
12. happy / sad	huān / peī	38	50	radostný / smutný	57	64	khush / ranjida	17†	38
13. hard / soft	kang / joı́	97*	83*	tvrdý / měkký	76*	96*	sakht / narm	61	64
14. light / heavy	chˈīng / chūng	93*	90*	lehký / těžký	66*	77	halka / wazani	36†	57
15. long / short	chˈáng / tuǎn	55	44	dlouhý / kratký	80*	70	lamba / chhota	93*	70
16. many / one	tō / yı̄	73*	57	mnoho / jeden	55	25	bahut / ek	88*	90*
17. strong / weak	chˈiáng / jò	37	64	silný / slabý	28†	64	mazbut / kamzor	34†	31
18. sweet / sour	tˈién / suān	58	51	sladký / kyselý	24†	25	mitha / khatta	88*	70
19. thunder / lightning	leı́ / tień	23†	31	hrom / blesk	92*	96*	garaj / chamak	62	77
20. warm / cool	nŭan / liáng	73*	50	teplý / chladný	69*	77	garam / thanda	66*	77
21. wide / narrow	kˈuān / chaı̌	37	90*	široký / úzký	43	57	chaura / tang	76*	51

*Choices are correct with $p \leqq .01$.
†Choices are incorrect with $p \leqq .01$.

equate members of all pairs in length. Examining the data we find no indications that performance is better when the words differ in length, and, furthermore, we find that performance with the Chinese language, where the translations are all monosyllables of almost exactly equivalent length, is superior to performance on Czech, where the words vary in length.

THE EXPRESSIVE QUALITY OF THE SPEAKER'S VOICE. Our translators did not know the purpose of the study but were aware of the meanings of the words they pronounced. How can we be sure that the correct translations of our Ss were not made possible by some expressive quality in the recorded voices? May they not have introduced some sharpness into their pronunciation of "sharp," some haste into their versions of "fast"? Since these are sensory words it would be possible to adjust the quality of speech so as directly to produce the sense quality in question.

To check this possibility we asked a control group of Ss (experimental condition B) to match words without the recorded pronunciation, using only the printed versions. These suggest a roughly correct pronunciation to most native speakers of English. The expressive quality of the voice is eliminated since Ss do not know the meanings of the words when they pronounce to themselves. The results for condition B, which appear in Tables 3 and 4, show that over-all performance in this control group was slightly more successful than in the experimental group. Correlating performances on individual items for the two groups we obtain an r of .59 for Chinese, .61 for Czech, and .55 for Hindi. All of these are significant ($p \leq .02$), and it seems to be clear that the words we have used have stable semantic implications which are not a consequence of expressive, nonphonetic aspects of pronunciation.

TABLE 4

Summary Data of Translations for 31 Pairs of Words in Three
Languages in Experimental Conditions A and B

Language and Experimental Condition	No. of Ss	Mean % Correct	No. of Pairs Significantly Correct	No. of Pairs Significantly Incorrect
Chinese				
A	86	58.9	11	4
B	16	61.9	5	0
Czech				
A	86	55.7	9	5
B	16	61.9	4	0
Hindi				
A	85	59.6	11	4
B	16	60.7	4	0

Interpretation of the Results

Since speech originated in prehistory, long before writing, there can be no record of the act or acts of origination. Traditional speculation on this subject has been trivialized with such titles as the "ding-dong theory" and the "bow-wow theory." The stale whimsy of this language has helped to make the subject distasteful. We shall avoid passing the standard theories in review, but will make one distinction among them. Some theories (especially Thorndike) (1933) suppose that symbols are arbitrarily assigned to their references. It is then only necessary to assume the random emission of vocalization and some such learning principles as the familiar "contiguity" and "reinforcement" to explain the perpetuation and social diffusion of particular vocalizations. Other theories assume that the earliest speech, like the earliest writing (Gelb, 1952), was "representational." There are three subvarieties of the representational position. The first two of these assume some kind of imitation. The onomatopoeia theory holds that vocal sound can suggest nonvocal sound. The gestural theory holds that motion and contour described by articulatory muscles can suggest motion and contour in the external world. Paget (1930) has contended that human communication began with such gestural imitation of the external world. The third theory holds that vocalization falling on the auditory sense will naturally arouse meanings associated with other modalities. Hornbostel wrote of the "unity of the senses." Students of synesthesia have claimed (Kouwer, 1949) that perception is not an act involving only a particular receptor but is an affair of the whole body. Of course hearing does not involve all parts of the organism in equal degree but reducing hearing to audition alone means ignoring essential components. We doubt that this third variety of representational vocalization should be assimilated to synesthesia for the reason that studies of synesthetic response have typically yielded large individual differences. We prefer to use Werner's (1948) term "physiognomic language" to name these universal, unlearned intersensory connections.

All of these speculations must be supplemented with a learning theory. They share, however, a belief that some sound-meaning connections begin with a little boost in habit strength that elevates them above the level of arbitrary connections. If languages all began by making use of these associations our data might be explained by the survival of some of these associations in modern languages.

The existence of onomatopoeia in modern, natural languages is widely accepted though it is considered to be far too infrequent to account for the origin of language. If we had selected our words for onomatopoeic possibilities no one would have been surprised at positive results. It would not be very interesting, for example, to demonstrate that subjects could distinguish the word for the cry of the rooster from the word for the cry of the cat in many languages. However, none of our words names an auditory experience and therefore onomatopoeia cannot account for our correct results. It is possible, however, that the origin of speech in gestural imitation and physiognomic language has left a residue of roughly translatable words in all languages and that we have tapped this residue in Chinese, Czech, and Hindi, while Allport tapped it in Hungarian, and Rich in Japanese and Polish.

TABLE 5

Frequency Distributions of Percentages of Correct Translations for
Three Languages in Experimental Condition A

% Correct	No. of Ss		
	Chinese	Czech	Hindi
88			1
83	1	1	2
78	3	2	8
73	11	3	5
68	8	9	15
63	18	12	14
58	20	24	7
53	9	11	15
48	7	12	10
43	7	6	5
38	2	5	1
33		1	2

The uniformity of performance among our Ss might alternatively be explained by the fact that they are all native speakers of English who naturally share a cultural conception of the sounds likely to express a given meaning. The fact that our Ss showed a significant amount of agreement in both incorrect as well as correct choices tends to substantiate this view. If the connections between linguistic sounds and meanings are arbitrary, however, the English speaker's cultural conception of phonetic symbolism should lead him to make correct translations of languages historically related to his native tongue but not to make correct translations of totally unrelated languages. Of the languages studied three are Indo-European (Czech, Hindi, and Polish) while three are not (Chinese, Japanese, and Hungarian). The Indo-European tongues should show a closer resemblance to English than the languages outside the family. However, there is no clear tendency favoring the Indo-European tongues. We are inclined to believe that most of our Ss did not usually translate an English word with the foreign word bearing the closer resemblance, but rather responded in terms of principles of phonetic symbolism imperfectly realized in all languages. The words "light" and "heavy," for instance, translate into Chinese "ch'ing" and "chung." As we might predict from the work of Sapir and Newman, 93 per cent of our subjects were correct on that pair.

Even if we assume a phonetic symbolism which is not a cultural acquisition, it does not necessarily follow that the presence of such symbolism in natural languages must be explained by the origin of speech in representational vocalization. Speech might have begun with the arbitrary association of sounds and meanings and then moved toward phonetic symbolism. A given speech form might have been aided in the struggle for survival if it chanced to be representational. Instead of assuming that speech has fallen away from a golden age of phonetic symbolism we may come to believe that, in the evolution of languages, speech forms have been selected for symbolism and that we are moving toward a golden millennium of physiognomic speech. Work is under way which we hope will decide between these interpretations.

SUMMARY

Three separate investigations, using three lists of English words and six foreign languages, have shown superior to chance agreement and accuracy in the translation of unfamiliar tongues. The agreement can be explained as the result of a "cultural conception" of the symbolic values attached to various phonetic combinations. This hypothesis does not explain the accuracy of translation. The accuracy can be explained by the assumption of some universal phonetic symbolism in which speech may have originated or toward which speech may be evolving. For the present we prefer to interpret our results as indicative of a primitive phonetic symbolism deriving from the origin of speech in some imitative or physiognomic linkage of sounds and meanings. We forsake conservatism on this occasion for the excellent reason that the thesis proposed is so alien to most thinking in psycholinguistics that it needs to be brought forward strongly so that we may see that its unpopularity has not been deserved.

REFERENCES

Allport, G. W. Phonetic symbolism in Hungarian words. Unpublished experiment, Harvard University, 1935.

Bentley, M. and Edith J. Varon. An accessory study of phonetic symbolism, *Amer. J. Psychol.*, 1933, **45,** 76–86.

Gelb, I. J. *A study of writing.* Chicago: University of Chicago Press, 1952.

Kouwer, B. J. *Colors and their character.* The Hague: Nijhoff, 1949.

Müller, H. *Eperimentelle Beiträge zur Analyse des Verhältnisses von Laut und Sinn.* Berlin: Müller and I. Kiepenheuer, 1935.

Newman, S. S. Further experiments in phonetic symbolism, *Amer. J. Psychol.,* 1933, **45,** 53–75.

Paget, R. *Human speech.* New York: Harcourt, Brace, and World, Inc., 1930.

Rich, Susannah. The perception of emotion. Unpublished honors thesis, Radcliffe Coll., 1953.

Sapir, E. A study in phonetic symbolism, *J. Exp. Psychol.,* 1929, **12,** 225–239.

Thorndike, E. L. The origin of language, *Science,* 1933, **77,** 173–175.

Tsuru, S. Sound and meaning. Unpublished manuscript on file with Gordon W. Allport, Harvard University, 1934.

Werner, H. *Comparative psychology of mental development.* Chicago: Follett Publishing Company, 1948.

Zipf, G. K. *The psycho-biology of language.* Boston: Houghton Mifflin Company, 1935.

5-3

Cross-Cultural Use of the Semantic Differential

HOWARD MACLAY
EDWARD E. WARE

Osgood and his associates (Suci, 1960; Osgood, 1964) have demonstrated that the semantic structure of concepts is invariant across cultures, and that factors of evaluation, potency, and activity are found with various cultural groups. Does the judgment of concepts against these three dimensions differ from one culture to another?

The present study shows that the Zuni, Hopi, and Navajo Indians vary in terms of the connotative meaning of different concepts on these semantic dimensions. The Osgood semantic differential test is thus shown to be useful in the study of cultural differences in the perception of meanings of concepts.

REFERENCES

Osgood, C. E. Semantic differential technique in the comparative study of cultures, *Amer. Anthropol.*, 1964, **66,** 171–200.

Suci, G. J. A comparison of semantic structures in Southwest culture groups, *J. Abnorm. Soc. Psychol.*, 1960, **61,** 25–30.

A central problem in research is the extent to which the methods

Reprinted from *Behav. Sci.*, 1961, 6, 185–190, by permission of the authors and editor.

and conclusions of one discipline can be applied to the data of another. We are concerned here with methods of gathering and interpreting data rather than with the transfer of general theories from one area to another. We propose to take a measuring instrument developed by experimental psychologists, the semantic differential (Osgood et al., 1957), and apply it to data that have traditionally been the primary concern of anthropologists. A double value may be derived from such an approach. Psychological instruments have most often been developed and validated in the context of Western culture. An important question involves the extent to which conclusions based on these instruments can be extended to human beings generally. This can only be studied by applying the instruments to a subject population consisting of persons with non-Western cultural backgrounds. An inevitable result of this approach is a fuller understanding of the limits within which the instrument is effective. The extensive use of the Rorschach test by anthropologists (summarized by Henry and Spiro, 1953) is an illustration of how a psychological technique can be refined and improved by cross-cultural application.

Anthropologists will also benefit if a technique developed elsewhere proves to have cross-cultural validity and produces results which bear on problems of culture structure and process. Traditional anthropological field methods, which commonly involve some sort of participant observation, are extremely laborious and time consuming. If one wishes to describe a functioning culture, there is clearly no substitute for an extended period of systematic observation. It may be, however, that some part of the data needed for an adequate description can be gathered more effectively by other methods.

Our focus here is on the possible utility of a particular measuring device for anthropologists. This implies first that its cross-cultural validity must be demonstrated and further that its usefulness as a specific anthropological tool be shown. A fully convincing demonstration of validity is not possible in a short paper. This can only follow from extensive use in the field. Our aim here is to present data which will contribute to a final decision as to the anthropological worth of the instrument in question along with some observations based on previous use of the semantic differential in a number of field situations. The estimation of validity requires that evaluation be based on criteria which are independent of the instrument being judged. We will regard an instrument as having cross-cultural validity to the extent that it reflects cultural differences known to exist as a result of previous ethnographic study. We first discuss the instrument and then the cultural criteria against which it is to be judged. An application to subjects from three American Indian cultures is described followed by a concluding section in which an estimate of the anthropological value of the instrument is presented.

THE PSYCHOLOGICAL INSTRUMENT

The measuring device under investigation is a form of the semantic differential developed at the University of Illinois by C. E. Osgood and associates and fully described by Osgood et al. (1957). The semantic differential is a technique for measuring the meaning of linguistic forms. Concepts, such as *mother* or *President Eisenhower*, are rated on a series of descriptive scales. Each seven point scale is defined by a pair of opposite adjectives (i.e., good-bad, hot-cold, active-passive, etc.). If we are interested in the meaning of the English word *man*, we might present native English speakers with the following form:

MAN

good	:	:	:	:	:	:	bad
strong	:	:	:	:	:	:	weak
fast	:	:	:	:	:	:	slow

It should be noted that this is a method of measurement and not a specific test. Particular forms of the semantic differential may vary in the concepts and scales used in terms of the research purposes of the investigator.

Subjects indicate the direction and intensity of the association between the concept and the adjectives defining each scale. The meaning of a concept is given by the positions it occupies on a set of scales. Factor analyses of semantic differential results have led to the establishment of three main factors which are regarded as the primary dimensions that organize semantic judgments. These are named *evaluative* (good-bad), *potency* (strong-weak), and *activity* (fast-slow). Any concept may be located in a semantic space defined by these factors.

A final assessment of the cross-cultural validity and utility of the semantic differential must rest on the answers to two questions: (1) Is there some set of basic semantic dimensions that is universal? (2) If this is the case, can the instrument organize and classify cultures in a scientifically interesting way? The dependence between these problems is obvious. We can compare cultures directly only if the dimensions of comparison are universal. On the other hand, a similarity in factor structure across cultures does not imply that the meanings assigned to individual words are the same but only that the scales are used in an equivalent way. While the first problem has not been finally settled, a number of studies have found factor structures the same or quite similar to English for Japanese and Korean (Kumata and Schramm, 1956; Kumata, 1957), Greek (Triandis and Osgood, 1958), and Hopi, Zuni, Navajo, and Spanish-American (Suci, 1960). Work in this area has progressed to the point where an exploratory study addressed to the second question seems profitable. We will assume the universality of the semantic space and focus our attention upon the specific meanings assigned to concepts by our subjects.

THE CULTURAL CRITERIA

We now consider the cultural distinctions which will serve as criteria in evaluating this instrument. These arise from the observational methods of cultural anthropology and are thus methodologically independent of any results which the semantic differential may produce. An effort has been made to select cultural distinctions that are compelling and obvious to the point where all anthropologists familiar with the cultures involved would agree that they do indeed exist. We then ask whether the semantic differential is able to reflect these known distinctions. We will regard as clearly distinct any two cultures whose ethnographic descriptions differ and whose members speak mutually unintelligible languages. This means that a significant proportion of translation equivalent forms should be located differently in the semantic space for the two cultures. More specifically, most of the concepts used should have different locations on the scales of the semantic differential. It is assumed that the scales are being used in the same way and that direct comparisons of the concepts can be made. The three American Indian groups studied are Hopi, Zuni, and Navajo. They are known to be distinct cultures and we ask if the instrument can distinguish them. If the distinction is made, it can then be asked if the instrument orders the three cultures in an acceptable way. Hopi and Zuni are usually classified as Western Pueblo (Eggan, 1950) and it was therefore predicted in advance of the analysis that they should fall together as opposed to Navajo. It was further predicted that Zuni should be closer to Navajo than Hopi on the less secure grounds of more formal and more amicable Zuni-Navajo contact than Hopi-Navajo as described by Vogt (1951).

SUBJECTS

The Hopi group consisted of 28 subjects, the Navajo of 29 subjects, and the Zuni of 26 subjects. The groups ranged in age from the middle teens to over 60 and included both males and females.

MATERIALS

The following form of the semantic differential was used:

Concepts	*Scales*
1. Coyote	1. light-heavy
2. Mexican	2. hard-soft
3. Corn	3. ugly-pretty
4. Male	4. cold-hot
5. Horse	5. dirty-clean
6. Rain	6. wet-dry
7. Female	7. industrious-lazy
	8. sad-happy
	9. poor-rich
	10. sweet-sour
	11. short-long
	12. fast-slow
	13. strong-weak
	14. crooked-straight
	15. good-bad

PROCEDURE

The semantic differential was translated into the three languages by linguists working with informants (c.f. Ervin, 1956 for a discussion of translation procedures). The typical procedure using a seven-point scale described above was modified somewhat by the requirements of the field situation. Suci (1960) has described the exact procedures and the following is a paraphrase of his discussion.

The subjects were nonliterate in their own language and had to be given the material verbally and individually. Preliminary investigation had indicated that the standard rating procedure was not understood by subjects and might have led to ambiguous results. Consequently, a six-inch line with the ends and middle marked was used for each scale. The order of the scales and of the concepts, and the polarity of the modifiers (e.g., *good-bad* vs. *bad-good*) was determined by randomization. The differentials were scored by measuring the distance, in one-tenth inches, from the left side of the scale to the check mark locating the concept on the scale. Thus, a concept could vary from zero to sixty on any single scale.

It appeared that almost all subjects readily grasped the nature of the task and performed it satisfactorily.

RESULTS

To simplify interpretations and limit the number of variables in any particular comparison, Hotelling's T^2 (Hodges, 1955) was obtained from the 15 scales for each concept. The three cultures were compared by pairs. Hotelling's T^2 is the multivariate generalization of Student's t test. The t test is used to determine the statistical significance of the difference between the means of two groups of subjects on a single variable. T^2 is a statistical test of the difference between two groups on a set of several variables. The results of these comparisons are found in Table 1. Of the 21 comparisons, 17 show significant differences beyond the .05 level. We conclude on the basis of these results that the instrument can discriminate among cultures.

TABLE 1

F Values Derived from Hotelling's T^2 Test of the Differences
Between Pairs of Cultures for Each Concept

Concept	Hopi-Zuni	Zuni-Navajo	Hopi-Navajo
1. Coyote	1.28	3.79†	3.74†
2. Mexican	1.76	1.54	1.80
3. Corn Ear	2.30°	4.96†	4.54†
4. Male	2.89†	2.64†	6.05†
5. Horse	4.50†	2.12°	4.54†
6. Rain	4.50†	4.83†	2.56†
7. Female	3.46†	2.24†	4.54†

°Difference is statistically significant beyond the .05 level.
†Difference is statistically significant beyond the .01 level.

Individual comparisons were made between pairs of cultures for each concept-scale combination using the t test. These results, presented in Table 2, give a detailed picture of the culture-pair comparisons. Here, 94 of the 315 comparisons show a significant difference. Due to the large number of statistical tests based on a single sample, interpretation of the results should be considered as hypothesis gathering rather than hypothesis testing. Any specific findings require some form of cross-validation.

It can be observed that individual concepts and scales vary greatly in their ability to discriminate. The concept *coyote*, for example, seems to have a similar meaning for Zuni and Hopi and a different and distinctive meaning for Navajo. We have not explored in detail the cultural correlates of these results but students of the three cultures may find it profitable to attempt this sort of study. With the aim of facilitating such

TABLE 2

Results of *t* Tests* of the Differences Between Culture-Pairs for Each
Concept-Scale Combination

Scales	Concepts† 1	2	3	4	5	6	7
			Hopi-Zuni Comparisons				
1.					2.14		
2.							
3.							
4.						−4.03	
5.		2.09				3.87	
6.							
7.							
8.							
9.		−2.87	−2.43	−3.50		2.27	−3.50
10.						−4.48	
11.		−2.96			2.09		−2.97
12.			2.21		−2.42		4.37
13.							2.40
14.					−4.24		−3.98
15.	2.66	3.39	3.51		2.16		
			Zuni-Navajo Comparisons				
1.	3.47					−4.53	
2.							
3.			−3.69	−2.84		−4.52	
4.					2.74		4.25
5.	2.08					−4.83	3.32
6.			3.94				
7.		2.68		−2.31			
8.		2.11					
9.	3.24	2.71	3.49	2.22			3.06
10.	−2.78	−2.88				2.02	
11.	2.85						
12.			−2.07	−3.64	−3.11	−2.82	−3.24
13.	5.83	−2.42					−3.27
14.	4.08						
15.	−2.53	−3.57					
			Hopi-Navajo Comparisons				
1.	3.74					−2.43	
2.		−2.38	−2.38	−2.92	−2.34		−2.29
3.	2.35		−2.86	−2.76		−2.90	
4.						−2.72	3.88
5.			2.19	2.15			3.17
6.			4.76				
7.				−2.57			−2.55
8.							
9.	3.33						
10.	−2.03					−2.04	

TABLE 2 (*Continued*)

Results of *t* Tests* of the Differences Between Culture-Pairs for Each
Concept-Scale Combination

				Concepts†			
Scales	1	2	3	4	5	6	7
11.	2.31						
12.				−4.26	−6.21	−2.85	
13.	−5.62	−3.09		−2.66	−3.39		
14.	2.67			−2.95	−4.83	−2.26	−3.75
15.			3.71				−2.38

*Only those values significant beyond the .05 level are given. Values greater than
2.68 are significant beyond the .01 level.
†Scales and concepts are in the same order as they are given in the section on materials.

an investigation we present the actual means of all concepts on all scales
for each culture in Table 3.

No statistical test of the ordering of cultural differences was available for this data. However, an intuitive measure of cultural distance may
be derived by adding the number of significant concept-scale differences
under each culture comparison in Table 2. There are a total of 23
significant differences between Hopi and Zuni, 34 between Navajo and
Zuni, and 37 between Hopi and Navajo. If these numbers are taken as
measures of cultural distance we can conclude that the trend in the data
is in the predicted direction: Hopi and Zuni tend to fall together as
against Navajo; Zuni is closer to Navajo than is Hopi. The lack of any
significance test makes this conclusion suggestive rather than final.

DISCUSSION

We have considered here only one of the several criteria that an
instrument must meet before it is acceptable as an anthropological field
tool. With respect to its ability to reflect gross cultural divisions, the status
of the semantic differential is promising. Zuni, Hopi, and Navajo were
distinguished at a statistically significant level and they were also
grouped internally as predicted.

Some advantages of the instrument lie outside the analyses performed for this study. The task required by this technique is a straightfor-
ward one that can be easily understood and accomplished by most
subjects regardless of wide variations in their age, intelligence, and

TABLE 3

Semantic Differential Scale Means* for Zuni (Z), Hopi (H), and Navajo (N) Cultures†

Scales	1 Coyote			2 Mexican			3 Corn			4 Male			5 Horse			6 Rain			7 Female			
	Z	H	N	Z	H	N	Z	H	N	Z	H	N	Z	H	N	Z	H	N	Z	H	N	
1. Light	28	29	17	37	33	36	26	24	21	39	40	39	39	48	45	22	32	43	37	32	36	Heavy
2. Hard	24	27	30	26	23	31	28	23	33	28	21	32	25	16	25	37	32	32	30	27	35	Soft
3. Ugly	21	25	16	37	34	31	36	39	47	36	37	44	37	39	41	31	37	49	38	38	42	Pretty
4. Cold	33	36	32	37	34	35	22	25	19	36	33	35	42	39	34	23	9	19	40	38	26	Hot
5. Dirty	26	24	18	35	31	31	39	46	39	37	40	34	34	38	34	31	46	48	44	43	33	Clean
6. Wet	31	28	34	26	26	29	33	36	19	30	24	26	27	27	24	13	7	10	28	24	23	Dry
7. Industrious	30	34	26	19	24	30	21	18	20	17	16	24	18	17	20	21	19	16	18	15	22	Lazy
8. Sad	27	30	23	10	36	33	43	38	39	42	40	39	41	42	39	39	43	45	43	40	39	Happy
9. Poor	21	18	9	39	29	29	42	34	28	45	34	36	36	31	32	32	41	41	42	32	32	Rich
10. Sweet	33	36	43	24	28	34	16	13	17	23	25	22	26	19	21	25	9	16	20	20	24	Sour
11. Short	23	20	13	37	27	32	29	28	26	33	35	34	30	38	35	34	31	38	33	23	28	Long
12. Fast	17	16	23	24	25	28	24	34	32	19	18	32	17	10	29	20	20	33	21	37	33	Slow
13. Strong	21	23	43	19	18	28	22	25	24	17	14	21	14	9	17	18	13	17	17	26	28	Weak
14. Crooked	32	27	18	37	33	33	40	39	39	37	30	39	40	25	40	39	32	42	42	29	40	Straight
15. Good	33	45	44	17	33	30	14	31	16	17	16	22	16	26	19	14	19	14	15	14	21	Bad

*Means were computed from a 60-point scale so that low values are toward left-hand scale term (e.g., light) and high toward right-hand term (e.g., heavy).

†Values for significant culture-pair differences are given in Table 3. Concepts and scales are numbered in this table to facilitate use of Tables 2 and 3 together.

degree of acculturation. Even if the tests are administered orally and individually an impressive amount of data can be collected in a relatively short time; Hopi subjects marked scales at the rate of about 250 per hour. The tests can be administered by moderately trained persons and need not occupy the time of the senior investigator. The techniques of recording and analyzing data are objective and standarized although interpretation of the results does, of course, rest on the judgment of the analyst.

An obvious application of such an instrument is to problems of covert culture. Most definitions of culture include nonobservable elements such as values, ideas, and beliefs. The semantic differential has the potential of serving both to gather data in these areas and to evaluate hypotheses derived from other data. The evaluative factor, for example, offers a way of ranking events, people, and ideas on a good-bad continuum.

Any research device may have either full or auxiliary status in the methodological repertoire of a discipline. Full status implies that it is an essential data gathering or analyzing technique whose results are to be weighted equally with those obtained by other methods. An auxiliary method has the function of supplementing more basic techniques. It may provide detail in areas whose general outlines are established on other grounds. In this case its results tend to be checked against other information and discarded if they vary too widely. It may also act as an opening wedge for the introduction of more highly regarded procedures. As an example of this function, the semantic differential tends to provoke little anxiety and puts the field worker in friendly contact with many members of the community in a short time. If the local group is bilingual its members are very much aware of linguistic differences and likely to become quite interested in problems of meaning in different languages. That the semantic differential was administered to a great many subjects in areas where field work is often extremely difficult (Hopi and Zuni) is testimony to its field efficiency.

We conclude that while this instrument has unquestioned merit as a general scientific technique its full acceptance as an anthropological method must await further research. We believe it can now function as an auxiliary method and, further, that it shows promise of becoming a useful device in studies of covert culture.

REFERENCES

Eggan, F. *Social organization of the western Pueblos.* Chicago: University of Chicago Press, 1950.

Ervin, S. Translation procedures. In J. B. Carroll and S. M. Ervin (eds.), *Field manual of the Southwest project in comparative psycholinguistics.* Cambridge: Harvard University, 1956. (ditto)

Henry, J. and M. E. Spiro. Psychological techniques: Projective tests in field work. In A. L. Kroeber (ed.), *Anthropology today*, pp. 417–429. Chicago: University of Chicago Press, 1953.

Hodges, J. L., Jr., Discriminatory analysis 1. Survey of discriminatory analysis. Report No. 1, Contract No. AF41 (128) 8, University of California, 1955.

Kumata, H. A factor analytic investigation of the generality of semantic structure across two selected cultures. Unpublished doctoral dissertation. University of Illinois, 1957.

Kumata, H. and W. Schramm. A pilot study of cross-cultural methodology, *Publ. Opin. Quart.*, 1956, **20,** 229–238.

Osgood, C. E., G. J. Suci, and P. H. Tannenbaum. *The measurement of meaning.* Urbana, Univ. of Illinois Press, 1957.

Suci, G. J. A comparison of semantic structures in American Southwest culture groups, *J. Abnorm. Soc. Psychol.*, 1960, **61,** 25–30.

Triandis, H. C., and C. E. Osgood. A comparative factorial analysis of semantic structures in monolingual Greek and American college students, *J. Abnorm. Soc. Psychol.*, 1958, **57,** 187–196.

Vogt, E. Z. Navaho veterans, A study of changing values. Papers of the Peabody Museum of Harvard University, 1951, **44,** No. 1.

5-4

The Cross-Cultural Generality of Visual-Verbal Synesthetic Tendencies

CHARLES E. OSGOOD

"The Sapir-Whorf hypothesis" that the structure of a language influences cognitive behavior is questioned in this study of comparability of experience in different sense modalities. Do the Navajo, like ourselves, see 'Happy' as more up and 'Sad' as more down? Do the Japanese, like ourselves, conceive of 'Excitement' as colorful and Calm as colorless? Do the Navajos and Anglos differ widely in their connotative meanings of the word "blue" and its correlate in Navajo, yet agree closely on their meanings for a specific Blue color chip? Here is a first attempt to demonstrate that the visual-verbal synesthetic relationships characteristic of our language/culture community are shared by peoples who speak different languages and enjoy different cultures. Perhaps there is a "world view" that is relatively stable despite differences in both language and culture.

In a previous selection (Chapter 5, Selection 1) Davis has shown that there is agreement between English and Tanganyikan children in fitting nonsense words to abstract drawings; his findings give additional evidence to the view presented here concerning the cross-cultural generality of synesthetic tendencies.

Reprinted from *Behav. Sci.*, 1960, **5**, 146–169, by permission of the author and the editor.

INTRODUCTION

This study was planned as part of the Southwest Project in Comparative Psycholinguistics (Casagrande, 1956) during the summer of 1955. This project as a whole was concerned with the ways in which language or culture, or both, may produce differences in cognitive processes; *or*, conversely, the degree to which certain cognitive processes may be independent of differences in language or culture, and hence general across language/culture groups. One area of cognition studied was that of *connotative meaning*; specifically, translation-equivalent forms of the semantic differential (Osgood, et al., 1957) were given to subjects in several Southwest Indian communities, as well as to Mexican-Spanish and Anglo subjects. Suci (1957) has reported the results of this work elsewhere.

The usual form of the semantic differential requires the subject to judge verbal concepts (e.g., HORSE, CORN, MAN) against verbally defined scales (e.g., *strong-weak, active-passive, good-bad*). Problems of translation equivalence therefore enter at two places. In the present experiment the concepts to be judged are verbal, but the 'scales' are visual—binary pictorial alternatives with which the subject must selectively associate the verbal concept being judged. Thus, instead of the bipolar words *thin-thick*, the subject sees a *thin* line paired with a *thick* line, and he simply points to whichever drawing seems to 'go best' with the concept being judged; instead of the bipolar adjectives *angular-rounded*, he sees a jagged, *angular* line-drawing paired with a *rounded* line-drawing. The difference between the drawings in each pair is restricted to a single dimension, e.g., angularity, size, nearness, etc. The verbal concepts judged against these pictorial alternatives included both concept-terms (e.g., MAN, YELLOW) and scale terms (e.g., STRONG, BAD, LIGHT, GOOD, WEAK) taken from the standard semantic differential used in the Southwest Project by Suci.

One purpose of the present study, then, was to check the generality of semantic factors in a situation where at least the 'scales' of judgment were non-linguistic. Another purpose was to study the cross-cultural generality of visual synesthesia itself (and, indirectly, of metaphors based on visual analogies). Do the Navajo, like ourselves, see HAPPY as more *up* and SAD as more *down*? Do the Japanese, like ourselves, conceive of EXCITEMENT as *colorful* and CALM as *colorless*? And if certain differences in visual metaphor do appear, can these be related to what we know about the differences in culture? A third purpose was to see if those terms in Navajo, Mexican-Spanish, and Japanese selected as translation-equivalent to verbal opposites in English actually function as opposites in the meaningful judgments of non-Anglo subjects. Treating our paired visual alternatives as a sort of projective device, can the choices for GOOD be shown to be the mirror-image of those for BAD, for example? A final, and somewhat supplementary, purpose was to study similarities and differences in the connotations of both color terms and actual color samples. Can it be shown, for example, that Navajos and Anglos may differ widely in their connotative meanings of the words "blue" and its correlate in Navajo, yet agree closely on their meanings for a specific BLUE color chip? This analysis was restricted to the Navajo/Anglo comparison.

METHOD

Subjects

The synesthesia experiment was run on four groups of subjects, each representing a different language/culture base. Two of these groups, 40 Navajos and 10 Mexican-Spanish subjects, were included in the Southwest Project on Comparative Psycholinguistics (SWPCP), and the data were collected during the summer of 1956. Dr. Susan Ervin obtained the Navajo data and Dr. Sol Saporta obtained the Mexican-Spanish data. These subjects were, for the most part, rural people with little formal education. During the following year, the writer collected control data from a group of 27 Anglos, graduate and undergraduate students in psychology at the University of Illinois. The 20 Japanese subjects were either staff or students at the University of Illinois, but had been in this country less than two years; Mr. Hiroshi Azuma collected these data, as a research project in the author's course in psycholinguistics. It should be noted, first, that all but the Anglo subjects were bilingual to some degree with respect to English, and, second, that there are marked differences in education (and perhaps intelligence) between the Anglo and Japanese groups on the one hand and the Navajo and Mexican-Spanish on the other. The phenomena of visual synesthesia with which we are dealing here may be largely independent of these variables, but nevertheless they should be kept in mind in interpreting the results.

Materials

The verbal concepts used in this study are listed in Table 1. They include some of both the polar terms and the concepts used in the completely verbal semantic differential developed by Suci for SWPCP. They also include some color terms, for purposes of comparison with

TABLE 1

Verbal Concepts Used in Synesthesia Experiment

1. HEAVY	*10. QUIET	*20. NOISY
2. GOOD	11. BLUE	*21. GREY
3. FAST	12. BAD	22. SLOW
4. HAPPY	13. LIGHT	23. WHITE
*5. UP	*14. DOWN	24. CALM
*6. ENERGETIC	15. BLACK	25. MAN
*7. LOOSE	16. WOMAN	26. YELLOW
8. STRONG	*17. LAZY	27. WEAK
9. EXCITEMENT	*18. TIGHT	28. SAD
	19. GREEN	

Pictorial Alternatives Used in Synesthesia Experiment
(see Figure 1)

1. Up-down	5. Thick-thin	10. Rounded-angular
2. Vertical-horizontal	6. Dark-light	*11. Diffuse-concentrated
3. Homogeneous-heterogeneous	7. Crooked-straight	12. Large-small
4. Colorless-colorful	8. Hazy-clear	*13. Near-far
	*9. Blunt-sharp	

*These concepts and visual alternatives were omitted in the materials given to Mexican-Spanish subjects.

other experiments in the Southwest Project in which actual color chips were judged. Although the concepts are given here only in English, in administering the experiment the translation-equivalent terms in the subject's native language were given by the experimenter or interpreter. The equivalents for Japanese were determined by the back-translation technique (using different bilinguals in the two stages). Despite the extreme care exercised by the SWPCP linguists and by Mr. Azuma in achieving close translation-equivalence, perfect equivalence is probably impossible, and this is therefore another possible source of apparent differences in visual synesthetic tendencies across language groups.

The visual alternatives, or 'scales,' used in this study are displayed in Figure 1 and listed *verbally* in Table 1. The labelling of these visual alternatives is somewhat arbitrary and is done only to facilitate talking about them. The subjects were given no verbal characterizations, although they may well have done some spontaneous labelling. Each pair of visual alternatives was drawn on a single card, so that the order of presentation could be varied if desired; the left-right orientation on each card was as shown in Figure 1.

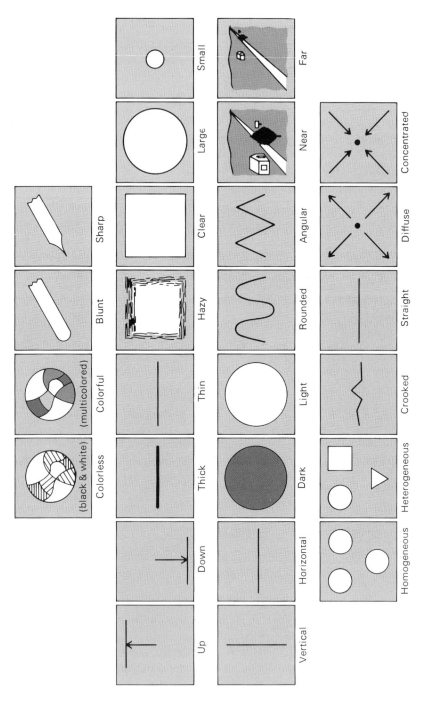

Figure 1.

Procedure

The general procedure was to name one of the concepts to be judged and then run through the series of cards, having the subject point to or otherwise indicate which of the two visual alternatives on each card seemed most appropriate to that concept. Then the next concept would be named and run through in the same fashion. Thus, in effect, the subject judged whether HEAVY (in his own language) seemed more *up* or *down, vertical* or *horizontal, homogeneous* or *heterogeneous,* and so forth through the 13 alternatives; then he did the same thing for the concept GOOD, and so on through the test.

There were some minor variations in procedure that may be noted, even though it is doubtful that they would have much effect on such a simple judgment process. For Navajo, Japanese, and Anglo subjects, the order of presenting the concepts was as given in Table 1; the order for the Mexican-Spanish subjects was different. Also, for the Mexican-Spanish group, certain concepts and 'scales' were omitted (those shown by asterisks in Table 1). The Navajo, Mexican-Spanish, and Japanese subjects were tested individually, each concept being spoken aloud before its series of judgments (and repeated whenever necessary). The Anglos were tested in two groups, the visual alternative cards being handed around from subject to subject in regular, repeating sequence; they indicated their judgments by marking "L" (left) or "R" (right) in the appropriate row, defined by printed concepts, and appropriate column, defined by number 1 to 13 for the 'scales.' For the Navajo and Japanese subjects the order of presenting 'scales' was randomized within subjects; for the Mexican-Spanish subjects the order of 'scales' was simply reversed on alternate concepts; for the Anglos the order was constant for all concepts. The direction, left to right, for each visual alternative card was constant for all subjects and groups.

RESULTS

Intra-cultural synesthetic tendencies

The first step in the treatment of the data was to compute the percentages of subjects in each group choosing each of the visual alternatives for each verbal concept. In other words, before comparing *across* language/culture groups, we want to determine the consistencies of synesthetic tendencies *within* each group. Table 2 presents these data. Since there were only two alternatives for each judgment, the proportion choosing one is always the reciprocal of the proportion choosing the other, and therefore only the percentage choosing the alternative listed at the top of each column is given, e.g., the fact that only .07 Anglos chose *up* means that .93 of them chose *down* as appropriate to HEAVY. To conserve space, the data for all four groups are included in this table, the first per cent in each quadruplet giving the Anglo data (A), the second the Navajo data (N), the third the Mexican-Spanish (S), and the last the Japanese data (J).

If we are to conclude that a particular synesthetic tendency is shared by the members of a cultural group, then we must show that a significant proportion of that group made the same choice. Accepting the 1% level of confidence as a conservative criterion of significant agreement within a group (except for the Mexican-Spanish, where the small N makes the 5% level seem more appropriate), then approximately 20/27 Anglo subjects (percentage values greater than .74 or less than .26 in Table 2), 28/40 Navajo subjects (percentages greater than .68 or less than .32), 8/10 Mexican-Spanish subjects (percentages greater than .79 or less than .21) and 16/20 Japanese subjects (percentages greater than .80 or less than .20) must choose the same way for the relationship to be considered nonchance.

Inspecting Table 2 with such criteria in mind, we find, for example, that Anglos agree among themselves that HEAVY is *down, colorless, thick, dark, concentrated,* and *near;* Navajos see HEAVY as *thick, dark, crooked, blunt, large* and *near;* Mexican-Spanish see it as *down, horizontal, heterogeneous, thick, dark, crooked, hazy,* and *large;* Japanese agree among themselves that HEAVY is *down, colorless, thick, dark, crooked, hazy, concentrated, large, near,* and *blunt.* The synesthetic associations for other concepts in Table 2 can be explored by the reader.

If these intra-cultural synesthetic tendencies were chance-like in their occurrence, we would expect about as many items to reach significance as the level of confidence we select, i.e., 1% of them. The fact of the matter is that 52% of all items for Anglos, 30% of all items for Navajos, 50% of all items for Mexican-Spanish, and 44% of all items for Japanese reach this conservative criterion. In other words, when 28 verbal concepts are judged against 13 different visual alternatives in all possible combinations (364 items), approximately half of the items yield evidence for consistent intra-cultural synesthesia.

Cross-cultural synesthetic tendencies

The principal purpose of this research was to explore similarities and differences in synesthetic tendencies across language/culture groups. To the extent that peoples in two cultures share a common basis for synesthesia, the deviations from a 50/50 selection of alternatives should be in the same direction. Thus if more Anglos judge EXCITE-

MENT to be *large* rather than *small,* more Navajos should make this choice rather than the reverse, and similarly throughout all items and all group comparisons. Our first test of shared synesthetic tendencies, then, is to compute, for each pair of groups, the percentage of items yielding the same direction of choice. For Anglo *vs.* Navajo groups we find 65% of 364 items agreeing in direction; for Anglos *vs.* Mexican-Spanish 72% of 190 items agree; for Anglos *vs.* Japanese 78% of 364 items agree; for Navajo *vs.* Mexican-Spanish 61% of 190 items agree; for Navajo *vs.* Japanese 71% of 364 items agree; and for Mexican-Spanish *vs.* Japanese 69% of 190 items agree in direction. Although these percentages may not appear impressive in size, they are nevertheless significant at beyond the .005 level of confidence. The most conservative test of significance was used here, counting items where choices were 50/50 with the disagree proportion and using a two-tail test.

The preceding test includes many items where the synesthetic tendency in one or both groups is essentially chance, and gives all items equal weight (e.g., a 19/21 split counts as much as a 2/38 split). A more meaningful test, therefore, is to count only those items for which *both* groups being compared yield significant within-group agreement. In other words, if the subjects in each of two different language/culture groups agree among themselves as to the direction of synesthetic association, is the direction favored the same for both groups?

For Anglos *vs.* Navajos there were 73 items where both groups yielded significant within-group agreement; of these 86% were in the same direction of synesthetic association. For Anglo *vs.* Mexican-Spanish, 67 items met these criteria and 100% of them were in the same direction of association. For Anglos *vs.* Japanese, 98 items were significant for both and 99% (all but one) were in the same direction. For Navajos *vs.* Mexican-Spanish, we have 49 common significant items yielding 96% agreement. For Navajos *vs.* Japanese 90% of 71 shared significant items show the same direction of choice. For the Mexican-Spanish/Japanese comparison, 97% of 58 common significant items agreed in direction. It is clear that when we count only those items for which the groups being compared both show *intra*-cultural consistency, the *cross*-cultural agreement becomes very impressive indeed. Although the Navajo group shows slightly lower agreement with the other groups, all of these percentages are significant at well beyond the .001 level of confidence.

Having demonstrated over-all generality of synesthetic relationships, we may now consider specific agreements and—particularly— disagreements. Table 3 summarizes this information. It is restricted to comparisons among Anglos, Navajos, and Japanese; not only does the small *N* for Mexican-Spanish limit the possible significance of comparisons, but the other three groups represent extreme variations in both language families and culture. While inspecting Table 3 it should be kept

TABLE 2

Percentages of Anglos (A), Navajos (N), Mexican-Spanish (S) and Japanese (J) Choosing the Visual Alternatives Defining Each Column as Being Appropriate to the Verbal Concept Defining Each Row

	Up	Vert	Homo	Color-less	Thick	Dark	Crooked	Hazy	Blunt	Rounded	Diffuse	Large	Near
HEAVY													
(A)	7*	37	37	78	93*	96*	30†	52	52	59	15	70	81*
(N)	33	65	48	50	95	85	73	63	75	45	35	87	80
(S)	10	20	20	40	90	100	100	90	—	70	—	100	—
(J)	20	40	65	85	100	100	80	00	90	55	15	85	95
GOOD													
(A)	74	37	81*	11	15	26*	37	30	56	59	74	78	52
(N)	60	45	75	28	33	23	23	33	35	28	45	70	45
(S)	50	60	70	30	70	10	00	00	—	30	—	90	—
(J)	45	25	90	35	25	5	00	10	45	40	50	70	95
FAST													
(A)	81	41	44	52	7*	22*	37	33	19	30	78*	22	22
(N)	50	38	50	60	30	23	40	25	43	40	70	58	58
(S)	60	60	90	80	00	20	00	40	—	30	—	10	—
(J)	55	00	50	70	00	20	15	40	00	15	95	00	5
HAPPY													
(A)	89	70	63	7*	22	11*	41	41	56	78†	85	93	59
(N)	48	50	68	28	25	10	25	33	38	28	68	62	43
(S)	90	70	50	10	10	00	50	20	—	30	—	90	—
(J)	60	25	95	10	45	5	00	25	95	15	45	70	80
UP													
(A)	96*	100	63	30	59	26	89	63	59	15	96*	52†	4
(N)	90	55	55	35	43	40	68	48	60	35	73	70	20
(S)	—	—	—	—	—	—	—	—	—	—	—	—	—
(J)	100	95	65	20	15	10	60	60	50	40	100	15	00

		1	2	3	4	5	6	7	8	9	10	11	12	13
ENERGETIC	(A)	93	89	15†	22*	48†	37†	81	56	4	26	70	52	48
	(N)	63	48	70	30	33	33	38	33	30	45	50	73	68
	(S)	—	—	—	—	—	—	—	—	—	—	—	—	—
	(J)	85	75	65	10	95	85	70	25	55	55	85	100	80
LOOSE	(A)	56	52	33	56	22	45	70	93*	81*	81*	93	70	70
	(N)	35	45	38	58	45	35	75	68	83	75	28	43	55
	(S)	—	—	—	—	—	—	—	—	—	—	—	—	—
	(J)	50	20	75	15	50	25	30	95	95	95	70	90	65
STRONG	(A)	41	74	74	81	100	100	22	4	44	22	15	37	59
	(N)	58	65	63	48	55	53	43	48	33	35	48	38	80
	(S)	30	80	80	60	100	80	30	40	—	40	—	70	—
	(J)	25	55	65	90	90	90	65	5	65	15	35	70	85
EXCITEMENT	(A)	89	89	7	7*	52	52	96	81	15	22	67	67	56
	(N)	44	53	51	26	51	36	53	51	36	47	44	75	56
	(S)	80	80	20	10	70	70	90	90	—	40	—	100	—
	(J)	95	95	25	5	65	70	90	65	00	15	70	75	50
QUIET	(A)	30	4*	93	81	22	41	00	37	100	96	41	37	26
	(N)	30	33	58	55	40	35	35	53	45	40	58	23	50
	(S)	—	—	—	—	—	—	—	—	—	—	—	—	—
	(J)	20	10	90	70	50	35	00	40	90	55	15	40	10
BLUE	(A)	44	33	70	52	70†	93†	30†	59	78	70	44	63	26
	(N)	53	50	41	15	47	29	73	70	44	44	44	50	56
	(S)	90	60	60	60	70	60	60	50	—	70	—	30	—
	(J)	45	50	65	25	20	35	45	55	30	45	50	50	25

*Items where all three groups (Mexican-Spanish excluded) make the same choices at the 1% level of significance.
†Items where one of the three groups (Mexican-Spanish excluded) makes a significant (1% level) deviant choice.

TABLE 2—*Continued*

Percentages of Anglos (A), Navajos (N), Mexican-Spanish (S) and
Japanese (J) Choosing the Visual Alternatives Defining Each Column
as Being Appropriate to the Verbal Concept Defining Each Row

	Up	Vert	Homo	Color-less	Thick	Dark	Crooked	Hazy	Blunt	Rounded	Diffuse	Large	Near
BAD													
(A)	4	52	26*	89*	93*	96*	89*	67	41†	22†	15	26	48
(N)	43	58	28	83	80	83	85	88	73	73	43	33	38
(S)	10	40	10	90	100	100	100	100	—	50	—	60	—
(J)	35	75	10	75	95	95	100	90	20	40	55	30	60
LIGHT													
(A)	100	67	52	15	00*	00*	41	70†	52	44	96	63	37
(N)	50	25	58	52	13	13	28	30	58	68	63	20	28
(S)	80	50	70	20	00	00	20	10	—	60	—	20	—
(J)	80	55	55	25	5	5	25	95	15	70	85	25	5
DOWN													
(A)	00*	52	15	89	89†	93	89*	48†	33	44	19	33	63
(N)	13	45	45	65	38	40	70	63	48	63	35	38	85
(S)	—	—	—	—	—	—	—	—	—	—	—	—	—
(J)	00	80	30	75	85	95	90	15	30	30	25	50	90
BLACK													
(A)	4	89	41	96*	100*	96*	52	37	19	48	00*	15	48
(N)	34	71	64	94	89	94	53	61	18	58	31	58	68
(S)	20	70	40	100	100	100	90	70	—	60	—	30	—
(J)	25	70	40	100	100	100	80	5	45	45	5	35	80
WOMAN													
(A)	74	41	81	4*	26*	19*	56	67	89	93	48	44	48
(N)	50	50	58	35	30	8	50	58	58	55	35	35	38
(S)	80	30	60	10	50	40	70	40	—	70	—	50	—
(J)	65	55	65	5	15	15	30	100	65	80	65	30	35

	1	2	3	4	5	6	7	8	9	10	11	12	13
LAZY													
(A)	48	70	41	89	100*	59	19†	48	44	67	70	15	15
(N)	55	38	43	55	73	65	70	68	55	75	38	43	40
(S)	—	—	—	—	—	—	—	—	—	—	—	—	—
(J)	45	80	70	90	95	95	60	65	60	40	65	35	25
TIGHT													
(A)	22	7†	7	7*	4	7*	33	74†	56	74	44	48	44
(N)	43	83	55	23	35	30	10	28	25	53	60	53	60
(S)	—	—	—	—	—	—	—	—	—	—	—	—	—
(J)	45	5	15	00	00	5	85	85	65	85	25	80	30
GREEN													
(A)	41	70	78†	56	59	56	44	33	33†	4*	59	48	48
(N)	66	53	32	43	36	50	58	43	62	25	50	53	47
(S)	—	50	—	40	—	20	60	30	20	20	90	50	60
(J)	50	50	75	90	60	55	30	5	15	5	80	40	40
NOISY													
(A)	70	78	85	15	7	81	93*	56	70	19	15	89	74
(N)	50	75	50	48	55	63	73	50	65	55	43	63	58
(S)	—	—	—	—	—	—	—	—	—	—	—	—	—
(J)	85	65	75	30	5	70	90	65	70	15	15	70	70
GREY													
(A)	41	67	52	74	81	93	48	37	37†	89	85	11	44
(N)	51	37	63	63	73	69	69	31	27	48	63	27	37
(S)	—	—	—	—	—	—	—	—	—	—	—	—	—
(J)	35	55	35	45	60	75	70	70	75	75	35	50	25
SLOW													
(A)	44	78	44	93	85*	70	44	67†	74†	63	81	26*	15*
(N)	58	45	43	53	73	45	38	13	28	53	53	35	35
(S)	—	70	—	80	—	80	70	80	80	50	30	20	10
(J)	80	90	25	95	100	85	55	60	90	40	70	10	20

*Items where all three groups (Mexican-Spanish excluded) make the same choices at the 1% level of significance.
†Items where one of the three groups (Mexican-Spanish excluded) makes a significant (1% level) deviant choice.

TABLE 2—Continued

Percentages of Anglos (A), Navajos (N), Mexican-Spanish (S) and Japanese (J) Choosing the Visual Alternatives Defining Each Column as Being Appropriate to the Verbal Concept Defining Each Row

	Up	Vert	Homo	Color-less	Thick	Dark	Crooked	Hazy	Blunt	Rounded	Diffuse	Large	Near
WHITE													
(A)	93	37	74	63	4*	4*	30	44	74	52	96	96	48
(N)	52	14	79	65	9	3	24	11	65	35	65	59	43
(S)	90	20	80	60	00	00	10	00	—	30	—	70	—
(J)	65	40	75	90	00	5	15	45	45	60	85	85	35
CALM													
(A)	41	7	100	59	26	15*	7	37	96	93	59	70†	30
(N)	29	29	64	42	39	31	39	51	72	51	53	34	47
(S)	50	10	80	60	30	20	10	30	—	60	—	70	—
(J)	25	30	80	95	25	20	5	5	45	45	15	40	35
MAN													
(A)	63†	96	30	85	89*	89	48	22	26	22	52	67	67
(N)	64	71	56	58	68	56	61	44	41	44	50	71	71
(S)	60	90	20	90	70	80	30	60	—	20	—	90	—
(J)	25	75	25	100	100	75	55	00	35	20	50	85	80
YELLOW													
(A)	74	56	37	15*	15	11*	59	78*	59	56	74	56	37
(N)	48	34	66	10	31	17	59	66	59	51	63	59	63
(S)	60	40	70	00	20	20	60	30	—	60	—	50	—
(J)	65	40	60	5	30	20	45	80	50	65	80	50	50
WEAK													
(A)	52	19	48	56†	19*	26*	81	93	67	70	74	52	48
(N)	34	36	34	66	20	36	71	56	64	66	49	31	36
(S)	30	70	60	30	10	10	80	50	—	60	—	30	—
(J)	60	70	45	00	10	10	50	100	65	75	80	30	20

SAD													
(A)	7	11	59	93*	70	85	41	85	78†	74	11	33	33
(N)	47	36	33	69	69	47	60	63	63	58	50	31	47
(S)	00	30	00	100	90	100	70	100	—	60	—	10	—
(J)	25	70	5	100	55	65	65	90	25	40	55	5	25

*Items where all three groups (Mexican-Spanish excluded) make the same choices at the 1% level of significance.
†Items where one of the three groups (Mexican-Spanish excluded) makes a significant (1% level) deviant choice.

TABLE 3

Significant* Synesthetic Agreements and Disagreements Among
Anglo, Navajo and Japanese Groups

Anglos, Navajos and Japanese Agree That:		Anglos, Navajos and Japanese Disagree on Whether:	
HEAVY	is down, thick, dark and near.	HEAVY	is crooked (A) or straight (N, J).
GOOD	is homogeneous and bright.		
FAST	is thin, bright, and diffuse.		
HAPPY	is colorful and bright.	HAPPY	is rounded (A) or angular (N, J).
UP	is up and diffuse.	UP	is large (A) or small (J).
ENER-GETIC	is colorful	ENER-GETIC	is heterogeneous (A) or homogeneous (N); is thin and light (N) or thick and dark (J).
LOOSE	is hazy, rounded and blunt.		
STRONG			
EXCITE-MENT	is colorful.		
QUIET	is horizontal.		
BLUE		BLUE	is thick, dark and straight (A) or thin (J), or light and crooked (N).
BAD	is heterogeneous, colorless, thick, dark and crooked.	BAD	is angular (A) or rounded (N); is blunt (N) or sharp (J).
LIGHT (weight)	is thin and bright.	LIGHT	is clear (N) or hazy (J).
DOWN	is down and crooked.	DOWN	is thick (A, J) or thin (N); is hazy (N) or clear (J).
BLACK	is colorless, dark, thick, and concentrated.		
WOMAN	is colorful, thin and bright.		
LAZY	is blunt.	LAZY	is straight (A) or crooked (N).
TIGHT	is clear and angular.	TIGHT	is dark and small (A, J) or bright and large (N).
GREEN	is colorful.	GREEN	is thin and diffuse (A, J) or thick and concentrated (N).
NOISY	is crooked.		
GREY		GREY	is thin (N) or thick (J).
SLOW	is down, horizontal and blunt.	SLOW	is thick (A, J) and dark (A) or thin and bright (N).
WHITE	is thin and bright.		
CALM	is bright.	CALM	is large (A) or small (N).
MAN	is thick.		
YELLOW	is colorless, bright and hazy.		
WEAK	is thin and bright.	WEAK	is colorless (N) or colorful (J).
SAD	is colorless.	SAD	is blunt (A, N) or sharp (J).

*Approximately .01 level.

in mind that *thick, near, homogeneous*, etc., refer to the visual alternatives shown in Figure 1.

A few of the significant agreements are artifactual, e.g., that UP is *up* and that BLACK is *colorless*. But most of the significant agreements across the Anglo, Navajo, and Japanese groups bring out what we feel intuitively to be appropriate synesthetic relations in our own languages of aesthetics and metaphor. Thus FAST is *thin, bright*, and *diffuse;* LOOSE is *hazy, rounded* and *blunt;* ENERGETIC and EXCITEMENT are *colorful;* BAD is *heterogeneous, colorless, thick, dark*, and *crooked;* NOISY is *crooked;* SLOW is *down, horizontal*, and *blunt;* and so forth.

The significant disagreements are open to a number of different interpretations: (1) Differences in the metaphorical extensions of the visual dimensions themselves. This may be the case as between Anglos and Japanese, on the one hand, and Navajo on the other, for the scales *thick-thin, dark-light* and *straight-crooked*. (2) Differences in the denotative meanings of verbal concepts, and hence unsuccessful translation. This is certainly the case for Anglo *vs.* Navajo meanings of BLUE (cf., results for color study below). (3) Differences in the connotative implications of translation-equivalent verbal concepts. This may be the case for Anglo *vs.* Navajo meanings of ENERGETIC, LAZY, FAST, SLOW, and TIGHT. It is obviously impossible to choose among these alternative interpretations on the basis of these data alone. In passing it may be noted that there were almost four times as many significant disagreements between Navajo and the other two groups as between Anglo and Japanese.

Correlations

One specific question that can be answered from the concept correlation matrices is this: do terms that are translation-equivalent to standard verbal opposites in English function as semantic opposites in Navajo, Mexican-Spanish, and Japanese? If they do function in this fashion, then the profile of choices for GOOD, say, should be reciprocal to that for BAD and hence yield a high negative correlation across the visual alternatives. Table 4 summarizes the data on this question, i.e., the correlations between concepts that are standard opposites in English for the various language/culture groups. The consistent negative r's in this table permit us to conclude with confidence that Navajo, Mexican-Spanish, and Japanese groups do treat these concepts functionally as opposites. If one visual alternative is chosen as appropriate to HAPPY (say, the *light* circle), we can predict that the other alternative will be chosen as appropriate to its opposite, SAD (the *dark* circle). Since the alternatives associated with the verbal concepts are not themselves verbal, and further, since the verbal opposites appeared independently and

TABLE 4

Correlations between Standard Verbal Opposites (in English) across
Visual Alternatives for Anglo, Navajo, Mexican-Spanish and
Japanese Subjects

	Anglo	Navajo	Mexican-Spanish	Japanese
HEAVY–LIGHT	− .87	− .82	− .81	− .96
GOOD–BAD	− .92	− .91	− .55	− .75
FAST–SLOW	− .61	− .47	− .73	− .52
HAPPY–SAD	− .73	− .66	− .89	− .85
UP–DOWN	− .39	− .72	—	− .58
ENERGETIC–LAZY	− .91	− .82	—	− .16
LOOSE–TIGHT	− .84	− .58	—	− .96
STRONG–WEAK	− .89	− .71	− .45	− .90
EXCITEMENT–CALM	− .75	− .21	− .54	− .72
BLACK–WHITE	− .82	− .47	− .75	− .55
MAN–WOMAN	− .86	− .35	− .70	− .91
QUIET–NOISY	− .95	− .62	—	− .92

widely separated in the test, this seems to be an adequate demonstration
of functional opposition. The oppositions are not as polar for the Navajo
as for the other groups, but whether this is due to lower reliability, to
inaccurate translation, or to a less clear conception of opposition cannot
be told from these data. Several exceptions to the rule may be noted in
Table 4: The glaring exception is the *positive* correlation between FAST
and SLOW for the Navajo; we will consider this in discussion. It can also
be seen that UP-DOWN functions less clearly as an opposition for Anglos
than for the other groups, that ENERGETIC-LAZY is hardly a functional
opposition for the Japanese, and that EXCITEMENT-CALM and MAN-
WOMAN are less clear oppositions for the Navajo than for the other
groups.

Highly significant agreements across all language/culture groups for
other than direct opposite relations are shown in Table 5 (A). Again,
because of the small sample and missing items, the Mexican-Spanish data
are not included (but inspection indicates that with no exceptions the
relations shown here also apply to this group). To facilitate visual
inspection, relations are repeated in clusters for each verbal concept
(e.g., the GOOD/HAPPY correlations appear both in the GOOD cluster
and in the HAPPY cluster). Some of these consistent relations seem to
reflect nothing more than we would expect from the commonness of
human beings and their physical environments: it is GOOD to be HAPPY
and BAD to be SAD; LIGHT (weight) things tend to be FAST and
EXCITEMENT tends to be NOISY; TIGHT musculature is associated
with STRONG and LOOSE musculature with WEAK; MAN tends to be
STRONGer than WOMAN, and WOMAN is LIGHTer (weight). Other

consistent relations across these cultures suggest 'true' shared metaphors: subjects tend to make the same synesthetic choices for WHITE as they do for GOOD, CALM, and FAST; opposed synesthetic choices are made for LIGHT (weight) vs. BLACK (i.e., BLACK has a "heavy" connotation); the choices for WOMAN are similar to those for YELLOW, but opposed to those for BLACK.

Table 5 (B) lists the most extreme cases of disagreement among these three language/culture groups in concept correlations. Since the disagreements clearly cluster in terms of certain key verbal concepts, the table is organized on the basis of such clusters. The Navajo use ENERGETIC in the same visual metaphors as they do GOOD, STRONG, HAPPY, and TIGHT (and the reverse for LAZY); for Anglos and Japanese these concepts are essentially unrelated, except that ENERGETIC goes with NOISY (and LAZY the reverse), which is not the case for Navajos. Similarly we find the Navajo using TIGHT and LOOSE in clearly different metaphorical relations than do Anglos and Japanese, TIGHT being used like HAPPY, GOOD, and WHITE (and the reverse for LOOSE); the other two cultures reverse these relations systematically. MAN behaves like DOWN, and WOMAN more like UP, for Anglos and Japanese, but there is no relation for the Navajo; yet Anglos and Navajos agree, in contradistinction to the Japanese, in seeing MAN as unlike CALM. The FAST/SLOW relations are confused—the Japanese are the divergent group in FAST/ENERGETIC, FAST/HAPPY, and SLOW/CALM correlations, but the Navajo diverge from the other two groups for the SLOW/LIGHT (weight) and SLOW/WHITE correlations. The Navajo see STRONG as most like the positive evaluators, GOOD and HAPPY, and like EXCITEMENT; the Anglos, surprisingly, see STRONG as more like negative evaluators; the Japanese treat STRONG as essentially independent of (uncorrelated with) evaluative concepts. On the color terms we find very systematic differences: the concept BLUE is clearly used differently by the Anglos than by the Navajos and Japanese; by the former it is used like QUIET, SAD, and LAZY and is uncorrelated with YELLOW or GREEN; by the latter it is used like the other color terms. The concepts GREEN and YELLOW, on the other hand, are handled similarly by the Anglos and Japanese, but 'deviantly' by the Navajo, who see GREEN as related to HEAVY, STRONG, and MAN and who see YELLOW as independent of STRONG and TIGHT (this color being significantly NOT-STRONG and NOT-TIGHT for the other two groups). Finally, the Japanese are 'deviant' in the use of GREY, failing to use it like CALM, WEAK, and WOMAN, as do the Anglos and Navajo.

VISUAL-ALTERNATIVE MATRICES. These correlation matrices indicate which visual dimensions tend to be used the same or different ways in differentiating the 28 verbal concepts. Table 6 (A) lists the

TABLE 5

A. Concept Correlations for which Anglos, Navajos and Japanese Display *Agreement* in Direction*

	A	N	J		A	N	J
GOOD/HAPPY	.88	.86	.81	BAD/HAPPY	−.93	−.87	−.87
GOOD/SAD	−.56	−.77	−.74	BAD/SAD	.57	.80	.80
GOOD/WHITE	.78	.59	.52	BAD/WHITE	−.82	−.63	−.64
HAPPY/GOOD	.88	.86	.81	SAD/GOOD	−.56	−.77	−.74
HAPPY/BAD	−.93	−.87	−.87	SAD/BAD	.57	.80	.80
				SAD/ENERGETIC	−.73	−.81	−.60
LIGHT (wt.)/FAST	.70	.50	.57				
LIGHT (wt.)/BLACK	−.82	−.55	−.81				
LIGHT (wt.)/WOMAN	.53	.53	.81				
FAST/LIGHT (wt.)	.70	.50	.57				
FAST/WHITE	.60	.82	.60				
ENERGETIC/ EXCITEMENT	.94	.65	.56				
ENERGETIC/SAD	−.73	−.81	−.60	CALM/QUIET	.90	.68	.61
EXCITEMENT/ ENERGETIC	.94	.65	.56	CALM/WHITE	.62	.52	.55
EXCITEMENT/NOISY	.95	.52	.88				
				LOOSE/STRONG	−.91	−.53	−.51
TIGHT/STRONG	.83	.66	.62	LOOSE/WEAK	.83	.75	.51

STRONG/TIGHT	.83	.66	.62
STRONG/LOOSE	-.91	-.53	-.51
STRONG/MAN	.71	.80	.83
MAN/STRONG	.71	.80	.83
MAN/WEAK	-.79	-.65	-.82
NOISY/EXCITEMENT	.95	.52	.88
WHITE/GOOD	.78	.59	.52
WHITE/FAST	.60	.82	.60
WHITE/CALM	.62	.52	.55
WHITE/BAD	-.82	-.63	-.64
YELLOW/BLACK	-.80	-.70	-.81
YELLOW/WOMAN	.65	.61	.87

WEAK/LOOSE	.83	.75	.51
WEAK/MAN	-.79	-.65	-.82
WOMAN/LIGHT (wt.)	.53	.53	.81
WOMAN/YELLOW	.65	.61	.87
WOMAN/BLACK	-.66	-.57	-.84
QUIET/CALM	.90	.68	.64
BLACK/LIGHT (wt.)	-.82	-.55	-.81
BLACK/WOMAN	-.66	-.57	-.84
BLACK/YELLOW	-.80	-.70	-.81

TABLE 5—*Continued*

B. Some Extreme *Disagreements* in Concept Correlations between
Anglos, Navajos, and Japanese

	A	N	J
ENERGETIC/GOOD	.05	.87	.30
ENERGETIC/STRONG	−.26	.76	.28
ENERGETIC/TIGHT	.02	.69	.06
ENERGETIC/NOISY	.89	−.08	.48
TIGHT/HAPPY	−.66	.78	−.73
TIGHT/BAD	.58	−.78	.69
TIGHT/DOWN	.52	−.44	.81
TIGHT/GOOD	−.56	.83	−.44
TIGHT/BLACK	.76	−.14	.82
TIGHT/WHITE	−.49	.62	−.48
TIGHT/SAD	.21	−.67	.53
MAN/BAD	.44	−.39	.37
MAN/DOWN	.49	−.10	.79
MAN/CALM	−.64	−.69	.20
FAST/ENERGETIC	.46	.54	−.46
FAST/HAPPY	.39	.68	−.16

	A	N	J
LAZY/GOOD	.14	−.84	−.10
LAZY/BAD	−.14	.84	−.13
LAZY/HAPPY	−.04	−.80	.27
LAZY/SAD	.65	.77	−.10
LAZY/NOISY	−.80	.04	−.27
LOOSE/HAPPY	.49	−.44	.72
LOOSE/BAD	−.44	.55	−.59
LOOSE/DOWN	−.39	.64	−.66
LOOSE/SAD	−.19	.57	−.53
WOMAN/DOWN	−.68	.16	−.80
SLOW/CALM	.64	.67	.06
SLOW/LIGHT (wt.)	−.45	.62	−.35
SLOW/WHITE	−.10	.67	−.21

STRONG/GOOD	-.44	.66	.12
STRONG/BAD	.48	-.68	.21
STRONG/HAPPY	-.56	.47	-.14
STRONG/SAD	.25	-.71	-.03
STRONG/EXCITEMENT	-.34	.69	-.13
BLUE/EXCITEMENT	-.55	.60	.26
BLUE/QUIET	.58	-.22	-.04
BLUE/NOISY	-.56	.50	.02
BLUE/SAD	.67	-.05	-.22
BLUE/ENERGETIC	-.67	.18	-.02
BLUE/LAZY	.62	-.14	.15
BLUE/YELLOW	-.38	.70	.64
BLUE/GREEN	.01	.66	.59
GREY/CALM	.73	.80	-.08
GREY/MAN	-.69	-.74	.32
GREY/WOMAN	.34	.61	-.40
GREY/WEAK	.65	.74	-.28

EXCITEMENT/SAD	-.63	-.56	.08
GREEN/HAPPY	.80	-.02	.70
GREEN/LIGHT (wt.)	.70	-.64	.57
GREEN/WHITE	.53	-.45	.46
GREEN/BLACK	-.78	.18	-.74
GREEN/DOWN	-.73	.20	-.66
GREEN/HEAVY	-.53	.55	-.45
GREEN/STRONG	-.63	.52	-.64
GREEN/MAN	-.55	.60	-.68
YELLOW/STRONG	-.89	.11	-.83
YELLOW/TIGHT	-.75	.10	-.77

agreements across groups in use of visual dimensions and Table 6 (B) gives the most notable *disagreements*. Since the data for the Mexican-Spanish seem particularly relevant here, and were based on correlations over 19 concepts, they are also included. The clearest relationships within the visual frame of reference for all groups are that *up* goes with *colorful* and *diffuse; dark* goes with *colorless, thick,* and *concentrated;* and *thick* goes with *dark* and *concentrated* (and the opposites of these terms, of course, showing the reverse relations). Other specific agreements: *vertical* functions like *sharp; homogeneous* is seen as being like *straight* (not *crooked*); while *blunt* is seen to be like *rounded* (not *angular*); and, quite reasonably, *large* goes with *near.* These relationships within the visual framework will be found (below) to contribute heavily to the major factors extracted from the visual-alternative matrices.

The disagreements among language/culture groups shown in Table 6 (B) are interesting. The largest number of disagreements separate the Navajo and Mexican-Spanish, on the one hand, from the Anglos and Japanese on the other—which could be due to either geographical (visual locale) or education-literacy differences. Navajos and Mexicans in the Southwest agree (in contradistinction to Anglos and Japanese): in seeing *homogeneous* as like *angular; colorless, thick,* and *dark* as being like *hazy; dark* and *crooked* as being like *rounded;* and *angular* as being *large.* Navajos 'deviate' from the other groups: in relating *vertical* with *large; heterogenous* (rather than *homogeneous*) and *crooked* (rather than *straight*) with *blunt; clear* with *diffuse;* and *sharp* with *large.* It is possible that the Mexican-Spanish would have agreed with the Navajo on most of these relations also, but they were not tested on most of these terms. Anglos 'deviate' from the other groups on three items: they do not see *dark* as being like *crooked,* or *diffuse* as being like *far,* but rather they see *diffuse* as like *large,* which the other groups do not. Japanese 'deviations' are restricted to the *hazy* dimension, this visual polarity being associated with *far* but not with *crooked* as in other groups (non-evaluative for Japanese?). Japanese and Navajo differ in seeing *colorful* as *rounded* (J) or *angular* (N). In interpreting these similarities and differences in the visual frame of reference, the reader should refer back to the diagrams in Figure 1 and keep in mind that it was these drawings, not words, to which the subjects were reacting.

Correlations between matrices

One way of getting an over-all picture of the similarities between groups in synesthetic tendencies is to correlate their intercorrelation matrices cell by cell. To the extent that the matched coefficients covary throughout the two matrices being compared, we have evidence that common variables are operating. This estimate of similarity has the

TABLE 6

A. Visual Alternative Correlations for which Anglos, Navajos,
Japanese and Mexican-Spanish Display *Agreement* in Direction

	A	N	J	MS
Up/colorful	.75	.36	.68	.51
Up/diffuse	.83	.44	.75	—
Vertical/sharp	.73	.44	.51	—
Homogen./straight	.74	.73	.78	.66
Colorless/dark	.64	.54	.51	.57
Thick/dark	.94	.90	.92	.91
Thick/concent.	.73	.54	.59	—
Dark/concent.	.84	.47	.55	—
Blunt/rounded	.87	.54	.73	.00†
Large/near	.36	.37	.65	—

°r > ± .35.
†M-S data not used as criterion.

B. Some Extreme *Disagreements* in Visual-Alternative Correlations
between Anglos, Navajos, Japanese and Mexican-Spanish Groups

	A	N	J	MS
N and MS vs. A and J				
Homogeneous/angular	− .65	.58	− .54	.22
Colorless/hazy	− .21	.16	− .52	.44
Thick/hazy	− .20	.58	− .31	.70
Dark/hazy	− .27	.56	− .32	.88
Dark/rounded	− .29	.26	− .45	.30
Crooked/rounded	− .48	.61	− .38	.53
Angular/large	− .33	.67	− .31	.31
N vs. A, J, and MS				
Vertical/large	− .04	.59	− .18	.05
Heterogeneous/blunt	− .77	.41	− .66	—
Crooked/blunt	− .49	.43	− .33	—
Clear/diffuse	− .33	.49	− .56	—
Sharp/large	− .35	.45	− .49	—
A vs. N, J, and MS				
Dark/crooked	.04	.56	.82	.63
Diffuse/large	.63	.03	− .09	—
Diffuse/far	.08	.48	.43	—
J vs. A, N, and MS				
Hazy/far	− .08	− .16	.46	—
Hazy/crooked	.52	.85	.04	.76
N vs. J (others neutral)				
Colorful/rounded	− .04	− .43	.49	.09

advantage of being independent of the absolute magnitudes of the *r*'s in the two matrices; it has the disadvantage that lack of independence between the rows and columns makes it impossible to estimate significance levels of the *r*'s. However, gross differences in the similarities of groups can be indicated in this manner. Table 7 gives such over-all correlations for both concept matrices and visual-alternative matrices.

TABLE 7

Correlations between Intercorrelation Matrices for Anglo, Navajo, Mexican-Spanish and Japanese Groups

	Concept Matrices		
	Navajo	Mexican–Spanish	Japanese
Anglo	.43	.75	.67
Navajo	—	.41	.24
Mexican–Spanish	—	—	.68

	Visual Alternative Matrices		
	Navajo	Mexican–Spanish	Japanese
Anglo	.37	.43	.76
Navajo	—	.81	.39
Mexican–Spanish	—	—	.42

The first thing to note is that all of these correlations are positive and, for the most part, of reasonable size. This supports the conclusion reached earlier on the basis of item analyses that there are considerable similarities in synesthetic tendencies across language/culture groups. The second thing to note is that whereas Navajo is the one deviant group for correlations of *concept* matrices (markedly lower *r*'s with all other groups), both the Navajo and Mexican-Spanish groups separate sharply from the Anglo and Japanese groups in the correlations of *visual-alternative* matrices. Another way of expressing this finding is to say that the Mexican-Spanish shift their 'allegiance' from the Anglo on concept relations to the Navajo on scale relations. This is a rather remarkable contrast.

CONCEPT MATRICES. It will be recalled that many of the polar scale terms used by Suci (e.g., *heavy-light, good-bad, happy-sad, fast-slow, strong-weak*) were included as *verbal concepts* in the present synesthesia study: If a stable semantic frame of reference is operating, one would expect the same or highly similar factors to appear in both cases. The first four factors in the unrotated Centroid Analysis accounted for 89% of the total variance for Anglos, 82% for Navajos, and 84% for Mexican-Spanish. Table 8 gives the indices of factorial similarity across groups for these rotated factors; the italicized values in the diagonals index the similarity among 'corresponding' factors for the several groups.

The first factor is quite well defined as *evaluative* by the concepts which load highly on it for all three language/culture groups: GOOD, HAPPY, and WHITE on the positive pole *vs.* BAD, SAD, and BLACK on the negative pole. The difference between Anglos and Navajos in what is "evaluatively relevant" is also well defined: STRONG, TIGHT, ENER-GETIC, and MAN are also positively evaluated by the Navajos (conversely for WEAK, LOOSE, and LAZY), whereas the reverse evaluation, with the exception of ENERGETIC, is given these concepts by the Anglos. The first factor for Mexican-Spanish corresponds almost perfectly with that for Anglos. The indices of factorial similarity for Factor I (A/N .60, A/MS .95, N/MS .64) are consistent with these interpretations. Inspection of the Japanese correlation matrix shows that the same concepts (with the exception of WHITE and BLACK) tend to cluster together. Suci interpreted the first factor in his analysis (of Navajo, Hopi, Zuni, and Mexican-Spanish groups) as being evaluative, the clearest scales across all groups being *good-bad, clean-dirty,* and *pretty-ugly.*

The second factor in our study is fairly well defined across all groups as a *potency* factor: STRONG and MAN have sizeable positive loadings for all groups and LIGHT (weight), WOMAN, YELLOW, and WEAK have sizeable negative loadings. The Japanese would probably add TIGHT *vs.* LOOSE, HEAVY *vs.* LIGHT, and BLACK *vs.* WHITE to the potency factor. The indices of factorial similarity (A/N .69, A/MS .75, N/MS .66) confirm the above picture. Suci's second factor included *strong-weak, heavy-light, hard-soft,* and *long-short* for all groups, but also *fast-slow* and *industrious-lazy* for some groups, and he dubbed it a *dynamism* factor.

Factor III is the least generalized across groups. For Anglos it is clearly an *activity* factor: UP, ENERGETIC, EXCITEMENT, and NOISY in contrast to QUIET, LAZY, SLOW, and CALM. But this pattern does not hold up satisfactorily across the other groups, as the low indices of factorial similarity (A/N .18, A/MS .52, N/MS .25) show. Inspection of the Japanese correlation data suggests that we would have ENERGETIC, EXCITEMENT, and NOISY in contrast with SLOW, LAZY, CALM, and QUIET—which is pretty close to the Anglo pattern. Suci also had difficulty demonstrating any consistent third (or further) factor in his study. Our Factor IV displays somewhat higher indices of factorial similarity (A/N .60, A/MS .54, N/MS .42), but it is difficult to come to grips with semantically. Its positive pole is best defined by

TABLE 8

Indices of Factorial Similarity for Concept Matrices

	Factor I			Factor II			Factor III			Factor IV		
	A	N	MS	A	N	MS	A	N	MS	A	N	MS
Factor I												
A		*.60*	*.95*	−.50	−.63	−.32	.13	.43	.04	−.11	.19	.34
N			*.64*	.25	−.09	.31	.30	.07	−.24	−.15	−.16	.09
MS				−.37	−.50	−.25	.20	.40	.04	−.14	.03	.34
Factor II												
A					*.69*	*.75*	.04	.38	−.53	.11	.17	.04
N						*.66*	.39	−.37	.02	.12	−.27	−.17
MS							.32	.29	−.30	.32	.05	−.03
Factor III												
A								*.18*	*.52*	.29	−.09	.08
N									*.25*	−.07	.11	.15
MS										.09	−.10	−.08
Factor IV												
A											*.60*	*.54*
N												*.42*

FAST, LIGHT, TIGHT, WHITE and its negative pole by HEAVY, EXCITEMENT, WOMAN. There is perhaps a Freudian flavor to this factor—something which touches on many shared myths—but the quantitative data won't bear much weight.

VISUAL-ALTERNATIVE MATRICES. In the unrotated factor matrices for visual dimensions, the first four factors extracted accounted for about the same proportions of total variance as in the concept factor analyses—87% for Anglos, 82% for Navajos, and 86% for Mexican-Spanish. However, the factors are not so readily interpreted (perhaps because all the variables are from a small domain). Table 9 gives the rotated loadings and Table 10 the indices of factorial similarity.

For Factor I the indices of factorial similarity only permit us to compare Anglos and Mexican-Spanish, where we seem to be dealing with a kind of *flatness* factor: *rounded* and *horizontal* best reflect the nature of the factor, with the Anglos including *homogeneous, straight,* and *blunt.* Inspection of the Japanese correlation matrix suggests that it would duplicate the Anglo factor closely. The Navajo Factor I is actually closer to Anglo II, as the indices of similarity show. Factors were grouped so as to maximize the sizes of the indices. In this case, Navajo Factor II has a higher similarity to Anglo II (.75) than does Navajo I (.62), and hence the apparently anomalous fact that Navajo I is assigned with Anglo I where its index is only .38.

Factor II for the visual alternatives displays the highest factorial similarities (A/N .80, A/MS .75, N/MS .75) found anywhere in this study. Perhaps surprising, since this is a visual domain, it seems to be essentially an *evaluative* factor connotatively. The defining characteristics are *colorless, dark, thick, down,* and *small* (vs. the opposite, favorable pole, *colorful, light, thin, up,* and *large*). An interesting difference is that Anglos would include *concentrated* in the definition of the negative pole, but not Navajo. Inspection of the Japanese data confirms this picture, *concentrated* being included with *dark, down,* etc. as with the Anglos.

Factor III for these visual dimensions also displays a high degree of cross-cultural correspondence (A/N .75, A/MS .62, N/MS .84), but one is hard put to label it. For all groups the positive pole of the factor is characterized by *hazy, crooked, rounded, heterogeneous,* and *down,* and the negative pole by their opposites, *clear, straight, angular, homogeneous,* and *up.* One possible interpretation would be that this is a *figure* vs. *ground* factor. Aspects of the visual environment that stand out as figures are *clear, straight, angular, homogeneous,* and *up* in perceptual experience. But whereas *thickness* and *darkness* is attributed to what we have called the "background" character by the Mexican-Spanish, this is not so for the Anglos.

TABLE 9

Rotated Factor Loadings for Visual-Alternative Matrices

	Factor I			Factor II			Factor III			Factor IV		
	A	N	MS	A	N	MS	A	N	MS	A	N	MS
Up	−30	−80	−30	−91	−28	−42	−15	−34	−68	01	16	07
Vertical	−86	−08	−88	−16	−08	−13	−21	00	03	24	92	−37
Homogeneous	85	08	−01	−13	−25	10	−41	−80	−87	−10	−18	−25
Colorless	17	15	01	82	89	74	01	23	46	−18	15	−22
Thick	−34	07	−17	83	15	26	−10	34	87	26	87	07
Dark	−24	08	−06	91	34	19	−12	36	95	13	81	−03
Crooked	−67	−06	16	−08	−09	−51	60	88	78	10	37	−08
Hazy	15	17	11	−22	−16	−08	89	86	94	13	32	−04
Blunt	94	−16	—	−08	23	—	10	67	—	11	−37	—
Rounded	90	33	75	−03	19	−28	16	81	36	18	−18	−20
Diffuse	−04	−61	—	−93	02	—	14	−34	—	15	−48	—
Large	28	−28	−39	−52	−20	−13	08	−55	10	72	63	85
Near	−26	61	—	22	−12	—	20	−09	—	78	56	—

TABLE 10

Indices of Factorial Similarity for Visual-Alternative Matrices

	Factor I			Factor II			Factor III			Factor IV		
	A	N	MS	A	N	MS	A	N	MS	A	N	MS
Factor I												
A		.38	.62	−.07	.05	.19	−.08	−.19	−.27	−.09	−.54	.07
N			.54	.62	.46	.44	.20	.45	.42	.20	−.16	−.40
MS				.16	.22	−.04	.35	.45	.16	−.35	−.60	−.16
Factor II												
A					.80	.75	−.11	.35	.59	−.17	−.28	.29
N						.75	−.05	.35	.46	−.23	−.12	−.29
MS							−.32	−.14	.15	−.30	−.02	−.15
Factor III												
A								.75	.62	.19	.10	.09
N									.84	.06	.25	−.31
MS										.35	.60	.00
Factor IV												
A											.69	.62
N												.14

Factor IV seems to be what might be called a *distance* factor, but the evidence is not very impressive—particularly since there is no correspondence between the Navajo and Mexican-Spanish factors. Common to all three groups we have *large* vs. *small;* Anglos and Navajos would include *near* vs. *far*—and so would the Japanese—hence the "distance" notion; but Navajos would include *vertical-horizontal, thick-thin, dark-light,* and to some extent *concentrated-diffuse.*

Addendum: Some data on color meanings

In the course of the Southwest Project on Comparative Psycholinguistics, Dr. Susan Ervin collected semantic differential data from 21 Navajo subjects when they were judging actual samples of colored paper. These were 2¼″ by 1¾″ rectangles of dime store colored papers: red, yellow, light green, blue, purple, brown, black, and white. The red was intensely saturated and bright, the green was very pale, and the blue was about the color of the non-carbon part of carbon paper, i.e., quite deep in hue but not too heavily saturated. These color chips were rated against the 27 scales given in Table 11. These scales were *verbally* defined and they were 6-*step* scales, the middle position being eliminated to force the subjects to indicate some directional choice in each case. Subsequently, Mr. Murray Miron collected equivalent data from 24 Anglos (students at the University of Illinois), using the same color chips and the same 6-step scales. Table 11 gives the mean scale positions for each color chip on each scale, Anglo (A) and Navajo (N) results being directly compared.

NON-DIFFERENTIATING SCALES AND SCALES USED DIFFERENTLY BY ANGLOS AND NAVAJOS. Inspecting Table 11 we can see that there are a few scales which, either for Anglos or Navajos or both, do not differentiate among the color chips—that is, are irrelevant with respect to this stimulus domain. The scale *long-short* fails to differentiate for both Anglos and Navajos. The scales *sharp-dull, up-down,* and *rich-poor* fail to differentiate for the Navajos. Asterisks between Anglo and Navajo values indicate that the difference in means is equal to or greater than 1.00 scale unit—an arbitrary unit that probably approximates a reliable difference (Osgood et al., 1957). Looking along the rows defined by scales, it can be seen that a few scales yield four or more (out of 8 possible) differences at this level: *happy-sad, sweet-sour, fast-slow, thick-thin, up-down,* and *white-black.* Whether these represent the dimensions along which Anglo/Navajo differences in color symbolism are most marked, or merely scales for which translation equivalence was not obtained, cannot be determined from these data.

OVER-ALL SIMILARITIES IN COLOR CONNOTATIONS.
Despite the occasional differences in connotation, indicated by asterisks in Table 11 the over-all similarities between Anglos and Navajos are quite striking, as inspection reveals. A rough way of estimating the significance of this connotative agreement is as follows: In each color column in Table 11 we note each scale for which the mean deviates 1.00 units from the midpoint (3.50) *for either group*—in other words, we count only those items where at least one of our two groups shows a probably significant connotation. Then we ask: on what proportion of such items do both groups deviate in the same direction from the midpoint? For RED we find that 12/15 go the same way, for YELLOW 14/15 the same, for GREEN 12/13, for BLUE 6/7, for PURPLE 4/5, for BROWN 11/14, for BLACK 16/19, and for WHITE 15/15 deviate in the same way from the midpoints. Since all of these proportions approximate or exceed the 5% level of significance (by a one-tail test, appropriate because we are predicting "same" rather than "different" directions), we can conclude that in general Anglos and Navajos have similar connotative profiles for these color chips. But is there anything systematic about these shared color connotations?

CONNOTATIONS OF BRIGHTNESS (WHITE VS. BLACK).
Table 11 is arranged to facilitate analysis in terms of semantic factors. From inspection of the WHITE and BLACK columns, it is clear that these chips differ sharply in evaluation for both groups, WHITE being *good, happy, pretty, sweet,* and *clean* as compared with BLACK. Other unclassified scales reflect the same tendency, BLACK being judged *rougher, angrier,* and *more crooked.* Brightness also connotes potency and activity, but less consistently; BLACK tends to be the more potent and masculine but WHITE the more active and feminine. Note that *hot-cold* reverses this trend in both groups, perhaps because of the specific association of WHITE with snow and ice.

CONNOTATIONS OF SATURATION (YELLOW AND GREEN VS. RED, BLUE, PURPLE, AND BROWN). Yellow is the least saturated region of the spectrum and, as noted earlier, the green used in this study was a pale, pastel shade; the other colors were quite saturated. The scales which differentiate among these two sets of colors for both groups are mainly along the potency dimensions. Thus we find the more saturated colors judged to be much *stronger, harder, heavier, larger,* and *thicker.* The same factor is reflected in the unclassified scales which differentiate these two sets: saturated colors are *angrier, dirtier,* and *more masculine,* as well as being judged *rougher* by the Anglos.

TABLE 11

Mean Semantic Profiles for Color Chips for Anglos (A) and Navajos (N)

	Red A	Red N	Yellow A	Yellow N	Green A	Green N	Blue A	Blue N	Purple A	Purple N	Brown A	Brown N	Black A	Black N	White A	White N	
†Good	3.9	4.2	3.0	3.0	3.0	3.5	3.3	3.5	3.8	3.5	4.4	3.8	4.8	4.4	1.8*	2.9	Bad
Happy	2.3	3.2	2.4	2.3	2.5	2.4	4.3*	3.2	4.0*	2.6	4.6*	3.3	5.1*	3.7	2.5	2.0	Sad
Pretty	2.3*	4.2	2.5	2.8	2.5	3.1	3.2	3.5	3.5	3.5	4.8	3.9	4.8	4.7	2.7	2.8	Ugly
Sweet	2.8	3.6	2.8*	1.8	3.7	2.9	3.9*	2.7	4.3*	3.0	4.3*	2.9	4.4*	3.4	2.5	2.2	Sour
Clean	2.7	3.4	2.3	2.2	2.0	2.2	3.6	3.4	3.8	2.9	4.8*	3.7	5.1*	3.5	1.4	1.5	Dirty
Strong	1.6	2.0	4.5	4.1	4.3*	3.2	2.0	2.3	2.3	2.8	2.7	2.7	1.8	2.1	4.0	3.3	Weak
Hard	2.4	2.6	4.1	3.2	4.0	3.5	2.8	3.1	3.5	3.0	2.8	2.8	2.2	2.0	4.6	4.1	Soft
Heavy	3.3	3.5	5.3*	3.7	5.4*	3.7	2.0	2.1	2.7	2.6	1.8	2.2	1.2	1.7	5.8*	4.1	Light
Large	2.5	1.9	4.3*	2.9	4.0	3.7	2.8	2.4	3.0	2.7	2.4	2.4	2.3	2.0	2.7	3.6	Small
Thick	2.6*	4.3	5.0	4.3	4.8	4.0	2.1*	3.9	2.6*	3.9	2.0*	3.2	2.1	2.7	4.1	4.2	Thin
Long	3.3	2.9	3.9	3.3	3.2	3.0	3.4*	2.4	3.0	2.5	3.2	2.5	2.8	2.7	2.6	2.7	Short
Fast	2.0*	3.4	2.7*	4.1	2.6*	4.3	3.8	3.3	3.9	4.1	5.0	4.1	4.5	4.4	2.8*	4.1	Slow
Sharp	2.0	2.7	2.6	3.4	2.7	2.7	3.9	3.1	3.3	2.8	5.0*	3.3	4.5*	3.3	2.8	3.4	Dull
Energetic	2.1*	4.0	3.0	3.6	3.0	3.7	3.7	3.3	3.5	3.5	4.9	4.1	4.5	4.8	3.4*	2.4	Lazy
Hot	1.5	2.4	2.9	3.0	4.5	3.9	3.8*	2.6	3.2	2.4	3.5	3.2	3.5	2.8	4.3	4.2	Cold
Young	2.1*	4.0	2.5	3.4	2.0*	3.4	3.8	3.6	4.0	4.1	4.7	4.4	5.4*	4.3	2.2	2.6	Old

	1	2	3	4	5	6	7	8	9	10	11	12	13	14	15	16	
Up	3.1	2.6	2.0*	3.1	2.7	3.5	3.3	2.6	4.0*	3.0	4.6*	3.5	5.6*	2.5	1.6*	2.6	Down
Smooth	4.0	3.9	2.3*	3.7	2.1*	4.0	4.0	4.3	3.5	4.4	4.9*	3.9	4.4	4.2	1.7	2.5	Rough
Happy	4.8	5.0	2.1	2.9	2.1	2.4	4.0	3.9	4.0	4.1	4.2	3.7	5.1	5.1	2.2	2.9	Angry
Ripe	1.4	1.7	2.5	2.9	4.6	3.9	3.4	3.4	2.9	2.8	3.5	2.6	3.3	2.4	3.5	3.0	Unripe
Rich	2.7	3.0	2.5	2.9	3.0	3.4	2.9	2.6	2.1	2.9	4.3	3.4	4.0*	2.7	2.4	2.6	Poor
Taut	2.7	2.2	3.8	3.3	3.2	3.8	3.3	2.4	3.3	2.7	3.8	3.5	3.3	2.5	3.7	3.1	Loose
Straight	3.0*	4.2	3.0	3.2	3.1	3.6	2.7*	3.8	3.7	3.8	4.1	4.3	3.9	4.0	2.9	2.8	Crooked
Noisy	1.5*	3.2	4.0	4.0	3.9	4.8	4.3	4.1	3.7	4.0	3.9	4.0	3.7	4.3	5.1*	4.0	Quiet
Male	3.3	2.5	4.7*	3.6	4.7*	3.6	2.5	2.7	3.6	2.8	2.7	2.8	2.2	2.3	4.6	3.9	Female
White	3.8	3.4	2.2	2.9	2.5	2.0	4.4*	3.3	4.4*	3.3	4.7*	3.5	5.9*	4.8	1.1	1.4	Black
Dry	3.2	4.1	3.4	3.5	3.8	4.0	4.0	4.4	3.5*	4.5	2.7	3.4	3.6	4.0	3.2	3.5	Wet

*Asterisk between Anglo and Navajo values indicates a difference $\geqq$ 1.00 scale units.

†Means were computed so that low values are toward left-hand scale term (e.g., good) and high toward right-hand term (e.g., bad).

CONNOTATIONS OF HUE (FOLLOWING THE SPECTRUM, FROM RED THROUGH PURPLE). Here we get evidence of differences between Anglos and Navajos. Anglos yield a number of activity scales which follow the spectrum (*fast-slow, sharp-dull, energetic-lazy,* and *young-old*), with RED being the most active and BLUE or PURPLE being the most passive. The Navajos have *noisy-quiet, taut-loose, hot-cold,* and *ripe-unripe* follow the spectrum, but with GREEN at the peak of *cold, quiet, loose,* and *unripe.* The Anglos show the same trend for *hot-cold* and *ripe-unripe;* Anglos also include some evaluative scales as following the spectrum, *happy-sad, pretty-ugly,* and *sweet-sour,* RED being on the favorable sides—but this may be an effect of the particular color samples used.

SOME SALIENT DIFFERENCES IN COLOR CONNOTATIONS. In the following summary, only Anglo/Navajo differences equal to or greater than 1.00 scale unit *and* with means falling on opposite sides of the midpoint (3.50) are counted. RED is *pretty, young, energetic, straight,* and *thick* for the Anglos, but not for the Navajo (who characterize it particularly as *taut, angry,* and *masculine*).[1] YELLOW is *small, fast,* and *smooth* and GREEN is *weak, fast,* and *smooth* for Anglos, but not for Navajo (who do, however, see these pastel shades as favorable evaluatively like the Anglos). Anglos and Navajos agree perfectly on the connotative directions of WHITE, with the single exception of *fast-slow*—Anglos seeing WHITE as quite fast and the Navajos as quite slow. The remaining colors, all dark hues, are judged less favorably by the Anglos: thus, for them, BLUE is the more *sad, sour, thick, cold, straight,* and *black;* PURPLE is more *sad, sour, thick, down,* and *black;* BROWN is more *sad, sour,* and *dull;* and BLACK is more *sour, dull, down,* and *poor* than for Navajos.

DISCUSSION

This paper began with a set of questions. The first was: *can the factors obtained by Suci (1957) for Anglo controls and for the Navajo* (and other Southwest Indian cultures) *with verbally defined concepts*

---

[1] In a personal communication, Professor Clyde Kluckhohn has pointed out that "color enters very prominently into Navajo ceremonialism, and therefore the reaction to such a color as red is culturally influenced in a very special way." Such ceremonial usages of color undoubtedly account for some of the differences found in this study. The fact that great similarities in color connotation are found despite such ceremonial usage may mean that the significances attached to colors in ceremonies themselves tend to follow the same rules of synesthetic translation.

and scales of a semantic differential be confirmed when his scales serve as concepts judged against 'scales' defined by purely visual alternatives? Suci obtained two clearly identifiable factors: an evaluative factor (*pretty, sweet, good*) and a potency factor (*heavy, rich, long,* and *strong*). Our own factor analyses of the concept matrices produced two clearly defined factors also—evaluation (GOOD, HAPPY, WHITE) and potency (STRONG, TIGHT, MAN). In both cases, the third and further factors did not yield satisfactory correspondence. To this extent, then, we have confirmed the factorial generality described by Suci, in a situation where the problem of translation equivalence of scale terms is minimized.

The second question was: *can cross-language and cross-culture generality of visual-verbal synesthesia be demonstrated?* There is ample evidence for visual-verbal synesthesia within our own culture. As early as 1921, Lundholm (1921) reported data on the "feeling tones" of lines: that SAD was represented by large, downward-directed curves; that MERRY was represented by small, upward-directed lines; that GENTLE was represented by large, horizontally-directed curves, and so on. Poffenberger and Barrows (1924) confirmed and extended the relationships reported by Lundholm. Kaworski et al. (1942) were able to demonstrate similar relationships between word meanings and the synesthetic drawings of photistic visualizers. More recently, Scheerer and Lyons (1957), Hochberg and Brooks (1956), and McMurray (1958) have reported Western intracultural consistencies in relating line drawings and/or verbally defined visual dimensions to connotative meanings or feeling-tones. As far as I am aware, the present study is the first attempt to demonstrate that the visual-verbal synesthetic relationships characteristic of our own language/culture community are shared by peoples who speak different languages and enjoy different cultures—the Navajo, the Japanese, and the Mexican-Spanish living in the American Southwest. The over-all similarities in synesthetic tendencies across these groups are impressive—when the synesthetic relationships that are significant (.01 level) intraculturally are tested for cross-cultural agreement, approximately 90% of the relationships prove to be in the same direction. We can conclude with confidence, then, that the determinants of these synesthetic relations are shared by humans everywhere—to the extent that our sample of "everywhere" is representative.

A third question in which we were interested was: *are terms which are translation-equivalent to functional opposites in our language also functionally opposed in other language/culture groups?* The answer to this question is important for several reasons: For one thing, the semantic differential as a measuring instrument is based on the assumption that 'true' opposites do 'slice up' the semantic space into meaningfully opposed regions; for another thing, the notion of logical opposition has always had a fundamental and primitive status in Western philosophical thought—is this merely a figment of our Western language structure, or is it really fundamental to human thinking wherever it may occur? Again, to the extent that our sample of human languages and cultures is representative, the answer is clear and compelling: peoples who use different languages and have grown up in different cultural settings also utilize meaningful opposition as a pillar of their logical constructions. This conclusion was obtained under conditions in which the verbal opposites were separated in time of judgment and were determined by association with purely visual alternatives. This over-all conclusion (see Table 4) is not countered by the occasional negative instances which were found: Landar's (1957) analysis of four Navajo folk tales implies that for the Navajo the logical opposition is between *moving-stationary*, the Anglo *fast-slow* as translated being degrees of moving; the failure of *energetic-lazy* to function as an opposition for the Japanese is also tagged as a translation problem. [Both Professor Seizo Ohe (at the Center for Advanced Study in the Behavioral Sciences, Stanford, 1958) and a Japanese friend agreed that the terms we used for "energetic" and "lazy" were not really opposites in their language.] For 11 of the 12 Anglo oppositions described in Table 4, functional opposition is demonstrated for the other language/culture groups as well.

The fourth question concerned the connotative meanings of colors: *do colors have similar connotations for Navajos as for Anglos, and is agreement greater for actual color chips than for color words?* A separate study of the connotations of colored papers, using verbally defined 6-step scales, revealed considerable agreement in connotation. For both Anglo and Navajo groups, the brightness dimension was shown to correspond to *evaluation* (WHITE favorable, BLACK unfavorable), the saturation dimension to *potency* (saturated colors being the more potent), and, with somewhat less agreement across cultures, the hue dimension to *activity* (RED being the most active and BLUE-PURPLE the most passive). These results agree generally with those of Ross (1938) on the effects of stage lighting on moods of the audience; of Odbert et al. (1942) on the relations of colors to verbally defined moods; and of Wexner (1954) on similar relations. The specific correlates between color dimensions and semantic factors found in our study agree with results obtained by Tannenbaum on the use of color in both abstract art and advertising (cf., Chapter 7 in Osgood et al., 1957). Our results extend these relations to at least one group differing in language and culture.[2] Because of lack of correspondence in the yardsticks used (verbally defined scales for

[2]A paper by Kimura (1950) indicates that Japanese subjects relate the hue dimension to a warm-cool scale (activity), red being the most warm; and saturation to a heavy-light scale (potency), black, blue, and red being the heaviest and green, yellow, and white the lightest. These observations are consistent with our findings for Anglos and Navajos.

color chips and visual alternatives for color words), direct comparisons of the connotations of actual colors with the connotations of color words were not possible. However, my own impression, based on the frequencies of disagreements on the meanings of color words [cf., Table 5 (B)] and on comparisons between word-meanings and chip-meanings where the scales were roughly similar, is that Anglos and Navajos agree more on the connotations of color chips than on the connotations of color words. For example, whereas Anglo "blue" refers to a relatively dark color close to Navy, Navajo "blue" refers to a region of the color space close to turquoise.

Dr. Susan Ervin, who collected the Navajo color data says: "The two terms that are most different in reference are the words for blue and for grey. Blue refers to any color within the range we would call green-blue-purple. The best Navajo blue is a bright aqua, about the shade of the turquoise popsicles they have in the Southwest (I think expressly for Indians!)."

Despite impressive over-all similarities across the language/culture groups studied in visual synesthetic tendencies, there are some clear-cut differences on particular relations [cf., Tables 3, 5 (B), 6 (B), and 11]. Such differences are open to a variety of interpretations—with no clear guideposts as to which applies in any single case. The Navajo data are somewhat less reliable throughout (which is understandable given the difficulties of communicating instructions under field conditions). This by itself could be the reason that Navajos display a smaller number of significant synesthetic tendencies (cf., Table 2), but this finding could also indicate a greater concreteness of cognitive processes in the Navajo. It may be that pre-literate peoples—peoples without a written literature—generalize less broadly through metaphor. Differences in the denotative reference of some of the verbally defined concepts (and hence, in a sense, inadequate translation) undoubtedly contribute to some of the differences described here also.

Nevertheless, there are probably some "real" cultural differences in visual synesthesia that cannot be explained away as artifactual on any of the above grounds. For one thing, it seems possible that the Navajo do not utilize an activity factor in connotative meaning to the same extent that Anglos do; in both the factor analyses of verbal concepts and the correlates of color dimensions (brightness, saturation, and hue), the Anglos clearly display a third, activity factor which is only suggested in the Navajo data. For another thing, we noted that both in terms of significant differences in correlations among the visual alternatives (Table 6) and in the over-all correlations of the visual-alternative matrices (Table 7), the Southwest-living Navajo and Mexican-Spanish agreed with each other as against the Anglos and Japanese. The shift of the Mexican-Spanish, from "allegiance" with the Anglos on concept meanings to "allegiance" with the Navajo on visual scale meanings, was particularly striking. Does this mean that growing up in the visual environment provided by the Southwest helps to organize the dimensions of the visual frame of reference in a somewhat different way than elsewhere?

This research obviously has bearing on the Sapir-Whorf "Weltanschauung" hypothesis—but in support of the converse. Most of the discussion and research relating to this hypothesis has been designed to demonstrate that differences in language do produce differences in "world view," and certainly there is both observational (Carroll, 1956) and experimental (Brown and Lenneberg, 1954; Lenneberg and Roberts, 1956) evidence for this view. The present study and others along the same line (Kumata, 1957; Kumata and Schramm, 1956; Suci, 1957; Triandis and Osgood, 1958) strongly support the position that, for certain aspects of cognitive behavior at least, "world view" may remain relatively stable despite differences in both language and culture. The apparent conflict between these two sets of findings disappears if one makes a distinction between two general classes of cognition—which, for lack of better terms, I shall call *denotative* and *connotative*. The phenomena which seem to display generality across human groups regardless of language or culture are essentially connotative—the affective "feeling tones" of meaning which contribute to synesthesia, metaphor and the like. The phenomena which display dependence upon the structure and lexical categorizing of language seem to be essentially denotative—the multitudinous and arbitrary sets of correlations between perpetual events and linguistic events (i.e., the "rules of usage" of any language code). The distinction I am making has the status of an hypothesis, not a conclusion, but the meager evidence available seems to be consistent with it.

Finally, we may inquire into the reasons behind similarities in connotative systems despite language/culture differences. First, by virtue of being members of the human species, people are equipped biologically to react to situations in certain similar ways—with autonomic, emotional reactions to rewarding and punishing situations (evaluation), with strong or weak muscular tension to things offering great or little resistances (potency), and so on—and hence they can form connotative significances for perceived objects and their linguistic signs varying along the same basic dimensions. Such connotative reactions enter into a wide variety of meaningful situations, are therefore broadly generalized, and provide a basis for synesthetic and metaphorical transpositions. Beyond this shared connotative framework, there are many specific relations between human organisms and their generally similar environments whose stability can be the basis for synesthetic and metaphorical translations. These may be either innate to the species or developed by learning under similar conditions. An example of the former (innate) basis may be the common association of the red end of the spectrum with warmth and activity and the blue end with coldness and passivity. An example of the latter (acquired) basis may be the common association of visually large with auditorily loud—it is simply a characteristic of the physical world that as any noise-producing object approaches or is approached, increases in visual angle are correlated with increases in loudness. These "homotropisms" and experiential contingencies may be expressed in language but are independent of the structure of any particular language.

REFERENCES

Brown, R. W. and E. H. Lenneberg. A study in language and cognition, *J. Abnorm. Soc. Psychol.*, 1954, **49**, 454–462.

Carroll, J. B. (ed.). *Language, thought and reality: Selected writings of Benjamin Lee Whorf.* New York: John Wiley & Sons, Inc., 1956.

Casagrande, J. B. The southwest project in comparative psycholinguistics: A progress report. Social Science Research Council, 1956, Item 10, 41–45.

Hochberg, J. and V. Brooks. An item analysis of physiognomic connotation. Unpublished study, privately distributed, 1956.

Karwoski, T. F., H. S. Odbert, and C. E. Osgood. Studies in synesthetic thinking: II. The role of form in visual responses to music, *J. Gen. Psychol.*, 1942, **26**, 190–222.

Kimura, T. Apparent warmth and heaviness of colours, *Japanese J. Psychol.*, 1950, **20**, 33–36.

Kumata, H. A factor analytic investigation of the generality of semantic structure across two selected cultures. Unpublished doctoral dissertation, University of Illinois, 1957.

Kumata, H. and W. Schramm. A pilot study of cross-cultural methodology. *Publ. Opin. Quart.*, 1956, **20**, 229–237.

Landar, H. J. Four Navajo summer tales. Report of the Southwest project in comparative psycholinguistics, 1957.

Lenneberg, E. H. and J. M. Roberts. The language of experience, *Suppl. Int. J. Amer. Ling.*, 1956, **22**, 33.

Lundholm, H. The affective tone of lines: Experimental researches, *Psychol. Rev.*, 1921, **28**, 43–60.

McMurray, G. A. A study of "fittingness" of signs to words by means of the semantic differential, *J. Exp. Psychol.*, 1958, **56**, 310–312.

Odbert, H. S., T. F. Karwoski, and A. B. Eckerson. Studies in synesthetic thinking: I. Musical and verbal association of color and mood, *J. Gen. Psychol.*, 1942, **26**, 153–173.

Osgood, C. E., G. J. Suci, and P. H. Tannenbaum. *The measurement of meaning.* Urbana: The University of Illinois Press, 1957.

Poffenberger, A. T. and B. E. Barrows. The feeling value of lines, *J. Appl. Psychol.*, 1924, **8**, 187–205.

Ross, R. T. Studies in the psychology of the theatre, *Psychol. Rec.*, 1938, **2**, 127–190.

Scheerer, M. and J. Lyons. Line drawings and matching responses to words, *J. Pers.*, 1957, **25,** 251–273.

Suci, G. J. An investigation of the similarity between the semantic spaces of five different cultures. Report for the Southwest Project in Comparative Psycholinguistics, 1957.

Triandis, H. C. and C. E. Osgood. A comparative factorial analysis of semantic structures in monolingual Greek and American college students, *J. Abnorm. Soc. Psychol.*, 1958, **57,** 187–196.

Wexner, L. B. The degree to which colors (hues) are associated with mood-tones, *J. Appl. Psychol.*, 1954, **38,** 432–435.

5-5

Language and TAT Content in French-English Bilinguals

SUSAN M. ERVIN

Since French-English bilinguals are able to communicate with social groups using either language, they tend to shift from one language to another depending on the reference group they are dealing with at a particular time. Does the shift of languages cause a shift in the individual's expressed emotional attitudes or social role? Do the TAT stories told by a bilingual reflect differences in the French and English cultures? Dr. Ervin presents some evidence to show the influence of French-English bilingualism and reference group on TAT stories.

Spoken language is, almost without exception, learned in a social setting. This setting includes material and behavioral referents for speech, rewards for speaking in a certain way about specific topics, and feelings towards those who hear and towards those who provide models of speech. Speakers in different language communities will have different things to say, and we may expect that learning a language carries with it learning of content.

Bilinguals provide a natural control for the investigation of content differences. Lambert et al. (1958) have shown that for "house," "drink,"

Reprinted from *J. Abnorm. Soc. Psychol.*, 1964, **68**, 500–507, by permission of the author and the American Psychological Association.

"poor," and "me," semantic-differential meanings differed for French-Canadian bilinguals. The pooled differences were significant only for those who learned the two languages in different physical settings. Since different social surroundings may occur in the same region, it is possible that the meanings of emotion or social-role terms might differ even for childhood bilinguals who learn two languages in the same physical surroundings.

With the purpose of studying content differences in speech, the present study compared two sets of Thematic Apperception Test (TAT) stories told by bilinguals about the same pictures at a French session and at an English session. The choice of languages was dictated by necessity (the author's ability to speak English and French) but it should be recognized that the languages and language community chosen were in some respects poor for testing the hypothesis of systematic content difference. The relationship of French and English makes generalization between them more likely; middle-class French and American cultures have many similarities; many of the bilinguals in the Washington, D.C., French community speak both languages with the same interlocutors. For all of these reasons content differences would be minimal.

Since economy precluded testing appropriate monolingual control groups, predictions regarding TAT differences were based on data about culture differences made available by Maccoby (1952) and by Métraux and Mead (1954), corroborated by other informants. Since that time, Wylie (1958) has confirmed some of the generalizations. A set of assumptions regarding the relation between TAT content and culture permitted specific predictions.

These assumptions were derived principally from Sanford's (Sanford et al., 1943) study of the relation between school children's TAT stories and ratings of their behavior. In interpreting his findings, he proposed that: behavior that does not conflict with social sanctions appears in fantasy only if there is insufficient ability or opportunity for overt expression (e.g., achievement and dominance); behavior conflicting with social sanctions appears more often in fantasy expression; ambivalent cultural prescriptions lead to more primitivism in fantasy than in nonfantasy expression.

Because of the possibility, suggested by experimental work with the TAT, that the testing conditions might influence the extent to which content conflicted with social santions, it was decided to conduct testing individually, orally, and face-to-face. In these conditions, while socially prohibited needs might be expressed, it seemed that the form of expression might be governed by cultural differences in preferred modes. Otherwise there was the risk that a greater prohibition of a certain form of behavior in one of the two cultures would have ambiguous implications for predicting TAT thematic differences.

Specific predictions of differences were these:

1. For women, greater achievement need in English. This difference was based on the ambivalence of American education for women toward the role of housewife, in contrast with the French view, and on the greater sex-role difference in France.

2. More emphasis on recognition by others in English. This prediction was based on Kluckhohn's (1949) remark that emphasis is less on fulfillment and more on external success in America than in Europe. Riesman (1950) has made a statement which implies the contrary: he states that other-directed persons (such as Americans) want to "cut everyone down to size who stands up or stands out in any direction." The hypothesis of culture difference between France and America is thus a weak one.

3. More domination by elders in French stories. Parents were said to be more influential in selection of wives and jobs in France.

4. More withdrawal and autonomy in French stories. A characteristic mode of aggression reported within French families was silent withdrawal to do as one wished, perhaps contrary to the wishes of another. Wylie (1958) reported that both children and adults after a disagreement tended to withdraw, and quoted a French child: "What we really do when we're angry is to go away from each other and not speak anymore [p. 199]."

5. More verbal aggression toward parents in English stories. Verbal attacks on elders are more strictly prohibited in France than in the United States, though Wylie reported considerable variation between families in the extent to which threats of punishment for verbal disrespect were carried out.

6. More verbal aggression toward peers in French stories. There is considerable admiration for verbal prowess in France. Wylie (1958) reports that this was true even in a rural village. French education emphasizes skill in oral argument, and children "are allowed to threaten and insult each other as much as they like [p. 50]."

7. More physical aggression in English stories. In France, children are immediately separated by adults if they begin to fight, and both are punished, according to Wylie, regardless of the culprit (p. 81). Presumably the culture difference would be greater for men than for women, since physical aggression is prohibited for American as well as French girls. However, there were too few men in the sample to permit a breakdown by sex.

8. More guilt in French stories and more frequent attempts to escape blame in English stories. This prediction was based in part on the age difference for acquisition of the two languages, on the assumption that a language learned in childhood would be more strongly associated

with internalized values than one learned during adult life. Further, Métraux and Mead's (1954) informants reported greater emphasis in France on internal control of behavior by adults, rejection of social pressure as a legitimate basis for action, and more strictness and consistency in child rearing.

In terms of the evidence of culture difference, the strongest evidence, most widely confirmed, concerns the forms of aggression preferred. The weakest evidence concerns the difference in the need for recognition.

METHOD

Subjects

Sixty-four adult French persons, raised in metropolitan France in middle-class families, were found in Washington, D.C. All had lived in the United States for more than 4 years and had learned English primarily from Americans. All of them spoke both languages fluently, the average number of years in the United States being 12. Forty were or had been married to Americans. The mean age was 38 years. Two-thirds were women.

Background Interview

An extensive interview determined how English was learned, how often and to whom both languages were spoken, and how much contact there had been with Americans. Scores from this interview were used to evaluate contact, amount of mixture, or switching of languages with the same interlocutors, degree of current French usage, education, and attitude toward linguistic interference. Details of this interview and other methodological information can be found in Ervin (1955).

Language Dominance Test

As a test of relative skill in French and English, a tape-recorded word-association test was constructed. The language of the stimulus word was varied at random in a list of words in various semantic domains, with frequency of the words in the respective languages matched. The subjects were instructed to offer orally an association to each word in the same language as the stimulus word. The score consisted of the median French reaction time in log seconds minus the median English time, when corrections had been made for translation responses and other language switches. The average subject, according to this test, was slightly French dominant. Superior language dominance tests have since been constructed. Literate subjects may use a machine devised by Lambert (1955) which measures reactions to printed words. A pictorial test, measuring time in naming simple objects, was used by Ervin (1961a).

Materials and Procedure

Nine standard TAT pictures which elicit themes related to the hypotheses were selected: 1, 2, 3BM, 8BM, 6BM, 4, 13MF, 7BM, and 18GF. They were presented in the above order. Subjects were given instructions to tell what was happening, what had happened in the past, what would happen in the future, and what the characters were thinking and feeling. In addition, at the second session, they were instructed to tell a different story if they recalled the first. Stories were to be 3 minutes long; a 3-minute glass was turned before the subject as he began each story.

The same examiner appeared at both sessions, speaking only French at the French session from the moment the subject appeared. The instructions were tape recorded in the appropriate language, and all responses were tape recorded. Analysis of content and of linguistic features was based on a verbatim typescript.

Design

Two groups were matched on the basis of sex, age, education, and language dominance. In addition, it was found that they were matched, on the average, in years in the United States, age at which English was learned, amount of contact with Americans, and amount of language switching. One group was instructed to tell French stories at the first session, and the other group told stories in English. There was a 6-week interval between the sessions for each subject.

Content Analysis

A quantitative system of analysis was adapted from those devised by McClelland et al. (1953) and by Aron (1949). Each time a theme appeared in a story with a new actor (hero) and target of action, it was given a quantitative score. Thus a theme might be scored several times if in a given story the actor or object changed. If a picture "pulled" a particular theme—e.g., physical aggression in 18GF—each occurrence of the theme received a lower base score than if it was a rare theme for that picture. If there was more than a simple occurrence of the theme—if there was adjectival or adverbial elaboration, addition of details, or repetition of the theme—the value might be increased by one or two points.

The reliability scores reported are product-moment correlations based on scores by picture for each theme. In the abbreviated category definitions below, reliabilities are presented in parentheses. The first is the reliability (product-moment correlation) of scores by two different coders, and the second the intracoder reliability with a 2-month interval. Since all coding in both languages was done by the author, the intracoder reliability is important.

ACHIEVEMENT (.77, .88). The hero is industrious. He fantasies hard work, studiousness, invention, attainment, accomplishment, reaching a career goal. He wants to accomplish great things. He prepares for or has achieved a profession, or a skilled occupation.

RECOGNITION (.90, .81). The hero fantasies greatness, public acclaim, recognition by others, applause, prestige, renown. He seeks approval, boasts, performs in public, competes, strives to rise in status as a primary goal. He is a master; he is great.

DOMINANCE (.84, .84). The hero tries to influence another by pleading or persuasion. He leads, directs, guides, advises, cajoles, but does not bring undue pressure, threaten withdrawal, or argue.

WITHDRAWAL AND AUTONOMY (.69, .74). The hero does something bad, violates moral standards, or acts in a way contrary to the wishes of love objects. He makes them suffer or knowingly disappoints them. He expresses anger or dislike by turning away from, snubbing, or rejecting a love object.

VERBAL AGGRESSION (.88, 87). The hero verbally expresses scorn, contempt, disdain. He quarrels, is involved in a misunderstanding or discussion (a more disputatious term in French than in English, but scored as verbal aggression in both languages).

PHYSICAL AGGRESSION (.81, .93). The hero fights, attacks physically, or injures, or kills another human being.

GUILT (.44, .73). The hero evaluates on the basis of moral principle. He avoids or regrets out of duty, moral standards, religious scruples. He resists temptation, or experiences anguish or regret. (The results will not be reported for this category because of the low reliability.)

ESCAPING BLAME (.70, .99). The hero seeks to avoid external censure or punishment by refraining from reprehensible acts, or by resorting to denial, deceit, or flight. He verbally defends himself against censure, proclaims his innocence, justifies his action.

Translation Control

Since there was a possibility of systematic bias in the scoring in the two languages, one of each subject's stories in each language was translated. These translations were given the appearance and style of originals, and were indistinguishable except by checking a code number. In the first phase of coding, the originals were removed, and the translations were mixed with the untranslated versions of each story for coding. In the second phase, 2 months later, the originals of the translated stories were mixed with other copies of previously coded stories for the intracoder reliability check.

Three kinds of checks were used to test coder bias. First, the intracoder reliabilities were compared for stories scored in the same language twice, and for stories scored in the original and in translation. It was found that achievement was scored more reliably when the story was in the same language both times. Reliability correlations differed at the .05 level. Escaping blame was scored more reliably in the same language at the .01 level. Thus it appeared that changing language might have led to different scoring standards. Such a difference might not be significant if it was unrelated to the hypotheses.

The total amount of each variable found in the originals and in the translations of the same stories were then compared to see if the differences in reliability were systematic. There were no significant differences.

Finally, the frequencies of the variables in all the stories coded in the first phase were compared to see if the stories coded in translation differed from those coded in the original language. There were no significant differences for any of the variables.

RESULTS

Content frequencies for each subject were weighted by the reciprocal of the total length in each language, since the stories in French were usually longer. The distributions of the variables were very skewed, medians of zero occurring for all but three variables. These distributions reflected the fact that some themes were readily elicited by the pictures, others not so readily. One might characterize the pictures as differing in their power to bring out thematic material above a threshold of overt speech. Presumably other pictures might have elicited responses from all subjects, and allowed a measure of session differences for all subjects for each theme. In order to make an analysis of variance possible in spite of the skewed distributions, the assumption was made that subjects who gave no responses relevant to a given theme at either session were randomly distributed as to session differences. Since the relative strength of their responses was in effect not measured, there was no way of knowing whether appropriate pictures would have elicited more thematic material in French or in English. In calculation of the analysis of variance, for each theme, subjects were removed who never used the theme at either session. For Physical Aggression and Withdrawal-Autonomy this adjustment was not necessary, and all subjects were included. The remaining frequencies were transformed to the logarithm of $X + 1$.

The analysis of variance was a Lindquist (1956) Type I design, with the group to which the subject was assigned a between-subject effect, and the session and language as within-subject effects. Because of the four-celled Latin-square design, there was confounding of certain types of interaction. The effects of language in this design appear as an interaction of session with group, since Session I is in French for one group and in English for the other. There is likely to be an interaction of language with session for certain variables, however, and this interaction cannot be isolated.

With these limitations, three variables showed significant language effects in the predicted direction: Verbal Aggression to Peers, Withdrawal-Autonomy, and Achievement. In addition, there was a significant group difference in Recognition, with no effect of language at all (see Table 1).

The following stories will illustrate the difference between the French and English versions by the same subject, a 27-year-old Frenchwoman, married to an American, who spoke English with her husband and child. Most of her friends were Americans. She was a full-time clerk, using English for the most part in her work. The stories were told for Picture 4 in the Murray series.

> [*French, first session*] She seems to beg him, to plead with him. I don't know if he wants to leave her for another woman or what, or if it's her who has . . . but she seems to press against him. I think he wants to leave her because he's found another woman he loves more, and that he really wants to go, or maybe it's because she . . . she's deceived him with another man. I don't know whose fault it is but they certainly seem angry. Unless it's in his work, and he wants to go see someone and he wants to get in a fight with someone, and she holds him back and doesn't like him to get angry. I don't know, it could be many things. . . .

TABLE 1

Weighted Content Differences in TAT Stories

Content Variable	N^*	32 French-First M†		32 English-First M		df	F for Language‡
		F_1	E_2	F_2	E_1		
Achievement (women)	21	14.3	26.6	21.1	25.1	1/40	6.148**
Recognition	24	4.7	4.8	7.3	8.3	1/46	—††
Dominance to younger	27	5.3	4.4	4.8	3.2	1/52	2.051
Withdrawal-autonomy	32	30.5	24.8	25.5	21.0	1/62	9.234‡‡
Verbal							
Aggression to elders	17	3.6	4.4	1.5	2.2	1/32	1.682
Aggression to peers	20	5.1	4.9	4.7	3.2	1/38	5.333**
Physical aggression	32	10.8	15.3	12.3	11.0	1/62	1.709
Escaping blame	16	2.3	3.2	2.3	3.8	1/30	3.926

*N in each group after cases with zero in both sessions had been removed.

†Means for the weighted raw scores of the total sample of 32 in each group.

‡Lindquist's Type I analysis, with Language as a within-subject effect, and a within-subject error term derived from the within-subject sum of squares minus Session and Language.

**$p < .05$.

††The group effect here had an F of 5.503, $p < .025$.

‡‡$p < .01$.

[*English, second session*] Oh, that one. In the past, well I think it was a married couple, average, and he got out of the Army and got himself a job or something like that or has decided he would go to college. He's decided to get a good education and maybe after he would have a better job and be able to support his wife much better, and everything would come out for the best. He keeps on working and going to college at night some of the time. Now let me see. He finally decided that was too much. He found he was too tired, he was discouraged and something went wrong with his work. The boss told him that, well, his production had decreased or something like that, that he didn't get enough sleep or something like that, that he couldn't carry on studies and working at the same time. He'd have to give something up, and he's very discouraged and his wife tries to cheer him up. Now, let me see. And eventually he'll probably keep on working his way through and finally get his diploma and get a better job and they will be much happier and . . . well, his wife will have helped him along too and as he was discouraged and all and was willing to give up everything, she boosted him up. That's all.

In French the picture elicited a variety of themes of aggression and striving for autonomy. In English the heroine supports the husband in his achievement strivings.

The subject below was a 33-year-old bachelor, with higher education in both countries. Most of his friends were Americans, but he used French in his work. The picture was 13MF.

[*English, first session*] Now this is a horrible story. This is one of those, one of those things that happen in married life when the husband suddenly finds out his own intelligence, his own way of living, his own . . . life altogether has gone to pieces. There is no weapon around in the room. But there is the hand which have murdered. There is the guilt of having in a moment of horrible passion, of aberration of mind when she was telling him that she loved the other, that he was more intelligent, that he was more beautiful, that he let himself go and put his fingers around her neck. And her laughter became more and more raucous. He had pressed down his thumbs and then he has gotten up, has dressed. The horror of the moment becomes entirely obvious to him. He knows that the next thing he will have to do is to go to the police and report it—maybe to flee, maybe to take his car and drive away. What kind of a life that will be. Constantly this thing in front of him. A dead body in the bed half-naked. Over the sheets. Police. Discovery. Warrants. Sirens. Shame. Flight. And perhaps prison and perhaps death. All this goes through his mind as he wonders where to go.

[*French, second session*] That's not a scene of a household but of a false household. There are sometimes false households with love, and there are those with hatred. This is a false household with hatred. They detest each other, and cannot separate. They are held together by physical attraction as much as by their quarrels, quarrels which change their life from an everyday life, a life which becomes infernal and at the same time different. If they had no quarrels they would be nearly dead with boredom, and when they are separated they desire only to see each other. He is still young, she already older, and it is she basically who holds him. He, too young, doesn't want to marry. She, older, wants only one thing, a home. Then, to oblige this man to live with her, to found this home she wants, she tries to hold him, to live with him at any price even if it is torture for both. Their joy, their only joy is physical contact, and even this joy has dangers of torture, of horror because for them this physical life is a bond, a terrible bond, of which he particularly is aware. This is how the woman holds him. He detests her and yet cannot detach himself. What we see here is the night when he has slept with her another time, dressed, and while she sleeps, he wants to leave, to leave forever, to forget this inhuman life, tear the bonds which . . . one becomes enslaved to this woman. He hides his eyes still, an instant of reflection, then takes his two books and goes out the door forever.

The last two stories contrast aggression by physical assault with aggression by quarreling and escape. Certain characteristics of the English story reflect mass media models.

DISCUSSION

There are several alternative explanations for the differences in content, none of which can as yet be excluded. One explanation is that the subjects interpreted the instructions to speak a particular language as an instruction to tell a story appropriate to that language. Such an alternative could be tested by giving instructions to give appropriate stories, while the language is held constant. No such control was used.

A second possibility is that language affects classification of stimuli (Ervin, 1961b) and presumably recall of experience through the classification (Brown and Lenneberg, 1954), and that bilinguals have systematically different recall of past experience in two languages. If we extrapolate findings from recall of simple pictured objects (Ervin, 1961a), we would expect that use of the weaker language would have a strong biasing tendency toward recall of experiences originally codified in that language and appropriate to its culture.

Third, the thematic differences may reflect the respective mass media. Those who use projective tests to assess individual differences usually dismiss this explanation and point out that selective reading, viewing, and recall are pertinent to differences. But such an argument cannot be used when cross-cultural comparisons are at issue, since exposure is not then entirely self-selected but is culturally imposed, and there is little doubt that there are systematic differences in thematic frequencies in the mass media in different countries.

A fourth alternative is that the differences are not due merely to contrasts in the mass media, but to more pervasive differences in the verbal preoccupations and values expressed verbally in the two cultures. Thus it may be said that story themes may reflect the gossip, verbalized personal experiences, and verbal evaluations of the behavior of oneself and others which have been experienced in the two cultural settings.

It should be noted that much value learning comes from verbal sources; condemnation of murder is learned not by punishment for murder, but by verbal learning of what is classified as murder (not killing in war, for instance), and by learning emotional attitudes toward verbal descriptions of murder and what happens to murderers; only in part is it learned by generalization of punishment for committed aggressive acts. Nobody concerned with education, propaganda, advertising, or the study of opinion change through role playing would dismiss the possibility that verbal sequences may affect other behavior as well, and thus create consistency with nonverbal behavior. Some of the effect of verbal sequences on other behavior may come through what has come to be known as verbal mediation. Self-control through verbal mediation has been studied in relatively few situations (e.g., Luria, 1961). Since the origins of such mediation may lie in verbal training conditions in early childhood, which vary widely, we can expect significant group and individual differences in the extent to which verbal training affects nonverbal behavior.

Finally, quite aside from such mediational effects, it is possible that a shift in language is associated with a shift in social roles and emotional attitudes. Since each language is learned and usually employed with different persons and in a different context, the use of each language may come to be associated with shift in a large array of behavior. Presumably such changes would have to be assessed nonverbally, at least in part through physiological measures, to separate changes in emotional state from the verbal statements by which attitudes are usually judged.

The above explanations can be summarized as attributing content changes with language to different interpretation of instructions, differences in perception and in recall of experience, to the effects of mass media; to differences in verbally expressed values; and to role or attitude shifts associated with contacts with the respective language communities.

Do these findings mean that our subjects have two personalities? The answer seems to be yes, at least to the extent that personality involves verbal behavior and perhaps further. This is a result no more surprising than any other shift in behavior with social context. It happens that bilinguals have available an additional dimension of potential variation in behavior in comparison with the alternative roles available to monolinguals.

But language is a very important dimension. It is not yet clear whether the differences found in bilinguals are merely a special case of biculturalism, or whether the fact that language is a medium not only for social behavior but for internal storage of information and self-control implies that bilinguals have a means of insulating sets of alternative behavior more pervasive than mere contrasts in behavior for different social situations or audiences.

Our basis for choosing between these explanations is at present slight. The fact that certain variables yielded stronger content differences than others may provide a clue. For this purpose, we may exclude Recognition, for which the evidence for an actual culture contrast on which to base a prediction was from the start precarious. The largest differences appeared in Autonomy, Verbal Aggression against Peers, and Achievement in Women. The smallest appeared in Physical Aggression, Domination by Elders, and Verbal Aggression against Parents. One feature that the first three share is that they are likely to be the preoccupations of adults, in contrast with the second three. Quite simply, adults who move to the United States from France may observe cultural contrasts in those domains of interpersonal relations that they observe directly in consequence of the roles into which they are cast as adults. If some of this learning is second hand, from the mass media, then it selectively reflects adult concerns. Physical aggression is certainly a common feature of the mass media in this country, yet the contrast in the amount mentioned in the French and English stories was not significant.

Not all of the subjects displayed content differences of the sort found in the averages. Too little data on individual acculturative experiences were available to account for the individual differences. Presumably some people are attracted to a second culture because they are already deviant in their own; others never adapt to a new culture but merely translate the familiar into a new language. Ervin and Osgood (1954) had suggested earlier that "coordinate" bilinguals who learned both languages in distinct settings should display these differences more than those who learn in one setting. All of the bilinguals in this study were coordinate bilinguals by this criterion but there was a wide range in their actual learning. Of all the variables measured—amount of switching with interlocutors, amount of linguistic interference in the stories from the other language, contact with Americans, attitude towards assimilation, having children reared here—none correlated markedly with the degree of contrast found. Thus the clarification of both the nature of the contrast we observed grossly and the individual process by which the differences develop must await later research.

SUMMARY

Adult French bilinguals told TAT stories on 2 different occasions for the same pictures, in French at one session, in English at the other. Predictions derived from studies of child-rearing practices and values in the 2 countries were made regarding expected content differences in the 2 languages. Of 9 predicted content differences, 3 were statistically significant. Achievement themes were more common in English in the women Ss. Verbal aggression against age peers, and autonomy or withdrawal from others were more common themes in the French stories. In these respects, content shifted with language, for the same individual at 2 different sessions.

REFERENCES

Aron, Betty. *A manual for analysis of the Thematic Apperception Test.* Berkeley, Calif.: Willis E. Berg, 1949.

Brown, R. W. and E. H. Lenneberg. A study in language and cognition, *J. Abnorm. Soc. Psychol.*, 1954, **49**, 454–462.

Ervin, Susan M. *The verbal behavior of bilinguals: The effect of language of report upon the Thematic Apperception Test stories of adult French bilinguals.* (Doctoral dissertation, University of Michigan.) Ann Arbor, Mich.: University Microfilms, 1955, MicA 55–2228.

Ervin, Susan M. Learning and recall in bilinguals, *Amer. J. Psychol.*, 1961(a), **74**, 446–451.

Ervin, Susan M. Semantic shift in bilingualism, *Amer. J. Psychol.*, 1961(b), **74**, 233–241.

Ervin, Susan M. and C. E. Osgood. Second language learning and bilingualism, *J. Abnorm. Soc. Psychol.*, 1954, **49**, (Part 2), 139–146.

Kluckhohn, C. *Mirror for man.* New York: McGraw-Hill, Inc., 1949.

Lambert, W. E. Measurement of the linguistic dominance of bilinguals, *J. Abnorm. Soc. Psychol.*, 1955, **50**, 197–200.

Lambert, W. E., J. Havelka, and C. Crosby. The influence of language-acquisition contexts on bilingualism, *J. Abnorm. Soc. Psychol.*, 1958, **56**, 239–244.

Lindquist, E. F. *Design and analysis of experiments in psychology and education.* Boston: Houghton Mifflin Company, 1956.

Luria, A. R. *The role of speech in the regulation of normal and abnormal behavior.* New York: Liveright Publishing Corporation, 1961.

McClelland, D. C., J. W. Atkinson, R. A. Clark, and E. L. Lowell. *The achievement motive.* New York: Appleton-Century-Crofts, 1953.

Maccoby, Eleanor. Some notes on French child-rearing among the Parisian middle class. Cambridge: Harvard Laboratory of Human Development, 1952. (Ditto).

Métraux, Rhoda and Margaret Mead. *Themes in French culture.* Stanford: Stanford University Press, 1954.

Riesman, D. *The lonely crowd.* New Haven: Yale University Press, 1950.

Sanford, R. N., M. M. Adkins, R. B. Miller, E. A. Cobb et al. Physique, personality, and scholarship: A cooperative study of school children, *Monogr. Soc. Res. Child Devel.*, 1943, **8**.

Wylie, L. *Village in the Vaucluse.* Cambridge: Harvard University Press, 1958.

5-6

Science and Linguistics

BENJAMIN LEE WHORF

Is our language related to our perception and behavior? Does the structure of our language affect the way we organize our world? In this paper, Whorf presents some linguistic instances to support his theory of linguistic relativity, and postulates a relationship between language and cognition. The concept of linguistic relativity discussed in this paper has been one of the most stimulating and significant contributions to the study of language and culture.

Brown and Leneberg (1958) tested the Whorfian hypothesis with English and Zuni groups. They found that color names consisting of single words (red) are more easily recognized and correctly designated than hyphenated words (blue-green). The codability level of color names appears to facilitate or hinder the perceptual recognition of English-speaking subjects. Data from the Zuni Indian group show the same trends. In the Zuni color vocabulary, orange and yellow have the same name. Zuni subjects tended to confuse these two colors, whereas English-speaking subjects did not make the same error.

Carrol and Casagrande (1958) have shown that differences between the grammatical structures of the Navajo and English languages have caused some differences in the behavior of these groups. They found that the verbal form of the Navajo language depends on the shape and other characteristics of the object and this tended to force the child to learn to distinguish the formal attributes of

Reprinted from *Technol. Rev.*, 1940, **42**, 229–231, 247, 248, by permission of the Massachusetts Institute of Technology Press.

objects at a younger age than persons speaking English. Similarly, verbs designating various kinds of physical action in the Hopi language are differently structured than in English. This is shown to affect the Hopi classification of photographs depicting action. Brown (1957) has also investigated the Whorfian suggestion that the grammatical structure of language affects cognitive behavior. He found that English-speaking children take the part-of-speech membership of a word as a clue to the meaning of that word. The grammatical characteristics of a nonsense word such as the verb "to sib" make the child associate it with a picture showing an action (someone kneading) rather than an object. If a nonsense word is a noun, "a sib," the child tends to associate it with the picture of an object (a container).

Studies investigating the Whorfian hypothesis suggest that language as well as other cultural factors, such as interest (the emphasis of the Eskimo culture on snow), tend to direct thought and perception of the speaker into certain habitual channels. However, the evidence reported by Osgood in Selection 5–4 does not support this hypothesis. Fishman (1960) has systematized some of the important work in this area and his conclusion is as follows: "Although evidence favoring the Whorfian hypothesis exists at each level, it seems likely that linguistic relativity, though affecting some of our cognitive behavior, is nevertheless only a moderately powerful factor and a counteractable one at that. Certainly much experimental evidence has accumulated that points to a large domain of contra-Whorfian universality in connection with the relationships between *certain* structures of particular languages and *certain* cognitive behaviors of their speakers. The time might, therefore, be ripe for putting aside attempts at grossly proving or disproving the Whorfian hypothesis and, instead, focusing on attempts to delimit more sharply the types of language structures and the types of non-linguistic behaviors that do or do not show the Whorfian effect as well as the degree and modifiability of this involvement when it does obtain." (P. 337.)

REFERENCES

Brown, R. W. Linguistic determinism and the part of speech, *J. Abnorm. Soc. Psychol.*, 1957, **55**, 1–5.
Brown, R. W. and E. H. Lenneberg. Studies in linguistic relativity. In E. E. Maccoby, T. M. Newcomb, and E. L. Hartley (eds.), *Readings in social psychology*, Third ed. New York: Holt, Rinehart, and Winston, Inc., 1958.

Carrol, J. B. and J. B. Casagrande. The function of language classifications in behavior. In E. E. Maccoby, T. M. Newcomb, and E. L. Hartley (eds.), *Readings in social psychology*. Third ed. New York: Holt, Rinehart, and Winston, Inc., 1958.

Fishman, J. A. A systematization of the Whorfian hypothesis, *Behav. Sci.*, 1960, **5**, 323–339.

Every normal person in the world, past infancy in years, can and does talk. By virtue of that fact, every person—civilized or uncivilized—carries through life certain naïve but deeply rooted ideas about talking and its relation to thinking. Because of their firm connection with speech habits that have become unconscious and automatic, these notions tend to be rather intolerant of opposition. They are by no means entirely personal and haphazard; their basis is definitely systematic, so that we are justified in calling them a system of natural logic—a term that seems to me preferable to the term common sense, often used for the same thing.

According to natural logic, the fact that every person has talked fluently since infancy makes every man his own authority on the process

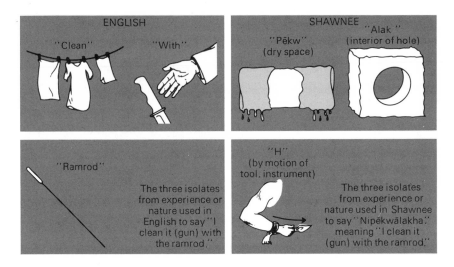

Figure 1. Languages dissect nature differently. The different isolates of meaning (thoughts) used by English and Shawnee in reporting the same experience, that of cleaning a gun by running the ramrod through it. The pronouns "I" and "it" are not shown by symbols, as they have the same meaning in each case. In Shawnee "ni-" equals "I"; "-a" equals "it."

by which he formulates and communicates. He has merely to consult a common substratum of logic or reason which he and everyone else are supposed to possess. Natural logic says that talking is merely an incidental process concerned strictly with communication, not with formulation of ideas. Talking, or the use of language, is supposed only to "express" what is essentially already formulated nonlinguistically. Formulation is an independent process, called thought or thinking, and is supposed to be largely indifferent to the nature of particular languages. Languages have grammars, which are assumed to be merely norms of conventional and social correctness, but the use of language is supposed to be guided not so much by them as by correct, rational, or intelligent *thinking*.

Thought, in this view, does not depend on grammar but on laws of logic or reason which are supposed to be the same for all observers of the universe—to represent a rationale in the universe that can be "found" independently by all intelligent observers, whether they speak Chinese or Choctaw. In our own culture, the formulations of mathematics and of formal logic have acquired the reputation of dealing with this order of things, i.e., with the realm and laws of pure thought. Natural logic holds that different languages are essentially parallel methods for expressing this one-and-the-same rationale of thought and, hence, differ really in but minor ways which may seem important only because they are seen at close range. It holds that mathematics, symbolic logic, philosophy, and so on, are systems contrasted with language which deal directly with this realm of thought, not that they are themselves specialized extensions of language. The attitude of natural logic is well shown in an old quip about a German grammarian who devoted his whole life to the study of the dative case. From the point of view of natural logic, the dative case and grammar in general are an extremely minor issue. A different attitude is said to have been held by the ancient Arabians: Two princes, so the story goes, quarreled over the honor of putting on the shoes of the most learned grammarian of the realm; whereupon their father, the caliph, is said to have remarked that it was the glory of his kingdom that great grammarians were honored even above kings.

The familiar saying that the exception proves the rule contains a good deal of wisdom, though from the standpoint of formal logic it became an absurdity as soon as "prove" no longer meant "put on trial." The old saw began to be profound psychology from the time it ceased to have standing in logic. What it might well suggest to us today is that if a rule has absolutely no exceptions, it is not recognized as a rule or as anything else; it is then part of the background of experience of which we tend to remain unconscious. Never having experienced anything in contrast to it, we cannot isolate it and formulate it as a rule until we so enlarge our experience and expand our base of reference that we encounter an interruption of its regularity. The situation is somewhat analogous to that of not missing the water till the well runs dry, or not realizing that we need air till we are choking.

For instance, if a race of people had the physiological defect of being able to see only the color blue, they would hardly be able to formulate the rule that they saw only blue. The term blue would convey no meaning to them, their language would lack color terms, and their words denoting their various sensations of blue would answer to, and translate, our words light, dark, white, black, and so on, not our word blue. In order to formulate the rule or norm of seeing only blue, they would need exceptional moments in which they saw other colors. The phenomenon of gravitation forms a rule without exceptions; needless to say, the untutored person is utterly unaware of any law of gravitation, for it would never enter his head to conceive of a universe in which bodies behaved otherwise than they do at the earth's surface. Like the color blue with our hypothetical race, the law of gravitation is a part of the untutored individual's background, not something he isolates from that background. The law could not be formulated until bodies that always fell were seen in terms of a wider astronomical world in which bodies moved in orbits or went this way and that.

Similarly, whenever we turn our heads, the image of the scene passes across our retinas exactly as it would if the scene turned around us. But this effect is background, and we do not recognize it; we do not see a room turn around us but are conscious only of having turned our heads in a stationary room. If we observe critically while turning the head or eyes quickly, we shall see no motion, it is true, yet a blurring of the scene between two clear views. Normally we are quite unconscious of this continual blurring but seem to be looking about in an unblurred world. Whenever we walk past a tree or house, its image on the retina changes just as if the tree or house were turning on an axis; yet we do not see trees or houses turn as we travel about at ordinary speeds. Sometimes ill-fitting glasses will reveal queer movements in the scene as we look about, but normally we do not see the relative motion of the environment when we move; our psychic make-up is somehow adjusted to disregard whole realms of phenomena that are so all-pervasive as to be irrelevant to our daily lives and needs.

Natural logic contains two fallacies: First, it does not see that the phenomena of a language are to its own speakers largely of a background character and so are outside the critical consciousness and control of the speaker who is expounding natural logic. Hence, when anyone, as a natural logician, is talking about reason, logic, and the laws of correct thinking, he is apt to be simply marching in step with purely grammatical facts that have somewhat of a background character in his own language or family of languages but are by no means universal in all languages and in no sense a common substratum of reason. Second, natural logic confuses agreement about subject matter, attained through use of language, with knowledge of the linguistic process by which agreement is attained; i.e., with the province of the despised (and to its notion superfluous) grammarian. Two fluent speakers, of English let us say, quickly reach a point of assent about the subject matter of their speech; they agree about

Hopi: one word (masa′ytaka)
English: three words

English: one word (snow)
Eskimo: three words

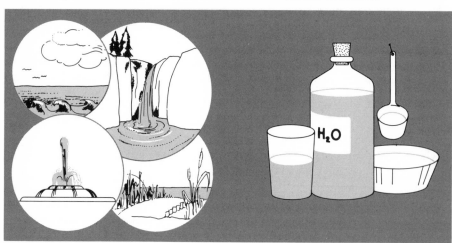

Hopi: pāhe
English: one word (water)

Hopi: kēyi
Hopi: two words

Figure 2. Languages classify items of experience differently. The class corresponding to one word and one thought in language A may be regarded by language B as two more classes corresponding to two or more words and thoughts.

what their language refers to. One of them, A, can give directions that will be carried out by the other, B, to A's complete satisfaction. Because they thus understand each other so perfectly, A and B, as natural logicians, suppose they must of course know how it is all done. They think, e.g., that it is simply a matter of choosing words to express thoughts. If you ask A to explain how he got B's agreement so readily, he will simply repeat to you, with more or less elaboration or abbreviation, what he said to B. He has no notion of the process involved. The amazingly complex system of linguistic patterns and classifications which A and B must have in common before they can adjust to each other at all, is all background to A and B.

These background phenomena are the province of the grammarian—or of the linguist, to give him his more modern name as a scientist. The word linguist in common, and especially newspaper, parlance means something entirely different, namely, a person who can quickly attain agreement about subject matter with different people speaking a number of different languages. Such a person is better termed a polyglot or a multilingual. Scientific linguists have long understood that ability to speak a language fluently does not necessarily confer a linguistic knowledge of it—i.e., understanding of its background phenomena and its systematic processes and structure—any more than ability to play a good game of billiards confers or requires any knowledge of the laws of mechanics that operate upon the billiard table.

The situation here is not unlike that in any other field of science. All real scientists have their eyes primarily on background phenomena that cut very little ice, as such, in our daily lives; and yet their studies have a way of bringing out a close relation between these unsuspected realms of fact and such decidedly foreground activities as transporting goods, preparing food, treating the sick, or growing potatoes, which in time may become very much modified simply because of pure scientific investigation in no way concerned with these brute matters themselves. Linguistics is in quite similar case; the background phenomena with which it deals are involved in all our foreground activities of talking and of reaching agreement, in all reasoning and arguing of cases, in all law, arbitration, conciliation, contracts, treaties, public opinion, weighing of scientific theories, formulation of scientific results. Whenever agreement or assent is arrived at in human affairs, and whether or not mathematics or other specialized symbolisms are made part of the procedure, *this agreement is reached by linguistic processes, or else it is not reached.*

As we have seen, an overt knowledge of the linguistic processes by which agreement is attained is not necessary to reaching some sort of agreement, but it is certainly no bar thereto; the more complicated and difficult the matter, the more such knowledge is a distinct aid, till the point may be reached—I suspect the modern world has about arrived at it—when the knowledge becomes not only an aid but a necessity. The situation may be likened to that of navigation. Every boat that sails is in the lap of planetary forces; yet a boy can pilot his small craft around a harbor without benefit of geography, astronomy, mathematics, or international politics. To the captain of an ocean liner, however, some knowledge of all these subjects is essential.

When linguists became able to examine critically and scientifically a large number of languages of widely different patterns, their base of reference was expanded; they experienced an interruption of phenomena hitherto held universal, and a whole new order of significances came into their ken. It was found that the background linguistic system (in other words, the grammar) of each language is not merely a reproducing instrument for voicing ideas but rather is itself the shaper of ideas, the program and guide for the individual's mental activity, for his analysis of impressions, for his synthesis of his mental stock in trade. Formulation of ideas is not an independent process, strictly rational in the old sense, but is part of a particular grammar and differs, from slightly to greatly, as between different grammars. We dissect nature along lines laid down by our native languages. The categories and types that we isolate from the world of phenomena we do not find there because they stare every observer in the face; on the contrary, the world is presented in a kaleidoscopic flux of impressions which has to be organized by our minds—and this means largely by the linguistic systems in our minds. We cut nature up, organize it into concepts, and ascribe significances as we do, largely because we are parties to an agreement to organize it in this way—an agreement that holds throughout our speech community and is codified in the patterns of our language. The agreement is, of course, an implicit and unstated one, *but its terms are absolutely obligatory;* we cannot talk at all except by subscribing to the organization and classification of data which the agreement decrees.

The fact is very significant for modern science, for it means that no individual is free to describe nature with absolute impartiality but is constrained to certain modes of interpretation even while he thinks himself most free. The person most nearly free in such respects would be a linguist familiar with very many widely different linguistic systems. As yet even no linguist is in any such position. We are thus introduced to a new principle of relativity, which holds that all observers are not led by the same physical evidence to the same picture of the universe, unless their linguistic backgrounds are similar, or can in some way be calibrated.

This rather startling conclusion is not so apparent if we compare only our modern European languages, with perhaps Latin and Greek thrown in for good measure. Among these tongues there is a unanimity of major pattern which at first seems to bear out natural logic. But this unanimity exists only because these tongues are all Indo-European dialects cut to the same basic plan, being historically transmitted from what was long ago one speech community; because the modern dialects have long shared in building up a common culture; and because much of this culture, on the more intellectual side, is derived from the linguistic backgrounds of Latin and Greek. Thus this group of languages satisfies the special case of the clause beginning "unless" in the statement of the linguistic relativity principle at the end of the preceding paragraph. From this condition follows the unanimity of description of the world in the community of modern scientists. But it must be emphasized that "all modern Indo-European-speaking observers" is not the same thing as "all observers." That modern Chinese or Turkish scientists describe the world in the same terms as Western scientists means, of course, only that they

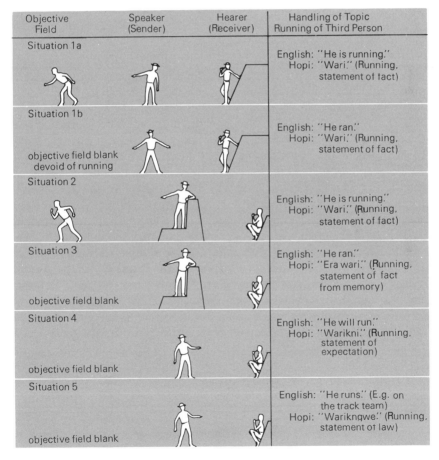

Figure 3. Contrast between a "temporal" language (English) and a "timeless" language (Hopi). What are to English differences of time are to Hopi differences in the kind of validity.

have taken over bodily the entire Western system of rationalizations, not that they have corroborated that system from their native posts of observation.

When Semitic, Chinese, Tibetan, or African languages are contrasted with our own, the divergence in analysis of the world becomes more apparent; and when we bring in the native languages of the Americas, where speech communities for many millenniums have gone their ways independently of each other and of the Old World, the fact that languages dissect nature in many different ways becomes patent (see Figure 1). The relativity of all conceptual systems, ours included, and their dependence upon language stand revealed. That American Indians speaking only their native tongues are never called upon to act as scientific observers is in no wise to the point. To exclude the evidence which their languages offer as to what the human mind can do is like expecting botanists to study nothing but food plants and hothouse roses and then tell us what the plant world is like!

Let us consider a few examples. In English we divide most of our words into two classes, which have different grammatical and logical properties. Class 1 we call nouns, e.g., "house," "man"; Class 2, verbs, e.g., "hit," "run." Many words of one class can act secondarily as of the other class, e.g., "a hit," "a run," or "to man" the boat, but on the primary level the division between the classes is absolute. Our language thus gives us a bipolar division of nature. But nature herself is not thus polarized. If it be said that strike, turn, run, are verbs because they denote temporary or shortlasting events, i.e., actions, why then is fist a noun? It also is a temporary event. Why are lightning, spark, wave, eddy, pulsation, flame, storm, phase, cycle, spasm, noise, emotion, nouns? They are temporary events. If man and house are nouns because they are long-lasting and stable events, i.e., things, what then are keep, adhere, extend, project, continue, persist, grow, dwell, and so on, doing among the verbs? If it be objected that possess, adhere, are verbs because they are stable relationships rather than stable percepts, why then should equilibrium, pressure, current, peace, group, nation, society, tribe, sister, or any kinship term, be among the nouns? It will be found that an "event" to *us* means "what our language classes as a verb" or something analogized therefrom. And it will be found that it is not possible to define event, thing, object, relationship, and so on, from nature, but that to define them always involves a circuitous return to the grammatical categories of the definer's language.

In the Hopi language, lightning, wave, flame, meteor, puff of smoke, pulsation, are verbs—events of necessarily brief duration cannot be anything but verbs. Cloud and storm are at about the lower limit of duration for nouns. Hopi, you see, actually has a classification of events (or linguistic isolates) by duration type, something strange to our modes of thought. On the other hand, in Nootka, a language of Vancouver Island, all words seem to us to be verbs, but really there are no Classes 1 and 2; we have, as it were, a monistic view of nature that gives us only one class of word for all kinds of events. "A house occurs" or "it houses" is the way of saying "house," exactly like "a flame occurs" or "it burns." These terms seem to us like verbs because they are inflected for durational and temporal nuances, so that the suffixes of the word for house event make it mean long-lasting house, temporary house, future house, house that used to be, what started out to be a house, and so on.

Hopi has a noun that covers every thing or being that flies, with the exception of birds, which class is denoted by another noun. The former noun may be said to denote the class FC–B, i.e., flying class minus bird. The Hopi actually call insect, airplane, and aviator all by the same word, and feel no difficulty about it (Figure 2). The situation, of course, decides any possible confusion among very disparate members of a broad linguistic class, such as this class FC–B. This class seems to us too large and inclusive, but so would our class "snow" to an Eskimo. We have the same word for falling snow, snow on the ground, snow packed hard like ice, slushy snow, wind-driven flying snow—whatever the situation may be. To an Eskimo, this all-inclusive word would be almost unthinkable; he would say that falling snow, slushy snow, and so on, are sensuously and operationally different, different things to contend with; he uses different words for them and for other kinds of snow (Figure 2). The Aztecs go even farther than we in the opposite direction, with cold, ice, and snow all represented by the same basic word with different terminations; ice is the noun form; cold, the adjectival form; and for snow, "ice mist."

What surprises most is to find that various grand generalizations of the Western world, such as time, velocity, and matter, are not essential to the construction of a consistent picture of the universe. The psychic experiences that we class under these headings are, of course, not destroyed; rather, categories derived from other kinds of experiences take over the rulership of the cosmology and seem to function just as well. Hopi may be called a timeless language. It recognizes psychological time, which is much like Bergson's "duration," but this "time" is quite unlike the mathematical time, T, used by our physicists. Among the peculiar properties of Hopi time are that it varies with each observer, does not permit of simultaneity, and has zero dimensions; i.e., it cannot be given a number greater than one. The Hopi do not say, "I stayed five days," but "I left on the fifth day." A word referring to this kind of time, like the word day, can have no plural. The puzzle picture (Fig. 3), will give mental exercise to anyone who would like to figure out how the Hopi verb gets along without tenses. Actually, the only practical use of our tenses, in one-verb sentences, is to distinguish among five typical situations, which are symbolized in the picture. The timeless Hopi verb does not distinguish between the present, past, and future of the event itself but must always indicate what type of validity the *speaker* intends the statement to have: (*a*) report of an event (situations 1, 2, 3 in the picture); (*b*) expectation of an event (situation 4); (*c*) generalization or law about events (situation 5). Situation 1, where the speaker and listener are in contact with the same objective field, is divided by our language into the two conditions, 1*a* and 1*b*, which it calls present and past, respectively. This division is unnecessary for a language which assures one that the statement is a report.

Hopi grammar, by means of its forms called aspects and modes, also makes it easy to distinguish between momentary, continued, and repeated occurrences, and to indicate the actual sequence of reported events. Thus the universe can be described without recourse to a concept of dimensional time. How would a physics constructed along these lines work, with no T (time) in its equations? Perfectly, as far as I can see, though of course it would require different ideology and perhaps different mathematics. Of course V (velocity) would have to go too. The Hopi language has no word really equivalent to our "speed" or "rapid." What translates these terms is usually a word meaning intense or very, accompanying any verb of motion. Here is a clew to the nature of our new physics. We may have to introduce a new term I, intensity. Every thing and event will have an I, whether we regard the thing or event as moving or as just enduring or being. Perhaps the I of an electric charge will turn out to be its voltage, or potential. We shall use clocks to measure some intensities, or, rather, some *relative* intensities, for the absolute intensity of anything will be meaningless. Our old friend acceleration will still be there but doubtless under a new name. We shall perhaps call it V, meaning not velocity but variation. Perhaps all growths and accumulations will be regarded as V's. We should not have the concept of rate in the temporal sense, since, like velocity, rate introduces a mathematical and linguistic time. Of course we know that all measurements are ratios, but the measurements of intensities made by comparison with the standard intensity of a clock or a planet we do not treat as ratios, any more than we so treat a distance made by comparison with a yardstick.

A scientist from another culture that used time and velocity would have great difficulty in getting us to understand these concepts. We should talk about the intensity of a chemical reaction; he would speak of its velocity or its rate, which words we should at first think were simply words for intensity in his language. Likewise, he at first would think that intensity was simply our own word for velocity. At first we should agree, later we should begin to disagree, and it might dawn upon both sides that different systems of rationalization were being used. He would find it very hard to make us understand what he really meant by velocity of a chemical reaction. We should have no words that would fit. He would try to explain it by likening it to a running horse, to the difference between a good horse and a lazy horse. We should try to show him, with a superior laugh, that his analogy also was a matter of different intensities, aside from which there was little similarity between a horse and a chemical reaction in a beaker. We should point out that a running horse is moving relative to the ground, whereas the material in the beaker is at rest.

One significant contribution to science from the linguistic point of view may be the greater development of our sense of perspective. We shall no longer be able to see a few recent dialects of the Indo-European family, and the rationalizing techniques elaborated from their patterns, as the apex of the evolution of the human mind; nor their present wide spread as due to any survival from fitness or to anything but a few events of history—events that could be called fortunate only from the parochial point of view of the favored parties. They, and our own thought processes with them, can no longer be envisioned as spanning the gamut of reason and knowledge but only as one constellation in a galactic expanse. A fair realization of the incredible degree of diversity of linguistic system that ranges over the globe leaves one with an inescapable feeling that the human spirit is inconceivably old; that the few thousand years of history covered by our written records are no more than the thickness of a pencil mark on the scale that measures our past experience on this planet; that the events of these recent millenniums spell nothing in any evolutionary wise, that the race has taken no sudden spurt, achieved no commanding synthesis during recent millenniums, but has only played a little with a few of the linguistic formulations and views of nature bequeathed from an inexpressibly longer past. Yet neither this feeling nor the sense of precarious dependence of all we know upon linguistic tools which themselves are largely unknown need be discouraging to science but should, rather, foster that humility which accompanies the true scientific spirit, and thus forbid that arrogance of the mind which hinders real scientific curiosity and detachment.

CHAPTER 6

CROSS-CULTURAL STUDIES OF MENTAL HEALTH

6-1

The Mental Health
of the Hutterites

JOSEPH W. EATON
ROBERT J. WEIL

The Hutterite sect originated in Germany in 1528. Its members lived together in neighboring European villages long before they migrated to the U.S. from southern Russia between 1874 and 1877. These immigrants settled in eastern South Dakota and are now spread over a wide area in the Dakotas, Montana, and the prairie provinces of Canada. They live in 98 colonies (hamlets), but they remain a remarkably cohesive group; each member is intimately acquainted with hundreds of other members in the settlements. As the Hutterites believe that it is sinful to marry outside the sect, all the present descendents stem from the original 101 couples who immigrated to the U.S. From the very beginning they endured persecution, including, in many cases, death at the stake. Among those so killed was Jacob Huter, the leader whose name the sect adopted after his martyrdom in 1536. A history of persecution and rejection in Europe and North America may have enhanced the cohesiveness of this group.

The Hutterite way of life is uncomplicated. Their culture stresses religion, conformity, and cooperation among its members rather than aggression and competition. To what extent is the mental health of the Hutterites affected by these values and beliefs?

Reprinted from *Culture and mental disorders,* New York: The Free Press, 1955, by permission of the authors and the publisher.

Contrary to common expectations, Eaton and Weil showed that the Hutterite society is not immune to the emotional and mental disorders known in the West. However, cultural and social factors were shown to be associated with the relative frequency of various disorders. The Hutterites, for instance, have a high rate of depression and a low rate of schizophrenia, reversing the pattern usually seen in the West. The Hutterite way of life seems also to provide an atmosphere within which emotionally disturbed members are accepted and encouraged to function within the limits of their handicaps. Thus the deleterious effects of institutionalization are avoided (e.g., extreme social withdrawal, deterioration, antisocial behavior). This study provides a good example of the implications of values and beliefs of a society for mental health.

In the study of the epidemiology of mental illness, it is common practice to examine hospital and clinic records. Results thus may only indicate the diagnosed prevalence of mental illness. Eaton and Weil obtained most of their information from direct contact with members of the Hutterite community and this gives an approximation to the rate of true incidence. The present excerpts give only some of the extensive data reported by the authors in *Culture and Mental Disorders* (1955).

In modern America, mental disorders rank high among the severely disabling illnesses in terms of cost, number of persons involved, chronicity, and suffering. Can this fact be a consequence of the pace of modern living? Were mental disorders less prevalent among past generations who lived in a simpler rural world? Are there some "ideal" cultures where psychic disturbances are relatively rare? These popular questions imply a common theory about cause—the theory that culture and social relationships are deeply involved in the multidimensional causal pattern.

This study was conducted in an unusual human laboratory—a society whose members share over four centuries of common history, tradition, and faith, and are bound together by many close kinship ties. They live in modern America, under the impact of its technology and its way of life, but sufficiently apart from it to constitute a miniature autonomous social system. The Hutterites were willing to co-operate in this scientific venture; they did so with a generosity and completeness rare in the annals of social science. Some of the cultural and social variables like educational level, income, migration, and others, which in other populations usually vary greatly, could be eliminated as factors because they vary little throughout the entire society. It has a relatively low level of social stress, in the sense that its way of life lacks many of the unresolved tensions and contradictions of the contemporary American melting pot cultural system.

The Hutterite sect, unlike American Indian tribes or other folk societies which have been studied by anthropologists in cross-cultural surveys, has a way of life which is much more similar to the larger American scene. Before we emphasize certain unusual features of the Hutterite social system, it must be noted that it is not "primitive" in the ethnographic sense. Hutterites employ some of the most up-to-date machinery. They are informed about the work of agricultural experiment stations and sometimes seek their advice. The people are literate in both their native Germanic dialect and in English. Their children attend school to the eighth grade. The schools are parochial but are staffed by licensed, generally non-Hutterite, elementary teachers. Nearly all the members are native citizens of the United States or Canada. They and their forebears have been exposed to American ways of living for over seventy-five years. They share with the majority of Americans the general Judaeo-Christian heritage of Western civilization. Hutterite values and beliefs have much in common with those of other contemporary orthodox religious groups such as rural French Catholics, ultra-orthodox Jews, Seventh Day Adventists, and Mennonites.

Hutterites believe in the communal ownership and control of all property. Like the Catholic orders, they live under economic communism in the classical and nonpolitical sense. Christ and the Bible are their ideological guides. Hutterites expect the community to assume a great deal of responsibility for each member. It is the community which buys clothing, doles out pocket money to each person, and pays a traffic ticket. No wages are paid. Each person is expected to work to the best of his ability. He eats his meals in the community dining room; the meals prepared by different women in rotation. If he is sick, the colony pays for all necessary care. In case of male death, widows and dependents have no financial worries; the loss of a breadwinner never means the loss of bread. The Hutterite way of life provides social security from the womb to the tomb. The religious creed of the group gives the members a further guarantee of security beyond the tomb. It promises absolute salvation to all who follow its precepts.

Provision for an intensive case count of mental pathology was made in a sample of the sect. Throughout our field work we were impressed with the prevailing overt atmosphere of relaxation, and absence of severe overt anxiety. Yet our sample showed more cases with serious psychiatric problems than seemed consistent with the Hutterite reputation for mental health. We then decided to check this trend of mental pathology by extending the case finding survey to the entire sect.

In the summer of 1951, 199 living persons, one of every 43 living Hutterites, were found who had had at one time in their life symptoms diagnosed by our staff as those of a mental disorder. About 57

TABLE 1

Lifetime, Active Case, and Recovery Morbidity Count of Mental Disorders Among Ethnic Hutterites Living in Summer of 1951*

	Lifetime Morbidity	Active Case Morbidity		Other Cases
Staff Diagnosis of Illness	Total Number Ever Ill	Ill in Summer 1951	Ill but Improved on Aug. 31, 1951	Recovered by or before Aug. 31, 1951	Status Unknown
Psychoses					
Schizophrenia	9	7	1	1	0
Manic-depressive reaction	39	3	5	27	4
Acute & chronic brain disorders	5	4	0	1	0
Total	53	14	6	29	4
Neuroses					
Psychoneurotic disorders	53	24	15	12	2
Psychophysiological autonomic and visceral disorders	16	7	3	5	1
Total	69	31	18	17	3
Mental deficiency					
Mild	14	14	0	0	0
Moderate	23	23	0	0	0
Severe	14	14	0	0	0
Total	51	51	0	0	0
Epilepsy	20	12	5	3	0
Personality disorders	6	6	0	0	0
Total number of cases	199	114	29	49	7

*The population was 8,542 on December 31, 1950. The classification of illnesses follows the system of the committee on Nomenclature and Statistics of the American Psychiatric Association, *Diagnostic and Statistical Manual, Mental Disorders* (Washington, D.C.: American Psychiatric Asscociation, 1952).

per cent of these were actively ill on August 31, 1951. Roughly 15 per cent were ill but improved. Twenty-five per cent were recovered. In about 3 per cent of the cases the investigators were unable to make a judgment concerning the recovery status (see Table 1). This study did not, therefore, confirm the Hutterite reputation of virtual immunity from mental disorders.

Depression was the most common reaction to stress in the sect. In 39 of the 53 cases, depression of mood with mental and motor retardation, perplexity, or agitation was prominent in the symptomatology. Most of the cases, 33 in number, were diagnosed as manic-depressive reactions of the depressed type. In one case there was enough excited behavior, flight of ideas, and elated effect to make the diagnosis of manic type. Five cases were recorded as mixed manic because of their restlessness, agitation, flight of ideas, extreme talkativeness, and occasional threat of violence. There were 4.6 persons per 1,000 Hutterites or 9.3 per 1,000 aged 15 and over who were diagnosed as manic-depressive. Included in this category were cases of involutional melancholia.

There were nine cases of schizophrenia among the ethnic Hutterites living in the summer of 1951. Four individuals were diagnosed as cases of chronic and undifferentiated schizophrenia, four as catatonic, and one as paranoid. The lifetime morbidity rate was 1.1 person per 1,000 or 2.1 per 1,000 persons aged 15 and over. These patients constituted 17 per cent of all diagnosed psychotics. This proportion of schizophrenics was close to the one in five ratio of such patients first admitted to United States state mental hospitals in 1928, 1938, and 1948. If there was anything unusual about schizophrenic cases in this culture, it was their ability to function socially at a moderate level of adequacy. Extreme antisocial acts, severe regression, or excitement, so common in the schizophrenic patients in mental hospitals, were not observed. One factor may be the excellent and generally thoughtful custodial care given by people who have some affectionate regard for the patient.

In Table 2 it is shown that the proportion of schizophrenics varies from a low of 16 per cent in the Arctic Norwegian Village to a high of 87 per cent in the North Swedish Area; the proportion of manic-depressives from a low of 2 per cent in the North Swedish Area to 74 per cent in the Hutterite group. All other diagnostic categories, including cases not diagnosed, vary from a low of 9 per cent in the Hutterite study to 79 per cent in Arctic Norwegian Village survey.

The Hutterite sect probably has the lowest frequency of psychoses among the four rural populations within the European and Judaeo-Christian complex of culture, but the experience of the population with this type of mental disorder is higher than that of the inhabitants of Formosa.

TABLE 2

Major Diagnostic Categories in Ten Studies of Psychosis

		Percentage of Cases Diagnosed			
Study	Number of Cases Diagnosed	Schizo-phrenia	Manic Depression	All Other Diagnoses	Total
Ethnic Hutterites	53	17	74	9	100
Formosa Area	76	57	17	26	100
North Swedish Area	107	87	2	11	100
Arctic Norwegian Village	38	16	5	79	100
West Swedish Island	94	43	27	30	100
Bornholm Island	481	31	25	43	100
Williamson County, Tennessee	156	27	26	47	100
Baltimore Eastern Health District	367*	43	11	46	100
Thuringia Villages	200	37	10	53	100
Bavarian Villages, Rosenheim Area	21	38	10	52	100

*Active and severe cases only. Recovered cases are not included, as no diagnostic breakdown is given for them.

In all except the Hutterite population there were more schizophrenic than manic-depressive patients. The highest ratio of schizophrenic to manic-depressive reactions was 46.00 in the North Swedish Area. The remainder were all above 1.00 (See Table 2). The same ratio was only 0.23 in the Hutterite sect. Patients with a manic-depressive reaction constituted 73.6 per cent of all Hutterite persons diagnosed as psychotic. Among patients first admitted to a reporting United States mental hospital in 1928, 1938, and 1948, a much smaller and a decreasing proportion of cases were so diagnosed: 14.4, 11.1, and 6.0 per cent, respectively.

The differences are startling. One of the first explanations considered in the analysis was the possibility that the manic-depressive reaction category was the unconscious favorite of the psychiatric collaborator in the study. But this we doubt. The psychiatrist did not make his diagnostic judgments in a vacuum. All cases and their diagnosis were repeatedly discussed in conference with one or more members of the senior field work staff; they could hardly have missed so systematic a "bias." There certainly was no general disposition to avoid critical review of the judgment of a staff member even in matters related to his specialty. The

Hutterite proclivity for depressive symptoms was not anticipated when the study was planned, nor did its extent become clearly apparent until most of the data had been collected. The full theoretical significance of this finding was not appreciated until much later.

Tietze et al. (1941) show that the proportion of manic-depressive psychosis patients is high, relatively to the number diagnosed as schizophrenic, among professional people, higher income groups, inmates of private mental hospitals, and residents of surburban areas. The reverse is true of persons with occupations of lower social status or lower income, inmates of public hospitals, and residents of the central areas of cities, where the population is more transient. Schizophrenia is the most common functional diagnosis among psychotic persons from these socially less integrated categories, and there is a significantly small proportion of cases of manic-depressive reaction. In general, many epidemiological findings of the frequency of functional psychoses show a high degree of internal consistency in support of the socio-cultural theory that manic depression is a disorder most common to persons who have a high degree of social cohesion and who are group centered. On the other hand, this diagnosis is much less common among persons who are social isolates and marginal. The latter category of persons is more likely to show symptoms of schizophrenia.

The Hutterites, who have the highest proportion of manic-depressive patients among the ten studies that have been compared, are also extreme in their emphasis on communal cohesiveness. There is much stress on religion, duty to God and society, and there is a tendency in their entire thinking to orient members to internalize their aggressive drives. Children and adults alike are taught to look for guilt within themselves rather than in others. The North Swedish Area, which has an unusually high proportion of schizophrenic cases and few manic-depressives, is populated by a much less socially cohesive population. Most inhabitants live in isolated farmsteads. There are many single males, particularly in the older age groups.

Social cohesion is certainly not the only socio-cultural element worthy of study to understand the etiology of psychoses. That there must be other significant constellations of factors is illustrated by the fact that psychoses associated with drug addiction, alcoholism, and syphilis, which are common in urban areas, were nearly absent in several of the rural populations. There were no cases among the socially cohesive Hutterites but these disorders also were virtually absent in three Scandinavian Lutheran populations who live in a much less cohesive social system: the Bornholm Island, the West Swedish Island, and the North Swedish Area. The rates were about 0.2 per 1,000 persons aged 15 and over. In Thuringia and in Bavaria the lifetime morbidity rate was larger, about 0.5 and 2.4 per 1,000 persons aged 15 and over. No case of general paresis, the most common mental disorder related to syphilis, was reported in both the Arctic Norwegian Village and the Formosa studies.

In 34 of the enumerated psychoneurotic cases, nearly 50 per cent, there was a multiplicity of symptoms which could not be classified clearly in any specific category. The diagnosis of *other psychoneurotic reaction* was made. Six patients showed enough general anxiety about specific problems to justify the diagnosis of *anxiety reaction*. Most of these cases also had vague neurasthenic complaints. We did not observe many symptoms typical of free-floating anxiety. This may explain the general impression that Hutterite colonies are populated by relaxed, well-adjusted, and mentally healthy individuals. It could be expected that free-floating anxiety would be rare in a culture where the individual has many close interpersonal relationships and is generally given a great deal of social and psychological support by his family and his community. A Hutterite usually knows how others will react to something he does. There is little of the deep uncertainty in social relations which is experienced by many people living in a metropolis with widely differing cultural expectations.

Eleven persons were found to have severe depressive symptoms. They were diagnosed as *neurotic-depressive reaction* cases. Two female cases diagnosed as *conversion reactions* manifested classical hysterical symptoms. One had a paralysis of the leg and the other had epileptiform fits following a miscarriage. The remaining sixteen cases were diagnosed as *psychopsysiological autonomic and visceral disorders.*

It was our impression that neurotic Hutterites react to most stresses with signs of depression rather than with anxiety symptoms or obsessive or paranoid tendencies as neurotic patients often do in the American culture. This rareness of obsessive and compulsive behavior may have something to do with the relative rigidity of the Hutterite culture. Persons who would seem to be compulsive in a loosely structured social system would be more normal in a Hutterite colony, where life is highly regulated by tradition. The Hutterite culture provides such persons with socially approved outlets for compulsiveness. They need only to be orthodox! Some Hutterites were regarded by their community as fanatical in their orthodoxy, but in no case seen by our staff did the psychiatrist think that a diagnosis of compulsive neurotic reaction would be justified.

The good mental health which has been ascribed to Hutterites by those who have observed them is not entirely contradicted by this finding. The sect probably does have a fairly low frequency of psychoneurotic disorders. What may be even more significant from the point of view of mental health, most Hutterite patients have fairly mild and benign symptoms. They are able to function in their communities and families with considerable acceptance for the limitations imposed by their psychoneurotic difficulties upon their social functioning.

Hutterite mental patients with a variety of functional disorders reflected Hutterite cultural values in their symptoms of illness. There was little free-floating anxiety among the people who had grown up in this highly structured social system. Dominance of depression and introjection rather than acting out or projection of conflicts was found in both manic-depressive reaction and psychoneurotic cases. Nearly all patients, even the most disturbed schizophrenics, lived up to the strong taboo against overt physical aggression and physical violence. Paranoid, manic, severely antisocial, or extremely regressive symptoms were uncommon. Equally rare or completely absent were severe crimes, marital separation, and other forms of social disorganization. People had interpersonal problems rather than antisocial manifestations. Hutterites showed evidence of having aggressive impulses in projective tests, but these impulses were not manifested overtly as acts physically harmful to others. Human brutality may be found in most social systems, but it is not a functionally necessary behavior; its repression seems to be possible.

The traumatic social consequences of mental disorders for the individual patient, his family, and his community were ameliorated by many Hutterite practices. The onset of a symptom of disorder served as a signal for the entire community to demonstrate support and love for the patient. He was generally approached with considerable sympathy and understanding. Mentally ill persons were treated as "ill" rather than "crazy." All but one case could be looked after in the home, usually by members of the immediate family. Patients were encouraged to participate in the normal activities of their family and community, and most of them were able to do some useful work. Rarely were their afflictions regarded as a social disgrace. No permanent stigma was attached to those who recovered. Symptoms of disorder were relatively bearable for the patient, his family, and his community. There seemed to be little need for the severely restrictive care which is so characteristic of many mental hospitals. This fact supports the theory that many of the severe disturbances of some psychoses and personality disorders are not an inherent attribute of these conditions. At least in part they seem to be a consequence of the methods of handling patients used by hospitals, families, and communities.

The Hutterite way of life was no antidote for severe mental disorders, but it provided an atmosphere within which emotionally disturbed persons were encouraged to get well or to function in a socially accepted manner within the limits imposed by their illness. While the prospects for recovery for Hutterites suffering from a manic-depressive psychosis were no higher than those of other American mental hospital patients in the same category, Hutterite colonies were therapeutic communities in the sense that the traumatic social consequences of being mentally ill were kept at a minimum.

Our findings contain no blueprint for a "perfect" social order. On the contrary, a mental health utopia is probably impossible. The strong social cohesion and clear-cut expectations which tend to protect Hutterites from having to face the uncertainties of life unaided and without normative guidance, can also be a source of psychological stress. Strong guilt feelings were found in Hutterites who feared that they might be unable to live up to the expectations of their group. Severe depressive moods were the most common psychopathological symptoms in neurotic and psychotic members of the sect. The emphasis on mutual aid, social security, friendliness, and nonaggression, which impressed the researchers and previous students of Hutterite life, also had negative consequences for social and psychological adjustment, particularly of individuals who were social deviants. It is probably valid to generalize that no cultural trait is inherently positive or negative for mental health. All tend to produce individual behavior which can be regarded as "good" or "bad," depending on the value standards of the people affected.

In a complex and diversified social system there can be no single mental health standard. There may be wide agreement that severe mental disorders are "bad," although in many primitive groups men who have hallucinations are given the high status of medicine men, and in our own American and other contemporary societies men with severe psychoneuroses and character disorders are sometimes elected to positions of leadership. There certainly is far less agreement on positive mental health components. The American Hutterite looks with self-satisfied complacency at his crop, the sunset, and his children who surround him in old age. He feels genuinely sorry for his "poor city neighbor who can't see a sunset because the houses are so tall, who earns his living while sitting behind a desk, and whose children will leave him to make their own way." On the other hand, the non-Hutterite visitor to a colony may wonder how men can be happy without education, music, art, and many of the creature comforts which technology can provide. Science can make some cross-cultural generalizations about severe mental disorders; it can generalize much less about mental health, which is a more normative and a less scientific concept.

REFERENCES

Tietze, C., Lemkaw, and M. Cooper. Schizophrenic, manic depressive psychosis and social-economic status, *Amer. J. Sociol.*, 1941, **47**, 167–175.

6-2

Social Stratification and Psychiatric Disorders

AUGUST B. HOLLINGSHEAD
FREDERICK C. REDLICH

Cultural and social variables such as education, income, residence, religion, migration, and others vary little in a primitive society. They vary greatly in Western communities such as the one studied by Hollingshead and Redlich in New Haven. The authors found a correspondence between social class and the proportion of individuals under psychiatric care. They also found that both types of psychiatric disorder (psychoses and neuroses) and the type of treatment received by the patient (private, organic, psychotherapy) also correspond with social class. Although these findings may add little to our understanding of etiology, they represent an important step in raising hypotheses. The authors hypothesized that the association between schizophrenia and the lower class may be due to the downward mobility of schizophrenic patients. This hypothesis was not supported by the results reported in their book *Social Class and Mental Illness* (1958) which show that 91% of the schizophrenic sample were of the same social class as their fathers. Hypotheses IV and V put forward by Hollingshead and Redlich in the present study have later been investigated by J. K. Meyers and B. H. Roberts (*Family and Class Dynamics in Mental Illness*, 1959). They found that differences in the rate of neuroses and psychoses

Reprinted from *Amer. Soc. Rev.*, 1953, **18**, 163–169, by permission of the authors and American Sociological Association.

in classes III and V correspond to differences in child rearing social-ization (drive level for upward mobility, repression of sexual and aggressive impulses, etc.). These authors, therefore, raise the question of whether factors associated with class may differentially dis-pose class members to psychoses or neuroses.

The New Haven study makes us aware of the pitfalls of making generalizations about the American "culture" or "society" without due regard to subcultures or different levels of social organization within the same culture.

The research reported here grew out of the work of a number of men, who, during the last half century, have demonstrated that the social environment in which individuals live is connected in some way, as yet not fully explained, to the development of mental illness (Rosanoff, 1916; Stern, 1913; Sutherland, 1901; etc.). Medical men have approached this problem largely from the viewpoint of epidemiology (Braatoy, 1937; Gerard and Siegel, 1950; Hyde and Kingsley, 1944; etc.). Sociologists, on the other hand, have analyzed the question in terms of ecology (Faris and Dunham, 1939; Dunham, 1947; Felix and Bowers, 1948; etc.) and of social disorganization (Faris, 1934; 1944). Neither psychiatrists nor sociol-ogists have carried on extensive research into the specific question we are concerned with, namely, interrelations between the class structure and the development of mental illness. However, a few sociologists and psychiatrists have written speculative and research papers in this area.[1]

The present research, therefore, was designed to discover whether a relationship does or does not exist between the class system of our society and mental illnesses. Five general hypotheses were formulated in our research plan to test some dimension of an assumed relationship between the two. These hypotheses were stated positively; they could just as easily have been expressed either negatively or conditionally. They were phrased as follows:

    I. The *expectancy* of a psychiatric disorder is related significantly to an individual's position in the class structure of his society.

    II. The *types* of psychiatric disorders are connected significantly to the class structure.

---

[1]Extensive bibliographical sources are provided by the authors for the various ap-proaches noted above. The reader is referred to the original publication.

III. The type of *psychiatric treatment* administered is associated with patient's positions in the class structure.

IV. The *psycho-dynamics* of psychiatric disorders are correlative to an individual's position in the class structure.

V. *Mobility* in the class structure is neurotogenic.

Each hypothesis is linked to the others, and all are subsumed under the theoretical assumption of a functional relationship between stratification in society and the prevalence of particular types of mental disorders among given social classes or strata in a specified population. Although our research was planned around these hypotheses, we have been forced by the nature of the problem of mental illness to study *diagnosed* prevalence of psychiatric disorders, rather than *true* or *total* prevalence.

METHODOLOGICAL PROCEDURE

The research is being done by a team of four psychiatrists, two sociologists, and a clinical psychologist. The data are being assembled in the New Haven urban community, which consists of the city of New Haven and surrounding towns of East Haven, North Haven, West Haven, and Hamden. This community had a population of some 250,000 persons in 1950. The New Haven community was selected because the community's structure has been studied intensively by sociologists over a long period. In addition, it is served by a private psychiatric hospital, three psychiatric clinics, and 27 practicing psychiatrists, as well as the state and Veterans Administration facilities.

Four basic technical operations had to be completed before the hypotheses could be tested. These were: the delineation of the class structure of the community, selection of a cross-sectional control of the community's population, the determination of who was receiving psychiatric care, and the stratification of both the control sample and the psychiatric patients.

August B. Hollingshead and Jerome K. Myers took over the task of delineating the class system. Fortunately, Maurice R. Davie and his students had studied the social structure of the New Haven community in great detail over a long time span (Davie, 1937; Kennedy, 1944; McConnell, 1937; etc.). Thus, we had a large body of data we could draw upon to aid us in blocking out the community's social structure.

The community's social structure is differentiated *vertically* along racial, ethnic, and religious lines; each of these vertical cleavages, in turn, is differentiated *horizontally* by a series of strata or classes. Around the socio-biological axis of race two social worlds have evolved: A Negro world and a white world. The white world is divided by ethnic origin and religion into Catholic, Protestant, and Jewish contingents. Within these divisions there are numerous ethnic groups. The Irish hold aloof from the Italians, and the Italians move in different circles from the Poles. The Jews maintain a religious and social life separate from the gentiles. The *horizontal* strata that transect each of these vertical divisions are based upon the social values that are attached to occupation, education, place of residence in the community, and associations.

The vertically differentiating factors of race, religion and ethnic origin, when combined with the horizontally differentiating ones of occupation, education, place of residence and so on, produce a social structure that is highly compartmentalized. The integrating factors in this complex are twofold. First, each stratum of each vertical division is similar in its cultural characteristics to the corresponding stratum in the other divisions. Second, the cultural pattern for each stratum or class was set up by the "Old Yankee" core group. This core group provided the master cultural mold that has shaped the status system of each sub-group in the community. In short, the social structure of the New Haven community is a parallel class structure within the limits of race, ethnic origin, and religion.

This fact enabled us to stratify the community, for our purposes, with an *Index of Social Position*. This *Index* utilizes three scaled factors to determine an individual's class position within the community's stratificational system: ecological area of residence, occupation, and education. Ecological area of residence is measured by a six point scale; occupation and education are each measured by a seven point scale. To obtain a social class score on an individual we must therefore know his address, his occupation, and the number of years of school he has completed. Each of these factors is given a scale score, and the scale score is multiplied by a factor weight determined by a standard regression equation. The factor weights are as follows: Ecological area of residence, 5; occupation, 8; and education, 6. The three factor scores are summed, and the resultant score is taken as an index of this individual's position in the community's social class system.

This *Index* enabled us to delineate five main social class strata within the horizontal dimension of the social structure. These principal strata or classes may be characterized as follows:

Class   I. This stratum is composed of wealthy families whose wealth is often inherited and whose heads are leaders in the community's business and professional pursuits. Its members live in those areas of the community generally regarded as "the best;" the adults are college graduates, usually from famous private institutions, and almost all gentile families are listed in the New Haven *Social Directory*, but few Jewish families are listed. In brief, these people occupy positions of high social prestige.

Class II. Adults in this stratum are almost all college graduates; the males occupy high managerial positions, many are engaged in the lesser ranking professions. These families are well-to-do, but there is no substantial inherited or acquired wealth. Its members live in the "better" residential areas; about one-half of these families belong to lesser ranking private clubs, but only 5 per cent of Class II families are listed in the New Haven *Social Directory*.

Class III. This stratum includes the vast majority of small proprietors, white-collar office and sales workers, and a considerable number of skilled manual workers. Adults are predominantly high school graduates, but a considerable percentage have attended business schools and small colleges for a year or two. They live in "good" residential areas; less than 5 per cent belong to private clubs, but they are not included in the *Social Directory*. Their social life tends to be concentrated in the family, the church, and the lodge.

Class IV. This stratum consists predominately of semi-skilled factory workers. Its adult members have finished the elementary grades, but the older people have not completed high school. However, adults under thirty-five have generally graduated from high school. Its members comprise almost one-half of the community; and their residences are scattered over wide areas. Social life is centered in the family, the neighborhood, the labor union, and public places.

Class V. Occupationally, class V adults are overwhelmingly semi-skilled factory hands and unskilled laborers. Educationally most adults have not completed the elementary grades. The families are concentrated in the "tenement" and "cold-water flat" areas of New Haven. Only a small minority belong to organized community institutions. Their social life takes place in the family flat, on the street, or in neighborhood social agencies.

The second major technical operation in this research was the enumeration of psychiatric patients. A Psychiatric Census was taken to discover the number and kinds of psychiatric patients in the community.

Enumeration was limited to residents of the community who were patients of a psychiatrist or a psychiatric clinic, or were in a psychiatric institution on December 1, 1950. To make reasonably certain that all patients were included in the enumeration, the research team gathered data from all public and private psychiatric institutions and clinics in Connecticut and nearby states, and all private practitioners in Connecticut and the metropolitan New York area. It received the cooperation of all clinics and institutions, and of all practitioners except a small number in New York City. It can be reasonably assumed that we have data comprising at least 98 per cent of all individuals who were receiving psychiatric care on December 1, 1950.

Forty-four pertinent items of information were gathered on each patient and placed on a schedule. The psychiatrists gathered material regarding symptomatology and diagnosis, onset of illness and duration, referral to the practitioner and the institution, and the nature and intensity of treatment. The sociologists obtained information on age, sex, occupation, education, religion, race and ethnicity, family history, marital experiences, and so on.

The third technical research operation was the selection of a control sample from the normal population of the community. The sociologists drew a 5 per cent random sample of households in the community from the 1951, New Haven *City Directory*. This directory covers the entire communal area. The names and addresses in it were compiled in October and November, 1950—a period very close to the date of the Psychiatric Census. Therefore there was comparability of residence and date of registry between the two population groups. Each household drawn in the sample was interviewed, and data on the age, sex, occupation, education, religion, and income of family members, as well as other items necessary for our purposes were placed on a schedule. This sample is our Control Population.

Our fourth basic operation was the stratification of the psychiatric patients and of the control population with the *Index of Social Position*. As soon as these tasks were completed, the schedules from the Psychiatric Census and the 5 per cent Control Sample were edited and coded, and their data were placed on Hollerith cards. The analysis of these data is in process.

SELECTED FINDINGS

Before we discuss our findings relative to Hypothesis I, we want to reemphasize that our study is concerned with *diagnosed* or *treated* prevalence rather than *true* or *total* prevalence. Our Psychiatric Census included only psychiatric cases under treatment, diagnostic study, or care. It did not include individuals with psychiatric disorders who were not being treated on December 1, 1950, by a psychiatrist. There are undoubtedly many individuals in the community with psychiatric problems who escaped our net. If we had *true* prevalence figures, many findings from our present study would be more meaningful, perhaps some of our interpretations would be changed, but at present we must limit ourselves to the data we have.

Hypothesis I, as revised by the nature of the problem, stated: *The diagnosed prevalence of psychiatric disorders is related significantly to an individual's position* in the class structure. A test of this hypothesis involves a comparison of the normal population with the psychiatric population. If no significant difference between the distribution of the normal population and the psychiatric patient population by social class is found, Hypothesis I may be abandoned as unproved. However, if a significant difference is found between the two populations by class, Hypothesis I should be entertained until more conclusive data are assembled. Pertinent data for a limited test of Hypothesis I are presented in Table 1. The data included show the number of individuals in the normal population and the psychiatric population, by class level. What we are concerned with in this test is how these two populations are distributed by class.

TABLE 1

Distribution of Normal and Psychiatric Population by Social Class*

Social Class	Normal Population†		Psychiatric Population	
	Number	Per cent	Number	Per cent
I	358	3.1	19	1.0
II	926	8.1	131	6.7
III	2500	22.0	260	13.2
IV	5256	46.0	758	38.6
V	2037	17.8	723	36.8
Unknown‡	345	3.0	72	3.7
Total	11,422	100.0	1,963	100.0

*Chi square=408.16, P less than .001.
†These figures are preliminary. They do not include Yale students, transients, institutionalized persons, and refusals.
‡The unknown cases were not used in the calculation of chi square. They are individuals drawn in the sample, and psychiatric cases whose class level could not be determined because of paucity of data.

When we tested the reliability of these population distributions by the use of the chi square method, we found a *very significant* relation between social class and treated prevalence of psychiatric disorders in the New Haven community. A comparison of the percentage distribution of each population by class readily indicates the direction of the class concentration of psychiatric cases. For example, Class I contains 3.1 per cent of the community's population but only 1.0 per cent of the psychiatric cases. Class V, on the other hand, includes 17.8 per cent of the community's population, but contributed 36.8 per cent of the psychiatric patients. On the basis of our data Hypothesis I clearly should be accepted as tenable.

Hypothesis II postulated a significant connection between the *type* of psychiatric disorder and social class. This hypothesis involves a test of the idea that there may be a functional relationship between an individual's position in the class system and the type of psychiatric disorder that he may present. This hypothesis depends, in part, on the question of diagnosis. Our psychiatrists based their diagnoses on the classificatory system developed by the Veterans Administration (1947). For the purposes of this paper, all cases are grouped into two categories: the neuroses and the psychoses. The results of this grouping by social class are given in Table 2.

A study of Table 2 will show that the neuroses are concentrated at the higher levels and the psychoses at the lower end of the class structure. Our team advanced a number of theories to explain the sharp differences between the neuroses and psychoses by social class. One suggestion was that the low percentage of neurotics in the lower

TABLE 2

Distribution of Neuroses and Psychoses by Social Class*

Social Class	Neuroses		Psychoses	
	Number	Per cent	Number	Per cent
I	10	52.6	9	47.4
II	88	67.2	43	32.8
III	115	44.2	145	55.8
IV	175	23.1	583	76.9
V	61	8.4	662	91.6
Total	449	—	1,442	—

*Chi square=296.45, P less than .001.

classes was a direct reaction to the cost of psychiatric treatment. But as we accumulated a series of case studies, for tests of Hypotheses IV and V, we became skeptical of this simple interpretation. Our detailed case records indicate that the social distance between psychiatrist and patient may be more potent than economic considerations in determining the character of psychiatric intervention. This question therefore requires further research.

The high concentration of psychotics in the lower strata is probably the product of a very unequal distribution of psychotics in the total population. To test this idea, Hollingshead selected schizophrenics for special study. Because of the severity of this disease it is probable that very few schizophrenics fail to receive some kind of psychiatric care. This diagnostic group comprises 44.2 per cent of all patients, and 58.7 per cent of the psychotics, in our study. Ninety-seven and six-tenths per cent of these schizophrenic patients had been hospitalized at one time or another, and 94 per cent were hospitalized at the time of our census. When we classify these patients by social class we find that there is a very significant inverse relationship between social class and schizophrenia.

Hollingshead decided to determine, on the basis of these data, what the probability of the prevalence of schizophrenia by social class might be in the general population. To do this he used a proportional index to learn whether or not there were differentials in the distribution of the general population, as represented in our control sample, and the distribution of schizophrenics by social class. If a social class exhibits the same proportion of schizophrenia as it comprises of the general population, the index for that class is 100. If schizophrenia is disproportionately prevalent in a social class the index is above 100; if schizophrenia is disproportionately low in a social class the index is below 100. The index for each social class appears in the last column of Table 3.

TABLE 3

Comparison of the Distribution of the Normal Population with Schizophrenics by Class, with Index of Probable Prevalence

Social Class	Normal Population		Schizophrenics		Index of Prevalence
	No.	Per cent	No.	Per cent	
I	358	3.2	6	.7	22
II	926	8.4	23	2.7	33
III	2,500	22.6	83	9.8	43
IV	5,256	47.4	352	41.6	88
V	2,037	18.4	383	45.2	246
Total	11,077	100.0	847	100.0	—

The fact that the Index of Prevalence in class I is only one-fifth as great as it would be if schizophrenia were proportionately distributed in this class, and that it is two and one-half times as high in class V as we might expect on the basis of proportional distribution, gives further support to Hypothesis II. The fact that the Index of Prevalence is 11.2 times as great in class V as in class I is particularly impressive.

Hypothesis III stipulated that the type of psychiatric treatment a patient receives is associated with his position in the class structure. A test of this hypothesis involves a comparison of the different types of therapy being used by psychiatrists on patients in the different social classes. We encountered many forms of therapy but they may be grouped under three main types; psychotherapy, organic therapy, and custodial care. The patient population, from the viewpoint of the principal type of therapy received, was divided roughly into three categories: 32.0 per cent received some type of psychotherapy; 31.7 per cent received organic treatments of one kind or another; and 36.3 per cent received custodial care without treatment. The percentage of persons who received no treatment care was greatest in the lower classes. The same finding applies to organic treatment. Psychotherapy, on the other hand, was concentrated in the higher classes. Within the psychotherapy category there were sharp differences between the types of psychotherapy administered to the several classes. For example, psychoanalysis was limited to classes I and II. Patients in class V who received any psychotherapy were treated by group methods in the state hospitals. The number and percentage of patients who received each type of therapy is given in Table 4. The data clearly support Hypothesis III.

At the moment we do not have data available for a test of Hypotheses IV and V. These will be put to a test as soon as we complete work on a series of cases now under close study. Preliminary materials give us the impression that they too will be confirmed.

TABLE 4

Distribution of the Principal Types of Therapy by Social Class*

	Psychotherapy		Organic Therapy		No Treatment	
Social Class	No.	Per cent	No.	Per cent	No.	Per cent
I	14	73.7	2	10.5	3	15.8
II	107	81.7	15	11.4	9	6.9
III	136	52.7	74	28.7	48	18.6
IV	237	31.1	288	37.1	242	31.8
V	115	16.1	234	32.7	367	51.2

*Chi square=336.58, P less than .001.

CONCLUSIONS AND INTERPRETATIONS

This study was designed to throw new light upon the question of how mental illness is related to social environment. It approached this problem from the perspective of social class to determine if an individual's position in the social system was associated significantly with the development of psychiatric disorders. It proceeded on the theoretical assumption that if mental illnesses were distributed randomly in the population, the hypotheses designed to test the idea that psychiatric disorders are connected in some functional way to the class system would not be found to be statistically significant.

The data we have assembled demonstrate conclusively that mental illness, as measured by diagnosed prevalence, is not distributed randomly in the population of the New Haven community. On the contrary, psychiatric difficulties of so serious a nature that they reach the attention of a psychiatrist are unequally distributed among the five social classes. In addition, types of psychiatric disorders, and the ways patients are treated, are strongly associated with social class position.

The statistical tests of our hypotheses indicate that there are definite connections between particular types of social environments in which people live, as measured by the social class concept, and the emergence of particular kinds of psychiatric disorders, as measured by psychiatric diagnosis. They do not tell us what these connections are, nor how they are functionally related to a particular type of mental illness in a given individual. The next step, we believe, is to turn from the strictly statistical approach to an intensive study of the social environments associated with particular social classes, on the one hand, and of individuals in these environments who do or do not develop mental illnesses, on the other hand. Currently the research team is engaged in this next step but is not yet ready to make a formal report of its findings.

REFERENCES

Braatoy, T. Is it probable that the sociological situation is a factor in schizophrenia? *Psychiatrica et Neurologica*, 1937, **12**, 109–138.

Davie, M. R. The pattern of urban growth. In O. P. Murdock (ed.), *Studies in the science of society*. New Haven: Yale University Press, 1937, 133–162.

Dunham, H. W. Current status of ecological research in mental disorder, *Soc. Forces*, 1947, **25**, 321–326.

Faris, R. E. L. Cultural isolation and the schizophrenic personality, *Amer. J. Sociol.*, 1934, **39**, 155–169.

Faris, R. E. L. Reflections of social disorganization in the behavior of a schizophrenic patient, *Amer. J. Sociol.*, 1944, **50**, 131–141.

Faris, R. E. L. and H. W. Dunham. *Mental disorders in urban areas.* Chicago: University of Chicago Press, 1939.

Felix, R. H. and R. V. Bowers. Mental hygiene and socio-environmental factors, *The Milbank Memorial Fund Quarterly,* 1948, **26,** 125–147.

Gerard, D. L. and J. Siegel, The family background of schizophrenia, *Psychiat. Quart.,* 1950, **24,** 47–73.

Hollingshead, A. B. and F. C. Redlich. *Social class and mental illness: A community study.* New York: John Wiley & Sons, Inc., 1958.

Hyde, R. W. and L. V. Kingsley. Studies in medical sociology, I: The relation of mental disorders to the community socioeconomic level, *The New England J. Med.,* 1944, **231,** No. 16, 543–548.

Kennedy, J. R. Single or triple melting-pot: Intermarriage trends in New Haven, 1870–1940, *Amer. J. Sociol.,* 1944, **39,** 331–339.

McConnell, J. W. The influence of occupation upon social stratification. Unpublished Ph.D. thesis, Sterling Memorial Library, Yale University, 1937.

Rosanoff, A. J. *Report of a survey of mental disorders in Nassau County, New York.* New York: National Committee for Mental Hygiene, 1916.

Stern, L. *Kulturkreis und Form der Geistigen Erkrankung.* Sammlung Zwanglosen Abshandlungen aus dem Gebiete der Nerven-und-Geiteskrankheiten, 10, No. 2. Halle a. S:C. Marhold, 1913, 1–62.

Sutherland, J. F. Geographical distribution of lunacy in Scotland, *Brit. Assoc. Adv. Sci.* Glasgow, 1901.

Veterans Administration. *Pychiatric disorders and reactions.* Washington, D.C.: Technical Bulletin 10A-78, October 1947.

6-3

Fear and Anxiety as Cultural and Individual Variables in a Primitive Society

A. I. HALLOWELL

Although all the traditional psychoneurotic disorders appear to occur in non-Western cultures, they may differ in form from their counterparts in the West. While traffic phobia seems to be frequent in Western big cities, the frog phobia described by Hallowell is seldom encountered by the Western clinician. Phobias are based on the individual's experience and his contact with the objects of fear in his environment.

In addition to the role of individual experience in the development of fears and anxieties, Hallowell suggests cultural beliefs are important factors in conditioning members of society to fear certain objects. Contrary to Western expectation, the Berens River Indians are not afraid of dangerous animals such as wolves and bears, but of harmless animals like toads and frogs or imaginary creatures like cannibals. The fears of these Indians appear to relate to local beliefs or the cultural meaning of certain stimuli.

Culture does not only define the situations that arouse certain fears and anxieties, but also determines the degree to which responses may be regarded as abnormal. Hallowell points to the difficulty of distinguishing between true neurotic reactions and fears and anxieties sanctioned by the society. This may either make

Abridged from *J. Soc. Psychol.*, 1938, **9**, 25–47, by permission of The Journal Press.

neurotic reactions less noticeable to members of the community itself, or may make the outside observer think that the whole culture is "neurotic." Dr. Hallowell draws our attention to cultural variables that are not given due attention by Western psychologists in the study of psychoneuroses.

The Indians whom I have been studying and whose fears and anxieties I wish to discuss with reference to their native culture, live on the Berens River in Canada. This river rises in Ontario and flows westward, emptying into eastern Lake Winnipeg at approximately 52 deg. N. Lat. There are 900 of these Indians today and they make their living by hunting moose, deer and caribou, by trapping fur bearing animals, and by fishing. Except for a few white traders, trappers and missionaries, there are no white people living in the area which they inhabit. It is still undisturbed bush country, of low elevation; a wilderness of rock, muskeg, and labyrinthine streams and lakes. Travel is by canoe in summer, and by dogsled and snowshoes in winter. The Indians living closest to Lake Winnipeg have been christianized, although they still retain many of their pagan beliefs, while many of those farther inland cling to the old native dogmas with great tenacity. During the course of several summers' field work I have visited all the settlements on the river in order to accumulate as much information as possible on all aspects of their lives.

I think that the relation between some of the characteristic fears experienced by these people and their traditional system of beliefs will become sufficiently clear if I discuss the former with reference to the situations in which they occur. Some of these situations, such as illness, are common to human life everywhere. Yet they do not give rise to equivalent affects. The psychological differentia, I believe, are to be sought in the content of the beliefs that are part of the cultural heritage of these Indians. These beliefs not only define each situation for the individual in a typical manner, they structuralize it emotionally. But at the same time it is interesting to note that there are usually traditional means available for the alleviation of culturally constituted fears. The individual is not altogether left at loose ends; he may obtain some relief and reassurance through the utilization of institutionalized defenses.

A. ENCOUNTERS WITH ANIMALS

The traditional attitude of the Berens River Indians towards animal life must be distinguished from our own. Animals, like men, have a body and a soul. Each species is controlled by a spiritual boss or owner that is of the nature of a transcendental being. Guns and traps are of no avail if this spiritual boss of the species is offended and does not wish human beings to obtain his underlings. Consequently, wild animals as a whole must be treated with respect lest their bosses be offended.

While this general attitude is characteristic, the affective responses of the Indians to different animals is not uniform. It would be impossible, however, to make any a priori judgment, based upon our attitude towards wild life, as to which animals are feared and which are not. Wolves and bears, for instance, are common in this region, but the Indians are never afraid of them. The creatures they fear most are snakes, toads and frogs, animals that are actually among the most harmless in their environment.

What then are the determinants of toad phobia? There are several etiological factors at work: (a) the generalized belief in the malevolent attributes of toads; (b) the notion that their presence in a dwelling was an ill omen; (c) the fact that a taboo had been broken, specifically indicated by the presence of the toads.

In addition, however, there was another factor peculiar to the personal history of individual Indians such as W. B. When a young boy, a toad had crawled up his pants and he had crushed it against his bare skin. This experience would appear to be an important differential factor which may account to some extent for the *exaggerated* fear reactions of W. B. to toads as compared with that of the other Indians. Judged by strength of affect, W. B. was abnormal in comparison with the other Indians observed. But etiologically viewed, his phobia cannot be fully explained by reference to his personal history alone. It needs to be related to the native beliefs in regard to toads and the situational factors already mentioned. The generalized fear of toads and frogs among these Indians is fostered by another fact. Monster species are reputed still to inhabit the country, the tracks of which are sometimes seen. If we take these factors into account, they evidenced a normal response to a danger situation as defined for them in cultural terms.

B. DISEASE SITUATIONS

Since disease situations occur and recur among all peoples, they provide excellent material for the investigation of the cultural differentia that may influence the individual's attitude towards his own illness and the quality of the anxieties that his relatives and friends may experience. Different human groups have different traditional theories of disease causation and when an indvidual falls ill, his emotional attitudes and those of his associates are intimately related to the theories held.

Among the Berens River Indians, broken limbs, colds, constipation, toothache and other minor ailments are considered fortuitous in origin and do not arouse any marked affective states. But a prolonged illness, which has not responded to ordinary methods of treatment, a sudden illness, or one that is characterized by symptoms that are considered in any way peculiar, arouses apprehension or even fear. Why? Because of the belief that the person may have been bewitched. The individual believes that some one is trying to kill him. He becomes more and more worried and begins to reflect on his past activities and associations in order to recollect who it is that may wish him out of the way. In such a situation institutionalized means of protection are readily available. A conjurer or seer may be hired to discover the person responsible and measures taken to counteract the evil influence. Jealousy is often the motive attributed to the witch, frequently arising out of rivalry situations.

The special form of sorcery that causes the most fear is based on the theory that material objects can be magically projected into the body of the victim. Sebaceous cysts, lumps of any kind, and other symptoms are evidence of the presence of such objects. They are removable by a pseudo-surgical technique in which certain medicine men specialize. It involves the withdrawal of the object by sucking. These men, of course, produce actual objects that they claim to have removed from their patients' bodies. This serves to allay the latter's fears and in cases where a recovery is made, empirical support is given to the native theory of disease causation. Examples of such disease-causing objects are magic shells, dogs' teeth, bits of metal, stone, etc. One Indian showed me a series of such projectiles that had been "sent" him. His body was strong enough to resist them and they fell at his side where he found them.

Feelings of guilt for past moral transgressions are also the source of apprehension in a disease situation. This is due to the fact that these Indians believe that sickness may be the result of such transgressions. Again it is the fact that an individual does not respond to the usual drug remedies that precipitates apprehension. The transgressions that fall in the panel of traditional sins are murder, incest, deceit, and sexual practices such as masturbation, fellatio, the use of parts of animals as artificial phalli and bestiality. Confession is the necessary preliminary to cure when it is thought that sickness is connected with sin. An interesting aspect of their theory, however, is the belief that such sins on the part of parents may be the source of illness in their children. Consequently the anxieties aroused in disease situations where some trangression is believed to be back of the illness, are not confined to the patient. His parents are likewise suspected and they may confess sins committed in childhood or adolescence. In a series of 15 cases illustrating the transgressions confessed, 12 were those in which sexual sins were involved (Hallowell, 1939).

C. ENCOUNTERS WITH CANNIBALS

The most intense fears the Berens River Indians experience are generated in situations that are emotionally structured by their beliefs concerning *windigow-a-k*, cannibals. They believe that human beings may be transformed into cannibals by sorcery, that cannibal monsters can be created "out of a dream" by a sorcerer and sent into the world to perform malevolent acts and that cannibal giants roam the woods, particularly in the Spring. Consequently, when some human individual is reputed to be turning into a cannibal, the Indians become terror stricken. They are similarly affected when it is reported that a cannibal, created by magic, is approaching their encampment or when some individual travelling in the bush discovers traces of a cannibal or claims that he has seen one.

Gastric symptoms are among those that the Indians interpret as evidence of incipient cannibalism on the part of human beings. When a person refuses to eat ordinary food or is chronically nauseated or cannot retain the food he ingests, suspicion is at once aroused. Even the individual so affected will develop anxiety and make the same inference. He may even ask to be killed at once. For this is the inevitable fate of reputed cannibals according to native custom. Usually they are strangled and their bodies burnt, not buried.

It is not surprising then to discover individuals who claim to have seen the kind of cannibal that is reputed to roam the woods, or to have been pursued by one. Such illusions are particularly interesting in view of the fact that these Indians are expert woodsmen, who not only have spent all their lives in the bush, but are familiar with the detailed topography of their country to an amazing degree, as well as with all the various species of fauna and flora. Consequently it might be expected that the whole gamut of possible sights and sounds would be so well-known to them that they would be insulated against false perception of any kind. I know from personal experience, at least, that many sounds that have startled me from time to time have always been explained by my Indian companions in the most naturalistic manner. It is all the more significant then to discover cases in which the perceptions of individuals have been so thoroughly moulded by traditional dogma that the most intense fears are aroused by objectively innocuous stimuli. It is the culturally derived *Einstellung*, rather than the stimuli themselves, that explains their behavior.

One old man, for instance, narrated the following experience.

> Once in the Spring of the year I was hunting muskrats. The lake was still frozen, only the river was open, but there was lots of ice along the

shore. When it began to get dark I put ashore and made a fire close to the water edge to cook my supper. While I was sitting there I heard someone passing across the river. I could hear the branches cracking. I went to my canoe and jumped in. I paddled as hard as I could to get away from the noise. Where the river got a little wider I came to a point that has lots of poplars growing on it. I was paddling quite a distance from the shore when I came opposite to this point. Just then I heard a sound as if something was passing through the air. A big stick had been thrown out at me but it did not strike me. I kept on going and paddled towards the opposite side of the river. Before I got to that side he was across the river already and heading me off. I paddled towards the other side again. But he went back and headed me off in that direction. This was in the spring of the year when the nights are not so long. He kept after me all night. I was scared to go ashore. Towards morning I reached a place where there is a high rock. I camped there and when it was light I went to set a bear trap. Later that day I came back to the river again. I started out again in my canoe. Late in the evening, after the sun had set, there was a place where I had to portage my canoe over to a lake. I left my canoe and went to see whether the lake was open. There were some open places so I went back to get my canoe. Then I heard him again. I carried my canoe over to the lake—it was a big one—and paddled off as fast as I could. When I got to the other end of the lake it was almost daylight. I did not hear him while I was travelling. I went ashore and made a fire. After this I heard something again. I was scared. "How am I going to get away from him," I thought. I decided to make for the other side of an island in the lake. I was sitting by my canoe and I heard him coming closer. I was mad now. He had chased me long enough. I said to myself, "the number of my days has been given me already." So I picked up my axe and my gun and went in the direction of the sounds I had heard. As soon as I got closer to him he made a break for it. I could hear him crashing through the trees. Between the shore and the island there was a place where the water was not frozen. He was headed in this direction. I kept after him. I could hear him on the weak ice. Then he fell in and I heard a terrific yell. I turned back then and I can't say whether he managed to get out or not. I killed some ducks and went back to my canoe. I was getting pretty weak by this time so I made for a camp I thought was close by. But the people had left. I found out later that they had heard him and were so scared that they moved away.

D. DISCUSSION

In the situations thus far passed in review I have attempted to indicate the cultural constituents of the fears of individuals and the institutionalized means available for their alleviation. In societies with different culture patterns the same situations would be emotionally structured in a different way, the affects of individuals would be qualitatively, if not quantitatively, different and other traditional defenses would be invoked.

To an outsider the fears of the Berens River Indians, and those of other primitive peoples, appear to be "neurotic," in the sense that they occur in situations where no actual danger threatens and for the reason that the sources of some of these fears are of the nature of fantasies. Can we speak then of "cultural neuroses" that are characteristic of whole populations? I think not. If we do so, as Karen Horney (1937) has pointed out, "we should be yielding to an impression based on a lack of understanding" as well as being guilty of a fallacy in reasoning.

In the first place, the Berens River Indian *is* responding to a *real* danger when he flees from a cannibal monster or murders a human being who is turning into a windigo, or when he becomes apprehensive in a certain disease situation. To act or feel otherwise would stamp an individual either as a fool or as a phenomenal example of intellectual emancipation. For, psychologically, the actual order of reality in which human beings live is constituted in a large measure by the traditional concepts and beliefs that are held. Furthermore, the Indians themselves are able to point out plenty of tangible empirical evidence that supports the interpretation of the realities that their culture imposes upon their minds (Hallowell, 1934). They are naive empiricists but not naively irrational.

Once we relegate commonly motivated fears to their proper frame of reference—cultural tradition—a fundamental etiological distinction can be made between fears of this category and those which arise in individuals from conditions primarily relevant to the circumstances of their own personal history. The *genuine* neurotic, in addition to sharing the culturally constituted fears of his fellows, "has fears which in quantity or quality deviate from those of the cultural pattern" (Horney, 1937). Any comparison, then, between the fears and defenses of such individuals and the culturally constituted fears and institutionalized defenses of whole human societies is not only superficial, it is actually misleading, since no account is taken of differences in etiological factors. Primitive peoples are sometimes accused of the logical fallacy that results from an inference that two phenomena are identical if one or more elements are shared in common. To seriously maintain that the culturally constituted fears and defenses of primitive peoples are evidence of "cultural neuroses" which are of the same order as the neurosis of individuals in western civilization, is just such a fallacy. Manifest surface analogies are compared whereas the underlying differences in the dynamic factors that produced them are ignored.

A further differentiation between the genuine neurotic and the person experiencing the "normal" fears of his culture is important. The former is inevitably a suffering individual; the latter is not.

There are individuals among the Berens River Indians, who manifest phobias that are quantitatively or qualitatively deviant from those of the other Indians. These persons are among the genuine neurotics. I have already mentional W. B. whose toad phobia was quantitatively distinguishable from that of the other natives. An example of a phobia which is qualitatively different is that of an Indian who could go nowhere unaccompanied by one or more companions. When alone he would always keep within sight of human habitations or people. This was the rule even when he had to urinate or defecate. If he had to relieve himself at night his wife would always get up and go with him. He rationalized his anxiety by saying that he once dreamed that a jackfish would swallow him, if this creature found him alone.

The manifest behavior of this individual suggests that the causes of anxieties are of a different order than the culturally constituted fears of the general run of the population. In contrast with the latter, the situations that provoke the fears of these individuals are emotionally structured by highly subjective meanings that are personal.

This differentiation, it seems to me, is of general significance. It indicates that a comprehensive account of the determining factors in the affective experience of individuals must include on the one hand an analysis of the influence of cultural patterns and, on the other, an investigation of the factors that determine quantitative or qualitative individual variations from a given cultural norm. In any particular society these two aspects of the problem are inseparable. But in western civilization a great deal of attention has been paid to factors thought to be relevant to individual deviation without reference to the influence of the characteristic culture patterns that mould the ideologies and affects of individuals in a common manner.

In clinical practice, cases have turned up more than once that necessitate an evaluation of such factors. Some years ago a negro committed to a mental hospital and thought to be suffering from private delusions was discovered by a psychiatrist to belong to a local religious cult of which his ideology was characteristic. In another case,

> an elderly Neapolitan cobbler comes to a hospital clinic with a rambling story told in broken English. His account wanders from headaches and listlessness to an old woman who has made him sick. He is referred to the neuro-psychiatric department with the comment: *Question of psychosis.* Examination brings out little more than irrelevant detail about the enemy and how long she has wished him ill, and why, and how she makes his head hurt. There is all the first indication of a persecutory delusion. The man is told to come back with an interpreter. He returns with a fluent Italian-American who explains apologetically that the old man is illiterate and believes the woman is a witch and has cast the evil eye on him. The apparent delusion dissolves into a bit of superstition typical generally of

the lower orders of Neapolitan society. What is a normal belief there is a psychotic symptom in one of our hospitals. If the writer or reader of these lines were to harbor the same conviction as this Neapolitan, it would be prima facie evidence of mental derangement. The norm of one culture is a sign of nervous pathology in the other (Kroeber, 1934).

Hence the necessity of taking the immediate cultural background of the individual into account as a primary frame of reference. It is only through the study of affective experience in a number of different human societies that the rôle of cultural variables can be thoroughly understood. Comparative data of this sort may also indicate that individual deviations themselves take on characteristic forms in different societies. But while the typical conflicts engendered by different cultures may vary and the symptomatology of individuals may reflect the traditions of their society, from an etiological standpoint genuine neurotics will remain comparable in so far as we can account for their behavior in terms of common dynamic processes.

REFERENCES

Hallowell, A. I. Some empirical aspects of northern Saulteaux religion, *Amer. Anthropol.*, 1934, **36**, 389–404.

Hallowell, A. I. Sin, sex, and sickness in Saulteaux belief, *Brit. J. Med. Psychol.*, 1939, **18**, 191–197.

Horney, K. The neurotic personality of our time. New York: W. W. Norton and Co., Inc., 1937.

Kroeber, A. L. Cultural anthropology. In M. Bentley (ed.), *The problems of mental disorder*, National research council. Committee on Psychiatric Investigations, M. Bentley, chairman. New York: McGraw-Hill, 1934.

6-4

The Symtoms of Depression — A Cross-Cultural Survey

H. B. M. MURPHY
E. D. WITTKOWER
N. W. CHANCE

Studies in the epidemiology of mental illness assume that psychiatric syndromes are reliable and valid. The conventional classification of mental illness is thought to be applicable to patients from different social, religious, and cultural backgrounds. This pioneer work in cross-cultural psychiatry reappraises the reliability of the concept of depression across different cultures.

The authors distinguish between primary and secondary symptoms. Primary symptoms that may be basic to depression occur early and constitute the essence of the disorder. Secondary symptoms are regarded as part of the individual's reaction to his illness; they develop because he attempts to come to terms with his changed behavior. Although it is found that some of the primary symptoms of depression are universal, other symptoms are dependent on the social and cultural background of the patient. The authors show that symptoms of depression are not equally important in both the diagnosis and treatment of depressive patients. Furthermore, the syndrome of depression may disguise differences and only emphasize some similarities between patients within or across cultures. This

Revised version of an article entitled "Cross-Cultural Inquiry into the Symptomatology of Depression" in *Transcult. Psychiat. Res. Rev.*, 1964, 1, No. 15, 5–18. Reprinted by permission of the authors.

study suggests the desirability of dealing with specific symptoms in the investigation and management of "depressive" illness taking cultural background into consideration.

Although the method used here is impressionistic and the results may reflect variations in the orientation and cultural background of the respondents to the questionnaire, many of the authors' conclusions have been confirmed by later studies.

The elucidation and understanding of depression has moved surprisingly slowly considering the volume and frequently high quality of writings since Kraepelin. There are numerous good descriptions of small groups of patients, and numerous theories to explain particular features observed. The theoreticians, however, repeatedly insist that there seem to be types of depression to which their theories may not apply, and the clinicians leave us in doubt whether they are describing a single common syndrome or several different ones. Accordingly, we remain uncertain whether depression is a single disease or multiple, and whether different features should be treated as primary or secondary.

Related to this lack of clarity is a different problem, namely whether depression is a disorder to which mankind in general is susceptible or one found in its true form only in certain peoples or cultures. Several serious and unbigoted investigators have suggested that true depression is rare almost to the point of non-existence in some parts of Asia and Africa, but it has been difficult to decide how limited a syndrome they are writing about, and whether a variety of this so-called true depression might not be present in some other guise. Especially it has been suggested that patients may so emphasize the somatic elements of their trouble that the psychiatrist may not be called to see them or if called may choose to regard the condition as neurotic hypochondria rather than as the depression it really is.

To explore the directions in which cross-cultural research might best help with this double problem, the Transcultural Psychiatric Studies section at McGill two years ago proposed to a number of widely scattered psychiatrists a survey of depression symptomatology similar to the survey of schizophrenia symptomatology which the section had previously conducted (Murphy et al., 1963). That is to say, no actual analysis of records was to be made, but each respondent was to give his impressions in a standard form of rating, along with certain other information which would make the interpretation of these impressions easier. The response was good, over a hundred reports being received from over sixty psychiatrists in thirty countries. In an earlier paper the countries covered, the questions asked and the method of rating employed are discussed, along with the first general findings (Murphy et al., 1964). The present paper will deal with three main questions, namely:

Is one form of major depressive illness to be found in all cultures, and if so, what are its basic features?

Are there within this single form discrete symptom clusters to be found irrespective of culture, suggesting different syndromes?

Are the variations in predominant symptomatology between one culture and another random, or can they be linked to basic cultural elements?

THE UNIVERSALITY OF PSYCHOTIC DEPRESSION

The target of the enquiry was intended to be depressive psychosis, as classically described. However, depression is a field where the boundary between the psychoses and the neuroses is most difficult to ascertain, some authorities believing that the division should depend on the detection of reactivity, others that it should depend on reality testing, and still others that a clear division is impossible or has no meaning. For this reason it was decided to focus the enquiry on a particular clinical picture, regardless of whether called psychotic or neurotic, and to ask respondents to restrict their comments as far as possible to that section of their patients exhibiting it. Since the enquiry was to deal with impressions and not with actual patient counts it could not be expected that the restriction would be strictly applied, but it was hoped that this approach would prevent respondents from ranging too widely in their ideas of what was appropriate. The picture chosen comprised the symptoms of

A mood of depression or dejection
Diurnal mood change
Insomnia with early morning waking
Diminution of interest in the social environment.

For only one patient sample was this picture reported to be "very rare", and the comment seems likely to have arisen from a greater strictness of definition than is customary, since reports by the two other psychiatrists on people of the same main culture—Polish—do not agree with it. Elsewhere, from tropical Africa, India, the Near East and other parts of Asia, it seems to be agreed that this form of depression is never either wholly absent or very rare. It can therefore be said that depression does not vary so much from one culture to another that a single syndrome cannot be detected in all.

However, this is not to say that this syndrome is common or is the predominant form of major depression everywhere. In three of the seven reports from India it is noted to be relatively rare, with diurnal mood swings being uncommon, and in two of the six reports from tropical Africa a loss of interest in the social environment is reported to be infrequent. The survey thus supports and augments what has been written from India and from some parts of Africa in the past, suggesting that the common forms of depression found there may not follow the classical pattern, but that, nevertheless, this pattern is still to be found. Since the distribution of secondary symptoms is also unusual in these samples, this probably explains why to some observers it has appeared that true depression was virtually not present at all.

THE BASIC SYMPTOMS

Since the great majority of reports indicate that the commonest form of major depressive illness in the studied culture is one which includes all four of the prescribed symptoms, it can reasonably be assumed that these comprise basic or primary symptoms. The one item on which there was some doubt was mood swings, but this is a symptom which patients may not report spontaneously and, with the aforementioned exception of India, its absence is more associated with individual psychiatrists than individual cultures. It seems probable, therefore, that it will usually be present where patients are sufficiently self-observing and sufficiently communicative to note and report it.

Of the twenty-three other symptoms specifically enquired about, there were four which merited consideration as basic symptoms, the grounds for this being that they were nearly always noted to be usual or frequent. They are despondency, fatigue, loss of weight and loss of sexual interest.

Regarding *fatigue,* there were eight reports mentioning it as being only occasionally found, but in most of these instances other reports on the same culture disagreed, and it seemed likely that the respondents involved were mentally comparing the sample with another in which the complaint was much more striking, or that they had unusually strict criteria for assessing its presence. For instance, three out of the nine reports from Brazil mention fatigue as only occasionally found, but these three reports come all from the same psychiatrist. Again, one of the reports from Greece mentions its low frequency, but reports on other Greek subcultures or social strata by the same respondent rated it as usual or frequent. It seems highly likely, therefore, that fatigue is a primary symptom for this syndrome, and that some degree of fatigue is virtually always to be found.

With despondency, weight loss and loss of sexual interest the picture is a little different, since there are indications that in certain cultural settings one or the other of them may be uncommon or at least be infrequently reported. Thus, although there are only eleven reports where *weight loss* is rated as less than frequent, three out of the four reports from Scandinavia (each by a different psychiatrist) are included in these eleven. It would seem, therefore, that in Scandinavia weight loss is not a regular symptom of psychotic depression and that in some way the Scandinavian cultures induce depressives to maintain normal eating, even though everywhere else weight loss seems routine. (The other samples for which weight loss is reported as only occasional are 1 Polish, 1 Greek, 1 Indian, 1 U.S. Negro, 1 West African and 2 Japanese.) Regarding *despondency*, there are only six reports indicating this to be less than frequent, but four of these six come from tropical Africa, and this does not seem to be a coincidence. Although one meets in the literature on West African mental disorders many descriptions of despondency associated with 'bewitchment', 'magical fright' and similar reactive states, that same literature suggests that hopelessness is not an obvious accompaniment of more conventional depressive syndromes, as it undoubtedly is in Europe. In particular, a reading of the depression case histories supplied by Field (1960) in her book *Search for Security* suggests that hope of cure or assistance usually persists. Whether despondency is to be treated as an invariable symptom or as a variable one allied to secondary guilt feelings must therefore remain in doubt.

Loss of sexual interest, the fourth of the symptoms meriting consideration as primary here, must similarly remain doubtful on the grounds that although only eight reports suggested that it was less than 'frequent' in particular patient samples, three of these reports relate to Japanese samples and none of the remaining six reports from Japan suggest that this symptom is 'usual' among them. Since seven out of the nine Japanese reports also indicate that amenorrhoea is a rare or only occasional symptom, the primary involvement of sexual functions in the depressive process must be held in doubt despite the frequency with which it appears as a symptom in other peoples.

The basic symptoms of the particular depressive syndrome studied must therefore be taken as depressive mood, fatigue, insomnia and loss of interest in the social environment, with diurnal mood swings as a probable fifth. Weight loss, despondency and diminution of sexual interest may prove to be primary symptoms also, but a decision on this must await their investigation in the particular cultures mentioned. All of the remaining symptoms enquired about vary so much from one reported sample to another that they cannot be considered to be essential features of psychotic depression as it was conceived for this survey, though they may be essential features of some secondary cluster or syndrome. This conclusion is not all original, being similar to those arrived at in many earlier clinical studies. Its discovery here, however, may add weight to the argument that any search for the origin of depression should focus on these basic features and not on the more dramatic features of self-accusation, hypochondria, preoccupation with poverty, etc. Investigation of the latter symptoms can certainly be valuable in elucidating the secondary processes in depression, but insofar as psychotic depression can frequently occur without these symptoms, they cannot be assumed to be part of the primary process.

SECONDARY CLUSTERS

Regarding these further symptoms, the second question to which this paper was addressed was stated to be whether they could be recognized to form stable clusters irrespective of culture. If this were so, and more especially if such clusters could be demonstrated to vary inversely with each other, then one could infer that definite secondary syndromes existed, possibly as alternative reactions to the basic process.

There are two methods whereby such secondary clusters can be investigated in the present material. One is to take the descriptions or patterns reported by earlier workers and see to what extent they predominate or at least are discernable in the global impressions which the reports represent; the other is to factor analyse the reports themselves and see what patterns they yield. In either instance it is going to be difficult to say anything positive about syndromes which do not predominate in any people, but something can still be learnt from the associations that occur most often.

Full factor analysis did not seem justified for the present and would have required a computer to push the completion. The total ratings for each symptom, however, were correlated with those for each other, and the resultant distribution was tested to see whether it was outside chance expectation. Figure 1 gives the results, with the symptoms so arranged as to make the presence of clusters obvious.

It can be seen that most of the associations fall into three clear groups, labelled here, for want of better terms, intrapsychic, somatic and expressive. One symptom, self-neglect, is found in association with all three; one other, anxiety, has almost no associations at all; and four more are too weakly attached to be attributed to any. The memberships of each of the three clusters are interesting, however, and as much for what they exclude as for what they include. For instance, *thought retardation*, which one might have expected to be associated with all three, like self-neglect, correlates strongly only with the self-depreciatory, intrapuni-

	Intrapsychic								Somatic											Expressive			
	1	2	3	4	5	6	7	8	9	10	11	12	13	14	15	16	17	18	19	20	21	22	23
1. Self depreciation	—	**	**	**	**	**	**	**					*										
2. Self accusations	**	—	**	*	**	**	**	**													*		
3. Feelings of guilt	**	**	—	*	—	**	**	*		**		*											
4. Suicidal tendencies	**	*	*	—	**	**	*	*											*				
5. Thought retardation	**	**	*	**	—	**	*	**	*														
6. Despondency, hopelessness	**	**	**	*	**	—	**	**				*				**					*		
7. Expectation of punishment	**	**	**		*	**	—	**	**	*											*		*
8. Self neglect	**	**	*		**	**	**	—		*		**	**			**		**			**	**	
9. Preoccupation with Poverty					*	**			—			*		*									*
10. Preoccupation with Religion			**					*		—								*	**				
11. Somatic preoccupation	*					*					—	—						*					
12. Loss of weight									*		—	—	**	**	**	*							**
13. Anorexia											**	**	—	—	**	*	**						**
14. Constipation											*	**	**	—	—			**					
15. Amenorrhoea									*			**	**	**	—			**					

	Intrapsychic									Somatic								Expressive					
	1	2	3	4	5	6	7	8	9	10	11	12	13	14	15	16	17	18	19	20	21	22	23
16. Fatigue						**		**				*	*		**	—	*						
17. Loss of sexual interest													**			*	—						
18. Ideas of influence					*			**		*	**				**			—	—	**	**	**	
19. Agitation										**									—	**	*	*	
20. Excitement																		**	*	—	**	**	
21. Theatricality of grief			*				*	**										**	*	**	—	**	
22. Semi-mutism, semi-stupor								**										**		**	**	—	
23. Anxiety							*		*				**										—

Level of significance: ** = beyond 0.01; * = 0.05–0.01.

Figure 1. Intercorrelations between investigated symptoms of *depressive psychosis*.

tive group. *Preoccupation with poverty*, on the other hand, is not significantly associated with self-depreciation or with feelings of guilt, but only with expectations of punishment. *Semi-mutism* or semi-stupor, which one might have expected to develop as the extreme picture of thought retardation, proves to correlate not with the latter but with excitement and the expressive group, as though it were an active gesture of the catatonic type rather than the end result of reduced activity. One must keep in mind that the data here represent impressions of whole groups, not of individual patients, but since the groups represent a vastly wider sampling of patients than any other study on depression has attempted, the correlations found here deserve attention.

It might be expected that such clear groupings of symptoms would represent recognisably distinct syndromes, perhaps negatively associated, but this does not appear to be the case. There were no negative correlations of significant strength between any two symptoms, and no groups of associated samples where the one cluster of symptoms were rated uniformly frequent and the other clusters uniformly infrequent. There are, of course, cultures where a majority of one cluster would be rated high and a majority of the other clusters' members rated low, but there are always too many symptoms not following their cluster for any simple theory of alternative channels of secondary process development to be plausible. Single symptoms appear to derive from more than one line of development, insofar as the majority picture in different samples is concerned, and it cannot be said this method of analysis has yielded distinct secondary syndrome complexes which could be taken as independent of cultural setting.

The second method of searching for symptom clusters has not yielded distinct, transcultural, syndromes either, but has nevertheless been instructive. The two studies which appeared best to provide likely patterns for such an approach were the factor analysis ones of Grinker et al. (1961) in Chicago, and of Hamilton (1960) in Leeds, England. Each had yielded four patterns or factors, and their quantitative analyses made it possible to assess how much weight to give to different symptoms. As might be expected from the bias built into the present survey, the more reactive patterns or syndromes described from each location find no reflection in the present material, but three potential syndromes, one from Leeds and two from Chicago, did turn up when searched for. The most widespread of these, the Chicago pattern "A," was approximated to sufficiently often to lead one to think that it was universal, had it not failed to be reflected in any of the fourteen reports on Moslem and on African Negro samples. This lack of reflection does not mean, of course, that pattern "A" does not occur in the latter groups, but it does suggest that something in Moslem and in Tropical African cultures may interfere with the development of the relevant constellation of secondary symptoms.

The other two patterns or factors were not widespread at all, but proved to be reflected best from the very areas from which the two papers derived. Factor 2 in the Leeds study proved to be more closely approached by the two reports stemming from Britain than by reports from anywhere else. Pattern "B" of the Chicago study was reflected rather more widely, but a majority of the reports coming closest to it derived from the U.S. Middle West, and only one of the eight reports from that region did not reflect it. These correspondences between the impressions of the present survey's informants and the much more strict symptom counts and analyses of researchers from the same societies are gratifying, but they do not give support to the belief that a study of depression in one society is likely to be valid for others. As was noted earlier, there are certain symptoms of what may be called psychotic depression which seem world-wide; but beyond these few symptoms it would appear that the picture of at least certain types of depression can be quite local. The question now can be asked whether these local pictures are related to cultural differences, derive from differing conditions of psychiatric referral and examination, or follow no logical distribution.

CULTURE PATTERNS

Some variation of symptomatology with local setting is to be expected, if from nothing more than differences in the psychiatrist's role and work load. One would hardly expect the same symptoms to be reported by a foreign doctor in an overcrowded African clinic as by a Boston analyst from his leisurely upper-class practice. And, without variation in setting, differences in reported symptoms are to be expected according to what individual psychiatrists choose to ask, to emphasise, to remember. The question must therefore be whether the main differences reported relate to differences in psychiatric practice, or whether they exist under conditions of relative equality of patient contact, and to an extent which over-rides the personal factor.

In the present material the importance of conditions of interview is, as far as could be analysed, less than expected (Murphy et al., 1964) whereas differences associated with culture are quite great. The strongest demonstration of the latter comes from Brazil and is related more to social class than to culture, although the two concepts overlap there. Nine reports were received from five psychiatrists in that country, and it so happened that there were three concerning mainly upper class patients, three concerning mainly middle, and three mainly lower. These nine reports, sent independently, show agreement regarding the directions in which depression differs in the three classes, for no fewer than thirteen of the twenty-three symptoms explored (Table 1). There can be little doubt, therefore, that the different social classes in that country present different pictures of depression, and that these differences arise not merely from economic disparity but from cultural traditions and outlook. However, it is difficult for the outsider to sense what these differences in cultural tradition are, and an easier illustration to follow relates to North-western Europe. Figure 2 shows the profiles reported for French, German, Polish and Scandinavian patients as respects certain symptoms. Each profile is derived from the averaged ratings of at least

TABLE 1

Relative frequency of different symptoms for depressive psychosis, in three social classes in Brazil*

BRAZIL	Socio-Economic Stratum		
	Upper	Middle	Lower
(Number of reports)	(3)	(3)	(3)
A. Symptoms predominating in Upper Class patients			
1. Suicidal tendencies	10	6	6
2. Feelings of guilt	16	8	10
3. Anxiety	18	14	12
B. Symptoms predominating in Upper and Middle Class patients			
4. Self-depreciation	14	14	8
5. Preoccupation with poverty	12	14	8
C. Symptoms predominating in Lower Class patients			
6. Ideas of influence	0	0	6
7. Excitement	2	2	6
8. Theatricality of grief	6	4	10
9. Semi-mutism or semi-stupor	4	6	8
10. Agitation	4	4	8
11. Preoccupation with religion	6	8	10
12. Somatic preoccupation	12	14	16
13. Self neglect	4	12	14

*The differences shown here apply only to Brazil and should not be taken as operating regardless of culture. In Colombia, similar differences are reported but in other parts of the world the total pattern is not followed.

The relative indices were obtained by giving a score of 6 for "usual," 4 for "frequent," 2 for "occasional," and 0 for "rare," and adding the three ratings for each social class.

three psychiatrists working independently of each other and sometimes in considerably different settings. For instance, the reports on the French samples came from Paris, Marseilles, Algiers and Canada. There was, nevertheless, considerable agreement regarding the relative frequency of different symptoms in groups of patients of the same culture and, as one can see, there are considerable differences in the resultant profiles. Some of these differences may arise from problems of semantics, but the Brazil illustration has shown that that cannot be a sufficient explanation. The question now arises whether these cultural differences in symptom pattern can in any way be made meaningful and thence contribute to our understanding of the means by which they arise.

There are two main approaches which can be taken to the problem of the origin and meaning of depressive patterns in different cultures. One is to consider the cultures individually in the hope of matching their symptomatology to basic elements in their life pattern. The other is to investigate whether the variations shown by a particular symptom across various cultures is paralleled by variations in some type of cultural

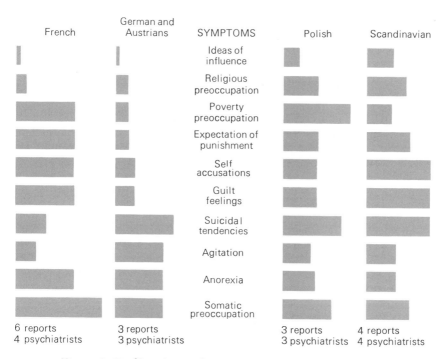

French	German and Austrians	SYMPTOMS	Polish	Scandinavian
		Ideas of influence		
		Religious preoccupation		
		Poverty preoccupation		
		Expectation of punishment		
		Self accusations		
		Guilt feelings		
		Suicidal tendencies		
		Agitation		
		Anorexia		
		Somatic preoccupation		
6 reports 4 psychiatrists	3 reports 3 psychiatrists		3 reports 3 psychiatrists	4 reports 4 psychiatrists

Figure 2. Profiles of French, German, Polish and Scandinavian patient samples as respects certain symptoms. (Profiles were prepared by giving regardless of culture. In Colombia, similar differences are reported, but in other quent," 2 for "occasional," and 0 for "rare," and adding the three ratings for each the results.)

orientation. The first is the easier but the less convincing. Numerous possibilities for it exist within the present material, but it will be sufficient to illustrate it with two cultures already mentioned, the French and the Japanese.

The striking features of the French depression profile given in Figure 2 were the routine presence of somatic preoccupation or hypochondria and the unusually low levels of agitation and suicidal tendencies. The somatic emphasis is paralleled in other fields of French psychiatry, and one could argue that it stems from the French mother's notable concern about her child's body and especially from her concern about his feeding. Françoise Dolto's comment on the latter suggests a clear association with depression, though not necessarily a one way connection only. She says, "During his first years the French child *must* eat. If he refuses nourishment (which in the countryside includes wine, cabbage and alcohol from the first months on) his mother gets depressed" (Dolto, 1955). We are also told regarding French childhood, however, that spontaneous expression and rebelliousness are strongly suppressed, so that many French children exhibit a "subdued, almost resigned attitude" in such matters as their play and artistic production (Wolfenstein, 1955). This restraint is lifted when the child becomes adult and is not merely permitted but is expected to rebel, but if one envisages the psychotic depressive patient as regressed, then the relative infrequency of expressive, communicative symptoms such as agitation and the suicidal gesture might be interpreted as a reflection of the repressed French childhood. The combination of high somaticity and low expressivity is not a common one, according to the present survey, and its presence in the overall impression yielded by French depressives to our respondents is therefore the more interesting.

There were six reports from four psychiatrists regarding French samples. There were nine reports by eight psychiatrists regarding Japanese samples. The Japanese picture is thus seen through many eyes, and there is unusual unanimity in the rating of many symptoms. In addition to the sexual function symptoms mentioned earlier, the reports suggest that excitement, theatricality of grief, religious preoccupation and agitation are relatively infrequent, while despondency and thought retardation are unusually common. There are thus sufficient features to seek explanation for. The simplest is the relative absence of expressive symptoms (with the possible exception of suicidal tendencies, about which the reports are in strong disagreement) since the submission which is expected of Japanese children from a very early age is still stronger than that expected of French children, and the same argument as with the French can apply. The most interesting feature, however, is the relative infrequency of sexual disinterest and dysfunction, since this is virtually the only culture from which this has been generally reported.

The most obvious explanation to come to mind is that the sexual role is in some way less important for personal expression and social intercourse in Japanese culture than it is elsewhere, being not repressed but merely devalued. This concept receives considerable support from the literature on the Japanese family. Caudill and Doi (1963), for instance, have noted that the intense, almost symbiotic, relationship between mother and child leads to a de-emphasis on the sexual gratifications which that relationship cannot provide and an emphasis on other forms of intimate pleasure-giving contacts. Provided the male child avoids any hint of a direct sexual claim on his mother, she remains his for as long as he desires, and the father arouses few oedipal rivalries since he is no threat to this attachment. Accordingly, these authors conclude that Japanese family life places major emotional emphasis on the "non-sexual satisfactions to be derived from every-day events (. . . such as . . .) sympathetic concern and care for the sick, pleasure in bathing in the company of others" (Caudill and Doi, 1963). Sexual intercourse, while completely sanctioned in itself, is kept outside this area of social warmth lest it reduce the simple pleasures obtained. Hence insofar as the problem of depression lies either in the area of emotional needs and supply or in that of self-esteem, it seems possible that sexual feeling would be less involved in Japanese culture than in most others.

On first hearing, explanations such as these may strike one as highly plausible, but to the careful researcher they are both unsatisfying and suspect. They are exceedingly difficult to prove, and as discussions of national character are notorious battlegrounds he knows that if he hunted long enough he could probably find quotations to support any hypothesis he could devise, however improbable. Until some method of objectively testing such hypotheses is found, therefore, explanations like the foregoing must be regarded as exceedingly tentative.

Explanations derived by following a single trait across many cultures would be much more satisfactory, could this only be effected, for they would avoid both the arbitrary character of the foregoing type, and the problems of priority which beset culture and personality studies such as the classic work of Whiting and Child (1953) or that of Kiev (1960). The latter have the difficulty of deciding whether the personality variable or the cultural one is the more basic, whereas the social psychiatrist knows that symptoms of an infrequent disease are not likely to affect cultural traditions. Unfortunately, however, the cultures covered by surveys such as the present one are more modern, more complex, and have more conflicting statements written about them than do those included in Murdock's Human Relations Area Files, on which Whiting and Child depended. Rating single traits is thus more difficult, and may be impossible and ambiguous for many of the so-called cultural samples on which psychiatric reports are available. Nevertheless, the approach can be demonstrated with respect to the important symptoms of self-depreciation and guilt.

These symptoms, and the intrapunitiveness which they seem to imply, have sometimes been considered basic to depression, and many dynamic theories of the disease depend on them. Yet it is known that there are major depressive syndromes in which no direct evidence of intrapunitiveness can be found. Sometimes these latter syndromes are considered to have a different genesis; sometimes they are believed to arise from denial or displacement of the basic intrapunitive process. It is therefore appropriate to ask in a survey such as this whether guilt feelings and self-depreciation are found least in those cultures in which denial and displacement could be expected to be most strongly indoctrinated, or whether they correlate with some other variable.

The present survey offers no support for the theory that self-depreciation is least associated with depression in societies that appear to lead their children through a phase of intrapunitiveness and on to extrapunitiveness or somatic dissociation; for such societies appear to be rare. Nor is there, to the writer's knowledge, clinical evidence to suggest that in societies where self-depreciation in depression is infrequent, probing uncovers this symptom as the cause of the more somatic or expressive ones. On the contrary, there is some evidence in African literature to suggest that the primitive secondary development in depression is projective, with introjection developing later. However, there is in this survey clear evidence that self-depreciation and guilt are associated with a different variable, namely religion, a variable which had been specifically inquired about.

In Table 2 it can be seen that both these symptoms are most common in patients from devout Christian communities, less common in Christian communities where religious belief and involvement is weaker, still less in non-Christian populations where religious involvement was casual or mixed, and least of all in non-Christian populations where the attitude was devout. At the one extreme, feelings of guilt were *never* reported as usual in the ten samples of patients from devout *non*-Christian communities, and in seven of these the symptom was reported as only occasional or even rare. At the other extreme, feelings of guilt *were* reported as usual in eight of the twelve samples from devout Roman Catholic communities, and in none of the twelve were they less than frequent. It is unclear from the data whether the association is truly with Christian belief or with modern European civilization, and it is also unclear whether it is likely to reflect the same influence as was reported for delusions of persecution in schizophrenics. In that previous study it was concluded that the frequency of such delusions "increases in step with the guilt-evoking character of the religions" (Murphy et al., 1963), and one would expect the same to apply to guilt feelings in depressives.

TABLE 2

Variations in Frequency of Guilt Feelings as Related to
Religious Involvement

	Roman Catholic		Other Christian		Moslem & Hindu		Other excluded mixed groups*		
	Devout	Other	Devout	Other	Devout	Other	Devout	Mixed	Non-rel.
Guilt feelings									
Usual	8	4	4	5	0	1	0	2	0
Frequent	4	7	3	8	2	3	0	6	3
Occasional, rare	0	8	0	4	4	5	3	3	0
Self-depreciation									
Usual	8	3	6	5	0	3	0	8	0
Frequent	4	11	0	4	4	4	1	2	3
Occasional, rare	0	6	1	8	3	1	2	2	0

*Samples which were predominantly Buddhist, Shintoist, Confucian, Hebrew, Pagan.

The data, however, do not at this time permit so clear a separation of different religious groups for the conclusion to be drawn. What is clear is that psychotic depression, as defined for this survey, is not basically associated with intrapunitive processes, and that the latter are probably a secondary feature of the disease, deriving as much from cultural emphasis on introjection as from the basic disease process itself.

CONCLUSIONS

The results of this survey, even though based only on impressions, are fairly clear. On the one hand there would appear to be a basic depressive disorder, here called psychotic, which is present and exhibits the same few primary symptoms in all cultures. This is not to say that it occurs with equal frequency in all cultures, and there are indications that it may be relatively rare in some; but it is to say that the basic disease process is probably not culturally determined. On the other hand, the majority of symptoms of depression, including some often considered basic, like thought retardation and self-depreciation, do appear to be culturally determined to a great extent. The distinction should be useful, because the reactions which a disease elicits sometimes outlast the original disorder and are more crippling than it ever was, so that there is an advantage in distinguishing the treatment of the one from the treatment of the other. Regarding the treatment and elucidation of the basic process, the present findings suggest that research can be pursued anywhere, and that a treatment successful in one culture should be successful in another. Regarding the treatment and elucidation of the secondary processes, however, the fact that symptom constellations change with culture suggests that their causes may likewise change, and hence that therapy appropriate in one setting may not be appropriate in another. This is already known, of course, just as it is known that in psychotherapy what succeeds with one patient must not blindly be applied to the next, but it may be an advance to emphasise that cultural background is likely to be important in deciding what technique to choose.

Regarding the causes of different symptoms, the survey has offered two main pointers. The first is the association between the intrapunitive features of depression and communal (not necessarily individual) belief in Christian teachings. What aspect of these teachings is involved, how far it is found in other traditions such as the Hebrew, to what extent it is basic to the religion and to what extent incidental is all unknown. Obviously, however, there is need for an exploration of the concepts of introjection, the superego and intrapunitiveness in suitable subjects from outside the Christian sphere. The second pointer lies in the associations and absence of associations illustrated in Figure 1; the fact that thought retardation, for instance, seems so much more frequently associated with the intrapunitive group of symptoms than with any others. There is every likelihood that such secondary symptoms can arise by more than one channel, but these associations may give a clue to common lines of development. For the rest, the differences in the symptom profiles from different cultures can obviously give food for thought, and there may be the possibility of associating individual symptoms with individual culture traits as in the case of guilt and religion. The former, however, should be viewed with caution until means of controlling and testing tempting hypotheses are better developed.

REFERENCES

Caudill, W. and L. Takeo Doi. Interrelations of psychiatry, culture and emotion in Japan. 1963, 51 pp. Mimeo.

Dolto, F. French and American children as seen by a French child analyst. In M. Mead and M. Wolfenstein (eds.), *Childhood in contemporary cultures*. Chicago: University of Chicago Press, 1955.

Field, M. J. *Search for security: An ethno-psychiatric study of rural Ghana*. Evanston, Ill.: Northwestern University Press, 1960.

Grinker, R. R., et al. *The phenomena of depression*. New York: Paul B. Hoeber, Inc., 1961.

Hamilton, M. A rating scale for depression, *J. Neurol. Neurosurg. Psychiat.*, 1960, **23**, 56–62.

Kiev, A. Primitive therapy; a cross-cultural study of the relationship between child training and therapeutic practices related to illness. In W. Muensterberger and S. Axelrad (eds.), *Psychoanalytic study of society*. Vol. I. International University, Inc., 1960.

Murphy, H. B. M., E. D. Wittkower and N. W. Chance. A cross cultural survey of schizophrenic symptomatology, *Int. J. Soc. Psychiat.*, 1963, **9**, 237–249.

Murphy, H. B. M., E. D. Wittkower and N. W. Chance. Cross-cultural inquiry into the symptomatology of depression; a preliminary report. *Transcult. Psychiat. Res. Rev.*, 1964, **1**, 5–18.

Whiting, J. W. M. and I. L. Child. *Child training and personality; a cross-cultural study*. New Haven, Conn.: Yale University Press, 1953.

Wolfenstein, M. French children's paintings. In M. Mead and M. Wolfenstein (eds.), *Childhood in contemporary cultures*. Chicago: University of Chicago Press, 1955.

6-5

Cross-Cultural Studies
of Symptomatology
in Schizophrenia

IHSAN AL-ISSA

The present review shows that the global concept of schizophrenia, as in the case of depression, encompasses behaviors and symptoms so differently described and manifested within as well as across cultures that it is difficult to call this concept schizophrenia at all. The author, accordingly, suggests that it would be more useful to concentrate on the study of specific responses and symptoms that are measurable transculturally. Responses and symptoms that are minimally influenced by culture (e.g., physiological responses, cognitive symptoms) may be taken as a baseline for the study of the interaction between different cultural variables on the development of abnormal behavior. The present paper as well as Selection 6–4 on depression highlights the unreliability of the present psychiatric classification system in the study of socio-cultural variations of mental illness.

Another topic discussed by the author of the present selection is the use of projective techniques as diagnostic tools of schizophrenia and abnormal behavior. The Rorschach Ink-Blot Test and the Thematic Apperception Test (TAT) are the most widely used techniques for the assessment of normal and abnormal personality.

Reprinted from *Canad. Psychiat. Assoc. J.*, 1968, 13, 147–158, by permission of the Canadian Psychiatric Association.

The Rorschach test consists of ten ink blots for each of which the subject is asked to tell what he sees or what the ink blot might be. His perception of the blot is assumed to reveal some inner personality trends. The present paper shows that the validity of a relationship between modes of perception of ink blots and personality seems to be doubtful when the Rorschach is applied to groups other than Europeans and Americans. Even if the Rorschach proves valid for Europeans and Americans, it should not be assumed that it is valid in other cultures. Concepts and terms used in the interpretation of the Rorschach are very much saturated with psychopathological implications. The alleged relationship between the Rorschach scores and abnormal behavior is mainly based on a theoretical rather than empirical approach. It is, therefore, not surprising to find in the studies conducted by anthropologists and psychologists that pre-literate societies appear abnormal. The same criticism applies to the TAT of Henry A. Murray. This test consists of thirty pictures and one blank card. These stimuli are more structured than the Rorschach ink blots and they mostly involve people in various situations. The individual is asked to tell a story about each card. Here, again, the validity of this test in diagnosis is questionable. Personality judgement based on the TAT or the Rorschach is often contaminated by the knowledge of the cultural background of the subject being tested. In general there is a paucity of well executed studies to validate these projective techniques. A detailed discussion of the use of projective techniques in cross-cultural research is provided by Lindzey (1961). It should, however, be noted that projective techniques are found useful when the researcher is investigating a specific hypothesis, using an objective system of scoring. The use of the TAT by Ervin in Selection 5–5 and by McClelland and his associates in the study of the achievement motive are both included in this category.

REFERENCES

Lindzey, G. *Projective techniques and cross-cultural research.* New York: Appleton-Century-Crofts, 1961.

Recently, there has been an increasing interest in the cross-cultural study of symptomatology in schizophrenia. A major aim of these studies has been to throw some light on basic processes or general principles pertaining to the aetiology and prognosis of schizophrenia as known in the West. It is thought that variations in the incidence and symptomatology of schizophrenia may give some indication of social and cultural factors contributing to the prevalence of schizophrenia in certain societies. Implicit in most of these studies is the view that some cultures are more stressful than others and cultural pressures and stresses may differentially dispose individuals towards schizophrenia. For instance, the early claims that schizophrenia is non-existent in some non-Western cultures (Lopez, 1932; Dhunjiboy, 1930) gave rise to the speculation that the incidence of schizophrenia may be attributed to the complexity of Western culture (Devereux, 1934). Although later studies have shown that the incidence of schizophrenia is almost universal (Wittkower and Rin, 1965) there is a good deal of evidence that symptoms of schizophrenia might occur with different frequencies or constellate into different patterns in various cultures. Since socio-cultural factors in the epidemiology of schizophrenia have been adequately reviewed by Mishler and Scotch (1963), the present paper will be devoted primarily to cultural variations of schizophrenic symptoms. Furthermore, the paper will be concerned with some of the major methodological problems involved in the field of the cross-cultural study of schizophrenia.

CULTURE AND SYMPTOMS

The cross-cultural study of schizophrenia has been directed to find out whether or not the classical schizophrenic symptoms are the same all over the world. Reports of schizophrenia in non-Western cultures tend to stress differences from, more than similarities to its counterpart in the West. For instance, it is reported that catatonic rigidity, negativism and stereotypy are more common in India than in other countries (Wittkower and Rin, 1965). Patients appear to be quieter in Africa, displaying more features which suggest deterioration such as blunting of affect or bizarreness of behaviour. African schizophrenia is claimed to be a "poor imitation of the European forms", showing less violence and aggression than in the West (Benedict and Jacks, 1954; Marinko, 1966). Schizophrenic patients in Iraq and Italy appear to show the opposite trends. They are more expressive and more aggressive than patients in the United States and other Western countries. Social withdrawal is relatively rare among these patients (Bazzoui and Al-Issa, 1966; Wittkower and Rin, 1965).

Comparing Japanese and Filipino paranoid schizophrenics, Enright and Jaeckle (1961–1962) found that ideas of reference and disturbances of thinking are more frequent among the former patients. Japanese patients also showed much more apathy, social isolation and loss of interest in their surroundings. Unlike Western patients the Hutterite schizophrenic does not show severe regression, excitement or any extreme anti-social acts (Eaton and Weil, 1955).

Among the most extensive cross-cultural studies of schizophrenic symptomatology is the one conducted by Murphy, et al. (1961). They sent a questionnaire to psychiatrists representing different cultures and their findings show some definite associations between the frequency of symptoms and certain cultural backgrounds. Delusions of destructiveness and religious delusion are frequently reported only among Christians and Muslims. Delusional jealousy is most frequent among Asians regardless of religion; visual hallucinations are reported most often in Africa and the Near East. Urban and rural patients seem to differ in their symptoms. While the presence of depersonalization is seen most frequently among urban patients, delusions of grandeur seem to occur among the rural patients. One important finding by Murphy, et al. (1961) is that symptoms such as social and emotional withdrawal, auditory hallucinations, general delusions and flatness of affect appear to occur frequently in all their samples. Since these data were collected by questionnaire, it is not certain whether their results reflect variations in the socio-cultural background of the respondents or variation in the symptoms of their patients.

Another cross-cultural study comparing symptomatology between Japanese and American schizophrenics was conducted by Schooler and Caudill (1964). They found significant differences between the two groups. The Americans, for instance, show greater disruption of reality testing and are more likely to show hallucinations and bizarre ideas. Physical 'assaultiveness' is found more prevalent among the Japanese. Since physical 'assaultiveness' involves breaking a highly valued norm in the Japanese culture, Schooler and Caudill suggest that schizophrenic symptomatology seems to appear in the areas of functioning which are stressed most by the culture.

Although non-Western patients sometimes show the familiar Western symptoms, these may differ in their onset and duration. Consider, for instance, the transitory psychotic states reported by Collomb (1966) in the Senegal. These psychotic attacks appear to be sudden and without any preliminary symptoms. They are characterized by transitory delusions with hallucinations and ideas of reference. Unlike Western patients, the onset of their symptoms have a clear detectable relationship to the patient's everyday life. They seem to occur when the individual faces a difficulty or as a means of avoiding a traumatic situation.

Similarly, cases of catatonia among the Eskimos seem to be a result of intense fear of the spirits which interfere with their motility but do not affect their human relationships such as having a gay conversation with others (Opler, 1956).

It should be noted that even in the West there are sub-cultural differences in symptomatology. Thus, Opler (1959) reported that there is more hostility, acting out, elation and bizarre mannerisms among Italian paranoid schizophrenics than among their Irish counterpart. Opler (1959) also reported that while Irish patients had sin and guilt preoccupations concerning sexuality, Italians had no feelings of sin or guilt in this area.

It appears from different surveys of symptoms of schizophrenia that it is the hebephrenic or catatonic rather than the paranoid type which is found by investigators in non-Western cultures (Kline, 1963a; Kline, 1963b; Pfeiffer, 1966; Loudon, 1959). However, it should be noted that the reliability of all these observations must be in doubt because of the doubtful reliability of the psychiatric classification system even when used in the West. The description of the African 'schizophrenic', for instance, makes one wonder whether it is true schizophrenia at all.

In addition to the finding that there are cross-cultural or subcultural variations of symptomatology, manifestations of schizophrenia seem to change during certain periods of time within the same culture. Linz (1964) studied such changes during the last one hundred years in Vienna. His data show that ideas of grandeur and aggressive behaviour are less frequent in the twentieth than in the nineteenth century. While visual hallucinations decreased during the period of study, there was an increase in auditory hallucinations. This result may be compared with the general finding that while auditory hallucinations are more predominant among Western schizophrenics, visual hallucinations are more present in illiterate non-Western patients. Diethelm (1956) has also described several changes in the characteristic symptomatology of the schizophrenias with the passage of time. These studies give the impression that symptoms of Western patients in the past, e.g., Middle Ages, are somehow similar to those patients in primitive cultures at present. Since studies over a long period of time use case histories, it is again difficult to decide whether the results indicate the different background of the psychiatrists over these periods or reflect true changes in symptomatology.

INTERPRETATION OF VARIATION IN SYMPTOMATOLOGY

Variations in specific schizophrenic symptoms such as paranoid delusions have been mainly attributed to the non-Western peoples' lack of education or contact with modern 'civilization'. Similarly, the shallowness of affect and gross deterioration of the patients' habits in a primitive, illiterate culture may be due to the poverty of their intellectual and cultural resources. Taking these interpretations as a starting point, the author (Al-Issa, 1967b) predicted that the frequency of certain classical schizophrenic symptoms should differ in literate and illiterate patients in a non-Western culture. Among ten symptoms investigated, only formal thinking disorder and flatness of affect were significantly related to literacy, the illiterates showing greater evidence of these symptoms. It is interesting to note that contrary to prediction from cross-cultural studies, paranoid delusions were not significantly related to literacy. Thus, the clinical findings that paranoid delusions are very rare among illiterate patients are not supported by this study. It is suggested that paranoid delusions in an illiterate culture may tend to appear in action, assulting or killing somebody, rather than in thought, e.g., during the clinical interview (Al-Issa, 1967b).

However, literacy may affect the contents of the patients' delusions. It affects, for instance, the tendency of urban Africans to develop ideas of influence of the European type such as grandiose delusions of identification with Christ and God or influences involving electricity or the wireless (Tooth, 1950). These tendencies are not evident with rural illiterate Africans.

Differences in cultural values are also suggested to explain differences in the manifestation of schizophrenic symptoms. While the quiet behaviour of the Indian has been explained in terms of cultural control of anger and aggression, the opposite behavior of Italian and Iraqi patients was thought to be a result of cultural encouragement of aggression and the lack of strong feeling of guilt. The absence of extreme anti-social acts among the Hutterite patients was attributed to the good custodial care and the affectionate regard for the patient (Eaton and Weil, 1955).

It should be noted that no objective studies have been undertaken to assess the normal personality or values of individuals in non-Western cultures. Therefore, the validity of the above observations is still in doubt.

METHODOLOGY

In the cross-cultural study of schizophrenia it is sometimes difficult to differentiate between unfamiliar but culturally acceptable forms of behaviour and the manifestations of genuine mental disorder. Behaviour which seems to indicate abnormal symptoms to a Westerner might well be in keeping with indigenous beliefs and practices. The West Indian society, for instance, supports the belief of possession by Christ and God as well as ghosts; and the patients' delusions may be similar to these beliefs, making diagnosis very difficult (Kiev, 1963). The confusion between normal and schizophrenic behaviour in a non-Western culture is well illustrated by Yap (1951). He reported that "if a Hindu Fakir behaves much like a catatonic schizophrenic in Britain he need not be necessarily insane, since not only can he begin or stop his apparently catatonic behavior at will, but such behaviour has a recognized place and possesses some degree of social approbation in his own culture" (p. 315). Thus, if the Western diagnosis criterion is inappropriately applied to other cultures, the clinician may be able to observe 'group psychoses' (Opler, 1959) or group paranoid delusions (Bazzoui and Al-Issa, 1966).

The difficulty in the diagnosis of mental illness in non-Western culture may be due in part to the wholesale application of Western criteria without due attention given to cultural factors or individual variations within the culture. It is, for instance, suggested by some workers in the field of transcultural psychiatry that some symptoms cannot be accepted universally as signs of abnormality because of differences in the degree of their acceptability from one culture to the other, e.g., hallucinations involving religion are accepted in some cultures. Buss (1966) has pointed out that this suggestion may be applicable to deviations where social evaluations are important in distinguishing between normality and abnormality (e.g., sexual deviations, non-conformity with the rules of society). Deviations involving cognitive symptoms which appear to be universal (c.f. Murphy et al., 1961) represent failure to adapt to the physical rather than the social environment. These cognitive abnormalities involve the inability to perceive correctly the nature of the physical world and do not depend on social environment. Whether a person is hallucinating or not is relevant to physical stimuli and can be studied objectively irrespective of the cultural background. Reality in the sense of recognizing the physical world is a universal issue and failure to be in contact with reality should be considered universally abnormal.

In addition to the attribution of abnormality to culturally accepted behaviour, atypical mental syndromes may be confusing to a Western trained psychiatrist. The diagnosis as well as the rating of specific symptoms is very much determined by the background and outlook of the psychiatrist. The fact that the concept of schizophrenia is very loosely defined in the West (Guertin, 1961) may add to the difficulty of diagnosis in non-Western culture. Furthermore, it is possible that in a culturally isolated environment, a patient may be able to achieve 'superficial adjustment' and his illness is less likely to be detected (Eaton and Weil, 1955). Adjustment may be possible for a schizophrenic in a primitive culture because the culture makes fewer demands on the individual. These factors will, therefore, influence results obtained by using the method of clinical observations or the questionnaire method referred to in the previous section.

Symptoms deviating from a Western description were thus regarded by Opler (1956) as atypical schizophrenic symptoms. Opler (1956, p. 133) believes that: "The lack of delusional systematizations in a wide variety of mental disorders of non-literate peoples: the 'running wild' of Fuegian tribes (Cooper, 1934), the Greenland Eskimos Piblokto, women running around naked (Cooper, 1934), the 'Arctic hysteria' of Lapps,

Eskimos, and Northeast Siberian tribes (Cooper, 1934; Yap, 1951), and the similar forms of psychosis, *Latah* of Malaya and *Imu* of the Ainu tribes of Hokkaido (Yap, 1951; Aberle, 1952) all point to atypical forms of schizophrenias varying from the Western standard. Like the 'frenzied anxieties' with hysterical elements of Carothers and Aubin, they remind us of schizo-affective disorders as discussed by Adolf Meyer, but more loosely organized, more episodic, and more bound to action modes of emotional expression than to fantasy." It seems to the present writer that the inclusion of these atypical symptoms into the concept of 'schizophrenia' gives no justification for calling it schizophrenia at all.

Data obtained from clinical observations may be misleading because only certain cases come into the psychiatric clinic. Traditional treatment is usually attempted before the patient comes to the psychiatrist's notice. In Iraq the mental hospital patients are admitted mainly by order from the religious court or when their symptoms are beyond the control of the family. That these conditions may affect clinical observations is suggested in a study by Vitols et al. (1963). Their finding that there are more hallucinations and delusions among Negro than among White schizophrenics was attributed to the Negroes' delay in coming to the hospital; thus, the predominance of these symptoms reflected only the degree of severity of illness among the Negro patients in the mental hospital. Similarly, the observation that Iraqi hospitalized schizophrenics are aggressive and noisy may not necessarily apply to patients kept at home. It is possible that selective factors may play a part in bringing aggressive patients to the hospital. Furthermore, social isolation and material deprivation within the hospital framework seem to be conducive to noisiness and aggression (Bazzoui and Al-Issa, 1966).

As the samples of cross-cultural reports of symptomatology in schizophrenia are confined to a limited group of the population, it is not surprising to find contradictory results in the literature, e.g., the traditional withdrawn, mute and negativistic picture of the Indian schizophrenic patient is contrasted with a recent report describing him as 'aggressive and boisterous' (Sharadamba, 1966). In countries where the mental patient is tolerated and kept at home, samples selected from hospitalized patients may not be representative of the whole population.

It should also be observed that data on schizophrenic symptoms obtained through the use of clinical observations or official records may be contaminated by linguistic and semantic misunderstanding. If the investigator is not familiar with the local language, it would be difficult for him to check on the reliability of his reports. Yap (1951) has observed that studies showing more catatonic than paranoid symptoms in non-Western cultures may be a result of linguistic misunderstanding or that the patient is discouraged to express his thoughts. The role of language in the diagnosis and observation of psychiatric symptoms is expressed by

Stengel (1961) as follows: ". . . certain symptoms which to psychiatrists using one language appear very important do not exist for psychiatrists and patients using another language, because there are no words for them. Take the example of the symptom of *Gedankenentzug,* which many German psychiatrists regard as a basic schizophrenic symptom. You find no reference to it in British or American textbooks, and patients using the English language do not complain about this experience" (p. 59). The linguistic problem is sometimes complicated by the unwillingness of the local population to co-operate. Moreover, it may be difficult to obtain information about their emotional or even their everyday life, e.g., in Nigeria and Haiti (Wittkower and Bijou, 1962). Topics related to mental illness may be classified as shameful and 'unspeakable'.

From this discussion the obvious solution to these methodological problems seems to be the use of standardized tools specific to different cultures for the assessment of symptomatology. Psychologists have been aware of this problem for some time, but their role in the studies reported in the previous section has been very slight. It is, therefore, of interest to discuss the possible contribution of the psychologists' cross-cultural studies.

THE PSYCHOLOGICAL APPROACH

It is generally recognized that the conventional diagnostic tests are inapplicable in non-Western cultures. Since these tests were validated on selected Western population of a certain age, level of income and education, it is not surprising that the application of these tests to non-Western patients is questionable. One solution to this problem by the psychologist is the use of the so-called culture fair tests such as the Cattell Culture Fair Test, the Porteus Maze, the Draw a Man Test and the Rorschach. These tests are thought to require minimal verbal abilities and to have little dependence on past experience. It is, therefore, assumed that they are applicable to different cultures, but the validity of this assumption appears to be doubtful. Relevant to the discussion of cultural variations in the criterion for abnormality is the finding that abnormal test responses as defined by Western criteria may be characteristic of a whole non-Western society. Take, for instance, the study by Bleuler and Bleuler (1934) showing that the desert Moroccans give a much larger number of fine-detail responses on the Rorschach than do Europeans. The interpretation of these Moroccan subjects of very tiny and hardly observable details in an ink blot seems to be bizarre, when judged by Western clinical standards. In the West, fine detail responses are regarded as an indication of compulsive tendency or mental disorganization, e.g., schizophrenia. The Moroccan results may be partly attributed to the obsessional concern with detail in the ritual of the Muslim religion. Henry (1941) has suggested that the use of rare detail in the Rorschach records of a jungle people in South America is a function of their need to observe their surroundings in order to survive. Henry's observation may be also applicable to the Moroccan Bedouin's keen surveillance of the desert environment. In contrast to the Moroccan Bedouins, Cook (1942) found that the Samoans give whole responses to the entire blot, e.g., an animal. Samoans also differ from Western subjects in giving more responses to the white space of the blots. According to Western criteria, the responses of the Samoans and the Moroccans would warrant the diagnosis of schizophrenia (Weiner, 1966, p. 314). Since it is difficult to assume that the whole Moroccan Bedouin community or the Samoans are abnormal, these results throw some doubt on the efficacy of the Rorschach as a diagnostic tool in the cross-cultural study of mental illness. There is also considerable evidence that it is not valid even in Western culture (Costello, 1966). Dennis (1960) has also recently shown that the Draw a Man Test is not suitable for diagnostic purposes. It is art tradition and experience rather than emotional state that determine the drawings of the human figure of the Syrian Bedouins. The analysis of the Goodenough scores of 40 groups from different cultures appears to support the hypothesis that variations in these scores are related to the amount of experience with representational art and the encouragement of members of these groups to engage in this activity (Dennis, 1966). Mensh and Henry (1953) commented on the use of projective techniques in cross-cultural studies as follows: "one of the most striking findings of projective testing of primitive people, and in general of people from cultures other than our own, is that they regularly turn out to show signs of deep-going psychopathology; and the anthropological works on projective tests are full of the language of psychopathology. It is difficult to understand why this should be so, unless we take the position that everybody is sick but the observer. One impression is that not only do such interpretations stem from preconceived notions of what is 'normal', but that something inherent in the instrument's past history in our culture compels us to see the responses of peoples from other cultures as psychopathological" (p. 469).

Abnormal perceptual processes as indicated by psychometric measures are also found prevalent among non-Western normal individuals. Shapiro (1960) found that illiterate Africans show more rotation of drawings than English brain damaged patients. Other perceptual anomalies are concerned with the African underestimation of figure size or the passage of time (Schwitzgebel, 1962), or his performance on the Müller-Lyer Illusion Test (Biesheuvel, 1952; Hudson, 1960; Jahoda, 1966). Verhaegen and Laroche's (1958) African Bush subjects who perseverate with the wrong response on a Form Board Test are reminiscent of responses given by schizophrenic and brain damaged subjects in the West. The authors, however, point out that their subjects' inability to differentiate between a cross and a five point star is the result of their unfamiliarity with these forms. Using Indian and British students, Thouless (1933) found that Indians show a greater tendency toward object constancy than his British subjects. It should be noted that experimental results show that Western schizophrenics tend to show underconstancy (Venables, 1964). However, paranoid schizophrenics show overconstancy, a result similar to that reported by Thouless concerning Indian students. Here again, non-Western subjects are found to respond in a similar way to schizophrenic subjects in the West.

In addition to schizophrenic responses observed in the perception of non-Western illiterate peoples, it is assumed that they are unable to form concepts. In the study of abstract abilities of Western schizophrenic patients, it has been demonstrated that they are less able than normals in forming abstract concepts on non-verbal classification tests (Goldstein and Scheerer, 1941; Hanfmann and Kasanin, 1942) and verbal tests requiring the definition of words (Chodorkoff and Mussen, 1952; Feifel, 1949; Flavell, 1956; Gerstein, 1949). Using the Draw a Man Test, Haward and Roland (1954) claimed that the Nigerian mental approach is characterized by a concreteness which is so rigid that it produced schizophrenic signs in the drawings. Similarly, Joseph and Murray (1951) also claimed that there is concreteness in the Rorschach responses of the Chamorros and Carolinians at Saipan. In general, the claim that non-Western peoples are characterized by concreteness of thinking is based either on little relevant evidence (Carothers, 1953; Haward and Roland, 1954) or it has disregarded factors that might be effective in determining the subject's level of abstraction. Jahoda (1956), for instance, found that literacy and familiarity with the test material (Goldstein Scheerer Cube Test) affect the African level of abstraction. Using some native material for classification (plant material, animal material), Price-Williams (1962) showed that in addition to literacy, motivation and interest may also be effective. Using a word definition test the author (Al-Issa, 1967a) obtained similar results with four groups consisting of literate schizophrenics, literate normals, illiterate schizophrenics and illiterate normals. These results show that both literacy and schizophrenia affect the subjects' level of abstraction. The author (Al-Issa, 1967a) reported that "significant differences between literate and illiterate subjects may reflect a difference in the frequency of usage of abstract concepts in the written and spoken Arabic. Spoken Arabic which is the main source of information for the illiterates, makes less use of abstract concepts, and this use is closely related to the practical situation and to the interest and motivation of the subjects. An illiterate may be aware of a complex system of family or tribe on the abstract level (his awareness that it is possible to live in different parts of Iraq, and yet belong to the same tribe) while at the same time giving . . . concrete or functional definitions" (P. 42). An interesting aspect of these results is that literate schizophrenics scored significantly higher than illiterate normals and illiterate schizophrenics. However, the relationship between the level of abstraction and literacy or schizophrenia does not hold when the presence of specific psychiatric symptoms and the level of abstraction are investigated within a schizophrenic population (Al-Issa, 1966). The inapplicability of Western norms for the assessment of schizophrenic symptoms might have affected the relationship between verbal abstraction and symptomatology. These studies clearly point out that under certain conditions, normal and schizophrenic subjects may equally show either concrete or abstract thinking abilities.

The search for abnormal signs in apparently normal subjects (e.g., illiterates) is also demonstrated by the study of Gallais et al. (1951). In their analysis of the EEG records of 100 normal subjects from Guinea, they found that about 58 per cent of these records were abnormal. Comparing 66 Bantus and 72 Whites in South Africa, Mundy-Castle et al. (1953) found no significant difference in the incidence of abnormal EEG between the two groups. Thus, it is concluded that there is no significant difference in the EEG patterns of normal Africans and Whites. If future research demonstrates that different cultural groups (Western and non-Western schizophrenic subjects) show similar abnormal patterns of the EEG in the case of schizophrenia, it would be plausible to suggest that similar processes may be responsible for their deviant behaviour.

The above EEG study is one of the few investigations which is in line with the 'behavioural approach' suggested by Zubin and Kietzman (1966) for the cross-cultural study of schizophrenia. (For further studies of physiological responses, the reader is referred to Nelson (1959, 1965) and Lazarus et al. (1966).) In contrast to the conventional measures used in cross-cultural studies their approach is based on the measurement of the initial components of the patients' response in the various modalities and under controlled experimental conditions. For instance, the speed and accuracy of responses to specified types of stimuli may be measured and contrasted in patients and controls. Zubin and Kietzman (1966) point out that there are differential influences of culture on the observed behaviour of the individual. In another report, Zubin (1966) described these influences as follows: "Though no measures can be said to be completely culture free, the way in which culture affects certain measures (as pupillary response to light stimuli) is indirect, unlike the direct way in which it influences primarily conceptual measures like vocabulary. The major way in which culture will tend to influence the culture-free or culture-fair tests is probably not in the function under measurement, but in the subject's approach to the testing situation, e.g., in the subject's understanding of the purpose of the test, in the degree of fear, in his motivation, attention and co-operation, etc. In other words, the influence of culture is specifically on those variables which also tend to contaminate comparisons of schizophrenics and normals even when they come from the same cultural background" (P. 66–67). The findings of Robertson and Batcheldor (1956) are relevant to the 'indirect' influences of culture in the test situation. They found that British subjects tended to stress accuracy at the expense of speed when compared with the American norms of the Wechsler Adult Intelligence Scale. However, these influences are controllable in the test situation such as by emphasizing speed or accuracy in the instructions.

　　If the experimental 'culture-fair' approach which is postulated by Zubin and his associates (Zubin, 1966; Zubin and Kietzman, 1966) is applied cross-culturally, similar patterns of responses (e.g., psychophysiological) may be found in schizophrenic patients from different cultures. This would suggest that although there are cross-cultural differences in the manifestations of schizophrenia, similar processes may underlie this illness. Similarly, comparing the responses of Western abnormal subjects with non-Western subjects who show the same response pattern, but without behavioral pathology, may give us some indications of the types of interactions between different variables (sociocultural, perceptual, physiological) which led to mental illness in one group but not in the other. At the present stage of these studies the best contribution to the understanding of mental illness and schizophrenia is to establish normative data for normal and abnormal processes which are already known in the West. These data would then be used as a basis for the cross-cultural comparisons of schizophrenic and mentally ill patients.

SUMMARY

　　This paper is an attempt to review some of the main cross-cultural studies of symptomatology in schizophrenia. Although it is shown that there are cultural variations of symptomatology, the reliability of these observations seems to be questionable. The inclusion of behaviour of different description into the concept of schizophrenia throws serious doubts on the usefulness and desirability of this concept as presently used in cross-cultural studies. However, problems of reliability or validity of observations at the cross-cultural level pose similar problems, encountered at the inter-individual. A more reliable and rigorous system of classification is needed to differentiate between normal and schizophrenic behavior in different cultures or within the same culture. Cross-cultural studies suggest that some responses (e.g., conceptual) are more amenable to the influence of culture than others (e.g., physiological). Thus if it is demonstrated that different cultural groups show similar responses on some relatively culture-free tasks (e.g., EEG pupillary responses) it would be plausible to suggest similar processes cross-culturally. These processes may underlie behaviour disorders such as schizophrenia despite the inter-individual or cross-cultural differences in their manifestations.

REFERENCES

Aberle, D. F. Arctic hysteria and *latah* in Mongolia. *Trans. New York Acad. Sci.*, 1952, **14**, 291–297.

Al-Issa, I. Word definition in chronic schizophrenia, *Psychol. Reports*, 1966, **19**, 934.

Al-Issa, I. Effects of literacy and schizophrenia on verbal abstraction in Iraq, *J. Soc. Psychol.*, 1967(a), **71**, 39–43.

Al-Issa, I. Literacy and symptomatology in chronic schizophrenia, *Brit. J. Soc. Psychiat.*, 1967(b) **1**, 313–315.

Bazzoui, W. and I. Al-Issa. Psychiatry in Iraq, *Brit. J. Psychiat.*, 1966, **112**, 827–832.

Benedict, P. K. and I. Jacks. Mental illness in primitive societies, *Psychiatry*, 1954, **17**, 377–389.

Biesheuvel, S. The study of African ability, *Afr. Stud.*, 1952, **11**, 105–117.

Bleuler, M. and R. Bleuler. Rorschach ink-blot tests and social psychology, *Charact. and Pers.*, 1934, **4**, 99–114.

Buss, A. H. Psychopathology New York: John Wiley and Sons, Inc., 1966.

Carothers, J. C. *The African mind in health and disease.* Geneva: World Health Organization, 1953.

Chodorkoff, B. and P. Mussen. Qualitative aspect of the vocabulary responses of normals and schizophrenics, *J. Consult. Psychol.*, 1952, **16**, 43–48.

Collomb, H. Bouffées délirantes en psychiatrie Africaine (Transitory delusional states in African psychiatry). Mimeograph, 87 pp. Abstracted in *Transcult. Psychiat. Res.*, 1966, **3**, 29–34.

Cook, T. H. The application of the Rorschach test to a Samoan group, *Rorschach Res. Exch.*, 1942, **6**, 51–60.

Cooper, J. M. Mental disease situations in certain cultures, *J. Abnorm. Soc. Psychol.*, 1934, **29**, 10–17.

Costello, C. G. *Psychology for psychiatrists.* Oxford: Pergamon Press, Inc., 1966.

Dennis, W. The human figure drawings of Bedouins, *J. Soc. Psychol.*, 1960, **52**, 209–219.

Dennis, W. Goodenough scores, art experience, and modernization, *J. Soc. Psychol.*, 1966, **68**, 211–228.

Devereux, G. A sociological theory of schizophrenia, *Psychoanalyt. Rev.*, 1934, **26**, 315–342.

Dhunjiboy, J. Brief resume of the types of insanity commonly met with in India, *J. Ment. Sci.*, 1930, **16**, 254–264.

Diethelm, O. Report of the Payne Whitney Psychiatric Clinic. New York Hospital (cited by Opler, 1956).

Eaton, J. W. and R. J. Weil. *Culture and mental disorders.* New York: The Free Press, 1955.

Enright, J. B. and W. R. Jaeckle. Ethnic differences in psychopathology, *Soc. process*, 1961–1962, **25**, 71–77.

Feifel, H. Qualitative differences in the vocabulary response of normals and abnormals, *Genet. Psychol. Monogr.*, 1949, **39**, 151–204.

Flavell, J. H. Abstract thinking and social behavior in schizophrenia, *J. Abnorm. Soc. Psychol.*, 1956, **52**, 208–211.

Gallais, P., G. Miletto, J. Corriol, and J. Bert. Introduction à l'étude d'EEG physiologique de Noir d'Afrique, deux mém, *Méd. Trop.*, 1951, **11**, 128–146.

Gerstein, R. A. A suggested method of analyzing and extending the use of Bellevue-Wechsler vocabulary responses, *J. Consult. Psychol.*, 1949, **13**, 366–374.

Goldstein, K. and M. Scheerer. Abstract and concrete behavior. An experimental study with special tests, *Psychol. Monogr.*, 1941, **53**, No.2.

Guertin, W. H. Medical and statistical–psychological models for research in schizophrenia, *Behav. Sci.*, 1961, **6**, 200–204.

Hanfmann, E. and J. Kasanin. Conceptual thinking in schizophrenia. New York: Nervous and Mental Disease Monographs, 1942, No. 67.

Haward, L. C. R. and W. A. Roland. Some inter-cultural differences on the Draw-a-Man test: Goodenough scores, *Man*, 1954, **54**, 86–88.

Henry, J. Rorschach technique in primitive cultures, *Amer. J. Orthopsychiat.*, 1941, **11**, 230–234.

Hudson, W. Pictorial depth perception in sub-cultural groups in Africa, *J. Soc. Psychol.*, 1960, **52**, 183–208.

Jahoda, G. Assessment of abstract behavior in a non-Western culture, *J. Abnorm. Soc. Psychol.*, 1956, **53**, 237–243.

Jahoda, G. Geometric illusions and environment: A study in Ghana, *Brit. J. Psychol.*, 1966, **57**, 193–199.

Joseph, A. and V. F. Murray. *Chamorros and Carolinians of Saipan: Personality studies.* Cambridge: Harvard University Press, 1951.

Kiev, A. Beliefs and delusions of West India immigrants, *Brit. J. Psychiat.*, 1963, **109**, 356–363.

Kline, N. S. Psychiatry in Kuwait, *Brit. J. Psychiat.*, 1963(a), **109**, 766–774.

Kline, N. S. Psychiatry in Indonesia, *Amer. J. Psychiat.*, 1963(b), **119**, 809–815.

Lazarus, R. S., M. Tomita, E. Opton, and K. Masahisa. A cross-cultural study of stress-reaction patterns in Japan, *J. Pers. Soc. Psychol.*, 1966, **4**, 622–633.

Linz, H. L. Verleichende Psychiatrie. Eine Studie Uber die Beziehung von Kultur Sociologie und Psychopathologie. Vienna: Wilhelm Mandrich Verlag, 1964.

Lopez, C. Ethnographische Betrachtungen über schizophrenia, *Ztshr. Ges. Neurol. u. Psychiat.*, 1932, **142**, 706–711.

Loudon, J. B. Psychogenic disorder and social conflict among the Zulu. In M. K. Opler (ed.), *Culture and mental health.* New York: The MacMillan Company, 1959.

Marinko, B. Psychoses in Ethiopia, *Transcult. Psychiat. Res.*, 1966, **111**, 152–154.

Mensh, I. N. and J. Henry. Direct observation and psychological tests in anthropological field work, *Amer. Anthropol.*, 1953, **55**, 461–480.

Mishler, E. G. and N. A. Scotch. Sociocultural factors in the epidemiology of schizophrenia, *Psychiatry*, 1963, **26**, 315–351.

Mundy-Castle, A. C., B. L. McKiever, and T. Prinsloo. A comparative study of the electroencephalograms of normal Africans and Europeans of Southern Africa, *EEG. Clin. Neurophysiol.*, 1953, **5**, 533–543.

Murphy, H. B. M., E. D. Wittkower, J. Fried, and H. Ellenberger. A cross-cultural survey of schizophrenic symptomatology. In *Proceedings of the Third World Congress of Psychiatry*, 1961, **2**, 1309–1315.

Nelson, G. K. The electroencephalogram in Kwashiorkor, *EEG. Clin. Neurophysiol.*, 1959, **2**, 73–84.

Nelson, G. K. Electroencephalographic studies in sequelae of Kwashiorkor and other diseases in Africa. *Proceedings of the Central African Scientific and Medical Congress*, pp. 777–787. London: Pergamon Press, Inc., 1965.

Opler, M. K. Cultural differences in mental disorders: An Italian and Irish contrast in the schizophrenias. In M. K. Opler (ed.), *Culture and mental health*. New York: The MacMillan Company, 1959.

Opler, M. K. *Culture psychiatry and human values*. Springfield, Ill.: Charles C Thomas, Publisher, 1956.

Pfeiffer, W. M. Psychiatrische Besonderheiten in Indonesien (Psychiatric peculiarities in Indonesia), *Transcult. Psychiat. Res.*, 1966, **111**, 116–119 (English abstract).

Price-Williams, D. R. Abstract and concrete modes of classification in a primitive society, *Brit. J. Educ. Psychol.*, 1962, **32**, 50–61.

Robertson, J. P. S., and K. J. Batcheldor. Cultural aspects of the Wechsler Adult Intelligence Scale in relation to British mental patients, *J. Ment. Sci.*, 1956, **102**, 612–618.

Schooler, C. and W. Caudill. Symptomatology in Japanese and American schizophrenics, *Ethnology*, 1964, **3**, 172–178.

Schwitzgebel, R. The performance of Dutch and Zulu adults on selected perceptual tasks, *J. Soc. Psychol.*, 1962, **57**, 73–77.

Shapiro, M. B. The rotation of drawings by illiterate Africans, *J. Soc. Psychol.*, 1960, **52**, 17–30.

Sharadamba, R. Culture and mental disorder: A study in an Indian mental hospital, *Int. J. Soc. Psychiat.*, 1966, **12**, 139–148.

Stengel, E. Problems of nosology and nomenclature in the mental disorders. In J. Zubin (ed.), *Field studies in the mental disorders*. New York: Grune and Stratton, Inc., 1961.

Thouless, R. H. A racial difference in perception, *J. Soc. Psychol.*, 1933, **4**, 330–339.

Tooth, G. *Studies in mental illness in the Gold Coast*. London: Her Majesty's Stationery Office. Colonial Research publication, 1950, **6**.

Venables, P. H. Input dysfunction in schizophrenia. In B. A. Maher (ed.),

Progress in experimental personality research. Vol. I. New York: Academic Press, 1964.

Verhaegen, P. and J. L. Laroche. Some methodological considerations concerning the study of aptitudes and elaboration of psychological tests for African natives, *J. Soc. Psychol.*, 1958, **47**, 249–256.

Vitols, M. M., H. G. Water, and M. H. Keeler. Hallucinations and delusions in White and Negro schizophrenics, *Amer. J. Psychiat.*, 1963, **120**, 472–476.

Weiner, I. B. *Psychodiagnosis in schizophrenia.* New York: John Wiley and Sons, Inc., 1966.

Wittkower, E. D. and L. Bijou. Psychiatry in developing countries, *Amer. J. Psychiat.*, 1963, **120**, 218–221.

Wittkower, E. D. and H. Rin. Transcultural psychiatry, *Arch. Gen. Psychiat.*, 1965, **13**, 387–394.

Yap, P. M. Mental diseases peculiar to certain cultures: A survey of comparative psychiatry, *J. Ment. Sci.*, 1951, **97**, 313–327.

Zubin, J. and M. L. Kietzman. A cross-cultural approach to classification in schizophrenia and other mental disorders. In P. H. Hoch and J. Zubin (eds.), *Psychopathology of schizophrenia.* New York: Grune and Stratton, Inc., 1966.

Zubin, J. A cross-cultural approach to psychopathology and its implications for diagnostic classification. In L. D. Eron (ed.), *The classification of behavior disorders.* Chicago: Aldine Publishing Co., 1966.

6-6

A Cross-Cultural Study of Correlates of Crime

MARGARET K. BACON
IRVIN L. CHILD
HERBERT BARRY, III

One advantage of cross-cultural research delineated by R. Sears in Chapter 3 (Selection 3–3) is the use of cultures for testing hypotheses and thus obtaining wider variations among many cultures than within a single culture. The present study is an excellent example of the use of 48 cultures as single units for the study of correlates of criminal behavior. The authors investigated the association of a wide range of child rearing practices, economic systems, and social structures with the frequency of crime. This study thus contributes to our knowledge of both methodology and theory in the cross-cultural investigation of crime.

As in the case of symptoms of psychopathology discussed in previous selections of this chapter, students of culture are interested in the study of cultural factors in criminal behavior and their effect on the frequency and manifestations of crime. A book edited by Gibbens and Ahrenfeldt (1966) is a review of research in this area.

REFERENCES

Gibbens, T. C. N. and R. H. Ahrenfeldt, *Cultural factors in delinquency.* Philadelphia: J. B. Lippincott Company, 1966.

Reprinted from *J. Abnorm. Soc. Psychol.,* 1963, **66,** 291–300, by permission of the authors and the American Psychological Association.

A number of researchers have analyzed the sociological and psychological background of delinquents and criminals and compared them with a noncriminal control population, in order to discover what conditions give rise to criminal behavior; for a recent review, see Robison (1960). The present paper reports on variations among a sample of preliterate societies in the frequency of crime, in order to determine what other known features of these societies are associated with the occurrence of crime. The cross-cultural technique (Whiting, 1954), in which each society is taken as a single case, is a unique method for studying crime and has certain advantages: The index of frequency of crime in a society represents the average among its many individuals and over a span of many years, so that the measure is likely to be more stable and reliable than a measure of criminal tendency in a single individual. Some of the cultural features which may be related to crime show wider variations among societies than within a single society, permitting a more comprehensive test of their significance. Results which are consistent in a number of diverse societies may be applied to a great variety of cultural conditions instead of being limited to a single cultural setting.

If certain cultural features foster the development of criminal behavior, they should be found preponderantly in societies with a high frequency of crime; factors which inhibit crime should be found largely in societies which are low in crime. Thus the cross-cultural method may help us discover psychological and sociological variables which have a causal relationship to the development of crime; the importance of these variables may then also be tested intraculturally. On the other hand, variables identified as possible causes of crime within our society may be tested for broader significance by the cross-cultural method.

The possible causal factors which we have explored are principally concerned with child training practices, economy, and social structure. Hypotheses concerning these factors, as they have been presented by other writers or as they have occurred to us, will be described in connection with the presentation of our results.

METHOD

SAMPLE. The sample used in this study consists of 48 societies, mostly preliterate, scattered over the world. They were taken from a larger group of 110 societies which were selected on the basis of geographical diversity and adequacy of information on aboriginal child training practices. The present sample of 48 consists of those societies whose ethnographies were searched and found to provide sufficient information to permit comparative ratings on criminal behavior by three independent research workers.[1]

RATINGS. We have included two types of crime in our study: *theft* and *personal crime*. These two were chosen because they are relatively easy to identify and almost universal in occurrence. Also, they represent two quite different types of behavior. Thus we are able to clarify antecedents common to both types of crime and those characteristic of only one. Judgments were always made in relation to the norms of the culture under consideration. Theft was defined as stealing the personal property of others. Property included anything on which the society placed value, whether it was a whale's tooth or a song. Personal crime was defined by intent to injure or kill a person; assault, rape, suicide, sorcery intended to make another ill, murder, making false accusations, etc., were all included.

The method of comparative ratings was used to obtain measures of frequency. Three raters independently analyzed the ethnographic material on each society and made ratings on a seven-point scale as to the relative frequency of the type of crime under consideration. Thus a rating of 4 on theft would mean that the frequency of theft in a given society appeared to be about average for the sample of societies. Ratings of 5, 6, and 7 represented high frequencies and those of 3, 2, and 1 were low. Societies in which the behavior did not occur were rated as 0. Each rating was classified as confident or doubtful at the time that it was made. No rating was made if the analyst judged the information to be insufficient. We have included all societies on which all three analysts made a rating, whether it was confident or doubtful, and we have used the pooled ratings of all three analysts. The reliability of these pooled ratings is estimated as +.67 for Theft and +.57 for Personal Crime. These estimates were obtained by averaging (using a z transformation) the separate

[1]The 48 societies included in the study are as follows: Africa—Ashanti, Azande, Bena, Chagga, Dahomeans, Lovedu, Mbundu, Thonga; Asia—Andamanese, Baiga, Chenchu, Chukchee, Lepcha, Muria, Tanala, Yakut; North America—Cheyenne, Comanche, Flatheads, Hopi, Jamaicans (Rocky Roaders), Kaska, Kwakiutl, Navajo, Papago, Tepoztlan, Western Apache; South America—Aymara, Cuna, Jivaro, Siriono, Yagua; Oceania—Arapesh, Balinese, Buka (Kurtachi), Ifaluk, Kwoma, Lau Fijians (Kambara), Lesu, Manus, Maori, Pukapukans, Samoans, Tikopia, Trobrianders, Trukese, Ulithians, Vanua Levu (Nakoroka). All information was obtained from ethnographic studies available in the literature or in the Human Relations Area Files. Ratings were, so far as possible, of the aboriginal practices of the group in order to reduce the influence of acculturation. All ratings used in this study have been filed with the American Documentation Institute. Order Document No. 7450 from the ADI Auxiliary Publications Project, Photoduplication Service, Library of Congress; Washington 25, D. C., remitting in advance $1.75 for microfilm or $2.50 for photocopies. Make checks payable to: Chief, Photoduplication Service, Library of Congress. All intercorrelations among variables for our sample of societies appear in the same document.

interrater reliabilities, and entering this average into the Spearman-Brown correction formula.

Most writers in this field make a distinction between delinquency and crime, largely on the basis of the age of the offender. The nature of our evidence does not permit us to make such a clear distinction. Ratings were made in terms of the relative frequency of specific types of criminal behavior in the adult population. Since the age at which adulthood is considered to have begun varies from one society to another, ratings may in some cases have included individuals young enough to be considered adolescent in our society and therefore delinquent rather than criminal. The distinction does not appear to be crucial in this study.

The measures of possible causal variables consist of ratings which have been derived from several sources. Each will be described in the following section. Except where noted (for certain variables in Tables 3 and 4), none of the three people who made the crime ratings participated in any of the other ratings.

HYPOTHESES, RESULTS, AND DISCUSSION

Our results will be presented under three main headings: Correlates of Crime in General, Correlates Specific to Theft, and Correlates Specific to Personal Crime. As this classification suggests, we have found it useful to consider the antecedents of crime as either general or specific, i.e., leading to a general increase in criminal behavior, or associated with only one major category of crime. A correlation of +.46 was found between frequency of Theft and frequency of Personal Crime. This indicates that the two variables show a significant degree of communality ($p < .01$) and also some independence.

Correlates of Crime in General

Our principal findings concerning common correlates of both Theft and Personal Crime are relevant to a hypothesis that crime arises partly as a defense against strong feminine identification. We will begin with an account of this hypothesis.

In our society crime occurs mostly in men, and we have no reason to doubt that this sex difference characterizes most societies. Several writers have called attention to the sex role identification of males as especially pertinent to the development of delinquency in our society. It is assumed that the very young boy tends to identify with his mother rather than his father because of his almost exclusive contact with his mother. Later in his development he becomes aware of expectations that he behave in a masculine way and as a result his behavior tends to be marked by a compulsive masculinity which is really a defense against feminine identification. Parsons (1954, pp. 304–305) notes further that the mother is the principal agent of socialization as well as an object of love and identification. Therefore, when the boy revolts he unconsciously identifies "goodness" with femininity and hence accepts the role of "bad boy" as a positive goal.

Miller (1958) has made a study of lower-class culture and delinquency which is also pertinent in this connection. He points out that some delinquent behavior may result from an attempt to live up to attitudes and values characteristic of lower-class culture. He also notes that many lower-class males are reared in predominantly female households lacking a consistently present male with whom to identify. He feels that what he calls an almost obsessive lower-class concern with masculinity results from the feminine identification in preadolescent years.

Whiting et al. (1958), in a cross-cultural study of male initiation rites at puberty, found these rites tended to occur in societies with prolonged, exclusive mother-son sleeping arrangements. Their interpretation of this relationship is that the early mother-infant sleeping arrangement produces an initial feminine identification, and later control by men leads to a secondary masculine identification. The function of the initiation ceremony is to resolve this conflict of sexual identification in favor of the masculine identification. The authors further predict that insofar as there has been an increase in juvenile delinquency in our society, "it probably has been accompanied by an increase in the exclusiveness of mother-child relationships and/or a decrease in the authority of the father."

The hypothesis that crime is in part a defense against initial feminine identification would lead to the expectation that all factors which tend to produce strong identification with the mother and failure of early identification with the father would be positively correlated with the frequency of crime in the adult population. The factor that is easiest to study is the presence of the father. It seems reasonable to suppose that successful identification with the father is dependent on his presence. Therefore, societies which differ in the degree to which the father is present during the child's first few years should differ correspondingly in the degree to which the boy typically forms a masculine identification.[2]

Whiting (1959) has made use of Murdock's (1957) classification of household structure and family composition to distinguish among four types of households which provide a range from maximal to minimal degree of presence of the father. They are as follows:

---

[2]The whole problem of the mechanism whereby identification occurs has been omitted from this study. In all theories it would appear that identification with the father would be in some degree a function of the frequency of the presence of the father.

MONOGAMOUS NUCLEAR. This household is the usual one in our society. The father, mother, and children eat, sleep, and entertain under one roof. Grandparents, siblings of the parents, and other relatives live elsewhere. The effective presence of the father in the child's environment is thus at a maximum.

MONOGAMOUS EXTENDED. Here two or more nuclear families live together under one roof. A typical extended family consists of an aged couple together with their married sons and daughters and their respective families. In such a household, the child's interaction with his father is likely to be somewhat less than in the single nuclear household.

POLYGYNOUS POLYGYNOUS. The polygynous household consists of a man living with his wives and their various children. Here the child is likely to have even less opportunity to interact with his father.

POLYGYNOUS MOTHER-CHILD. This type of household occurs in those polygynous societies where each wife has a separate establishment and lives in it with her children. In these societies the father either sleeps in a men's club, has a hut of his own, or divides his time among the houses of his various wives. The husband usually does not sleep in the house of any wife during the 2 to 3 years when she is nursing each infant. Thus the mother may become the almost exclusive object of identification for the first few years of life.

Table 1 shows the number of societies with low and high frequency of Theft and Personal Crime within each of the four categories of household type. As the opportunity for contact with the father decreases, the frequency of both Theft and Personal Crime increases. This result agrees with our hypothesis. If the family structure and household is treated as a four-point scale, it yields a correlation of $+.58$ with frequency of Theft and of $+.44$ with frequency of Personal Crime: both correlations are statistically significant ($p < .01$). If we compare the extremes of the distribution—contrasting Monogamous Nuclear households (which provide the maximum opportunity for identification with the father) with Polygynous Mother-Child households (which provide the minimum opportunity for identification with the father)—this relationship is clearly demonstrated: 18 of the 21 societies fall in the predicted quadrants for Theft, and 14 out of 21 for Personal Crime.

Several results of empirical studies in our society appear consistent with this finding. One is the frequently reported relationship between broken homes and delinquency, since in the majority of cases broken homes are probably mother-child households. Robins and O'Neal (1958), for example, in a follow-up study of problem children after 30 years, refer

TABLE 1

Frequency of Theft or Personal Crime in Relation to Family
Structure and Household*

Family Structure and Household†	Frequency of Theft		Frequency of Personal Crime	
	Low	High	Low	High
Monogamous nuclear	7	2	5	4
Monogamous extended	7	3	6	3
Polygynous polygynous	7	6	3	7
Polygynous mother-child	1	11	3	9

*Each entry in the table gives the number of societies in our sample which have the particular combination of characteristics indicated for that row and column.

The total number of cases in the left-hand and right-hand parts of this table and in the various divisions of succeeding tables varies because lack of information prevented rating some societies on some variables. In testing each relationship we have of course been able to use only those societies for which the relevant ratings are available. The division into "low" and "high" was made as near the median as possible.

†See Murdock (1957).

to the high incidence of fatherless families. Glueck and Glueck (1950) report that 41.2% of their delinquent group were not living with their own fathers, as compared with 24.8% of a matched nondelinquent group. These data suggest that a relatively high proportion of the delinquents came from what were essentially "mother-child" households.

A recent book by Rohrer and Edmonson (1960) is also relevant. Their study is a follow-up after 20 years of the individuals described in *Children of Bondage* by Davis and Dollard (1941). The importance of the matriarchal household typical in a Southern Negro lower-class group, and its effect on the emotional development of the young boy and his eventual attitudes as an adult, are stressed throughout. The following passage summarizes, in its application to their (Rohrer and Edmonson) particular data, an interpretation consistent with those we have cited in introducing this hypothesis:

> Gang life begins early, more or less contemporaneously with the first years of schooling, and for many men lasts until death. . . . Although each gang is a somewhat distinct group, all of them appear to have a common structure expressing and reinforcing the gang ideology. Thus an organizational form that springs from the little boy's search for a masculinity he cannot find at home becomes first a protest against femininity and then an assertion of hypervirility. On the way it acquires a structuring in which the aspirations and goals of the matriarchy or the middle class are seen as soft, effeminate, and despicable. The gang ideology of masculine indepen-

dence is formed from these perceptions, and the gang then sees its common enemy not as a class, nor even perhaps as a sex, but as the "feminine principle" in society. The gang member rejects this femininity in every form, and he sees it in women and in effeminate men, in laws and morals and religion, in schools and occupational striving (pp. 162–163).

Correlates of Theft

Although we shall consider correlates of Theft in this section and correlates of Personal Crime in the next section, each table will show in parallel columns the relation of a set of variables both to Theft and to Personal Crime. This will facilitate comparison and avoid repetition. How each of these variables was measured will be described in the section to which it is most pertinent.

The first variables to be considered are concerned with child training practices. Most of the child training variables have been developed in our research and described in an earlier paper (Barry et al., 1957). These variables may be briefly described as follows:

OVERALL CHILDHOOD INDULGENCE. The period of childhood was defined roughly as covering the age period from 5 to 12 years, or to the beginning of any pubertal or prepubertal status change. In making ratings of childhood indulgence, factors relevant to indulgence in infancy—such as immediacy and degree of drive reduction, display of affection by parents, etc.—if operative at this later age, were taken into account. In addition, the raters also considered the degree of socialization expected in childhood and the severity of the methods used to obtain the expected behavior.

ANXIETY ASSOCIATED WITH SOCIALIZATION DURING THE SAME PERIOD OF CHILDHOOD. This was rated separately for each of five systems of behavior: Responsibility or dutifulness training; Nurturance training, i.e., training the child to be nurturant or helpful toward younger siblings and other dependent people; Obedience training; Self-reliance training; Achievement training, i.e., training the child to orient his behavior toward standards of excellence in performance and to seek to achieve as excellent a performance as possible.

In rating the training in these areas, an attempt was first made to estimate the Total Pressure exerted by the adults in each society toward making the children behave in each of these specified ways (Responsible, Nurturant, Obedient, Self-Reliant, and Achieving). The *socialization anxiety* measures were based on an estimate of the amount of anxiety aroused in the child by failing to behave in a responsible, self-reliant, etc. way, and they reflect primarily the extent of punishment for failure to show each particular form of behavior. The measures of Total Pressure reflect both this and the extent of reward and encouragement.

Wherever boys and girls were rated differently on any of the above variables of socialization, we used the ratings for boys.

The relation of the crime ratings to these and other variables of child training is presented in Table 2. It is clear that Theft is significantly related to several variables of child training.

First, Theft is negatively correlated with Childhood Indulgence, i.e., societies with a high rating of Childhood Indulgence tend to have a low frequency of Theft in the adult population; and, conversely, societies with a low rating of Childhood Indulgence show a high frequency of Theft.

Frequency of Theft is also positively correlated with socialization anxiety during the period of childhood with respect to the following areas of training: Responsibility, Self-Reliance, Achievement, and Obedience. It should be emphasized that Total Pressures toward those four areas of socialization are not significantly correlated with Theft. Therefore it is

TABLE 2

Child Training Factors Associated with Theft or Personal Crime*

	Theft		Personal Crime	
Factor	N	r	N	r
1. Childhood indulgence	45	− .41**	42	− .10
2. Responsibility socialization anxiety	43	+ .48**	41	+ .20
3. Self-reliance socialization anxiety	43	+ .35†	41	+ .24
4. Achievement socialization anxiety	36	+ .41†	35	+ .20
5. Obedience socialization anxiety	40	+ .32†	39	+ .06
6. Dependence socialization anxiety	31	+ .14	28	+ .56**
7. Mother-child sleeping	20	+ .40	19	+ .46†
8. Infant indulgence				
9. Age of weaning				
10. Oral socialization anxiety				
11. Anal socialization anxiety				
12. Sex socialization anxiety				
13. Aggression socialization anxiety				
14. Nurturance socialization anxiety				
15. Total pressures toward responsibility, nurturance, self-reliance, achievement and obedience				

*In this and the following tables the correlations are Pearsonian coefficients, thus reflecting all available degrees of gradation in score rather than simply classifying societies as high and low.

Factors 8–15 showed no significant relationship with either Theft or Personal Crime.

†$p \leq$ .05.

**$p \leq$ .01.

apparently not the area or level of socialization required which is significant, but rather the punitive and anxiety provoking methods of socialization employed.

These findings on child training in relation to Theft may be summarized and interpreted by the hypothesis that theft is in part motivated by feelings of deprivation of love. Our data indicate that one source of such feelings is punitive and anxiety provoking treatment during childhood. Such treatment during infancy may tend to have a similar effect, as suggested by a correlation of $-.25$ between frequency of Theft and Infant Indulgence. This correlation falls slightly short of significance at the 5% level. It is of special interest that substantial correlations with socialization anxiety in childhood tended to occur in the areas of training in Responsibility, Achievement, and Self-Reliance. These all involve demands for behavior far removed from the dependent behavior of infancy and early childhood and close to the independent behavior expected of adults. If we assume that lack of adequate indulgence in childhood leads to a desire to return to earlier means of gratification and behavior symbolic of this need, then we would expect that pressures toward more adult behavior might intensify this need and the frequency of the symbolic behavior. Theft, from this point of view, would be seen as rewarded partly by its value as symbolic gratification of an infantile demand for unconditional indulgence irrespective of other people's rights or interests.

The results of the early study by Healy and Bronner (1936) seem directly pertinent to our findings and interpretation. They found that a group of delinquents differed from their nondelinquent siblings primarily in their relationships with their parents; the delinquent child was much more likely to give evidence of feeling thwarted and rejected. It seems reasonable to assume that such feelings would often, though not always, indicate a real deprivation of parental love. Glueck and Glueck (1950) also found that their delinquents, compared with matched nondelinquents, had received less affection from their parents and siblings and had a greater tendency to feel that their parents were not concerned with their welfare. It was also noted that fathers of the delinquents had a much greater tendency to resort to physical punishment as a means of discipline than fathers of the nondelinquents. This agrees with our observation that more punitive methods of socialization are associated with an increased frequency of Theft.

Compulsive stealing (kleptomania) has been interpreted by psychoanalysts (see Fenichel, 1945, pp. 370–371) as an attempt to seize symbols of security and affection. Thus this form of mental illness, in common with more rational forms of stealing, may be regarded as being motivated by feelings of deprivation of love.

Table 3 summarizes the relationship between our two measures of crime and a number of aspects of economy and social organization on which we were able to obtain ratings. Theft shows a significant relationship with only three of these measures: Social Stratification, Level of Political Integration, and Degree of Elaboration of Social Control. Social Stratification was treated as a five-point scale ranging from complex stratification, i.e., three or more definite social classes or castes exclusive of slaves, to egalitarian, i.e., absence of significant status differentiation other than recognition of political statuses and of individual skill, prowess, piety, etc. Level of Political Integration was also treated as a five-point scale ranging from complex state, e.g., confederation of tribes or conquest state with a king, differentiated officials, and a hierarchical administrative organization, to no political integration, even at the community level.[3] Elaboration of Social Control is concerned with the degree to which a society has law making, law enforcing, and punishing agencies.

Our findings indicate that Theft is positively correlated with each of these three measures. In other words, with an increased Level of Political

TABLE 3

Socioeconomic Factors Associated with Theft or Personal Crime[*]

	Theft		Personal Crime	
Factor	N	r	N	r
1. Social stratification	44	+ .36†	40	+ .16
2. Level of political integration	43	+ .34†	39	+ .02
3. Degree of elaboration of social control	43	+ .46**	40	+ .04
4. Accumulation of food				
5. Settlement pattern				
6. Division of labor by sex				
7. Rule of residence (patrilocal, matrilocal, etc.)				
8. Extent of storing				
9. Irrationality of storing				
10. Severity of punishment for property crime				
11. Severity of punishment for personal crime				

*Ratings of Factors 3, 10, and 11 were made in connection with the analysis of crime by two of the three raters (H. Maretzki and A. Roman). Ratings of Factors 8 and 9 were made by one of the raters (H. Maretzki) but in connection with an analysis of food and economy.

Factors 4–11 showed no significant relationship with either Theft or Personal Crime.
†$p \leq .05$.
**$p \leq .01$.

[3]Both variables are taken from Murdock (1957). Our manner of treating his data is described in Barry et. al. (1959).

Integration, Social Stratification, and Elaboration of Social Control there is an increase in the frequency of Theft. These variables show no significant relationship with frequency of Personal Crime. Each of these institutional conditions seems capable of arousing feelings of insecurity and resentment, and hence may be similar in this respect to parental deprivation. Therefore the correlation of these institutional conditions with Theft might be tentatively interpreted as consistent with our hypothesis about motivational influences on Theft. It is obvious that other interpretations might be made from the same data. For example, a high frequency of crime may give rise to increased elaboration of social control.

Table 4 presents the relation of both Theft and Personal Crime to certain adult attitudes on which we were able to obtain ratings. Frequency of Theft is positively related to Sense of Property and negatively related to Trust about Property. This may indicate merely that the greater the importance of property, the greater the variety of acts which will be classified as Theft, or that a high frequency of Theft gives rise to an emphasis on property. But it may also mean that the greater the importance of property, the more effectively does Theft serve the personal needs to which it seems to be related.

Frequency of Theft is also negatively correlated with Environmental Kindness in Folk Tales. This folk tale measure requires some explana-

TABLE 4

Adult Attitudes Associated with Theft or Personal Crime*

	Theft		Personal Crime	
Attitude	*N*	*r*	*N*	*r*
1. Sense of property	43	+ .45**	40	+ .25
2. Trust about property	43	− .31†	40	− .27
3. General trustfulness	42	− .28	40	− .40**
4. Environmental kindness in folk tales	23	− .47†	21	− .30
5. Environmental hostility in folk tales	23	+ .36	21	+ .56**
6. Communality of property				
7. Competition in the acquisition of wealth				
8. Generosity				
9. n Achievement in folk tales				

*Attitude 3 was rated by one of the three raters (A. Rosman) in connection with the analysis of crime. Attitudes 1, 2, 6, 7, and 8 were rated by another of the three raters (H. Maretzki) in connection with the analysis of food and economy. Attitudes 6–9 showed no significant relationship with either Theft or Personal Crime.
†See Child, Veroff, and Storm (1958).
†$p \leq .05$.
**$p \leq .01$.

tion. It was taken from an analysis of folk tales made by one of the authors (MKB) without knowledge of the societies from which the sample of folk tales was taken. In making the analysis, each folk tale was divided into units of action or events as they related to the principal character or the character with whom the listener would be expected to identify. Each unit was then classified in one of a number of different categories including that of environmental kindness. Classification in this category means that the particular unit involved action or state of affairs definitely friendly or nurturant to the principal character. Thus our results show that societies high in frequency of Theft tend to have folk tales which do not represent the environment as kind. Thinking of the environment as lacking in friendly nurturance seems entirely consistent with the relative absence of parental nurturance which we have already found to be correlated with frequency of theft.

Correlates of Personal Crime

Inspection of Tables 2, 3, and 4 reveals that the significant correlates of Personal Crime are different from those for Theft. In no instance does a variable in these tables show a significant correlation with both Theft and Personal Crime.

Frequency of Personal Crime shows a significant positive correlation with Dependence Socialization Anxiety, a rating taken from Whiting and Child (1953). In making this rating, an estimate was made of the amount of anxiety aroused in the children of a given society by the methods of independence training typically employed. This estimate was based on the following factors: abruptness of the transition required, severity and frequency of punishment, and evidence of emotional disturbance in the child.

Ratings on mother-child sleeping are taken from Whiting et al. (1958). In this study societies were placed into two categories: those in which the mother and baby shared the same bed for at least a year to the exclusion of the father, those in which the baby slept alone or with both the mother and father. According to our results there is a high positive relationship between prolonged exclusive mother-child sleeping arrangements and frequency of Personal Crime. The variable of mother-child sleeping might be considered to favor feminine identification. In that event, the fact that it shows correlations in the positive direction with both types of crime tends toward confirmation of the findings in our earlier section on Correlates of Crime in General.

Inspection of the child training factors associated with frequency of Personal Crime suggests that the conditions in childhood leading to a high frequency of Personal Crime among adults are as follows: a mother-child household with inadequate opportunity in early life for identification with the father, mother-child sleeping arrangements which tend to foster a strong dependent relationship between the child and the mother, subsequent socialization with respect to independence training which tends to be abrupt, punitive, and productive of emotional disturbance in the child.

We would predict that this pattern of child training factors would tend to produce in the child persistent attitudes of rivalry, distrust, and hostility, which would probably continue into adult life. The results obtained with ratings of adult attitudes (Table 4) support this view. Frequency of Personal Crime is negatively correlated with General Trustfulness. Frequency of Personal Crime is also positively correlated with Environmental Hostility in Folk Tales. Classification of a folk tale unit in this category means that the particular unit involved definite deception, aggression, or rejection in relation to the principal character. This variable was not highly related to that of environmental kindness, although the results obtained with the two are consistent with each other. The correlation between them was only −.34, most folk tale units not falling in either of these categories. Our results indicate that societies which are rated as relatively high in the frequency of Personal Crime have folk tales with a high proportion of events representing the environment as hostile. If we may infer that the content of folk tales reflects the underlying attitudes of the people who tell them, then this finding, as well as those with our other measures of adult attitudes, supports the view that personal crime is correlated with a suspicious or distrustful attitude toward the environment.

An analysis by Whiting (1959) of the socialization factors correlated with a belief in sorcery is relevant to this aspect of our results. He points out that a belief in sorcery is consistent with a paranoid attitude. According to Freudian interpretation, paranoia represents a defense against sexual anxiety. Whiting presents cross-cultural data in support of a hypothesis, based on Freud's theory of paranoia, that a belief in sorcery is related to a prolonged and intense contact with the mother in infancy followed by a severe sex socialization. The same hypothesis might be applied to frequency of Personal Crime, since we have evidence that Personal Crime is correlated with a suspicious, paranoid attitude in adult life, and sorcery is after all one form of Personal Crime. Our results for Personal Crime, in common with Whiting's for sorcery, show a correlation with mother-child household and prolonged mother-child sleeping. However, we found no significant correlation with severe sex socialization but rather with severe dependence socialization. We do not feel that these findings negate the Freudian interpretation, because dependence socialization, bearing as it does on the child's intimate relation with his mother, necessarily is concerned with the child's sexual feelings in a broad sense.

GENERAL DISCUSSION

We would like to emphasize the value of the cross-cultural method for exploring the possible determinants of crime. When each society is used as a single case, and is classified according to crime and other variables for the entire society over a period of years, the measures are likely to be reliable; comparison among societies provides great diversity in frequency of crime and in the other variables to be related with it.

The cross-cultural method may help us to identify variables with a causal relationship to crime. For example, our cross-cultural data suggest that high differentiation of status within a society is a favorable condition for a high frequency of Theft, and that a high frequency of Personal Crime is associated with a generalized attitude of distrust. These relationships should be subjected to more systematic and intensive tests within our own society than has hitherto been done.

Variables which have been suggested, whether in empirical studies or theoretical discussions, as possible causes of crime within our society may be tested for broader significance by the cross-cultural method. It has been argued, for example, that within our society delinquent or criminal behavior is likely to develop if the boy has been raised without adequate opportunity to identify with the father. These suggestions have often been made in connection with family patterns that are said to characterize certain classes or groups within our society; the cross-cultural findings indicate that a high frequency of both Theft and Personal Crime tends to occur in societies where the typical family for the society as a whole creates lack or limitation of opportunity for the young boy to form an identification with his father. Therefore the cross-cultural method supports the theory that lack of opportunity for the young boy to form a masculine identification is in itself an important antecedent of crime.

Another instance of such confirmation in a broader sense is the following: In our society delinquents have been reported to express feelings of alienation from their parents. It is unclear, however, whether this reflects their parents' actual treatment of them, or merely their own subjectively determined perceptions. Our cross-cultural data (in common with some of the findings within our own society) indicate that a high frequency of Theft is correlated with an actual low degree of indulgence during childhood.

Other theories about the antecedents of crime, when tested with the cross-cultural method, have not been confirmed in this broader framework. For example, pressures toward achievement were not significantly related to frequency of crime, although such a relationship is implied by theories of delinquency which emphasize the discrepancy between culturally induced aspirations and the possibility of achieving them. This negative result in our sample of societies does not deny the existence of such a relationship within our society, but it does indicate a limitation on its generality.

SUMMARY

In a sample of 48 nonliterate societies, frequency of Theft and Personal Crime were separately correlated with a number of variables which were suspected to be causal factors in the development of crime. Lack or limitation of opportunity for the young boy to form an identification with his father was associated with both types of crime. A high degree of socialization anxiety in childhood and a high degree of status differentiation in adulthood were significantly associated with Theft only; a general adult attitude of suspicion and distrust was more decidedly associated with Personal Crime.

REFERENCES

Barry, H., III, I. L. Child and Margaret K. Bacon. Relation of child training to of some sex differences in socialization, *J. Abnorm. Soc. Psychol.*, 1957, **55,** 327–332.

Barry, H., III, I. L. Child and Margaret K. Bacon. Relation of child training to subsistence economy, *Amer. Anthropol.*, 1959, **61,** 51–63.

Child, I. L., J. Veroff, and T. Storm. Achievement themes in folk tales related to socialization practice. In J. W. Atkinson (ed.), *Motives in fantasy, action, and society,* pp. 479–492. Princeton: D. Van Nostrand Company, 1958.

Davis, A. and J. Dollard. *Children of bondage.* Washington: American Council on Education, 1941.

Fenichel, O. *The psychoanalytic theory of neurosis.* New York: Norton, 1945.

Glueck, S. and Eleanor Glueck. *Unraveling juvenile delinquency.* New York: Commonwealth Fund, 1950.

Healy, W. and A. F. Bronner, *New light on delinquency and its treatment.* New Haven: Yale University Press, 1936. (Republished 1957.)

Miller, W. B. Lower class culture as a generating milieu of gang delinquency, *J. Soc. Issues,* 1958, **14,** 5–19.

Murdock, G. P. World ethnographic sample, *Amer. Anthropol.*, 1957, **59,** 664–687.

Parsons, T. *Essays in sociological theory.* Revised ed. New York: The Free Press, 1954.

Robins, L. N. and Patricia O'Neal. Mortality, mobility and crime: Problem children thirty years later, *Amer. Sociol. Rev.*, 1958, **23**, 162–171.

Robison, Sophia M. *Juvenile delinquency: Its nature and control.* New York: Holt, Rinehart and Winston, Inc., 1960.

Rohrer, J. H. and M. S. Edmonson (eds.). *Eighth generation: Cultures and personalities of New Orleans Negroes.* New York: Harper & Row, publishers, 1960.

Whiting, J. W. M. The cross-cultural method. In G. Lindzey (ed.), *Handbook of social psychology.* Vol. 1. *Theory and method*, pp. 523–531. Reading, Mass.: Addison-Wesley Publishing Company, Inc., 1954.

Whiting, J. W. M. Sorcery, sin and the superego: A cross-cultural study of some mechanisms of social control. In M. R. Jones (ed.), *Nebraska symposium on motivation:* 1959, pp. 174–195. Lincoln: University of Nebraska Press, 1959.

Whiting, J. W. M. and I. L. Child. *Child training and personality.* New Haven: Yale University Press, 1953.

Whiting, J. W. M., R. Kluckhohn and A. Anthony. The function of male initiation ceremonies at puberty. In Eleanor E. Maccoby, T. Newcomb, and E. L. Hartley (eds.), *Readings in social psychology*, pp. 359–370. (Third ed.) New York: Holt, Rinehart and Winston, Inc., 1958.

6-7

Alcohol and Culture

D. G. MANDELBAUM

Studies of Western society indicate that alcoholism is a more common social problem among the Irish than among the Jews and is more prevalent with the French than with the Italians. It seems that Jews and Italians permit the use of alcohol while regulating the occasions on which it may be used (religious ceremonies, celebrations, mealtime, etc.). Another observation is that the pattern of alcoholism tends to vary from one Western country to another. Gamma alcoholism, which involves an inability to control the amount of drinking, is more prevalent in Anglo-Saxon countries in which whiskey consumption predominates; delta alcoholism, which involves inability to abstain, is more prevalent in Latin countries in which wine consumption predominates. Social class also appears to be associated with alcoholism (McCord, McCord, and Gudeman, 1959).

On the wider cultural scene, the present review shows that alcoholism as a problem is associated with cultural values and attitudes rather than with the amount of alcohol consumed. The behavioral consequences of the use of alcohol seem to have some association with the cultural beliefs and expectancies about the effects of alcohol.

Although the present paper emphasizes cultural variables that may explain the origin of alcoholism, it should be emphasized that

Reprinted from *Curr. Anthropol.*, 1965, **6**, 281–293, by permission of the author and the editor. (The reader is referred to the original source for comments on the present selection from the following international scholars: Vera S. Erlich, Khwaja A. Hassan, Dwight B. Heath, John J. Honigmann, Edwin M. Lemert, and William Madsen.)

excessive drinking in all cultures (through individual learning, imitation, and cultural attitudes and values) may bring physiological changes in the individual; and these changes may account for the maintenance of this habit (alcoholic addiction).

REFERENCES

McCord, W., J. McCord, and J. Gudeman. Some current theories of alcoholism. A longitudinal evaluation, *Quart. J. Stud. Alcoh.*, 1959, **20**, 727–749.

There are a great many substances that men have learned to ingest in order to get special bodily sensations. Of them all, alcohol is culturally the most important by far. It was anciently the most widespread in use, the most widely valued as a ritual and societal artifact, the most deeply embedded in diverse cultures. Tribal peoples of all the major parts of the world (save Oceania and most of North America) knew alcoholic drink; it was of considerable interest in the principal civilizations, in most of them from their early beginnings onward. In some languages, as in English, the very term "drink" takes on the connotation of drinking alcoholic liquids.

Where alcohol is known, patterns for its use and for abstention are prescribed, usually in fine detail. There have been very few, if any, societies whose people knew the use of alcohol and yet paid little attention to it. Alcohol may be tabooed; it is not ignored.

In many societies, drinking behavior is considered important for the whole social order, and so drinking is defined and limited in accordance with fundamental motifs of the culture. Hence it is useful to ask what the form and meanings of drink in a particular group tell us about their entire culture and society. In a complex modern society, made up of many subgroups, the drinking patterns of each subgroup or class may reflect its special characteristics as well as the cultural frame of the whole society.

The same kind of question can be asked about the drinking patterns of an individual. Given the cultural definitions for drinking in his society, what does his characteristic drinking behavior tell us about his personality? Within most cultural prescriptions there is leeway for individual choice and manipulation. But before we can learn much about the configuration of his personality from a person's drinking activities, we must understand what choices about drinking are possible in his culture. These encompassing cultural factors are not often made clear in studies of drinking behavior and figure little in the literature on drinking pathology.

CULTURAL VARIATIONS IN THE USE OF ALCOHOL

Cultural practices in drinking range from avid immersion to total rejection. Anthropologists know this well, but those who study the social problems of the use of alcohol do not always take this fact into account. Even a brief mention of the varied social functions of alcohol and the different cultural expressions of these functions points up the central importance of viewing the act of drinking as part of a larger cultural configuration. Alcohol is a cultural artifact; the form and meanings of drinking alcoholic beverages are culturally defined, as are the uses of any other major artifact. The form is usually quite explicitly stipulated, including the kind of drink that can be used, the amount and rate of intake, the time and place of drinking, the accompanying ritual, the sex and age of the drinker, the roles involved in drinking, and the role behavior proper to drinking. The meanings of drinking, its relation to other aspects of the culture and society, are usually more implicit. Thus drinking in a particular society may be either a sacred or a profane act, depending on the context, and the people may not be aware of the basic principles and meanings that are actually involved. These may become apparent only after studies have been made of the contexts of drinking and the behavior of drinkers.

At the extremes of the range of cultural practice the meanings are relatively clear. For example, among the Kofyar of northern Nigeria, "people make, drink, talk, and think about beer." In the religious sphere, "the Kofyar certainly believe that man's way to God is with beer in hand" (Netting, 1963:1–5).

In contrast with those who consider alcohol to be essential and blessed are the people who regard it as destructive and dispensable. The Hopi and other Pueblo Indian tribes of the American Southwest felt that drinking threatened their way of life. They abhorred the use of alcohol so greatly that they successfully banned it from their settlements for many years (Parsons, 1939:22–23; Benedict, 1959).

The range of religious usage is great. Among the Aztecs, for example, worshipers at every major religious occasion had to get dead drunk, else the gods would be displeased (Thompson, 1940:68). In sharp contrast are those Protestant denominations which hold that alcohol is so repugnant spiritually that it is not allowed even symbolically in the communion rite (Cherrington, 1924:2:669–670). Yet another contrast is that provided in India, where a villager may pour an alcoholic libation in the worship of one type of deity (usually of the locality), while to do so at a temple of one of the deities of the classic pantheon would desecrate the place and disgrace the worshiper.

Cultural expectations regulate the emotional consequences of drink. Drinking in one society may regularly release demonstrations of affection, as is common among Japanese men; in another it may set off aggressive hostility, as frequently occurs among Papago Indians (Joseph et al. 1949:76–77). Among Japanese, drinking is part of the fine ambience of pleasant physical sensation—when done at the proper time and place— and so is quite devoid of guilt or ambivalence. Conversely, there are other people among whom drinking is often accompanied by a flow of guilt feeling.

The act of drinking can serve as a symbolic punctuation mark differentiating one social context from another (cf. Honigmann, 1963). The cocktail prepared by the suburban housewife for her commuting husband when he returns in the evening helps separate the city and its work from the home and its relaxation. In more formal ritual, but with similar distinguishing intent, an orthodox Jew recites the Havdola blessing over wine and drinks the wine at the end of the Sabbath to mark the division between the sacred day and the rest of the week. Drinking may be quite purely symbolic, as it is in the Havdola rite and in the sacrament of communion, or it may be substantive as well as symbolic, as in the heavy drinking at Aztec religious ceremonies.

Among other symbolic uses of drinking are its diacritical functions, as when one group or class within a larger society follows drinking patterns that serve as a badge marking them off from others. Such a badge may be deliberately adopted by the members of the group or may be ascribed to them by others, but when a sectarian group forbids drinking to its devotees, the prohibition is often deliberately taken as a counterbadge to separate the elect from the forlorn.

The physiological effects attributed to alcohol vary just as greatly among different peoples. Some are ready to feel high effect from a modicum of drink. Thus it has seemed to more than one Westerner that a Japanese man feels the convivial glow almost before the first sip of sake can reach the stomach. Among Aleut Indians, drinking leads more to surly drunkenness than to mellow conviviality, but among them also a drinker becomes intoxicated after he has taken relatively small amounts of a fairly mild beverage (Berreman, 1956:507). In other societies a man must absorb a large amount of alcohol before he shows that the drink has affected him. So is it also with hangovers and addiction; both are heavily influenced by cultural interpretations. A people who drink as heavily and as frequently as any group yet known, the Camba of eastern Bolivia, attribute no ill effects to their drinking other than the irritation caused to the mouth and throat by their liquor, an undiluted distillate of sugar cane that contains 89% ethyl alcohol.

Most Camba men participate in recurrent drinking bouts, which may last for a whole weekend. A drinker may pass out several times in the course of a bout and, upon reviving, drink himself quickly into a stupor again. Dwight Heath, the anthropologist who has studied Camba drinking, observes (1962:31): "Hangovers and hallucinations are unknown among these people, as is addiction to alcohol." In general, addiction to alcohol seems to be quite rare outside certain societies of Western civilization. Among most peoples whose men are expected to drink heavily and frequently, a man does not do any solitary drinking nor does he have withdrawal symptoms if he cannot get alcohol. He may not like to do without it, but he does not feel gripped by an iron compulsion to get a drink in order to be able to keep alive.

There is, however, a full description of the behavior of an addict in one of the ancient Aztec codices. It is given in a discussion of the astrological sign "under Which the Drunkards were Born" (Dibble and Anderson, 1957:11–17).

The chemical and physiological properties of alcohol obviously provide a necessary base for drinking behavior; the same kinds of behavior are not socially derived from other widely used drugs, such as coffee, tea, or tobacco. But the behavioral consequences of drinking alcohol depend as much on a people's idea of what alcohol does to a person as they do on the physiological processes that take place (cf. Washburne, 1961:267). When a man lifts a cup, it is not only the kind of drink that is in it, the amount he is likely to take, and the circumstances under which he will do the drinking that are specified in advance for him, but also whether the contents of the cup will cheer or stupefy, whether they will induce affection or aggression, guilt or unalloyed pleasure. These and many other cultural definitions attach to the drink even before it touches the lips.

SIMILARITIES ACROSS CULTURES

Cultural variations in drinking practices are well documented, but there has been little notice of similarities in the use of alcohol across cultures. One such regularity is that drinking is usually considered more suitable for men than for women. It is commonly a social rather than a solitary activity but is done much more in the society of age mates and peers than with elders or in the family circle. In France and even more so in Italy, wine is assimilated into the definition of food and the delight that good food brings. Hence wine is drunk by all around the family dinner table. But other kinds of drink, cognac for example, are classified in a different way and drunk in non-family contexts (cf. Lolli, 1958; Stoetzel, 1958). Drinking together generally symbolizes durable social solidarity—or at least amity—among those who "share a drink" (cf. Washburne, 1961:270).

Drinking is more often considered appropriate for those who grapple with the external environment than for those whose task it is to carry on and maintain a society's internal activities. This distinction was anciently symbolized in India by the difference between the god Indra, the scourge of enemies, the thunderer, the roisterer, the heavy drinker, and Varuna, the sober guardian of order and morality (Basham, 1954:233–238). In ancient Greece, the worship of Dionysius could transport the worshiper into an extraordinary, even frenzied state; that of Apollo encouraged only social morality. The Greeks successfully combined the two by assigning certain functions and occasions to the one deity and a different jurisdiction and festivals to the other. Drinking was a prominent feature of the Dionysian rites but not at Apollonian ceremonies (Dodds, 1956:69; Guthrie, 1950:146–149).

In general, warriors and shamans are more likely to use alcohol with cultural approval than are judges and priests. A priest is generally the conserver of tradition, the guide and exemplar for his fellows in precise replication of ritual in ways that please the gods. Drinking rarely goes with the priestly performance of ritual, except in symbolic usage, as in the Mass. But a shaman has personal relations with the supernatural, must directly encounter potent forces beyond ordinary society. Drinking is not often considered as interfering with this function.

When the fate of many hinges on the action of a single person, that person is usually not permitted to drink before performing the critical activity. The high priests of the Old Testament, beginning with Aaron, were particularly forbidden to drink "wine nor strong drink" when discharging their priestly duties in the Sanctuary (Leviticus 10:9). American pilots today are forbidden to drink for a number of hours before flying as well as during the flight. (French pilots have wine with their in-flight meals, but, as we have noted, that kind of alcohol is defined as food by the French.)

Yet another ban that appears in various cultures is imposed when it is considered dangerous to heighten the emotions of large numbers of people who gather at the same occasion. To give but one eloquent example, there is an inscription dating from about the year 5 B.C. near the stadium at Delphi which forbids the carrying of wine into the stadium on pain of a 5-drachma fine. The classical scholar who comments on this also notes that similar signs are to be seen now at the football stadia of Harvard and Southern Methodist Universities (McKinlay, 1951).

Drinking patterns give one set of answers to fundamental questions that must be answered in every culture. Drinking is inescapably relevant to attitudes toward bodily sensations. It is made relevant by most peoples to relations between man and woman, to the proper interchange between man and man, and to the nexus between man and God.

CHANGE AND STABILITY IN DRINKING PRACTICES
AMONG CIVILIZATIONS

As a whole culture changes, so do the drinking mores of the people change. We can best see evidences of change and also of long-term stability in drinking practices over the long careers of the ancient civilizations.

In India, for example, changes in alcohol use reflected major changes in social structure. Drinking was done by all men in an early, egalitarian period. Then, as the motif of hierarchy pervaded and stratified Indian society, drinking was accommodated to this social theme. Liquor was prohibited for certain castes and permitted for others, just as other social functions were specialized according to caste. Within very recent years there has been a shift to a more egalitarian though alcoholically less permissive social code. Under the law of several state governments of the Republic of India, drinking is prohibited to all in the state.

The earliest Indian literary sources, the Vedic hymns, make frequent mention of intoxicating liquors. One ritual drink was Soma, used only in sacrifices, and described as having inebriating effects, although it may not have been alcoholic, since it was pressed from the juice of a plant, mixed with milk, and drunk on the same day. Sura was certainly alcoholic. It could be prepared from molasses, or rice, or possibly honey, and certain kinds were made only for use in sacrificial ritual. But there was a good deal of drinking outside the ritual occasions, and such drinking is condemned in the Vedic literature as leading to quarrels and misleading men from the path of virtue (Prakash, 1961:22–26; Renou, 1954:169).

Later there came a change in the social meaning of strong drink in India. It was eliminated from the rituals for the high gods; it became polluting to those who sought to follow the edicts of scripture. The rise of Buddhism may have had some influence on this shift of Hindu religious practice, since early Buddhism discounted mere ritual, including the ritual use of alcohol.

But alcoholic drinks were not prohibited for all society. The code of Manu says only that the Brahmans should totally abstain. Those of other strata of society need not take any disgrace in drinking but also could not attain, for that and other reasons, a high state of religious purity (Jhā, 1926:70–71, 419). Since the time of Manu, drinking has been socially and religiously compartmentalized in India. It is totally excluded from the worship of the high, universalistic gods and from the way of life of the religiously purest people. Many Brahman groups are strictly abstinent, and even among those Brahman communities in which the men may drink liquor occasionally, they must abstain from drink when they prepare to approach the high deities.

The men of the *Kshatriya*, warrior tradition, customarily drink heartily. Since this class provided most of the rulers and executives of the state, there was no more thought of total prohibition under indigenous Indian princes than there was under the later regime of the British. Yet the Kshatriyas also acknowledge that the high gods dislike alcohol, and they abstain when they seek to be in a state of ritual purity.

Scotch whiskey is put in a special category. It is so costly that its main use is as a prestige symbol for the wealthiest, and so it is not nearly "as defiling as is country-made liquor" (Srinivas, 1955:21).

There is another set of deities, local godlings who preside over local illness and misfortunes, whose ritual is carried on mainly by those of the lower castes, though all in village society, high and low alike, may seek their intervention for personal aid. In the ritual for these deities, liquor is often applied, externally as libation, internally as invigorant. Thus there has long been a rigid separation of alcoholic use in Indian civilization. It was tabooed for those gods and men who were immersed in cosmic concerns. The influence of drink in that sphere was considered disruptive for the whole universe of religion and society. But in the more parochial domain, for local blessings, for village solidarity, for personal benefits, strong drink was liberally used.

Gandhi was strongly in the ascetic tradition, and, when the political party that he led took over the government of the country, the ascetic mode was respected. Many of the political leaders held the belief that an independent India had to be a pure India, and one way to advance national purity was by legal prohibition. This seemed to be quite in the sacred tradition, but in fact it was in one respect a radical departure from it. The Sanskritic tradition did not rule out alcohol for all in society but only for the most spiritually elevated. Yet the recent statutes prohibit alcoholic drink absolutely, for all who are within the territorial bounds of the state.

A modern example of the ancient specialization in drinking is given in Carstairs' study of a town of Rajasthan in western India. Alcoholic drink is still readily available there, but the Brahmans of the place do very little drinking. A good many of them openly drink an infusion of hashish (*cannabis indica*) which gives them a feeling of detachment quite compatible with the religious meditation enjoined in their scriptures. But the Rajputs of the town, as inheritors of martial tradition, spurn hashish and drink an alcoholic brew called daru. One Rajput explained that hashish "makes you quite useless, unable to do anything. Daru isn't like that; you may be drunk but you can still carry on" (Carstairs, 1957:119). Those of military heritage choose alcohol because it helps maintain their traditional posture; those of the priestly heritage prefer hashish because it helps them to pursue their eternal verities. The legal arm of the state may, in time, influence such internal controls; it does not alter them quickly and directly. In India, as elsewhere, drinking practices are tied into fundamental themes of a people's life. While these practices change as the conditions of that life change, legislative acts are only one part, and not always a critical part, of the total change.

In Mesopotamia wine was known at Jemdet Nasr, dating from some time before 3000 B.C. As Sumerian civilization became established around the temple, beer became an integral part of temple ritual and economy. It was the popular drink, indeed a staple of diet, throughout two millenia of the Sumerian-Akkadian tradition. Some 40% of all cereals grown, one estimate has it, went into brewing at one period (Forbes, 1954:279). Not only was beer offered as part of the temple service, it was also drunk copiously in beer shops, and there the drinking was not necessarily seen as being morally benign.

The code of Hammurabi (who came to power about 1720 B.C.) laid down strict regulations for tavern-keepers and tavern servants, who were mainly women. Taverns and inns are marks of civilization; they provide anonymous travelers and customers with food, drink, and shelter, not because of kinship or personal obligations, as is usually the case in tribal societies, but because the customer can pay. Taverns help maintain a complex society, and Hammurabi was concerned that they be operated properly. His code specified the price, the quality, even the credit terms for beer.

But, because taverns are places where anonymous people can gather, they could be dangerous to the regime. One danger was from conspirators and outlaws. A tavern-keeper who tolerated such characters on her premises could be put to death. Even more stringent were the liquor laws for women who were dedicated to the gods. Such a woman could not keep a beer shop or frequent one. If she was convicted of doing so, she was burned to death, the direst form of capital punishment. It was imposed only for this beer crime and for mother-son incest (Lutz, 1922:127:130). Prostitutes also gathered at the beer-houses; since alcoholic euphoria could be had there for money, so also sexual pleasure. Though alcoholic drink in Sumer was used in worship and served as a means of consolidating society, in certain contexts its use was potentially antisocial and immoral, so the state tried to eliminate the disruptive side effects of alcohol.

In Egyptian civilization wine and beer were also staples of diet and ritual. One inscription states that a good mother provides her schoolboy son with three loaves of bread and two jars of beer every day (Lucas, 1948:19, 24; Lutz, 1922:107). Heavy drinking, to the point of insensibility or illness, is frequently depicted in sketches and descriptions of banquet scenes. Egyptian taverns, like those in Mesopotamia, were supposed to be avoided by the social elite.

The ancient Egyptian writings include a number of warnings against drunkenness, among them a touching letter, perhaps from the equivalent of a student's copybook, written by a teacher to his student. The teacher writes that he hears that his former student is forsaking his studies and is wandering from tavern to tavern. He smells of beer so much that men are frightened away from him, he is like a broken oar, which cannot steer a steady course; he is like a temple without a god, like a home without bread. The teacher ends by hoping that the student will understand that wine is an abomination and that he will abjure drink (Lutz, 1922:105). In ancient Egypt as in Sumer, alcohol was an essential element for human welfare when used in one context, a dangerously disruptive force in another. But there seems to have been little attempt by Egyptian state officials to regulate drinking in the manner of the Hammurabi code.

Both the moral and the immoral uses of alcohol are set forth in the Old Testament. Wine is specified for use as libation in the temple service (e.g., Numbers 15:5–10, 28:7–8) but drunkenness is depicted as leading to shame and abomination, as in the accounts of Noah and Lot. Several passages in the Book of Proverbs warn against wine's dangers, and others mention its benefactions; one passage refers to both (31:4–7). According to one biblical scholar, the antagonistic view of alcohol is from an earlier, simpler stage of Hebrew history and the more tolerant view from a later period (Jastrow, 1913).

In the New Testament wine is mentioned as a festive drink (John 2:3–10), as a medicament (Luke 10:34; I Timothy 5:23), and as supreme symbol (Matthew 26:27–29; Mark 14:23–25; Luke 22:17–18). But wine must be drunk in moderation. There are several disapproving references to excessive drinking (I Timothy 3:8; Titus 2:3; Ephesians 5:18). There is considerable continuity in attitudes toward drinking in Old and New Testaments, though the symbolic use of wine becomes greatly elevated in Christianity.

Continuities in style of drinking suggest clues to cultural stabilities. There is another kind of continuity that is of interest; it is the similarity in drinking practice over a large culture area, among many separate societies.

CULTURE AREAS IN DRINKING PATTERNS

The functions of beer-drinking that we have noted among the Kofyar of Nigeria in West Africa are important also among the Tiriki of Kenya in East Africa (Sangree, 1962). Beer is a constant medium of social interchange for men, beer-drinking is a preoccupying activity that few men reject. Drinking beer together induces physical and social mellowness in men. Very little aggressive behavior is ever shown as a result of drinking, and that little is promptly squelched. Pathological addiction rarely, if ever, occurs. The supernaturals are as fond and as interested in beer as are mortals, hence worshipers regularly offer beer for the spirits.

This is quite different from the style of drinking in many Central and South American societies; that drinking pattern allows or requires men to drink steadily into a state of stupefaction. Drinking is social, often done when there is a religious celebration, but not so much poured out for the supernaturals as poured into the celebrants, and always done at fiestas. Though drinking is frequent and heavy, no problem of addiction arises. This pattern has been remarkably consistent through time and place. It was maintained by the peoples of the ancient indigenous civilizations, the Maya, Aztec, and Inca. It is followed in contemporary societies, both Indian and Mestizo, from Mexico to Chile, in highlands and lowlands. (See Cooper, 1948; Morley, 1956:236; Thompson, 1940:68. On modern communities see Simmons, 1962; Stein, 1961; Mangin, 1957; Bunzel, 1940; Metzger, 1963; Viguera and Palerm, 1954.)

This style of drinking is widespread but is not followed everywhere in Central and South America, as is indicated in the study by Sayres (1956) on three Colombian villages and by Viguera and Palerm on Tajin, a Totonac Mexican village. While the modern distribution of this pattern has yet to be traced in detail, the data suggest certain avenues of analysis.

CULTURE AND PERSONALITY ANALYSIS OF A DRINKING PATTERN

To take the extreme case of the Camba of eastern Bolivia, why does a normal Camba man regularly drink himself into a stupor, and on reviving promptly want to drink himself right back into alcoholic oblivion? There are some 80,000 Camba in all, living in a remote but fertile geographic enclave. They are mostly Mestizo peasants, who have little contact either with the neighboring Indian tribes or with the centers of Bolivian national life. Camba men are among the heaviest drinkers on record for normal members of a functioning society.

Drunkenness for them is not an unfortunate by-product; it is the explicitly sought goal of drinking (Heath, 1962:30–31). Alcohol is supposed to have some medicinal value as an internal parasiticide, but no other beneficent properties are attributed to it. The Camba could easily make wines or beers of lower alcoholic content, as do their Indian neighbors, or use other means to prolong a convivial state while drinking. But what they choose is a highly potent drink with very quick effect, and that effect is gross inebriation.

What explanation can we find for this behavior? It seems to require some further exploration. Camba men gulp down quantities of a drink that they dislike in order to attain a state in which they feel nothing. Certain conditions help maintain the pattern, though they do not explain it. Alcohol is cheap and easy to get; it is the main product and export of the region. The region is naturally bountiful, so the simple economy can be maintained even though the drinking absorbs much time and energy.

Heath offers a tentative interpretation based on the nature of Camba social relations. These are fragmented, tenuous, and atomistic. Marriage bonds are brittle, families notably unstable, and kinship ties meager. People shift residence a good deal, there is little cooperative enterprise, and enduring friendships are rare. Heath notes that all people in the world value association with others and the Camba choose to get such association in drinking parties rather than in other ways (pp. 32–33).

This seems true enough, but there arises the question why they choose to have such brief conviviality associations outside the aura of alcohol. Perhaps a single answer can be postulated for both questions, based on what seems to be a deep-seated personality characteristic. The Camba individual seems to be self-isolated, quite like individuals of another South American group about whom we have more personality data (Simmons, 1959, 1962).

The men of Lunahuaná, a Peruvian town in the Andean foothills, also drink frequently, often into drunken oblivion. While their drinking practices differ in detail from those of the Camba, the grand pattern is quite the same. Simmons notes that the adult male Lunahuaneño may be characterized, in part, as timid, evasive, shy, indirect, at a loss for words, uncertain of his behavior when in the company of others, inordinately concerned with "correct" behavior, always preoccupied with what others may think of him, and always timorous lest there be unfavorable criticism. He sees other people as potentially dangerous and is characteristically suspicious and distrustful even of people he knows well.

These attitudes are instilled at an early age. Children are taught to keep to themselves, close to home, and are punished if they go into neighbors' houses. They are kept away from any visitors to the home for fear that they will not behave properly (Simmons, 1962:41, 44). Each person's social relations are "marked by a profound sense of distrust of others and a lack of confidence in his own ability to control the outcome of a given episode of interaction."

If we assume that the Camba have similar fear and distrust of others, similar doubts about their own abilities to cope with social relations and hence a constant attitude of defensive self-isolation, we can begin to see an answer to the questions raised above. It is that a Camba man wants to have two different kinds of relations with his fellows. He wants to insulate himself from them, and yet at the same time he wants some safe interaction with them. He achieves both through drink. From the normal isolation of the week, he comes to the drinking bout of the weekend. For two or three hours then, in the first stage of the drinking cycle, warmed by the liquor, he has pleasant interchange, is voluble and sociable. But since his fear is great and intrusive, he does not want protracted sociability. He needs the protection of isolation. This he gets through the narcotizing effect of alcohol. He regularly proceeds from normal self-isolation, through a brief episode of non-isolation, promptly into alcoholic isolation.

Two features of Camba social life give evidence in support of this formulation. Both are circumstances under which Camba men do not drink. One is at the annual reunion of the Veterans of the Chaco War, one of the bloodiest conflicts of the twentieth century. There is no drinking then, "the presence of a prevailing atmosphere of genuine camaraderie stemming from a past of significant shared experience, and a common characteristic pride may be sufficient basis to unite the veterans, during their reunion, in a way which allows warm and easy fellowship without dependence on alcohol to overcome initial reserve" (Heath, 1962:33–34). The trust born of having endured great hardship and danger together dispels the normal distrust. Hence the participants feel no defensive need to drink, and when they do not have to, they do not drink.

The second instance is that of the relatively few Camba who belong to fundamentalist Protestant sects. Abstinence is part of the denominational doctrine, but there is another reason that helps explain why these few are able to deviate from the normal pattern of drunkenness. Heath observes that these Protestant converts have a stable primary group, which other Camba do not have. Three or four nights a week they meet for religious purposes, call each other "brother," and interact under favorable conditions in which each one is encouraged to take active part (1962:33). The members of one of these Protestant churches form a tightly knit group, consolidated by both their internal interchange and their common opposition to the Catholic majority. So bolstered, a Protestant Camba does not need to preserve social isolation among other Protestants, he does not have the same need for alcoholic isolation, and he is able to uphold the non-drinking doctrine of his denomination.

Normal Camba drunkenness thus seems to arise from a fear of one's fellows and a desire not to interact much with them even when in their presence. This is quite different from the attitudes of Jews or Italians, whose childhood training teaches them to need social interchange and to fear social isolation. Among these people, convivial drinking is condoned, but isolated and isolating drinking is strongly disapproved.

Some interesting implications are suggested by this analysis. One is relevant to studies of the use of alcohol, and adds to the thesis ably presented by some students of the subject, namely, that drinking behavior is best understood as an outcome of fundamental social relations and that the nature of these relations must be known before the meaning of drinking, to the group and to the individual, can be recognized and any alcoholic debilitation efficiently treated (cf. Bacon, 1944, 1945; Bales, 1946, 1962; Pittman and Snyder, 1962: *passim*).

The other opens up new queries in the study of South American cultures. The Camba, as mestizos, have kept only a very few, minor elements of the tribal Indian culture that their ancestors carried on. Yet in their drinking bouts, and presumably in their attitudes toward their fellows, they share fundamental ideas with the surrounding tribesmen. It is as though all the surface, manifest, superficial traits of Indian culture had been abandoned but certain of the basic, structural concepts retained. If this is so of the Camba, what then of all the other Latin-American peoples who follow drinking patterns that are similar in certain main respects? Could the widespread importance of "machismo," the imperative necessity felt by men of these societies to defend and validate their manly qualities, be a general manifestation of fear and suspicion of others which seems to be at the bottom of Camba drinking practices?

STUDIES OF THE USES OF ALCOHOL

Both change and stability in drinking patterns have occurred within the frame of those ways in which alcohol tends to be used everywhere. If we should find a people in which women must drink more than men, in which drinking must be done alone or in the company of one's mentors and dependents, or in which the upholders of scripture (whether theological or political) are expected to drink more heavily than do others, we should know that we have encountered a society basically different from others so far known.

Drinking practices can be studied as expressions of pervasive behavioral themes. A pioneering effort in this direction is Donald Horton's study (1943) on the functions of alcohol in primitive societies. It was based on a survey of reports of drinking in 56 tribes. Horton concluded that the amount of alcohol used was related to anxieties created by food scarcity, acculturation, or war. That is, peoples who were habitually subject to these stresses drank heavily to reduce the anxieties that were so generated. Horton also noted that heavy drinking can create anxiety, and he said that the amount of drinking allowed in a culture is the outcome of the interplay between the anxiety-reducing and the anxiety-creating functions of alcohol.

This formulation has been found wanting as a valid explanation both in general and in particular cases. Two intensive studies of drinking, by

Lemert among Northwest Coast Indians (1954) and by Mangin among Andean Indians (1957), found that drinking among these people was a means of social integration, a way of providing needed primary social relations, rather than a response to anxieties of the kind Horton mentions. And, from the case examples noted above, it is clear that the use of alcohol in a society cannot be explained simply as either a solvent or a source of anxiety. The Camba evidently have none of the major anxieties postulated by Horton. In the Indian village studied by Carstairs (1957), the Rajputs who drink have not been under any greater anxiety than the Brahmans who do not. The description of the beer-centered Kofyar culture gives no hint that Horton's three sources of anxiety have much to do either with heightening their continual thirst for beer or with quenching it. It well may be that where alcohol is culturally defined as a means of relieving anxiety, those groups and individuals who feel themselves under greater stress will drink more, but we must note that drinking is not necessarily so defined nor is tension relief necessarily sought through drink.

A more recent study by Peter B. Field, entitled "A New Cross-cultural Study of Drunkenness," gives a critique of Horton's methods and offers a different explanation. "The general conclusion indicated by the findings to this point is: drunkenness in primitive societies is determined less by the level of fear in a society than by the absence of corporate kin groups with stability, permanence, formal structure, and well-defined functions" (1962:58). The presence of such group organization provides controls over heavy drinking that are not available to peoples who have looser, less well defined kinship organization (p. 72).

To be sure, if a society has strongly integrated kin groups whose members closely control each other's behavior, and if heavy drinking is seen as something to be kept in check, their drinking will be so controlled. But not every people considers heavy drinking as something to be controlled by kinsmen. Drunkenness is the normal goal of drinking in a good many South American societies, some of which have tight unilinear kin organization and some of which do not. Conversely, drunkenness is minimal in many African societies, some of them with strong corporate kin groups and some with quite loose kin organization. In India, there are both Rajput and Brahman groups that have all the social features (save only bride price) postulated by Field (1962:72) as being positively correlated with sobriety, yet some of the Brahman groups are teetotalers and the Rajputs are generally heavy drinkers.

Edwin Lemert has proposed yet another approach, that drunkenness need not be considered as a symptom of either personal deprivation or defective social organization. "There is an alternative way of viewing drunkenness, which is to say as an institutionalized pattern operating in a relatively autonomous way and only tenuously related to other aspects of the culture" (1956:313). There probably are some societies in which, as Lemert says, drunken behavior is fenced off from other areas of behavior and is considered to be outside the context of morality; perhaps this occurred among the English gentry when there were alcoholic remittance men and drunken squires whose condition was politely ignored. But in most societies drunkenness is not disregarded; it may be deliberately sought, as with the Camba, or deliberately discouraged, as with the Kofyar. In either case it is closely related to the general pattern of drinking, and drinking, as has been noted above, is not culturally ignored. Most certainly it was not ignored among the English upper classes, whatever may have been their social techniques for dealing with drunkards.

One difficulty with these and some other theoretical contributions to the studies of alcohol is that their focus is so greatly on drunkenness and alcoholism. Their scope then becomes too restricted for them to be able to explain well even the phenomena on which they concentrate. Inebriety is not really dissociated from the general pattern and standards of drinking, even where drunkards are overlooked. Hence drunkenness cannot be understood apart from drinking in general, and drinking cannot be understood apart from the characteristic features of social relations of which it is part and which are reflected and expressed in the acts of drinking. At the American cocktail party, for example, participants not infrequently take in much alcohol rapidly. It has been suggested that if more food were eaten with the drinks or if drinks of lower alcoholic content were served, the social benefits of such occasions would be enhanced because the deleterious effects of the high intake of alcohol would be minimized (Lolli, 1961). But whether food is taken or liquor of low alcoholic content is offered is in a sense irrelevant. We know that persons can get drunk on beer as well as on distilled spirits if they intend and are expected to do so; they can mix food and alcohol and still get intoxicated. Even more importantly, many cocktail parties seem to be mainly occasions during which one can interact gaily and superficially with a number of others in a way that precludes being relatively serious and intimate with any. If this is indeed the real social purpose of the occasion, rapid alcohol intake helps rather than hinders it.

Alcoholism in the sense of abnormal, addictive, pathologically compulsive intake of alcohol is not the same as drunkenness, which can be quite normal culturally, and should not be confused with the standard drinking practices of any society. In a paper entitled "Alcoholics Do Not Drink," Selden Bacon (1958) shows how very different are the typical practices of alcoholics in the United States from the usual American ways of drinking. Both drunkenness and alcoholism, and the manifold social, economic, and medical problems involved in them, will be understood better than they now are to the degree that they are seen in relation to each culture's normal ways of drinking.

SUMMARY

The extensive literature on drinking practices raises some interesting anthropological problems. This paper is not a review of that literature or of any major part of it, but it is rather intended to bring to notice certain problems which merit further attention.

The use of alcohol is generally a matter of considerable cultural interest. It may be tabooed; it is not ignored. Even a brief account of the range of drinking practices shows that cultural expectations define the ways in which drinking, both normal and abnormal, is done in a society. This is well known to anthropologists but often glossed over in the medical and behavioral studies of the subject.

Cultural variations in drinking have been more often noted by anthropologists than have the cross-cultural similarities. Where drinking is culturally approved, it is typically done more by men than by women. Drinking is more often a social affair than a solitary act, and the social group in which drinking is done is usually composed of age mates and social peers. Where alcohol is used at family meals, it tends to be defined as a food rather than as a stimulant (cf. Ullman, 1958). Once we have a clear conception of these patterns, we can assess the themes of personality that lead an individual to make certain choices in drinking, and we also can appraise the motifs of culture that become expressed in the kind of drinking that a people customarily does.

Changes in drinking customs may offer clues to fundamental social changes. This is the case in the history of Indian civilization. The use of alcohol in Sumerian, Egyptian, and Judeo-Christian civilizations could usefully be examined from this point of view.

The distribution of drinking practices is another promising field for investigation. The kind of drinking done over large parts of Africa stands in contrast to the drinking patterns used over a large part of Central and South America. Among a good many South American peoples, drinking is done at frequent intervals in prolonged bouts of drunkenness. One of the most extreme cases in this pattern is that of the Camba of Bolivia. A tentative analysis of Camba drinking suggests that it is a way of controlling interaction with others under circumstances in which such interaction is feared or mistrusted.

Drinking patterns can usefully be studied as manifestations of pervasive cultural themes. Some of the earlier studies in this vein can now be supplemented with more ample data. Cultural studies of the use of alcohol have important implications for the medical problems of alcoholism.

REFERENCES

Bacon, Selden. *Sociology and the problems of alcohol.* New Haven: Yale University Press, 1944.

Bacon, Selden. Alcohol and complex society. In *Alcohol, science and society.* New Haven: Yale University Press, 1945.

Bacon, Selden. Alcoholics do not drink, *Ann. Amer. and Soc. Sci.,* 1958, **315,** 55–64.

Bales, Robert F. Cultural differences in rates of alcoholism, *Quart. J. Stud. Alcoh.,* 1946. **6,** 480–499.

Bales, Robert F. Attitudes toward drinking in the Irish culture. In D. J. Pittman and C. R. Snyder (eds.), *Society, culture, and drinking patterns.* New York: John Wiley and Sons, Inc., 1962.

Basham, A. L. *The wonder that was India.* New York: Grove Press, Inc., 1954.

Benedict, Ruth F. Psychological types in the cultures of the Southwest. In Margaret Mead, *Anthropologist at work.* Boston: Houghton Mifflin Company, 1959. (First published in 1930 in *Proceedings of the Twenty-Third International Congress of Americanists.*)

Berreman, Gerald D. Drinking patterns of the Aleuts, *Quart. J. Stud. Alcoh.,* 1956, **17,** 503–514.

Bunzel, Ruth. The role of alcoholism in two Central American cultures, *Psychiatry,* 1940, **3,** 361–387.

Carstairs, G. M. *The twice-born.* London: Hogarth Press, ltd., 1957.

Cherrington, E. H. (ed.). *Standard encyclopedia of the alcohol problem.* Westerville, Ohio: American Issue Publishing Co., 1924.

Cooper, John M Alcoholic beverages. In Julian H. Seward (ed.), *Handbook of South American Indians.* Vol. 5, pp. 539–546. Bureau of American Ethnology Bulletin 143. Washington: U.S. Government Printing Office, 1948.

Dibble, Charles E. and A. J. O. Anderson (eds. and trans.). *Florentine codex, Book 4 and Book 5.* Santa Fe: School of American Research, 1957.

Dodds, E. R. *The Greeks and the irrational.* Berkeley and Los Angeles: University of California Press, 1956.

Field, Peter B. A new cross-cultural study of drunkenness. In D. J. Pittman and C. R. Snyder (eds.), *Society, culture, and drinking patterns.* New York: John Wiley and Sons, Inc., 1962.

Forbes, R. J. Chemical, culinary, and cosmetic arts. In Charles Singer et al. (eds.), *A history of technology.* Vol 1. New York and London: Oxford University Press, 1954.

Guthrie, W. K. C. *The Greeks and their gods.* London: Methuen and Co., Ltd., 1950.

Heath, Dwight B. Drinking patterns of the Bolivian Camba. In D. J. Pittman and C. R. Snyder (eds.), *Society, culture, and drinking patterns.* New York: John Wiley and Sons, Inc., 1962.

Honigmann, John J. Dynamics of drinking in an Austrian village, *Ethnology,* 1963, **2,** 157–169.

Horton, Donald. The functions of alcohol in primitive societies: A cross-cultural study, *Quart. J. Stud. Alcoh.,* 1943, **4,** 199–320.

Jastrow, Morris, Jr. Wine in the Pentateuchal codes, *J. Amer. Oriental Soc.,* 1913, **33,** 180–192.

Jhā, Ganganatha. Manu-smrti. Calcutta: University of Calcutta, 1926.

Joseph, Alice, R. B. Spicer, and J. Chesky. *The desert people.* Chicago: University of Chicago Press, 1949.

Lemert, Edwin M. *Alcohol and the Northwest Coast Indians.* University of California Publications in Culture and Society, 1954, No. **2,** 303–406.

Lemert, Edwin M. Alcoholism: Theory, problems, and challenge. III: Alcoholism and the sociocultural situation, *Quart. J. Stud. Alcoh.,* 1956, **17,** 306–17.

Lolli, Giorgio. MS. Physiological, psychological, and social aspects of the cocktail hour. 1961.

Lolli, Giorgio et al. *Alcohol in Italian culture.* New York: The Free Press, 1958.

Lucas, A. Ancient Egyptian materials and industries. Third ed. London: Edward Arnold & Co., 1948.

Lutz, H. F. *Viticulture and brewing in the ancient Orient.* Leipzig: J. C. Hinrichs, 1922.

McKinlay, Arthur P. Attic temperance, *Quart. J. Stud. Alcoh.,* 1951, **12,** 61–102.

Mangin, William. Drinking among Andean Indians, *Quart. J. Stud. Alcoh.,* 1957, **18,** 55–65.

Metzger, D. MS. Drinking in Aguacatenango. 1963.

Morley, Sylvanus G. *The ancient Maya.* Third ed. Stanford: Stanford University Press, 1956.

Netting, Robert M. MS. A West African beer complex. 1962.

Parsons, Elsie Clews. *Pueblo Indian religion.* 2 vols. Chicago: University of Chicago Press, 1939.

Pittman, David J. and Charles R. Snyder (eds.). *Society, culture, and drinking patterns.* New York: John Wiley and Sons, Inc., 1962.

Prakash, Om. *Food and drinks in ancient India.* Delhi: Munshi Ram Manohar Lal, 1961.

Renou, Louis. *The civilization of ancient India.* Calcutta: Susil Cupta Ltd., 1954.

Sangree, Walter H. The social functions of beer drinking in Bantu Tiriki. In D. J. Pittman and C. R. Snyder (eds.), *Society, culture, and drinking patterns.* New York: John Wiley and Sons, Inc., 1962.

Sayres, William C. Ritual drinking, ethnic status, and inebriety in rural Columbia. *Quart. J. Stud. Alcoh.,* 1956, **17,** 53–62.

Simmons, Ozzie G. Drinking patterns and interpersonal performance in a Peruvian mestizo community, *Quart. J. Stud Alcoh.,* 1959. **20,** 103–111.

Simmons, Ozzie G. Ambivalence and the learning of drinking behavior in a

Peruvian community. In D. J. Pittman and C. R. Snyder (eds.), *Society, culture, and drinking patterns*. New York: John Wiley and Sons, Inc., 1962.

Srinivas, M. N. The social system of a Mysore village. In McKim Marriott (ed.), *Village India*. Chicago:University of Chicago Press, 1955.

Stein, W. W. *Hualcan: Life in the highlands of Peru*. Ithaca: Cornell University Press, 1961.

Stoetzel, J. Les caractéristiques de la consommation de l'alcool. Rapport a Presidence du conseil. Haut Comité d'étude et d'information sur l'alcoolisme, 1958. (Seen in MS of abstracted translation.)

Thompson, J. E. S. *Mexico before Cortez*. New York: Charles Scribner's Sons, 1940.

Ullman, Albert D. Sociocultural backgrounds of alcoholism. *Ann. Amer. Acad. Pol. and Soc. Sci.* 1958, **315,** 48–54.

Viguera, Carmen and Angel Palerm. Alcoholismo, brujeria, y homocidio en ros comunidades rurales de México, *América Indígena*, 1954, **14,** 7–36.

Washburne, Chandler. *Primitive drinking*. New York and New Haven: College and University Press, 1961.

6-8

The Importance of Cultural Factors in Psychiatric Treatment

T. A. LAMBO

The practice of psychiatry in the developing non-Western countries requires not only the introduction of new methods of treatment but also the utilization and evaluation of local ones. Non-Western psychiatrists returning home after training in the West tend to find it difficult to accept traditional methods and downright embarrassing to apply them. The therapeutic village in Nigeria started by Dr. Lambo is an interesting example of the successful integration of local therapy with modern psychiatric treatment. He has divided psychiatric care between himself and the local Ju-Ju medicine men who are employed on his hospital staff. Dr. Lambo is credited by the patients for giving symptomatic treatment. The Ju-Ju men are considered by the patients to be responsible for dealing with the causes of abnormality (e.g., magic, possession, evil eye). This practice is useful in giving Dr. Lambo the opportunity to evaluate local treatment and in making his medical treatment acceptable to the patients. It should be noted that the evaluation of native psychological and drug therapies may be a valuable contribution to our knowledge (e.g., the Rauwolfia Alkaloids have been used for thousands of years in Asia, but were only recently introduced in the West).

Reprinted from *Acta Psychiatrica Scandinavica*, 1962, 38, 176–179, by permission of the author and Munksgaard.

Many primitive societies are more tolerant of the mentally ill than is usual in the West and patients are, thus, enabled to function in the community. Work responsibilities are simple and non-demanding and members of the extended family are ready to take over when an individual is unable to carry on with his work. This native communal care and support has been made part of Dr. Lambo's therapeutic village in an attempt to avoid the negative effects of institutionalization as known in the West (e.g. Goffman, 1961). There is at present a movement in the West that encourages patients to remain part of the community both through liberal hospital policy and the use of outpatient treatment and day hospitals.

REFERENCES

Goffman, E. *Asylums*. New York: Doubleday & Co., Inc., 1961.

I should like to emphasize at the outset that I propose to tackle this subject in the light of our experiment in Nigeria, among the Africans of various social and cultural backgrounds.

Our observations in societies that are not "Western" or literate have forcibly demonstrated the importance of cultural factors in the entire management of the patient. The concept and practice of medicine in these non-literate societies is bound up with the whole interpretation of life. Thus a disease, its prevention and healing play a tremendous social role. A knowledge of the culture (and the prevailing attitudes) is not only essential in epidemiological studies within a community, but it is the culture which determines the acceptability, the success or failure of a particular treatment orientation. It is also the culture (including attitudes and social experiences) which either permits or hinders the readiness of the relatives to adjust to the sick person and his emotional needs. Community attitudes as outlined by the culture, clearly permit the bulk of African mental defectives with varying degrees of insufficiency and some psychotics, who keep themselves at some sort of functioning level, to live as tolerated members of the general community.

Analysis of data collected from various parts of Africa has clearly demonstrated that indigenous African culture has not yet accepted Western methods of treatment in their present forms (especially institutionalization) and our people seek medical help with a considerable degree of ambivalence, but paradoxically with such a degree of dependence and often a despair of resignation, that increases both the effectiveness and the difficulties of the physician to the point where he may earn undue credit or undue blame. The realization of this fact caused me and my colleague (Dr. Tigani El Mahi, 1960) to recognize the part played by indigenous psychotherapeutic approach in the total management of the patient, without lowering the standard of medical practice. Even though by customary Western standards, this approach is indefensible and some indigenous cultural factors may be caricatured as primitive and antediluvian, they are nevertheless emotionally reinforced and, as an historical and traditional legacy, the psychiatrist working in this cultural setting must be sensitive to their implications and reckon with them.

Experience in various parts of Africa has shown that even in non-literate societies, with their own pre-literate causal formulations, the greater the confidence of the community in the *nature* and *form* of treatment they could obtain and in the *people* who would treat them, the more readily would they come forward for treatment or encourage their ill relatives to do so. Consequently the *nature* and *form* of treatment has to be defined within the cultural framework.

Before going on to describe our approach in Nigeria, which has made full use of the social environment, I should like to stress that one of the most important cultural factors which influences or determines the nature of treatment is community attitudes. Community attitudes towards emotional disorder, especially in cultures outside the West, have been found to be complex, and have been described by some observers (Tooth, 1950; Lambo, 1956). They are, of course, to be reckoned with in the emotionally disturbed as in the healthy members of the community. Such attitudes may considerably influence what action the patient takes about his disability, and even the content and evolution of his neurotic symptoms. They may impede free communication of his emotional (inner) experiences without the knowledge of which proper diagnosis of his condition is impossible.

Due to our recognition of the fact that there is a great need in our entire management of the African patient to consider and treat him within the social environment, an experiment to treat the patient within the framework of the community was started in 1954 at Aro, Abeokuta, Nigeria. (For details of the experiment see: Lambo, 1956.) It would seem sufficient here to mention that the scheme consisted of four traditional villages on which we grafted our therapeutic unit which was able to accommodate between 200–300 patients.

Our patients come from various parts of the country, accompanied by their relatives, usually either mother, sister, brother or aunt, who should be able to cook for them, wash their clothes, take them to the hospital in the morning for therapy and collect them in the afternoon. Patients and their relatives, as well as the villagers, are invited regularly to attend church services, cinema, plays, dances and many social functions in the hospital proper. Many social group activities are also promoted in the villages.

One of the most important lessons learned during the course of our experiment is that this form of treatment provides the best avenue of dealing satisfactorily with the family attitudes to the patients from the outset of treatment. In many cases, personal experience gained by relations accompanying the patients to therapy has changed materially the social attitudes not only within the family group, but also within the community. Such personal experiences have proved to facilitate the readiness of the relatives, who are in constant contact with the patient, to adjust to the sick person and his emotional needs.

The entire hospital labor force (daily paid laborers, gardeners, craftsmen, etc.) is drawn from the four villages. Consequently, they are in turn the landlords of the patients who are boarded in the villages and with whom they are in constant contact both in the hospital grounds and in the villages. A market, which was started near the villages a few years ago, is now flourishing, and this has proved a useful way of promoting wider communication with the outside world.

In this therapeutic experiment, the villages are looked upon as hospital wards as far as the internal administration is concerned, but every effort is made to impart to the nursing personnel and other mental health workers an intelligent appreciation of the conditions of those who are under their care.

It is the contact which the patient has with his social environment that we highly value as the most important therapeutic factor in this scheme. Through this social interaction in the heterogeneous group (normal villagers and patients) our patients receive help and support from other patients as well as from people who are emotionally healthier than they are. We have observed that the rapidity with which a patient effects a compromise in his emotional attitudes which is suited to his impaired level of function is greater in the village (i.e., within this therapeutic community).

There is no doubt that under conditions which we have not yet been able to define satisfactorily, the community group influences in the village make life richer and healthier. We know that the social responses to this therapeutic environment are positive and therefore some socio-psychological elements, however embryonic, must be postulated. Many of the socializing and therapeutic factors inherent in certain environments (e.g., cults, divination, native religions, sacrifices, etc.) are manifold, and would seem to work with great precision and we have, as a result, utilized some of these cultural factors as therapeutic factors of great potency. Much of this is still empirical and intuitive, but one cannot escape the findings of well-recorded and systematically made observations.

Even though in a way, our village system in Nigeria has become a self-treating, self-propelling and progressive therapeutic community, with constant but unobstrusive supervision and direction in terms of the emotional needs of the individual patient, it must be emphasized that any system of community care, however, requires skilled social psychiatric help in the form of guidance, supervision and direction, if it is not to flounder. Merely leaving patients in the community and treating them on an out-patient or domiciliary basis, without offering any extra service, is placing an undue burden on the families and the community at large, and increasing the tension to which the patient must be subject in his interpersonal relations.

In any group situation (tribal, family, religious, etc.) in Africa, transference is a vital problem. In traditional African societies, group has been the spontaneously evolved and fundamental basis of human relations. We have found in our practice in Africa, that where recovery is probable, the success of all other measures towards re-adaptation depends upon an effective transfer. Even when an unfavorable prognosis is recognized, a positive transfer of affect, under the social conditions of the village, may be used to prevent patients from deteriorating. This approach in our experience has been the only answer to the problem of preventing disability from chronic psychosis, and may well be responsible for the rarity in Africa of deteriorated and disabled psychotics one frequently meets in European and American institutions.

There is nothing sensational or spectacular about our approach. This experiment has allowed for the fullness and complexity of the social and cultural processes inherent in the environment. Such influences or processes help to make changes or recovery permanent and do not merely relieve symptoms. Our practice in Nigeria, from consideration both of experiment and expediency, has been increasingly towards putting the patients into the center of the community to enable them to have full and adequate social participation in an environment loaded with sincere emotional bonds.

References

Lambo, T. A. Neuropsychiatric observations in the Western Region of Nigeria. *Brit. Med. J.*, 1956, **2**, 1388–1394.

El Mahi, T. Roundtable participant: Psychiatry in the underdeveloped countries, report of roundtable meeting, Atlantic City, N.J. American Psychiatric Association, May 12, 1960, p. 21.

Tooth, G. *Studies in mental illness in the Gold Coast.* London: Her Majesty's Stationery Office, 1950.

Name Index

Subject Index